Praise for *Michael Palin's Diaries*

'If anyone writes a diary purely for the joy of it, it is Michael Palin'

The Times

'Charming and vastly entertaining'

Irish Times

'Palin's style is so fluid, and his sincerity so palpable, that it is often easy to underestimate just how talented he is as a comedian, broadcaster and writer ... [the Diaries] are just too good and he is too modest'

Sunday Express

'These diaries record an astonishingly successful career ... they are remarkably good company, always dependable, never upsetting: safely enjoyable, page after page. And that's quite a triumph of tone'

Evening Standard

'Palin reminds me of Samuel Johnson: driven, intellectually formidable, and spurred on by self-reproach and the wholly irrational idea that he's not really getting on with it ... Palin is a seriously good writer. These diaries are full of fine phrases and sharp little sketches of scenes'

Daily Mail

'Delightful and often extraordinarily funny ... An entertaining and at times deeply moving read'

Mail on Sunday

'At first you think how lucky Palin is to be living his life. Then, gradually, you see the dark side. He connects with you in a lovely way, which is very calming'

Spectator, 'Books of the Year'

'It's clear why Cleese later nominated Palin as his luxury item on *Desert Island Discs* . . . he makes such unfailingly good company'

Guardian

MICHAEL PALIN has written and starred in numerous TV programmes and films, from *Monty Python* and *Ripping Yarns* to *The Missionary* and *The Death of Stalin*. He has also made several much-acclaimed travel documentaries, his journeys taking him to the North and South Poles, the Sahara Desert, the Himalayas, Eastern Europe and Brazil. His books include accounts of his journeys, two novels (*Hemingway's Chair* and *The Truth*), several volumes of diaries, *Erebus: The Story of a Ship* and *Great-Uncle Harry*. From 2009 to 2012 he was president of the Royal Geographical Society. He received a BAFTA fellowship in 2013 and a knighthood in the 2019 New Year Honours list. He lives in London.

Also by Michael Palin

Fiction
Hemingway's Chair
The Truth

Non-fiction
Around the World in 80 Days
Pole to Pole
Full Circle
Hemingway Adventure
Sahara
Himalaya
New Europe
The Python Years: Diaries 1969-1979
Halfway to Hollywood: Diaries 1980-1988
Brazil
Travelling to Work: Diaries 1988–98
Erebus: The Story of a Ship
North Korea Journal
Into Iraq
Great-Uncle Harry: A Tale of War and Empire

MICHAEL PALIN

There and Back

DIARIES 1999–2009

W&N

WEIDENFELD & NICOLSON

First published in Great Britain in 2024 by Weidenfeld & Nicolson
an imprint of The Orion Publishing Group Ltd
Carmelite House, 50 Victoria Embankment
London EC4Y 0DZ

An Hachette UK Company

1 3 5 7 9 10 8 6 4 2

A CIP catalogue record for this book is
available from the British Library.

ISBN (Hardback) 9781474612753
ISBN (Trade paperback) 9781474612760
ISBN (eBook) 9781474612784
ISBN (Audio) 9781474612791

Printed and bound in Great Britain by Clays Ltd, Elcograf S.p.A.

MIX
Paper | Supporting
responsible forestry
FSC® C104740

www.orionbooks.co.uk

To Helen, who was always there when I got back

Contents

Acknowledgements xi

List of Illustrations xiii

Who's Who in the Diaries xv

Introduction xxi

1999 I

2000 53

2001 107

2002 155

2003 205

2004 251

2005 299

2006 349

2007 395

2008 441

2009 493

Index 541

Acknowledgements

As I keep my diary in longhand, the task of deciphering my scribbles is always a mammoth undertaking. The basic transcription was completed by Katharine Du Prez and later editing work was done by Alison Sieff.

Without their patient and dedicated work, the Diaries would never have come together.

Huge thanks too, to my editor Jenny Lord for taking on the job of editing, sorting and sifting the ton of material into readable shape, and to her team at Weidenfeld & Nicolson – Lily McIlwain, Steve Marking, Lucinda McNeile, Virginia Woolstencroft and Lindsay Terrell.

And, as ever, my voluminous gratitude to Steve Abbott, Paul Bird and Mimi Robinson at Mayday Management for looking after me.

List of Illustrations

Section One:
Last day of filming *Michael Palin's Hemingway* Adventure, July 1999[1]
Michael Katakis[2]
At the premiere of a 30th anniversary screening of *Life of Brian*, 1999[3]
Behind the scenes of *30 Years of Monty Python*, September 1999[1]
Publicity shoot for *2000 Today*, December 1999[4]
With Sherrie and friends, 2000[1]
With Terry Jones, September 2000[1]
At the Yorkshire Awards, 2000[5]
On the phone to Helen, May 2000[1]
With Helen at home, July 2001[1]
With cockerel in Morocco, 2001[6]
In Agadez, 2001[1]
Outside Lagavulin distillery, April 2002[7]
With Keith Miller at Lord's cricket ground, July 2002[1]
Unveiling the Virgin Super Voyager in Sheffield, August 2002[1]
With David Attenborough in publicity photo for *A Life on Air*, 2002[4]
With Alan Bennett, February 2003[8]
Tom, Will and Rachel, May 2003[1]

Section Two:
Birthday celebrations, 2003[1]
Birthday cake[1]
With great-niece, April 2004[1]
Himalaya team with the Dalai Lama, 2004[1]
With the Dalai Lama[7]
With Imran Khan[7]
Billboard for *Himalaya with Michael Palin*, 2005[9]
Neighbours with their Himalaya project, 2005[1]
Family photo with motorbike and sidecar, 2005[1]
Edith and Elsie the cats[1]
Helen with Granny G, 2006[1]
With baby Archie, 2006[1]
With baby Archie and Barry Cryer, April 2006[1]
With HRH King (then Prince) Charles[10]

At a book signing for *New Europe* in Tewkesbury, December 2007[11]
With Marcus, Morag and Camilla, 2008[1]
With Terry Jones, 2009[1]
Helen with Terry Gilliam[1]
Family at street party, 2009[1]

1   From the author's private albums
2   Kris L. Hardin
3   PA Images / Alamy Stock Photo
4   BBC Photo Library
5   Jack Hickies Photographers Ltd
6   Vanessa Courtney
7   Basil Pao
8   Dave Bennett / Getty Images
9   John Pritchard
10   Shutterstock
11   The Photo Studio Tewkesbury

Who's Who in the Diaries: 1999–2009

FAMILY

Mary Palin, mother, lived at Southwold, Suffolk. Died in 1990. Father died in 1977.
Helen, wife
Children:
Tom born 1968, married **Rachel Winder** in 2006, son **Archie** born 2006
Wilbur born 2009
William born 1970
Rachel born 1975
Angela, sister. Married to **Veryan Herbert** of Chilton Hall, Sudbury, Suffolk. Died in 1987.
Children:
Jeremy born 1960, wife **Melanie** and children **Eugene** and **Esmé**
Camilla born 1962
Marcus born 1963, wife **Morag** and daughter **Louisa**
Helen's family:
Anne Gibbins, mother
Elder sister, **Mary**, married **Edward Burd** in 1964, daughter, **Catherine**, born 1966. Catherine the mother of **Eve** and **Esther**.
Younger sister, **Cathy**
Nigel Greenwood, cousin and art dealer. Died 2004
Judy Greenwood, cousin and antique dealer

FRIENDS AND COLLEAGUES

Terry Jones, formerly married to **Alison Telfer**, married **Anna Soderstrom**
Terry Gilliam and wife **Maggie**
John Cleese, formerly married to **Connie Booth**; married **Barbara Trentham** 1981
Graham Chapman, died 1989, partner **David Sherlock**
Eric Idle, married **Tania Kosevich** in 1981
Robert Hewison, contemporary of MP at Brasenose College, Oxford,

1962–5, during which time he persuaded MP to perform and write comedy for first time

Simon and Phillida Albury. Simon met MP after Oxford in 1965. Television journalist, producer and gospel music fan.

Ian and Anthea Davidson. Ian met MP at Oxford. Encouraged him to perform in revue and gave him early work at the BBC. A writer and director and occasional Python performer.

Neil and Yvonne Innes. Neil, ex-Bonzo Dog Band. Worked closely with the Pythons, especially on their stage appearances. Collaborated with Eric to create the Rutles. Sons: **Miles** and **Luke**.

Richard Loncraine, film director (*The Missionary*, *Richard III*). First wife, **Judy**. Married **Felice** in 1985.

George Harrison, musician, ex-Beatle. Married to **Olivia Arias**, son **Dhani**, born 1978.

Chris Orr, artist and printmaker

Tristram and Virginia Powell. Tristram was director/collaborator on *East of Ipswich* and *Number 27* and co-wrote and directed *American Friends*.

André Jacquemin, recording engineer, Python recordist, composer (with Dave Howman) of some Python songs. Founder of Redwood Studios.

Trevor Jones/John Du Prez, musician and composer (Python songs, *The Meaning of Life*, *A Private Function* and *A Fish Called Wanda*)

Ray Cooper, legendary percussionist who became important go-between and general troubleshooter on all the HandMade films

Alan Bennett, playwright and author

David Attenborough, broadcaster and biologist

Eleanor Yule, writer/director, on MP's arts films

Mhairi McNeill, producer, MP's arts films

Ion Trewin, editor of the Diaries at Weidenfeld & Nicolson

Michael Dover, editor of the travel books at Weidenfeld & Nicolson

Jonathan Clyde, record producer and friend of George Harrison

Michael Katakis, writer and photographer and manager of the Ernest Hemingway literary estate

Rita Gardner, director of the Royal Geographical Society

John Goldstone, producer of Monty Python films – *Holy Grail*, *Life of Brian* and *Meaning of Life*

AT MAYDAY MANAGEMENT/PROMINENT FEATURES

Anne James, management

Steve Abbott, financial management. Film producer (*A Fish Called Wanda*, *American Friends*, *Fierce Creatures*, *Brassed Off*).

Paul Bird, personal assistant to MP
Roger Saunders, management
Mimi Robinson, secretary/assistant
Alison Davies, secretary/assistant
Kath James, secretary/assistant
Anouchka Harrison secretary/assistant

IN AMERICA

Nancy Lewis, publicist for Python in the USA, deserves much credit for getting them on US TV in the first place. Married actor **Simon Jones** in 1983. One son, **Timothy**.
Sherrie Levy, New York-based representative of MP in America
Al Levinson, writer, poet, close friend. After wife **Eve**'s death, he married **Claudie** in 1979. One daughter, **Gwenola**.
Paul Zimmerman, screenwriter (*King of Comedy*), married to **Barbara**

HEMINGWAY ADVENTURE, SAHARA, HIMALAYA AND NEW EUROPE

David F. Turnbull, director of *Hemingway Adventure*
Martha Wailes, producer on *Hemingway Adventure*
Roger Mills and **John-Paul Davidson**, co-directors of *Sahara*, *Himalaya* and *New Europe*
Nigel Meakin, cameraman on all four series
John Pritchard, sound recordist
Alex Richardson, editor on *Sahara*, *Himalaya* and *New Europe*
Vanessa Courtney, location manager on *Sahara*, *Himalaya* and *New Europe*
Basil Pao, photographer and fellow traveller
Nicola Moody, executive producer, *Sahara*
Eddie Mirzoeff, BBC executive producer

'The farther one travels, the less one knows'

George Harrison

Introduction

There have been signature years in my life which, like swollen rivers or wind-swept mountains, I've approached with wary respect. Nineteen eighty-four was one. George Orwell's book had fixed in my young mind a dark and sinister threat, that seemed, at one time, awfully real. But all was well as the year dawned, free of menace.

The other year that came with an association close to such significance is covered in these diaries. 2000 AD. Not just my son's favourite comic, but a truly landmark year. The end of a millennium. Something that only happened every, well . . . every thousand years. William the Conqueror was not even born when humans last experienced a year like this. But my diary on this epoch-shifting day merely notes 'I walk up to South End Green for a paper'.

By far the most significant day in these diaries is not January 1st 2000, but September 11th 2001. On that day I'm in a small Saharan town in the 144th poorest country in the world. The first thing I hear on my arrival in this remotest of places is that the Twin Towers in New York have been attacked and destroyed, with the loss of hundreds, possibly thousands, of lives. Re-reading my diaries around that dreadful event I'm struck by descriptions not just of what happened on that world-changing day, but what it felt like on the day before and the day after. The great thing about a diary is that it is all about continuity, about time moving on. Few other literary forms exist to show what it's like to survive. How bad things can change with perspective, and good things too.

There and Back is an account of an increasingly restless life, darting and dodging about the planet. But I never assumed that one journey would follow another, and these diaries show the squirming indecision between each one, as I try to prioritise the rest of my life and do all the other things I want to do.

Though I seem constantly on the move, there and back, most of my time is spent at home, because for me, the real attraction of going to new places is the joy of coming home and realising the sheer satisfaction of looking at the world out of your own windows.

Asked to write a snappy strapline for this new volume, I came up with 'There and Back: Eleven Years on and off the Road as Michael Tries to Grow Up'.

And there's not much I can add to that.

Michael Palin,
London, April 2024

My travels underscore this volume of Diaries. In the period from 1999 to 2009, I follow Hemingway from Cuba to Uganda, cross the Sahara, climb the Himalayas and explore Eastern Europe. All of these journeys have a book to themselves, which is why they remain on the periphery of this volume.

The travel books covering this period are all available, recently reissued in a newly designed edition. What you have here is the infinitely more complex saga of what I did between check-in desks.

1999

Friday, January 1st

The grey clouds of Christmas have rolled away and it's a scintillating start to '99. A great calm has descended after the efforts and the visitings of the past week and I feel wonderfully relaxed and rested, and also in one of those receptive and responsive moods in which everything around me looks its best – the house, the vase of flowers and the bowl of fruit catching the light on the oak table, with Redpath's 'Menton' looming above them.

Saturday, January 2nd

A long, full sleep would seem to have been the logical consequence of a serene and restorative New Year's Day, but once again that worry about being really good at anything (even sleeping) seems to have risen from somewhere, and I slept quite lightly, waking often, listening to the wind as another low-pressure system blows in from the west.

Ken Cranham and Fiona [both actors] come round for tea and pictures. Ken knows painting – it was either art school or drama school for him when he was young, 'like Ralph Richardson' – and we look at my paintings and enjoy discussing them. He was lined up for a new TV series that had been written for him, but Peter Salmon [Controller of BBC One] judged him to be too old. 'Just as well, really,' says Ken, 'there was an awful lot of sex in it.'

Monday, January 4th

To the Travel Clinic in Harley Street. Voluble Irish doctor/pathologist has lined up all the jabs I need for the Hemingway trip. Typhoid and tetanus and meningitis. 'It's the meningitis season in Uganda,' she assures me. (And in Yorkshire too if the news is anything to go by – two students in Rotherham died of the disease over New Year.) I'm also given a booster of polio vaccine on a lump of sugar – more uncomfortable than any of the jabs which are now administered with such fine needles that you hardly feel the penetration.

Feel quite depressed by current state of Python, and as there is no one taking a leading role in organising us, I imagine things will drift on.

Watch 'Lolita' – Adrian Lyne's film with Jeremy Irons. Not bad, not bad at all, though they've cheated a little by making Irons look almost younger than the nymphet. Dyed hair, sweet clothes, all chirpy, camp winsomeness, it's 'Brideshead' all over again.

Wednesday, January 6th

Picked up by cab to go down to the Royal Academy. I've been asked to record an appreciation of one of the pics in upcoming Monet in the Twentieth Century exhibition, for a series of one-minute progs on BBC One.

My cab driver is a soft-spoken black man who rather shyly asks if I wouldn't mind him asking me a question. There is an odd pause before he begins, which, as it turns out, is what the story is all about. His nine-year-old son has developed such a bad stammer he can now hardly speak and his four-year-old daughter, with no previous problems at all, has suddenly begun to stammer too. Both he and his wife stammer. He'd seen me talking about it on television and wonders if I have any helpful advice. His lack of self-pity and yet his obvious pain at what is happening to his children is very moving; I forget all about the painting and what I'm going to say about it, and just make sure that he has the number of the Stammering Centre and knows where it is. It's rarely that you have a real chance to change things and strangers' hard-luck stories are sometimes not what they seem, but I hope that encounter this morning will benefit both of us.

Arrive and am led upstairs to a gallery whose walls are empty except for the one painting I'm to talk about – a view of the Thames, from the Savoy. Around me, yet to be unpacked, the rest of the Monets, 80 of them. Just arrived from Boston. An extraordinary thing to behold. The backstage work of an exhibition. The paintings are not yet in costume and make-up, they're fine paintings, but not yet stars. I feel privileged to witness all this, as I record my short interview and try my best to say what *I* like about the picture and not what the producer is trying to push me into saying. 'Lots of enthusiasm,' she urges. 'Remember, it's BBC One!'

Friday, January 8th

Clear skies. To Harmood Street, where, at No. 104, a delightfully enthusiastic lady called Josie takes a mould for the mask we need for the Venice Carnival sequence. Have to lie flat and have my hair and all superfluous areas covered in cling-wrap, a couple of straws for breathing inserted in my nose, and a soft, cold mud of dental plaster layered onto my face. The whole process takes an hour and she and her assistant are so sunny that I barely feel discomfort.

The next twenty days were spent filming for the Hemingway Adventure *series in Africa. In 1954 Hemingway, always accident-prone, had been involved in two plane crashes within 36 hours. We had something of a scoop when we reached the small town of Butiaba in Uganda, where his second crash took place. A local man, who had never been interviewed before, had not only witnessed the Dragon Rapide bursting into flames on take-off but had picked up some of the remains of the plane, one piece of which he insisted I keep. I found myself returning to London with a certain amount of apprehension. What would be the security implications if they found aeroplane wreckage in my bags?*

Monday, January 25th

Slept around nine hours, which must have recharged the batteries. Just as well for a busy day ahead. To the office for a meeting with the 'HT' ['Hemingway's Travels', as it was called at the time] production team. Italy and France both imminent and have to be discussed as virtually one continuous stretch of filming. Unlike Africa, which was largely retracing, in quite a linear fashion, we have to be more creative in Italy, and there are several contrived 'comedy' sequences in both Italy and France which will have to be tried before we know if they work and are at all necessary.

The masks are ready. Hemingway's good – MP less so. Which I think confirms my impression of the two of us side by side in the book. He does make me look very ordinary.

Tuesday, January 26th

Awoke, as if still on East African time, in the dark hours. Mental safari – leaves me exhausted by the time I get up.

Car over to the Stammering Centre. Normally, a bevy of children and therapists overwhelm me as soon as I set foot in the place, but today Diana [de Grunwald, employee at the Centre] keeps it low-key, so only one autograph and three therapists.

Luke Jeans [filmmaker for the Centre] is able, efficient and knows what he wants. I have to introduce the film and ask for money, etc. at the end. Quite a lot to say and I just have to concentrate and say it and mean it. He wants to do a longer documentary piece about the Centre. Would I be prepared to do a voice-over? Of course I say yes – this is one cause for which I always make a priority. And there is a big brass plate on the wall with my name on it!

Up to Moro in Exmouth Market where I have arranged to meet Basil [Pao, my photographer friend] for a Bunter-ish lunch. At a round table by the door is Nick Elliott [head of drama at ITV] and, amongst the others, Prince Edward, who still seems absurdly young. He rises to shake my hand and I congratulate him on his engagement. Nick, very much the old warhorse, greets me with a poignant cry of 'Brownlow!' Of course it's his people who are financing the Bleasdale 'Oliver Twist'. I'm slightly thrown as everyone round the table seems to be quite familiar with the intricacies of my involvement, or *non*-involvement in the project.

But I do try out my idea of post-cooking programmes – eating programmes. 'Eat the World' was, of course, Katakis's [writer/photographer and manager of the EH literary estate] idea. Much laughter – Prince Edward, a paragon of politeness, remains standing and listening attentively.

Friday, January 29th: Venice

At our hotel close by the Rialto. This morning we came into the city from Caorle, where Hemingway used to go on duck shoots – and wrote about it in one of his worst books, 'Across the River and into the Trees'; wild, windswept lagoon scenery. Mid-morning to the Palazzo Tron to meet Alberto Franchetti, from one of Venice's most famous families. His dad took EH shooting and composed operas in his spare time. Alberto, a chain-smoker, talks to us on a balcony looking down over the Grand Canal. Quite stunning location. But it doesn't seem to make him particularly happy. The increase in outboard motors on the canal has made life in what would seem to me a paradise almost intoler-able. 'My mother was the last of the family to sleep on the Grand Canal – now it's impossible.' He remembers EH in Venice. He didn't seem like a happy man, he says. Nor did he seem much interested in La Serenissima. 'He sat in his room in the Gritti Palace and drank.' I bring up the slightly awkward subject of how the book was received by the locals. He smiles fleetingly. 'The truth is that nobody read it.'

Tuesday, February 9th: Venice–London

Much water under the bridges since last entry. North Italy criss-crossed suc-cessfully. A spell of cold, clear weather throughout the filming period has broken this morning.

My aching right side gives me a quick reminder, as I pull myself out of bed at the Hotel Ai Due Fanali, of my suffering last week. Bicycle filming on the straight roads of Noventa, involving repeated falling. Possible cracked rib.

By mid-morning sleet is coming down hard and driving across the Campos.

Hurry to the Scuola Grande di San Rocco to take in the Tintorettos. The movement above me of the massive forces he disposes reminds me of the passing over of the spaceship in '2001 [A Space Odyssey]'. I'm beginning to feel a strong, fresh response to the big Venetians and can't wait to come back here. A lovely, private prowling morning. I think I'm the only one of the crew who hasn't been shopping.

Friday, February 12th

Run in late morning. No fierce resistance from ribcage, but the jolting gradually intensifies whatever discomfort is there, and I shorten the course. All being well should be able to cope with the sporting demands of the Paris shoot.

Into the West End to buy boxing shorts and gumshield at Lonsdale in Beak Street. Droll manager asks if I'm busy. I tell him I always seem to be busier than I want to be. 'Well, I'm glad to hear that, Frank [Bruno]'s got nothing coming up after he finishes panto.' Is there any other country in the world in which boxing champions do Christmas pantomimes? I choose a red and white pair of real satin boxing shorts. 'Red's a good colour,' he assures me. 'Doesn't show the blood.'

Saturday, February 20th: Paris–London

Everyone is very tired after six days on the run, and the grey, misty drizzle doesn't raise spirits. Then a lot of walking and GVs [general views] in the crowded marketplace of the Rue Mouffetard. The smells of the food from the various stalls is agonisingly, achingly tempting and irresistible, but we keep on the move until midday – then across to Les Invalides for the last sequence of the week, and the one I'm least looking forward to.

I'm to join in a game called Ultimate Frisbee, which is played largely by young Americans in Paris. I have the wrong shoes, so slip and slither in the mud whilst Nigel [Meakin, cameraman] and David [Turnbull, director] film on with broad grins. The players are a decent lot, caught between the highly competitive game and wanting to know about 'A Fish Called Wanda'. I run around with them – though cautiously mindful of what another heavy fall might do to my recovering ribs – for about half an hour. And that is the end of our Paris shooting, and the end of nearly five weeks' intensive filming and travelling over the past month and a half.

Monday, February 22nd

It's a good feeling to be doing just what you want to be doing, and odd that it happens so rarely. I want to be exactly where I am – at home, among my books and shelves and plants and tables and chairs and garden walls. I'm entirely happy with this late winter weather – cold enough to make the house warm and attractive, bright enough to send sunlight and sharp shadows across my desk, and changeable enough to make staring out of the window less of a waste of time.

In the afternoon I begin work on the Chicago and Michigan sections. I love prowling about the room checking on facts, figures, finding quotes – immersed in my own, wholly controllable activity.

Tuesday, February 23rd

Brisk walk over to Kenwood at half past twelve. First time I've been in the house for a while. It's squeaky clean now and the English Heritage staff are in bottle-green uniforms, and younger women have replaced the silent guardians in black.

The trio of Hals's van den Broecke, Van Dyck's Duke of Richmond and Rembrandt's self-portrait gives me great pleasure – all the more for not having seen them for a while. A small group of early pre-Renaissance work in the Housekeeper's Room – a Memling portrait and a Dieric Bouts and Paris Bordone and a Botticelli amongst them. Culturally recharged I walk back home – the whole round trip in less than two hours.

Amanda from John's office rings – 'poor John' has been misinformed about the fiscal implications of his residence in the USA, and has had to leave the country sharpish; he's currently, Trotsky-like, in Mexico. Lucky man, is my re-action, but Amanda says this is not the way John sees it, 'things don't work there, quite as well as he's used to'.

Then, surprise, surprise, she asks my advice on places John might stay if he were to go to Havana. 'You know he likes his comforts.' The Ambos Mundos is clearly out, but I remember another place on the other side of the Plaza de Armas which was dauntingly expensive and air-conned and posh. She seems very happy with that. 'The other place is Iceland, but there don't seem to be *any* suitable hotels there at all.'

I find this idea of John tax-avoiding his way round the world irresist-ibly bizarre. All he needs is a camera crew and he'd have the money to pay for it.

Wednesday, February 24th

The pleasure of post-filming is still seductive, and the routine I've returned to still feels fresh, so I remain in good spirits and happy to be working at the Hemingway book. By 6.30 have pushed a further 1,000 words on.

To supper with neighbours Mary and Sebastian Taylor, who've also invited Ron Lendon and Thelma.[1] So much Gospel Oak Primary chat. Sebastian hoots with laughter as he remembers Ron's head-lice lecture — the screen dominated by a hugely magnified slide of a head louse, and Ron berating the parents. Stories of the psychiatrist mother whose continual demands for special treatment of her son drove Ron to distraction. Later her son lost his teddy bear and she put posters up all over the Heath asking for information leading to the recovery of the teddy. Ron revealed that it had been in his study all the time.

Friday, February 26th

A sad call from Alan Bleasdale, 'just checking one last time' that I haven't changed my dates and can do Brownlow after all. Usual rather appealingly maudlin tone – 'I was talking to Lindsay [Duncan] in New York at six o'clock this morning and she's the same' – and a touch of self-dramatisation. 'I wouldn't worry if this was one of my entertainments – you know, like "Melissa" – but it's one of my biggest, most important things I've ever done.' I can't help. If anything I've less time.

Saturday, February 27th

To Liverpool Street for the 10.30 train to Norwich. We're guests of Mike W-J and Delia[2] at the league game against Sheffield United. Easy journey on efficient, friendly Anglia, then met by Delia and M's driver who whisks us to Carrow Road Stadium.

Meet fellow guests and enter the intricate and convoluted world of football finance. Mike and Delia have sunk a lot of their own money into the club. Through their food industry contacts they have recruited the former Number Two at Sainsbury's as full-time chairman (although he admits to being a Villa supporter).

Quite a good lunch – rillette of pork, fish pie, mango ice cream, Beaujolais

---

1 Ron was the Head of Gospel Oak Primary School during the time our three children were there. Thelma was his partner.
2 Mike Wynn-Jones was a friend from Oxford University days. He married Delia Smith, and the two of them bought Norwich City Football Club.

– then, after coffee, long walk through smoky rooms where the comparatively privileged supporters congregate, and to our seats in the directors' box.

The game is not of great quality. Norwich on top in first half and United do well to hold them to a single goal. Second half United strengthen and an equaliser ten minutes after the start brings the game to life. Any prospect of a return to the Premiership this season looks unlikely for either side.

Sunday, February 28th

Gales and rain forecast so have justified a lie-in. But Helen, on her way out to nine o'clock tennis, proclaims it 'a lovely day' and I know I should take some exercise, especially as I can feel a cold settling in and getting me down.

Ablutions whilst listening to Alastair Cooke on the role of President Wilson at Treaty of Versailles. Thesis – idealist who didn't really know Europe and whose plan laid the seeds for an almost imminent conflict. And he did, apparently, invent the term 'self-determination'.

News in the paper of a report saying the first flowers are blooming six days earlier on average than they were 30 years ago seems reasonable to me. Winter in London seems to have become just a dilution of late autumn and early spring.

Monday, March 1st

March comes in mild and wet and windy. Concentrated day and most productive (in words rather than ideas!) since I began the Chicago, Michigan section of the book last week.

Pick H up outside the Bereavement Service office at King's Cross, and down to TJ and Al's for supper. They've just returned from Wales – 'It *really* rained,' says Terry enthusiastically. We sit in the kitchen over a glass of Cloudy Bay and mull over the wreckage of Python. Terry reminds me that no one officially told Allen Tinkley [American promoter] that the Las Vegas event was off and he sounded a little bruised when TJ called him.

He asks what plans I have after Hemingway. I know he'd like to work on something together. I surprise myself at how little I've thought about it. I suppose my first priority is another novel.

Wednesday, March 3rd

Call JC in Mexico. He's in a hotel on the very southern tip of Baja California ('You know Mexico . . . it's a frightful dump.'). He's 'very fed up' with the people who do the Sainsbury's commercials. They've now cancelled the remaining ones he had to do.

He's intrigued when I tell him TG may be doing a film of 'Don Quixote'. 'I think after "Fear and Loathing" he won't find it easy to raise the money.' I tell John he's been offered 40 million dollars and there's a brief pause and a sharp intake of breath – or perhaps the other way round.

Later in the evening call Allen Tinkley and try to repair some of the damage over the Las Vegas show – which he's twice tried to set up for us, and has twice been let down. Allen is LA-positive about it all so he has not taken it personally and I think regards my call as increasing the possibility that the Pythons might get together again, whereas in fact it's probably the opposite.

Thursday, March 4th

Read through revised Chicago–Michigan section. Run. To Grey Flannel to buy a suit for tonight's dinner with American ambassador.

Police (armed) in the little tiled patio at bottom of steps when we arrive in Holland Park. Met by the Laders (Philip, ambassador, and Linda) with a certain formality from him and easy affability from her. I didn't know that the evening news had been full of the 'Banana Wars' story. US slapping restrictions on imports from UK and Europe in retaliation for European favouring of Caribbean (i.e. non-American) banana producers. Lader had been summoned to the Foreign Office only this afternoon to be ticked off.

A lot of businesspeople there. H and I are in different rooms. She talks to Michael Buerk's wife, and I'm sat between two wives of tycoons. One is Swedish and married to the founder of the Tetra Pak empire (they made huge amounts from inventing the wholly irritating pull-apart milk carton sealings). She lives in East Sussex and loves it. Doesn't want to go back to Sweden, where, she says, 'there are no villages'. Paints a picture of a pretty grim country – without village communities, or easy access to alcohol! Run by Social Welfare (which she seems to regard as a negative).

After the change-round find myself next to Joanna Lumley on one side and a very spirited lady, married to a diplomat, who comes, to my delight, from Wath-upon-Dearne.

Introduced to a huge Swedish paper magnate. He is tall with snow-white hair, and I see, with some apprehension, wears a hearing aid. So he can talk, which he does with great confidence – this is clearly a man used to being listened to – but cannot necessarily hear your reply. 'What do you think of taxis?' he booms at me. I'm about to launch into a diatribe against Dial-a-Cab, when I realise he means taxes.

So never much chance to talk to JL, though H has met her husband Stephen

[Barlow] and they've sort of bonded as those who are left behind. Stephen says he *is* jealous of Joanna's travels – which is I suppose where he differs from H.

Lader says Blair and Clinton talk three times a week.

We're the last to leave – after banter with Michael Buerk which has Philip Lader shaking his head in admiration. 'You English just say what you like to each other.'

Friday, March 5th

I'm padding into the bathroom in time for pre eight o'clock weather forecast when the phone rings. A couple of minutes later Rachel calls out from the stairs – 'Jeremy's had a baby, a boy.' Whereupon I burst into tears. It just happens. Because the only person I can think of is Angela. My sister, and Jeremy's mother. It's as if the news of what would have been her first grandchild has hit, like an acupuncturist's needle, upon a pressure point that has been untouched for a long time. The wrongness of the baby being born, with Angela not here to share the happiness. It really is too much for me.

Talk briefly to Jeremy, congratulations gush. He sounds exhausted. At the ripe old age of 55 and three-quarters, greatness has been thrust upon me for the first time. I'm a great-uncle. Try it on for size. Don't think I'll use it a lot.

Monday, March 8th

To the gym for the first time since the rib injury. It's now five weeks since the fall and though I'm aware of a slight tenderness if I press the spot, it doesn't stop me. Much encouraged.

To Screen on Baker Street to see 'Festen – the Celebration'. In the end the strength of the acting and the compulsiveness of the story carried it through against all the odds. It packed quite a punch and left a deep impression. The father, the suicide of a daughter, the confession of child abuse – all in polite, respectable middle-class company touched a raw nerve. What do I really know about the cause of Angela's depression? Drive home thoughtfully.

Wednesday, March 10th

Work at book a.m. Run over Heath at midday, and drive down to Spital-fields to see work in progress at the house.[1] Scaffolded back and front and

---

1 In 1997 our son Will, with my help, bought a former Huguenot silk weaver's house in Spital-fields. It dated from 1717 and the aim was to restore it.

corrugated-iron frame over the roof. After two weeks of clearing out the skeleton is now stark and exposed. The ribs, beams and rafters of the roof are a revelation. Foreman says that not only are most of the rafters original (i.e. 1717), but many of them would have been second-hand at the time – so possibly mid-seventeenth century. Very little deterioration and you can see how they've been sawn – planed only on one side to save time, and some of them, which are structural and not intended to be seen, haven't even had the bark taken off.

Thursday, March 11th

To Freud Museum in Maresfield Gardens for launch of Alyce Faye Cleese's book 'How to Manage Your Mother'. It's drizzling as I walk up from the corner of Fitzjohn's Avenue where Helen dropped me off on her way to badminton. As I reach the neat privet hedge outside the house a shining black vintage Rolls-Royce pulls alongside. Two white bouffant hairdos in the back. Wonder if the Queen Mother is coming – which would be the publicity coup of the century.

Nip in ahead of whoever it is. Find TJ bent over a cheque book buying a copy of the book. He looks just like his mum – as he admits in the book. Then the Queen Mother appears, only it's not the Queen Mother, it's Michael Winner, and a blonde of 22 or 23.

Richard Eyre is there, and carefully avoids talking to Winner, who is telling me some story about his meal with Lucian Freud last night and whether or not Freud will paint the Queen. Freud's family inescapable – not only in the museum, but also as Matthew Freud is running the publicity.

Terry O'Neill is very taken with my new haircut – I explain it's Markos's special and that I've given up going to expensive salons and I now have it done at the end of the road. 'For 20 quid,' says Terry, helpfully. Well, £8.50 with tip actually.

Dougie Hayward – big, portly and very friendly – says I'm lucky to have hair to style. He's introduced as the man who makes John's suits. 'Mainly for commercials,' adds Dougie.

Saturday, March 13th

For the first time this year I feel the sun's warmth as I step out into the garden.

In the late afternoon we leave for the Neil Diamond concert at Wembley Arena. This is something I've rather dreaded – so uncool! – but know that I must do for Sherrie's [Levy] sake.

Arrive backstage soon after six o'clock. The band, many of whom have been with him 25 years, seem pleasantly laid-back, like members of a rather exclusive gentleman's club. They're not remotely fazed by Neil-bashing. 'The Bronto-saurus of Slush' the Guardian called him today – whilst grudgingly admiring his chutzpah.

Neil appears in his black sequined shirt and trousers. Even the towels he dabs himself with on stage are black. He is freshly made-up and walks as if he may have just been prised into a corset. He's chatty and informal, but in that slightly detached, pre-performance mode.

The concert itself is as big and noisy as they can make a one-man show. The Arena is packed with 12,000 people who think he's God – well 11,998. The stage revolves, lit by 200 lamps from above – like some huge restless spaceship. We like the later, better known songs, but the whole mass audience experience seems to work against the singing – there can be no intimacy. It's an all-out assault on the senses.

Wednesday, March 24th

Look at a tape found in the NBC vaults of EH being interviewed in The Finca around the time of his Nobel Prize. He's like a rabbit in car headlights. Stiff, unnatural, answering questions like a soldier under interrogation – even reading the commas on the cue-cards. Very sad.

Thursday, March 25th

A BBC crew comes to the house to record my memories of the Python shows in Germany.

Annie [Chamberlain, a New Zealander working temporarily at the office] comes round to do letters and at a quarter to four I go down to see Debbie and Kieser [Bernard Kieser my dentist, Deborah his nurse] for regular check-up. Kieser is a little worried about some new areas of puffiness and asks if I'm under stress at the moment. My answer is not more than usual, and, as I'm enjoying what I'm doing, it is constructive pressure I'm under. Book in for one month's time. I need a period when I won't have to move my jaw too much.

Home, only to find as I check on the word processor, that the corrections I've spent half the day doing have not been saved. Fortunately, we've been in-vited round to the Loncraines' [film director Richard Loncraine]. Very good food, cooked by Richard and much laughter. Meg Ryan and Dennis Quaid were at his table quite recently. Dennis ate the entire chicken dish which was meant for everybody.

Second night of NATO bombing action against Milosevic. Like the contin-ued air-strikes in Iraq, absolutely no one knows what will be achieved.

Friday, March 26th

Dream that my teeth are falling out due to worry! Wake unrested, but to my relief discover that my corrected copy for the Italy chapter has not been entirely wiped, and is on the disk after all.

Spend evening in trying to bone up on history of Kosovo as my country attacks their country (on their behalf) for the third night.

Sunday, March 28th

Listen to news and views on the war in Kosovo. People speak out freely on either side and every opinion represented – which I suppose makes it different in some way from most other twentieth-century wars. Most eloquent testimony is from a Serbian playwright, sacked from her job by Milosevic, who reads excerpts from a diary she has kept since the raids began last Wednesday – quiet, calm, resigned but above all confused – 'Killing to stop the killing?'

A man from a charity organisation quotes the statistic that since the end of the First World War there have only been 14 minutes when a war was not being fought somewhere in the world.

Monday, March 29th

To work on the next section of Hemingway Adventure book – France, well Paris, specifically. A well-trodden area and one I'm least looking forward to. Requires a lot of reading, too. Once again, I'm aware of the weight of Hemingway research and published material leaning against my door.

Break off at half past four and go to the gym. Longer session than usual. Time to try all the tortures.

More bombings, more destruction in Kosovo. No solutions or climb-downs. Milosevic, like Saddam Hussein, survives and is, if anything, strengthened in his own country.

Tuesday, March 30th

Warning of a new computer virus, affecting Microsoft Word, and called Melissa – the other strand is called, ironically, Papa. The virus strikes through unsolicited email which comes labelled 'important message' and containing the name of someone I know. If I click and accept its offer I receive pages of pornographic sites. Delete and hope I've done the ~~wrong~~ right thing. (Freudian slip!)

Saturday, April 3rd

Around 5.10 in the afternoon the doorbell goes, it's the Kentish Town police. H and I are both here. I expect it to be some small-time Oak Village matter but they look solemn and ask if they can come in.

'Is anything wrong?' H asks.

'Well . . .' says the older, taller copper, with a trustful, pleasant, tanned face. He's holding his cap I notice.

'Is it the children?'

He nods. It all seems to be going in slow motion.

'It's Thomas,' he says next.

For a moment mangled bodies and wreckage spin into my mind, but it's not an accident. His wallet and credit card have been found near Swanage and his car has been located, locked, in a car park overnight. He cannot be found.

I tell them he's gone climbing and camping and when I mention that he's with three friends they are visibly relieved. They will try and glean more information from the Wilts and Dorset force, such as where the wallet was found, and let me know.

The police depart. Both of us are a little unsteady, mentally and physically, and try to make sense of what might have happened. The already grey day darkens fast. There's nothing we can do but wait.

About 55 minutes after the police have gone there's a call from Kentish Town. Tom has been found, he's safe. An hour after the whole scare began, I hear Tom's voice. He sounds a little bewildered by the fuss. He was watching a chopper prowling the cliffs when a coastal rescue man came by. Tom asked him what was going on and received the memorable reply – 'They're looking for someone called Tom Palin.' There had been no danger and no emergency. His coat had been picked up where he had left it – beside their tents at the top of the cliff – as they went for a short climb. So normal service resumed at No. 4 after this frightening hiccup.

But it's not quite over. First the Sunday Times, then the Sunday Telegraph call for details of a wire story about my son. Am as polite and informative as I can be and play down the whole incident. Hope it works.

Sunday, April 11th

I look at the assembly for the first of the Hem programmes. Pleased by the quality of the shooting and the editing and some unusual and idiosyncratic direction. But the bad jokes are still bad jokes, and there are too many of them. At the moment though, my feeling's one of relief.

In early evening out to present a BAFTA Film Award. A stretch Mercedes blocks most of Julia Street. H and Rachel and Elsie (one of our cats) wave me off.

The bash this year is at the Islington Design Centre. It's a big, soulless place, which has the room, but lacks the curious intimacy of the Dorchester or the Great Room at the Grosvenor. This is more like a political rally, everyone in serried ranks.

Jonathan Ross presents the whole thing like a naughty schoolboy. I'm called from my table after the first few awards and taken to an 'assembly point' back-stage. Tall black drapes, a table full of what look suspiciously like non-alcoholic beverages, a big fruit basket, lots of women with headsets and Martin Clunes and Andie MacDowell.

'I need a cigarette,' growls Andie MacD, Clunes obliges with a deft flick of a pack – the sort of gesture you don't see much in these healthily correct days. 'I gave up for seven months,' says MacDowell, unasked.

Then, down the steps, clutching an envelope and someone else's BAFTA. A lot of people out there – filmmakers and freeloaders as far as the eye can see. My Best Original Screenplay Award goes not to Tom Stoppard for 'Shakespeare in Love' but to Andrew Niccol who wrote 'The Truman Show'. He's a short, very young New Zealander who despite winning an award for words seems quite uneasy delivering them.

Friday, April 16th

Lots of marks on the desk diary today. Our 33rd wedding anniversary, Spike's [Milligan] 81st birthday, delivery day for Paris and Spain copy. I'm prepared for all of them, except Spike's 81st which I've missed by a day.

Mary and Edward come round and we have takeaway from the Fleet Tandoori. A toast to our 33 years together. I worked out that it is 40 years ago this August since we met. I told Rachel this on the phone today. 'Forty years since our first snog.' She was rather disgusted. 'I don't want to know that!' Edward replied wittily, 'How long since your last one?'

Tuesday, April 20th

To BAFTA in Piccadilly, for an RTS dinner in honour of John Hendricks of Discovery Channel. David Attenborough at the door looking young – he got my tickets by mistake. 'You'll have to go, I'm afraid,' he says. We talk books – and circulations and sales figures, as ever. He jokes that three shows isn't enough to sell a book. I tell him we've got orders already, which he seems to find remarkable.

When we're all suitably warmed up, the doors are opened and we're herded through from the claustrophobic reception area to the only slightly less claustrophobic dining area. Three fellowships are awarded (after the first course) followed by another orgy of buttonholing. Paul Hamann [producer] comes and talks business to Yentob, right across me. Jaci Stephen assaults David Attenborough – grabbing him by the head and pushing his face into her cleavage. It starts by being very funny and becomes rather grotesque.

Hendricks's speech is affable, full of good intentions and the wonderful promise of new technology – interactive TV being the 'third great communications revolution'. Can't remember the other two.

Saturday, April 24th

Last two days of the Ingres exhibition at the National so decide to catch it at opening time. Will comes along with me for the ride, though he's already seen it. Queues of people with same idea as mine, and Will's reaction was that it wasn't worth a half-hour wait; so miss Ingres, but take in a small Rogier van der Weyden exhibition. Further evidence that painting was big business in the late Middle Ages – Rogier and his family produced steady output from a big workshop in Brussels – and (favourite theme of mine) how much change the paintings we see now have gone through – underpainted, overpainted, recoloured, restored, cut up, separated from other elements of the work – as in fragments of triptychs and diptychs and altarpieces.

Then to the East Gallery – Cézannes and blazing Van Goghs. An hour of solid pleasure in the gallery and no queues.

News of a nail-bomb explosion in Brick Lane, a further nasty twist in a month of dreadful news.

Monday, April 26th

Helene [our cleaner] calls. Have I heard the news? Oh, no, here we go again, I hardly can listen. Jill Dando murdered at the door of her house. It's outrageous, barely believable. The month has gone out of its mind surely. But it's true. Jill Dando, that comfortable, slightly anodyne, likeable figure seemed as immortal as anyone. A newsreader who announces tragedies doesn't get involved in them.

Friday, April 30th

Up before seven, to visit the site at Hanbury Street with Will. Odd feeling to arrive knowing that since last Saturday it is more than just another part of London, but now known nationally as the place where the second terrorist bomb of the right-wing blitz of April '99 went off. Mick, the foreman, told me that originally the bomb was left in a bag on the corner of Hanbury and Wilkes, less than 50 yards from the house.

But this morning all is calm – rubbish left out all night for the early morning collection has been tipped over and broken into, neither of the parking meters I try work, but the building team are at their breakfast, and afterwards Mick shows me round.

The scaffold will be down in the next week. The roof is ready to be tiled, and much work has been done on the back wall, new brickwork blended in with the old by a process called sooting – 'Quite common,' says Mick with infectious enthusiasm – 'we get the sweep round, ask him to leave the soot and we brush it onto the walls.'

Back home by 9.30. Rachel brings us the last ghastly bit of April news. A bomb has exploded in a pub in Old Compton Street (one of my favourite parts of the new lively London); people killed. Third of the racist bombs confirms their trilogy of hate – blacks, Pakistanis, gays.

To the King's Head to see 'A Saint She Ain't' – latest Denis King/Vosburgh show. The show is consistently funny, with lovely surreal lines like Snaveley Bogle (W.C. Fields played by Barry Cryer), 'I wouldn't drink that with a pair of rented lips.'

Thursday, May 13th

Apparently the viewing for Eddie [Mirzoeff, Head of Documentaries] yesterday went very well. He was shown big episode two and felt moved enough to call the scheduler then and there to ask how they would view the possibility of an extra show. Their response was positive and apparently word was that the series will be slotted in sometime during October, probably Sunday nights. All good news – tapes are to be sent round to me. David has come up with a title, which is the first one that has caught my fancy, 'Michael Palin's Hemingway Adventure'.

A quick look at the trailer for PBS that Martha [Wailes, our producer] has helped assemble. Good, bright, lively – only one shot of me looking seriously old.

Monday, May 17th

To Broadcasting House to read an appeal for a small charity called Prisoners' Families Support Groups. Heavy security following Dando murder and threats to high-ups in the Corp re: Serb retaliations, etc.

Two readings and they're happy. Walk to Tavistock Street, passing the Admiral Duncan pub in Old Compton Street for first time since the bombing. Lilac painted wooden screen behind which I can see hard-hatted figures working away by the light of bare bulbs. They're smiling, cheerful as builders are – working in what was so recently a deathtrap.

At the office – the crew all together again, for first time in nearly eight weeks. Discuss the new title. Seems a slow burner, but no strongly negative responses. I'm wary of 'MP's Hemingway Adventure' for the book, but I'm not quite sure why. Michael Dover [my publisher] will talk to his people and gauge reactions.

Then some letters with Anne [James, my manager] and off to Ladbroke Arms for a beak dip with Roger [Mills, co-director of Around the World in Eighty Days, Pole to Pole and Full Circle]. In the course of our conversation – as usual bemoaning the state of TV generally (Roger is finding Channel 4 frustratingly vague – 'We want it to be about race, but not about race, if you see what I mean,' one said about his Army prog) – talk turns to the Sahara idea and I realise that Roger wants to do it with me, and for a moment it seems so easy – work on new novel in 2000 whilst all recces are being done, then shoot Sahara in 2001 for 2002 transmission. Because of the change of millennium the date talk sounds faintly ridiculous, as if we're planning something light years away.

Tuesday, May 18th

Wet and windy morning. Take Rachel to work as I have a Python Night meeting with Ralph Lee a few floors above her at the BBC's new office block at White City.[1] I find the size of the place quite alarming. Crowds of workers pour out of White City Station heading for the newly built aluminium grey block; the car parks spread wide – much wider than anything at old TV Centre, over the ground on which the White City Stadium once stood. High security; so bags checked, passes issued and stamped – to be worn at all times with instructions to staff to challenge anyone not wearing one. And everyone seems so young – roles reversed from 33 years ago when I first joined the crowds at TV Centre.

1 Python Night was a 30th anniversary documentary, directed by Elaine Shepherd. Ralph Lee was one of the producer/directors assigned to gather material.

A good viewing of the possible sketches we can use next month. At the end of it, it seems clear to me that we have quite enough to do in West London without trekking up to Scotland, Yorkshire or Norfolk. But the It's Man walking into the sea at Poole Harbour is eye-catching and unusual enough to stay in consideration.

At midday, along the corridors past 'Timewatch' and 'Reputations' to see Paul Hamann. His office is tidy, spacious and decorated and furnished almost entirely in black. It's like a rather sophisticated cave and I'm not terribly comfortable sinking back on a squeaky black sofa to say my bit about our proposed new series title with Paul sprawling at me opposite. But I bring him up to date – mention possibility of a fourth show and float the Sahara idea again – he wants to meet and talk this over with Peter Salmon in June.

Then down to the ground floor to see where Rachel works. It isn't a pretty place at all, with much less light down here, and the same cramped, functional set-up of workstations in a limbo-land of partitions and floor space. Meet her colleagues – all female. Her boss Sue seems very bright and sparky.

Friday, May 21st: Paris–London

Push aside the long thick curtains and look out over narrow quiet Rue Christine with its arthouse cinema and sought-after Jacques Cagna eatery opposite.[1] Lean out and peer up – overcast but dry skies.

I think I have enough material to write up the walk, so will treat myself to some art before catching the train home. Rumours of strikes – which already affect the major national collections, but reception tell me the Modern Art Museum of Paris, over on the Right Bank, is open.

The collection, just down the road from Iéna station, is housed in a partly abandoned pavilion in '30s modernist style, built for an exhibition. A cold, rather abrasive space, but the big white walls offer room and air and the paintings look very good here. Huge Delaunays, fine Légers and Picassos. My eye much taken by a painting of barges on the Seine by Derain; from a bridge looking down as the barges emerge into a rich, complicated, beautiful spread of colours.

Back to the hotel and cab to Gare du Nord. Finish the stimulating, rewarding V. Woolf biog. As Virginia slipped under the Ouse, we slip under the Channel. The way her death was treated was oddly comforting in view of my sister Angela's death. No judgements made. The suicide as a rational act of an intelligent woman. Her last note to Leonard W showed how sharp and direct and crystal clear her writing could be, even in extremis.

1 I'm in Paris to research and write a Hemingway walk for *Time Out*'s Paris guide.

Sunday, May 23rd

To the Springsteen concert at Earl's Court. The compromises you have to make for even the best organised pop concert – distorted sound, hard seats, unpunctuality and the sheer weight of numbers, is just about worth it tonight. But only just. Bruce's energy, at 50, is demonic. He's a driven man and though he moves less about the stage, his voice is pushed to the limits. Unfortunately so are the Earl's Court acoustics.

Still, to see the E Street Band in full glory is quite something. Five guitars, at one point, arrayed along the front of the stage like gladiators. The audience was enthusiastic but never dangerous, quite a few Sloanes mixed in with the crop-headed workers round us. We leave as 'Born to Run' is being thrashed out, but though H is bewildered, I've been happy enough just to see and hear Clarence Clemons' sax solos, live after 23 years!

Monday, May 24th

To Covent Garden for a meeting called by Martha to talk about future filming plans. Difficult to pin anything down until we know if we are to push for three or four shows. General feeling is that we have four, but the protocol seems to demand a delay until Eddie M comes back from holiday to look at an assembly.

Wednesday, May 26th

Peter Salmon called around six and has agreed to the 'Hemingway Adventure' title and seems accommodating over the extended series. So, I think from now on we're thinking of four programmes – and all the extra work that that entails.

Thursday, May 27th

To the office. It's the nearest we've had this year to a hot day, mid to upper 70s – everyone suddenly driving as if they're in a Hollywood movie – roofs open, stereos blaring, fat forearms hung over the doors, corners taken just a little wider than usual.

Upstairs first to the Hemingway office. They have made up a new schedule to cover the extra Key West filming needed for the extra programme. September is now full, three more weeks added to my schedule, but if we are serious about four programmes then there is little option.

Watch first of the 'Windrush' series on West Indian immigration. Very good and quite hard-hitting.

Sunday, May 30th

Basil here at ten with the first layouts of the book. I have a real feeling, as I turn the pages, of being enveloped by the visual material – just the right feelings and atmospheres come through – and apart from a tiny number of pictures that could be better placed, they harmonise well with the text. Some big spreads are quite breathtaking.

Monday, May 31st

Tom Dunne [publisher at St Martin's Press] comes to lunch. We talk about the future. I realise that Tom, urbane and intelligent and experienced as he is, is not really interested in angst or revelation or anything 'dark or deep' as he puts it. He's firmly of the opinion that if I write another novel it should be about the English and Englishness and should be funny and should possibly be historical too.

It sets me thinking – maybe it would be much easier if I took a 'Ripping Yarns'-style approach to a new novel. Maybe the Biggles in retirement idea that I talked to David T [Turnbull] about in Kenya.

Rewrite, learn, rewrite, learn, the opening lines which we shoot, weather permitting, on Southwold beach tomorrow.

Tuesday, June 1st: London–Southwold

Basil can't believe Southwold and immediately christens it Pleasantville. It certainly does seem to have exactly the same sort of people wearing exactly the same sort of clothes (no shell-suits here) as it did when I met H here 40 years ago.

Running with the horns after me goes well – we even film in the churchyard, only a few yards away from Mum and Dad's grave. However, whilst making one spectacular leap through the crowd into the High Street I feel a muscle pull at the top of my right thigh. Very irritating as there is a lot more running to do. Whilst crew lunch at the Lord Nelson, I sit up in Room 19 with a bag of ice on my thigh.

In the afternoon we break off from the running to shoot me reading Hemingway in a deckchair opening sequence on the beach. The sun is out and children build sandcastles and run into the sea, but the east wind is sharp and quite cold. The camera is on the end of a remote control rig. It takes forever to get a fairly simple move right. Nineteen takes eventually.

The pain in my leg is increasing. Much talk over dinner in the Swan as to whether it's a groin or thigh injury. The word 'groyne' appears all over the beach, causing much amusement – especially one which warns: 'Beware, Derelict Groynes'.

A walk round the old haunts after dinner – up Godyll Road and across the Common. The way I went on the night Mother died. Sit on the seat that bears her name, outside the Red Cross hut.

Wednesday, June 2nd: Southwold–London

Did I dream or was I awake when I was trying to remember my mother's voice, and found it elusive and regretted very much that I had no recording of her, or my father?

My thigh muscle has responded to the ice pack, and the first running shots we do – up the stairs of the Swan Hotel – pass by without further damage.

Back up to London with Laura [Tutt, our researcher] and Martha, traffic heavy.

Phone rings constantly for an hour or so. JC is back in London and asks me to watch the England–Sweden game with him on Saturday. I assume this involves a trip to Wembley and can't really face crowds and stadiums, but JC laughs – he's one week away from his hip replacement and in no shape to move from his sitting room chair. So, agree to meet.

Friday, June 4th

To Three Mills Island just beyond Bow. A complex of good-looking Victorian brick buildings, once a gin distillery, beside the River Lea. Bought up and restored by Edwin Shirley, transporter of rock bands. There is a tall hangar beside the buildings where the acts which will fill the Millennium Dome are being rehearsed. Find our studio, where the lavatory set is being rigged for the Hem skylight sequence. [EH pulled what he thought was a lavatory flush, but it was a skylight. He tugged so vigorously it fell onto his head, wounding him quite badly.]

There is much jesting about the falling camera shot and I suggest (without mentioning his name) that it might have been easier to do it the way TG suggested last night – pull the camera up and out and reverse the film.

Long time setting up the first shot, through the skylight. Fortunately I've brought work to do and I sit in the canteen by the river, looking out at a big spreading willow tree, an Underground railway line and the monolithic silver needle of Canary Wharf beyond. Squally rain and wind spatter the windows, a group of young female dancers chatters away at another table. Members of the unit appear at regular intervals to apologise for the delay.

Charlie Higson passes as I'm waiting outside the studio. He's written and is directing a 'Randall and Hopkirk (Deceased)' remake with Vic [Reeves] and Bob [Mortimer]. I like him. He's pro-BBC and cares a lot about the quality of the work. Laura interrupts to ask me in for the shot.

The moment of truth arrives. Feel quite uncomfortable with this contraption thundering down towards me but get on with it. A good take. They want one more, without my arms going up to shield my face. On 'Action!' down it comes. There is a thud and I feel a sharp pain as the camera hits my head.

I don't fall, but reel out of the set into the surrounding darkness with blood spilling through my fingers. Laid on a chair, head back to stop the bleeding. Aware of the awful awkward silence around me. This is the Special Effects man's nightmare and he's on the verge of tears. 'Never . . . nothing like this ever happened before,' he blurts out, and I feel more sorry for him than myself. 'No one's fault, no one's fault,' is all I can say to him, but it can't mean that much. He knows it is his fault.

JJ [Odedra, our assistant cameraman] rushes off to fetch the unit nurse from 'Randall and Hopkirk'. He arrives within five minutes, examines the wound which is about four and a half centimetres long, curved in the shape of the lens, and running from just above my hairline down across my left forehead. The same damn spot as Hem's!

Martha and Laura take me in the car to the Royal London, a mile or two down the Bow Road (having first taken me to the Royal London Psychiatric Hospital by mistake!). A large Scottish nurse called Liz takes a look at me and decides stitches are needed if they're to minimise the damage. So I lie back and she chatters on about how she *loves* stitching, and by the time I'm done there are eleven stitches (two more than Hemingway's!) *and* some glue.

Discharged within an hour. They have all been calm and good-humoured and the neatness of the stitching is quite beyond reproach. Back to the studios to complete the sequence and try and reassure all concerned that I'm fine.

Saturday, June 5th

Slept well without headache or any other discomfort – that end-of-filming sleep when all the stresses and strains recede.

Over to Holland Park to watch the England–Sweden Euro 2000 qualifier. Is it my imagination or is Portobello Road twice as busy since 'Notting Hill' opened?

The tension between John and the world around him is palpable even before we've said hello. It's all to do with gates and buzzers and instructions. One gate works but JC is upstairs and has to come all the way down to open the other so I can bring my car in. A fan is somehow involved in this pantomime. 'I can't believe it,' he goggles. 'I've just been swimming and I was walking home . . .'

'Are we into autographs?' John hisses rather testily at me from the front door. Autographs given, car driven inside – but fan *also* inside and has to be let out.

The house has been altered yet again, it is very comfortable and soft and woody and I glimpse a dressing room with partitioned open shelves each stacked with expensive knitwear, sweaters, shirts. At the very top is the television room. Under the eaves, with a small workroom next door. Enveloped by a soft, multi-cushioned sofa is Steve, a professor from Los Angeles who looks earnest and is earnest..

The game is awful. England truculent and ineffective, lacking skill, co-ordination and passion. Swedes tolerate dreadful fouls without much retaliation. Scholes becomes first English player ever sent off in a home international. It comes on to rain at the end. JC's masseur arrives and the afternoon is wound up.

Not before JC has announced that he's fed up with Terry Gilliam being rude about him in the press. 'He called me a control freak,' JC complains, 'which is pretty good coming from a director.' Then he smiles his winning smile and becomes lovely and friendly and asks me to sign a copy of 'Full Circle' for him. I leave him two bottles of wine and a book called 'Eccentric Explorers'.

Sunday, June 6th

Ate up hours of sleep, but a great brown/black stain has appeared on my right thigh at or near the point where something went 'ping!' last Tuesday in South-wold. A blood vessel must have burst and sent its contents spilling and spreading beneath the skin.

I watch the assembly of what is likely to be prog four of the 'Hem Adventure'. If I had wanted this to confirm once and for all that we have four shows then I'm disappointed. Cuba looks good, is well-edited, but very little happens and people might well get irritated at MP just being there.

Monday, June 7th

Tender was the night. Right thigh still marked by great slab of aubergine.

Have promised TJ and the BBC two or three days' work on the Fegg radio script this week, and of course, now this long-delayed moment has come it's the wrong moment. The Hemingway series hasn't conveniently stopped its demands during May and June. It lurks and seems to grow – the shape of the series, Basil's requirements for the book – captions, intros, etcetera. My speech, various bits of writing. And here I am, at 9.15, stuck in traffic between the British Library and St Pancras for more than ten minutes. Almost an hour after setting out to get down to TJ's.

I don't know when we last wrote together, but it doesn't feel that long once we get down to it, and the pattern of co-operation establishes itself quite easily and naturally.

Wednesday, June 9th

Call JC who goes into hospital tomorrow to have his hip replacement. Wish him well. He's watching his side Somerset being mangled by Gloucestershire and is in mental and physical pain.

Pick up and swift delivery to 6 Hamilton Place, off Hyde Park Corner, where I'm to be honoured with a Soap Box Award. Small, wedding-style atmosphere. Most guests of our age or over.

Barry Cryer (one of the previous winners – along with Maureen L [Lipman] and David Frost who has come along as a guest. He casts a slightly bored and misanthropic eye around.

The occupational hazard of after-dinner speaking (which is why I so rarely do it) is that you can only ever half-enjoy the pre-speech proceedings, as you have to remain relatively sober and a little tense all evening. Tonight, what with drinks, the meal, a long-drawn-out raffle and two prior speeches, I'm in this hot, noisy company making polite conversation for three and a half hours before I'm finally called to my feet.

Barry chats up H and tells her how he'd thought when he first met me that I was far too nice to succeed in the hard showbiz world. I suppose he was right in a way. Pythons created our own world, which I did again with the travels.

My speech starts wonderfully then takes a dive and I'm stuck in a central section which for one reason or another (too personal, too reflective, too gentle for this audience boozed and hyped-up by the auction) doesn't play. It irks me because I know I could and should have done better. Helen says it was fine, and the evening raised £32,000, the highest ever, so the organisers are pleased.

Thursday, June 10th

Have my stitches removed by nurse at the Health Centre. She's a perfect complement to Liz Prentice at the Royal London who sewed me up. 'I love taking stitches out,' she says. She also checks my blood pressure. Down to 115/68 (which compares to Hemingway's at 56, of 158 over 68 – which was his best for some time!).

Sunday, June 13th

To see John who is having a hip replacement. Collect some goodies from Villandry, then, as instructed, get him a caffé latte at Patisserie Val.

By the time I get back to the King Edward VII Hospital for Officers and Comedians, as we've dubbed it, the coffee has overflowed and burst the bag and JC is on the loo. When he emerges he looks enormous. Combination of voluminous hospital gown and mighty pair of crutches make him look like some Mayan god-priest. Iain Johnstone, his Boswell, is in attendance and it's a bit of a squash for us in a cubicle of a room with plaque of some officer over the bed.

Whilst we're there TJ calls and delights John by telling him that ten months of hip pain came to an end the very day JC went into hospital.

Friday, June 18th

Driven to Sloane Square for WHSmith signing. A lively signing – lots of tourists – Japanese, American, Belgian, Italian, Polish (when will you come to Poland? Very soon, I hope), and afterwards to Harvey Nick's fifth floor for lunch and a chat with Zsuzsanna [Zsohar, my BBC Books publicist] about the rest of the year.

Eric Idle is coming over in early October for a week's publicity on his novel – 'Road to Mars' – and with the connivance of his publishers would like to do some event with me.

So to the two radio interviews for the BBC books. Walk up scummy pavements of East Oxford Street to Talk Radio where a hopeless interview is conducted by a giggling lady, giving every appearance of being high on something. Inane piece, in filthy surroundings, with not so much as a tea or a coffee offered. Truly appalling place, but at least I didn't have to meet Kelvin MacKenzie [editor of the Sun].

Walk backstreets to the BBC for Des Lynam interview. Des not as comfortable with radio as TV, and with his grey hair disarranged by the headset looks more like a mad professor than a sex god. It's his last show for a while and he's quite demob happy. We have an amiable chat but I'm a little fuzzy from the day's activity, and find it hard to get the words out smoothly.

Sunday, June 20th

After breakfast down to Marylebone, collect a couple of coffees and drop in on JC. He's with the nurse, would I wait in the library. There is a plaque above the door which notes that I am sitting in the room in which Queen Elizabeth II accepted the resignation of Harold Macmillan in October 1963.

Up to see John. He's on his own; wind blows through the net curtains and out the open door into the corridor, cleanliness before privacy. He comes out tomorrow. He occasionally notes down some thought that's occurred to him or some remark I've made. Turns out he's keeping notes for a book to be compiled 'over the next two or three years' to be called 'So Anyway' – little memoirs, a few funny stories and 'some of the little tricks they play on you in television interviews; like the size of the chair'.

Monday, June 21st

Prepare for the Monty Python Week filming which begins tomorrow with 'Pythonland'. My own contribution to the Python Night. A little nervous – a lot of different aspects to the exercise. I hope they will all gel and it won't be a mishmash of styles.

Tuesday, June 22nd

Bright sunshine as I'm collected at 7.30 and driven to Ham House where we all assembled for Day 1 of Python's on-screen existence on July 8th 1969. Just two weeks short of 30 years ago.

Rest of the day we revisit sites like Ullswater Road ('Seduced Milkman') and South Ealing Road ('Climbing the Uxbridge Road').

Bleasdale has called and I ring him back. He's at home. 'Oliver T' is going well. Michael Kitchen is playing Brownlow. Alan waxes sentimental over me and how much he wanted me – he apparently let Kitchen know he was stepping into my shoes (which seems unfair – especially as Kitchen is a wonderful actor). I ask him if he got to Prague for the filming. He rumbles painfully. 'Almost. I got as far as Brussels.' Evidently there had been some Channel port blockade and this had rattled AB's already tenuous faith in the transport process – so he just turned round and came home.

Wednesday, June 23rd

Swept through maze-like backstreet run to Thorpebank Road W12 to begin day's filming at the shop from which JC emerged and gave the world the first view of a Silly Walk. Now it's a house (the shop burnt down in '86) and we doorstep the tenants – a lovely, lively art student and her somewhat more Sloaney friend. They make my job very easy.

Then on around London – use a Routemaster Bus to recreate Bicycle Repair Man moments.

Finish at 5.30 in a launderette near Shepherd's Bush. Meet an Ethiopian outside – he shakes my hand vigorously – he and his Ethiopian friends have a great deal of praise for my 'Pole to Pole' visit to their country. They were especially grateful for the fact that we were so un-slanted. Usually people, he says, only make films about Ethiopia if there's a famine or a war.

Thursday, June 24th

Last of our three-day shoot on 'Pythonland'. Collected by Mark the PA and Ralph Lee, the director, and driven down to Poole to recreate the first It's Man at Shell Bay. Takes us an hour to get out of London and three and a half hours to the ferry at Poole.

Across on the ferry. Shell Bay Beach is part of National Trust – we cross reed-beds and dunes before we get to the spot.

This is a tricky sequence as I have to get my suit completely soaked and really want to complete it in one take. All works well, except that I find it hard to stay submerged at the end of the walk out to sea, and I float to the surface just a little too early for the joke. Decision taken to go with what we have, after running it back on the video screen (would Python have been any better if we'd had instant video replay at Shell Bay in 1969?).

Monday, June 28th

Warm, bright morning. Am filling up the car with various recycling treats. There has been an ambulance and a police car in Elaine Grove for about half an hour. A black van is parked on the corner of Elaine and Oak, and cars have to squeeze very carefully past it.

As I take out one load, I almost bump into two men emerging from the Browns' house with a stretcher, to which is strapped a grey bag, with someone inside. It's a rather chilling moment – everyone and everything involved is in black or dark grey. A sudden monochrome moment. Indoors to tell Helen who is pretty sure it's Mrs Brown.

When I get back from recycling this is confirmed. The dear, jolly, frequently tired and emotional, Irish neighbour we've known 30 years, died in the night, peacefully, and was found by the lodger. I was always bumping into her on that corner. Never again.

Wednesday, June 30th

To the Frost garden party. We take Lin Cook. She's touched that David still invites her now Peter's gone – 'Most people don't,' she says, making me feel a twinge of guilt.

Carlyle Square is like a war zone, with police controlling access as huge Jaguars ease their way in and out, depositing the High and Mighty. It's impossible to describe – for the diarist this is the equivalent of Crewe Junction for a trainspotter.

Heseltine behind me as I go in – doesn't return my smile. Lady Tebbit, in a wheelchair, grasps my arm and tells me how much she loves the programmes. I took to her immediately, and not just because of that.

It's like Madame Tussauds come to life. Tim Brooke-T makes a joke about Margaret Thatcher – only here, the real thing is less than a dozen yards away. Try to make sure Lin is introduced to everyone and to avoid Widow of Famous Person syndrome, but it isn't easy for her.

On the way out, Prince Andrew and the royal princesses rush by, Fergie in tow. 'We love all your programmes,' she gushes at me, 'I don't care what anyone else says, *we* love them!'

Ronnie Corbett is very funny about the present spate of 'tribute to' programmes. 'I've had enough. I can't do any more praising,' he says.

And I can't get out of my mind the image of crippled Lady Tebbit, her immediate warmth and liveliness, and the photographs of the man who planted the bomb that had done the damage being let out of prison in Ireland earlier in the week.

Thursday, July 1st

Up at ten past seven. Cab to the new Tate Gallery of Modern Art site at Bankside for one of the pre-opening breakfast visits.

Rosie Boycott's mobile goes off in the middle of the Swedish curator's opening remarks. Rosie then moves into a room behind and carries on a conversation more deafening than the original call.

The building is terrific. Massive, blank walls of dark brick. A huge interior space – the Turbine Room, the galleries stepped up around the walls, so this great central space is preserved. A broad view directly out towards St Paul's. The new footbridge will enhance the drab waterfront on the North Bank and the gardens will do the same for the South. The Globe Theatre nestles beside the power station down to the east.

Walk back along the river and am much excited by the way London feels and looks now. I think we're entering one of the best times for city building – enhancement of existing good buildings, like Somerset House, imaginative conversions like Bankside plus prospect of new and original work like the City offices down by Tower Bridge. Knock-on effect of regeneration and liveliness in the areas surrounding.

To Leicester Square, to talk about 'MPHA' at a BBC Video launch. Unfortunately they get the trailers muddled up and having announced a wonderful new programme about dinosaurs they show me walking into an office. I leap out from behind the curtain and shout 'I'm not a dinosaur! Yet.' Young audience, quite hard to make them laugh. I realise that I'm growing away from these people. Our references aren't the same. I'm an old person.

Friday, July 2nd

Lots of glum voices. Evidently Sinn Fein has given an historic commitment to peace and decommissioning by May 2000, much more positive than anything so far. The Unionists once again are shown to be negative in their response and Drumcree comes up on Sunday with the Orange Order determined to resist the law once again. I'm afraid it all has Custer's Last Stand written across it. The extreme Unionists are moving resolutely against change like an army marching bravely on to the enemy guns. How long it will take to finish them off as a serious political threat remains to be seen.

Saturday, July 3rd

Flurry of telephone activity. An interview re Hem book with Corrine Gotch, who organised the Network conference in Cambridge last Monday, forces me into first serious consideration of what I'm going to say to all these Hemingway questions with which my life will be filled from now on.

Zsuzsanna calls. She met with Radio Times editor (Sue Robinson). They want to do a 'Hemingway Adventure' cover. More intriguingly, they have had word that 'MPHA' will premiere in week of October 5th – the same week as

Python Night on BBC Two. It will be very rum if I scoop the cover on Python's 30th Anniversary.

Friday, July 30th

Round to André's [Jacquemin, composer and soundman] to record a special version of 'Finland' for Dhani Harrison on Sunday. André locates and isolates the backing track to the original 'Finland' which fits my new version 'Henley! Henley! Henley!'

Sunday, August 1st

H and I gird up our loins, despite enervating heat, and make our way to Henley for Dhani Harrison's 21st.

I think the 'formal' meal, in a long, white, windowed pavilion of a marquee at the front of the house, is the hardest bit for George. He's not easy with large gatherings and hates having to behave in what he sees as an unnaturally conventional way.

George now spends nearly all his time in the garden; he's spent weeks moving boulders around with a forklift truck to prepare it all for Dhani's great day.

Food is wonderful and original and Gordon Murray, who selected George's wine cellar, has called up a 1978 Margaux and Chateau Montrose, the former heavenly. At the end of the meal there is a hush and a pause and down the steps leading from the house comes a young girl wearing Dhani's present from George. His Sgt Pepper Album costume.

For some reason, around one o'clock, we're all together in a Viking boat plus sail which stands among the trees. George is being very droll, if a little repetitive, and it's all very nice beneath the gibbous orange moon. It's Lammas Night, George tells us, an ancient pagan festival and the night that Dhani was born. The whole evening becomes more and more fairytale-like as we repair to an Arabian tent by the swimming pool for a birthday cake – which arrives about 1.15.

Friday, August 6th

Have organised some tickets for Eddie Izzard's 'Lenny' which is at the end of two weeks of previews. Terry G and Maggie give us a lift down into the steamy, seething West End, and we meet TJ and Al at the theatre.

Elaborate staging – jazz band, big cast, lots of clever lighting and slide effects – for what is basically a vehicle for Eddie to do Lenny Bruce's stand-up act – which is often indistinguishable from the sort of thing Eddie likes to do anyway.

The biographical element promises well at the beginning. The second half is split between Peter Hall's gimmicky staging and Eddie's wonderful monologues. As they say in American TV show previews – some nudity. Well, quite a lot, really. Eddie Izzard's willy is prominent. And often not necessary!

Backstage to see Eddie. He looks small without his heels. Peter H is giving notes. He seems big, slow, moves with difficulty and one of his eyes is half-closed. 'There are still bastards out there telling us what we should or shouldn't say,' is his comment on the relevance of the play to a 1999 audience. But this production doesn't tell us anything new about who they are and why they do what they do, and there's a whole other play to be written about Lenny's drug addiction and the reason why he wrote what he wrote.

It's raining softly as we leave and Shaftesbury Avenue is crowded and damp like a 'Blade Runner' set.

Tuesday, August 10th

In the evening we're invited round to the Cleeses'. Met at the door by Alyce Faye, rather than the maid, as happened for a while and rather put me off. Humphrey Barclay,[1] who is working with JC on some project, is fresh back from LA, unaged apart from a little grey in the curls. David Hatch, a nice, solid, ruddy-faced, decent Englishman is there with his new wife (very new) – Mary, a lovely, likeable lady with a deep raspy voice, independent ideas and great humour. Trevor Nunn, on his own at the moment, Imogen coming later.

During the course of a long, comfortably appointed evening – everything immaculate, well-chosen and looking marvellous – I discover that Trevor Nunn loves to talk. A potentially discussable theme like relativity in artistic appreciation becomes in his hands a 15-ton weight dropped on the dinner table. Even Alyce Faye, with whom I'm enjoying a subversive moment at our end of the table, falls silent, urging me to listen to the wisdom.

On way back H says JC noticed that I hadn't said anything for a while when Trevor N was going on, and he wondered if I might have had a stroke!

1 TV producer who gave me a break in *Do Not Adjust Your Set*.

Wednesday, August 11th

Eclipse day. There is a crowd assembling on Parliament Hill. Mostly young, with picnics. Keen schoolboys cycling up to the Hill, a small number of mothers with children in tow – 'It's going to get dark in a minute!'

H has prepared the pin holes and cards and by 10.40 we can clearly see a slice of the sun's surface being eaten away. By eleven there is cloud cover gathering and within five minutes a thick black cloud has materialised from nowhere, and is heading rapidly for the only patch of sky in which we're interested, the bit with the sun in it.

H and I are up on my roof – and people are popping up on rooftops all over Gospel Oak. No one seems quite sure which way to turn. We've been instructed by the government's advisers not to look at the sun directly, and yet it's unnatural not to want to face the source. As the exact moment of the first total eclipse in Britain since 1927 arrives, I notice, appreciatively, the postman working the street oblivious to the watchers on the rooftops.

To Groucho's for Python script meeting. Terry G has come from an aborted street interview, during which an annoying busker had his guitar smashed by the interviewer who chased him off into Wardour Street and never returned.

We work through the script. Within half an hour TJ is humming loudly as JC politely refuses to see the point of one of his suggested changes. On the whole, though, it's a good session with much laughter and many silly ideas, though I can see JC holding back as the three of us get into wilder excesses – gorillas putting TVs running Eric Idle's monologue up their bottoms, etc.

Thursday, August 12th

Lunch with Rosie Boycott at Christopher's. I'm early, she's late. She's a pixie-like woman who gives the impression of being far too delicate physically to edit a tabloid newspaper. But she doesn't drink and I notice quite distinct bicep bulges beneath her plain white jumper.

As a good editor should, her eyes sweep the room before getting down to a softly delivered hard sell about me being the sort of person people trust and look to as a guide. To where and what?

The millennium is what she has in mind. Would I like to write a weekly diary for the Express as I travel the country and the world on the build-up to the millennium? One side of me thinks it might be interesting to see if my presence on the paper might make a difference, but afterwards my thoughts veer to the very cautious. Why the Express? A paper I never read and have no feelings for. Buy a copy to look at in the taxi home.

Sunday, August 15th

Watch the last 'Larry Sanders Show' – Seinfeld makes appearance halfway through Hank's emotional farewell piece. Inspired. Its gentle, subtle playing makes me despair slightly of the tired old Python ranting which we're lining up for October!

Tuesday, August 24th

In a rapid half-hour's scribbling I pull together the remaining Python links in time for four o'clock meeting at Radical Media.

Arrive early, chat with Ray, then JC and Terry J arrive (Gilliam cannot be traced, but is believed to be in Spain) and we plough through the script once again. JC in generally ameliorative mood; he likes the new links I've written and I seem to have sold the gorillas idea to him.

Roger S [Saunders, from the Python office] comes round for a business catch-up. JC gets a little testy over new demands on his time but is generally a picture of co-operation and conciliation. (He's vexed though about the amount of newspaper space devoted to the Turkish earthquake – despite the fact that nearly 40,000 are feared dead – 'There's nothing I can do. It's happened.' I ask him what he would like to read about in the paper. 'New things, new ideas. Things that can be changed.')

Wednesday, August 25th

Out in the evening to see 'Copenhagen' at the Duchess. A marvellous, tight, well-played, intelligent and funny play. Three characters, one set, no staging gimmicks – two and a half hours, completely riveting. Made me proud of London theatre. Thoughtful and thrilling. A play you feel in your bones.

Saturday, August 28th

To the National Gallery for the Rembrandt portraits exhibition, called, neatly, 'Rembrandt by Himself'. Down in the bowels of the Sainsbury Wing, so artificial light gives tomb-like feel to the display. And it is quite melancholy. Like Lovis Corinth, Rembrandt was unsparing in his depiction of himself in hard times – though his early portraits show a bit of a dandy.

At the very end of his life Rembrandt looked like W.C. Fields – and it's part of the strength of his painting that he does not have a conventionally attractive face – yet one that is unforgettable.

Drive to the South Bank to catch the Chuck Close exhibition at the Hayward and find a modern up-to-date equivalent of Rembrandt's scouring self-scrutiny. Chuck Close, like Rembrandt, is no oil painting, and unlike Rembrandt he works exclusively on portraits, but his rigorous examination of every detail of the face – every unheroic, distressed detail, has echoes of the powerful later Rembrandts. Less painterly, perhaps, more powerful and, to coin a phrase, in your face, but in some cases equally thrilling.

Work at clearing desk then to Broadcasting House to appear on Radio 4's Saturday afternoon chat show 'Live from London', hosted by Simon Fanshawe. A motley collection we are too – myself, Rosemary Leach, the actress who used to be Ronnie Corbett's mother in 'No, That's Me Over Here' and Jay McInerney, hip New York high-lifer and Brat Pack novelist. I'm sort of a bridge between the two, though I think that how you bridge Rosemary Leach and Jay McInerney is something only God can explain.

Rosemary gets very agitated about the fact that light comic farces are not still played in rep in Britain whilst Jay M is urbane and I talk about eating bull's testicles.

Afterwards Jay and I trade Updike quotes – apparently he's given up drinking, something which he (Updike) described as 'like living in the Midwest'.

Sunday, August 29th

A boy rings the doorbell. Helen holds him at bay for a while. Does Michael Palin live here, sort of thing. Gradually Helen warms towards sending me out with an autograph, then his friend screams 'Michael Palin fucked my bitch' and they run off.

In the evening Rachel's friend Karen's mother comes for dinner. She's a doctor in Northern Ireland. Well-educated, Protestant. Reluctantly she accepts the reality of a United Ireland, and seems to think it will be no more than ten years before the 'demographic' (buzz word in NI) shows a majority of Catholics in the Province, so if Sinn Fein can be patient they will quite quickly win what they want. But, she sighs, in Northern Ireland, the 'psychopaths' can upset any patient, sensible solution.

Wednesday, September 1st

Down to Telecine. New commentary studio. As I squeeze through to my booth I see the rumpled, unshaven figure of Kenneth Branagh in the sound-proof box next door. He's narrating the BBC's 'Dinosaurs' series.

We've had quite a cautious response from PBS [Public Broadcasting in

America, who broke Python in the States in 1974] to prog four. They adamant-
ly reject the 'bullshit' ending at the graveside. Martha suggests we say 'bull',
which is a neat way, hopefully, of keeping both sides happy. They're nervous at
one or two other points – such as me being thrown out of a bar!

Thursday, September 2nd

To the Savoy for lunch with Michael Dover, John Mitchinson, Annabel Merullo [from Orion] and Anne. Michael's thank-you to me for the book. The talk
comes round to future plans.

Mitchinson pitches heavily for a new novel, or any kind of travel writing.
Michael floats the Basil Pao picture book, 'Travels with Palin', on which I'm
not very keen. So much of the ground already covered in photo books and the
existing BBC vols. But I do like the idea of doing some travelling with Bas,
and suggest short books might be the answer – 'Off the Beaten Track' guides
– Burma, Mongolia. Anne immediately sees a TV series and I rather swiftly
knock this one on the head. Just travelling to write would be the point and
pleasure of this one.

Catch a cab in Shaftesbury Avenue. Aware of smoke and smell of something
like a bonfire. Fire engines out in force. It looks as if smoke is drifting up from
the Phoenix Garden area.

Friday, September 3rd

To the gym. Frank Skinner (his name fits his body so well) comes up to me
as I pedal my way through a warm-up. He's been in the paper this week. His
company, Avalon, asked the BBC for £20 million for a five-year contract with
him. Yentob pulled the plug on negotiations.

Comedy has such clout now. Harry Enfield (as mainstream BBC as you
could get) has just signed to do his new series with Sky. Not ITV, Sky. They can
offer huge money for, as yet, very small audiences.

I want to ask Skinner if it was his decision or his management who pushed
him – but a certain etiquette operates amongst the muscle-straining and
grunting.

Talk to TG later. 'Radical Media is no more' – this was where the fire was
last night. It began in the facilities house below them and has burnt the place
out. Lots of TG work on 'Quixote', and Ray Cooper's desk, have gone up in
smoke. Though TG says he's got nearly all of it duplicated. He's now shooting a
one-minute commercial, for which he says he's paid a third of his total fee for
'Fear and Loathing'.

Monday, September 6th

Feel mightily tired. Taking foot off the accelerator this weekend probably to blame. Nevertheless, gird loins, pack bag and take a cab to Frontier Post to fit Commentary 3 and view Prog 4. Work on and through lunch to finish both tasks by 3.30.

An hour to kill so walk across to Tom's studio in the Heal's building. I know Ray C [Cooper] is there with him doing the music track for Terry Gilliam's commercial, and I buy a couple of bottles to cheer him up after the Radical Media fire last week.

Ray gives me graphic account of the fire at Earlham Street and of watching it with co-owner of the business, Jon Kamen.

When the roof of Radical caught alight a fireball rose 10 or 20 feet above Covent Garden – this at about 2 a.m. The fire brigade lost it at one point and Ray feared for a much wider conflagration – 333 years to the day since start of Great Fire of London.

Sunday, September 12th

Out in the evening to the Haffmans' [my Swiss publishers] London author party. Stephen Fry, their star author, isn't there, he's off playing Wellington to David Suchet's Napoleon in Spain, but he's sent his parents. Both of them very complimentary about my work. Stephen's mother raves about 'East of Stowmarket', then apologises and blames the wine – proceeds to effusively tell the story of 'Private Function' to Gerd Haffmans who nods for quite a while before she pauses and asks 'Do you know the word chiropodist?' 'No,' says he, quite matter-of-factly.

Tuesday, September 14th

In the evening to see Will Boyd's first film as director – 'The Trench' at John Brown's (Viz founder) studios in Bramley Road, Notting Hill. Noisy echoey anteroom, but comfortable theatre off it.

The film is gripping from start to finish. Set, like the great 'Das Boot', in a claustrophobic world with violence and danger always impending. Action and camera confines itself to the trench just before the Somme attack on July 1st 1916. No false heroics, no martial music, no sentimental harmonicas, a direct, matter-of-fact observation of the young lives about to be expended.

The silence at the end of the barrage. The solitary singing of a bird before the attack. Images we know, but presented with great control and maintained with finely paced tension.

Silence at the end. Quite shocking still to see the reality of the botched attack, read the figures of lives lost and wounded (60,000 in first day of the battle). Why do public schoolboys recapture this stuff so well? Graves, Faulks, now Will Boyd – they seem to be able to understand the awful futility and nobility of it all.

Later, around 10.45, I'm called by The Times, a brisk, American female voice asking if I have anything to say about Charlie Crichton, who died today. Very sad. I was fond of Charlie. He put Ealing Comedy values into John's 'A Fish Called Wanda' and it paid off handsomely.

Friday, September 17th

Take a postponed run. Aware of how tired I've been this week. Have to make a real effort to look like a runner. Survive. Feel better. Back home to various calls re Python and Hem. TJ notes that JC has said no to a '60 Minutes' CBS prog on Python. TJ happy to do it as it might help A & E [Arts and Entertainment Channel] who put out a lot of his stuff. I promise to have a word with JC and leave a message.

With H to Zsuzsanna and Michael [Ignatieff]'s wedding party in Clere Street. Festive atmosphere in the small converted industrial building on whose top floor they live, balloons, bright lights, chatter echoing out on the silent and dark office blocks that surround them.

Quite a throng. Jonathan and Rachel Miller, on the edge of the noise, at the back. Michael and Zsuzsanna (she dressed in white robe like the Pearl and Dean woman) marvellous hosts. Ruth Rogers is instantly and unselfconsciously friendly to both of us. Just the way she is, I think. The ageing brat pack of English writers – Amis, McEwan and Rushdie – meet and hug like Pythons might. As a team. And slightly unwelcoming to outsiders.

The trouble with a roomful of achievers is that everyone's far too cool to be the first to go up to anyone and express enthusiasm for their work. So one begins obliquely, like talking to Richard Eyre and Sue Birtwistle about the Will Boyd film, which leads on to what Richard is doing now. That is, being a TV presenter! Walking along cliffs with waves breaking (for a history of theatre) and having to keep talking to a camera he can't see.

Later, this image in my mind, I toy with the idea of a book about the absurd world of television presenting – 'Foreground Attraction' is a nice title.

Speeches – very eloquent. Simon Rattle proposes the bride, Michael Ignatieff's chunky, bearded brother is good too. Then a Mexican group and we all dance – apart from the Millers. Jonathan, face locked in mock horror, is driven out by the noise.

Thursday, September 23rd

Woken by the alarm at twenty to seven. Can hear the dripping and pattering of rain which has been falling most of this week. And today is our one day of outdoor filming on the Python Night links that have occupied most of my waking hours since I began learning the lines on Sunday evening.

Start round by the BBC rubbish bins at TV Centre with the Ken Shabby link – JC in DJ at desk, me as the ghastly Ken looking through dead cats and old condoms on a skip. Then the rain comes down and we're held up half an hour or so. Once there is a break we work very fast. Finish Shabby and are into Pepperpots link and finally Gumbies.

Home – look through papers for first time in three days; there is a list published by the BFI of the Top 100 British Films ever made, rather chuffed to see that I'm in three of them ('LOB' at 28. 'Fish Called Wanda' at 39! and 'Brazil' at 54!).

Bas rings. He's back from Frome. The last pass, the last sheet was cleared at 3 a.m. This morning they bound up eight copies by hand and he has one for me.

We have our last meal before he returns to Washington. Discuss future plans with pleasantly boozy enthusiasm. 'The Good Buddha Guide' seems suddenly attractive. I've seen the Buddhas in Burma and know how wonderful they look and I'd like to know a lot more about Buddhas and Buddhism.

The Hemingway book is a great achievement. In one year we've produced something of value, of dazzling good looks and hopefully, of readable content. A last embrace by the cabs then off on our separate ways.

Friday, October 1st

The great nine-week blitz that began the day we returned from Key West is now virtually over. In August and September I've finished the book, written and recorded four commentaries, written and filmed new material for Python Night, read the 'Hem Adventure' for Orion recorded books, done a few days of publicity and spread the word at a clutch of sales conferences. The book is ready for distribution, two out of the four shows are ready for transmission, the audiotapes and the videotapes are being prepared.

The general buzz is positive. Booksellers clearly expect decent sales, and Peter Salmon's decision to place us at nine on a Sunday is a sign of his faith in the project. Things could always throw us off course, but I've the general feeling that the first show has been seen by the powers that be and judged to be good, which is a relief, and that there aren't any horrible shocks ahead.

Wednesday, October 6th

To the gym for a bit of hard work before off to record the Clive Anderson Show down at the South Bank. Clive doesn't like to greet the guests before-hand (so as not to lose the spontaneous moment of greeting as he or she steps out) – which makes for slightly farcical behaviour backstage, with curtains being drawn and redrawn as he goes by.

I'm aware of being comfortable, but not as sharp, fluent or articulate as I'd like to be. I can foresee problems like this until I can pin down my thoughts. My reasons for doing the Hemingway subject are explicable, but what I've learnt – and how and why I went about it the way I did, are less easy to ex-plain. The usual Palin weakness, instinct over intellect, heart before head – do something appealing and hope people don't ask too many awkward questions, like why?

Thursday, October 7th

The Paramount Comedy Channel 'LOB' screening. We're driven round to the Empire in rickshaws – pedalled by sturdy young women. JC and Gilliam in one (they're talking to each other now), myself and TJ in another. I think there is a crowd – but mostly we're besieged by the strange, wild, staring-eyed nutters who seem to be our most intense fans – pushing autographs and photos at us with unsmiling urgency.

The press take photos; then we give interviews to a bank of TV crews and retreat eventually to a back room to be fitted with mikes and to sign some of the range of Python wines. TJ very critical about the design of the labels – but this is party wine – all from Pays d'Oc and not really worth making a fuss about – Norwegian Blue Red is passable.

Then we're introduced by Jonathan Ross and, as planned, we all talk at once for at least one and a half minutes before being led off by Roman centurions.

When I get home I watch my appearance on Clive Anderson. It's adequate but not remarkable. My trouble is that I don't really believe in anecdotes, in telling jokes in that rather confident way, presuming your audience will be fas-cinated. I believe doubt is much more interesting than assertiveness.

Saturday, October 9th

A missive from Eric – addressed to us all, rather than personally – prompted by his worries that he has been seen as the Python who – as TJ put it at a press conference at the 'LOB' screening – 'doesn't want to play any more'. It's conciliatory and blames any misunderstanding on the media's inability to appreciate irony.

In the evening round to TJ's with H to watch Python Night. The new material – the new linking material – is fine but seems to lack something (are we all a little self-conscious, or a mite unrelaxed, at doing what we did so apparently effortlessly 30 years ago? Or is it the lack of a studio audience?)

Monday, October 11th

Publication day for my fourth travel book in ten years. Breakfast overshadowed by a Mark Lawson piece which says most of the things I feared might be said about the series – even though he's only seen the first episode. Headlined 'Farewell to Charm', it's an inescapable full-page complete with photo basically bemoaning the fact that the programme is more about travel than Hemingway, and even then it is less good than my previous programmes.

Run before lunch. Paul Hamann on phone soon after I return, with good news on Python Night ratings. BBC Two's average Saturday-night audience doubled – better figures than any other themed evening. Ralph Lee calls later – I feel very pleased for him and Elaine and Selena, hard work rewarded.

Saturday, October 16th

To the St Martin's Lane Hotel. Big, wide, airy foyer. Hard, yellow feel to it all. Austerity chic. Am there to talk to Rob van Scheers, for a Dutch magazine, who want to do a big feature on me, Hem and Python.

There's always a slight asymmetry with a Dutch – and a German – interview, as though we are mentally just out of synch. His laughter comes at times I don't expect – usually unrelated to the joke. But he's thorough and I have to work hard for my breakfast. 'You seem to be, out of all the Pythons, the . . . how shall I say . . . the most relaxed,' he ends.

I rush off to seek some peace and quiet away from my own views, until all this starts again on Monday. Check some of the papers. Previews largely friendly, if neutral; though The Times calls the first show 'self-indulgent'. Wait till they see the others.

Sunday, October 24th

Rachel has left home. The last of the children we first began bringing into the world 31 years and two weeks ago, has left Julia Street.

Monday, October 25th

Waiting for Adam to collect me at eight, I'm idly scanning the Guardian Review and run slap-bang into one Desmond Christy in bilious mood. A short, sharp, deeply unpleasant little piece. Like someone who'd heard there was a beating going on and arrived late, just as the victim was getting up.

His criticism, at heart, is about the 'attempts to be funny', and my anger is compounded by my own awareness that these were the areas in which I felt we were weakest. David encouraged any silliness and my battles only curbed a few of the excesses of comic taste for which I'm now being punished.

Still, it's my fault in the end. No one else's. So for the second week I set off on a tight-packed publicity tour for a series that has been given a critical drubbing. News of the overnights not much better. Down to 4.2 – but apparently all BBC One progs suffered. 'Ballykissangel' dropping from 7.5 to 4.5, and 'French and Saunders', after me, mustering no more than 3.5. But Zsuzsanna is upbeat, as ever, and the punters (especially in Nottingham) are out in force and generally very happy with the series. The patient is bruised but not beaten yet.

Sunday, October 31st

Anne J rings to tell me that there has already been one recanting review – by Stephen Pile in the Telegraph on Saturday, off his 'high horse' onto 'a very small pony'.

The book is slowly making a mark on the charts. The Observer has it at No. 6 in its second week – this on returns at end of our first signing week, and after one, controversial, programme. Should rise on the next chart.

Monday, November 1st

Gloomy day that gradually turns wetter as Atlantic weather blusters across during the morning. At last, a chance to spend a day without leaving home.

Anne rings with the figures, about midday. I've been trying to suppress my deepest anxieties – that the series could free-fall down through the ratings, so my initial response to a raised figure of 4.5, up from 4.2 for prog two, and a share of 18.4 per cent is a relief.

Talk later to Eddie M. I think we've failed to please either audience sufficiently – those who would follow MP anywhere, by bringing Hemingway into the equation and by making the programme deliberately difficult to follow, and those who expected Hemingway's presence to lift MP into a sort of arts prog for the masses, by treating the material too lightly.

Complete 'Disgrace' by Coetzee, a deeply depressing book, but sort of relevant. All about change, about comfortable certainties being turned on their head.

Wednesday, November 3rd

Another, and final, dig at the series, this one in Time Out – 'he's more concerned with making bad jokes than telling us about . . .' etc., etc., this morning has me thumping the walls in helpless anger and frustration. I know! I know! But leave me alone, for God's sake. The jokes are a tiny part of a series of beautiful photography (not mentioned in a single review this time, strangely enough), some underplayed and telling observations and, particularly last week, some genuine revelations, but no, it must be dragged down to the level of personality. If Michael makes a few bad jokes it invalidates the whole.

I'm only strengthened by remembering Virginia Woolf's wonderful phrase about 'the queer, disreputable pleasure of being abused'. The rage passes quickly – what can I do about it now?

I clear some of my room. TV repairman comes. I've booked a massage. Dawn at Face To Face in Chetwynd Road thought the series 'brilliant'. Helen comes back with a similar reaction from the man in the gym.

Friday, November 19th

Feel wide awake enough to get up at half past six, as H is preparing to go into hospital at seven.

H calls at eleven, sounding very drowsy. Bright spells and dark, violent showers alternate. Potter round, settling myself; trying to reduce the amount of paper, letters, requests, demands that drift about.

By taxi to London Bridge Hospital at three. Traffic sluggish along Cannon Street. Not quite a hotel, but the general lack of clattering trolleys and stretchered patients, and the soft pile of carpet everywhere, makes it seem more like one than a hospital. Cheerful lack of security. If I wanted to get rid of an inmate I'd have no problems.

Up to the second floor and locate H in a small, functional room. She looks in good colour, but has difficulty keeping her eyes open. An oxygen tube runs across both cheeks and up her nose, and a morphine drip runs into her arm.

Stay for about an hour and a half, during which time I go down to the hospital shop for an Evening Standard. Told by the girl who runs it that they only have a limited selection of papers. Limited indeed – there isn't a single one that isn't in Arabic.

Home on the Northern Line and buy Will a book at Belsize Park for his birthday today.

Will and Heather are waiting at the house. Presents are opened. Glass of champagne then we all take a taxi to the 29th birthday party that Will has organised in South Ken, collecting Rachel on the way (she's just back from spending a week in Oldham filming 'The League of Gentlemen' at work). Unpretentious Italian. Reminds me of the sort of places we ate in in the Piave Valley. They serve us Prosecco as we wait for the guests to arrive.

Despite my fears of being overtaken by jet lag I survive quite happily until eleven – talking with Will's friends Dan about Northern Ireland (he's on the Bloody Sunday enquiry, which has run for a year, and he argues for more understanding of the Protestant position) and Jim Bobin about dubious editing techniques in the new Ali G series. I'm glad Will keeps such a diverse collection of friends, that's how it should be.

I'm still perfectly awake and compos when Big Ben strikes at twelve. So far, no serious after-effects of the two-week door-to-door trip down under.

Monday, November 22nd

Strange nights. Waking in the silence of the small hours as if it's morning. Pass ideas for novels through my mind, audition prospects for new travel series, before drifting off to elaborate dreams, these in turn broken by the subdued roar of the first big jets coming into Heathrow – then more unconvincing sleep. H and me, both in our different ways, suffering the effects of major interference in the normal routine of our healthy lives.

Zsuzsanna rings with her demands. Today programme wants me to be on tomorrow morning to talk about British image abroad – feel I should do it for the book, though in my gut I know these things never work out as well as you'd hoped.

Tuesday, November 23rd

Wake again in the early hours with headache, gut-ache and general system emergency. Feel like getting up, think a lot, then back to sleep which is quite deep by the time H nudges me to remind me that I have a car coming at a quarter to eight to take me to Broadcasting House, a down-the-line interview for Today.

Now Today is centralised at White City, the foyer of BH is like a ghost town. Security personnel are the only other occupants this morning. I'm escorted by a woman with a pleasantly guttural Central European accent – to the area where the small, cubicle-like studios are guarded by three men. I'm shown into mine and left there. No tea, coffee or even water offered.

Sit around listening to details of Jeffrey Archer's downfall on cans until, when it's almost my time to take part in a discussion about the British Council and how the British are seen abroad, I realise my throat's dry. Halfway through my contribution frogs take over my throat and most of my interview with Sue McGregor is spent clearing it.

No word at the end. I let myself out of the booth and out of the building, this time unescorted. There is no car waiting to take me home. Wish I'd never done it. I didn't have much to say, or time to say it.

To lunch with Anne J. Amongst a bundle of requests she passes over to me before we go to Orso's is a letter from Downing Street offering me a CBE. My immediate reaction is good, honest surprise, incredulity and a twist of pride as well. My citation is for 'Services to: Television drama and travel documentaries'. Well, I'm certainly chuffed. Should I accept it? Obviously yes, less obviously, but worth considering, no.

Some shopping then home. Tell H about the CBE. She thinks I should accept. So I tick the 'I Do' box and send it off.

To Ladbroke Arms to meet up with Roger and Alex Richardson [editor of most of my travel shows]. They're both gently critical of the 'MPHA' series. Good things along the way but something wrong in tone and pitch. Rog says nothing new I did that involved travel would be accepted easily after success of the long journeys. Maybe this is a necessary part of the process – distance myself from the old travel shows (after ten years) and draw a line under the past – with CBE as my epitaph?

Wednesday, November 24th

Lie awake in my almost habitual waking interval sometime in the dead of night and worry about accepting the CBE with such alacrity. Decide in the end that it would be much more of a palaver not accepting it – I would have had to tell everybody I hadn't accepted it and I can't think of a good enough reason to go with such a decision. Back to sleep.

Thursday, November 25th

Feel sudden, unfamiliar apprehension about the book-signings today. Comparing the 'Hemingway Adventure's performance with any of the three big travels is pointless. Ridiculous to have expected exactly the same; nevertheless I occasionally get a whiff of real disaster – if the book doesn't excite, because of mixed feelings and low audience for the series, and if I can't sign it back into the charts by Christmas, then the promise of the massive first printing will end up as an embarrassment. Mighty machines that poured out pages for eight days will be replaced by mighty machines that may have to destroy the same pages.

To Books Etc in Broadgate. Small, well-run store. A rather well-dressed, middle-aged woman secures my autograph but says in that acceptably frank way which the upper class have, 'I didn't enjoy your "Hemingway's Travels" as much as the others.' We talk and it is the style which she took exception to – not as easy as my previous series. Trying too hard.

Saturday, November 27th

Work on my Sheffield speech. Adam collects me at half past one. To Books Etc, now Borders, megastore, in Charing Cross Road. I'm installed up in the Religion department – not far from Erotica, one of the assistants tells me, consolingly. It's quiet, but I have a steady queue for an hour and a lot of foreign buyers – Danes, Germans and French.

Sunday, November 28th

Run, soft underfoot but more sunshine than cloud and quite warm. The BA/ Millennium Wheel, now up, makes a dramatic impact on the classic London skyline. I like it. The circle adds a good shape, breaks down the dominance of rectangular plinths.

The book is hanging in at the very bottom of the Top 10, and, as there is very little difference between those at five and ten, I am hopeful.

Wednesday, December 1st

Write out and edit the Sheffield speech. To the gym for a workout; grab a sandwich then to St Pancras for the train to Sheffield.

I talk to the woman opposite. She used to work for the Labour Party and refers to their leaders by their Christian names. She's also going to the Made In Sheffield dinner. She assures me that the Chancellor, Gordon Brown, star guest, will speak before the dinner – 'he never sits through the meal' – then leave – and that he'll not be wearing black tie as requested. 'He never does.'

We share a car to the Stakis Hotel, two years old and built on Victoria Quay, a canal-side location just off the approach to what I remember as a trainspotter, was Victoria Station. Time to change, check the speech one last time, and down to pre-drinks at 7.15.

Gareth, the university vice-chancellor, mutters about the football clubs, both in dire straits this season, merging together. Proud of new university figures that show Sheffield taking highest proportion of state school entrants in the country.

Gordon Brown appears, moving unfussily into the room, preceded by a young PPS, looking rather anxious and much less at ease than his boss. We're introduced. He gives me a very warm, soft hand to shake. No grip, no pressure. Amiable grin; talks about being my warm-up man. Very easy, relaxed manner.

Then I notice Lord Rogers, Richard Rogers – whose presence on the bill is a surprise to me. He's not wearing a DJ either. Instead a collarless black shirt – beautiful he looks, like a Roman emperor.

Brown speaks early – usual government line, occasionally mentioning Sheffield, as if the references are fed in to a speech he's given many times. He tells quite a few jokes, stories against Tony and teasingly against New Labour's image. He seems comfortable, almost smug, as if he knows an awful lot that none of the rest of us do – which is of course true.

Then he finishes and the meal grinds slowly on. It's almost half past ten when the first after-dinner speaker is announced and Lord Rogers takes to the podium. He has some of Gordon Brown's lordliness and he makes a few opening remarks about 'this beautiful city', which I assume aren't architectural – for the much messed-about centre of Sheffield contains some of the dullest of all modern buildings. Then he settles in to develop his thesis about cities, about how important they are, how brownfield sites must be developed before greenfield sites, how the government density guidelines are absurdly low, about how we have the least undeveloped land in Europe, outside the Netherlands. All good stuff but he speaks for 45 minutes and delivers to me a tired audience desperate for some jokes. So my 20 minutes goes down a storm. One of the most enjoyable deliveries I can remember.

Sunday, December 5th

Helen brings a Mail on Sunday back from one of her tennis friends. Interview with Alan Whicker in which he has a good go at his 'imitators' as he calls people – well *anyone* really – who travels and talks to camera. Clive James 'can't interview for toffee' and sending Michael Palin – 'a man who hates guns, doesn't hunt, doesn't drink!' – to do Hemingway was ridiculous – I should have been sent to do Barbara Cartland!

Evening. Girl sobbing and shouting in the street below our bedroom window. Then she kicks a front door. Silence. A bitter silence, then more moaning.

And on the Browns' corner a couple kiss beneath the old lamppost. He's in a big, dark suit, close-cropped hair, like a bouncer. She's well-wrapped against the cold, a slash of red scarf in there. They're locked in a passionate embrace throughout the time it takes me to have a bath, then they both get into a shiny black sports car with elevating headlamps and drive away.

Monday, December 6th

At nine o'clock give a quick interview to Woman & Home books page. My three favourite books – of course I have to make choice of *some* of my favourites, impossible to narrow down one's pleasures – so Jan Morris on Venice, Primo Levi on concentration camp survival ('If This Is a Man') and Virginia W's diaries. 'Interesting choice,' she says, on the other end of the phone.

Up to the Screen on the Hill for 'The Straight Story' – David Lynch's latest. A delight – most beautiful, painterly images of the Mid-west and fine music too, all fill out a slim tale with great charm and dignity. Uplifting in the best sense. Walk home a happy man – affected, as one should be, by a good piece of work.

Monday, December 13th

Appalling signing at Sloane Square with WHSmith's. Quite the worst so far. Only one pre-order. A queue of three at the start of the signing. However, Robin Cook does come browsing by. He doesn't buy my book but tells me he has just bought the video of 'A Fish Called Wanda' – 'the best comedy ever'. We talk of signing. He says he's done a thousand Christmas cards at the weekend. Quite surprised at how well-cut is the Foreign Secretary's suit.

Wednesday, December 15th

To Guildford for a lunchtime signing. Smooth journey, bright sunny day. They have a glass elevator in the centre of the store in which I descend to the signing position. Unfortunately the doors won't open and much to the bemusement of the waiting queue the lift eventually rises up again. More tinkering with the buttons and we descend once again. It still won't open. I'm trapped in full view. It's like the pod sequence in 'Spinal Tap' – and I'm the Harry Shearer character. We rise up again. Thank God this is Guildford – anywhere else we'd have had ribald cheers at the very least. Finally we prise the doors open and walk down via the steps.

Friday, December 17th

To Waterstones, Piccadilly, for the final signing of the year. Twenty, ten, even five years ago, the prospect of Simpsons of Piccadilly closing down and being transformed into a five-storey bookshop would have been unthinkable. But now books have become as irresistible as snacks, and indeed allied themselves with the new snack-bar culture – coffee shops and bars and restaurants share the space. Bookshops are now bookstores, as they always were in America and with five floors of them it seems the sky's the limit.

The signing is typical of most of those in London – polite interest, well short of hysteria. A man in black paramilitary outfit stands guard in case anything should get out of hand. If only. When I ask for coffee and water it is fetched on a tray by an immaculate Prada-garbed young man. There are lots of books and plenty of space but this is not really a friendly place and there is no heart or core to it.

Monday, December 20th

To TV Centre to be briefed for the millennium show. Shown a model of the set, complete with gallery area where I will be plonked down to assemble my short pieces about what's happening around the world, between two and seven on the last day of the millennium. David Attenborough, Tony Robinson and Fergal Keane will be fellow 'eyes on the world'.

Tuesday, December 21st

Shopping a.m. Then to Engineer for lunch with Terry G. Still waiting for the deal on his 'Quixote' movie but has another lined up for the summer. Most interestingly – he wants to get me back into comedy writing. Says Johnny Depp is very keen to play Le Pétomane.[1] It sounds an instantly attractive proposition – my mind whizzing on to thoughts of shooting it with the same elegance and style of a 'Liaisons Dangereuses'. Keeping the farting itself very sparing – like the appearance of a ghost in a good horror film.

1 Joseph Pujol (1857–1945) – also known by his stage name Le Pétomane – was a French flatulist (professional farter).

Christmas Day

A landmark Christmas for the family – the first one run by the younger generation, and the first one in the East End. Temporary parking problems, for despite it being Ramadan there are plenty of Bengalis shopping and parking. Helpful Dutch neighbour of Will happens to be coming out of the chapel next door and gives me his place. His parents can't believe their eyes. 'We know you. We have seen all your journeys, and the one with Hemingway. You are nice!'

Tuesday, December 28th

Pale dawn light, cold, clear morning, and at ten I take Helen's mother back to Abbotsley. She's been, as usual, an essential part of Christmas, happily plunging into a series of boisterous events, from our Christmas Eve party onwards. In the car on the way up north I've time to listen and we talk about all sorts of things. About the changes in our lifetimes – about education and the declining importance of rules and formality in personal behaviour. And so on. I learn a lot.

Wednesday, December 29th

At a quarter to four I'm collected and whisked off to TV Centre to be shown the set for the millennium programme on Friday. Lots of ground support, ladies with headsets and mobiles and clipboards. The producer shows me to the 'Crow's Nest' which has a bank of monitors and which looks out over a sort of Bluewater Shopping Centre set with water bubbling and flowing down a ramp in the middle.

It's a cosy, closeted world in Studio TC1, and once I'm in it I can see the attractions of being there throughout the event. Just to say you were there. I shall only be on for three hours or so between Tony Robinson and David Attenborough (who I think refused to stay on for the midnight shift).

Driven home by a burly man who tells me I'm his 'last job of the millennium'.

Thursday, December 30th

Wake to rain which continues for most of the day. After breakfast down to Conran to buy various presents for tomorrow night's party. When I get back H tells me the phone has been ringing almost constantly. Some mad fan has broken into Friar Park and taken a knife to George (who has either one, two, or four injuries to his chest) before being laid out by Olivia with a desk lamp.

H has rung Rachel [George and Olivia's assistant], and it sounds as if the wounds were not serious and George will be out of hospital within a couple of days.

Friday, December 31st

Wake to the feeling of a heavy day ahead. The CBE will be announced publicly. I shall be live on national television without a script for most of the afternoon and then we have our New Year party with the added emotional and psychological baggage of the great millennium experience.

I'm not at all hooked on this millennium stuff. In fact I've grown to hate the word. Its resonance and significance has been diminished, reduced to commercial cliché. I don't really have any feelings about the change of century – not like I felt about becoming 21, or 30, or at the end of Thatcher, or the assassination of Kennedy, or the moon landing. These all had real impact on me. Like John Lennon's shooting. Which brings me to the spectre at the feast – the horror story of George's wounding at Friar Park.

I call Dhani [his son] – George is stable but in pain. Dhani arrived a minute after it happened. They had struggled with the man, he says, for almost 20 minutes. He sounds on the edge, and at one point his voice chokes to a silence. I send a message from us both – praising their bravery, saying we're thinking of them all the time – which is pretty much true.

Car into TV Centre at 1.30 – taking Will and Heather as guests.

Tony Robinson is packing up after his first shift on the 'Crow's Nest' – as they call the raised gallery from which the PRPs (Presenter Review Packages) are presented. He confirms my worst suspicions – that you don't know what they'll throw at you, when or for how long.

The very prolixity of the picture sources is also the problem. It's like flicking the pages of a book. Leaping from place to place, without time for information or anecdote – barely enough time for identification.

An hour later the pace is increasing. The ambition of 'Today 2000', or '2000 Today' is exceeding the delivery and the number of communication glitches and stillborn links is proliferating. I'm told to stand by, then a few notes are thrust into my hand and up come the pictures and off we go.

Actually, by the time I finish my last piece, after five o'clock, I'm thoroughly enjoying the Python-ness of it all.

Rolf Harris and Peter Salmon lurk at the back of the studio. Rolf is extremely friendly and congratulates me on my CBE. 'You've got one already haven't you?' Peter asks him. '*MBE,*' Rolf replies curtly, then adds, 'I've lost mine. It was in a red box, I know that.'

Back home – prepare for the dinner party. H cooks wonderful salmon steak with salsa, preceded by watercress soup.

At 11.15 we set off for Parliament Hill. A few thousand people, but not threateningly crowded. The River of Fire[1] doesn't materialise, we don't think, but the pyrotechnics along the Thames are pretty good – even from up on the side of the hill. Some of the fireworks, especially the crimson flashes, go up in massive formations – creating the illusion of a sunset in the middle of the night.

Television and radio bring no messages of doom – no collapse of computer systems, or terrorist outrages, or ends of the world, even. The millennium celebrations seem to have gone according to the marketing plan – apart from the River of Fire, perhaps.

H and I not to bed until 4.30.

I write this in 2000 AD, and I do feel a touch of sadness at the passing of the 19s – after all, all my life has been lived in 19 this or that. Look back over 1999, then. One to be proud of? Hemingway dominated – filming, writing, editing, transmission and publication. A lot of hard work.

The initial buffeting by some critics – and friends too – did not prove to be the harbinger of disaster. In fact the programmes themselves seemed to please people more as they went on and I feel relieved, because we did have problems in deciding what kind of show we wanted it to be. So a year in which I snatched some success from what could be seen as another 'in-between travel series' failure. And as Paul Jackson, head of BBC Light Entertainment, said when we met at TV Centre this p.m., 'A CBE – for you and Richard Curtis – you'll have to fight it out between you for nicest man in England.'

1 The midnight pyrotechnics that were supposed to create the illusion of a wall of flames running down the Thames.

2000

Saturday, January 1st

2000 was one of those almost mythic, fantastical, science fiction dates which thrilled us when we were young. Even as 1984 did when I was a teenager. Now it's here. A reality. I've lived to the year 2000. I feel a curious numbness where perhaps significance, realisation, assessment and point of perspective should be. It's another day. Throughout my life I've gradually whittled away the tyranny of the great, mass-experience, expected Moment. A Sheffield United win tomorrow will give me far greater pleasure and a far keener sense of where I am when it happens.

Walk to South End Green for a paper. With no sunlight to sharpen outlines and bring surfaces to light the streets look damp and tired. From one of the housing blocks comes the angry scream of a voice in an upper room. 'You left me alone! On New Year's Eve!'

Though there are hardly any cars on the road, two have managed to hit each other at the junction of Southampton and Mansfield Road, glass scattered across the tarmac. The shutters drawn down on normally welcoming corner shops are scored with graffitied tags. The huge, glum, grey bulk of the Royal Free Hospital – one of the greatest architectural disasters to be visited on Hampstead, looms over South End Green. But I know from my newspaper that the first British baby of the new millennium was born there as midnight struck. More alarmingly, 15,000 will be born in Britain by the end of the day.

Cleese calls from Santa Barbara to thank me for sending him the 'Hem Adventure' book – he particularly liked the dedication to the Dalai Lemur. He's working on his BBC series about the Human Face which will take up much of the next year. His tax problems of two or three years ago have been solved, so he sounds dangerously close to being happy.

He hasn't heard about the CBE, but when I tell him that part of the citation was for Services to Television Drama he goes into one of his long wheezy chuckles and says he's going to write to Tony Blair and point out that 'that was supposed to be comedy'. He does reveal that three years ago he was offered a gong and turned it down – said he felt it was too much like a pat on the head from the headmaster at speech day.

Much navel-gazing in the papers and on TV. I do sense that people seem to want the new millennium to be some sort of new beginning.

Call Friar Park again. George's brother picks up the phone. George is on his way home. Which is the best news of the New Millennium.

Monday, January 3rd

Quite mild, low skies, persistent rain. At eleven, Mark – computer expert – comes round to sort out some of the problems I've had over last year – and to update the system. We start with a lesson on how to organise files and folders – I feel an almost physical pain at my inability to grasp the logic of each procedure, as if trying to learn Spanish grammar or medieval English. But he is remarkably patient and good-natured and gradually I begin to understand why I'm doing what I'm doing.

Wednesday, January 5th

George H rings mid-morning and I hear the full story of the attack. The man appeared crazed, screaming and shouting in from the kitchen and into the hall. George had been told that the best way to deal with such aggression was to return it – so he yelled 'Hare Krishna' at his adversary at the top of his voice. A more bizarre confrontation, in the oddly Agatha Christie-like setting of Friar Park's galleried hall, is difficult to imagine.

A Veda healer is coming to cleanse the house. George takes refuge in a mixture of his Indian beliefs – his Vedantist side – and a fury at the state of a country which can't pay its nurses and ambulance men a decent wage. 'Every cabinet minister should be stabbed on New Year's Eve and have to go into hospital; then they'd realise how hard these people have to work!'

On a lighter note, Tom Petty sent George a fax – 'Bet you're glad you married a Mexican girl.'

Friday, January 7th

Visit George and Olivia at Henley. Dhani had warned me that the press were camped at the gates (even eight days after the attack), and I caught sight of a little coven of them, across the road, squatting down beside bags of rubbish.

Olivia comes down, barefoot, tiny and insubstantial, but eyes shining. We go into an ornate Regency-style sitting room – full of light – and sit and talk. George appears. Though they both look strained, he talks (as only George can) without rancour or bitterness, except at the politicians who underfund the Health Service; he has lots of ideas – a documentary about the house, incorporating music, musicians and his love of Indian philosophy.

Olivia goes and George rambles on with his message about the wonders of Indian spiritualism, the origins of the world, the meaning of life and the universe. I think he must have sensed my reaction for at one point he broke off, realised he was talking to someone, not lecturing, and gave me a bristly, unshaven kiss!

Thursday, January 13th

Ring Rachel at breakfast time. She's 25 today. Haven't seen her since last century. Her ski trip to St Anton was a great success; have given her a globe that lights up and a big A-Z map of London for their flat.

Friday, January 14th

A marathon session of intense concentration – this time on myself – for the Playboy 20 question column. I find it very hard at times to be plunged straight into the hot oil of sassy, snappy US magspeak. Such a gulf between my room, reeking of fresh paint, dusty with fine particles from the stripping of the walls and ceiling and still half under siege from our decorator Pat Winstone, and the hip, smart reporter from New York (who for all I know might be in a room just like this). I fight his witty questions with solid straight-bat answers – occasionally going for a big hit, and either sneaking a four or missing the ball completely.

Saturday, January 15th

An email from Eric asking me to go and see George, but adding the sort of friendly, conciliatory remarks that we used to exchange before the Python tour disagreements. The drama of the Friar Park attack has brought us closer again – as if acknowledging how trivial by comparison are our own differences – and perhaps also, how much we need our friends.

Monday, January 17th

To Euston to catch 9.15 to Birmingham. Met at Birmingham International 85 minutes later and taken, via M6 and M42 – great strips of lumbering trucks – to Walsall.

The New Art Gallery, already a much-talked-about building, has an uncompromisingly cube-like, unadorned exterior which I'm pretty sure the locals must find as alienating as I did when I first saw the photos, but what it lacks in amiability it makes up for in approachability – right in the centre, with no walls, steps, fences or any obstacle – it's rather like the keep of a castle – rising abruptly, and I daresay glowing a bit when the sun's around.

At lunch beside the canal basin when two women come in, bearing a beautifully stitched travel bag which has been made in the small factory next to the gallery. They present me with this bag, compliments of the management, and I feel duty bound afterwards to pay a call on the makers – Whitehouse Cox. They're a small family business specialising in saddlery and leather (Walsall's football team is called The Saddlers) since 1875. Buy another shoulder bag – just what I needed – and feel I've got to know more than one aspect of Walsall.

Catch a train to London just before four o'clock. I feel uncomfortable with playing the role of unofficial royalty and the constant attention is quite wearing too. Fall asleep, woken by a member of the train staff asking for my autograph.

Tuesday, January 18th

Sift through letters and business calls. Ring Rachel at Friar Park to check on visit to George tomorrow – she says George has had a sharp psychological and emotional reaction and feels he cannot stay in the house. They've gone to stay with friends nearby.

To the Imperial War Museum to take in the C.R.W. Nevinson exhibition.

Feeling I've had since the start of a new century – that this mere date, the over-playing of whose significance I've instinctively resisted, is beginning to mean something to me. It's as if the twentieth century has gone quite suddenly from being a synonym for modernism and progress, to a piece of the past. Joining a new century at the age of 56 poses the question of what relevance people of my age are to anything new – are we not just guardians of the past, relics of a pretty unpleasant century full of ghastly mistakes?

This thought emphasised by the excellent Nevinson exhibition. Many of his pictures capture the futility and brutality of the First World War – not just in the trenches, but on the streets where a boy lies dead on a pavement, or in the dressing stations and hospitals. He captures a prevailing feeling of exhaustion.

Wednesday, January 19th

Grey, wet, scouring cold. Walk up to Markos to have my hair cut. Notice a picture on the wall of Markos and George Michael – signed by the man himself.

Organising my diary before trip to Oxford to hear Robert Hewison's first lecture as Slade Professor of Fine Art. It's on Ruskin, so very suitable that it should take place at Ruskin's great contribution to Oxford – the Natural History Museum, the spiky, distinctive, unusual Gothic palace on Parks Road. The structure reflects the purpose of the building in a literal way. Columns are ornately topped with leaves, the marble-supporting pillars in the gallery are each made of a different type of British rock. Robert lectures for an hour (56 mins 05 secs he tells me later), with well-chosen slides.

Back to the Old Parsonage for supper. I'm amongst Ruskin aficionados and opposite a man called Michael Wheeler who runs the Jane Austen house at Chawton. We talk about Victorian morality, how a rigid moralism was imposed on a more relaxed eighteenth-century society. Gladstone put a reference mark in his notebook every time he masturbated, Ruskin and his wife may never have had penetrative sex, but masturbation took place in the marital bed – 'Shall we talk about this *after* you've eaten?'

A bracing midnight walk with Robert across the centre of Oxford clears my head – except of course of nostalgia, which flourishes, as we walk alongside the walls of the Bodleian, past Brasenose, past the hamburger vans in the High (which we often used to supplement, or substitute for, college food). And so on down to the Examination Schools, by the gates from which we emerged after our last Finals Exam nearly 35 years ago.

Walk back through almost empty streets. Along Bear Lane and past Oriel. The moon, two days from full, shines on the lead pate of the Radcliffe Camera, stars sparkle, and old Oxford looks magical.

Thursday, January 27th

Read through the reviews of 'Hemingway Adventure'. Dispiriting – such abuse, such bitter vitriolic stuff. There's definitely an irritation factor to my popularity which has spilt out in many reactions to the series. Chris Dunkley in the Financial Times even saved his kicking for the end of the year – awarding me the Worst Programme of the Year award. It's unsettling, and a little frightening, this bilious wrath. It goes, in some cases, way beyond criticism and reveals a dark delight in biting someone hard. Anyway, it's over, done, finished – and all the most ugly attacks were from men anyway.

Head down to Camberwell. Squash with TJ – I win today, Terry's hip is a problem for him. He says he's also been persuaded by a friend to have an angiogram to ascertain state of his heart, bearing in mind his family history of heart disease and his high cholesterol tendencies.

Friday, January 28th

To lunch at Langan's Bistro with Tristram Powell, who's currently learning to swim – properly. 'It'll come,' his instructor tells him – 'like riding a bicycle'.

Bottle of Sancerre and herb risotto and cod. Tristram asks how Harold P is in 'Mansfield Park'. Pinter had apparently been much pleased by a review which called his performance 'frightening'. Apparently he and Antonia [Fraser] – 'the great socialists' – have gone to Barbados for two weeks on Concorde. Tristram clearly amused at Harold's 'man of the people' role. He plays tennis with them and a bottle of white wine on ice and a meal is always spread out waiting at the end of the game.

Tuesday, February 1st

Up early for an energising run across the Heath before appearance on Trevor McDonald chat show. Joanna Trollope also on. She has an almost regal bearing, but a spiky leanness which doesn't look too healthy. (I find out later that she has been through some painful marital split.) I find her smart suit and immaculate but over-effusively dressed stack of hair a little intimidating. I think she's quite nervous as she waits, but very good and articulate as befits an ex-teacher.

Later she asked what I'm up to. A little sheepishly (because I've read none of *hers*) I mutter about writing a novel. 'Oh you *must*,' she enthuses. 'I *loved* "Hemingway's Chair"' – which surprises, pleases and embarrasses me even more.

Thursday, February 3rd

Up in Glasgow by half past ten to begin day's research on 'Glasgow y V'.[1] Everything works out with almost eerie neatness. The address I have for Mc-Naughton and Sons in 1904/5 is five minutes' walk from my hotel – the Malmaison.

On to West of Scotland Water HQ up in Possilpark. They're all very helpful and I'm lunched by the chairman *and* CEO and afterwards meet an 'old-timer' with good stories. They're all amused but also not without interest in my interest. Also good political issues. Water industry in Strathclyde never privatised, after referendum went 96 per cent against.

Having talked and listened for three and a half hours I need to go back and digest the info. Feel enormously satisfied as I walk, in brisk wind and glowering

---

[1] Idea for a novel set in the sewers of Glasgow, prompted by a manhole cover in Segovia with the name of a company based in 'Glasgow y Valencia' inscribed on it.

sky, back across the motorway and along past 'Greek' Thomson's exceptional church to the Malmaison.

Wednesday, February 23rd

I check my Amsterdam schedule and worry about the lengths of the proposed interviews. An hour seems quite sufficient for all I want to say – some run on for two with a half-hour for photos.

The re-marking of the streets outside goes on. A well-planned operation, cars are swung from one side of the road to the other by a lifting vehicle, or given hydraulic shoes and rolled along pavements. The word 'Disabled' takes its place on the surface of the road outside the deaf lady's house. Perhaps I could have 'Major Star' outside mine. 'Shy, Withdrawn' at another and so on.

Get back to find H on phone, face lit up. Will has been offered the job as assistant director (in charge of Education) at the Soane Museum – 11,000 initial applications.

Thursday, February 24th: Amsterdam

Chris the publisher meets me. Tall, upright, quite serious. Beer and sandwich lunch and an afternoon of interviews.

First interview for Volkskrant is conducted at the Maritime Museum. Am interviewed by a tall, intelligent woman in the Admiral's Room with its beamed ceiling and portraits of the great Dutch naval commanders gazing down. Photos of an old steamship – 100 years old, beautiful and functional wooden interior reminds me how much I miss my river/sea trips.

To the Red Hut (Rode Hoed) to check the slide screen, sound and projection. The Dutch regard it as a very old-fashioned form of presentation – they associate slideshows with family evenings in winter. All 450 tickets are sold and by the time I return for my Hem talk at a quarter to eight, they're turning people away. Have trimmed the number of slides – but find resources of energy to match a 75-minute presentation, followed by a one-hour book-signing.

Friday, February 25th: Amsterdam

I woke about four and as shoulder pain threatened to keep me awake I took two painkillers. As I cross through the foyer to breakfast, a tall man accompanied by a middle-aged blonde lady with a squint gets to his feet. He's the first interviewer – an hour early. Traffic not as bad as he thought, etc. He's not the same name as on the schedule either, a Sven not a Hans, and she certainly doesn't look like a photographer.

He has no small talk, no lead-in questions, and is not concerned with putting me at ease. In fact the opposite. He fixes me with a steely, inquisitional gaze and fires out, not really questions, but suggestions, like a hostile lawyer in court. I'm afraid I have no way of dealing with this, other than to get flustered, then a little resentful, and as the broadsides hit, reactive. The losing of my cool at least has the effect of turning a cross-examination into a conversation. He seems surprised that his 'technique' should have hurt. By the time the photographer comes and takes me on the first of many visits to the nearest canal bridge, we can laugh and seem to have made it up.

The rest of the day is easier, but there are long, detailed, personal lines of questioning, and I find handling them, keeping my guard up, fencing and parrying, quite exhausting.

A drink with Chris and Wendy at six, after the last interview – a curious affair with a heavy plodder of a Belgian from the Standaard, pock-marked face, no sense of humour. He mystified me with reference to a friend who had crossed Europe on a monkey. Despite my obvious amusement, he repeated this several times until we worked out he had meant donkey.

Monday, February 28th

Quite sharp pains down upper right arm in the night. Take another painkiller. Later in the morning drive down to Devonshire Street for some laying on of hands from Tracy [Maunder, my physio]. I should, ideally, have come to see her last week, she says. The muscles in my shoulder and side of my neck have gone into spasm, and are trapping nerves and tissues, hence the pain. She thinks that with three sessions this week she should be able to release me back to mobility by the time I leave for Vermont on Sunday.

Tuesday, February 29th

Cab to Moro at Exmouth Market for discussions on a possible TV adaptation of 'Hem's Chair'. Caroline Reynolds, a businesslike, confident woman of middle years, is the instigator. She picked up the book at a New York bookstore, liked it and passed it on to her script editor – younger, thin, wide face, given to smiling, whose name I don't catch.

We discuss adaptors first. I confirm I'm not interested in going back to it myself and that I'm rather looking forward to seeing how someone more experienced might sort it out. Alan Bennett is their first thought. Lovely if he *did* want to do it, but I don't think it's quite his thing – and Alan is someone whose *own* thing is not only particular and precise but also very successful. Why on earth would he want to do 'Hem's Chair'?

Suggest Simon Gray and Jack Rosenthal. 'And what about the master adaptor himself, Andrew Davies?' I have to ask. Caroline jumps in quickly, her script editor blushes lightly. 'He's her father,' she explains.

Later, back home and doing letters, Anouchka [at the office], who used to have him as a client, nods sagely . . . 'He's a very naughty man.' But a fine adaptor!

Wednesday, March 1st

To the Russell Hotel to give a luncheon talk to the Air Force Officers' Wives' Club – something Liz Johns [close college friend of Helen's] had manoeuvred me into. Not that I'm unwilling – I always enjoy a ladies' audience, can trip a little lightly, be a bit fanciful, not rely on the nudge-nudge quite as much. The organisers had expected 180, but 270 have homed in on Russell Square from all over the country.

The lunch is ordinary and the long wait to speak which is endemic to such affairs (and keeps reminding me not to do too many of them) drags on. Give them my 'Indecision' talk – the quick why am I here and how did I get into all this. Things are moving well and the audience warming up when an alarm sounds and moments later the doors swing open and the portly figure of the maître d' appears and asks us all to leave the building as soon as possible.

Much laughter – and uncertainty – a lot of people seem to think it's something I've engineered. Gradually it dawns that there is a real emergency and the crowd of ladies ('Shall I take my wine?') moves slowly out towards the sunlit Russell Square. There is, of course, no fire – everyone would have moved a lot faster if there were – and one waiter tells me the alarm goes off once a week at the moment as they have builders in.

Sunday, March 5th

Time yesterday to pack and prepare after lunch with Will and Heather and look at most recent work on 24 Hanbury. Usual threats – a restaurant on Brick Lane wants a late licence, Will says the behaviour of the City boys, and girls, is so bad at these places – drunkenness, vomiting – that any extension would just encourage them. Otherwise the church, the market, the interesting houses, the Bengalis – their long white coats flapping out from beneath anoraks as they emerge from the mosque into the bright sunlight – is as magical a mix as ever.

Saturday, March 11th: Boston, en route Vermont–Washington

It's a quarter past four in the afternoon. I'm at Logan Airport in Boston, six days after arrival here with Tom. It's raining and I'm a few minutes away from boarding UA 1685 to Washington to spend three days with Basil.

Tom has decided to stay up in Stowe [with our friends the Taylors] for the full time – his ticket back is for next Thursday – as the weather is set to get colder and to snow, offering good ice-climbing through the week. It's been a pleasure doing this journey with him. Quiet pleasures, just doing things together – vicariously enjoying his many happy attacks. Tom is one of those people predisposed to happiness. The sun does seem to shine when he's around.

He can be desperately, frustratingly indecisive – slow to make up his mind, sometimes seemingly unaware of the effect of his vacillation on others, but he does have a magic quality that seems to seduce and delight as much as it infuriates. He *is* a great person to have around. I felt his absence quite poignantly at the airport just now. The poignance, the stab of pleasant pain coming I suppose from regret that we shall not have this week again, and that Tom is 31 and not 21.

Thursday, March 16th

My mind has been working energetically on future plans. I can see things more clearly and am determined to simplify the elements of my working life. Have my writing, travelling and art as main interests. Must not get sidetracked by my CBE into thinking I'm good at chairing committees – so write back to Dept of Environment to turn down chairmanship of Committee on Sustainable Development – or that I can be a 'wise man'. Nor must I let myself be Rottweilered by various charities beyond the ones I already support. I want to be less committed, rather than more, as I get older.

Have come around to the conclusion that I should do one more journey. Peter Salmon's letter asking if I would front a big, new BBC Science prog on Space Travel, was waiting on my desk. But it's terrestrial journeys I prefer. I think I've one more big adventure in me before I'm 60!

Friday, March 17th

Some letters, then with Anne to Livebait [restaurant in Covent Garden]. Round-up of significant thoughts that have clarified this week – the website and potential book, the novel (now 60 per cent likely) and 'Sahara'. I've scribbled a route and divided it into six episodes, Cairo to Cairo anti-clockwise. We agree to put in some research before approaching anyone. but at least we have time on our side. I'd like to start filming in late spring 2001, with completion a year later, for screening in autumn 2002.

Saturday, March 18th

To lunch with Tom Dunne at St Martin's Lane hotel – which I asked Anouchka to book without realising coincidence of hotel and publisher. I have omelette Arnold Bennett. Neither of us drinks alcohol (Tom having renounced both booze and cigarettes). We marvel at the way the fellow diners conform to the style of the hotel. In what is almost a uniform they wear mainly black, close-cut shirts and tank tops and the men have partially shaved heads and designer stubble and the women look fit and slim and understated.

I tell him my idea, so far, for 'Glasgow y Valencia', and he immediately starts to put his mind to plot for me, though he doesn't think it a good title. Plotting is what he loves. He likes the sound of the 'Good Buddha Guide' very much. I feel able to exchange such candid detail of my various projects with him because he doesn't seem as calculating or commercially driven as most publishers. He affects a curious, genial amateurism which maybe disguises a hard, ruthless, tough fighting unit (Golden Gordon[1]) beneath, but I think not.

Monday, March 20th

A late afternoon beak-dip with Roger. I can't not tell him about my revived interest in the Sahara project, and I can't tell him without implicitly inviting him to be part of it. His experience with people, his reputation within the industry and his steadfast, honest friendship with me over the years outweigh my concerns about his age, state of health and general stamina. He is, as Basil was when I told him of the possibility of 'Sahara', very excited. I am too. As I drive back across the comfortable London of Notting Hill and Maida Vale, I project myself forward a year to Cairo and the Western Desert and my heart begins to speed up.

Tuesday, March 21st

With relatively few minor distractions, I can get on with the two projects that now look likely to occupy the remainder of my fifties – 'Glasgow y Valencia' and 'Sahara'. Work at a story for 'GYV' and move the action and characters healthily on to a point, a third of the way in (or more) where the manhole is

1 Episode of *Ripping Yarns* about a football team that never won.

discovered. I can't, at times, wait to get writing. I'm longing to put the characters together and see what happens.

I take advantage of generous sunshine with a lunchtime run over the Heath. As my shoulder heals, most of my stiffness, which I worried might be a permanent old-age factor, has cleared and I feel back to the sort of mobility I remember before the Mnemba wave threw me around [I had been thumped onto the beach while body surfing on the island of Mnemba, Tanzania, months earlier].

Wednesday, March 22nd

Call TJ. His angiogram revealed no plaque on his arteries, so, as I tell him, vineyards, abattoirs and dairies of the world can breathe a sigh of relief. He's rewriting 'The Dog Who Saved the World'.

Thursday, March 23rd: London–Sheffield

Taxi to St Pancras, meet Anouchka, who is coming on the road with me to help with all the Sheffield arrangements. We're in First Class, but when I ask if lunch is available I'm told that it's only served in Premier Class. Another of these ludicrous new hierarchies – obviously copied bad example of the Premier League and the First Division. The sparkling sunshine of the past week is gradually replaced by murky cloud and, as we near Sheffield, by rain.

To the Children's Hospital. They're very pleased with press turnout. Two TV stations, two radio stations and several papers – and that's before the hospital radio and the children's radio and the staff and the autograph hunters.

The press poke around lining up shots of me and tiny, very sick, lovingly cared-for children. I find it's the parents that interest me more. Some of them are not from the area, but because of the expertise the hospital provides, this is the only place for their children (born with bowels outside their body, squashed heads and inability to breathe through their mouths). So the parents are accommodated near the hospital. They are so involved with their children's condition that they have a strange, rather enviable calm. Life is refined down to the very basics. It's touching and I find myself, in the middle of this media zoo, benefitting from their aura of calm.

Friday, March 24th: Sheffield

To another photocall, this time at the site of the soon to be completed Millennium Galleries in Surrey Street. An interesting and I think potentially attractive building to add to all the others going up around this area. Don hard hat and wellies and try not to look like the Prince of Wales as I gesture interestedly and nod as if I'm taking it all in.

Two women in charge of the arts side of the project waffle on about the first exhibits. I'm afraid they seem to represent the worst aspect of middle-class art-babble, and when I hear that their first exhibition is to be called 'Precious', I fear for them and for Sheffield. Sheffielders are deeply suspicious of any new 'improvement' to their city. Their mindset is still honest, conservatively socialist, industrial working class. After an hour's tour and photos, I'm a free man and taxi up to Fulwood to see Marjorie [Stuart-Harris, mother of my oldest friend, Graham]. Her 'retirement' home development is, like a lot of modern work in Sheffield, cheap and undistinguished, but her flat is spacious and has views out over green hills. Talk of Angela and how she told Marjorie that she wished she had been able to be like me and not have been so easily provoked into arguments with my father. She argued with him, I always had the Stuart-Harrises to escape to. Interesting how I've always done everything to avoid confrontation. Maybe this is where it all began.

Tuesday, March 28th

To the MP Stammering Centre to do my bit for a documentary for Meridian TV's 'Esther' prog. They use me talking to young stammerers and parents and also a spontaneous, unprepared meeting with the Agostin family who all now attend the Centre – after the father picked me up in his cab and told me how they all had a problem. This was a very happy encounter. Father, mother and son Rafael, all confirming how much confidence had improved since coming to the Centre, and it was clear they are a much happier family.

Little Charlie, aged six, watched me sign one of the many autographs of the day. As I wrote it I was saying it out loud for the young ones. 'Michael . . . Palin.'

'You've missed out "Centre",' says Charlie.

Thursday, March 30th

More distillation of 'Glasgow y V'. Tightening the plot, identifying the key elements.

Satisfied with progress and realise, as I make a writing schedule which will deliver by December 31st, and dovetail into the 'Sahara' project, that I must make some final decision on 'G y V'. Oh, and Prince Charles's office called Anouchka to see if we had a copy of 'Tomkinson's Schooldays' [first episode of 'Ripping Yarns'], which the heir to the throne has requested to see!

Saturday, April 1st

Back home and out to Dan and Laura Patterson's [Dan, comedy writer and director] joint 40th. 'Big Bash' it says on the invitation and 'Carriages at 1.00'. Sounds formal, and I'm never really comfortable in black tie.

A crowd already there when we arrive. Find Richard Wilson and we exchange banter. He's directing a play at the Court. Any nudity, I ask. (Revelation of Kathleen Turner's nude scene in revival of 'The Graduate' has increased ticket sales 50 per cent!) Richard laughs and nods emphatically. Three! I leave it to David Baddiel to ask what sex they are (2W, 1M).

Baddiel, an unashamed Python groupie who knows everything we did and is particularly enamoured of 'Spanish Inquisition', analyses his appreciation wonderfully and makes me chuckle at it all over again.

At the end of the evening guests are divided into those who are sweating profusely after dancing to a ceilidh band (Clive Anderson, Lise Meyer) and those – like Stephen Fry – who are cooler but have probably had more to drink. He's writing a novel. I tell him I'm thinking of writing a second novel. 'I skipped straight to my fourth,' says Stephen – quite seriously.

Monday, April 3rd

To BH to record thoughts on 'My Favourite Programme' for Radio 4. I choose 'From Our Own Correspondent' by a short head from Frank Delaney's excellent 'Poetry Please' (erudite, never patronising or pretentious).

Wednesday, April 5th

Lunch with Ion Trewin. Ion is nice, almost apologetically so, and it's difficult to be absolutely sure whether he likes the novel or not. 'Original' and 'some wonderful characters', he says, but I feel he thinks, to quote the word of the day, it might be unfocused. He loves the fact that I got the whole idea from a manhole cover. Good meal, but I can't enjoy a glass of wine as I'm driving up to Southwold later.

Long, tedious slog out of London. The M25 a great glutinous mass, sticking fast every now and then. It's a lovely evening. Southwold and east coast at their best. Cool-tipped east wind, clear warm light of sinking sun. Everything serene and quietly gleaming.

Thursday, April 6th: Glasgow

Onto the 9.15 Glasgow flight, after a very useful half-hour in the airport lounge during which time I rethought the start of the novel.

Lunch with Robert Bell, the foundryman who sent me a fax after reading of my last novel-researching trip in the Scotsman. He's 42, though looks older, physically, and in his dress reminds me of a Unionist politician. He's very interested in architecture and the historical background to Glasgow's prosperity. He's extraordinarily accommodating with his time – and drives me to my next appointment at West of Scotland Water and points out the Clyde–Forth Canal which passes over the road and along which the raw materials would be shipped for the foundries.

Alan Thomson (with his slightly naughty-boy smile) gives me an hour and a half of his time, and it is all quality stuff. Flesh out a story for my hero Chellerby, Trade Effluent Adviser, living within 15 minutes' drive of his office (which would be on a trading estate). The small town of Milngavie (pronounced 'Mill-guy') seems a possible.

Friday, April 7th: Glasgow–London

Spend most of the morning exploring prospects for Chellerby's world in my nifty rented Alfa Romeo. Poke about Possilpark which is run down and rather shabby, then on to Milngavie which is quite neat and tidy and prosperous. Have the idea he and his wife would run a B&B.

My greatest find is the Applecross Canal Basin. It's off Possil Road and though much reduced from its former glories it still has the canal, the stones of the canal walls and a sensational view of the towers, spires and cupolas of Glasgow – and it's right alongside some of the biggest and most uncompromising '60s blocks. The elements seem to be fitting together and feel, as a result of researches here, that I really do have a novel.

Back in London; call Anne J on my mobile before end of week's business at the office. Apparently Prince Charles and his sons so enjoyed 'Tomkinson's Schooldays' that they've asked for all the other 'Ripping Yarns'!

Best news of the evening though is from Rachel – who presented her laboriously re-edited Luther King film and received a fax full of praise, encouragement and admiration from her head of department.

Friday, April 14th

Today is typical of a week in which I have tried to cover all my bases before three weeks away in Canada and USA. More phone interviews for US papers, a visit to Peter Salmon to pitch 'Sahara'. He was cautious at first, worried as to what the BBC's audience, and, by implication, the MP audience, might be in three years' time. I was full of energy and surprised myself at my own confidence in the project. In the end he seemed rather easily won over, and quite relieved, he said, that he now knew my intentions, as he had four or five people a month after my services!

Went round with H to see Rachel's 'Great Speeches' effort. Fifteen minutes, or less, but packed and very well done. I'm so proud of her. She has a producing and directing credit, and after seeing this I think she can only go onwards and upwards.

Complete a synopsis of 'G yV' to be sent to Ion Trewin while I'm away. Two or more phone interviews and to the Ivy, at the invitation of Greg Dyke [chairman of the BBC] with his chirpy, wonderfully indiscreet partner Sue, to meet John Hendricks, founder of the all-conquering Discovery Channel, and his wife. Dyke quite open about his desire to change emphasis at BBC from John Birt's managerial bureaucracy to programme making. He and Hendricks and their partners are off to Man United tomorrow. They all love football.

Saturday, April 15th

11.50 on a very wet Saturday back at what feels like my second home – LHR. Settled into seat 2A for flight to Toronto – my ninth air departure from London this year.

Yesterday 'Glasgow y Valencia' took giant step forward with completion of my first synopsis and first written account of the story I've slogged out over last two weeks. From Monday the ball will be in Weidenfeld's court. 'Sahara' has been accepted in principle by BBC after last Monday's meet with Salmon.

I leave for the Hemingway tour reasonably confident that next three years of my life are, sort of, sorted. By which time I'll be sixty and will have done quite enough.

Sunday April 16th: Toronto

5.10: The brunch lectures a success. Michael Dibdin, huge head, Hemingway chest, v. funny. Alison Wearing good on Iran – only women can really discover what women go through in those countries – good on the discomforts of the chador, and how naked she felt without it in Paris on way back.

Edna O'Brien nervous before but magical at the podium – after consternation, as she asks for a barstool to sit on. She likes to cause a little fuss. Edna is asked why is Ireland such a breeding ground for writers. E: 'One word. "Turbulence".' She goes to London for peace and Ireland for her ideas. She reminds me of Maggie Smith. Wonderfully, eloquently, rude about people. She liked Hemingway's work, 'Poor Hemingway.' She likes hotel rooms with absolutely no noise, so is doomed to disappointment except in certain cases – like the Wyndham in NYC (where I went to see her in '92).

Tuesday, April 18th: New York

Air Canada lounge at Toronto. I'm off early to New York. Asked about tobacco at US customs here, of course I said yes – and was sent around to the search area. Had to dig out the 25 Romeo y Julietas I bought for Sherrie. 'If they're Cuban, sir, I'm afraid I'm going to have to take them and send them to Chicago to be destroyed.' Big man, thick glasses, hot face – but my celebrity, and checklist of all things I'd been in, helped. 'Put 'em back in your case, and don't give them to *anyone* in New York. I'll be watching your eyes on the next documentary.'

Saturday, April 22nd: New York

Midday: Hopper room at the Whitney. Unblinking dawn light, stillness, edge of the unseen/unknown always present. Light shines yet reveals little. Subjects almost seem petrified by the light. Taken too, with Charles Sheeler – River Rouge Plant. Celebration of power and confidence of American industry. 'Precisionism'. Also Charles Demuth – beauty and harmony in industrial detail.

Later, by way of complete contrast, to 'Waiting in the Wings': Noël Coward's wobbly but endearing story based on the Actors' Home at Denham, outside London. Lauren Bacall (entrance received with rapturous applause) drifts through making no effort at an English accent and completely misunderstanding how her role was written and how it should be played. She almost deliberately goes against the grand old actress supported by charity – by wearing New York designer fashions. Still, it's very enjoyable.

Friday, April 28th: Peninsula Hotel, LA

Short story idea as I'm lying in bed. The Grim Reaper comes to fetch someone. V. agreeable. Not at all grim. Good chat.

Massage at Peninsula – she asks if I would mind if she worked on my face. 'Not at all, I love it.' 'Well you have to ask,' she says, 'especially in Beverly Hills, or you could find a nose coming away in your hand.'

I spend morning in the sunshine at the Los Angeles Times Book Festival – a huge literary encampment on UCLA campus. The sun shone beneath a smog, scouring Santa Ana, and I spoke at Barnes & Noble's arena for 35 mins before Cybill Shepherd then signed for two hours. Enormous demand – and everyone well-drilled by B&N staff into bringing books, not memorabilia.

Later meet George Plimpton, whom I follow in the interview seat for PBS Book Talk prog. Thick white hair, he's slow and awkward in his movements. A pen has run in the top pocket of his shirt leaving a deep blue ink stain and his hands fumble at the mike lead in his belt like those of an old man. So, a first impression of disappointment. A flawed hero. I introduce myself. He doesn't appear to know me. He goes into a beautifully recounted, mellifluously spoken anecdote about his being out fishing with EH on the Gulf Stream and asking him why there were always birds in the sexual scenes in his stories. EH set down a tray of drinks he was carrying, fixed Plimpton with a glare and rejoindered, 'Could you do any better?'

Another shooting in the paper today. A man in a Pittsburgh suburb goes round to several locations shooting various minority group citizens – 'He just snapped'. Not good for the gun sequence in Chicago which will air next Wednesday.

Sunday, April 30th: Seattle

Good, generous preview in Seattle Post. A sleek, tidy city. The munificence of the computer barons – Gates, Paul Allen – investing in the city, invites comparison with Florence and the Medicis, but neither Gates nor Allen seem overtly interested in art.

To Third Place Bookstore. V. heavy signing. Another 200 HA books and lots of HC and travel book list. Hard work, but lovely comments and wobbly girls, 'Can I touch you?', and bores and intense men, and the usual, 'I'm from Yorkshire's.

Wednesday, May 3rd: Chicago

Six thirty departure from the Burnham hotel in sunshine. Best spell of weather in Chicago this year. Magic of May. Up to 80° predicted today.

Transmission day for Hem Adventure in USA. Pre-publicity has been friendly; New York Times leads with a review (by Don Westheimer), which I read in limo to O'Hare. With relief. Driver is chatty. 'My name is Joaquin. I'm a Mexican. We're lower than the Jews' – all said with great humour. American demotic at its best.

Thursday, May 4th: Washington DC

About to be flown by US Airways on their eight o'clock to Boston – last point on the itinerary. A man at check-in had seen last night's show and was complimentary.

Sherrie, over her cigar in the bar last night, criticises PBS decision to show series in Sweeps Week [when TV stations put out all their big hitters to max-imise ad revenue]. 'Instead of a 5.6 share, you'll end up with 2.6.' We'll see. Nevertheless, pleasant feeling now that we're up and running, book and series have come together, as from last night the HA is public property. The website is available. Two more signings and I can forget Hemingway for a while.

Sunday, May 7th

Slept until some clatter awoke me at twenty past nine. H out playing tennis so it must have been cat activity. Edith [sister of Elsie] eyes me owlishly from the end of the bed. It's been a warm and muggy night. Yesterday was hottest day of the year in London – as had been my previous days in Chicago, Washington and balmy Boston.

So, once again, back to earth. Ken Livingstone is Mayor of London.

Succession of visits from my children. Rachel, with Sam, to borrow H's car for a trip up to Suffolk. They've just returned from a break in Barcelona, and Rachel has had two weeks' holiday prior to Sam's departure for San Francis-co for six months on Wednesday. She looks good, slim and hair blonder than I remember. She's pleased to see a laudatory preview in Time Out for the 'Speeches' series, which starts on Choice this week.

I make inroads into the formidable and depressing pile of letters, mags, faxes and so on that has accumulated over last three weeks. As I feared, 'Glasgow y Va-lencia' has slipped from the forefront of my mind and is no longer as crystal clear as it was three weeks ago, after Madrid. Fax from Tom Dunne feeds my insecurity. He knows there is something wrong in the synopsis, wants to meet and discuss.

Monday, May 8th

The PBS overnights come in for 'Hemingway' parts one and two. Sweeps week clobbered them. Though I pushed up the numbers after ice skating it was substantially less watched than any of the other shows I've done.

Tuesday, May 9th

The day begins, cool, cloudy and damp. Take advantage of these conditions to make my first assault on the Heath in my 58th year. Hard work. Side of right knee quite tender towards end of run – slows me on descent of Parliament Hill. I feel very mortal.

Shower and take car up to South Hill Park where I have agreed to talk on camera about Mr Heeley's sex talks for a programme on Sex Education which Sally Doganis is producing for Carlton. The programme is produced and directed by a lady. They're far more relaxed about these sort of sexual reminiscences than the camera crew (both men). I talk of our innocence about my prep school headmaster's gropings. Sally D agrees – in those days we kept all these things quiet. Her doctor prescribed a vibrator for her at the age of 17 and said that next time she came in he'd show her how to use it!

All over by midday. Over to Assaggi's for lunch with Louise Moore – dynamic Penguin editor (of Sue Townsend among others). Louise's general view is, I think, that though anyone would make an offer for *any* Michael Palin book, this one should be a huge seller, with 'large' publicity and that though she likes the character of Chellerby [hero of 'Glasgow y Valencia'] she clearly is not interested in manholes and the Spanish side of the story and in particular big conglomerates. She thinks I have a big novel in me, but, as I say to H later, I'm not sure how much I want to get it out.

Food for thought in cab to Tavistock Street. Much of what Louise says has touched a raw nerve, leaving me feeling unsettled. How good a novel *could* I write? How happy would I be trawling as close to my own experience, as she recommends, in order to create a 'hero for our times'?

Wednesday, May 10th

To Liverpool Street Station by ten o'clock. Meet up with Jonathan Denby of Anglia for a farewell to Wally Rose the breakfast steward who I forever associate with my 9.30 departures for Ipswich on the way to see parents. He's retiring today after almost 50 years' service and I've been asked to come up to Norwich and make a presentation. In a nice twist they surprise him by getting me to serve him breakfast on the train. TV crews are on hand – from both BBC and Anglia evening news shows, plus a smattering of other reporters.

I'd forgotten just how well-mannered and gentlemanly Wally was, and as I

remember sometimes imagining him a lonely man, I was glad to meet his sparky wife and know that they have six grandchildren. And he wears an elegant
dark suit. In short, an apparently very happy man.

Back to London after presentation of a silver tray from Anglia Railways and
an '80 Days' book (in which he features, anonymously, on Day 79!).

Home. Deskwork, letters and exhaustion. Martin Amis's 'Experience' has
been serialised in the Guardian and I felt reassured as he described coming
down from a three-week US book tour. 'The après book tour condition, I
think, would be indistinguishable from extreme jet lag, with or without the
extreme jet lag that usually accompanies it.'

Thursday, May 11th

To the opening of Tate Modern. We are dropped off beside a police barrier within walking distance of the rejuvenated Bankside Power Station. (The
Queen and Tony Blair have both been in today.)

Photographers out like a BAFTA night, then past them and into the real triumph of the building, the leaving-alone of the great long, wide, cathedral-like
space of the turbine floor. A huge area in which to wander, progress interrupted
only by intriguing sculptures, Louise Bourgeois's towers wrapped by mirrors
– all very good jokes on us self-regarding fashionable folk. There is a lot of
noise for the unadorned walls create bouncing soundwaves. A ballet is being
performed amongst what looks like a row of desks.

Bump into Will and Susan Boyd and are bemoaning the poor film distribution that dogged 'The Trench' when Mick J and entourage come through. Mick
slim, lean and lined like a piece of old biltong, but he does have a good smile
and quick, bright eyes. I introduce him to the Boyds and an attendant group of
photographers flash away. Then Mick, in a wonderful, impatient gesture, shoos
them all away, and they dutifully scuttle off like household pets – used to being
ordered about but secure in the knowledge that their owner needs them.

There is a feeling of this being a great moment for London, the creation of a
huge new public area, a huge new asset, and something which will extend and
enlarge public access whilst the great white ghostly shape of St Paul's across the
river looks indulgently, protectively on.

Friday, May 12th

I work at home, tidying up loose ends, writing endorsements, checking letters,
conjuring up some thoughts for the Observer on, what else, the Tate Modern.
I've been asked if I will contribute to a biog of Alan Bennett, but feel I should

ring Alan first (Anne J. cautioned this).

He has exactly the same attitude as I had with Margolis [Jonathan, my biographer]. He would rather the book were not written, not entirely out of dislike for the author, but because if he's going to do it, he'd rather do it himself. I ask how long 'Lady in the Van' will play – he says Maggie [Smith] has agreed to stay in it until July 9th. According to Alan she refers to it affectionately as 'that fucking play'.

Down to the South Bank for our first ride on the Wheel (I can't really get used to calling it the 'London Eye'). Unfortunately the thick, smudgy blanket of cloud that's hovered all day thickens and there are spots of rain. Our 35-minute 'flight' is, even in this sullen, colourless gloom, a delight. The pod is spacious, there is room at the rail for all of us, and a wooden (not plastic, I'm pleased to see) bench in the middle to rest on. There's time enough to spot the landmarks and dwell on the view. Best decision the operators took – *no* recorded commentary.

Monday, May 15th

A very warm night, waking and falling asleep again – my insatiable appetite for sleep since the end of the tour sees to that. More letters, then try to focus on the novel. Is it the one I want to write, can I write it in time, should I take a commission or leave it loose? Must say that my resolve is weakening.

Wednesday, May 17th

To the office. Tell Anne and Anouchka of my most recent thoughts. I don't have enough confidence in the story or the 'weight' of the novel to be sure of completing something by the end of the year, for publication in the spring. As 'Sahara' grows, into what I now estimate to be a seven-part series, so the novel becomes less of a pleasant task and more of a millstone. I think I should begin to write – maybe write as much as I can, but should there be an offer of a commission, I shall not take it.

Back home, a late fax sent on from the office. It's from Ion Trewin confirming that Weidenfeld very much want to go ahead and commission my novel.

May 24th to May 28th: Filming the Scottish Colourists documentary for BBC, in Glasgow, Iona and Fife

Wednesday, May 31st

To Fleming's Bank in the City to be photographed with assorted Colourists for the article I'm going to write for the Sunday Telegraph. Photo sessions and heavy traffic are not my favourite combinations even without the sogginess of a cold dragging me down, but the pleasure of seeing the tremendous array of Scots painting power around the walls at Fleming's brightens my mood considerably.

I'm photographed, sniffing and snuffling, in front of an elegant Fergusson, jonquils in a vase, silvery grey palette, sinuously applied, and then a joyful Hunter.

A quick visit to see some of the rest of this wonderful collection, which is soon to be dispersed as Fleming's are absorbed by Chase Manhattan. This much art in this free, open, office style of display will never be seen again, though I'm told it will be made available to the public regularly, but in smaller doses.

June 1st to June 4th: Colourists filming in Paris and St Paul de Vence and Cap d'Antibes

Tuesday, June 6th

On to the eight o'clock to Ipswich. The cancellation of the connecting train to Woodbridge is announced. Ring the production and take a taxi.

Crew are squeezed in a small house on Stockford Street, whose door is opened to me by an elderly woman with bright eyes and a round, intelligent, welcoming face. She has an elegant Chinese-style linen suit, cornflower blue, loose-fitting trousers and wide top. She wears a matching sort of turban, very eighteenth-century artist. This is Gill Cadell, whose husband John, now dead, was Bunty's nephew.[1] Various Cadell paintings have been brought in to add to those she already has. Over the fireplace is her mother-in-law Jean, with a teacup and black hat; also hung around are his oddly gruff and choleric self-portrait of 1922, 'My Parents at Gotha' of 1906 and the 'Red Fan' of 1923 which had belonged to Simon, the actor son of Gill who died only two years ago.

She has a wonderful presence and a natural poise and easy eloquence which enables us to run swiftly through the long single interview, out in her tiny garden under a vine-covered pergola.

Our final sequence is to be shot at 10 Downing Street, and from here on the day becomes increasingly surreal. We cannot take the backdoor directions to Downing Street as Horse Guards Parade is closed for Trooping of the Colour

---

1 Francis 'Bunty' Cadell was a Scottish painter renowned for his depictions of Edinburgh, where he spent most of his life.

rehearsals; we're eventually let in through the Thatcher Gates (put up during the Poll Tax Riot period, I'm reminded) and allowed to park at the end of the street, opposite Number 11.

If there is such a thing as a psychic forcefield created in places of high emotional significance, the doorstep of No. 10 and the ten yards outside should crackle with it. But it seems oddly mundane. And yes, somehow, comforting that access is so unprotected and so ordinary.

We film upstairs, as the PM is expected to be coming and going downstairs. In the Small Dining Room are a number of very interesting Colourists – Hunter's little lively oils of Venice, a Fife-scape and a couple of Peploe still lives.

I'm allowed to prowl around, I scan the portraits of all the PMs since Robert Walpole which adorn the walls of the main stairs. I lean for a moment on William Pitt's writing table. Outside the window in a clear, windy sunlight the bands in their red tunics and bearskins (reminding me of my lead soldiers I played with so often – and probably poisonously!) practise their steps and formations in the sand of the Horse Guards, separated from the intimate and modest rose garden of No. 10 by a high brick wall.

I hear my name called, and someone approaching up the stairs. It's the prime minister – we shake hands between Lords Aberdeen and Derby. I'm struck by his tan, and by how similar he is in private to the way he behaves in public. Eager beaver look in the eyes, strong handshake, nothing superior or affected in his attitude; an easy natural encounter.

He confesses that he knows very little about the collection and that the lord chancellor, Derry Irvine, is responsible for the choice. Blair touches his tie and collar with a hint of apology. 'It's Tuesday night, I've got to go for my audience.' He grins, apologises once more and disappears off to see the Queen.

By eight o'clock, we're almost finished when there's more commotion, a flurry of activity around the door and Tony is back from the palace. Quite unfazed, he picks his way through our light-stands and cables and walks towards me down the passageway.

He has to begin work now on a speech for 10,000 women he's addressing tomorrow. 'Not the biennial conference of the WI?' I ask. The same. When he hears I've done that, he can't believe his luck. He asks what they're like and seems genuinely concerned about the task. I tell him that all they're interested in is having their own area mentioned. He asks if I have any jokes. I tell him I don't usually do jokes, I can never remember them. He agrees, says he's the same.

As he doesn't seem to be in a great rush I ask him if he would be at all prepared to say a word or two about the Colourists. He seems genuinely unsure about this, makes a move towards us, but by now advisers have appeared. 'I tell you what,' he says, 'I'll do an interview with you about the Colourists, if you'll talk to the WI tomorrow.' And then he's off down past the Fergusson of white-capped Côte d'Azur seas and the Peploe portrait of a woman without a hat and into a downstairs room to prepare his speech.

We take our leave of 10 Downing Street – which resembles half hotel, half private clinic and a little bit of a home – but one in which we've all felt strangely comfortable and quite unintimidated. The press officer confirms that this is how Blair likes it. It's clear they all like him.

Thursday, June 8th

Tony's speech to the WI seems to have already earned its place in history. Tony, after a nervous start (reference to the nude calendar) had clearly not expected the reaction from some of the 10,000. Some of them walked out, others heckled, the applause at the end was unenthusiastic. Amidst much amused comment, there is a general feeling that this was a seriously misjudged speech. Too obviously political. Well, he should have listened to me and just called out a few names!

Friday, June 9th

To Shaftesbury Avenue to see 'Lady in the Van'. Beautiful image at the beginning. The window of A's house, elongated at night against a black background, A's face peering anxiously out into the night. An unforgettable image of Alan, private, internal man with an insatiable appetite for, and instinctive sympathy about, whatever's happening outside.

It also creates an ominous tension which is very effective. The play never really delivers on a dramatic and emotional level. It's a feast of surreal humour, with Maggie in fine form as the Lady, and a sort of discussion on the Alan-ness of Alan, by two men playing Bennett (a clever, very well-executed idea).

Champagne in a very hot little room at the interval, then escorted backstage to see Maggie – who promptly produced another bottle for us all. She looked well – had freed herself from the bodystocking which Alan had warned me about this morning ('She sits there, with her legs apart. I think she forgets she's not dressed'). She was in her most enchanting form. Fluffing around with her hair – always one of Mag's most eye-catching features. She hugs Rachel – and cannot believe she is the shy six-year-old on the 'Missionary' set.

Peeping from her dressing gown on an elegant lower leg is a bloody gash of make-up against a half-scrubbed black background. ('I think she makes herself far dirtier than Miss Shepherd ever was,' Alan tells me later.) She agrees it's athletic – physically gruelling, but she looks so much stronger than when I last saw her.

Monday, June 12th

Mouthwatering prospect of England's first game in Euro 2000 tonight. As ever, the hope that they will rise to an occasion and help everyone interested to feel better about life.

The new Millennium Bridge, meanwhile, has been a sad embarrassment, another little humiliation. It's unstable with a lot of people on it.

Spend most of the day on synopsis for the 'Sahara' filming. I begin reorganisation and de-Hemingway-ification of my workroom. Break off to watch the England–Portugal game. Portugal look all-round sharper, more inventive team, but England score (unbelievably) within three minutes.

Put the supper on and by the time I've clicked the TV there's been another goal. McManaman being mobbed. Two–nil looks, at last, a securable position. But euphoria doesn't last. A brilliant Portuguese goal, followed by wave after wave of Portuguese attacks and England suddenly look familiar – slow, frightened, clumsy in the tackle. Portuguese score again and by half-time it's back on level terms. H comes back and we eat and the by now almost inevitable happens, the Portuguese go ahead. Adams is substituted, Ince gets a caution and there is nothing but gloom and awful anti climax.

I go back to clearing my room. Whether it's being deprived, yet again, of the pleasure of confidence and pride in my national football team, or reaction to being off the work treadmill for a while, my mind slips into negatives. I have misgivings about 'Sahara'. I miss Clem [Vallance, co-director on '80 Days', 'Pole to Pole' and 'Full Circle'] and his instinctive geographical sense. I worry, more fundamentally, about tying myself up, after these next few months, until I'm nearly 60.

In quite a melancholy mood by bedtime. Haven't felt like this for a while – as the roller-coaster rolled on, there hasn't been much time for introspection.

Wednesday, June 14th

Our dull lives immeasurably enhanced by the arrival of a singing fish from the Paos. The idea of creating a trophy fish on a plaque that sings 'Be Happy' could probably only have come from the USA. But it's made in China. Anyway it makes us laugh for at least two minutes.

Friday, June 16th

Begin the day with the delicate process of faeces-sampling. The technology for these frighteningly named haemoccult tests hasn't yet changed and involves fetching samples of jobby from different parts of one's evacuation, and spreading a 'pea-sized' fragment onto a card. This is part of the preliminary work ahead of my 20th anniversary BUPA check-up on Monday.

To Ladbroke Arms to meet Jean-Paul Davidson [potential director for 'Sahara'], and Roger M. Davidson is easily the most confident and engaging of those we've seen. Charming and enormously easy to get on with. He has a smile always at the corners of his mouth, but can also see and talk quite authoritatively about the importance of reflecting the political and cultural life of the countries. He's experienced, but does seem to have a lot of other work on his plate. He has more weight, somehow, than the others.

Monday, June 19th

Hot night. I worry that I'll be dehydrated by the time I get to Battlebridge House for my medical.

BUPA Centre has changed very little – poky rooms into which various business people disappear and from which you can hear their death-rattle wheezes as they undergo the lung function test. I've been coming here for 20 years, figures can be compared, bearing the unavoidable truth about my condition from the age of 37 and the days before 'Time Bandits' and 'The Missionary' to the present day. I approach each test as if it might bite me, but in the end all is still well. I'm heavier, heavier even than last visit, two years and three months ago, but even allowing for my spurt of corpulence, I'm still below the average weight, and above average in heart and lung function and general fitness. I have little trouble walking 15 minutes on the treadmill, with wires trailing off my body, whereas the average at my age gives up at between 10 and 12 minutes. Dr Witchalls feels my balls and my prostate – neither lumps nor enlargements to be found – and pronounces himself very satisfied.

Home to begin first tentative steps on the novel. But after lunch the heat in my room (it's just short of 90 outside) defeats me, and I end the first day's account at 461 words. 'Summer's a discouraging time to work' wrote Hem to Scott Fitzgerald, so I don't feel so bad!

Tuesday, June 20th

My 'Sahara' treatment has been discussed with Salmon, who likes it, wants to do it, but has 'gut feeling' that it is a five-parter. Not the seven we've suggested. The day of the long series is over, apparently. Apart from Attenborough, of course – oh and Simon Schama who's doing a 16-part history of Britain! Quite a lot really, as TJ used to say in the Python 'Rat Tart' sketch.

Rumours filter through of the progress of England's 'vital match' (again) being played against Romania in Charleroi. In the midst of all the noise and excitement and general mayhem, our 3–2 defeat (penalty given away two minutes from the end) and exit from the competition at the first stage, is barely noticed.

Wednesday, June 21st

The Longest Day. My father would be 100 years old today. Get to work on the novel, but still can't push beyond 1,000 words. Partly because no deadline, partly because I'm going through that strange, drifting, occasionally quite low mood that follows hard work and heavy expenditure of adrenaline. A readjustment of time and pace.

All the news and books I read of the Sahara seem to make it sound very grim.

Lunch with TG at Odette's brightens my mood. He's doing a German, French co-prod in Spain, so he's good on Europe. The French make life very difficult for him. They're hierarchical, and inflexible when it comes to rewarding those who do the work. Their cultural superiority and the manifest greatness of French history, art and civilisation is the unstated excuse for such patronising behaviour. The Germans, on the other hand, are nervous of anything to do with their Nazi past, even to the extent of expressing fondness for Goethe or Wagner. Their past is still perceived as so irrevocably tainted, so tied to their fascist history, that it is better not to be acknowledged. So, unlike the French, they are defensive about every aspect of their success.

Thursday, June 22nd

Walk round Hoxton Square with Will. A strange feeling of an old landscape being reclaimed by the young. The buildings are an interesting mix and some are derelict, others like the Lux Cinema and bar, on adjacent corner to the White Cube Gallery, are full of life and noise. A tiny colony of modern London life in an otherwise dark and silent world. I find this exciting, the first feelers of change, of a place with a dying past being reinhabited, slowly at first then with increasing confidence. In ten or twenty years the change will have happened, modern development will not be the tentative presence it is tonight. It will be the norm.

I'm accosted at various points; people shout at me or loom out of the darkness. None of them are as threatening as I first take them to be. One is the chef from the Lux who rushes after me in full white outfit wanting an autograph for his mother. Another man sticks his head out of a car, 'John Palin isn't it?', and as I make my way down an alley flanked with particularly dark walls and bricked-up entrances, a car stops, reverses and then slowly comes towards me. An Indian boy leans out. 'Nice to see you in the East End, Michael!'

Feel a great surge of elation and excitement. This is a wonderful place to have a house. Magical, messy and mysterious.

Sunday, June 25th

My Colourists piece is in the Sunday Telegraph. Seems a bit of a jumble – and according to the subhead the Colourists are 'a new love' for me. Which is not strictly true — a new interest, perhaps, but I'm finding that the more you look at them the less exceptional some of them become. It started with Fergusson's women, and now it's the flowers and vases of Cadell and Peploe. Only some of the Hunters – especially his beach scenes – remain 'loves' of mine.

Wednesday, June 28th

Work on what was intended to be the start of 'Glasgow y Valencia', now re-named 'Scottish Waste'. It's turning itself into a short story. Not a bad thing, I think; maybe this is what my summer book should be. It's clear that I no longer believe I shall write this up into a novel – and once you lose belief in the final outcome, I think there's something wrong.

On the other hand, short stories is a good new discipline – helping soak up a lot of the half-formed ideas for novels, giving my imagination greater freedom, enabling finished work to be produced more quickly, improving confidence, etc., etc. Feel better and push on with 'Scottish Waste' into the afternoon.

Thursday, June 29th

Vividly disturbing dream. As if in slow motion, a building across the street from where I am eating with, I think [my old New York friend] Al Levinson;

someone American being jokey with the waiter as we watch this black sil-houette across the road sway as if in the wind. Then I see people on the roof jumping off as the building starts to break up. The awful truth becomes clear, it's an earthquake – beyond the black, disintegrating block opposite are others breaking up, clouds of smoke and dust rising. Apocalypse. I run up the street, knowing I must stay in the open. Then from the low-rise, open side of the street comes a shower of rubble, spraying through the air. I dive to the ground – and this is the most intense moment of the dream – I feel the wholly accu-rate, realistic physical sensation of debris thudding onto my body, along with the equally intense emotion of surprise that mere rubble could kill – that this is how people died in earthquakes.

Saturday, July 1st

To the Royal Academy for a second look at the Colourists, away from the dis-tractions of a first night.

A Gay Pride march is coming along Piccadilly soon after twelve. Very re-laxed atmosphere. Gay couples at the barriers, smiles, laughter, policemen who less than 40 years ago would have been arresting homosexuals are now keeping the streets clear for them.

Hundredth Test Match at Lord's. Cliffhanging climax – but solid Gough and brilliantly unintimidated Cork see us through by two wickets. West Indies are dignified and generous in defeat. The English, wearing their tacky red Vodafone caps instead of their team caps, romp with laddish self-congratulation. It seems that we no longer know how to win with dignity.

Thursday, July 6th

Sit in Terminal 1 lounge and make final changes to my speech in Belfast in the light of the upsurge in street demonstrations following the barring of the Drumcree procession down the Garvaghy Road. Seems calm enough as we fly in, though our driver from the university said last night was bad for movement round the city. 'We'll get ye there, one way or another.'

To Queen's as sun struggles to push away the clouds. Welcomed by George Bain the vice-chancellor – determined, almost pugnacious jut of the jaw, a Canadian from Winnipeg who has lived in the UK for 17 years and was prin-cipal of the London Business School. He introduces me to the chancellor who will be conferring the doctorate upon me.

A shock of recognition. The man in the gold-trimmed robes with the fine grey hair and glasses is Senator George Mitchell, architect and arbitrator of the most recent peace moves, the honest broker between Prots and Catholics, Loyalists and Republicans and a man who seems to have emerged from it all with nothing but credit.

At lunch I'm sat between George Bain and George Mitchell on the same table as Rabbi Julia Neuberger, who received an honorary degree this morning. Mitchell is quietly spoken. He listens well and talks thoughtfully and quite seriously and without resorting to hyperbole or rhetoric. He is insistent that the RUC should not back down over the Drumcree ban. The last time they backed down after Loyalist violence was one of the most damaging moments in the entire process. And when *he* says that, I believe it.

Otherwise his views are as you'd expect. Minds cannot be changed overnight. It's not until a new generation which has only known peace has grown up that there will be hope for lasting change. So much, he says, is about face and attitude and street cred; which is why every move in the process is so sensitive. Then he grins and tells me that wherever he's been in the world, dealing with these sort of situations, knowledge of Monty Python has been a great help.

We line up after lunch and process, in robes and mortar boards, from the main door of the Gothic portals of Queen's to the more recent, more bland Whitla Hall. My citation is read, then Senator Mitchell shakes my hand and hands me my scroll. A satisfying moment, even if it does all feel like a cross between 'Tomkinson's Schooldays' and 'American Friends'.

Then my speech. Early satirical references to Gordon Brown and Tony Blair receive unpromising silence, but it picks up after that and my message about travelling with respect and humility goes down well, it seems, and perhaps the continued exhortations to open minds through exposure to other cultures hits home in view of the recent expression of extreme Loyalist paranoia.

Home and to bed. Exhausted, but a Doctor.

Remembered a statistic I'd read in today's paper earlier and laughed again. In a survey of attitudes to male kissing in public – 67 per cent of men were not comfortable with the thought of it and 53 per cent of Yorkshiremen said they would punch a man who tried to kiss them.

Friday, July 7th

To the Ivy for supper organised by Peter Benchley, who I met at Paul Zimmerman's [American writer who wrote De Niro's 'King of Comedy'] a while ago. He arrives with his wife Wendy (environmentalist and very jolly) and two save the world friends with whom he is doing publicity for 25 years since 'Jaws' and the Endangered White Shark.

Benchley is lean and oddly yellow of complexion. He and I reminisce over Zimmerman – Benchley was in a restaurant when someone came up and told

Paul he reminded him very much of our Lord Jesus Christ. Without missing a beat Paul replied, 'No he was the one with the famous father.'

Peter, who must be approaching 70 I would think, tells good stories of speechwriting for Lyndon Johnson – like not spelling Nepal phonetically for LBJ, an oversight that almost cost Benchley his job when Johnson referred to his host as 'The Prime Minister of Nipple'.

Tuesday, July 11th

I feel the experiment with Chapter One of 'Scottish Waste' as short story has failed. Most of the writing is bad – straining for some kind of consistent tone. But I've learnt from this three-week experiment, and, going back to basics, I assemble in my mind all the initial strengths of the story. Chellerby's character and his Scots world (much filled out by my researches in April) seem to be the richest seam.

Ask Anouchka to try and book me a trip down the sewers when I visit Glasgow.

In the evening to the Royal Court, now reopened and restored with Jerwood and Lottery cash. Interesting rough-hewn walls – at certain points unplastered to reveal all the layers of the past. V. effective. Meet [nephew] Jeremy there who says there is one unsolved problem and that is the presence of a large sewage pipe which on occasions renders certain parts of the theatre almost uninhabitable.

We're here to see '4.48 Psychosis', the last play by Sarah Kane, which has been well reviewed, especially Jeremy's design, and playing to packed houses. Jeremy has produced another excellent, thoughtful, eye-catching set – the great mirror suspended at 45° above the stage, in which the patterns of the action can be seen almost diagrammatically, as if we are watching a laboratory experiment, is typically bold. Back projection floods the set at times. Maybe a little cool and detached, but it counterpoints the emotional intensity of the play.

When Sarah Kane committed suicide she was younger than Tom and Will are now. Some of the lines ring very familiar – Angela came to mind with the line 'each compliment I hear takes a part of my soul'. What powerful poetry is 'the web of sanity' into which the characters try to resist being drawn.

Thursday, July 13th

I sifted back to my diary entry this time six years ago – after 'The Weekend' and before 'Hem's Chair', and found almost identical state of ennui and aimlessness. Since then I've written three bestselling books and fourteen 50-minute TV documentaries, so perhaps I shouldn't feel so bad. Difference is that I don't feel so bad. I'm that much older; a part of me feels I've paid my dues, put my head on the line often enough, done everything I might want to do and I shouldn't feel so driven.

I talked to [the writer] Gordon Burn last night about these days before and between bursts of creative energy. He sounds to be like me. Taking books from the shelves at random, sampling, looking at how others do it. Not a time, he says, to be frightened of.

Tuesday, July 18th

To the office for a day on 'Sahara' before I leave tomorrow for a brief break in France. The gist of Laura's research is that there are people who will take us anywhere in the Sahara if we're prepared to pay for it. The plan I made a few weeks ago and submitted to the BBC is about right in number of programmes and route – though we're taking Robin Hanbury-Tenison's [great traveller and travel writer] advice and avoiding Nigeria.

Wednesday, August 2nd

To lunch at the Engineer with [director] Phil Agland – he of 'Beyond the Clouds' and 'Shanghai Vice'– the man whose detailed, intimate studies of people in communities round the world I always use as my yardstick for the way I should like to make documentaries. (I realise, with a pleasant shock, how little it would matter to me to give up the front of camera role. Such a pleasure to be freed from being 'a personality'.)

He's younger than me (which is nowadays less and less surprising!), a neat compact man with unlined, olive skin, and very energetic blue eyes. He smiles easily but seems to prefer seriousness – and he talks about his work with an articulate intensity, he's proud of what he does but never oversells himself. He's just returned from Bangladesh, 'wonderful people', and hopes to make another film there. Whereas some people are all blather, I feel that Agland sets out to achieve what he wants and does so.

He asks me about the Sahara – from what point of view will we be approaching it? This flummoxes me. I don't know yet.

Monday, August 7th

Comparatively easy day's work ahead on JC's 'Human Face' prog, but still wake with a gnawing edge of anticipation.

Collected at 8.15 in a freshly polished Mercedes with a navy-suited driver and copies of The Times, Hello and OK! in the back seat and an electronic computer navigation system. Indecipherable lines and squiggles on the screen and every now and then a robotic voice issues from the speaker. 'A-4-0-6, west-bound-con-gestion' etc. We get to High Wycombe and despite the technological marvels on the dashboard I look up to discover we are halfway up someone's drive and about to reverse. The robot voice is silent.

The sketch is dealt with efficiently. We know our lines and we know how to play them. J suggests lunch. 'Come with me, Mickey, in my car, and Michael will find something for us.' JC's florid-faced, white-haired driver really doesn't have a clue what we want, so we coast through Gerrard's Cross, passing a sign for 'Thai Country Food' on a half-timbered pub, which JC thinks might be a wonderful idea. I spot a 'Contemporary Indian' sign in Chalfont St Giles. Though we are the only two customers the food is excellent – tender, delicately tasty ingredients. We have a couple of Kingfisher beers each and talk about the world.

John doesn't want to be considered a permanent exile, even though he's spending September to June back in Santa Barbara. After that 50–50, UK, US. If he could find a like-minded group of say six people who could write and perform a satire show in London, he would be tempted. 'But it would have to be something *incredibly* savage,' he adds, with relish.

A day of little pressure and good companionship.

Friday, August 11th

Muggy night. More helicopters overhead these days. Taxi to the Foreign Office. Late neoclassical courtyards, pale stone facades, freshly scrubbed and restored; decorative William Morris tiles line the floor of the long passageways. Sadly the office we repair to is like any office anywhere, a let-down from the grand approach.

About ten 'advisers' gathered together; we squeeze round a table. I tell them what we're doing, they reply that they are all delighted that we're doing it. The Sahara needs some publicity, they feel! Their advice is impressively clear and well-delivered, though a few gaps in their intelligence – namely Niger and Chad. There is no trace of colonial loftiness or disapproval. They are enthusiastic about all the countries, and do not attempt to talk down to us. Cautionary where necessary, they feel that it is possible for us to film and enter all the countries on our list, with Algeria (and Northern Chad) being the most potentially dangerous.

Monday, August 14th: London–Glasgow

To West of Scot Water; meet up with Alan who drives me over to the South Side and there waiting for me around a hole in the middle of a busy main road is the reception committee for my sewer visit. I'm put in protective clothing, boots and hard hat and, secured by a harness, am lowered 25–30 feet beneath the street into a wonderful Gustav Doré world of shimmering damp walls, streaked and slicked with sediment and various accretions. Beautifully constructed brick vaults rise above the Styx-like flow of a six-foot-wide stream of filth. My minder's voice echoes round the chamber. 'This is just about the entire sewage content of South Glasgow.' The smell is quite bearable, far less offensive than Venice in winter. I take notes. We're down for maybe half an hour.

Photos with the team, then Alan and his engineering director take me round to Partick Pumping Station. This handsome edifice, set amongst equally elegant and impressive university buildings, exists to pump sewage from one level to another 40 feet up.

Back to the hotel. Very good meal indeed and now I know where it all goes.

Saturday, August 19th

The summer goes bowling on. The air is cooler and more pleasant and eventually the sun predominates. After a frustrating hiccup with my laptop I begin work, again, on the novel. Having produced only a fragment so far, I have thought through the problems and find Glasgow and Chellerby appealing. I want to start again and make serious but leisurely progress until the end of the year. Feeling my way to a story. This afternoon I'm full of enthusiasm and enjoy working at the description of Chellerby's visit to the sewer chamber I saw in Glasgow five days ago.

H and I look at diary for next week. A glorious emptiness, which one day would have made me feel insecure, but now offers tantalising prospects of tranquillity – and opportunities of more time to do what I want to do. Whatever that is.

Saturday, August 26th

Brighten up the morning with a visit to Tate Britain, wonderfully quiet and peaceful since the hordes were lured away by Tate Modern. Spend most of my time among the Turners, my most recent enthusiasm. Especially drawn to any vaporous mists, early morning fogs and struggling sunrises. I derive as much pleasure from the way others see the world as I do from seeing it myself. The fresh eye of the artist, in paint or words, heightens the intensity of the pleasure; going to art galleries gives me a chance to indulge in all sorts of emotions and sensations physical and intellectual, which leave me stirred and often inspired.

More and more determined to pursue the idea of an art series of some kind, after 'Sahara'.

Monday, August 28th

Watch Terry J in a prog on gladiators; he argues well that the so-called civilised Romans came up with death as a spectator sport and the much condemned 'Barbarians' brought the show to an end, but he seemed to be walking round in circles a lot of the time – and the short, wacky section where TJ strips off to 'learn to be a gladiator' added no new information, made TJ look a bit daft and confirmed my determination to avoid the 'funny' set-ups in future.

Tuesday, August 29th

Wake before seven and lie brooding over things until it's time to get up. Consumed with negatives this morning – almost achingly so at times. What have I done with the summer – where is the novel going? Why did I do this and that and not do the other? Generally demoralise myself. Perhaps I should just have got up and spent an hour writing.

It's cooler today but the sun comes through and I apply myself to the novel again and, as often happens, a rich seam comes to the surface from nowhere and when I leave it aside for a run at lunchtime, I've regained some optimism. Glasgow itself, or my feelings for Glasgow projected onto Chellerby, is becoming one of the motors of the story.

To Daunt Books to seek out material on Glasgow. 'Very badly served,' says the proprietor.

Thursday, August 31st

Maria A has invited us to a publication launch of Patrick McGrath's new book 'Martha Peake', and the invitation goes on, 'to celebrate . . . the birthdays of Maria, Jonathan and William Aitken'.

Taxi drops us at the end of Lord North Street, and one of the most perfect Georgian prospects in London. The houses, all original, leading the eye up to the fine church of Smith Square in the background. Jonathan A's house is No. 8, but it may not be his for much longer as the Receivers are at the door – as Maria puts it.

Considering Jonathan is one of the most spectacularly disgraced English-men of his time, there is quite a good turnout; many seem to be friends of Maria and Patrick. Norman Lamont is near the door at the centre of a very small circle. A man with a big face, glasses and wild hair is introduced to me as a book editor for the Spectator; we have nothing much to say to each other. Nic Kent [Director, Tricycle Theatre] gives H a big kiss and praises her tennis with great enthusiasm; Maria rushes past, offers an apologetic greeting but says she's heard that Harold Pinter hasn't had a drink for 15 minutes and she has to chivvy the staff.

Jonathan A, suit, plain shirt, no tie (on him, an ex-government minister, this does not look merely informal, it looks as if he's just returned from a rather rough police interrogation – which of course, might well be true) smoothes his way through a group of people.

'Do you know Jonathan?' someone asks, which is a bit like asking if you know Madonna or the Duke of Edinburgh. His face, close to, is revealingly free of lines and his complexion is that of an overripe apple. 'We were at Oxford together,' says JA smoothly, before I can reply.

Later, after food, we end up talking more. He talks about prison, about the 'diamonds' and the 'plastics'. 'Diamonds' being decent coves who you can trust, plastics being flaky and unreliable. I assume he was seen as a diamond. The whole thing sounds remarkably like boarding school. He agrees with this but says the one big difference is drugs. The prison he was in was 'awash with drugs', many of which get in during visiting time. Prisoners are allowed a short physical embrace with their loved ones, and he observed clinches of consid-erable intensity in which packets of drugs were passed mouth to mouth. Soft drugs are more easily detectable as the evidence can stay in the bloodstream for a week, hard drugs for three days (and even then they can be flushed out using large amounts of water). Prison officers do not test for drugs on Saturdays or Sundays, so the heavy stuff is taken on Friday morning.

Sunday, September 3rd

Watch the 'Colourists' tape – without titles and colour grading. Very rich. Paintings speak for themselves, the new music richly compatible. I talk as if I'm about to be electrocuted – could have said less and not conveyed same feeling of rush. But as a celebration of the Colourists' world, it works well.

H and I have supper with Robert Hughes's documentary on Oz 'Beyond the Fatal Shore' playing beside us. Even on the tiny kitchen TV it impresses.

Visually splendid. Hughes crusty, funny, opinionated and tells a familiar story with unusual skill. His face is marvellous too – in fact his whole body, broken, battered, bruised by his car accident, seems like some ancient god-like figure. Mischievous and immortal! The easily conveyed, lightly dispensed depth of knowledge that accompanied his verve rather depressed me!

Sunday, September 10th

Leisurely day; bask in the late summer sunshine, scan the papers. Begin to dig into Thubron's 'In Siberia'. He is a marvellous writer, but there is a Thubron tone which rarely changes – it's ascetic, sombre, elegiac and sad, and doesn't change gear very often.

About 7.30, Rachel, returned this a.m. from Dallas, drops by. Her 'Conspiracies' filming was very good in Dallas, more of a rush in Los Angeles. I'm full of admiration for what she takes on and the way she deals with it. She finds just talking to people, keeping them relaxed, whilst at the same time having to organise yourself and your own contribution, to be the most demanding. I agree. But it doesn't seem to be putting her off this kind of work – in fact quite the opposite.

And news, late, that, as from four o'clock this afternoon I'm a great-uncle again. Melanie, Jeremy's wife, has had a little girl.

Monday, September 11th

A slow push forward with the book. Compared to 'Hemingway Adventure', 'Scottish Waste' is developing slowly – I'm around 8,000 words after two weeks of writing – but it is evolving into something interesting and quite rich. It's allowing me to say a lot.

In the evening [my cousin] Nigel Greenwood, the gallery owner, comes round to talk over paintings, where and how to hang them. His advice useful, especially about my over-ornate frames, put around the picture by galleries anxious to give them some status (I'm aware that I'm a bit too much of a frame-buyer – well, frame-influenced anyway). Looking at my collection in No. 2 with Nigel I realise what an eclectic mess it is. Nothing wrong with liking lots of different work, but I accept N's point that you don't have to put all of it up on the wall at the same time.

Wednesday, September 13th

Big story is the petrol price protests. Sparked off by the blockades in France three weeks ago, the British farmers and hauliers are currently blocking supplies getting out of refineries and according to the Herald Tribune our country is 'paralysed'. Dire warnings that hospitals may have to turn people away, food will run out in two days. A series of legal blockades has been hugely successful. The army is being readied for action!

Thursday, September 14th

Collected by cab at a quarter to eight to go on to a supper at Michael Dover's home in New King's Road. The driver takes me past a garage in St John's Wood which he points out as being 'the only garage open in the whole of north-west London'. The cars stretch in an orderly queue, patrolled by yellow-jacketed police, for a mile or more. A television crew is set up, with a besuited Sky News presenter illuminated in a white, semi-religious glow with the filling station behind him. Petrol pumps are showbusiness.

An excellent evening at the Dovers'; the guests are 'adventurers' in some shape or form. [Mountaineer] Chris Bonnington, very slim and immaculate in a suit and tie, hair cut very short, eyes sparkle, but he's older and frailer than I expected. Julie Summers, who's writing a book on Irvine – of Mallory and Irvine – who died on Everest at 22. He was a Salopian so she's been working up at the school. Mallory and Irvine would make a great film.

The beef we eat comes from a beast by the name of Kiz of Dabrieda and has a family tree supplied with names of its beefy Scottish forebears.

Sunday, September 17th

H's mother came last night and is staying until Monday. After my Sunday run, I take her to see Somerset House. The fountains spurt and sag rhythmically as a small group of us watches and a child who can only just have learnt to walk runs in amongst the performing waterjets, in a distinctive little red waterproof (which no one who's seen 'Don't Look Now' can ever take in without a frisson of fear).

We drive on to St Paul's and walk down the newly laid steps towards the sadly impotent Millennium Bridge. I, like Granny, had never seen it in situ before, and it is a beautiful thing – soaring gracefully up and across the river. The tragedy is that it is so tantalising, it's like a magic carpet, instantly exciting and appealing – but of course it is at present dead as a dodo, a barrier of functional silver-painted fencing mocks its light, soaring appeal. It reminds me of Concorde, too good to be true.

We take some photos and back up the steps and home. The fallout from the petrol protests is still beneficial, streets and roads much emptier, cleaner and less noisy. Very strong feeling I had as I ran this morning that this country is in a mess. Blair, having done much good – especially in Ireland – seems to be slipping. I think of his glass-eyed weary stare as I told him about the WI – the look of a man who can't take much more, of anything.

Why not do a series about Britain? Why not call it 'Ten Million' and deal with the ten million on the poverty line whose voice is never heard in these shrill, greedy times? Talk to them, meet some of them, make them into people not just statistics.

Sunday, September 24th: Glencoe–London

Woke in Hamish's [MacInnes, Scottish mountaineer and friend] spacious upper room. Have not slept as well as might have been hoped after yesterday evening's walks and exercise. Hamish told me he only needs four hours' sleep a night (legacy of his rescue work he says) and I'm complaining about six and a half?

A peremptory breakfast. Weetabix and a cup of tea. The skies look very unfriendly over Glencoe. We climb up a gully down which a stream runs between two of the Three Sisters' summits. Quite a scramble over big boulders but we emerge, after about 40 minutes' climbing from the road, into what Hamish calls the Lost Valley, a natural amphitheatre, quiet and sheltered, about a quarter of a mile across and half a mile long.

Here the MacDonalds hid their cattle from marauders. It does have a peaceful quality to it, protective but grand at the same time. Prompts Hamish to suggest that I should make a programme about another, much more impressive hidden valley, now a reserve, near Nanda Dir in Kashmir – this time about 16,000 feet up. Access restricted but Hamish says he could sway it for me.

Since I heard from Anne two days ago that the BBC are offering only four one-hour films about the Sahara, I've been keen to see the positive side, and one way of doing that has been to appreciate that less time in the Sahara could mean other opportunities elsewhere.

Monday, September 25th

A letter from Peter Salmon – confirming the 4 x 1 hour offer, referring to me as 'one of the most important presenters at BBC One and we want you to feel appreciated and inspired to do more wonderful work here'. 'Sahara' would be 'one of our biggest blue-chip series going forward'.

Tuesday, September 26th

We beat out a new schedule more suited to four 1-hours than seven 50s, and at every step I feel relieved that we have been forced to concentrate and conserve rather than expand the series merely to match its predecessors.

Friday, September 29th

Eleanor Yule [director of our Arts films] calls. BBC Two have rejected 'The Bright Side of Life' as a title and want the show to be called 'Michael Palin . . . on the Colourists'. Only glimmer of hope from this tired but expected reaction is that it opens the way for a whole series of 'Michael Palin . . . on's and E and I trade ideas for future arts progs. I suggest women painters – much neglected but fascinating to find out how much and why.

Saturday, October 7th: Leeds

At the Dragonara, the morning after being honoured as 'Yorkshireman of the Year'. Breakfast in my room. The engraved glass rose-bowl will clearly be my cross to bear today. The hotel has no carrier bag which will go round it, so I shuffle out into the rain about an hour later with my award uncomfortably under one arm and both bags in the other.

Up a flight of steps to the station, which is full of people. A number of them look to be heading for Wembley, where England play Germany in a World Cup qualifier that has also been deemed the last game to be played at the old Twin-Tower stadium. We lose to a single German goal – generally felt to be a soft one – early in the first half.

Some half-hearted fireworks afterwards, but nothing as dramatic as Kevin Keegan's decision to resign as England manager – an awful, candid confession of failure by the man who, as Yorkshireman of the Year 1999, would have had to carry the rose-bowl home last year.

Wednesday, October 18th

Sour weather again after night-time rain. Sara Jane Hall, who is to be my producer and travelling companion in Trieste and Szczecin, comes round at a quarter to ten to discuss ideas for this series of radio travels following the route of the Iron Curtain. She's probably in mid-thirties, bright and quick-witted, and seems to enjoy the life as well as the work – as befits someone who made a series on great bars of the world with Arthur Smith. We discuss a rough approach. She has some interviews lined up. The Trieste–Stettin will be made into two half-hours.

Thursday, October 19th

Collected by a UNICEF lady at half past ten and driven to Waterside, BA's new environmentally and user-friendly HQ built on the site of an old rubbish tip tucked in the armpit formed by M25 and A4.

Meet various luminaries including Sir John Waite who I believe is head of UNICEF in UK. White hair, guardsman's manner, but mischievous sense of humour – and arrived via public transport!

Children from Diepkloof township in South Africa (beneficiaries of all the loose change collected on BA aircraft over last six years, amounting to £10 million in total) put on a half-hour show – music, dance, some jokes, some serious messages about life in new South Africa. Considering nearly all of them have never travelled before, let alone all the way to Europe, it was engaging and confident stuff – a remarkable event to happen in the middle of a huge corporate headquarters with people milling about in their lunch hour.

I thank them and then say my bit about the Change for Good campaign, which is easy to praise, then photos with the children, with various cabin crew and so on. Then a tree-planting ceremony to mark Ten Million Day – with Sir John Waite's speech appropriately broken by the roar of ascending jets.

Monday, October 23rd

Oldie magazine at the Guildhall in Winchester. Richard Ingrams, who does have one of the most wonderful faces in the whole world, and like so many irascible commentators is touchingly soft and gentle off the page, says they've over 200 people. Best turnout for any of their out of London lunches so far.

They seem old, rather upmarket and opinionated, the audience. One or two smiles, and a number of odd conversations as I sit between Bill Cotton and Brian Blessed at tiny round signing tables.

'My cousin's children were at school with your children.'

'Oh yes.'

'Yes, at Eton.'

'No, my children went up the road to the state school.'

'Winchester?' says her friend, cupping an ear and looking confused.

After an hour's mingle, lunch is announced and we all move through. I'm the only male apart from Blessed without a tie. He is the first to go, eschews the mike and prowls the room. He says his house is an animal sanctuary and I think he has become one of them – half lion, half OT prophet. Certainly OTT.

Then Bill C, who does not have a carrying voice and has every word prepared and is frequently interrupted with shouts of 'Speak up!' delivered in that unpleasant talking-to-the-servants kind of upper-class voice. He soldiers on, but I think detects that this is not the perfect audience for showbiz reminiscing.

I'm glad I cut loose from my written text. A little bit choppy at the beginning, but comparing bearded Brian B to Hemingway goes down well, as does my request for anyone who thinks I'm talking too loudly to say so.

Saturday, October 28th: Trieste–London

Breakfast, then walk out onto the seafront, weather bright and clear for first time. Record a last piece to mike – Sara [Hall, producer of this Radio 4 documentary on the Iron Curtain] rather impressed that I didn't say 'um' once in a one-minute-thirty piece – then interview the mayor at the messily grand neoclassical pile looking out over the Piazza d'Unita (Trieste's St Mark's Square).

He is Riccardo Illy – rich and successful head of Illy coffee empire. Slim, well-groomed (as Sara puts it), built like a jockey. Good English even if he does snap into a Trieste sales pitch. We've been told he's popular and has for the first time in 80 years offered Trieste a realistic vision of a rosy future, and started to deliver by spending money on the look of the city.

Back to the Duchi d'Aosta, grand in name and renown, but in reality, a cosy, almost intimate Grand Hotel run by the family who own it. Meet and talk with Claudio Magris, writer and historian of Trieste (of whom his fellow author John McCourt said 'he's good, but not as good as he thinks he is'). He plays the intellectual star card. 'I can't answer about the cafés – I don't want to. I've done it all before.' Lots of looking at watch.

I've enjoyed my first exposure to radio reporting. I like the concision – the lack of clutter, but also the new challenge of having to convey all by words. My vocabulary is not big enough for me to do this with absolute confidence – but I hope I will get better as I get more familiar with the technique. Sara is very easy to travel with and keeps the pressure on gently.

Thursday, November 2nd

Start the day with two interviews for Scottish media, ahead of 'Colourists' opening tomorrow. The weather is once again apocalyptic, turbulent skies, swaying trees, darkness at noon stuff. In fact, in the middle of one of my replies about the sunny, life-enhancing qualities of the C's, there is a sudden, blinding light in the sky above me, not fork lightning, just a flash powerful enough for me to yelp down the phone. A great splitting crack of thunder. I expect a godly finger to poke through.

TG called yesterday sounding grim. He's back from Spain, the film abandoned at least until the new year, after Jean Rochefort, his Quixote, had to pull out – unable to ride a horse for medical reasons. We arrange a lunch at the Engineer, mull over things and taste the best ham and pea soup I can remember. Another swift shower hisses across the patio outside where the garden chairs are piled rather forlornly on one another.

TG is to talk to Nigel Hawthorne tomorrow, but even if he can replace the French star, he may lose Johnny Depp. 'And the problem is,' says Terry, 'it looks good.'

'How much have you seen?'

'About three minutes.' TG praises Depp's commitment, wit, improv skills and reiterates that he thinks he'd have made a perfect Python.

Saturday, November 4th: Edinburgh

Shave, shower, exercise, pack, snatch some breakfast then leave for London at 7.30. Another glorious autumn day – the serious classical facades of Edinburgh brushed with gold.

The cabbie drops me at the airport with a variation on the usual 'I enjoy your work' theme. 'I've had a shit at sea, Michael, and believe me I know how difficult it is!'

Monday, November 6th: London–Szczecin

Lie awake listening to the rain popping against the windows and running water in the gutters outside. It eases by the time I get up but I've not slept well and have to deal with the now familiar combination of fatigue and hard work ahead.

Meet up with Sara and onto BA flight to Berlin. A bus transfers us from the airport to the Zoo station on the S and U-Bahn systems. As we lug our bags up the steps I'm approached by a German news crew. Can't understand their question, so smile and apologise. As soon as they hear I'm English, they snap, with embarrassing fluency, into English. 'That will be interesting,' says the reporter. The issue is that there are proposals to sell off the German rail system and some of the bidders may be British. What do I think? Well, of course I can't miss this one. Don't do it, I say. Look at the railways in Britain since privatisation – chaos. Your railway system is the envy of Britain – it's something we admire.

I'm quite amused by the thought that, although this team have no idea who I am, there are thousands of Python fans in Germany who will find this one of the great TV surprises!

Sara gets out the mike, puts her headphones on and we record my impressions of crossing a border into Poland, a country new to me. Szczecin station is kind of what I expected. Dimly lit – the Eastern half of Europe has always been a few watts short of the West, and there is not the money for display advertising and ambient lighting.

Friday, November 10th: Lübeck–London

Back in Germany, in Lübeck, in a tiny room in the Hotel Jensen, with the sound of traffic on wet streets below me and a view of the great hulk of the Holstentor and the more graceful narrow, step-gabled roofs of the old salt warehouses.

I've set the alarm for 7 but since 6.30 I've been turning over in my mind thoughts of what I need to say in my final summary, out at the end of the Iron Curtain. Write down one or two phrases, knowing that these programmes work best when I'm on the spot, adapting to what I find.

Click the TV on. The American election still stymied by the re-count and general irregularities in Florida, where it seems less than a thousand votes will decide for Bush or Gore.

At eight our mini-bus arrives and, having checked out, we're driven to a small town called Schlutup where the most northerly checkpoint on the old Iron Curtain is now to be a museum. Photos of the old fortifications seem scarcely believable now. Mesh fences, guard posts, ditches, trace detector strips, dogs, mines; a fearsome paraphernalia of security keeping Germans away from fellow Germans.

Saturday, November 11th

Terrible tunnel fire in the Alps, 170 people thought to have been burnt at temps of 1,000°C. Just on their way up the mountain for a day's sport.

Monday, November 13th

Supper with Rachel who shows us her latest BBC Choice prog – on assassination conspiracies. I'm very impressed. With tiny budget (£20,000 in all) and less editing time than on her 15-minute 'Great Speeches', she's put together a fast, coherent, densely packed but watchable survey of the subject. Good catchy television, her talents of organisation and conscientious dogged commitment have given the BBC an extraordinary bargain. She has no further work offered her at the moment.

Saturday, November 18th

Call George and Olivia. The case of their attacker was up in court last week. He was found not guilty on grounds of insanity, which means, says Olivia, that they have no further rights to know anything about him – his release dates or whatever. She's deeply hurt by a Deborah Orr piece in the Independent, criticising George and O for fighting off their attacker!

Friday, November 24th

Long, complicated day ahead. Need to have it well plotted. Picked up at 8.15 to go down to Tracy for more physio and a short session up in the torture chamber. To Great Portland Street and onto the Circle Line to Liverpool Street. Turn off Bishopsgate and walk up Birchfield Street, towards the church – from Mammon to God. Meet Graham Simmonds of Trees for London in a coffee bar in Brick Lane, opposite the corner of Quaker Street on which I'm to help plant a tree. Some journalists, a camera or two as we all raise the Himalayan birch and help local children throw a few shovelfuls of pretty unhealthy-looking soil around it. Stay and chat a while, do a short interview for BBC South East News – who now only send one person to shoot, interview and record.

Pick up a few things at the market, then onto the train to Blackfriars to look for something original for Gilliam's upcoming 60th birthday.

To Zwemmer's [bookshop] – find a good-looking book of photos (b and w) of world cities, all unusual and personal insights. Also organise a voucher from the sister health club of the Hyde Park Hotel and have Terry's name put on and hopefully biked up to me by tomorrow.

Back onto the Underground – east to Old Street, then a brisk walk across Hoxton to the Geffrye Museum in Kingsland Road for a short celebration with T2000 [transport lobby] people of [our director] Suzanne May's OBE.

Tea and update on the hideous mess that the railway is in – current feeling in the industry is that Hatfield derailment (coming so soon after Paddington) caused a panic reaction and ridiculously unnecessary safety measures which have been punitively expensive and caused huge defections from the trains to overcrowded and much more dangerous roads.

Home, via Kentish Town. Find the Dorchester Health Club voucher has arrived. Amazing efficiency – v. impressed until I note that it has been made out to Terry Jones by mistake.

Sunday, November 26th

Terry G's 60th. Terry J and Al come to the house at 6.30 and we have a glass of wine and a gossip, then the four of us walk up to Cucina in South End Green.

Terry G looks heavily tanned, but on closer look appears nastily burnt. Poor man, he has to explain to everyone who might want to make some festive contact with his glowing face that he scorched it in Italy last week, after pouring petrol on wet branches and igniting them with a cigarette lighter. He was treated in an Italian hospital, and I just hope it all heals up. Bits look very raw.

George and Olivia on very good form. George bought Terry a ukulele, and both of them strummed away on it. George, anxious as ever to fight against formality, turns the evening into a very jolly musical cabaret. He sings a silly version of 'Something' and encourages Ray [Cooper] to accompany him on the spoons.

Terry, bashful and apologetic at first, but forced by public pressure to speak after he's blown out his candles (another potentially dangerous manoeuvre!), gets his head down and delivers some wise, well-expressed thoughts on being 60. 'I'm as old as a grandfather, with the mind of a grandson'.

Frustratingly, his Quixote film seems to have little chance of survival now. Irene [Lamb, Terry's casting director] has no doubts that Johnny Depp will go elsewhere – 'he's ditched Terry in the past and he will do again'.

Wednesday, November 29th

Roger Mills rings at breakfast. He's somewhere in the Sahara, and the reception is not very clear. He sounds as if he's about to peg out, but when I can make out his words they sound almost ecstatic . . . He's slept under the stars last night and never seen anything like it.

The series is gaining momentum. This morning I take my old passport down to the office to give to Janina [working on the production side]. Sad to part with it – the last of the solid, dark blue British passports, easy to identify, much less easy to lose than their drab EU counterparts.

Saturday, December 2nd

Leisurely afternoon at my desk. Enjoy the pleasures of having time to be side-tracked, pursuing a reference through my books, following up on where exactly my great-uncle Harry, H.W.B. Palin, is buried in France, after someone sent me details of his grave.

I should be putting the novel in order or beginning on 'Sahara' research, instead I find myself writing to Ion Trewin giving reasons why I shall not get the novel completed for at least two years. Truth is, this is not a year for con-centrated work on big projects. It's a fallow year – a year to let myself breathe, let my mind clear and regenerate.

Edith sits behind me gazing out of the window, watching what goes on outside and presenting quite an acceptable image for this last year. Watching the game, that's what I've been doing. It's been so pleasant – travelling without a series depending on it, investigating things like the Colourists and Szczecin and Trieste on a whim, digging into Glasgow, absorbing painting, helping charities whilst satisfying the dormant urge to perform – so pleasant that I wonder if I still have the will to commit to more very hard work.

Monday, December 4th

Begin some reading on the Sahara. Anne reports that Roger has written off Chad completely after 24 hours there. Civil war makes it impossible to move anywhere . . .

We have new weekly recycling collections now – a green box provided for us to put papers, cans, bottles, books, old clothes in, is now to be picked up every Monday, and the line of them becomes another new addition to the streetscape.

Friday, December 8th

Write Christmas cards. A session at the gym, then the cats to be taken to the vet for annual booster. Not Albert, thank God, so we don't need buckets and kitchen-roll, but Edith and especially Elsie fight hard and Elsie keeps popping up and out of her box. In the end I just have to manhandle these lithe, elegant, beautifully constructed bodies like a bunch of old rags. In the evening write more cards whilst H wraps presents. Feel unrushed and listen to Bach's cello suites till quite late.

Monday, December 11th

To Holland Park Comprehensive for eleven o'clock. Have agreed to speak to the drama class who are putting on 'Cabaret' this week. Big, modernist, pioneeringly liberal comprehensive, tucked away on smart Campden Hill.

Children of all creeds and colours, as they say, and quite a lively session. I talk for 15 minutes or so about the joys of acting – then questions. A moment of real surprise when I begin my answer to the 'What is your favourite film?' question by saying 'It's a Swedish film . . .' only to be met by an oo-ah! ew, whoar, nudge-nudge barrage worthy of a rugby club in the 1950s. Rather refreshing to know that to today's multiracial, liberated, mobile-phoners 'Swedish' is still a synonym for sex.

Tuesday, December 12th

Home to Zafferanos restaurant in 40 minutes, with a vigorous walk and a chance to read the New Yorker thrown in; Eddie Mirzoeff arrives, breathless and apologetic, 15 minutes later. He's been called back to the BBC, but has no office or secretary. He's making a programme on John Betjeman.

I show him an email which came through from Presentation at the BBC ahead of the screening of 'Full Circle' on BBC Two over Christmas. As it's going out in the afternoon some smutty mind has been through it itemising a litany of shits, the use of the word penis and even 'Michael appears to utter the word "arse-fuck"'. A bizarre and depressing example of the way the censor's mind works. And, as Eddie points out, the series went out before the watershed, at eight o'clock, with none of this fuss. A pleasant lunch – Eddie very agreeable company.

By now the wind is rising and rain being flung around. Horrible conditions. No, not really, I rather like them. Weather with passion.

Wednesday, December 13th

Anne says the BBC, when challenged, have dropped most of the objections to my language in 'Full Circle', but I shall keep the document, which is hilarious and sinister at the same time.

Roger rings around ten. 'One thing's for sure, Michael, after this series no one will ever be able to accuse you of staying in five-star hotels. There aren't any.'

Thursday, December 14th

News that Gore has conceded and Dubya Bush is to be next president – news that I should have heard five weeks ago in Szczecin.

Walk down Drury Lane and cut through to the office. Roger M is upstairs with Anne and Janina. I've bought him a colourful pocketbook of 'Erotica in the British Museum'.

Leave them to talk schedule, then do letters with Anouchka and have my photo taken on the streets of Covent Garden to accompany a Norwegian TV piece.

Briefly home and just about to go out to the first of my Christmas book-signings when Anne J calls. In one of those casual 'just to let you know' tones she adopts for significant news, she says that Louise Moore and Penguin have increased their offer for the 'Sahara' book advance to double what BBC offered.

My immediate reaction is instinctive irritation. It's ridiculous, irrational, silly money. I feel like a ping-pong ball. Batted about. Anne, somewhat taken aback by my reaction, says it shows how high an opinion they have of me. I can't immediately see it as clearly as that. To me it means trouble, the way silly-money increases always have. How can they just slosh another half a million my way without sort of admitting that it doesn't really matter much to them.

Ring Anne later from the car and apologise for sounding churlish. The more detail I hear, the less I'm inclined to dismiss it out of hand, especially as Louise had told Anne that the increase in offer would probably 'irritate Michael'!

To Selfridges. Sign for two and a quarter hours. All the hardbacks are gone and a lot of paperbacks too. Michael Dover, scarcely able to walk after putting his back out in New York a week ago, arrives at the end of the signing and I'm delighted to see him.

Over a drink before I go home he shows me the illustrated cover of Orion's proposal for the 'Sahara' book, which he will pitch to Anne tomorrow afternoon. Our decision to stay with the BBC, that seemed to be the easiest and most sensible thing a week ago, now appears less certain. Louise and Penguin's intervention has upped the ante and there is a limited bidding war on. Exciting times.

To Battersea after that, as guest of George and Olivia at a charity performance of Cirque de Soleil (who hope to take over the shell of the power station for a permanent London base). The Cirque organisation now employs 3,000 worldwide, Ray Cooper tells me. The show is efficient, some acts like the diabolo-wielding Chinese girls breathtaking, the clowns tedious. It's long, a little in love with itself. A cool, almost detached cast, stare out unblinkingly at the wildly applauding audience at the end – I reckon the sight of a man leaping backwards, off another's shoulders, to land on top of three men standing on each other's shoulders behind him, was worth a bit of self-congratulation.

Monday, December 18th

Catch up on cards and diary for the week, then to Tristram's party at the Polish Health Club. Mixed crowd of showbiz and aristos. Melvyn B, of course, but newcomers to Tristram's events like Ken Cranham. Alan Bennett is leaving almost as everyone arrives. He slips out, clutching his face and trying not to stop – 'Oh, you look so well,' he waved as he went past me, craggy Ken and Harold Pinter, 'so pink!'

I complimented Harold on 'The Caretaker', but when I made a lightly ironic remark about the truth of the story that Michael Gambon was in possession of a fart machine which he planned to use on stage, Harold didn't see the funny side and delivered a venomous attack on all who write such garbage in the papers and, looking aside at me with his hard stare, 'those who believe them'. This was quite a punch and intended to hurt rather than entertain. I was bemused. I haven't been bullied like that for a while.

Tuesday, December 19th

To meet Richard, now Baron, Faulkner at the House of Lords for dinner. A remarkable place. The lushly decorative Pugin interiors, the whiff of high church Gothic seems unusual, un-British – a sense of slightly naughty overdressed decadence pervades, alongside a sumptuous sense of national grandeur. It's the complete opposite of modern and adds a theatricality to everything.

Richard (who introduced me to T2000) is a newly created life peer. He meets me at the Peers' Entrance, inside which is an area of coats and old-fashioned hooks and pegs, which reminds me instantly of my first day at school. We wander the corridors, Richard every now and then nodding to people who nod back, politely but, I feel, sometimes uncertainly. He says the Lords is a much happier place than the Commons, even though, so far, he only has half a desk and no secretary. He's always been one of the most regular attenders, Lord Lloyd Webber being one of the worst. He shows me into the bar and we have a pre-dinner drink and I'm introduced to four very jolly female peers.

Richard is Labour – works quite closely with Prescott and Gus MacDonald.

A most unusual evening – very enlightening – but I can sense how narrow one's horizons can be inside such a seductive institution. Status assured and history welling up all round you.

Wednesday, December 20th

Things moving rapidly on the book front – Orion have upped their offer to three-quarters of a million.

Have promised Cathy's Michael [Stratton, partner of Helen's younger sister] that I will visit the company that supplies his trucks for the Christmas mobile canteen. Cathy drives me across East London to Canning Town. The company collects and processes second-hand and cast-off clothes and sends most of them out to countries in Africa. The boss is a self-made, confident East Ender called Laurence. He employs 100 people sorting through the garments, and has an impressive acquaintance with countries he's actually been out to – Uganda, a pal of Museveni, a house in Togo. A seriously interesting set-up here and I have a coffee and am shown round but not paraded or shown off at all. Most of the workforce are from Third World countries.

Walk back to the office for a meeting with Anne on the book offers. After about 45 minutes' chat, I decide to go with Orion – Penguin unknown, and the BBC is much too 'corporation' minded. The personal touch wins.

Thursday, December 21st

Another run. Holiday walkers already out making ripples of dogs across footpaths. I so much prefer the world when it's working.

About mid-morning, after comparatively little rethinking I called Anne and confirmed my decision to go with Orion. Apparently they had been in contact this morning upping their offer to a million. I sigh and call Anne to make sure she lets Michael Dover know that I'd decided on them before the million carrot was dangled. I know that however much money I'm paid now makes no difference at all to the quality of what I shall be able to provide them with in the future. In my experience, the quality of the work is more often than not in inverse proportion to the amount of money invested. Still, mustn't be too puritanical. I feel a spring in my step as I walk through Notting Hill, which must be something to do with being worth a million.

Christmas Day

The rain has moved away south and the murk of yesterday has lifted to give a pleasantly bright morning – but with an occasionally biting wind giving uninviting running conditions.

The turkey is in by 9.30 (to find its weight H had to stand on scales in the bathroom, then be handed the turkey. Bizarre!) and preparations begin for family Christmas at Julia Street. All goes very smoothly. Edward and Mary round by 1.30 – bringing goose and gravy and pears and prunes to go with it; Rachel has organised Japanese tour guide style flags to mark the piles of presents which are laid out before lunch.

From the first glass of champagne, to the last glass of Slovenian Chardonnay at 9.30, the day follows familiar pattern. Very good presents – mostly books for me. Sahara book from Tom, book on the design of London Underground lettering in the '20s and '30s from Will, Derek Jarman's diaries – follow-up to my favourite 'Modern Nature' collection – from Mum. The sharper, cooler weather means fires all blazing and the house looking its very best.

Only three for the post-prandial Parliament Hill leg-stretch. Me, Rachel and Mary. We have the Hill virtually to ourselves. The wind tight but bearable and it has swept away the low cloud and revealed a wide, clear, glittering panorama of London – the city which in all its perversity, makes me feel comfortable and protected and stimulated – and yes, almost a Londoner.

Wednesday, December 27th

Cleese returns my call of yesterday. He sounds businesslike. I ask him what he's doing and he recounts a dream in which he found himself in a roomful of men in suits wishing that he should have been born German. He woke up, thought of how much influence Germany has had on his life and has decided to spend next summer 'cracking it' – living in Germany.

Friday, December 29th

Take GG [Helen's mother, Granny Gibbins] back home to Abbotsley [near St Neots in Cambridgeshire]. Five degrees below F last night and have to take it carefully. Settle Granny with her various presents; as if a bag lady had invaded the kitchen. Make some coffee, wind her clock, walk upstairs and try to see if memories of Christmas morning with the boys here, 26 years ago, are recoverable. Not really, just the illusion that nothing has changed and their little faces pressed against the long window looking out over the snow-spread lawn could have been there yesterday.

At last, as this fifth afternoon after Christmas begins to fade, I have time to myself – no more clearing, preparing, serving, collecting, delivering, wrapping, arranging – time at last to look through my clutch of Christmas books at leisure. The trouble is I can't decide which, what and how best to choose to read.

Have begun Derek Jarman's 'Smiling in Slow Motion' – it's a series of diary entries so I can always dip in and out – and read Richard Ford's short story in the New Yorker, but what should I really get stuck into? The Coleridge biogs? The latest Linda Grant, 'Modern Times' novel, tantalisingly slim, or the Peter Biskind 'Easy Riders, Raging Bulls' that Rachel gave me, or a trawl through Kingsley Amis's letters? Or should I make a start on Saharan research? And if so, where? I choose the Coleridge and fall asleep in front of the fire after a couple of pages.

Sunday, December 31st

The year 2000 has been one of those interval years for me. No major project has dominated. H and I have had real holidays – Kenya, Tanzania, Zanzibar, Minorca, Roques – and I've sampled a few places long on my list – Trieste, Poland, Vermont. A year of input rather than output. Despite modest output, what I've done has found fertile ground – 'The Colourists' being a delight to make, and a great success with viewers, opened up an arts strand for me at BBC Two whenever I want to make use of it.

I feel revived, mentally and physically, by a year off the treadmill. Time to catch up with myself. Think, without demand of instant commitment, what I really want to do next.

I've been very happy with the house and with living in London – much less psychological restlessness. This has perhaps been the best feature of an in-between year, the discovery that I'm pretty much content. I feel curious, but not driven. If I were told there was nothing more for me to do, I'd be happy surrounded by what I already have. But to be honest, that happiness comes from knowing that there is still a lot for me to do.

So, the Sahara beckons. I must take care with this one. Make it very good. Avoid accusations of repetitiveness or laziness.

2001

Monday, January 1st

As I write a new year date for the first time, every one seems to become more resonant. Must stem from some retroactive memory pushing me back into childhood when anything beyond 1984 seemed impossible to contemplate – and now we've reached 2001. A Sahara odyssey.

A mild start to the New Year, the steely discipline of ice and snow, flushed away by a return to Atlantic wet and warmth. Am living in extreme times for weather – six out of the warmest years for the country since reliable records began have happened since 1989. And last year's rain the highest since they kept measurements in the 1670s.

Make list of all the must-do's, for departure now not much more than a month away.

Tuesday, January 2nd

I spend an hour on Michel Thomas's French course – it is easy to absorb, and the comfort of hearing two others struggling to learn on the recording itself makes it very different from the more severe, characterless, language tuition I remember. Listening to Michel is like being in a schoolroom, part of a small class with a quietly charismatic teacher. Four more hours to go.

Over to Notting Hill to meet Roger at the Ladbroke. Both of us thinking along the right lines. I feel the fewer stunts we pull this time the better, and Rog has himself decided to drop the Marathon de Sable – which, being another forum for adventurous Westerners, never interested me that much. Like me, Rog feels we must look for Africa and Africans wherever possible.

It's a good way to start the New Year – with one of my most valuable friends, who has stayed that way despite also being my director, talking about an all-encompassing project which generates real excitement between us. Happy times, sharpened by expectation and anticipation.

Friday, January 5th

Richard Ingrams, my new friend and buddy, has asked me to contribute my six candidates for the Oldie's Pin-Up page. Choose Captain W.E. Johns,

Luis Buñuel, Virginia Woolf, Keith Miller, Glenys Kinnock and Harrison Marks.

To the gym to try out the new circuit which Daniel [my trainer] has planned for me. It's turning into the comedian's gym. Baddiel was thumping lugubriously away on the treadmill on Tuesday and today I see Rhona Cameron being bent double by the lovely Sam [another trainer].

Down to meet Terry J and Al and Mark Wexler [son of Haskell Wexler, and like him, a documentary director], who's passing through, at the Groucho. A short, but mostly jolly evening. Wexler, who arrived from Bali and Singapore yesterday and leaves for Chicago tomorrow, is painfully jet-lagged and Terry in a more asperous mood than usual.

As I make for my cab two young men approach – they're big, vaguely menacing, but have disarming Oxford accents. 'Excuse me,' both rather drunk, enormous admirers, want to shake hands, 'and that'll be the end of it'.

My driver is Ethiopian and we talk about the situation there as he drives back through Camden Town. He thinks there will be no winners in a war against Eritrea.

Wednesday, January 10th

Desk work. Listen to the last of Michel Thomas's French tapes. Impressed to the end by their effectiveness and simplicity.

Begin typing up the foreword for Brian Roylance's 'A Time to Live' – book of photos of twentieth century. For some reason he's asked me to write an introduction covering the last 2,000 years of history – 'but it can be quite short!'.

Saturday, January 13th

To Rachel's party at 7.30. She's 26 today, the age I was when I started Python. She certainly has acquired a thick-skinned confidence over the last couple of years (which she needed) and she is in good form with her friends. There are 25 or 26 of us at a long table in a burgundy-painted upper room at the Vine.

I enjoy myself and though I have happy memories of Rachel's childhood, I love to see her and her friends growing and, in most cases, maturing as the years go by. I learn more about the way the world works for them and they in turn are less defensive with me.

Monday, January 15th

Tiresome prospect of the Health and Safety day, inflicted on us by the BBC and without which we cannot qualify for their insurance cover. Entire Sahara crew assembled at 34 Tavistock.

Chairs arranged in front of a screen in Anne's office. At 10.30 the various presentations begin. Straight away I have the impression that we are to be talked down to and that the Rubicon Company are much more interested in themselves than they are in us. A languid, tall, youngish man begins, after a plug for his company, with the political background to the countries and ends by grading them all as to potential danger – with Algeria 'Extreme Caution' at one end of the list and Libya, Morocco and Tunisia 'security aware' at the other. Killings have begun again in Algeria this last month and the Polisario has declared war on Morocco!

After him is Gary, an ex-regular soldier on various high-level protection squads. He's never actually been to any of the countries we're visiting, but this doesn't really matter, they're all foreigners. His presentation is full of basic spelling errors, which hang embarrassingly magnified, on the screen in front of us. He deals with the possibility of capture, what to do if you suspect surveillance, how to ram a car through a roadblock and what to expect when arrested by border police. He goes into interrogation techniques – and I make a mental note to re-read Brian Keenan's book which deals with all this much more eloquently.

Return from lunch to find Anne's desk is covered with an assortment of landmines, both anti-personnel and anti-tank, together with the red skull and crossbones signs which mark out some minefields. It's like the setting for a rather violent Tupperware party.

The man from MAG, a mines dispersal charity, gives his stock talk making no attempt to tailor it to our needs. For almost two hours he bellows on, stopping only for a nasty cough; then he in turn is followed by a short, podgy blonde from Liverpool who gives a talk about stress which is toe-curlingly wrong for us – much of the material is self-evident common sense. She seems unaware of where we're going and who we are and what we've done before.

At the end of this dreadful, jargon-littered lecture, which she's 'cut down' to an hour and 20 minutes, Roger takes me aside and says with feeling that he doesn't expect we'll have any days worse than this on the entire shoot.

Thursday, January 18th

Up at 7.30 for another RA breakfast view. H decides to join me as the icy weather means that play not poss on the tennis courts.

It's 'The Genius of Rome' 1592–1610. It's grand in scale and conception and the big works fit the galleries well. I know Caravaggio and, of course, Rubens, but not much more about this intense period of patronage and exuberant experiment, which was begun by the new Pope ClemVIII in 1592 and continued with a brief but intense flourish until 1610, by which time Caravaggio and Elsheimer, two of its leading lights, were dead.

The curator, a confident, clear-voiced American, has been working for the last six years to get these gems together and she is articulate and enlightening about the themes and allusions without which the paintings can seem like overwrought melodrama.

I told one of the organisers afterwards that the exhibition could have been called Sex andViolence without contravening the Trades Descriptions Act, and he agreed much of it was more shocking than the 'Apocalypse' exhibition (which set out to appear shocking).

Artemisia Gentileschi's 'Judith and Holofernes' another inspiration for a Women Painters prog.

Monday, January 22nd

Out to lunch at Odette's with EleanorYule and May Miller – who is now 'creative director' at BBC Scotland (new Greg Dyke branding). What do I want to do next?

In the case of Redpath and the Colourists we've looked at artists and their life and work, and have not attempted to do overviews of the state of the arts or heavy academic examinations of the subjects.We've chosen work that we are enthusiastic about and tried to convey this enthusiasm to the audience. And it's worked. I'm sure the high profile we gave to the Colourists is a considerable element behind the success of the exhibition – it's been the best attendance for any exhibition at the Scottish Gallery of Modern Art. So in the end I agree to a single or maybe two progs with filming no earlier than May 2003 – which at least guarantees work for me when I reach 60!

Eleanor suggests the St Ives school – Nicholsons et al. – which I like. I also would still be interested in women artists – why so few? It does seem we're best when focusing on artists themselves and drawing wider conclusions from the particular.

Tuesday, January 23rd

To John Lewis-land to begin buying my clothes for the journey, plus drug supplies, electricals, etc. The rain blows in late morning so can't do as much as I'd hoped. Discover that the excellent, perfectly fitting 'pantalons de voyages' that I was so pleased with myself for finding at Gap make a dreadful noise when I walk. The cotton is brittle and crackles at every step. Edith runs away when I approach.

In early evening up to Belsize Park to catch 'À Bout de Souffle' at a one-off screening at Screen on the Hill. Romaine herself bustles around selling tickets and introducing Derek Malcolm who introduces the film, which is one in a series he's chosen as 'Films That Change Your Life'. He admits this may be a grand claim for 'Breathless' ('À Bout de S'), but says it is a film which changed the way people made films. The first of the Nouvelle Vague, handheld, doc-style, fragmented, shock-editing which we now take for granted.

It's quite charming considering it's a story of an unrepentant thief and murderer trying to bed a young American student in Paris in 1960. But Belmondo is attractively amoral and Jean Seberg so irritatingly moral that it does send your sympathies into a spin.

Thursday, January 25th

Meet J-P [John Paul Davidson] for breakfast on the corner of Sloane Square at what used to be a pub where I received my first professional payment – £50 from Willie Donaldson as an advance on my work for 'The Love Show' in 1965. Today it's a café, brasserie, staffed by disdainful French waiters. We eat – baguette, marmalade, coffee – and discuss the series. J-P is resourceful and slightly mad, reminds me of Richard L[Loncraine]. He takes me into the office on the back of his motorbike, and as we speed along Millbank he shouts back at me that he used to have a small inflatable boat that he'd drop into the river every now and then and ride the waves to work.

One of the many appealing things about J-P, apart from an apparent and total lack of censoriousness, is his enthusiasm for food and drink – no agonising over wine at lunch, or even in this case, foie gras at lunch. He has an attractive candour too. I think he might be quite serious when he says that the series should perhaps feature a brothel sequence.

Sunday, January 28th

I lie awake from seven onwards trying to decide on the pros and cons of our planned naughty weekend in Paris. The pros are – tickets booked on Eurostar and a suite awaiting us at L'Angleterre in Rue Jacob, and promise of a good evening tomorrow with Mick [Sadler, friend from Oxford] and [French wife] Lulu. There is, in the back of my mind, the advantage of being somewhere French for two days, a sort of linguistic acclimatisation before the Sahara.

The cons – well, just my body really. It's not sending out the right signals. It doesn't want to go anywhere, least of all a long journey with a lot of people around to a city renowned for its food and drink.

Decide to stay. H is sympathetic and quite happy not to go. I email Mick and the hotel and when that's done I feel better. H goes to play tennis.

Throughout the day wisdom of my decision made clear. There is a lot more of this cold to come out. Its effects, apart from occasional fierce sneezes that seem to turn my whole respiratory system inside out, are just heaviness of head, complete instability of ventilation system and a slow process of attrition which reduces me to a snuffling, nasally incontinent lump.

Complete Linda Grant's excellent 'When I Lived in Modern Times' and read New Yorker and the Observer in depth – the Mandelson resignation is taking on a life of its own, and this time it seems less about government, sleaze or whatever and more about Mandelson himself, who's clearly not mourned by any of his colleagues. What did he do to make himself so loathed? Just not a team player?

Watch 'Jackie Brown' again. *This* is comedy, Bobby, not 'Meet the Parents'.

Thursday, February 1st

Manage a short run – into thick, icy fog, with paths treacherous underfoot. Then a cab down to meet Anne and Basil at the office and on to an introductory meeting with the Orion team at Wellington House. Their office looks as impermanent as ever – with sacks of rubbish and boxes of authors' discarded life's works waiting to be collected.

Squeeze round a table. Photos taken for the Bookseller to go with the announcement of my signing. Basic agreement on title – 'Sahara' by Michael Palin, 100,000 words, delivery by mid-May 2002. Afterwards, Basil, Anne and I celebrate with sausage and mash at Joe Allen's.

Friday, February 2nd

Most relieved at the purchase of a suitable hat – the 'Namibia' at Lock's in St James's, where my head is measured by some Victorian device, the shape and size of a birthday cake, squeezed on to my head and holes punched to outline my size. I have to sign the result, which they will keep for their celebrity board – currently filled with such as Laurence Olivier, Princess Diana, Edward VIII and Larry Hagman.

Have to hurry home as two of my paintings are coming back from Stewart Heslop after being reframed. Both now much less intimidated by the frame – the paintings, especially the Sickert, almost shockingly undressed. Heslop loves the Sickert and just to hear him describe the colours used is to be aware of how rarely I actually look closely at my own pictures.

At 7.30 we go round to Tom and Rachel's [his partner Rachel Winder, later his wife] for a meal – Rachel makes sweet potatoes with vine tomatoes and gorgonzola as a starter, and Tom a prawn risotto – both very tasty, clean, light and satisfying. We talk music a lot, then watch Flash their hamster getting about in his mansion of tubes and turrets.

Sunday, February 4th

Struggle to re-familiarise myself with Spanish, prior to the Tindouf Polisario camps. A BBC tape. They're all geared to communicating with businessmen, not families in refugee camps.

Jeremy, Melanie, Eugene and Esmé [wife and children of my nephew Jeremy Herbert] come round for tea. Both children in very good form. No sooner in the door than Eugene immediately sets up a set of Lego men on the hall floor. He talks a lot now – mostly to himself. Esmé is delightful, smiling so much she shakes all over. Jeremy may design the next Ben Elton show – 'For the money,' he says quickly, 'It's about time I did something for the money.' Married life has shaken him up!

Marcus [Herbert, my other nephew] comes by later and Basil arrives hot foot from taking tea with Bernado Bertolucci. Bas reports him as looking in bad shape, old and ill. A boisterous evening and a great send-off. Will last to leave, soon after eleven.

Twelve and a half years since I settled down to a nervous night before setting out on '80 Days', I take my last night's sleep before another big journey. Another big test.

Tuesday, March 13th

A short night in the air. Flying north from Bamako, across the Sahara. Mali, where the shortest land journey between its cities takes several hours, is only five and a half hours' flying time from Paris.

We're scattered around the club class cabin of a wide-bodied Airbus, a functioning but exhausted group – having covered the ground from Tindouf to Timbuktoo in a 35-day slog in often basic conditions. In overhead racks are 40 rolls of the 139 we've shot. The rest have already gone back to London.

I'm at the window and no one has come to close the shutter, as they do on somnofascist BA night flights. As I wake from physically awkward, sprawling sleep, I look down into the darkness and there are lights – clusters of them, small towns or large villages, star-shaped, and separated by pitch blackness.

A map on the screen helpfully indicates that we are over Rognon. Can there really be a town called Kidney? Reach for my glasses – it's Avignon. Such a wonderful part of the world. Saint-Exupéry comes to mind, the romantically evocative images of flying at night. I feel very much back home, grateful perhaps for the reassuring order and familiarity of Europe.

The last five weeks have, I think, been the toughest and most relentless days of filming I can remember. Only two clear non-working, non-travelling days and everything new, strange, often astonishing and rewarding, but nearly always a price to pay in heat, discomfort and accessibility.

I try to run it through in my mind as my car moves slowly into London along the A4 – the windows flecked with rain, the doleful tones of John Humphrys spreading the latest grim news on the foot-and-mouth outbreak. What with BSE, gauge corner cracking and depleted uranium poisoning, it's hard to condemn Africa for its lack of progress.

But H is home, just, and the cats scuttle and run around my feet, and the clouds pass over and the sun shines.

Wednesday, March 14th

Slept long and well, but loose bowels in middle of night, and stomach feeling upset this a.m. Fine morning, up to dry cleaners. 'You are a different colour,' he says.

To the office, by Tube. London seems spotlessly, almost obsessively, clean. Clothes drab, colour comes from buildings, ad hoardings, etc. The opposite in Africa. The office buzzes – Vanessa [Courtney, producer], through one of her contacts, has a foot in the door in Libya, which will involve flying out there in about five weeks' time to cover the 60th and final war veterans' gathering at Tobruk.

Agree series title should be the simple 'Sahara with Michael Palin' and that if Libya does not work out, we should have a plan B – possibly involving the Red Sea coast and a boat up to Sinai.

Talk of the increasing problems of carting film stock round the world, and how much easier it would be if Nigel shot on tape. General sense that the quality argument is less relevant now digital video has improved and is so flexible in the edit, but I was aware that certain apparent advantages – the much longer interviews made possible with digital – would really drain him.

Thursday, March 15th

Diarrhoea persists, which is a nuisance – take charcoal and rehydration preparations but my stomach will not settle, despite my appetite being largely unaffected. So stay at home and hope it will sort itself out.

Day grows cloudier and milder. It starts to rain. Watch football. Liverpool very lively and impressive as they beat FC Porto on way to semi-finals of UEFA Cup, on same day as three English clubs make it through to last eight of Champions League.

That's the good news. The bad news, hanging like a shroud over everything else, is the latest devastation to be wrought on British agriculture – after BSE, GM crops, now foot-and-mouth – our once-vaunted farming industry has made us international pariahs again. The French have gone bonkers over one confirmed case. We have 230 and rising daily.

Monday, March 19th

Bright morning. Try not to dwell on images of cows, sheep and pigs burning across the country, and after breakfast take Granny to the train – make sure she's on and has a seat, then back home. Read outline script sent through from Mike McCormack for my T2000 documentary appearance next week.[1] First reaction is near fury at the amount I'm expected to learn. But it's good stuff; important too, and I watch 'Car Sick', which we made seven years ago and was impressed by Mike's work.

JC rings from Santa Barbara. Wants to compare notes about experience with BBC on documentary series – his 'Human Face' running at the moment and John (doing silly walk!) is on front of Radio Times. He blames his series editor and originator for appointing as one of the directors someone who was clearly not focused on the job – 'He may have been experiencing some change in sexual orientation,' jokes John airily. 'The footsoldiers were marvellous.' Lions led by donkeys it seems. BBC Science at Bristol took over the series halfway through and wanted less humour. And so on. I advise him to control it from the ground up next time – pref as independent prod.

Catch Chris Guest's 'Best in Show' at an underpopulated Everyman. Marvellous wit, observation and the joy of comedy played serious.

---

1 A film I'd agreed to front as part of my involvement with the pressure group Transport 2000. Mike McCormack was writer and director.

Tuesday, March 20th

Ron the painter, elderly, moustachioed, the way a painter might have been portrayed in a 1950s schoolbook, comes to finish the new front door (put in to replace the old one after it was violently kicked in the early hours when I was away). The wind is rising, it's cold and from the east and is forecast to bring rain and even snow on this vernal equinox.

I clear the desk and manage, a little late in the morning, to get my head down on the 'Sahara' book. The effort required to overcome initial inertia is familiar, and, because I have more than a year to go before delivery, it occasionally feels a rather academic discipline. But persevere and am rewarded by that nice feeling of the ball rolling.

Wednesday, March 21st

Steady morning's work on 'Sahara', the rain eases and has stopped by the time I set out for a run. Water spilling down the flank of Parliament Hill as if it had just risen from the sea.

The news is of CJD and foot-and-mouth – almost literally sickening. Keep my spirits up by reading 'The Plague'.

Thursday, March 22nd

TJ calls. He's working on 'Who Murdered Chaucer' and about six or seven other things; has bad experiences at BBC to report. A radio prog he was asked to do refused to send him script to look over in advance, and they don't seem at all keen to employ Alan Ereira as director, who TJ likes to write and work with so much. They made 'Crusades' and 'Gladiators' together.

Sara Jane sends a nomination certificate from the Travelex Awards confirming that the Iron Curtain progs came second in Best Radio Travel category.

The Jeremy Novick biog proofs lie on my desk.[1] The tone is embarrassingly sycophantic most of the time – though Terry J, Robert H [Hewison] and Roger's quotes add an edge. There's a promising chapter on the 'dark side' of Michael Palin, but it peters out after a page and a half.

---

1 *Life of Michael: An Illustrated Biography of Michael Palin* by Jeremy Novick, published by Headline. A previous biography, by Jonathan Margolis, had come out in 1997.

Friday, March 23rd

Sit and work at 'Sahara' and watch the rain, again. Newspapers quote official figures as showing April 2000–April 2001 already wettest twelve-month period since records began – around the time of American War of Independence.

A quick visit to the gym and then down to meet Nicola Moody [our commissioning editor] at Union Café for a diplomatic update on our progress so far. Will there be any sequences where you drink yourself silly, she asks, worrying that an Islamic non-alcoholic environment will not be conducive to the Russian vodka-style sequences in 'Pole to Pole'. Otherwise not much of an inquisition. She won't immediately accept 'Sahara with MP' as title, though. Rather wearily see some future problem looming here – but at least it's been aired and I've made my feelings very clear.

Monday, March 26th

A dull morning with light drizzle – perfect for the Brent Cross flyover. A sharp wind scours my inadequate clothing as I walk around the network of sinister, rusting pedestrian ways beneath the flyover. It's like upturning a stone. The mess and neglect under here is comprehensive and depressing.

Throughout the day as we make our way from one desolate road-blighted location to another, horns sound and thumbs go up as people pass on their recognition from the very speeding cars and trucks that I'm, officially, getting so steamed up about. The jams melt away as we approach. For a unit dependent on congested traffic, this is not good news.

Hanger Lane Hell is the description of our last location and even that is an overstatement today. Traffic flows freely and we find a sheltered garden in the very midst of the famous gyratory system.

Tuesday, March 27th

Picked up by TG to go down to TJ's for supper. He's just back from a horror and fantasy film festival in Luxembourg, where the most popular phrase was 'We want a shrubbery'.

Terry and Al show great curiosity about where I've been and open up the atlas. Geoff Burgon, composer, is there, and a quiet, boffiny man from the armoury at the Tower of London – 'the Middle Ages brought us together', he says of Terry, rather sweetly.

Terry provides an abundance of food, shows off his new wood-smoking tray, and his hip X-ray which shows a deterioration of cartilage on his right side which, he's pretty certain, will lead to him becoming the second Python to seek hip replacement.

Wednesday, March 28th

To a reception given by Cherie B at 10 Downing Street for the Medical Foundation. It's nice to be able to climb into my scruffy mini cab from Priory Cars and ask for 10 Downing Street.

Greeted by the staff as if I live there – 'Where've you been, Michael?' The Colourists in the hall have been replaced by some other interesting work – a small Sickert and a large realist painting of a railway refreshment room by a man called Bell, which I like very much. Lowrys in the passageway.

John McCarthy [one of the Iraqi hostages, now a broadcaster] is there – ruddy-faced and decent and self-deprecating – and Kathy Lette's hubby, the celebrated [barrister] Geoffrey Robertson. They took their son to the MP Stammering Centre. He was dyslexic and we talk for a while about the various causes of a stammer. Having Kathy and Geoffrey for parents reminds me of Nicholas Mosley's story that his stammer came from having to keep his end up in a household where everyone was talking!

Cherie is rather a surprise. She talks easily, mostly about her father (the actor Tony Booth) – much raising of eyes heavenwards – and listens. Her children are great Python fans. 'We had John Cleese to Chequers and they loved it.'

She gives a short speech introducing John McC who introduces Helen Bamber [founder of the Medical Foundation for the Victims of Torture. At the age of 20 she had been one of the first to enter the Bergen-Belsen concentration camp]. She tells us in the nicest possible way that we're here to be tapped to fill a gap between the 4.7 million needed for the new centre and the 3.8 million collected. And there is some urgency. People having to wait six months to be seen is unacceptable, she says.

Ralph Steadman [the cartoonist] introduces himself. He was at TG's 60th. I note that Benicio del Toro, who was in 'Fear and Loathing', won the best supporting actor at the Oscars this week. 'He was completely wrong in "Fear and Loathing",' thunders Ralph. I say I presume Gilliam cast him. 'He *can* be wrong. Gilliam can be wrong. Geniuses can be wrong!'

Out of No. 10 at a quarter to eight. A 24-hour Tube strike begins at eight. No cabs. Stand in the rain outside the Horse Guards, opposite the Banqueting House, until Big Ben and a chorus of subsidiary bells chime eight o'clock. This must be one of the best-located bus stops in the world. Onto a 24 at five past eight.

Friday, March 30th

To the Roundhouse to see a show called 'Because I Sing'. Amateur choirs from all over London, representing different interests, areas, ages, ethnic groups, etc., all drawn together for two performances. Starts rather respectably with groups tackling quite serious stuff and Armenian church music, but warms up as soon as we get black groups on – the Congolese Christian Choir and small, beautifully modulated close harmony choir, eight black women and one man.

Then it all becomes surreal, with the WI from Bexley or somewhere alternating with the London Gay Men's Choir, a fearsome crowd of 40 or so, in black, nearly all with shaved heads, singing 'Keep Your Lamps Lit' – 'and your wicks trimmed'. By now the audience is warmed up and 'Keep It Gay' is greeted with roars of applause.

There's a deaf choir, who sign in rhythm and a rather sweet group of ladies in velvet dresses and scarves who treat us to a muted and quite powerful version of the 'Internationale'.

Friday, April 6th

Al and Terry round early evening. Show them a glimpse of 'Sahara' rushes. TJ v. complimentary about material. Then up to King's Head to see 'Two Beards and a Blonde' – latest Denis King, Dick Vosburgh offering. Dick's irresistible attraction to old films, old compilations and torturous puns is sometimes marvellous to behold. Specially liked his creation of Ifields Moor Hospital (instead of Moorfields Eye Hospital) as the tag of some elaborate question about Frank Ifield working with Muslims in North Africa. And liked very much the phrase 'usurer-friendly'.

We all have a lovely time and eat afterwards at a Turkish in Theberton Street. Upper Street still buzzing at 12.30.

Thursday, April 12th

Have wrestled with decision as to whether or not I should drive up to Southwold today and leave some flowers at the parental grave. I haven't been up for at least a year. H and I discussed it over supper last night. Am I going up for the parents, who are dead and won't notice, or am I going up because I am embarrassed that my lack of filial devotion will be noticed by those who visit the graves nearby? For some reason I can't accept that five hours in a car on crowded roads just to be at the grave is the best use of the day. We agree to go on my next filming break.

Having laid my guilt I sleep well until roused at five past seven by BBC Wales who want me to take part in their morning news piece on the death of [actor and comedian] Harry Secombe. Wait by the phone at eight, on at 8.10 with Barry Cryer and Rhodri Morgan, senior minister of the Welsh Assembly.

Barry C calls me afterwards – Secombe once told him that Spike had said of him, 'he's the only one pretending to be mad, the rest of us are mad'. He'd spoken to him only two weeks ago. Secombe characteristically not revealing how serious things were until there was a noise on the line which he said was 'the wife tripping over the wheelchair'.

Friday, April 13th

My knee is well enough to tempt me, or perhaps force me into a run this morning. And it holds up for an outing, as long as I've done for some time.

Michele Hanson [friend and Guardian columnist] is out walking her dog. She has with her an older lady who also has a bulldog – but as Michele points out in her delicate ladette voice, 'The trouble with that one is, she eats shit.' To which her older, grey-haired companion replies, patting the coprophagic dog in question, 'I don't mind that, really, it's just that he sicks it all up again.' Leave these two disgusting women and run on back to Parliament Hill.

I'm caught up in the latest volume of Derek Jarman's diaries, when, with a sudden shock I see my own name there – his entry for November 30th 1992 noting that 'Michael Palin recommended "Modern Nature" as his book of the year . . .' It gives me a touch of grateful pleasure that he saw my recommendation because I find such wisdom in his writing – expressed hotly and temperamentally sometimes, which makes the opinions human and fragile and spontaneous.

Saturday, April 14th

Revise the twelve thousand plus words I've completed on 'Sahara'. Am reading in the kitchen at half past eleven when I hear a dull crump, a compact thud of sound which I feel certain is an explosion. No sound follows it though. An hour later, I hear that a bomb has gone off up in 'North London'.

Sunday, April 15th: Easter Sunday

The papers – well the Observer – trails its parade of gloom. Foot-and-mouth still out of control, the disposal of slaughtered cattle now threatening the 'environment' (wherever that is), railways will not be back to pre-Hatfield levels for another year. A Real IRA bomb suspected at Hendon. As I read Jarman I'm surprised how strong a theme is the terrorist activity in London in 1992. It all seems so long ago – and yet it was a constant in his descriptions of Central London life.

Thursday, April 19th

Woke early, thinking about sand and deserts. The usual trickle of anxiety, or is it anticipation? Going on the road again never seems to get any easier. It's still an abrupt change of way of life. I have never learnt how to segue into it with Zen-like mental and physical ease. It's always a kickstart. Work on thoughts for opening to be delivered at Gibraltar. Sleep very fitfully. Off we go again.

April 20th to May 3rd: Filming in Gibraltar and Libya

Friday, May 4th

The news not as relentlessly gloomy as it has been these past few months. Foot-and-mouth still active but effects much reduced – burning of animals almost at an end. Crossrail (that eminently sensible rail connection between Paddington and Liverpool Street, recommended by T2000 15 years ago) has finally received the go-ahead. The Tube strike planned for yesterday was called off, and my Szczecin programme has gone out again – last-minute replacement after some hitch with another prog.

A sniff of better times ahead.

Friday, May 25th

Off to Royal China – the service is as rushed and curt, the sound level as high and the food as deliciously tasty as ever. H turns out to be the only woman. John [Pritchard, sound recordist on our journey] and J-P both there and Gilliam comes later.

Terry G warms up – like a big affable bear but with a growing manic intensity he seizes the chance to fill the air with his stories, observations, groans and moans. Always entertaining but monstrously excitable, like a whirlwind. He talks as others breathe – to stay alive.

Mind you he has just been a judge at the Cannes Film Festival and he has good material. Twenty-two films in ten days, of which only six were any good. Being on the panel – which included Liv Ullman and Charlotte Gainsbourg

– was like being in a hostage situation. But there were perks. 'I came within three feet of Liz Taylor,' he boomed. 'The head was OK, but make-up stopped at her neck.' He then described Liz Taylor's breasts as if they were some ancient mummified organs, recently discovered.

J-P in good form. Thinks early September for twelve days shooting in Niger, then a three-to-four-week break and last big filming dash in mid-October.

Wednesday, May 30th

Organisational morning. Call Nicola Moody to thank for birthday hamper. She says that she and Lorraine Heggessey [Controller BBC One] have discussed titles and come up with 'Palin's Sahara'. It's déjà vu. Back to the 'Full Circle' ('Palin's Pacific') debate all over again. I shall press for 'Sahara with Michael Palin' but I don't feel quite as rigidly against the possessive 'P's Sahara' as I might. Still, worth a struggle.

Sunday, June 3rd

Ran this morning. A fine day, stopped to talk to Valerie Grove [journalist and writer]. She unpicks her earpiece (Andrew Motion on Bob Dylan at 60) and we have a swift chat. She was one of the chosen who got to meet Bill Clinton at Hay last week. She admits that she did ask him for his autograph and was surprised that he was left-handed.

'I didn't know you were a southpaw,' she said. To which Bill smoothed, 'Left-handed people have more interesting thoughts.'

Arthur Smith apparently sang a Leonard Cohen song with him. Surely it won't be long before Bill has his own show – BBC One, Two, or Radio 4?

My left leg tweaks painfully as I ascend Parliament Hill, pulling at the hamstring that last went on a Moroccan beach (on camera!) the day after my birthday. I'm hobbling a little as I come back up the Hill an hour later, only to run into the lady walkers who stare at me as I begin the painful last few yards and wave and shout 'We love you!' as I grimace to the top. Like being watched on the lavatory.

Monday, June 4th

To the Ladbroke for a catch-up with Roger. Lovely late afternoon sunshine so most of the clientele are outside, leaving us a bit more space at our usual table. Editing began this morning. Discuss various details like the Dakar–Bamako train journey. Two key pieces to camera are not usable after the Charles de Gaulle airport scanner zapped the film, and it looks as if we must reshoot.

Tuesday, June 5th

A meeting at the Ivy. On the agenda is Orion's proposal to do a 'Pythons' definitive history rather like the 'Beatles' definitive history they published last year, and which sold 180,000 in the UK, apparently (at 35 quid). Terry J has been sent to the wrong restaurant and is sitting waiting for us in Sheekey's. He eventually arrives. He's off to play the voice of a chicken for some animated film this p.m. and confines himself to one glass of St-Véran. TG points out Joan Collins, but I only ever see her back view.

There seems to be nothing to object to, though TJ likes big books and I don't as much. TG suggests we provide the book with legs so it can become a coffee table.

Wednesday, June 6th

Call from TG to say Johnny Depp is in Mexico but would have *loved* to have been a non-speaking assistant office manager in a Python DVD film about coconuts.

Thursday, June 7th

I have to sort out some dates and decisions on finance and meetings with the BBC on 'Sahara'; and I must cast my vote.

Much jollity as I enter the polling station, which is also the school hall at Gospel Oak – heart of my children's education. A policeman asks me if I'm going to make any more travel programmes, the polling officers chat away and my crossing of the paper for Glenda Jackson just seems like a short break in a conversation.

Friday, June 8th

I stay awake, interested as much by the TV presentation as the election itself until around 2.30, by which time it's clear that the Conservatives have received another thumping – and Blair is in with around 170 majority, on a much-reduced voter turnout – around 58 per cent.

Up at 7.45, hearing from the radio in the bathroom the odd 'ee-eck' sing-song of William Hague making not just a speech of defeat but of resignation too – and nobody forecast that last night. So after four years of being generally unsuccessful with the public, Hague has made his last speech as party leader. He never felt right – nor did the Widdecombe/Coe axis that led him on to the right-wing ground where they stood alone.

Michael Heseltine suddenly back in favour again – because he always made it quite clear how much he disliked what Hague was doing to the party. Now Hague has achieved nothing – the old Tarzan not only looks good but sounds pretty smug too.

Saturday, June 9th

As usual before a demanding day's filming I'm awake before the alarm; however much I try not to, I can't help running through the day ahead, estimating and assessing what's required of me. And all this worry for a short addition to the stock of material to be available only on the 'Grail' DVD.

A very affable crew, all very young. I wish I could recapture the ease with which I approached these things in the first series of Python, before anything was expected of me. Now I am an august senior figure of comedy, a presenter with an awesome reputation – and I find it much more difficult to come from there. I know that I'm best when being spontaneous and in-stinctive – with as little fuss and expectation as possible – which is why I find this morning daunting. I've got to live up to, rather than create, a reputation.

Sunday, June 10th

Slept, greedily, until nine. My calf strain the perfect excuse to catch up on sleep I feel I need. Don't feel quite right this morning. A little fuzzy-headed and a touch of the breathlessness I noticed as we filmed yesterday. As soon as I men-tion that to H she sounds alarmed. 'Heart!' she says. Well, it's not so bad, but I'll keep an eye on it.

Monday, June 18th

Work away at a pile of personal letters, which occupy most of the morning. Congrats to Bill Cotton [Head of BBC Light Entertainment in Python era], now Sir Bill, and Barry Cryer, OBE, in the honours lists. Compose a letter to

Nicola Moody in defence of my original 'Sahara with MP' title before we meet next week.

To eat with Will P at Café Marché in Charterhouse Square. W looks good in new suit and rather natty shirt (American) and tie. He's giving lectures every day this week and he has a good moan about the difference between Berlin where he was last Friday and London. Mainly about the efficiency and competence of the transport infrastructure in Germany compared to here. He also found Berlin more soothing, a less hectic pace.

Tuesday, June 19th

Meet Caroline Reynolds and Stephen Mallatratt from Yorkshire TV to push the 'Hem Chair' adaptation a little further along the line. Mallatratt is a tall, striking figure, with close-cropped grey hair and rather well-chiselled features, he's standing in the bar looking a bit lost when I come in. He's soft-spoken, almost apologetic.

We reach some useful conclusions. Prompted by Stephen (who has written over 100 'Coronation Street's) we decide that simplifying the whole plot may be the way forward. Hopefully when he's finished writing his musical about Lady Godiva he'll be able to tackle a screenplay.

Caroline Reynolds, who lives up north of Manchester, I like very much. She's the enthusiast, having bought 'HC' at an airport in America – and she seems determined to give it its best shot.

Wednesday, June 20th

Previews of 'Road to Hell' aka 'Counterblast' [the T2000 documentary about cars]. Picked as choice for the day everywhere so there will be close attention. To BBC at 12.30 to talk about it on Steve Wright show. After which profound lethargy descends.

At six o'clock I force myself into action – shower, change and taxi down to Bush House where I am to do a website 'appearance' after transmission. Over three thousand people try to log on. Mike McCormack has to select and highlight questions for me to answer. A typist waits for the oracle to speak and Stephen Joseph and Lynn Sloman [who run Transport 2000] are there to advise me what to say. An impossible task. We put together maybe 25–30 replies in the hour I'm there, most of them rushed and banal.

Home around 11.30. H amused by my appearance on the show – the old brown Donegal tweed coat making probably its last appearance. 'Collar half up, collar half down,' says H, 'made you look like a tramp.'

Thursday, June 21st

Fine, cool morning. Become involved in Village issues – graffiti, and the mess in Lismore Circus. The new saplings which I expected to bear the brunt of local vandalism, have succumbed instead to neglect; nearly all seem to be dying.

Better luck with graffiti – a couple of lads who form the local 'Grimebuster' team help out. One of them says he's lived here all his life but is getting out to go and live 'somewhere by the sea in Essex'. 'There's all them Kosovans now,' he nods darkly off toward Barrington Court, 'and they're moving paedophiles into the flats.'

At the Ablemans' [Sheila Ableman was our main contact at BBC Books] summer drinks I meet John McCarthy [five years a hostage in Lebanon], who's off to film round the Middle East in the steps of St Paul. He says they asked if he wanted to begin the re-creation with Paul's years in prison. McCarthy laughs heartily at this. 'I told them I thought I'd done that.'

Monday, June 25th

A year ago I was struggling with the second novel, today I am looking forward to solid week of progress on a much less tricky proposition – the fifth travel book. The core material is all there, in notebooks, transcripts, even photographs and menus. The way forward takes care of itself, the narrative can be tweaked and adjusted but basically it sustains itself. So, a lot less intimidating than a work of fiction, the crucial difference being that I know whatever I produce each day will be part of the completed work. Or just about.

Tuesday, June 26th

To BBC for a meeting with Nicola Moody. The Wood Lane entrance still scarred by the bomb explosion in spring, a scaffold and partition boarding across the front. Modest, standard Beeb exec's office is set off an open area where various secretaries and assistants sit; not a male face to be seen.

We get nowhere on the important matters of title or series length, other than that Palin must come before Sahara because of the digital menus that guide people to progs having no room for more than one word. Everything is to be sacrificed on the wretched altar of choice – the public are not thick (that's heresy) but they are assumed to be fickle.

Thursday, June 28th

Up and out by 8.15 to breakfast view of Ingres to Matisse show at Royal Academy. It's a show that's come in from Baltimore, where the art gallery is being renovated and comprises excellent paintings from three Baltimore collections – Walters, George Lucas (sic) and the Cone family – so for me this breakfast view is more than just a chance to see some fine paintings, it's also an opportunity to learn more of Claribel and Etta Cone, the Baltimore spinsters whose lives I might be entering this time next year.

Mary Anne Stevens who has curated the exhibition is delighted at my enthusiasm. She says that the Cone sisters' taste was particular – more modern than the others and that you can sense which canvases are theirs because they relate in an almost physical way to the Cones themselves. Big women, big pictures. Bold nudes by Matisse, a beefy and wonderful Cézanne of a quarry near Mt Ste-Victoire, substantial canvases.

One thing friends have been very positive about is that 'Palin's Sahara', the BBC's choice of title, was worse than 'Sahara with MP' and this morning, lying in bed, I realised that I not only absolutely agreed but that I had been far too amenable at the meeting with Nicola. Resolve to state my preference more firmly and write a letter to that effect. I have to deal with this now because I can't go on promoting a show I've dreamt up with a title that's been forced upon me. Watch this space.

Sunday, July 1st

Robin and Jadzia Denselow [he a journalist, she a producer] come over. Ex-neighbours. Robin is comfortably unchanged, has been to three concerts this week – all African bands; I saw his 'Newsnight' report on the Congo last week, made by himself and one cameraman. He had an exclusive interview with 'Baby' Kabila, who's only lived in the Congo four months and is now its president. I ask Robin about his education. 'Mainly in a bar in Tanzania.' Long, lazy afternoon out in the garden, hot sun and cool, heavy cloud alternate. Chilled rosé and salmon. The cats have had a wonderful afternoon as all our guests are cat-lovers and no allergists.

Tuesday, July 3rd

I hear Terry G's appearance in 'On the Ropes' with J. Humphrys trailed and though I start with it on in the background I end up listening through the whole half-hour, so good is TG's storytelling of the 'Munchausen' and 'Quixote' fiascos. The great thing about TG is that he, as he admits, thrives on conflict and chaos, he likes to have his own war zone around him (which is why his working methods and aims are so different from my own) and he keeps going back to 'Quixote' because he sees himself as Quixote. Well-told and revealing.

Drive over to Ace Editing to see first assembly of 'Sahara with'. The location is the unprepossessing light-industrial side of the West Coast Main Line. I rather like the fact that our exotic African adventures are being put together in such unexotic surroundings. Bamako to Scrubs Lane.

Dakar is a bit of a mess. It's shapeless and stutters along through a series of performances – the band at the club, the modelling display, the wrestling. But they all work in their own right. The train journey is fine (with damaged foggy stock shots removed).

After Bamako some strong sequences draw me in – Dogon, Djenné, the boat trip and right up to Timbuktu, this feels like the best of the old travel shows. No new tricks, no new gimmicks, just new people and new places well observed. I think this will be the heart of the series and I'm pleasantly reassured – no, to hell with it, fucking delighted.

We all follow Alex, our editor, in convoy through faceless streets at the back of Willesden Junction to the Grand Junction Pub beside the canal. 'Hello Mike,' says a man on a bar stool, cheerfully. 'What you doing in 'ere? This is a sad place.' Yes it is pretty rough, scrawny, scraggy faces, long hair, red eyes, no one chic or smart. I like it. Couldn't think of a better place to be after a viewing like that. Back in the real world.

Wednesday, July 11th

Call Anne and hear that she has already seen a response from Nicola to my letter about the title. They are intransigent but offer little justification for this intransigence. Instead a sop. 'We know you don't like apostrophes, so how about "Palin in the Sahara"?' They also as good as admit that Sahara may be an evocative word and image, but 'we also believe that it actually will not inspire viewers to watch'. Tergiversation aside, it's great to know I'm working on such an uninspirational subject.

Thursday, July 12th

I call Simon [Albury, long-time friend] for his thoughts on the title. He's very good devil's advocate. Devil being the BBC. I'm a brand, my name sells programmes and in an increasingly competitive world it's absolutely natural that a popular channel would want to push my popularity first and foremost. I'm what they've bought, not the Sahara. It's a bracing argument and leaves me less certain about my opposition to 'Palin's Sahara'.

Saturday, July 14th

Have been invited to share Sir Paul Getty's box at Lord's for the Benson and Hedges Final. This arose from my pin-up page in the Oldie in which I selected Keith Miller, the great Australian all-rounder, as one of my all-time heroes. Sir Paul read the column and as Keith Miller was coming to Lord's as another of his guests I was invited. Helen couldn't bear the thought of a whole day of cricket so I asked Roger M to come along instead.

Stephen Fry arrives, looking heavy and dishevelled, as if he'd dressed in a hurry in the dark. I thank Sally Munton, Paul Getty's PA, for facilitating the exchange of ticket from Helen to Roger. 'Ah, bringing your boyfriend today?' Stephen asks, stirringly. Roger, when he arrives, is referred to throughout as 'Mrs Palin', which seems to amuse everyone greatly.

The rain holds off but it's dark and cool and gloomy as Gloucestershire begin to pick off the Surrey batsmen and a fifth consecutive B and H win looks on the cards. The Hollioake bros have stemmed the decline and are scoring quite consistently when, on my way to the loo, after a champagne or two and some unexciting lunch, I encounter my childhood hero, in the flesh, for the very first time. Keith Miller, with a posse of companions and attendants around him, is leaning on two crutches as he's helped through the swing doors from the lift.

I hold the door back. He's just about recognisable as the charismatic figure that so captured my imagination. The head is erect, defiant almost, the hair, though almost completely silver, is copious and swept back from that strong forehead, his blue eyes are a little rheumy but still strong. The complexion is that of a very old, frail man. It's delicate, like parchment, with age spots, and drawn tight around his cheekbones. I'm aware, with some relief, that he's still a bit of a character; his eyes shine with a humorous, ironic vitality, he takes people's hands, holds arms, touches shoulders, clocks the waitress.

I'm introduced to him and as has happened to me before when meeting heroes of my youth (viz Edmund Hillary), they get their reaction in before mine. 'Michael,' says Keith Miller (who hit six sixes in one innings on this ground when I was two and a bit) 'it's wonderful to meet you.' He keeps hold of my hand with his own bony, thin-skinned left hand. Well, I eventually blurt out my hero-worship, rather self-consciously as I'm aware of people watching anxiously. His reply is reassuring – 'Oh, that's all bullshit you know. You're more famous in Australia than I am.' His hearing and speech is not good. 'Doctors buggered up the op,' he says tapping a long white scar by his left ear, but considering we're in a crowd, at a game, he concentrates well and makes sense. He has a direct mental energy – a relish of the situation, an appreciation of the silliness of it all, which completely counters his physical condition.

Sir Paul Getty arrives a few minutes later. He is in a wheelchair, bent up, head leaning on to chest. He wears a straw hat and an MCC tie and is neatly dressed. Another introduction, another expression of gratitude from him before I can get mine out. His face spreads into a smile, a little constricted perhaps but all the more charming for that. He's wheeled up beside Keith, who is 82 to Getty's 60-odd, but looks the haler and heartier of the two.

The Gloucs bowlers give a few away at the end and are left 245 to win. The low clouds have passed and a crisp, clean light adds to the pleasure of the occasion. I talk mainly with Stephen and Roger. Always amazed at Stephen's encyclopaedic knowledge and most of all by his ability to retrieve it. Names, stories, situations, books read, whatever; he seems to be able to lay his hands on the essence of it. But, despite making much of being a Gloucester sup- porter he has no idea where they are in the Championship and leaves before the end.

I'm spotted by Sky TV and asked if I'll go up to the press box and spend five minutes on air with Ian Botham. It's all too much. First Keith Miller, now one of the few cricketers of recent years to play with the same spirit and power. The press pod is hermetically sealed from the game – none of the crowd noise or even sound of leather on willow permeates its glassy shell. Botham is good company, but I feel he's on good behaviour and the real richness of anecdote and experience would probably come out after a sharpener or two.

The game is now swinging Surrey's way. Miller with a cry of 'Michael!' and an upraised hand, is about to leave. We talk a little more – he was a big mate of Trevor Howard and Helen Cherry, his wife. I tell him I'll come and see him in Sydney.

Home by 8.30 and regale H with all I can remember of an extraordinary day. In which I forgot I was 58 and reverted to between 12 and 20, very happily.

Monday, July 16th

Shopping in the p.m. Meet Roger Katz [of Hatchards] on the corner of the street. He clearly felt that the 'Hemingway' book sales were affected by poor reaction to the programme. His customers, he said, were quite happy with the more serious Michael Palin, they went along with that and were disappointed by the need for jokes. I feel a dull pain somewhere far back in the brain. En- thusiasm, passion and a clear goal and objective is what sells books says Roger.

Wednesday, July 18th

Basil, who flew in from HK at half past five, is at the door at ten and we look through photos for the Tindouf–Nouakchott section. Impressive and reassuring – not only that Bas is on form but that the Sahara has such a powerful visual appeal. I know by looking through this latest cull, crouched over the lightbox, that we are, as they say, on to a good thing and that Basil has delivered the qualities he's quite generously paid for. So all sweetness and light.

An email from Michael D, full of encouraging praise for the first draft material I sent him last week. Roger says that the Algeria recce has had to be postponed because of visa problems. Dates for Niger filming have been put back again as rains have come late!

Thursday, July 26th

Among the letters and faxes is one from Nicola Moody, dated 23rd July, thanking me for my last letter and going on to say 'I admire your passion and determination on the title, so let's go with your request: "Sahara with Michael Palin".' So, a battle won just as I thought it lost.

Call Roger who has good news too – the Algerians came through with visas (too late, but the principle established should make it easier from now on) and Libya looks good.

Watch Chris Morris on the subject of paedophilia – or rather paedophile hysteria. Privately, I thought it brave and mad and wonderfully exhilarating, but when H came in halfway through, I found some on-screen images hard to justify. Extraordinary, uncompromising and probably far too long, it does rail brilliantly against the rabid reaction and manipulation of the media.

Saturday, July 28th

Leave home around 9.30 to be at Tate Gallery, sorry, sorry, Tate Britain, by opening time. The general cleanliness of London's landmark buildings strikes me positively as I drive down Whitehall, and the number of buildings being improved and spaces being filled in. Though recession is now talked about almost daily, London has sprung forward over the last few years and I pray that the change is not just superficial. There are signs that the real needs of Londoners – affordable housing and efficient transport – are being seriously neglected.

Because of the perverse 'genre' hang I don't really know where to begin looking for Wright of Derby's 'Iron Forge', which I want to see before I write my thoughts about it for the Tate Centenary Development opening in

November. Do I look for a room dedicated to 'Iron Forges'? or even 'Indus-trial Subjects'? Well, I never find it and as a number of the galleries are being re-hung it could be in store. The helpful, colour-coded people at Information can't tell me either – their computer is apparently 'affected by the heat' and taking ten minutes to come up with any information.

I'm happy poking around. Discover the delights of Constable once again and this time notice the importance of his skies – always cloudy; the more clouds the better for him.

A Michael Andrews retrospective is almost empty of visitors, which seems unfair, for his work is accessible (if a little psycho-babbly at times) and often big and dramatic and bold. From the 'Colony Room Crowd', a claustrophobic cluster of egos which he was clearly awed by, to the spare immensity of Ayers Rock, sorry, sorry, Uluru, which represents, it seems, the end of the arc of his life – from people at parties to great empty spaces without any people at all. Quite understandable!

Sunday, July 29th

Heat builds through the morning, both outside and on the Chris Morris 'Brass Eye' reaction. It being nearly August and no serious news deemed to be happening, unless of course you include the prospect of world recession, the collapse of the peace accord in the Middle East and the increased violence in Northern Ireland, stories like the paedophilia prog and the engagement of 'Sir' Paul McCartney swell and grow distended in the heat. Our new and pious Culture Secretary [Tessa Jowell] and the government have weighed in, making the fatal mistake of not having seen the programme first.

All of course is irrelevant. If you have no sense of humour or delight in the spectacle of our 'celebrities' making fools of themselves, you will not have enjoyed the programme. Bad luck, but you don't have to watch it. Press the button and go back to BBC One.

No, this is now a crusade. The hysteria satirised in the programme has result-ed in another wave of similar hysteria. The Daily Mail is doubtless preparing the foam for the mouth even now. Nothing has changed since the 'Life of Brian' or Jonathan Swift.

Monday, July 30th

This morning Radio 4 featured the 'Brass Eye' story. I could scarcely believe my ears when a pious, moralising minister – having castigated and reproved those concerned with the programme – was asked if she'd seen it. 'Not all of it no,' was her reply and I howled, partly with outrage, but mostly with disbelief that this on-message, spin-sensitive government should have learned nothing since the days of Malcolm Muggeridge and the Bishop of Southwark. Fortunately, Jim Naughtie – God bless him – pinned her down and wouldn't let her wriggle off the hook. Result, embarrassment for government, which seems to have few supporters on this one other than the predictably apoplectic Daily Mail.

Ray C rings. He has been in touch with the ailing George and our plan for a day trip to Switzerland seems to have gone down well with him. Now just the dates to be finalised.

Wednesday, August 1st

A near-definite schedule for the rest of the shoot has been agreed. Subject to Algerian and Libyan visas we will be away for a total of eight weeks between early September and end of November. By then, apart from the ending (I still favour a boat back across the Straits of Gibraltar) and possibility of shooting the Paris–Dakar rally, we will have completed the filming, leaving me five clear months to concentrate on second half of the book and commentary.

Thursday, August 2nd

Write until midday when a cab comes to take me down to pick up Judy [Greenwood, my cousin] for lunch. Throughout the journey the driver, a member of the Middlesex Bowls team, conducts his own monologue, Going on holiday this year? I've been on holiday, you know where I went? Portugal. You should go there! Have you been there? You should go – this mixed with an unhealthy curiosity about who I might be meeting or why as we near Judy's house in Fulham Road. Will the lady be ready? Very Fast Show.

Take Judy to the River Café. Soon the heavens open and rain is pouring off the sun blinds. Judy talks of mutual friends – unexpected ones like Harry Enfield and John Watts [actor friend from Oxford] – of the number of gay men she knows, of the problems with her father, who I knew and wrote to in awe-struck Christmas thank-you letters as Commander Hilary Greenwood RN. He had a bottle in his workroom marked Kerosene which was full of sherry. [Brother] Nigel is the one she doesn't understand. She feels he's wasted himself – he should be an academic not a part-time art dealer.

Ruthie [Rogers, co-owner of the River Cafe] comes up, we chat, Judy knows her wine buyer, and we have had a marvellous Friulian Sauvignon. We're offered a drink on the house. J has nothing, I have a grappa – which according to the waitress earns me brownie points in the kitchen!

To Tricycle Theatre to see Pieter-Dirk Uys's one-man show. South African satire – this one all geared to Aids. He is able to attack left and right, white and Black and is remarkable, skilful, audacious and highly intelligent. Oh and funny. A sort of Edna Everage character called Evita dominates second half and has made him a big star in SA.

Friday, August 3rd

Leave for Heathrow at half past eleven. Meet Ray C in the lounge. He's already agitated as George, having got wind of the fact that we are really coming out to see him, wants us to stay longer and they've enquired if I could extend the visit until Sunday.

Flight to Milan Malpensa, which is all I know of the arrangements so far. A driver in a big black Mercedes meets us and we drive north. About 6.30 we find the hotel – a luxuriously dressed lake and mountain view called the Villa Principe Leopoldo – drop our bags off and wait for Olivia to collect us. She arrives ten minutes later in a small VW and drives south into the village of Montagnola, round a few tight bends and we're in front of two gates – with weathered sheets of metal covering them. They jerk open at the press of the remote control and we're in a very green and woody garden with a semicircle of cypresses and a short drive up to a dark front porch.

The spirit of Friar Park lives on here – it is a late nineteenth-century Alpine rustic mountain villa with a porch that's clearly come from an Indian temple, and once inside even more evidence of Hindu bounty. Low elaborately carved doors, leading to wine cellars, or passageways to washrooms. Just like Friar Park there is a feeling of dark mystery. Voices heard somewhere, doors slam but everything infuriatingly concealed.

Olivia seems in no hurry to take us upstairs but eventually, clutching our gifts (I've brought them two books, one the book of the TV series 'Meetings with Remarkable Trees' and the other a coffee-table collection of photographs of Lutyens houses), we're taken up the gloomy staircase where George is waiting for us. My immediate reaction is one of relief. His face is not drawn, in fact quite the opposite, it's round, a little too round, and puffy from steroids, but his eyes shine out a welcome and he's up and quite nimble. Then he does a mock drum roll and removes his floppy all-weather hat to reveal an almost entirely bald pate with just a tiny black tuft at its crown and some patches of hair running asymmetrically down the back of his head to his neck. The sight of George without hair is perhaps not as traumatic for me as it is for him. After all, I've spent all day with Ray Cooper who doesn't have a hair on his head.

He undoes the presents – 'We nearly bought a Lutyens house,' he says. Then we meet Dhani and [George's assistant] Rachel and have drinks outside. It's a suffocatingly close evening but can see fine views down the dramatic valley filled with Lake Lugano. Then the wind begins to blow and drops of rain come down and we move inside to eat, round a small round table in a room painted with a mural of what looks like Fatehpur Sikri.

George had massive surgery on his lung at the Mayo Clinic in March. He likens it to being attacked by a shark. Mayo recommended a Swiss clinic and it was here that he had his most recent bout of surgery and a preventive course of radiotherapy in May, which burned his hair out but will hopefully have killed off any cancers in his neck and throat.

He's a little slower in movement and speech but remarkably well considering and we end up fired by his enthusiasm, listening to music from Hoagy Carmichael CDs in what they call the ballet room, a tall white room with dancing bars, mirrors and a basketball hoop. He laughs and sings along with the music, then tires a bit, as if he's momentarily surprised by his own weakness, but it's after one o'clock when Olivia drives us out through the heavy metal doors and back to the hotel.

Saturday, August 4th: Lugano, Switzerland

Breakfast and then up to the house. No sign of George, so we saunter around the garden. I have a swim in a pool made murky by the night's rain. Afterwards, draped in a towel, Ray and me are peering through a gap in the trees at Lugano's small airstrip down below when there's a hiss and there's Dhani up on a balcony, miming a newspaper being opened and soundlessly indicating us to retreat.

A reporter from the Mail on Sunday has evidently rung the bell at the gates and asked if George is there and how he is. I feel immediately responsible for this lapse of security, as no one has found the house until today, but Olivia absolves us from blame, and says there had been a man following Rachel's car last week. But whatever the reason this casts a baleful shadow over the whole day.

Plans for a boat trip and a meal out are abandoned. We're advised to stay away from windows and Olivia renews attempts to have the security people deal with the journalist. George comes down at lunchtime. He's relaxed about it all but will not consider any pre-emptive public appearance to draw the sting of all the stories. The reaction from the family is that they've had enough, they've given statements and it's time they were left in peace. But George seems most concerned about the revelation of his hairlessness and much discussion centres around the possibility of making this public as part of a campaign for his new album 'Brainwashed'. The word 'Brainwashed' would be written across his head. At least George's playfulness has not abated, but I think the stakes are higher now and it will be difficult for him to escape a press fired up by recent statements that suggest he is dying.

Ironically, there can be no way of finding out if he's dying or not until he has an MRI scan to check the success of the radiotherapy and Olivia revealed that they can't take him to have his scan for fear of giving away his whereabouts — because the clinic in Bellinzona is staked out.

After lunch all seems to subside a bit. Dhani plays a motor-racing video game, George, tired by the talk at lunchtime, retires to sit and watch him. Olivia takes Ray and I for a walk in the gardens. Everything seems to grow here: weeping beech, gingko, oaks, larches, cypresses, alongside flourishing palm trees; geranium and hibiscus everywhere.

I remember an image from the long, aimless day and that's the discovery in mid-afternoon of a strong fir tree that had clearly taken the brunt of a direct lightning strike this morning. Its trunk was split down the middle and pieces of bark lay scattered 50 or 60 yards away. Unless the family can somehow reduce the tension of their lives and defuse some of their anger and resentment and begin to be like ordinary mortals again then anything could strike at any time. The trouble is that George is not an ordinary mortal.

Sunday, August 5th: Lugano

A clear, cool, beautiful morning. Breakfast out on a terrace with a tremendous view down the lake, intersected with sharp-edged mountainsides knifing down into the water. Peace and quiet. Sit, drink coffee and take it all in.

I find myself very much at home here. Am often asked where I would live if I didn't live, etc., etc. Today, Switzerland would come close to the top of the list. It is measured, efficient, discreet, unhysterical and very beautiful too. I must be getting old!

My car arrives at ten. Bid farewell to Ray, who is going up to the house and will urge George to go and have his MRI scan, even if it means breaking cover. Good flight back, am asked up on to the flight deck as we head straight for Mont Blanc. Think of Edward P, first setting eyes on my great-grandmother somewhere down among those plunging mountainsides and tight valleys, 140 years ago.

Friday, August 10th

Start on 'Sahara' and push on till break for interview for a New York paper on HandMade Films. Talk to TG. Says Ray is anxious for him to go out to see the Gardener. TG finds Ray's touches of conspiratorial secrecy quite amusing. 'Your last chance to see George before he recovers,' mimics TG — at which I laugh a lot.

Wednesday, August 15th

The house is heating up again. Shorts and T-shirt writing weather. The Hemingway look. Push on with the book.

A rather sad round robin email from Rachel. 'I'm leaving the Beeb today. My new email is . . .' She has learnt so much there – and I think put so much in. She and her department are now without work, and I think it is both sad and wrong that the BBC cannot find something to help keep this nucleus of talent, hard work and initiative on board.

Just H and me for supper outside. Quiet days, which I rather like, knowing that this time next month I will be in the heart of the Sahara.

Monday, August 20th

To the Lord Palmerston for a meal. I never have entirely happy experiences there. The clientele are rather sinister and the place itself, almost deliberately drained of colour, is quite dispiriting. An Australian girl with a laugh like a hyena brings across her mobile phone and asks if I'll speak to her mother in Sydney; a jolly waitress has to tell me that 'A Fish Called Wanda' was the best thing she ever saw and a very disturbing man with cool slits of eyes mutters 'mediocrity' at me as I join the jostle at the bar to try and pay. Though he looks a little psychotic I do go back and ask him what the problem is. He rattles off something to the effect that whilst Stalin, Hitler and Mussolini are ignored, mediocrities like myself are given television time. A quite nice, Pythonic twist this, but he's not being funny. He begins to raise his voice and looks hard at me. So, probably my last trip to the Lord Palmerston – for another few years anyway.

Tuesday, August 21st

Have my photo taken for Tate Britain's exhibition in November. The photographer tells me that John Cleese, who was asked to be part of the same exhibition, also chose Wright of Derby's 'Iron Forge' – only to be told I'd already done it.

I think of John affectionately today. He gave a good interview on the Today prog counteracting claims in the Mail (where else?) that he was turning his back on Britain for good. 'They're absolutely right. I haven't done any decent work since I was 35 years old.' There's a fan letter Alison [Davies, in the office] has out for me to reply to which asks plaintively if John and I could come back and do something 'as you work off each other so well'.

Thursday, August 23rd

Write to Wendy Woods, trying to sum up, as economically but honestly as possible, my fondness and respect for her husband Donald [South African journalist on whom the film 'Cry Freedom' was based] who died at the weekend. A wonderfully lively, alert, enthusiastic and energetic man who was easy and immensely likeable company. It's so difficult writing these letters – so much to say, and so hard to say it originally.

Do some letters with Alison. Have been approached to do a series on New Zealand wines which sounds remarkably like those documentaries on the relationship between gin and tonics and hotel swimming pools we used to fantasise about on Python.

Around eight, Simon, Nancy and Tim [Jones] come over. Tim has a huge appetite and is very sweet and good-natured and loves what he calls 'the bubble' – which is the plastic hatch cover from the spiral staircase in my workroom onto the roof. Simon spills raspberries on his pristine white trousers and spends much of the evening pant-less as Helen washes and spin-dries them. Nancy looks very well – like a younger Shirley MacLaine tonight.

S has discovered an unpublished and unperformed Noël Coward play called 'Long Island' which he is very excited about and is putting on in NYC – off Broadway, 20 characters.

We sit out and eat from the barbecue. The mugginess decreases but it's still warm through to midnight.

Sunday, August 26th: London–Washington

Both up at ten to eight after another sheet-only night. H off to tennis, me to America. A thick blanket of low, damp cloud shrouds the city. Picked up by Virgin Upper Class driver and once again have to admire their fast check-in system. Nothing could be easier and I'm in the Club Lounge by 10.15.

Easy passage through the airport at DC and only a 20-minute drive out to Basil's house in Earl's Court off Covent Garden off Liverpool Street (all thus named by the English developer Carisbrooke Homes).

I'm put to work on the book straight away, checking Basil's captions, and writing a word or two for the back cover. Basil cooks a sensationally good paella, which we all eat out on the deck. It's as balmy as it has been at home and I hardly feel I've crossed an ocean.

Tuesday, August 28th: Ashburn VA

Bas and I make an early start down in the basement with a view of the pond. Very comfortable place to work. Basil has all the right chairs, gadgets, desk accessories and is a wonderfully attentive host, always bringing me cups of tea and nibbles. He sits at his desk sorting out photos to fit the text, I sit at mine selecting, with little red sticker dots, my own favourites from that selection.

Wednesday, August 29th: Washington–Baltimore–New York

Driven by [Basil's wife] Pat on the next stage of my American week – up to Baltimore [to check out the possibility of using the Cone sisters' collection as the subject of another arts documentary]. Despite great swathes of highway, we are slowed down by jams on the Beltway, until at last we coast into Baltimore – usual mane of downtown skyscrapers to announce the virility of its city status – and park in an underground lot by the waterfront.

The waterfront has been developed, without much inspiration – just tourist dross grafted on to the end of a rather fine harbour – but we find a friendly place for lunch where the young waiter recognises me and where they serve good crab cakes and salad. 'This has made working here worthwhile,' says the waiter who insists on giving us a bottle of wine on the house.

The art museum is in a traditional neo classical style. The Cone collection has very recently been reorganised and is in a well-lit, woody area. Plenty of room to enjoy the work and a virtual reality tour of the Cone apartment is part of a recreation of the cramped, art-filled space the sisters lived in. Altogether promising place to work if the show gets the go-ahead. And some fine modern work here – Warhol's 'Last Supper' and a powerful and pleasingly puzzling Motherwell called 'Africa'.

Get to Baltimore Penn Station on time for 6.00 high speed to NYC. The station is handsome too with three stained-glass rotundas in the main hall. Once on the track though you enter another world. Glaring strip light, basic refreshment, cheap plastic fittings – and that's in First Class. But I do enjoy the scenery – soft pink glow over the wooded bays and inlets and on the terraced houses with their corniced flat roofs, creating a succession of Hopper-ish images.

Friday, August 31st: New York

Cloudier now and the hot, heavy weather is forecast to end with rain and storms this evening. Americans use the word 'storm' liberally – it can mean anything from a weather front bringing some light rain to a full-scale tempest, so you're not really sure what to expect.

Rain seems about to fall, and by the time I've walked down Madison and been lured into the likes of Armani and Barneys, the predatory side of New York has taken over, and I never reach my goal of the Museum of Modern Art. Instead, laden with bags, I survey the hot, sticky blur of Midtown and turn back, via the Madison Ave Bookstore which is small and helpful and on a human scale, and on to the hotel.

It rains, eventually, accompanied by tremendous thunder that seems to re-bound off the canyon walls of Manhattan. When it's over, I walk to the Met, then back through hot, green, steamy pathways of Central Park, to the hotel.

Saturday, September 1st: New York–London

Porridge in the Virgin Clubhouse. The waitress apologises that they're out of 'soldiers' to have with the boiled eggs.

One of the most crucial – or perhaps another of those regular crucial tests – for the English football team tonight, a World Cup qualifier against the Germans, in Munich. The captain is listening in on the flightdeck and reports, after six minutes, that Germany are a goal up. Groans of the usual, familiar kind. Then he interrupts again to bring the news that England are level. Nothing more for quite a while – presumably whilst we negotiate the densely packed skies around the UK, but as we are making our final approach the captain, whose name, incidentally, is Howard Hughes, proffers the casual information that England are 4–1 up. Finally, in the queue at immigration I'm grabbed by a complete stranger – 'Heard the news, Mike – 5–1!' There is really no other story in town. Will rings from Berlin to express his shock, horror and delight – and said the Germans were being very sweet and buying him drinks.

Sunday, September 2nd

Slept through until ten, after a night ruptured by another kick at the front door, around 4.30, the same time as the much more serious last attack, when I was away in the Sahara and H was here on her own. This time just one kick and by the time we were up whoever delivered it had moved on.

Despite overcast skies, around 16 of the local gardens were open and various groups of people trickled in and out throughout the day. H had worked very hard and the jungle, as she called it, looked both lush and still colourful, and the creeper is just on the turn.

Many people who run a mile from street parties turned out for the gardens.

The dark-haired man who runs on the Heath and never speaks as we pass becomes quite voluble – 'I shouldn't run. My knees are ruined. I keep getting told to give up. But I have to. I can't sleep if I don't run.'

Meet an elfin-slim lady and her equally slim lady friend who has just moved two Steenbeck editing machines into their upstairs room – she's an editor and filmmaker and I'm pleased people like her are coming in to Oak Village, which has always attracted more creative than City folk, thank God.

The family from Côte d'Ivoire also come by. Well-educated, well-behaved children, parents, sisters, uncles all speak some English and seem curious and interested; and at the end of it all I'm reassured to see how richly mixed a community this is. And it makes up for the boot on the door last night.

Saturday, September 8th

Tomorrow we leave for more desert filming after three and a half months' summer lay-off. Always, in the back of my mind, lurks that reluctance to uproot from home comforts, from my garden and workroom, from the regular visits to and from Rachel and Tom and Will, and the mornings at the National or the Courtauld, and onto aeroplanes and into heat and dust and sand and the hard work and long hours that must be put in to bring back something that's worth watching. It's the same feeling as not wanting to get out of a warm bed on a cold morning after a particularly nice dream.

I try to work out how to put up the tent I have to take. Erect it in the garden, with H in attendance, and it does seem awfully fiddly, with an inside and an outside and lots of hooks and eyes. I, predictably I suppose, lose my patience with it, and kick it and stomp off. Return later, but it is a fiddle and H calls Tom who says he will consult his friend Simon and bring round an easier one, and help me to erect it.

Then H and I tackle the mosquito net, which seems equally awkward, but H works it out, whilst I pack next door. In both cases the instructions are completely hopeless. They make the mistake of assuming that because it *is* quite easy, they don't need to tell you anything – what they forget is that there are such things as novices, who don't put up tents every day. However, I'm beginning to feel I've made the first faltering steps towards joining the secret world of Those Who Know These Things.

H and I eat pasta from Giacobazzi and Tuscan sausage. In bed, heart generally at ease, by midnight and a quarter. Tomorrow Paris, the next day Niamey and the day after – Insh'Allah – Agadez.

September 9th to September 25th: Filming in the Sahara. This was no ordinary trip. The heart of the desert was spectacular, but we were in one of the most remote parts of our

journey, in the town of Agadez, in the heart of the Sahara, when the Twin Towers were
destroyed. When we returned, the world had changed utterly.

Wednesday, September 26th

The sky is still, with low white clouds slowly breaking and a thin blue haze
above slowly growing. The creeper is a mixture of sombre maroon and streaks
of yellowed scarlet. I've just opened my email and found a plea from Terry
Gilliam to sign a 'Petition for a Thoughtful US Response' – a bid to steady
America's reaction, to avoid the emotive language of 'war', which was the tone
of George W. Bush's initial rhetoric. On the floor lie copies of newspapers of
September 12th which H saved for me. They show images of the catastrophe –
in a city I'd strolled happily around one week earlier.

It is as hard to believe now as it was when J-P came down the stairs at the
Pension Tellit in Agadez when we arrived after a 13-hour drive from Niamey,
and gave me the news.

For more than a week we saw none of the visual images of the events which
we heard about on shortwave radios in the heart of the Sahara. Not until the
evening of Wednesday 19th, when two French microlite pilots descended on
our camp in the Ténéré, did we see any of the photos of the attack, the flying bodies, the burning and collapsed Towers, the sight of Lower Manhattan
engulfed in smoke, dust and flame. Even now, as I write, I've seen no video
footage of the attacks, now referred to succinctly as 'September 11th'.

The sheer scale of the destruction and the terrible power wielded by those
prepared to die for their beliefs, has left the world shocked and still trembling.
The destruction of two of America's mightiest commercial icons was completed so thoroughly and comprehensively that everything now seems possible.
Never have I felt such collective nervousness – since perhaps the Bay of Pigs
and the nuclear stand-offs in the '60s.

I'm glad I was working in Niger, away from the regular diet of news, for I
doubt any of us would have been able to concentrate our minds on the work if
we had been near televisions and newspapers. As it is, we achieved a lot.

Not without its own pressure though. Since leaving London two weeks
ago last Sunday, I've spent 16 nights in different places – packing and unpacking every day for over two weeks. As much of the travelling involved
overnight camping, there was little time to catch up on notes, and the powerful
heat reduced daytime concentration, leaving me struggling just to keep going.
Physically, I survived well, but the largely supine style of desert life made even
relaxation an effort. I tried to make sense of it all but found my lack of fluent
French stifled my natural ability to communicate, and I envied J-P's ease and
affability with the people we met.

As we stepped off the plane in London, Basil reminded me that this was the same date, 13 years on, that I left London on 'Around the World in 80 Days', and the day his daughter was born.

A meeting at 11.30 at the office to discuss Algeria plans. Then to Joe Allen's for lunch. It's busy enough, but rest of Central London is quieter than usual and there are dire warnings of an almost complete collapse of US tourist trade over foreseeable future. The fat and secure days of the nineties seem to have come, temporarily at least, to an abrupt halt. Insecurity and economic crisis is in the air. As they say.

Thursday, September 27th

A day of clearing up – checking through the Niger notebook to make sense of my Saharan scribbles and demolishing the pile of letters and magazines and invitations and expectations. Some easily processed, others stick awkwardly, not fitting on any pile. Some encouragements – two Scottish geog teachers want me to address their annual meeting and become some sort of patron, believing that I've done for geography what 'David Attenborough has done for biology and Simon Schama has done for history'.

Friday, September 28th

The smoke still rises from the rubble in New York, and the shockwaves ripple out in a spate of opinions, forecasts, predictions and attempted explanations, but militarily all is eerily quiet. A phoney war, some are calling it. I pray that reason and patience and intelligence triumph over emotion or the grand gesture. America has to maintain the moral advantage that it still holds as the injured party – injure others and the balance will tip again. Worryingly, there is hysteria out there – not so much American as Muslim. Those who carried out and supported the attacks seem to relish the 'war of civilisations' that some are talking of.

Drawn to the TV. Nothing much to watch. 'Ab-Fab' is so formulaic now. But a short appreciation of John Le Mesurier is a treat. Sends me to bed happy, with his words of advice to young actors in my ears – 'always play exactly the same character, and if possible, wear the same suit'.

Saturday, September 29th

Catch up on papers and news – my reaction to being without either in the Ténéré desert. Mostly saying the same thing – new kind of enemy; who are they, where are they and how is it possible to defeat suicide attackers. All in all, a great sweep of negativity across the world. The good thing I suppose is the belated realisation that it's time to think about our attitudes to others, that we in the West have become used to having things our own way for too long. Like the intelligence services, we have misread the signs.

Thursday, October 4th

Swissair and Sabena have both gone bust since September 11, and BA's passengers down by 22 per cent. Strange things happening in the aftermath of the attacks. Read report that the towers of the World Trade Centre were built for height and lightness, with practically no reinforcing of the steel frame. And another report that bin Laden has a degree in civil engineering.

Friday, October 5th

A bright day, blue skies and sharply clear October sunshine.

   To Christie's for a private view of the modern art collection of a man called Gaffe, which his wife has bequeathed to UNICEF. We gather in the room in which 'Sunflowers' was auctioned for 26 million in 1988, starting an art boom – or a boom for Christie's anyway.

   Speeches. Roger Moore as Chief Ambassador to UNICEF – he's always exactly what he is, a sort of ersatz James Bond, a pleasant, amusing actor cursed with good looks, so conventional as to be unreal. Other Famous Person is Martin Bell, the absolute opposite of Moore – his face is becoming increasingly lived in and with his belly pushing hard against the trousers of his crumpled (trademark) white suit he reminds me of the later Rembrandt self-portraits. Passionately pleased to be out of Parliament (he lost his Independent seat at last election). Away from all those meetings and committees – he spits the words out. Says he was supposed to be in Afghanistan now, accompanying an aid convoy but someone had cocked up. He seems to be caught between celebrity and journalist and not sure which he enjoys most.

   Back to find faxed page of NY Post from Sherrie. 'Hemingway Son Found Dead in Women's Jail' – young Gregory gone. Right next to it an ad for the 'M-17 Style Gas Mask'.

Sunday, October 7th

Over to Roger M's for supper and to meet Said Chitour, our Algerian fixer who has flown in from Algiers this afternoon. The rain is heavy, puddles by the roadside and strong side winds along the A40. We're glad to arrive in the warmth of West Lodge Avenue.

Rog greets us with the news that the Allied attack on Afghanistan has begun – 'missiles streak across the clear night sky' – TV coverage of indistinguishable lights and blurs which could be Kosovo or the Gulf War. For a moment or two it all sounds exciting but soon the feeling of foreboding grows. The hawks have won – every life destroyed in 'collateral damage' will be another martyr, a chip off the smooth surface of America's moral superiority. And offering propaganda on a plate with the spectacle of the world's richest country bombing the world's poorest.

Monday, October 8th

Tom is 33 today. News comes in of the first night's raid on the Taliban. I'm confused but generally anxious. Why do it now? Why not wait until there is more intelligence, more unsettling of the regime by outside pressure? Is there a plan? The answers to these questions are infuriatingly vague and smug. We're told to prepare for a long campaign – nights, weeks, even months of . . . something or other. Well, How shall we prepare O Lord? Just carry on as normal, especially shopping, don't let the economy suffer and er . . . well, just prepare.

I ring Roger to express doubts about the wisdom of going into a country with a known, and violent, Islamic fundamentalist minority at this time and perhaps we should consider postponing the Algeria, Libya and Tunisia filming until the spring. Roger promises to take soundings and to listen to all the relevant advice from Algeria.

I accept Roger's assurances and his assessment that we should go ahead as planned, and am comforted that the crew appear to do so as well.

Tuesday, October 9th

Lunch with H at Moro to meet Wendy and Peter Benchley (author of 'Jaws'). Peter recounts the apocalyptic experience of his son-in-law who was near enough to the Trade Center to witness the collapse and its aftermath. Peter tells the story well – the sudden wall of dust careering towards him, the dense and utter blackness that it brought, the only light source being the green screen of his cell phone. Crawling across a road, feeling his way by the various signs – a water-hydrant, a parking meter – reaching swing doors of the Chase Manhattan to find them piled with bodies, dead or alive he didn't know, pushing in through an emergency side door to a lobby thick with dust, but at least some light.

The latest scare is anthrax in Florida, one man died, another confirmed in some newspaper office. That's all, but it's enough to add to the hysteria. And there's 'Holy Grail' just re-released in the States with me in Castle Anthrax!

Peter has been on TV screens throughout summer after the two or three shark deaths provoked earlier, pre-September 11 hysteria. In one case a man had a shark on his fishing line and actually urged his kids into the water to be photographed with it. It took one of their arms off.

Thursday, October 11th

A sour sky, some drizzle trickles down. Nothing to raise the spirits. I leave for the viewing of Part 1 of 'Sahara'.

Not a happy morning. The opening worries me, but then openings are always tricky ('80 Days' and 'Full Circle', for instance). What worries me slightly more is my own performance, which seems to be too often frivolous and dismissive at the expense of enquiry and information. My references to Yorkshire and Sheffield began to irritate. In fact I got on my nerves quite frequently.

Sunday, October 14th

Slept badly. No confidence in my ability to sleep, the concerns and problems of the day ahead, days ahead, preoccupy me and seem much stronger than the powers of calm and relaxation. Maybe it's not having H beside me. Glad to be up. Greyish skies but dry.

Run, then field various birthday phone calls for H, put the flowers I bought yesterday in a vase and arrange her presents around them on the kitchen table.

Collect H from hospital at a quarter to eleven. She's fine, but he's missed one area of her left leg and will have to complete it in outpatients. A small mystery on the way in. The security guard/receptionist said that a young man asking for Mrs Palin had come in an hour before. He was wary of saying where she was because, as he said, 'you never know quite what it's like with people who are a bit well known'. Eventually solved by call to ward sister. The mystery visitor was her surgeon.

Good homecoming. She loves her presents, and an unwrapping like Christmas follows. H, who's supposed to be taking it easy, ends up cooking a lamb leg – Will and Rachel join us for her birthday supper.

Finish watching 'The Battle of Algiers'. So many parallels with any terror-ist offensive – and so many lessons. Tempting to see Rumsfeld and his hawks in the damaged Pentagon as making exactly the same clumsy and ultimately unproductive response as Mathieu/Massu in Algiers. For two years repression seemed to have worked, then the tide of anger and resentment swept the re-pressors away.

Saturday, October 27th: Oran, Algeria–London

My clean bill of health on the last two filming trips comes to an end in early hours of this morning, with diarrhoea and mild but morale-sapping stomach cramps. In addition I'm tormented by a rogue mosquito that seems impervious to the cloud of Autan which hangs over me, and keeps buzzing back.

The Hotel Adef is a mysterious mess of a place. My bathroom ceiling has been partly removed to accommodate, or gain access to, a waste pipe, and strange half-human, half-animal cries issued from the hole this morning. The usual collection of faults – bath with no bath taps, only a shower, a balcony door handle hanging on by a thread. A trail of water comes out from under the door of one of the rooms on the third floor and runs slowly down the corridor.

Assemble in the lobby of the Adef at nine, and our police motorcycle escort leads us into the main square – the Place des Armes, around which are some fine colonial buildings. The one we concentrate on is the Municipal Theatre and Opera House, a striking, richly detailed copy of the Paris Opera House. It appears in Camus's 'La Peste' in a scene in which one of the actors collapses on stage.

At the airport later, a tall, middle-aged Algerian who has a family in Stock-holm, becomes the first person since we've been here to raise the subject of September 11 and the American bombing which began on the 30th September. It's colonisation by another name isn't it? Don't I realise that the Americans and their allies are making a big mistake and that the killing of innocent Afghans only strengthens the hand of those he calls 'Islamists'? I have to agree but I try to widen the argument, and I put to him something which has worried me in the days since I last watched and admired 'The Battle of Algiers'. Why are the FLN, who won independence and became national heroes, now running the government which my friend criticises so much for being a tool of the Amer-icans? What went wrong with the revolution?

He can't give me any better answer other than that 140 years of colonialism cannot be destroyed straight away – mistakes will be made. This was not, I'm sure, a slogan of the FLN at the time. They offered a new, free, liberal Arab state in Algeria, and none of that, apart from the increasingly resented 'arabisation' ever happened. They cruelly and brutally consolidated power, split one from the other, as happens so often, and have now, 40 years on, created a military and police state which relies for 90 per cent of its income on oil and gas sales to Europe and America. Little of that seems to have been reinvested in his country.

We are sped through the airport to the VIP lounge with cries of 'Délégation!' Leave on time, on an almost empty flight, and are back over England, what joy!, by five o'clock.

Eamonn, our action man protector from Stirling, has been a tower of strength. He takes justifiable pride and pleasure in the fact that I was the first Western journalist to be filmed in the Casbah for several years. Even John Simpson, here two years ago, couldn't get permission.

Farewells at Terminal 2. We're all exhausted again.

Thursday, November 1st

November comes in in a blaze of light. Another morning of blue and gold.

Drive to various errands around Belsize Park and South End Green and Kentish Town ending up at Alan B's for early tea.

He makes tea and we drink it upstairs in amongst accretions of books, papers, paintings, photographs that seem as if they have been like this for many years. Alan is finding writing difficult – he's surprisingly affected by the events of September 11. 'I mean what is there to write about. Everything seems so . . . trivial.' He keeps at the diary, has his daily visits from Dr Jonathan across the way. 'You know he's got an exhibition of paintings on at the moment,' says Alan, in a tone of voice which seems to set up my reply 'Asking for trouble, I would have thought' – and Alan's rapturous agreement, laughter and hands entwined.

He talks of moving, which I must say seems inconceivable, like a tortoise jettisoning its shell. He's living now with Rupert, editor of Interiors. 'Youngest ever editor,' adds Alan with a touch of pride.

We talk of stage acting, and Alan's reluctance to play himself in 'Lady in the Van' – which was apparently one of the conditions of taking it to New York. 'I just couldn't do it. It'd terrify me.' He's rather lost confidence in his acting and yet feels quite at ease reading or talking on stage. I know the feeling. Things he'd have done without thinking in 'Beyond the Fringe' days and I'd have done without thinking at the Edinburgh Festival back in 1964 no longer seem as easy.

As I leave, a taxi arrives to take the much-loved recluse to a signing at Selfridges.

Late in the day Mhairi [producer on the arts programme] rang from Scotland. Roly Keating [BBC Director for Arts] has accepted the Cones/Matisse programme and plans will now be laid to shoot next June.

Tuesday, November 13th

Work on the book with few interruptions. Unexpected (for me) news of Taliban collapse continues. The Northern Alliance is in Kabul and Mullah Omar is berating his followers for running like chickens. Kites can now be flown again freely in northern Afghanistan.

Wednesday, November 14th

Continuing uncertainty over Libyan visas blights plans for next trip. It now looks more and more likely that we will have to return from Tunisia, have two days back in London and fly out again to Tripoli – though even that cannot be guaranteed.

November 18th to November 25th: Filming in Tunisia

Monday, November 26th: Tunisia–London

Woken by alarm just before six. Still dark outside. As so often this week, the world outside looks chill and inhospitable. Wind tosses the palm trees. Washed and packed by 6.30. Breakfast before the crowds here at the Palm Marina, a forgettable tourist factory of a hotel.

Khalifa, our old, charmless driver, is lashing bags to the roof rack at seven and after much coughing, hawking and grinding catarrhal intakes, he pulls us away from the hotel at ten past seven, and we rocket along the coast road past a string of hotels, spreadeagled along the beach. A few miles east from Houmt Soukh they run out and a magical marshy shore stretches, unmolested, for a kilometre or two. Flamingos, herons, plovers scattered along the shoreline, sorting and picking.

Friday, November 30th

Around eight fifteen Sue McGregor announces 'some news just in'. George Harrison has died in Los Angeles. Ten minutes later it's confirmed and there is a short report and a dignified statement from the family.

Within a cup of tea of the confirmation the phones start to ring. Today – the programme I'm listening to, wants me to talk later, Breakfast News want me to talk before that. I pour another cup of tea and take it upstairs to my desk and try to focus my mind. There is not much time and once the floodgates are open the tide is unstoppable.

BBC TV news comes to the house, a German TV crew just turns up, un-announced on the doorstep. The fax machine clatters behind me, spewing out a list of all those who have tried to contact me through the office. There's no question of being able to go anywhere – even a trip to the loo isn't easy, as both phone lines buzz constantly.

In all the clamour there are still small voices of people I want to hear from. Ray rings; he has just come out of hospital after a spine operation, which pre-vented him from being able to fly out to LA to be with George. He breaks off and in a choking voice tells me he can't say any more now. Rachel – George, Olivia and Dhani's closest support – manages to get through and calmly de-scribes the situation in LA.

George died at about two o'clock in the afternoon LA time, ten o'clock in the evening UK time. She and Olivia and Dhani were with him as were other friends, including Brian Roylance [producer and publisher] who has been a stalwart over the last few weeks. They were chanting and the place where he died was quiet. Rachel apologises for describing what happened then. 'I'm not religious or even that spiritual,' she confesses, 'but a nurse who was present drew their attention to 'a sort of golden aura' that hung over them all as George's body finally gave out. And they all noticed it, she said, and 'silly as it sounds', it was true.

He had come to America, she said, because Americans don't want anyone to die – and so he'd had the most up-to-date and thorough treatment in New York and LA, but in the last two weeks he had become steadily worse, weaker and in increasing pain.

I felt duly grateful to Rachel for the call and for her equanimity and good sense. After that it was back to the circus.

I must have done a dozen interviews in the morning, maybe more, and I decided to go down to the office in the early afternoon – just to get me out of the house, and away from the same phone. In one of my interviews I'd referred to George three times as John, so it was time for a rest.

The office was under siege. Calls coming in even as TV crews were setting up in the conference room. Channel 4 and CNN, Dutch TV, People magazine, Time interviews in the cab on the way in. I extricated myself about five and was home in time to be interviewed by Robin Denselow for Newsnight. I had nothing new to say by then.

As I turned down Hanbury Street for a meal with Will just before eight o'clock, a white ITN news van with sat dish pointed towards Hawksmoor's steeple was already in position for a live input to ITN's evening special at 10.30. This was something like my 24th interview of the day and the piece I was looking forward to most of all still remained to be done. I'd agreed to write

500–1,000 words for the Independent on Sunday by first thing tomorrow and was looking forward to being able to say something different and something of my own more considered thoughts. I began work on it at midnight.

Saturday, December 1st

Wake, around nine, to more slow, steady rain and end of year gloom. Put finishing touches to the 'IoS' piece and emailed it off. Snatched a bowl of muesli and a cup of tea then H drove me up to Belsize Park to catch a train to Leicester Square.

Met up with Rachel at the Empire to see 'Apocalypse Now Redux' (as the re-release is pompously called). A long film made even longer and done few favours in the process. Still, it occupied me and kept me away from phones, and when I got home I scanned the papers and there was much about George and my name cropped up as the only Python spokesman available. I felt good for George as the comment was generally admiring and positive. And I'm glad I was able to tweak the clichéd myth of the Quiet Beatle – 'he never stopped talking when I was with him' one paper reported me as saying.

Friday, December 7th

Walk to Belsize Park, buy my macchiato from the coffee cart outside the station, read Tom Seger on Palestine on the train to London Bridge. Today's headlines carry the story of the fall of the last bastion of Taliban resistance with the surrender of Kandahar. Al-Qaeda, being much less well-defined, is another matter. No sign yet of Mullah Omar or Osama BL, so although there has been a rapid collapse of Taliban resistance, the real plums are still unpicked.

To Tate Modern, and the Surrealist exhibition – 'Desire Unbound', it's called – which centres around Surrealists' obsession with sex. They held serious group discussions about things like onanism, homosexuality, anal sex, bestiality, and reported their findings in earnest journals.

It's quite a rude exhibition and I'm not surprised to see a respectably dressed 40-something couple snogging hard on the terrace overlooking the Thames afterwards.

Sunday, December 9th

To Carlton School at ten. Evidence of much money spent on new facilities – especially security. The buzzers and electronic doors which used to be on banks and prisons and are now everywhere.

Dalu Chowdhury the headteacher is a remarkable example of calm and patience and tolerance and enthusiasm, in a school which deals in hope and despair in equal measures. Heavily multi cultural – 52 per cent do not have English as their first language – it is a rich and successful mix, an example to all who are blaming last summer's riots on separation of cultures and religions in education. But many children will not be here in two or three months as their families, desperately seeking asylum, are moved around the country. Eighty children have moved since September.

Despite these problems, the spirit of the school is good and the atmosphere encouragingly positive. Q and A about my travels with second assembly. Lots of questions, much participation. 'What country are you going to next and how old are you?' 'Have you ever eaten sick by mistake?' (This last from a very demure little girl.)

Tuesday, December 11th

After lunch prepare thoughts for my introduction of the National Film and TV School auction at Christie's this evening.

Michael Grade [chairman of the NFTS], his golden hair turned silver grey, is there. Michael says Alan Bleasdale is very low and can't get anything commissioned – he (Michael) is very critical of 'the pap' that passes for TV drama nowadays, and I can't help thinking that of the three writers who've written the best things I've ever done, one has writer's block, another can't get work and the third has left the country. I hope the demise of Bennett, Bleasdale and Cleese will only be temporary. We need them.

Home by 8.30. Glass strewn all over the pavement outside the house. Appears to have come from a half-dozen smashed milk bottles. Sweep it all up.

Watch Louis Theroux's curious and sad film about the Hamiltons, and then, hearing noise outside at the end of it, go and find Bernie helping a neighbour pick up cardboard boxes and rubbish that had been pulled off their bins and flung around. Bernie says it was a group of young kids, who ran off as soon as her door opened. Probably the same ones who threw the milk bottles. This and the door-kicking incidents of last year and the recent increase in graffiti lead me to the glum conclusion that for all the money spent, Gospel Oak is still its own worst enemy.

Friday, December 14th

The New York Times has turned down my piece on George, which irritates because I spent a weekend on it, but then I suspect that the reason why I had to spend a weekend on it was that it was so contrived to fit their brief, rather than flowing naturally and spontaneously, as my best pieces always do.

To Hanbury Street for supper with Will and Ruth Golding [colleague of Will's at the Soane Museum] and her husband A. N. Wilson. He's a surprise. He looks and talks establishment but has a wicked sense of humour and is not at all pompous or patronising – just entertaining, and good listener too.

Both good on Jonathan Miller and the Gloucester Crescent Set. Ruth tells of Dr Jonathan insisting on carrying her shopping for her whilst talking on about myth and reality, how we see ourselves, the birth of Renaissance art, whatever, right up to the doorstep.

'He is a polymath, we must remember that,' Andrew points out, mischievously, before describing the latest development in the doctor's career – 'he's a sculptor now'. Apparently he had asked Andrew to come and see his recent work and showed him what looked to Andrew like an old boiler. 'Walk round it, get to know it,' the doctor had offered, generously.

Saturday, December 22nd

Late lunch. Wrap some presents, then a short sit by the fire with H and a crossword – me and my Seger, before striking out into the icy night on our way to an ex-neighbour's Christmas party. Seemed a touch quieter this year. Same carols played and sung a little chaotically.

Sebastian [Taylor, journalist son of the historian A. J. P. Taylor] is interesting – a socialist by instinct, a left-winger making money from observing the City and the money markets. He explains to me the difference between mortgage here and in Europe and it's quite significant. Mortgages here can vary according to rise and fall in interest rates, whereas in Europe they are largely long-term and on a fixed, say, 7 per cent interest repayment. So with interest rates now down to 5 per cent here, more money is being saved and released into the economy, hence a UK economy that is more buoyant than other G7 countries, all of whom, apart from France, are in recession.

Sebastian thinks we are on the verge of being the new Germany – the original perpetrators of the 'economic miracle'.

Monday, December 24th

A child's voice rings out from Barrington Court, shouting 'Osama bin Laden shall live' louder and louder, over the eerily quiet neighbourhood. Very chilling.

Gear up for third party in three nights. This time it's our usual Christmas Eve open house for the neighbours.

Bruce Robertson [neighbour] is the first to arrive, and I'm surprised to see him as they're usually busy with family. His bright eyes, white beard, red waistcoat makes him look like an impish old Santa. Prowls my bookshelves, jots down the odd name. Farson's 'Soho in the Fifties' catches his eye. He knew many of those people – like the Bernards. Jeffrey did nothing, according to Bruce R, but his brother Bruce had a real job, worked hard and was much the preferable of the two.

I only learn later from Granny that when he sat and talked to her, he asked her if she was incontinent. 'Asked me twice, dear.'

Monday December 31st: New Year's Eve

A brilliantly cold morning. Quiet, settled, high-pressure weather to see my 58th year out.

End of year report: my hunch is that 'Sahara' will be less popular in terms of audience numbers than previous shows. 'Hemingway' upset the momentum – how severely we'll have to wait and see. On the positive side I feel generally happy and content. I have less angst about work and recognition and competition. I've paced myself a little better and apart from the angry mindlessness of the door kickers and window smashers, am very settled and oddly secure here in Oak Village. And Helen and I really get on pretty well.

2002

Thursday, January 3rd

To John Lewis early – car sliding on ice as I turn up into Grafton Road – to return Christmas gifts that didn't find favour, buy some DVDs to send Terry J as diversions during his post-hip recovery, then on to the office to catch up on arrangements for Mauritania. Home by two when Bas comes over with jet lag, Tunisian photo selection and dim sum.

Deal with all three with the help of a bottle of Cloudy Bay 2000, then I take him back into town on my way to see [dentist] Bernie Kieser. Generally good mouth report, but two persistent problems on right side. 'Access,' says Bernie and advises a new refinement to the usual brushes. At one point, noticing a blister on the bottom right lip, he asks 'Do you dribble?' 'When watching television, sometimes?' Somewhat shaken by this full and frank oral encounter I head home.

Watch some of 'Shackleton' – Charles Sturridge's epic recreation of a voyage in which no one said very much. But there were some great cold sores!

January 4th to January 8th: Mauritania, Dakar Rally Filming

Thursday, January 10th

At Orion, in the round-table conference room looking out over the busy junction of Aldwych, Waterloo Bridge and the Strand, Michael D has laid out the various cover mock-ups. Basil has improved the two much stronger, simpler images he submitted before Christmas. 'The noble profile' as Bas refers to my conk, with sun catching the outline of the face, a smile, and stretch of Chinguetti sands spread out beneath.

Make my way across the Strand to the office. A damp, smudgy drizzle coming down. A call from Helen to say that my Filofax has been found in a skip outside the Strand Palace Hotel. The couple who found it have been told where the office is and a few minutes later they appear. Only then do I realise, as gratitude and relief clouds into doubt, that what they are handing over to me is not the Filofax I lost before Christmas, but the Filofax which was with me as I stepped out of Orion's offices twenty minutes earlier.

In that time it has been removed from my bag without my knowing, riffled through in great haste by the looks of things – money stolen and one credit card removed together with a PIN number form, which I'm grimly happy to see is not the right one for the card. I've been pick-pocketed, on the street, for the first time in 36 years of living in London.

Ironically, my Evening Standard carries news of the Met Police chief's decision to take 250 officers off traffic policing to deal with a serious rise in street crime. Of course, when I tried to report what had happened on the Strand tonight, I couldn't get through to the police station.

Friday, January 11th

To the office for letters with Alison. She says there has been a very good response to the Christmas screenings of '80 Days' and 'Pole to Pole'. 'Mostly elderly couples,' she adds, sweetly.

Taxi across town to see Terry J at the EdVII Hospital. He's lying asleep as I peer round the door but wakes quickly and seems pleased to see me. Terry asks me to help put his slippers on as he swings out of bed in his pale blue hospital robe. I pass him his crutches; he shuffles off to have a pee. He's feeling good now, he says, and amazed that he can move about with relative ease after only three days. I'm shown his X-ray, with the chrome cap that now covers his offending joint a bright white image against shady bone. 'I'd rather hoped for titanium,' he mutters.

There's a bowl of fruit from JC with a note to the effect that he hopes all's gone well – 'if not please send the fruit back'.

Saturday, January 12th

Walk into Kentish Town to buy a present for Rachel. Almost opposite the Owl, there is a cry and a car, front door swinging open and window smashed, is driven hard and fast out of a side turning and down Kentish Town Road; a man races out into the street in pursuit, takes number. I'm watching this drama, a little dumbstruck, when the man comes up to me. 'Michael Palin?' I nod, a touch confused. 'Could I have your autograph?'

Tuesday, January 15th

Visit Terry. He looks like something out of Hogarth, with his white knee-length stockings and hospital robe. Take him a copy of Variety, a book about Iceland and a copy of GQ which has lots of semi-naked lovelies inside. Terry is grateful. Says he had his first erection since the operation, so the arrival of the magazine was timely.

Waste time watching 'Footballers' Wives' which is base and riveting.

Wednesday, January 16th

Up to La Provençale in Belsize Park to buy some food for tonight; the nor-mally salty Turkish Cypriot lady who runs the place is nervous. A middle-aged roué of a rep is hanging around the shop, casting shifty looks out at Haverstock Hill in case wardens appear. When he's out of earshot she asks me not to leave too soon. 'He has wandering hands, you know, and I don't like that.'

Run before lunch and afterwards set to work on the Dakar Rally piece. Have not got far when the screenplay of 'Hem's Chair' by Stephen Mallatratt[1] arrives and of course I have to put everything else aside. It starts very well, with more substantial rewriting of dialogue than I expected; some nuances lost but generally quite excited by what he's done.

Break off from the reading when Anne calls to tell me that BBC Worldwide have sold 'Sahara' in America. A very good deal of 200,000 dollars a show to Bravo, a cable channel which is investing in quite a lot of quality British work. 'Cold Feet', 'Crime and Punishment', etc. They're reportedly very keen on purchasing the earlier series – 'Full Circle', '80 Days' and 'Pole to Pole' and will be over at the Brighton TV Fair in February to meet me.

Thursday, January 17th

Most of the morning spent completing my read of Mallatratt's 'Hem's Chair'. I like the work he's done, but am aware that the shades of meaning, the subtleties, inflexions and ambiguities which a novel gives you time to indulge are ironed out in a TV film and this makes it occasionally disappointing. There are some suggestions I'd like to make before I would be happy to give it the go-ahead.

Friday, January 18th

At the Post Office in Mansfield Road. A man with his son approaches. He's a fan, a Kosovan who has lived here for nine years. 'It's a good country. People kind to me here. Your government is good.' Said without any trace of ingrati-ation – it came out so naturally I felt grateful myself for his remarks. In the light of our struggling NHS and hopeless transport systems it's good to know

---

1 Mallatratt's adaptation of Susan Hill's *A Woman in Black* was a long-running hit at London's Fortune Theatre.

there are those who appreciate us, more than we appreciate ourselves. It's all about perspective.

Saturday, January 26th

Wind and rain from quite early on. Good weather for writing, not so good for the day on which the RSPB has organised a nationwide birdwatch. There's not a bird to be seen in the garden below me or the roofs beyond as the wind and rain grow heavier.

J-P has invited me to a Burns Night party in Chiswick. The haggis is played in by accordion and Nigel Williams reads a Burns poem as dedication. A smaller, vegetarian haggis appears, without ceremony.

Monday, January 28th

Make a solid move forward today, over 2,000 words.

H and I out to the theatre to see 'Privates on Parade' – much-praised production by Michael Grandage of the Crucible, with newly composed music by Denis King. A squeeze around the entrance (not a phrase you could have used in the play without hoots of laughter); a slim blonde woman beseeches me to do more travelling – 'We want to see you back on our screens.' She introduces her partner – it is none other than the author and broadcaster F. Forsyth. His angular, hawkish face (and views) slightly gone to seed, as if his head has lost its shape, but he beams, in, I hope, endorsement of his partner's sentiment.

Entertaining first half – dominated by Roger Allam's well-controlled, but joyfully over-the-top campery as Terri Dennis – and imaginative staging by Grandage, including a superb – and really wet – rain sequence. The problem with the play is that Dennis dominates everything.

Tuesday, January 29th

Up to Markos for a haircut. I sit on his uncomfortably narrow bench and read my Herald Tribune. Eye caught by a story from Washington Post of 60 Israeli reservists – many of them officers with previous combat experience – who have refused to serve in the occupied territories. 'We will no longer fight beyond the Green Line for the purpose of occupying, deporting, destroying, blockading, killing, starving and humiliating an entire people,' they say. I cannot exaggerate how much this news raised my spirits, flagged and depressed as they are by the wretched belligerence of the bin Ladens, Bushes, Rumsfelds and

Sharons whose fire-breathing anger seems to be so fashionable now. I know that reason and human decency will not fill the earth in my lifetime, but it erupts at moments like this and makes you realise we are not all mad or stupid or cruel.

By coincidence an elderly Jewish man is on the bench next to me; he's 94 and lives in Gordon House Road. He used to be in the rag trade and loves London. He's full of positive, Rabbi Blue-ish, aphorisms. 'Live each day as if it was your last' and so on. We chat away and I like him very much. Daren't ask where he stands on the occupation of Palestine. It might spoil everything.

Monday, February 4th

Strong winds and rain sweep in from the west, again. Sit tight and write.

Feel very strange for a few minutes after finishing work and before going out for Nigel Walmsley's party for Terry J. A strange but unspecific feeling of system under stress. It passes and I arrive at the Century Club off Shaftesbury Avenue at half past seven.

Terry has a lot of difficulty ordering a small, starter-size portion of linguine. He's told that he can only have it as a main course. Couldn't you just use a smaller spoon, says Terry, plaintively, which becomes the joke of the evening.

Nigel W seems a little wary of Terry – as if dealing with a small but probably safe explosive device. They reminisce about Oxford and how hard they found it to fit in. I like Nigel, he's very clever and articulate and witty and should write – he says he'd love to write a play – but there is a side to him that is quite enigmatic. He's a consultant now, no longer top man at Carlton. Has been to Warsaw already this year. I think he'd be the perfect spy. He's interested in people and motivations and is also good at systems and management. And he has that cool, ironic gaze.

Nigel W finds us a cab but refuses to join us, insisting he'd rather take the Tube. Very suspicious!!

Wednesday, February 13th

Lunch with Terry G at Moro. He hadn't been there before and it's particularly good today with a Caldo Gallego, a thick ham and bean broth which is delectable. We compare our Milosevic-style haircuts and talk about every sort of news, films, the usual very easy chat which makes TG one of the best one-to-one dining companions.

Letter asking me if I'll present a 50-year tribute to David Attenborough being planned by the Natural History Unit. I'd love to be involved but I fear it's going to be overwhelmed by 'Sahara' and Cones.

Thursday, February 14th

The head of Natural History Unit at Bristol calls to talk about the Attenborough prog, which I might be able to fit in in August. Apparently David was nervous about the whole idea of a special devoted to him, but visibly relaxed when my name was mentioned! I should like to get a little bit closer to him – as he is one of the examples I use of someone uncompromised by fame and celebrity, and the best advert for public service TV.

Re-read Mallatratt's adaptation of 'Hem's Chair' before our meeting this p.m. Very good two-hour session. Stephen looks rather rock-like and serious, but he's a fine touch for comic dialogue and when stirred is witty and quite wicked. I like Carolyn Reynolds, very straight, direct and unmanipulative. Agree on some rewrites, notes given and taken and as we all feel that the Post Office situation is as ludicrous now as it was when I wrote it – Consignia, cut-backs 'to offer a better service', union opposition, mass closures – there is a certain added urgency to seeing the script filmed. For TV, we generally think.

Monday, February 18th

I have had my head down throughout the weekend, sprinting for the finish. Few interruptions, though H had a nasty fall at tennis yesterday and I had to take her up to the Royal Free. She was seen within a couple of hours, no breakages, but she'll have bruising. Both of us are hobbling on our left legs now as I have pulled or strained muscles in my buttock.

By 7.30 the ostrich-like three days on the book have paid off and I type out the last line. Many changes and adjustments still needed, but it's come in at around 95,000 words.

Tuesday, February 19th

Viewing of prog five. At the end, Nicola says, without any great drama, that she thinks four programmes will be better than five. I feel relieved. Though a side of me feels regret that this is the first time in five travel series that we've failed to sell an extra episode to the BBC, I recognise that what she's saying is probably fair.

The pace is slow in places, but that's the nature of the beast – the Sahara is a desert of wide underpopulated spaces. It moves to a very stately rhythm, more so than anywhere else we've been, and things have changed – peak-time BBC TV now demands a tighter, more focused and, I'm afraid, more presenter-led approach.

Sunday, March 3rd: London–Washington

I'm on my way out of Heathrow, a little after midday, devouring a short but engaging book called 'Five Days in May: London 1940' [by John Lukacs], which describes in detail how Churchill won the argument in that crucial stage of the war when it seemed to some to be sensible to start suing for some sort of peace. Churchill stood out against compromise and put himself and the country at great peril but, of course, pulled it off. Late in the American afternoon we touch down at Dulles, only to be confronted by a 50-minute, slowly winding wait at immigration.

Monday, March 4th: Ashburn, Va.

It's a beautiful morning – ducks and geese on the pond. A kite circling, and the grass grey-brown and dry.

Reports of most serious US casualties of the post 9/11 action in Afghanistan are coming in. A helicopter shot down. And we'd been led to believe that al-Qaeda and the Taliban had had their hides whipped at Tora Bora (though this now sounds to have been a failure in which the enemy were allowed to get away). All seems relevant to Churchill and 1940, but what Bush, or anyone, lacks is the sort of rhetoric Churchill used – viz London 'this strong city of refuge which enshrines the title deeds of human progress'.

Friday, March 8th: New York City

Quiet breakfast in the Mercer Kitchen, looking out on the almost quaint streets of the cast-iron district – about as close to an Old Quarter that New York has.

Though I fear it may be a little oversentimental, even vulgar to go down to Ground Zero, I banish such silly, uptight considerations and walk down towards where the Twin Towers used to be. On Church Street I'm aware of a stinging in my eyes, though the air itself doesn't look dusty and there is no wind blowing. I notice windows and shopfronts covered in dust and eventually am picking my way over wooden cable duct guards.

The signs of destruction are on the sides of surrounding buildings. Some have sections missing, bare frames of iron girders showing like ribs on a skeleton – a Stars and Stripes blows limply, one end serrated and torn, wire mesh covers some buildings, black stains spread across others. Makeshift shrines of drying flowers, photos, sad little inscriptions lean against the fencing.

Walk where I'm allowed to walk, picking my way across cables, mud and past boarded-up windows until I've come round to the east, to Trinity Church, which has in its wall a cherub's head, a fragment from a church called St Mary le Bow in London, blown to pieces by German bombs in 1940 – a fragment of a disaster so close to another disaster and yet untouched by any damage.

The dusty, sticky facades of surrounding buildings – the fenced-off atrium of the Millennium Hilton (so much hope in that sign) with its glass porch cracked and splintered, a surviving piece of twisted metal moulded into a crucifix. The dust stings, the diggers dig; it's a huge site and huge scar. Try to find a subway but the one I find is still boarded up.

Eventually find a cab and within the hour I'm in the Pierpont Morgan Library looking at a Gutenberg Bible, surrounded by a feeling of serenity, security, continuity with the past. The library is a more eloquent symbol of defiance, I think, than the metal cross. It represents everything we think is worth defending – art, culture, freedom of expression, freedom to make money and defend freedom of expression.

From Morgan to the Flatiron to see Tom [Dunne]. They watched the Towers' destruction from their windows. Tom saw people falling and says it will never leave his mind.

Lunch at nearby Bolo. Secret service activity outside this modest Catalan bistro – Laura Bush, wife of the Pres, is eating at the back with a group of African ladies. She's dressed in a suit, cut like those air-crew wear, the Africans all loose and colourful, Laura tight and boxy.

Back to the hotel. Damian Hirst in the lift. His eyes shine as he tells me that he's just about 'to make some money over here'. Which reminds me of the other thing that struck me about Ground Zero – that amidst the trauma and the wreckage, huge new developments are under construction. The Jersey shore gleams like the Promised Land of capitalism – shining new skyscrapers defiantly thrusting skywards. America is not going to let al-Qaeda get in the way of making money.

Wednesday, March 13th

In the afternoon we have to go to the funeral of Shirley Russell who died last Monday week.[1] I called Jonathan Benson [her partner] when I heard the news in NY on Friday. She had cancer which had spread, very swiftly, to her liver. J said that he was in a way relieved that there was an end to both their sufferings. 'She loved life,' he said in his curious half innocent, half loaded delivery, and rarely could such a cliché have been better applied. That's my memory of Shirley, into everything, but without any side – paintings, churches, costumes, France, railways, a wonderful melange of interests with which she was able to enthuse others and which she could share with others. With her knowledge and experience she should have been intimidating but was exactly the opposite. A sharer and a motivator.

Mortlake Crematorium is raked by a scouring east wind, cruelly cold for such a warmly remembered soul. Familiar figures greet each other as we stamp our feet and slap our sides and try to stay warm. Charles Sturridge [director and screenwriter] reads a brisk rundown of her life and achievements. He hurries it a little and at one time pays tribute to her as 'a great crook; sorry cook'.

Saturday, March 16th

Coffee and yesterday's papers to work through. My interview for the Mail on Sunday's 'Night and Day' is predictably vexatious. Not necessarily the piece but a bold subhead to the effect that 'The Death of MP's closest friend George Harrison changed his life'. Untrue, fabricated and so I shall have to write yet another protest note to the newspaper that can't stop making things up.

Notice the September 11th effect on my pension funds. Around 8 per cent of value wiped off over last year.

Saturday, March 23rd

Weather settled into soft north-east cooling breeze and sunshine to match. To Tate Britain for the 'American Sublime' exhibition. Artists dealing with huge, epic, immense landscapes; the sort of scenery that has the power to silence, which makes it difficult for painters and indeed writers to package it up within a frame or between book covers. Worth a try, though, and there are some impressive canvases. Some Turner-inspired I would think. Sky as important

1 Shirley Russell was an award-winning costume designer. She was married to the director Ken Russell, with whom she collaborated on several projects. She then lived for many years with the director Jonathan Benson.

as land; sunsets and sunrises framing tiny figures emphasising the majesty of nature. Interesting for me as I have been attempting to capture the boundless desert in words. Here at least there is an armoury of subjects – trees, various coloured rocks, water, wildlife – with which to fill the canvas.

Altogether a good experience which sharpened my appetite to travel again and made me aware of how fortunate I've been to see so many landscapes as grand and grander than these.

Monday, March 25th

New video, new commentary – this one with J-P. It looks and feels a little smoother than programme one, especially as the train leaves Dakar. It's Black Africa too – so much more open friendliness and general extrovert behaviour away from the control systems of the Islamic north.

Rachel rings, sounding full of beans, to thank me for suggesting David Pugh [theatre producer, who had put on my play 'The Weekend' in 1994] as a possible source of enlightenment on Madonna and bringing foreign stars to West End generally. She secured gems – such as Madonna's demand for a sunken bath and Patrick Swayze's Buddhist altar – missing, believed lost.

I call David and thank him. He's blithe and quite self-deprecating at the same time: 'I don't get interviewed because I'm not very good.' I say Rachel thinks he's a natural. 'Oh well, she was very sweet, but did ask me not to use the word wanker and Madonna in the same sentence.'

Wednesday, March 27th

To Tracy for 3.30 appointment. She cannot extract much pain from my left buttock, so we both agree it is healed, for now, and I can begin 'light jogging' in a few days. To celebrate my recovered mobility, and a delicately lit spring afternoon, I walk home – across Regent's Park and Primrose Hill. Feel virtuous, refreshed and have seen the camels at the zoo – now relocated to the Elephant House, as the elephants have been moved after a keeper was crushed.

About seven o'clock the phone rings. Express reporter introduces himself – heart sinks. Tells me Dudley Moore has died, heart sinks further. Must avoid the clichés, but there's not time, the phone rings again and again as the remorseless tide of media demand rolls in. Only much later do I reflect on the casualty rate of my comic heroes. The Goons and Pete and Dud all gone, and with the exception perhaps of Spike, all before their time.

Saturday, March 30th

The phone rings, H takes it and buzzes through 'You won't believe this but . . .' It's the News of the World breaking the news that the Queen Mother has died. Have I a comment? My mind bucks and rears, I feel a certain madness coming on – what if I get her muddled up with Dudley or Spike?

I offer some well-worn clichés – long life, did a lot for the country – and put the phone down, dazed more by this apparently unstoppable series of celebrity deaths than any real feelings about the Queen Mum as she was irreverently and lovingly known.

End of an era? The reporter had asked. I demurred from endorsing yet another cliché, but I can't help thinking that Rupert Murdoch, proprietor of his paper, would be delighted to have seen the end of the single most loved member of the family he has done so much to undermine.

In the evening am sucked into a long, archive-rich BBC appreciation of the QM. Some marvellous old aristos appear, including one who reckoned that Mrs Simpson was so hated by the rest of the Royal Family that they'd wanted to 'kill her'. He looked as though he would have approved.

Easter Sunday, March 31st

No Broadcasting House [BBC Radio 4 topical morning show] this morning, which I've become rather fond of, as it's Easter Day and church service time, but shave to the accompaniment of Alastair Cooke banging on about how the British education (and I think he's referring to the education of the Great and the Good, as riff-raff don't really show up on Big Al's screen) favours the literary at the expense of the scientific and what's more takes pride in the fact. Yet another reason, Cookie implies, why he thinks America a much more successful country.

H takes a call as we're about to set off for Granny G's. It's from BBC Radio 4. Barry Took has died, they want something for the One O'Clock News. H has promised I'll call them when I get to Abbotsley, which I do, but they're no longer interested as they've talked to Barry Cryer.

Oddly enough, Barry T influenced me far more than either Spike or Peter – or Dudley for that matter – and without him Python might well never have happened. He was a patron of myself and John and saw the potential of our working relationship. I've a lot to thank him for.

Back home the children have been rushing around inventing new games and no more comedians have died.

Wednesday, April 3rd

Lunch with Gilliam. He's always on best form when he isn't doing a movie, when his imagination is on the prowl and he's not confined to a single purpose – so we have an excellent ramble around old and new times.

Cleese called him the other day which, Terry thinks, is probably the first time he's done that for at least two years. It's Eric's 'Spamalot' musical idea that's exercising John now.

No movies coming TG's way at the moment, but he must have resources from somewhere as he's off to Italy at the weekend to 'fix the swimming pool'.

Bas and I walk across to Leather Lane Market and try a trendy bar called the Camberwell Room or something – full of the sort of moulded plastic tables and plastic and chrome chairs that would have filled motorway service stations in the 1960s and are now retro-chic. Quite intense discussion on the Buddha series. In an ideal world Bas suggests starting to shoot in September 2003.

Thursday, April 4th

Mad rush of a morning. Al rings in some distress as Terry has been admitted to St Thomas's after some blockage in his gut. X-rays will be taken this a.m. and only then will they know exactly what it is.

Friday, April 5th

The month has come in like a whirlwind, and I barely have time to catch breath than I'm down at BH to be interviewed for 'Brief Lives' on Radio 5 about Barry T. I'm reasonably eloquent except that I twice call him Basil.

To lunch at Moro with David L [Leland, director]. Before I left home this morning I had a chance to look at David's contribution to 'Band of Brothers'. I was very impressed – particularly by the wholly convincing French forest in winter created just off the A1 at Hatfield. Plenty of good character work and emotional punch delivered in an understated way.

Saturday, April 6th

A bracingly chilly east wind but skies clear. Down to see Terry at St Thomas's. I drive almost up to the Palace at Whitehall where the Queen Mother's body lies, then over Westminster Bridge. Beside the river a line of mourners stretches along the river path where it runs in front of St Thomas's Hospital.

Terry is in a room of his own, which, grubby windows notwithstanding, has a fine view of the Thames and the warm sunlit flanks of the Houses of Parliament. Terry is standing, draped in various intravenous devices, looking out at this prospect, and Al is sitting on the other side of the bed.

He's indignant, and if Terry's indignant, I know there's not too much to worry about. The staff here don't seem to know how to deal with Terry's need to know – about his drip-feed rate, about the process of passing urine through a tube. They don't know that when it comes to any form of equipment, Terry's natural instinct is to both understand and deeply question its capabilities at the same time.

We all appreciate the coincidence, or juxtaposition, of TJ and Queen Mum on either side of the river and I tell Terry that I came to see him only because he had the shorter queue. We talk for half an hour or so, but his eyes occasionally close and, after he's pressed a towel against him to help with the uncomfortable business of coughing, I leave him some magazines and make my way out.

Drive over Lambeth Bridge, past the queues for the lying-in-state. Good-natured, lots of families, mostly white, a decent crowd. Occasionally a television reporter rakes the line. There seems to be none of the weepy hysteria that marked the Diana reaction.

Tuesday, April 9th

Queen Mother's funeral. All very well done. The colour and dash and style of the uniforms that appear at a time like this make me wonder why this so rarely filters down into everyday life and the look of the place we live in.

Wednesday, April 10th

Mourning over. Funerals not over however. Today is Barry Took's day, and we drive up to a cemetery in Southgate. Barry and Terry Cryer, Alan Coren, Marks and Gran (protégés of Barry) and about 30 others, plus family, gather for a non-religious service. Cold east wind, a huddle of men and women in black. Faces set against too much grief, taking the tone from the family.

I deliver my thoughts standing at the top of the steps beside the coffin. Afterwards Paul Fox [ex BBC One controller], now Sir Paul Fox, came up and said that I had hit just the right tone. I'd told the story of Michael Mills [Python commissioner] giving Monty Python's Flying Circus 13 shows and Paul said he was relieved that I'd stopped there and 'not gone on to mention the man who put you on at 10.20 at night in the regional opt-out slot' who was, of course, our arch enemy at the time – Paul, now Sir Paul, Fox. So, after 33 years, a bit of truth and reconciliation! Afterwards, awkward hellos and goodbyes to the family members. We try to avoid using what Joyce Grenfell called 'Sunday voices'.

To see Terry at St Thomas's. He makes sure I have a cup of tea and shows me exceptionally lurid photos of his bowels. They lie resting on his stomach, great crimson coils spotted with the black stains of, wait for it, gangrene. In another photograph, a pair of green gloved hands holds up the intestines for the camera.

Whether they do this automatically or whether Terry had asked specially for them to be taken I don't know, but this seems to have the same quality of desperate physical honesty as his picking up of one of his turds one day – 'just to see what it was like'.

While I'm there the doctor comes by and I end up, at his request, having my photo taken with him, Terry and the photo of Terry's insides.

Saturday, April 13th: Glasgow

Collected by a unit car and taken up to the film set on which Basil is working. The movie's called 'Young Adam' – a Jeremy Thomas production of an Alexander Trocchi story. Am taken to Ewan McGregor's caravan. He's eating his lunch in a fug of heat, having spent a scary morning in the Clyde Canal doing a scene in which he rescues a nine-year-old boy. The boy was left in the water for too long, Ewan found it very difficult to get him up on to the bank and for a moment was worried for the both of them.

Leave him to lunch and meet his chirpy co-star Peter Mullan. He's a hero of mine since 'My Name Is Joe', and I'm evidently a hero of his. He's very warm and physical and stands quite close and beams at me. He's also in a state of perpetual smile.

Tilda Swinton, in fifties pinny and poor ladies' frock is all ease, confidence and politeness in a middle-class sort of way. Very friendly but none of the Python-worship bit.

Tuesday, April 16th

Our 36th anniversary, and still very happy to be together. 'I just take your money and run,' says H, evaluating our long relationship!

Wednesday, April 17th

Dry, bright weather continues, so does the nagging pressure of appointments and commitments which is beginning to weigh heavily on me as the commentary remains unfinished. Some time ago I agreed to attend one of the Commonwealth War Graves Commission lunches, and today's the day. Leave at 11.30 for their HQ in Maidenhead.

Interesting talk with Richard Kellaway, the director general. The cemeteries that are least easy to keep tidy are the ones in the UK. 'A disgrace,' he says. Somalia is one country to which they have no access, but others, like Iraq, surprisingly, allow our people in and look after the graves immaculately.

Afterwards their computers gave me a print-out of all Palins in war cemeteries. My only relative was Great-Uncle Henry William Bourne Palin. He's buried near Longueval on the Somme. He died at 32, and, coincidentally considering the Kiwis present, fought in the New Zealand Expeditionary Force. Now there's a lead to follow up. Why did he end up in NZ?

Sunday, April 21st

A good return to Sunday running – though the Heath is much busier than usual, perhaps the result of a terrific morning. No aches, pains or over-exhaustion, just a fine feeling of relaxation.

To the Phoenix Theatre for a re-opening ceremony after refurbishment. Great jostling crowd – celebs include Victoria Wood, Maureen Lipman and Tom Wilkinson, whose contribution to the raffle is the jockstrap he wore in 'The Full Monty'.

The bidding is poor – very little activity from the audience. I decide to make a run for the jockstrap and succeed in getting the bidding up to £200. Whereupon I'm left high and dry with Tom Wilkinson's jockstrap. Later I give it to the lady beside me in the row who had *so* wanted it and obviously thought 50 quid would be more than enough.

Wednesday, April 24th

Email becoming an increasing burden. As I suspected, far from making life easier, it only adds to the workload. One reply, or one appearance by me generates twenty more. People hear you're around, and are persuaded that the 'nothing ventured, nothing gained' approach should be adopted.

Exercise keeps me sane, as much by physically removing me from computer screens and telephones, as by the physical efforts I myself have to make. Escape onto the Heath at eleven and run as briskly as I can over Parliament Hill and round Kenwood.

Thursday, April 25th

To lunch at Sheekey's with David Pugh – first time we've met for years. He's in the bar, wearing T-shirt and knee-length shorts as if he's on the beach in Barbados; he greets me with a hug. He looks, reassuringly, exactly the same as he was before he became very successful. He won't drink wine as it sends him to sleep, but nurses a very cold vodka. We laugh a lot, he smokes a lot, I drink a couple of glasses of Sauvignon Blanc and over oysters and wonderfully light smoked haddock some very interesting things unfold.

I tell David that I'm off to meet Terry G and Terry J to discuss Python attitude to Eric's proposed musical 'Spamalot' which he's hoping to stage on Broadway. David would like me to come up with a way of staging 'The Life of Brian' in the West End. Whilst trying to digest this, and my oysters, a third strand is added to the saga when David tells me that MGM came to London to gauge if any impresarios/producers wanted to buy any of their film catalogue to adapt for stage. David's eye was caught by only one item, 'A Fish Called Wanda'. The success of 'The Producers' has obviously sparked a feeding frenzy between stage and film. David P's initial move on 'Brian' was, he says, inspired by Mike Nichols [American director of 'The Graduate'] who thinks that it's the one Python piece that would work best.

Taxi to Grove Park. Sit out in the garden. Terry hoists his shirt a few times to show his latest scar which looks like a piece of Aboriginal art. He's lost a stone, but looks pretty good. General feeling is that we have no objection to Eric going forward with the project, though I myself, and later John, on the phone, object to it being called Monty Python's 'Spamalot'. It's Eric Idle's 'Spamalot'. David P's proposal re 'Life of Brian' doesn't get much of a look-in. One thing at a time.

Friday, April 26th

Five o'clock at the Queen's Crescent Community Centre. I've agreed to say a few words of help and encouragement to a team which has been working for four years on a Camden scheme called Breaking the Links – a community effort using young local people to try and break the drug–crime connection. Seems worthwhile to me.

They're having a party – balloons, caps and T-shirts issued. Lots of excited children, very noisy, very hot. Earlier in the afternoon two young door-to-door salesmen from Npower came to the door and one, after taking a long, hard look at me, asked 'Aren't you Zoë Ball's dad?' I put this in my speech and it goes down very well with the children – who are for the most part, jolly, vivacious, polite and either Black or Asian.

Right July 1999. Sixty-six days of 'Hemingway' filming come to an end and at last I catch something.

l-r: Martha Wailes (producer), David Turnbull (director), MP (with fifteen pound mahi-mahi), Nigel Meakin (camera), John Pritchard (sound), Jay-Jay Odedra (assistant camera).

Below Michael Katakis: huge helper on the 'Hemingway' filming. Now a writer himself, he became a good friend. Pictured here with his bike by the Pacific.

Top The Pythons attempt silly walks in Leicester Square on their way to a 30th anniversary screening of *Life of Brian*. Eric still in America. *l-r*. JC, MP, TJ, Carol Cleveland, TG.

Above September 1999. Python 30th anniversary filming group. Eddie Izzard (centre, kneeling) made honorary Gumby for the occasion.

Left Not a hair out of place. Publicity shoot for BBC *2000 Today*. Michael Parkinson surrounded by stars at the start of a new millennium.

Above American friends. *l-r:* Simon Jones, Sherrie Levy, Tim Jones, Nola Safro (ABC news producer and Python fan), Nancy Lewis Jones (who – more than anyone – helped introduce Python to the States).

Right September 2000. Terry and myself with the climber Hamish MacInnes in Glencoe revisiting *Holy Grail* film sites.

Below Yorkshireman of the Year. A great day for a Sheffield lad.

May 2000. Falls of Dochart at Killin in the Scottish Highlands. On the phone
to Helen, whose postcard from here back in 1962 brought us together into
an eventual marriage which lasted 57 years.

July 2001. Holding the foot that hung outside my shop in the film *A Private Function*.
In the background, 'A Fish Called Wanda' painting by Lucy Willis.

Right 2001. Filming for *Sahara* at the apartment of Jonathan Dawson in Tangiers. His vicious cockerel 'Birdie' was known and feared throughout the expat community.

Below 11th September 2001. On our hotel roof in Agadez in Niger, John Pritchard desperately tries to get information on the disaster in New York.

April 2002. Malt whisky heaven; on Islay outside one of the legendary producers.

July 2002. Meeting my boyhood hero, the Australian fast bowler Keith Miller, at Lord's.

Top August 2002. Channelling Richard Branson. Train-naming ceremony at Sheffield – the heavy metal sign unceremoniously removed when Virgin later lost the franchise.

Above Looks as though we're in the Amazon together - but David Attenborough and I are in his garden, making *A Life on Air*.

Right February 2003. Presenting a 'Nibbie' to Alan Bennett at the British Book Awards.

May 2003. For my 60th birthday, my children Tom, Will and Rachel regroup
for a photo in their favourite childhood playground on Parliament Hill.

Monday, April 29th

Reading most of the Prison Reform Trust short story entries before the eyes begin to close. Generally a sad and sobering collection – all by prisoners, and half dealing with drugs. Drugs as a way of anaesthetising themselves against grim reality, and putting them at the same time even further out of reach of the rest of society. Reading them can only strengthen deepest misgivings about the criminalisation of drug use.

Tuesday, April 30th

Read the remainder of the Prison Reform Trust stories. All on the theme of failure – of people, relationships, justice, etc. A weird sense of comfort from reading them – not just from the Schadenfreude angle, but also because of the effort that must have gone into writing about their own suffering. A vindication of the act of writing and the exercise of the imagination.

Wednesday, May 1st

On the six o'clock news there are pictures of the day of protest – which we are reminded is now 'traditional' on May 1st. Generally good-natured, but scuffles breaking out in Piccadilly and round Shaftesbury Avenue. Cab driver who takes me down to Hatchards' Author of the Year party worries about the image of the country. I suggest that the sight of peaceful protests, escorted by police, does London more good round the world than bad. It is democracy in action (if you believe in democracy, that is).

The protesters (who seem to be an amorphous group, complaining about almost anything) have already won the psychological battle – with most of the smart West End and Mayfair boarded up. Galleries, car showrooms, the Ritz Hotel, all have retreated behind wooden boards, except Jack Barclay, the luxury car people, who've opted for fresh, shiny, corrugated iron. Hatchards itself is completely boarded up, except for a narrow rectangle of light beyond which the party is in progress, glasses of champagne going down like there's no tomorrow.

Meet Justin Marozzi – Libyan camel voyager – but am interrupted by someone else, who's then interrupted by someone else, so I rarely have much of a conversation. Kathy Lette is reliably lubricious, lots of patting of my stomach, feeling my bottom and clutching me – 'He's a love god.'

I talk to Ann Widdecombe. 'I'm Ann Widdecombe,' she says chirpily, a bit like Big Ben having a sign 'This is Big Ben' hanging from it. But, again, she gets lost in the crowd.

My driver home is partially deaf and can't hear anything said to him from behind, which I would have thought would have been an almost terminal problem for a cabbie. He seems determined to drive me into the one area of London where there is trouble. Shaftesbury Avenue is closed, but he doubles around Trafalgar Square and back up Shaftesbury Avenue. Police in yellow jackets at every intersection. We get through and there seems to be no sign of trouble; evidently it's cost £4 million to keep London safe. If indeed it was ever in danger.

Sunday, May 5th

Looking back at my diaries, I see this is the first birthday I've spent at home for six years.

Last few days have been uneventful, each one spent chipping away at the 'Sahara' rockface. The last commentary is the largest and in some ways the hardest – things that don't tie together have to be artificially bonded, and for some reason, it lacks grip, coherence and well, too much of too little at times and too little of too much at others.

Never really think of being 59. I can still run a few miles over the Heath (though left buttock may be showing signs of muscle strain again!) and survive. I'm happy writing, but anxious to get 'Sahara' over and begin something quite new. Strong urge to scribble some fiction. Something from my imagination not from an edited TV tape.

Monday, May 6th

Most of the day picking through the first draft of the fourth commentary – trying to match some unpromising shots to witty, perceptive insights. Too often I settle for the simple, direct approach. I have a real fear of sounding clever. Not that this is usually a problem.

Thursday, May 9th

Meet the equerry who accompanied Princess Margaret to the showing of 'The Missionary' at the Odeon Haymarket, almost 20 years ago. He confirmed that she had enjoyed the film, but, as he hints darkly, 'we both got her on a very good day'.

Monday, May 13th

Lousy forecast and it's already spitting and blowing as H and I set off on the Northern Line to Tate Modern.

We make our way to the Tate, passing the Millennium Bridge, up and running, wobble paralysed and everything looking in very good working order.

The Matisse–Picasso exhibition has been so praised in the press (Jonathan Meades, of course, being among the few dissenters) that we enter it with strong weight of expectation – as do a few hundred others. I never really like having to manoeuvre my way through crowds or rubberneck my art, but this is what you have to do. It's not hugely irksome but sometimes I become more aware of the people than the paintings. But then, I think, there's nothing wrong with that. Most of the paintings are of people and looking round at the wonderfully rich fizzogs of my fellow humans I appreciate Picasso's deconstruction of the human form particularly.

Tuesday, May 14th

Earlier than usual to VideoLondon for commentary recording. It's a very tough session, and at times I feel playing King Lear would be easier than being stuck in the box, battling with rewrites, strange 'clicks' in the voice, baffled discussion in the studio about the meaning of a link – Roger adopts quite a severe persona on these occasions.

Finally home about 6.30. I flop down in my chair and am subsumed with a delicious feeling of contentment and relief. As if similar moments like these over the last 15 months (end of difficult shoots, completion of book, completed commentary recordings) have all accrued enough good energy which has waited until now to spill over. It really is just about done – it is what it is, the time for tampering and adjusting and negotiating about content is over. It's a wonderful feeling, a surge of relief that transports me, briefly, I'm sure, onto a cloud which reminds me more than anything of having finished Schools at Oxford.

Tom cooks a great stir-fry, studded with rather good vegetarian sausage – but then everything's wonderful tonight!

Thursday, May 16th

A two-day heatwave forecast. Certainly steaming up when I set aside the text and go for a run.

To River Café at invitation of Jonathan Clyde [record producer and friend of George]. He's 20 minutes late and I sit quietly at the bar with a glass of water only to be nobbled by some diner, a young man who happens to be an Arctic explorer. Some friends of his are out there on the ice, would I be prepared to talk to them on a radio telephone. It would mean so much. Much more, clearly, than my privacy, but I realise I've not much right to that – what with being on television and that – so I try to be evasively pleasant.

We sit in the garden and the service is rather slow and the sun hits me full face as it moves round out of the shade of a tall fir tree. But JC good company – Olivia is coming back soon to Friar Park. George has left instructions for a new album to be completed.

Sunday, May 19th

Read a piece by Malcolm McLaren in the Observer saying that we should be celebrating 25 years since Punk, as much more relevant than 50 years of Eliz II. I quite warm to McLaren. I identify with people like him and Derek Jarman, because of their freshness, cheekiness, audacity, mischief – all elements of my own life which, CBE or no CBE, I can't, and don't want to get away from. I believe in order, public duty and all those things, but I have a sharp and intense distaste for deference.

Thursday, May 23rd

My core study days complete, real life rolls in. David Pugh and Dafydd [Rogers, also a West End producer] here at half past ten. Talk over their ideas about 'Life of Brian' and I promise to discuss it with the others. David is of the opinion that it is such a strong story it needn't be a musical. He has some nicely silly ideas like involving the audience in the stoning sequence by issuing them with polystyrene missiles as they come in, and parking a camel outside the theatre every night.

Call TJ. He doesn't see any point in doing 'Brian' on stage without new music, though I can't think why. It's perfectly strong – we could put in the shepherds, etc.

Tuesday, May 28th

Downing Street for a Stammerers Evening Fundraiser. Cherie Blair's impressive – makes it sound genuine and natural, minimum of politician's oratorical tricks, and as it's our tenth anniversary at the Centre, everyone, including me, rather proud.

To the Travellers Club for a reception to mark publication of a new book by Peter Matthiessen, whom I've never met, but whose account of descending the Pongo de Mainique gave me sleepless nights in Peru six years ago. Matthiessen is every inch the weathered American traveller. A big, slightly lugubrious, heavily grooved face, strong and sensitive. We chat. He's now very much involved in work in Antarctica. Americans who do travel take their travel very seriously, and for me, it's only rarely I can say that I've just hurried away from 10 Downing Street.

Friday, June 21st

The longest day. Out of bed at 7.15 to prepare for the England–Brazil quarter final. The first England game in this World Cup which I shall have seen right through.

Starts superbly with a perfect opportunist Owen goal which gives me the chance to vent my joy with such leaps and shouts that H hurries into my study, naked from the shower to see what's happened. Then a deep, familiar, ominous draining of the emotions takes me to the other extreme, like a tide running out – and with the same inevitability. We give away an early second-half goal and after that are tired, formless and unthreatening – even worse when Brazil are down to ten men. By half past nine the last rites have been given to England's most promising World Cup in years. Seaman looks like some wretched, haunted penitent as he's consoled in the centre circle.

Bas has organised an evening out to Royal China, Queensway. The Terrys have been rounded up. Terry J jokes that we should 'do all our talking before Gilliam arrives'. Quite astute. TG, last to join us, barely pauses for breath as he takes on the world, history and religion. Terry J announces that he is doing a show on sex for Discovery. 'Every religion is, when it starts, based on a celebration of sex,' says TJ, with the look of one who knows.

Wednesday, July 10th

To work on completing the Shrewsbury Speech.

Arrive about 7.15 at the new Haberdashers' Hall in Smithfield. First penguin-suited figure I see climbing out of a cab is Michael Charlesworth – my form master in the year I met Helen. He has a stick but his face, features, hair colour and general appearance belie his 83 years. He looks as I remember him, and as I had a special fondness for him as a teacher, it's a good start to the evening.

Try not to drink too much. Learn that Shrewsbury, along with Eton, Harrow and a mere handful of others, has resisted admitting girls. Michael's view is that they don't need them. Rolls and admissions are high. It's all working well, why fix it. He becomes quite animated about it which is revealing in such a cool customer.

I enjoy delivering the speech. I felt that I created a shape, talking about my own children and why they didn't go, and contrasting the old-fashioned values of the public school with Shrewsbury's tradition of liberal, sceptical free-speech mavericks, as instanced by 'Private Eye', Richard Hillary, Darwin, etc., with the more conventional values of the public school – finishing with my thoughts on what Shrewsbury could provide in an area which I feel most strongly about – our relations with the rest of the world. A call for Salopians to become the new ambassadors for a more compassionate Britain. Anyway, it seemed to go down a treat and afterwards Mike Popham [old Salopian and BBC World Service producer] grasped my hand and whispered 'You stuck to your guns, excellent.'

Friday, July 12th

By Tube to Leicester Square to meet John Lloyd [producer of 'Not the Nine O'Clock News' and 'Blackadder', among others] for lunch. He looks more gaunt than I remember him – receding hair cropped short and there's precious little extra flesh around his skull. He has the same dazzling smile but it's less relaxed, more fleeting. He gives off an air of wariness. He looks, I have to say, less like the big, confident blond and more like a medieval penitent. We sit in the window watching life on Dean Street.

He has something he wants me to do, but as it seems to boil down to being a TV quizmaster, I politely but firmly decline. John is a skilful operator, good talker and probably saw my refusal as a challenge.

With money from Pearson, John has set up a company called QI – Quite Interesting (a clever reverse of IQ, he tells me in case I didn't get it), which will dispense, market and popularise interesting information about life, things, philosophy, etc., etc., in contrast to the dull clichéd info we are fed every day. And that's about it. I know I'm uncomfortable with abstract concepts, but I can't understand why what seems like an extension of his clever word games with the late Douglas Adams can be seen with the zeal of one proposing a new way of thinking.

We leave without my being asked again to be a TV quiz game host and his big blue eyes seem to fill with a certain sadness. Still, he's persuaded Marjorie Scardino ('Marge') at Pearson to go along with it and he is toweringly clever and well-read, so maybe he was looking at me thinking 'poor sod, he's missed the break of a lifetime'.

Sunday, July 14th

Drive over to West London for an evening with JC at Cibo. I find to my great relief, fellow humourists David Hatch – now Chairman of the Parole Board – and Hugh Laurie. There's a round table on the pavement so we sit ourselves around it and a very jolly evening of much laughter ensues.

Hugh has obviously been talking to John Lloyd, for he comes up with the information that 'camels have three vaginas'. 'Not *camels,* kangaroos,' corrects Jo [Green, Hugh's wife]. I'm able to add what detail I can remember from my lunch with JL. Two horizontal and one vertical. 'No,' Hugh's brow furrows, 'two vertical, I think.' It's that sort of evening.

Monday, July 15th: London–Buxton

At the Palace Hotel in Buxton by seven. Change my shirt in a side road outside the town and am ready for the opera, 'La Périchole' by Offenbach, which I'm to be taken to see. It is good fun. Foot-tapping music and libretto in English; lots of current jokes and some awful gags – some Marx brothers – even one pinch from 'Fish Called Wanda' when the hero sniffs at his armpits. Morris dancers outside in the interval.

I'm driven back to where I shall stay tonight – Roy [Hattersley] and Maggie's house in Great Longstone. The literary events are his contribution to the Festival, and he admits, quite candidly, to the fact that they are the real money-spinners, 'because we pay people like you so little'. Well, nothing, actually. However, Gore Vidal, who was here two days ago, did invoice them for two nights in a suite at the Connaught. He was very good and popular, says Roy, but reckons Vidal has to 'have someone he can pick on; then he's happy'.

I'm privileged to have been invited to stay with Roy. He won't have any smokers, so Beryl Bainbridge can never be invited.

Tuesday, July 16th: Buxton–London

Down for breakfast at a quarter to nine. Am struck by how clean and tidy the house is – no plastic bags lurking, unpacked, as at Julia Street, no silly or frivolous ornament, or boxes of old biros. Roy is in shirt, tie and jacket and slacks, and about to go off for a physiotherapy appointment where, he admits, 'I'll just have to take all my clothes off again.' He's amusing is Roy. He can tell a joke well and can be appealingly self-deprecating, whilst at the same time maintaining that solipsistic confidence of the politician.

His latest pride and joy is a newly laid and levelled croquet lawn. I think he fancies the country squire's life. When they arrived here seven years ago the gardener politely warned him 'We're all Tory here, including me.'

Thursday, July 18th

Latest news of 'Hem's Chair' TV adaptation. It's gone to Nick Elliott who's read it and apparently rejected it on the grounds that the ITV audience won't know who Hemingway is!

Olivia H calls. She's been back at Friar Park three weeks, sounds strong. She asks if I'll say something at the lunchtime gathering for George next Wednesday.

Wednesday, July 24th

George's memorial service/ceremony is at one o'clock and despite clogged traffic in Baker Street, we're out on the M4 with time to spare. Then for some inexplicable reason we miss the Henley turning. Well, explicable in a way – I'm still looking for the numbers A423, which have been changed to A404, and the name Henley which doesn't appear on the sign. Mild, followed by concentrated, panic sets in. By now it's almost 1.30. I have this dreadful stomach-plunging feeling that we shall never get there, that we shall be trapped on the M4 for the rest of the day. Pray that Junction 8/9 is familiar. It is. We're on the right road at last. The road to Henley cannot be hurried and by the time we roll through the gates it's ten to two.

Shown across the lawn to the sunken garden where a quiet, dignified gathering are sat in neat rows beneath a cotton covering. Dhani is at the front speaking. Then Ringo is called upon. He's in full flow when I'm led up to the front to wait my turn to speak, and as I pass at a low, hopefully discreet crouch in front of him he interrupts his speech briefly to welcome me. 'Late again, Eric.' Excellent icebreaker.

Ringo is dry and funny – calls George the most social recluse he ever knew, voice cracks as he describes his own son's diagnosis with a brain tumour, but he ends on the right combination of affection and honesty. 'At least we won't have to listen to that bloody ukulele again.'

Then the soothing tones of the American who is conducting the ceremony, in a brown robe over smart trousers and Church's leather shoes, prepares the way for me to speak. So frazzled have I been in the last 45 minutes that I've been unable to think of rehearsing my remarks, so I have to rely on an indulgent audience and a wonderful subject. It goes fine and I get through all I wanted to say and end up reading the 'Four Yorkshiremen' spoof postcard which George sent us from the Lake Palace Hotel in Udaipur.

Some prayers. Very beautiful Vedic chanting by two monks. Can't help but be admiring of George's long commitment to Indian spirituality. No passing phase for him. Boxes of tissues are handed around to those who are moved to tears.

It's a dry, warm day, cloudy but soft and gentle light. Around us the fruits of George's devotion to his garden. Dhani puts on a cassette of some of George's very last work. 'To listen to as you leave,' he says. But no one moves. We sit, all thinking our own thoughts and let the music drift through us, as if sharing George, all together at the same time, is what we really want and need.

Friday, July 26th

With many misgivings I pack my bag with 'Sahara' clothes and props and leave in a BBC car to be photographed for the Radio Times cover.

A warm day that could end up hot. To studios beside the Westway and another effective Sahara back-cloth, as well as a rather threadbare camel, called Sarah (doesn't seem a suitable name for a camel) provided by two of the team who did 'Fierce Creatures'. Terry the Tarantula [the spider that was my co-star in the film] is alive, well and working, they tell me.

Make-up lady, who has been in business, she says, since 1971, makes polite conversation. 'So, I hear you were once with the Monty Python team.' This is followed up after a bit of a pause with the classic 'Tell me again, who were the others in the Python team?' 'Well, John Cleese was the best known.' She nods emphatically but I have the impression that I might as well be talking Mandarin Chinese. 'And Eric . . .' She brightens here. 'Eric Secombe?'

The camel seems thankfully a lot more on the ball. Her head comes as close to mine as they can make it. Occasionally Sarah burps and it's as if the gas from decayed remains of everything she's ever eaten is funnelled out.

By midday the photographer is satisfied. Sarah is given another carrot and I'm driven to Radical Media in Wardour Street to be interviewed for the DVD of 'Time Bandits'. Two old farts on the sofa reminiscing. Not for the first time I'm impressed by Terry's memory and his extraordinary energy.

Saturday, July 27th

To Lord's where, for second year running, Roger and myself are guests of Sir Paul Getty. This year it's for day three of the First Test Match against India.

High cloud, but enough to keep the sun at bay. The ball is swinging and India, up against an England 'reserve' attack, don't have much luck. Tendulkar is out for 16 and by lunchtime England's first innings of 478 looks unassailable.

Keith Miller and Marie arrive after lunch. Keith bubbling, very pleased to see me, so much to talk about that he spills white wine on his suit. His face reminds me of Spike's at the end of his life. Like that of an ageing saint. His eyes, wide and bright but unable to co-ordinate with the rest of his ailing body, look out with fierce intensity, as if imploring the rest of him to come to his rescue.

The Indians are trying desperately hard to stay in. 'Did you ever stonewall, Keith?' I ask him. He twinkles at the thought and leans his cadaverous face towards me: 'Only when I was pissed.' He also revealed that whenever possible he signed his autograph across Don Bradman's photo, because he knew it would irritate him. Hopefully, if I go to Oz in January, we will meet up in Melbourne.

Peter O'Toole, another great friend and fan of Keith Miller's, comes to pay homage and raise a glass. His face is pale, his skin light and delicate, but he looks a boy beside Keith. He tells of Noël Coward's remark to him after seeing 'Lawrence of Arabia' – 'Peter you looked so lovely. It should have been called Florence of Arabia.'

Throughout it all Sir Paul G, with physio and nurse in attendance, presides impassively. Wheelchair-bound, grey-skinned, but, like Keith, once you're close in, he's lots to say. Invites me to come and see his library for which he's just bought another 1603 Shakespeare Folio edition. I think he is quite fond of me, but as he can't move, other than to shake hands, his friendship has to be conveyed by discreet signs.

The weather is good, the Test is going England's way. We're attended to constantly with offers of tea and coffee, wine, beer or champagne, Pimm's, canapés and so on. 'A day in heaven' as Roger sums it up.

Monday, July 29th

Down to Richmond [to film 'Life on Air' documentary about, and with, David Attenborough]. Attractive house with its Strawberry Hill Gothic window and door frames. David A looking ageless in check shirt and chinos. He's barefoot. We're soon bantering about books – David has two out this autumn – 'Life on Air' and the 'Life of Mammals' – and is quite distracted by the amount of work still to do. He shakes his head as he describes the BBC marketing meetings. 'All they do is nod to each other and say "This'll be big" and after a bit of a pause . . . "Very big".'

Filming gets underway with David producing a couple of his artefacts (which adorn every shelf and surface of the house) and challenging me on camera to guess what they are. I do pretty well with the obsidian mirror (Mexican/Peruvian 2,000 years BC) and the dinosaur egg and he awards me nine out of ten for both. David is a compulsive collector, not just of tribal objects, but ceramics (Lucie Rie) and antiquarian books. I can't help but notice rows of Victorian and Edwardian travel books – about a dozen on Papua alone, all in excellent, mint condition. 'I have to have them,' he says simply. 'Don't you?'

After lunch we begin work on the interview. It's dreadfully hot and stuffy up in David's study with its dinosaur footprints and clusters of crystals from the Antarctic and Dogon masks and the great curved control-centre desk.

David is articulate, if a little routine in his answers to start with, but once we've got the measure of each other – and he realises I'm not just asking for funny stories – he, and I, relax and the last two rolls are considered to be the best.

We have quite a lot in common apart from our presenting styles – travel, learning as we go, exotic places, marriages that began in our early 20s, same house for 30 years or more. Love of books, especially reference books, and awkwardness with the internet.

David likes to tell stories – which he does very well. As a Beeb executive he attached much importance to how someone could tell a story, and narrative and storytelling is very important in his programmes. He, like me, wants the subject of the programmes to be given top billing, not the presenter. And I notice he's a Guardian reader.

Tuesday, July 30th

Second day's filming. David has a little of the faux-naif about him. 'I just do my job because I enjoy it' sort of thing, but I know he's sharp as a tack and picks up all hints and glances. He's proud of his talents and skills, though never to your face – but I notice it in the flickers of irritation when he's asked to repeat something, or even when he's asked to go again because he's unwittingly banged the microphone on his shirt.

I learn today of his antipathy to commercials, the fact that he travels on the Underground quite happily and that his next project is 'Life in the Undergrowth'. He describes this with delightful enthusiasm, at the same time grumbling 'I shouldn't have done two books at the same time, it's ridiculous.'

A photographer arrives from the BBC and I, who am as alert to nuances as David, have the feeling that this has a touch of Radio Times cover about it. David becomes a little prickly and impatient. 'This is the bit I really hate,' he confides. 'Being photographed', and adds a quick sketch of an over-demanding snapper, 'Left leg a little further right, right leg a little further left. Smile.'

Wednesday, July 31st

Collected 10.15 and taken to Twickenham Studios, approach along the staid suburban avenues and in the back entrance. 'Park in Lord Attenborough's spot' the gateman assures Mike. I'm dropped off and up into the cutting room where we are to shoot a sequence of David and myself looking at rare footage of his work on a Steenbeck (now so rare they have to be hired in).

'I see you've been upgraded to Lord today, David.' David shrugs. 'I've no idea what he's doing here,' he replies when I ask him if Dickie's making a film. He rather likes, or certainly affects to like this bewilderment about his estimable brother's activities.

Three sequences are cued up for us to watch and comment on. In between takes we talk about writing. David is a little frustrated with, as he calls it, 'the way it comes out'. He has plenty of stories and much to describe but it all comes down to 'he said, he replied, said he, replied so-and-so'. He mistrusts literary style but I think wishes he had it. 'Now commentary,' he says, 'that's a different thing. That does interest me, and I find writing it much more satisfying.'

Then onto another piece of film. A South Sea island. David criticises the length of his hair, but has no comment to make on the vaguely homoerotic sequence as he's led out of a hut having had to shed his Western clothes and wear only a thong-like leaf affair. From behind his near-naked white body, jostled by black South Sea Island bodies, feels more like a scene out of Pasolini.

Friday, August 2nd

Around one o'clock we walk home, cutting across the edge of the Heath, and I find a fax waiting for me from Paul Thomas Anderson.[1] 'This is Mr Anderson writing from Tarzana, California. I have a huge crush on you and would like to go eat when I'm in London . . . I would also like to enquire about your status as a working actor in the movies. I don't eat meat, but I do like vegetables. With tons of affection – Paul Thomas Anderson.' Well . . .

Friday, August 9th

To Moro for lunch with Paul Thomas Anderson. I'm there first, at the window table, my head deep in Boyle's 'A Friend of the Earth' when I look up to see a slight, slim, bearded but boyish figure looking down at me. He holds out both his hands and clasps mine. I make sure I get my praise in before his. He accepts my bouquets with quiet good grace and we find we have much in common. Like working with small crews, valuing actors, and wanting to do something fresh and different if possible.

---

1 Paul Thomas Anderson is the American director of *Boogie Nights*, *Magnolia*, *Punch-Drunk Love*, *There Will Be Blood* and many more very distinctive films.

He says that I could probably talk to any actor he's worked with apart from Burt Reynolds (who was apparently an old-fashioned hammy nightmare on 'Boogie Nights') and they would all still be his friends. He says he's been thinking about me for two years. The focus of his enthusiasm is my travel programmes. 'They're inspirational . . . inspirational.'

We do get on very well. In response to his enquiring about whether I want to act again I tell him that I'm not interested in cameo, but in being deeply involved – at the heart of a picture, like I'm at the heart of the travel programmes. He nods, smiles, almost shyly. 'That's OK. That's OK.' We finish a bottle of Galician white and take another glass.

I feel a bit like a Dirk Bogarde figure being wooed to make a return to the screen, but this doesn't really do justice to his gentle, humorous ease and calm. I have to keep reminding myself what he's done, but there is precious little glimpse today of the steel that must lurk beneath.

I want to go out and do something without a safety net, he says. That's what interests me. And in a sense I do too. That's what I respond to in him. I've a hint that this could be one of those meetings that turn me in quite a significant direction.

Sunday, August 11th

Another flat, mild, damp morning. Onto the Heath, then back to dally with the wording of an invitation to the 60th birthday gathering that I'm planning for H. I rather like 'The Helen Palin Preservation Society invites you to celebrate 60 years of their work'.

Friday, August 16th

Collect Billy's [Connolly] present. It's by Sarah Hill – a wonderful figure of a fantasy devil, colourful and rather rude, and so like Billy – I was so happy to have found it last Monday.

Saturday, August 17th: London–Candacraig

Our preparations and departure for the Connolly weekend reach smooth climax as we leave Julia Street, with the long, carefully packed box with Sarah Hill's figure in it, sheathed in protective John Lewis bags.

At Aberdeen we're met by middle-aged men in full Scottish outfits. Taciturn but agreeably unflustered, they escort H and me and Chrissie Hynde to a waiting helicopter. By mistake the pilot whisks us, not to our hotel, but to Candacraig, the Connolly home and castle. We're then flown back over the moors with lines of deer streaking away below us like rain hitting the windscreen.

Thirty-five minutes is all we have at the hotel to unpack and for me to be dressed in my muted Macdonald tartan. This is done by two lovely ladies who have been fitting almost solidly for two days and are near exhaustion point.

I've decided not to wear anything under the kilt. It's not often that you're not only allowed but encouraged to walk around with no knickers on, so I'll take advantage. The kilt is heavy, straight and voluminous, unlike my wedding tackle, so it's all quite safe.

An electrifying moment as Chrissie H, Helen and myself are told that there will be one other in our helicopter on to C'craig. Brian Wilson. 'Brian Wilson!' – even Chrissie's excited. It turns out to be Brian Wilson, the local MP. We find ourselves turning over the turreted roofs of Candacraig and then out and up through some woods and a lawn to a courtyard on which guests are sipping champagne as a somewhat intimidating double line of pipers and drummers flanks the way to the door.

In the library Prince Charles, rubicund as a weathered stick, is the first person I'm introduced to. He's friendly and charming, smiles his odd smile – he's one of the few people I've met whose mouth turns down as he smiles. 'It's awfully decent of you to wear all this,' he says, eyeing my togs. We're about to have a decent conversation when someone else is pushed into the library and H and I are moved inexorably towards the centre of a very warm room.

That's when I notice Eric, and we embrace – the first time for what, two years, that we've been in each other's presence. Eric is talking to Prince Andrew. He's equally amiable and straightaway interested in the fact that I might not be wearing anything under the kilt. He stoops and bends toward me and for one moment I think he might be about to flick aside the muted Macdonald and have a look, but he points to my toecaps. 'Not polished enough, that's how you have a look,' he says.

Eventually we're all allowed to move out of this hot little room to meet other mortals – and the range on offer is wonderful. I find myself hugging dear Anna (Friel) for the first time since she played my daughter in GBH, almost ten years ago. Then Steve Buscemi, my favourite American contemp actor – well, up there with the top half-dozen – is introduced.

Billy speaks later and is quite muted – as if not wanting to hog the limelight (and he makes clear his birthday is not until November, which checks the mood a touch). Everything carefully thought-out from the replica Finnieston cranes at the centre of each table to the stick-on black Billy beards which fall out of the crackers. There's dancing, to the Tartan Amoebas, and I get very hot at the Gay Gordons and the Dashing White Sergeant. Steve Buscemi joins us for Strip the Willow.

We're finally driven back to the hotel, exhausted, at two o'clock. Through dark, unlit strips of forest, slowly in case deer leap out and smash the car (as they often do). Can't do much but sit and stare at each other and contemplate the emotional roller-coaster of the last 14 hours.

And no knickers to take off before bed.

Sunday, August 18th

A coach leaves for Candacraig at half past twelve. Light drizzle. Umbrellas with Billy's face on them and the legend 'Sexageniality' are issued. No newspapers are allowed at Candacraig. Someone staying here went out to buy some and they were politely confiscated. Pam keeps them away. 'It's Brigadoon here,' as someone put it.

As if dampened by the drizzle the day drifts on and we drift amongst this rich and diverse gathering of the clans. Helen learns from Jackie Stewart, one of the world's great racing drivers, that he's dyslexic and can't always tell left from right.

[Television playwright] Peter McDougall, straw hat matching his droopy yellow moustache, swaps stories of Glaswegian street life with Billy on the veranda of the food tent, and gradually sucks in an audience of 40 or 50, as all conversations nearby fall silent, unable to compete with the gales of laughter. Most stories seem to involve vomiting and general lack of continence.

Best thing of all is making silly jokes with Eric as the rain spatters down, as if no time had passed since the days of 'Do Not Adjust'.

Smelling of wood-smoke and venison sausages we're all summoned to the climax of the celebrations, as a band of pipers, illuminated by torch-bearing Highlanders, lead us, Pied Piper-like, up the hill to be treated to a marvellously timed, brilliantly orchestrated fireworks display, accompanied by a loud and joyful mix of the Archers theme. A tour de force, defying the rain and giving everyone the chance to roar with approval as the words 'Happy Birthday, Billy' blaze and burn out.

Tuesday, August 27th

My BUPA medical exam – the first test of the system for over two years. I know the pattern of these examinations now; the only difference today being much more explanation and info from my medical 'adviser', a young lad called Ben who looks disconcertingly like Gary Lineker, and a lean young Australian doctor.

Though initially I worry that he's far too young and attractive to be sticking his finger up my bottom and grasping my prostate ('If you put your finger in it, you won't put your foot in it, we were taught'), he explains all sorts of things from prostate function to bowel habits and seems quite sad there isn't more I want his advice on.

Down to Tate Modern, to meet Robert Upstone, curator of Modern British Paintings, who is to take me to the Tate Store to look at their hidden collection of Camden Town Group artists.

It's a long single-storey modern warehouse in Mandela Way beside the Old Kent Road flyover. Impressive in its scale. A series of huge sliding doors open onto floors the size of football pitches. Along each side are narrow panels which slide out to reveal dozens of paintings hung on both sides of a mesh frame. It's the contrast between the clinical and the decorative that makes the process of looking at paintings here so bracingly unusual. It's almost as if we're visiting paintings in prison.

Only 25 per cent of the Tate's collection is on display to the public at any one time. Some are best kept out of sight, but lots of others are remarkably good – there's a Drummond portrait of a lady in a hat, looking boldly and unblinkingly at the viewer – which it's a privilege to see, and any number of Sickerts and Gilmans and Ginners and Bevans. It's a friendly place, and has that inside-the-business feeling; like being at the back of the shop, sharing the secrets.

Wednesday, August 28th

To St Pancras to catch the 9.25 for Sheffield where I am to unveil a Super Voyager [train] called 'Michael Palin'. The Midland Mainline train is shabby and badly in need of sprucing up but I'm the only one in the breakfast car and am served an excellent spread of potatoes, black pud, bacon, eggs, fried bread – breaking almost every dietary rule so thoroughly dinned into me at my BUPA medical yesterday.

The lineside is quite depressing – almost every bridge graffitied. I try to think less aggressively about graffiti – isn't it just a fairly harmless fact of life? – but it doesn't convince. To me it's still generally a mess, the work of very few imposed on the rest of us whether we like it or not.

The sight of Sheffield Midland Station is heartbreaking. A half-modernised system of glass and steel walkways and partitions unsatisfactorily grafted onto the old, decorated canopies. Nothing attractive to relieve the gloom. I'm introduced to the station manager – a blonde who looks to be in her early 30s – and am tempted to express my disappointment, but, to quote the King of Swamp Castle, 'this is a happy time'.

The gleaming new Virgin Super Voyager has drawn up at Platform One and a dais, red carpet and mike installed. Haven't prepared anything but manage a fluent two or three minutes then draw back the red curtain and there is Michael Palin, a good, solid plate; not bronze sadly, but some chunky-looking alloy.

Lots of interviews – how does it feel? Well . . . it's like something out of a movie. Local ex-trainspotter returns to the same station which he roamed, solitary and unnoticed, 47 years ago.

Sunday, September 1st

Soon after eight, set off for Parliament Hill and Kenwood. Perhaps it's because this is the first September since the Trade Center attacks, perhaps it's press headlines about a gun being found at Heathrow in the baggage of a young Muslim who had taken a course of flying lessons in America, but the clear blue sky seems ominous. It reminds me of the backdrop to the events of that morning in America – the cloudless, remorseless, precise clarity of the light which made the attackers' purpose and execution so brutally, clinically observable. And a morning like this should raise the spirits.

Tuesday, September 3rd

To the office to be interviewed for the Telegraph. Cassandra Jardine is my imposing interviewer. She occasionally affects naïve surprise at something I say, but I feel she's pretty shrewd. She's also candid in that slightly lofty upper-class way. 'I *loved* your book . . . no, I did really . . . and I didn't expect to.' 'Out of every ten people I speak to about you, nine will say you're the most admirable person they know, and one will see you as, well, rather smug.'

I notice, rather smugly, that she has a copy of 'Hemingway's Chair' in her bag, with a bookmark in the last few pages. 'And I'm really enjoying your novel. Are you going to do another . . . I mean you'll *have* to.'

Cassandra, not the best name for someone one hopes will carry forth the good news of Michael Palin and the Sahara, draws me into talking for 75 minutes; then a 30-minute photo session with an Australian lady who keeps muttering, encouragingly, that she just can't seem to get it right.

Wednesday, September 4th

Work on Sellers review. I've already spent two and a half days on close examination of the book and barely begun. I'm painfully aware that the New York

Times turned down my last contribution – on George's garden, and what with distant echoes of Nora Ephron's dumping my perf in 'You've Got Cut', I've lost some of my confidence in being able to gauge what New Yorkers want from me.

To the tiny Jermyn Street Theatre (all run by volunteers) where Annabel and John Watts are performing Sheridan Morley's theatrical biog 'Noël and Gertie'. Once again, I'm made aware how clever Coward's writing is, the way it seems so light and easy and yet underneath is dealing with every kind of emotion and situation. His duologues are masterly whilst seeming effortless. In fact, quite the opposite of my New York Times review!

Tuesday, September 17th

To Millbank for a breakfast view of the Lucian Freud exhibition. Bill Feaver, the curator, a wonderfully loose, bendy figure with a good suit hanging on a thin frame and a tie-less shirt, speaks with some amusement about his pal Lucian.

I'm not entirely sure what to make of Freud's attitude to his sitters – well, liers and sprawlers. They all seem to be reflections of himself – he takes away their right to give anything away. I feel his controlling, vaguely malign influence reducing my pleasure at his technical skills. His mother, suffering from depressive illness, is thoughtfully treated, otherwise it just seems he uses individuals as mounds of flesh or great gawping fannies. I feel inadequate because they make me feel uncomfortable.

Freud paints his figures and indeed himself, lumps, bumps and all against distressed walls and bare floors, but when I talk to Bill Feaver he smiles tolerantly. 'Oh he's not monastic,' he laughs. He lives in Notting Hill, loves his celebrity and likes to eat well and go to parties. I ask how he chooses who he paints – is there a way of auditioning for a part in a Freud painting? 'Well, if you're a woman, just go to a party he's at and stand on the other side of the room.'

Friday, September 20th

To the office at ten, having read and been irritated by the Cassandra Jardine interview in the Telegraph. Beneath an in-bold subhead: 'I'm not smug . . . I'm just nice' – quite blatantly made up – is a long, slightly sniffy, patronising piece which I can't think will do either myself, or the Telegraph who will be serialising the book from tomorrow, much good at all.

An urgent phone call put through from Terry Jones. Would I ring Alan Bennett and try and persuade him to reconsider his decision not to take part in the Peter Cook Foundation evening next weekend?

Ring Alan. When I ask him how he is, he laughs. 'Still here . . . and what more can you ask?' He's quite adamant in not wanting to do it. 'I couldn't honestly face it . . . I'd be such a bag of nerves.' He asks me to drop round for tea and, as ever, we part in general agreement about life.

Sunday, September 22nd

Alan and Julie Bleasdale come for supper. Alan goes outside to smoke every now and then. He's completed a film version of 'The English Passenger' for Nik Powell ('he's a Cockney scallywag') but is gloomy about its prospects of getting made. The collapse of 'Running Scared' (which he says he saw as the 2002 successor to 1990's 'GBH' and 1982's 'Boys from the Blackstuff') and his Henry VIII adaptation have knocked the spirit out of him and he looks more nervous and ill-at-ease than I remember. He always was such a supremely confident misfit. His ailments, once so proudly carried, now seem to genuinely dog him – latest is psoriasis of the ear.

But when I show them both the clapperboard mix of 'Sahara', they watch it – Alan especially – with a wonderful childlike enthusiasm. Direct, uninhibited delight. He is a remarkable man, and still one of our sagest and most original playwrights. Why he isn't working is a mystery. Is it just ageism?

Tuesday, September 24th

As some key moments of self-exposure loom, I find myself preoccupied by unanswerable anxieties – about what I have to say, about the long publicity period in which I have to keep giving an account of myself. Of being the observer observed. As I roll out of bed at a quarter to eight, to be irritated by 'Thought for the Day's' nerveless good intention, I feel deeply tired and the day hasn't begun.

Deborah Ross from the Independent arrives, with a photographer. Whereas Cassandra Jardine plonked herself down in the office and regarded me like a specimen in a lab, Deborah moves in as if we've known each other for ever. She's small, a little older perhaps than I'd imagined, quite direct, but not in any way aggressive, despite a habit of firing out questions like – Which author would you like to have been? Whose books do you look forward to buying? Halfway between providing coffee, parking permits for their two cars, trying not to notice the photographer manoeuvring me into a better light, I find such simple questions completely floor me.

At a reception at the Earth Gallery of the Science Museum I find myself in the good company of Alan Parker and Jack Gold. Jack and I reminisce about

'The Late Show' – and the trouble he got into using Holman Hunt's 'Light of the World' as an advert for paraffin (a Barry Humphries sketch I think).

Thursday, September 26th

Parky day. It's been on my mind for a while. Start of the campaign on TV and radio. Haven't done much of this exposure for some time and Parky still considered the most influential of TV plugs – sorry, interviews.

My dressing room is full of gifts – a goody bag, videos of Michael Parkinson's greatest interviews (none of mine included) – fruit, flowers, sandwiches. But no cool white wine, which is what I could really have done with.

Kate Adie arrives about the same time and I meet third guest – Ricky Gervais – as I'm being shown the studio set-up. He says he's very nervous and has been humming the theme tune for about a week. I tell him that a performance on a show like this can make or break a career. He enjoys hearing that, I think. A good, apparently uncomplicated, clever man.

Mike steers me on to the more serious areas – starvation in the desert, stammering, H's tumour. I feel quite happy dealing with all this and he pats my hand appreciatively as the interview ends and the lights go down on us and up on Ravi Shankar's daughter at the piano.

Friday, September 27th

With Tom and Rachel to Gospel Oak Primary 50th anniversary party. It's an odd feeling to be taking my two children to school again. One of them 33 and the other 27 – walking down the road together.

Alastair Campbell, now lean and mean, clutching a loveless plate of banana and salad, glances over at me. He's wearing a weird puce-green shirt. He says that the gates of the school (recent, florid and one of the few new and visually interesting touches to appear or survive, in this stretch of Gospel Oak) were paid for by his winnings from a libel action against the Daily Mail. He promptly gets into some verbal tussle with his companion about how many libel cases he's won and how many he's lost. He really can't resist a scrap.

Sunday, September 29th

To the Prince of Wales Theatre for a Peter Cook Tribute Show – wittily billed as a Post Humorous Tribute.

Terry J, who's directing, and Peter Luff, who's producing, are having a series of running spats with the BBC television production team – which has enveloped the place in cables and added lights and generally made life the way they want it, whilst almost totally ignoring the fact that there is an audience in who have paid upwards of £50 each for tickets.

David Frost – sorry *Sir* David Frost – arrives, fresh from interviewing the prime minister on his Breakfast prog (will Blair change his mind about going to war? No, he's made his mind up). Frost then takes over the role of narrator (reading old jokes off auto-cue) and executive producer. He establishes himself firmly at the centre of the evening – the friend of Peter's who, more than anyone else, can sum up the legacy we are all sharing tonight! And this is the man who Peter Cook saved from drowning and claimed it was the only regret of his life.

David Baddiel who is at once bright *and* nerdy, certainly has chutzpah. He thinks it would be good to mention the saved from drowning story, and I think I'm the only one who sees him disingenuously approach Frost and ask if he'd mind. There is some intense close-quarter confrontation – David hunched almost menacingly over Baddiel, heads are shaken, nods exchanged, and it's never mentioned again.

Tuesday, October 1st

Mike Griffin [my driver] picks me up at a quarter to eleven. He has thoughtfully provided me with a copy of The Times, in whose 'Review' section I can scan the latest revelations from naughty Edwina Currie. 'Edwina. Another Lover Revealed', is inked on the Evening Standard boards as we ride into the West End. (A reference to a Mr Clarke, a junior minister who seems to have come forward with relish – 'She was very physical. I just shut my eyes and thought of Scotland.') Couldn't make it up.

Saturday, October 19th

Signing at WHSmith in Reading. A phone call from Nicola Moody, reporting viewing figures of eight million and 30 plus share – hardly dented by 'Coronation Street'. Everyone at the Beeb delighted.

I go to the shabby staff loo and thump the air. This is the finest moment. The audience figures are, in the end, all that really matter in judging whether or not 'Sahara' was a good or bad idea. Out of the grubby loo and into the store to face the first of many signings. The weight of work is amply compensated for by the feeling that, after all my worries, the Sahara desert has proved far from being just my own fascination.

Saturday, October 26th

A cold has clung on all through this week of hugely attended signings. Tuesday's
talk at the Assembly Rooms in Edinburgh a grinding ordeal, then just when I
think it's all over – it attacks again. Yesterday evening, at the depressingly naff
Hilton in Sheffield, I avoided dinner with the Documentary Festival people
and after a drink in the bar I went to my room, ordered chicken and couscous
and went happily to bed early. An hour and a half later, I was up, coughing and
thumping my chest to try and root out whatever was causing the irritation.

Unlike the Sheffield Documentary Festival appearance this a.m., there's not
a spare seat to be had at the Lyceum tonight. Glorious theatre, scene of many
childhood panto visits. Behind my screen of slides is the big pink V of the set
of 'Vagina Monologues' – which is apparently packing them in, though very
few men. This is the first wholly enjoyable 'Sahara' talk I've given, and it stretches to almost 90 minutes as a result. My voice survives, though very husky and
strained by the end.

Meet Miriam Margolyes backstage. She's on her way to prepare for a 'Vagina' matinee. 'Three old cunts, you can't go wrong!' she booms.

Sunday, October 27th

Lie-in. No question of running. Cough a bit, return to bed and listen to the
wind and rain whacking away at the windows. It rises to gale-force levels.
Leaves swirl and race and chase each other round in spirals before settling, apparently, outside our front door. And these are big, chestnut tree droppings from
Lismore Circus. H goes out and clears the garden – emptying pots and window
boxes and tubs of their summer flowers and lining up a column of green bags.
I battle with my own clearances. Mostly letters, magazines, the usual.

Rachel comes round in the evening and we watch the third show – just the
three of us. It's lovely – my favourite. Timbuktu and Touareg; a more leisurely
pace, time to enjoy being drawn into the heat of the desert, and the building
up of relationships.

Monday, October 28th

The overnight figures aren't through until early afternoon. All sorts of things
had been going through my head, could the circumcision theme and the sheep
sacrificing in the last programme have dealt the sort of blow which bullfighting
delivered to the 'Hemingway' series? Eventually, the details come through: 7.9
million, 30.6 per cent share. We've not achieved the mighty heights of week

one, when we actually pulled in more viewers than 'Antiques Road Show', but we're ahead of 'Monarch of the Glen' and any other BBC programme of the day.

Eddie M calls with congratulations. He has a sage comment when I hint that I may follow the Buddha trail. 'Remember it's not themes that people turn to your programmes for', he warns. 'That was the trouble with "Hemingway". They want a journey.'

Sunday, November 3rd

To Roger's to watch the last of the 'Sahara' series go out. Nigel and John P come in from a shoot in Sussex. Afterwards Nigel fiercely advocates film again. 'It *has* to be film!' We stay a while after most people have gone. Roger opens a bottle of champagne. He and I embrace – job done. Series over. On to the next.

Monday, November 4th

Lunch at J Sheekey's with Eric, Terry and Terry G. One of the best group lunches I can remember. Eric is in town alone after some filming in Dublin (about which he's mysterious and self-deprecating) and shopping uncontrollably, he says.

Terry J is relieved to have sent 'Who Murdered Chaucer?' off to Methuen at last. TG, torn between Brothers Grimm and John Cusack/Dustin Hoffman films, is in an agony of indecision.

But much laughter and silliness, largely stoked by Eric. The food is excellent – oysters and smoked haddock. He goes back to shopping and I walk across to the office to collect my bags. Sharp, slanting sunlight making the streets interesting.

Saturday, November 9th

Filled with energy last night after a week away [in Paris and Antwerp], and replenished with two or three long nights' sleep, I have something of a reaction this morning. I haven't slept so well – nocturnal noises, as so often, from the house opposite. They call, toot horns, at 5 a.m. So, from being full of life and beans and the sheer joy of existence in Antwerp, I'm now sluggish in London – trying to steer my way through the commitments and obligations that dot the calendar almost every day till Christmas.

I haven't had any epiphanic insights into what I should do next, or how and with whom, and much of the day is spent on mundane activities like rewriting and rehearsing my 'Plankton' piece for tomorrow's gorilla concert.

Sunday, November 10th

Yet another charity evening. Cab arrives at five and I'm amongst the stage-door johnnies at the Opera House in Floral Street by 5.35.

A grand amount of space, wide corridors, a contrast with the pokey, back-stage areas of most London theatres. Money has been spent. First inkling of who my fellow performers will be is the billing on my dressing room door – 'Mr Alan Bates', 'Mr Jeremy Irons', 'Mr Terence Stamp' and 'Mr Michael Palin'. None are in. The door to the dressing room is opened by a four-number code and swings open to reveal, very little. One bottle of water, a small bowl of crisps, one orange, one apple and one banana between Messrs Bates, Irons, Stamp and myself.

Press a buzzer to let myself out and check names on other doors – Eileen Atkins, Rula Lenska, Sinéad Cusack and Nickolas Grace who is directing us all. Pour myself a cup of tea from a communal table at one end of the corridor and back to my high-security garret. Have just started to read 'The Afghan Amulet' when the door buzzer goes. I leap up and let in a galaxy of talent, who all seem to have come straight from some gala event. Or at least Jeremy does – he's in a complete DJ outfit and looks very soignée and 'Brideshead'. Alan Bates on the other hand is in a much less elegant suit and has a spectacular shiny grey clamp around his waist and knee. Supporting him is Joanna Pettet, actress from the '60s. With Jeremy is his feet-on-the-ground, straight-from-the-hip-shooting consort Sinéad.

There's a fluttering of recognition and greeting when Eileen Atkins comes in just behind them. I feel like a Grimsby fisherman at the Turner Prize-giving. They all have letters from Dian Fossey to read. Sinéad is the first to confide to me that they are dreadfully boring.

Terence Stamp is the next to arrive and there's a lot more fluttering and cooing and, of course, no one mentioning anyone else's work. Jeremy by this time realises that he's overdressed and loosens his black tie and opens a few buttons at the top of his shirt, checking the effect quickly in the mirror.

By now there's general agreement that they're all onto a loser with these letters. 'Nothing you can do with them really,' admits Alan. 'I fear it might all have to come down to gestures,' Jeremy suggests, as he rearranges his long legs picturesquely on an inexpensive little chair. No one has touched the crisps.

With only 15 minutes left before the audience comes in, we're led down to the stage. It's clear that there have been problems – stemming primarily from Bryan Adams and his ensemble, but also with a group of Rwandan dancers who arrived four hours late. Quick soundchecks. Nickolas Grace keeps shout-ing 'Next!' from the back of the stalls as Irons, Stamp, Lenska, Atkins and Co are cut off after a few lines.

Back in the dressing room Jeremy decides he's going to smoke and throws open the windows and is halfway through a roll-up when a special announce-ment over the Tannoy reminds us all that smoking is strictly forbidden and may set off the alarms. This seems to take the edge off Jeremy's pleasure and he despatches the remains of his cigarette onto the Piazza and pulls the windows to, dislodging as he does so one leg of a small heater which tilts to a crazy angle but doesn't actually fall over.

'What are you wearing, Michael?' he asks me.

'I'm wearing a long brown Mac and a pair of funny spectacles.'

'You're not reading a letter then?'

'No I'm doing a comedy sketch.'

'Ah . . .' Jeremy takes this in, but still appears puzzled as if the idea of my doing comedy is something he can't quite deal with.

Alan Bates has removed his eye-catching brace and is practising walking without it. He had a hip replacement a month ago but it slipped out of its socket a week later and had to be pushed back into place. He seems in awfully good spirits considering all this. 'I always say yes to these things,' he muses, 'I suppose we all need to feel we've done some good.'

'You're such a romantic, Alan,' says Terence S, visibly cheered by Alan's sweetness.

'Yes, I suppose I am. Yes . . . I suppose I am a romantic.'

Eventually most of them leave as they're not on until the second half, and I'm left alone with Stamp. As I close the door on Alan and his lovely muse, I tell him how much I once fancied Joanna Pettet. He nods reflectively. 'We had quite a little thing going once. We were filming together. We'd finish work, smoke some of the strongest stuff in the world, and just get on with it.'

Then he told me of her marriage, to a violent man who treated her badly, and how her son died, of an overdose, and he thinks that's what brought her together with Alan, whose son also died young. We both fall silent at this, until a buzz at the door means leaping up again to press the button. It's one of the young stage management assistants. He looks up at me like a startled rabbit. Someone's talking at him through his headphones. He checks a clipboard.

'You're Mr . . .' he hesitates, 'Pallin?'

'Palin, yes.'

His gaze turns towards Terence. 'And you are . . .?'

'Terence Stamp.'

'Right!' He nods, offers a glassy smile and retreats.

Terence and I go back to what's feeling increasingly like a very relaxed university tutorial. 'Alan's a nice man . . . lovely man. But he's so . . . so . . .

disorganised.' I can see Terry as being quite meticulous, putting his shoes to-gether very carefully.

We talk about the sixties, about how fresh and dangerous and exciting everything seemed to be, about where he lives now – mostly with a girlfriend in Australia. He enjoys work, but generally says no to things like this. Nik Grace talked him into it. 'I was supposed to be in America having a face mask mould-ed for the new Eddie Murphy film.'

Then it's time for me to go on stage. There's one last crisis. Rula Lenska is at the microphone but appears to be making up her letter; the stage manager can find none of what she's saying in the official script.

'And now someone who I would give my eye-teeth to travel with.' Much hysterical eye-rolling and fang exposing between me and Nick G, and I'm onto the stage of the Royal Opera House and give my 'Save the Plankton' sketch (a counterpoint to the fashionable glut of Save the Whales fund-raisers)'. As it's the only intentionally funny piece in the show, it goes well and I get it all right, and I'm home by a quarter to nine and telling all this to H.

Monday, November 11th

One of those glorious, innocent, butter-wouldn't-melt-in-its-mouth sort of days in between the ragged-sky downpours. A real tonic. Have shaken off weekend inertia and a clear day ahead at home is tantalising.

David Leland calls and the ominous rumble of another, yet another, charity/tribute evening. This, hopefully the last of the season, is for George H at the Albert Hall. Eric Clapton organising the musical side.

Then must call David Pugh and pass on the news that all Pythons present at our recent lunch felt that we should make no further moves on the 'Brian' stage show for now. Eric and John not keen on even talking to Pugh and Eric preoccupied with trying to further 'Spamalot'.

But in amongst the calls, some rewards that cheer a Monday morning – a reply from Keith Miller, to whom I sent a book. 'What a grand chap you are,' he writes in stroke-affected hand, wobbly but firm in spirit.

Tuesday, November 12th

The Grierson Award ceremony is the latest thing to hang over me. I don't much like 'taking charge' of proceedings, but am quite good at playing the role of school monitor. And this is what hosting awards is all about – keeping every-one in order, making sure that cues are hit and clips are smoothly integrated and that award presenters are hyped-up and recipients calmed down and eased off stage.

It ends on a high note with David A, clambering up on stage in a creased suit to collect his Lifetime Award and delivering a perfectly pitched speech of passion – for Grierson, for a regular re-running of some of the great documentaries which the BBC are, he implies, hiding away in their archives.

Talk to him afterwards. He's very complimentary about 'Sahara'; a difficult journey which I made seem so accessible. I tell him about thoughts for where to go next. Looks as if it will have to be somewhere testing. Like Tibet. 'Tibet!' David's eyes narrow in delight. 'I'd love to go to Tibet, but I can't because they've eaten all the animals.'

Friday, November 15th

One of the shimmery, shiny mornings that have interspersed the long spells of rain this past couple of weeks. Carrot and stick weather.

Walk down to Carlton School to speak to two groups about 'Sahara'. Show some clips on the TV, which not all of them can see, and then I have to try and keep their interest. The little ones, cross-legged on the floor, some yawning, but most thrusting hands up for questions.

Then an hour session with the older children. Great interest and good questions. Why do you travel? How do you make friends? Is language a problem? Basic, simple questions, that are rarely asked so directly by grown-ups. In the downstairs hallway, before I leave, a couple of children approach, still wanting to ask questions. One asks rather sweetly and bashfully: 'Are you shy?'

Sunday, November 17th

To the West End as guests of the distributors of PTA's latest film 'Punch-Drunk Love'. Find myself gulping down champagne and chatting to Emily Watson, co-star of the movie, with Adam Sandler. Her declarations of admiration for Paul slip quite quickly into 'gut-acting' talk and images of hanging off cliffs and jumping out without parachutes. She does confirm that he can get wound up, even angry, which is a relief.

Paul moves around with an almost cat-like softness, incredibly polite – introducing me to Daniel, his producer, slim, English, his publicity agent, also English, indeed a tight anglophile family.

More wine and eventually to the movie which is an extraordinary visual treat, has a terrific central performance by Adam Sandler, but left me a little dissatisfied, as if I'd been hit over the head rather than teased into the story.

We talk afterwards. I know now that the way he picks people is from some inner conviction that there could be a powerful working relationship, and I know he feels that about me. The 'family' drop hints, as if they too know that I am about to join them. Helen says be careful.

Tuesday, November 19th

I'm out of the house soon after nine. To Carlton for opening of various school improvements. A half-hour entertainment in the hall. Very lively and well done. Children wave to me. They slip their hands unselfconsciously into mine and I think about the culture of fear and litigation in many schools which has resulted in rules that teachers can never touch children, etc. I blame the phobic hatreds fanned by our bestselling newspapers.

To BBC TV Centre for an appearance on 'Later . . . with Jools Holland'. Unlike the decorous, celebrity ego-massage of something like 'Parkinson', I'm picked up in a minicab and without dressing rooms, make-up or any preamble, led onto the set and sat at a table and given a beer. Huge noise as Moby's band is warming up, so can barely hear any instructions, but the instant party atmosphere and the cameras swooping and swirling and twisting about is exciting and the music strong – Badly Drawn Boy and Dave Brubeck, two months off 82 and looking delicate, but sounding as strong as ever. And somewhere in the middle of all this Jools finds time for a five-minute plug for 'Sahara'.

Wednesday, November 20th

To South Kensington for an Art Fund lunch. First of all a photocall for a campaign to encourage reading. Have to choose a book I'd like to be seen with (not my own). Take Hogarth edition of V. Woolf's diaries. Turn a page or two in the taxi and am reassured I've made a good choice. Rich, well-observed, gossipy, analytical, funny, introspective, bitter and celebratory.

David Barrie, tall, youngish, enthusiastic and unstuffy, is hosting and two other guests are Michael Frayn and Brian Sewell. Sewell is eloquent and affected and persistently and unswervingly negative. On almost every subject he has to pronounce some waspish criticism. Simon Jenkins is 'incredibly styoopid'. The department of Culture Heritage and Sport is perverse and hopeless. It's embarrassingly monotonous to listen to.

I try to make some practical suggestions – like pitching my old provincial art galleries idea to TV with a prominent local celeb selecting and enthusing about something in their local gallery/museum. This to counteract David Barrie's tendency to London-ise everything.

On the way back I share a cab with Michael F who not surprisingly in-
timates that he hadn't liked Sewell at all. He thinks he's adopted a character,
tone and stance from which he can't escape. M thinks it probably comes from
insecurity at having been humbly born. Maybe he was just shy.

Wednesday, November 27th

Picked up by Mike to go to Methvens in Windsor for a talk and signing. We're
late leaving – Elsie rushes out and hides under the car, which doesn't help. It's
one of those days.

Good news on the way out. Angela [Martin, my publicist] says the Waterstones promotion has pushed 'Sahara', temporarily, ahead of *all* non-fiction
hardbacks, including reference book/manuals like 'What Not to Wear' and
'The Guinness Book of Records'. Another Number One position as Christmas approaches.

At Windsor Angela and I are dropped off at the shop whilst Mike takes
Helen up to the castle, where we've arranged to stay the night, with Liz and
Dick [Elizabeth and Dick Johns, now Sir Richard and Lady Johns. She one of
Helen's oldest friends, he an Air Chief Marshal].

A Bacchic post-talk signing as the punters have been fuelled with at least
a glass of red wine and so much more intimacy, and some long tedious tales
to listen to. Work over, I walk up to the castle. One genial copper on duty, no
obvious signs of heavier security. I make my way to the two Norman gate-
towers, one of which is the governor's residence. Pull on a long iron bell lever
(the sort which would have had a cat on the other end in Python).

As Dick says, they lead a 'vertical existence' as the rooms are stacked beside
a labyrinth of staircases. Sit and drink a glass of wine enclosed by walls built by
Edward III's masons. Dick shows me the rather elegant graffiti left by prisoners
during the Civil War. A black Labrador, Sheba, follows us around with either a
small pillow, or a length of draught excluder in her mouth.

Thursday November 28th

The planes coming out of Heathrow in quick succession. Her Madge suffers
much more noise pollution than we do in London. Comfortable bed, small,
irregular-proportioned stone-walled room above the gate from which the old
portcullis used to be lowered.

Out at eight. Dick uses a heavy old key to unlock various cast-iron gates
which lead us eventually to a terrace, from which we walk down to the paths
of Home Farm Private – the Queen's own estate – before climbing up again

to the East Terrace. The strength of the position of the castle very clear to see; it dominates the approach to London, and is 20 miles as the crow flies from the Tower of London – William the Conqueror's double defences.

A sylvan mist over the fields. It can, from certain sides, especially with the view to the south, feel as if the castle is a medieval time warp, but the smoking chimneys of Slough and the constant line of climbing aircraft spoil the illusion. Mike collects us at eleven and we drive out through the Henry VIII Gate.

Quick turn round at home then to the Cinnamon Club at the invitation of Nicola and Lorraine Heggessey to discuss their reactions to 'Sahara'. Lorraine is already there, a diminutive figure looking rather lost at the edge of big round table. She and I talk for a while before the others arrive. 'What do you want to do?' she asks. So I tell her about Hammershoi (with a nice sense, as I do so, of the change in my circumstances since 'Sahara' – the fact that I have the power to pitch a film about an obscure Danish painter to the head of BBC One) and she wants Eleanor and me to come in and talk to her about it. Curiouser and curiouser, the power of the ratings.

Friday, November 29th

Another stage performance tonight, at the Albert Hall, to celebrate George. New, untried material, and the familiar, but tricky to relearn, 'Lumberjack Song'.

I take an hour's hard labour at the gym, then down to the Albert Hall in the company of Terry Gilliam. Terry seems to have decided to put all his eggs in the Brothers Grimm basket and has seven weeks to put final script in order before deal is, hopefully, signed.

The names on the dressing room door today are Monty Python and Tom Hanks. Eric, doing some celebrity trawling at Friar Park last night, has pulled in Hanks to be a lumberjack.

We rehearse on stage after Tom Petty and the Heartbreakers, and by half past four we're rehearsed, miked, choreographed and costumed and there is nothing more for us to do before the concert starts at 7.30.

Quiet, spiritual opening with Olivia lighting a flame on stage, then Ravi Shankar and orchestra conducted with crisp authority by his daughter Anoushka. We are to open the second half and with 'good luck' greetings all round, the boys drop their underpants and I'm taken round to the other side, in my glittery, gold-sequinned jacket, to await my entrance beside one of the audience doors.

Eventually the lights go down and 'Sit on My Face' hits the Albert Hall with full force. The quadruple mooning is greeted ecstatically. 'Lumberjack Song' goes fine, and by the time I deliver the final chorus I find myself feeling right on top of it. I've always been haunted by Mr Biltcliffe's [prep school music master] verdict on me as a non-singer, and have lacked all confidence when singing in public. Tonight, as I try to raise the roof of the Albert Hall, I feel I've finally conquered a considerable fear, and with Tom Hanks in the choir behind me. We turn and salute the big photo of GH. Thank you, George.

A wind-down drink then into the wings to watch the last hour of the concert. It is powerful stuff. Paul, Ringo, Eric Clapton out front backed up by Tom Petty, Andy Fairweather Low, Jim Keltner, Ray working the tambourine, turning one song after another into concentrated, intense, urgent and rousing tribute to George.

The audience springs up in salute. 'While My Guitar Gently Weeps' is huge; makes the hairs stand up on the back of the neck. For all my grumbling about charity shows and tributes, etc, I realise I'm intensely fortunate to be here, for it is a night that will never be repeated. George was greatly loved, but he also wrote some very fine, rich, complex music which brings the best out of this stellar cast. The mood is good and the music stupendous.

Well-judged finale, for which we all step out onto the stage, is Joe Brown playing 'I'll See You in My Dreams' on his ukulele. The petals descend onto the audience, and this massive event ends with the curious intimacy that has distinguished it throughout. A feeling of being round the fireside at Friar Park.

Saturday, November 30th

During the afternoon I plan out a possible follow-up to 'Sahara' and plot a route. Call it 'Himalaya', beginning in Kabul and ending in Dhaka at the mouth of the Brahmaputra. Contains some great adventure potential, and chance of some good Indian footage as well as the possibility of Bhutan and Tibet.

Gripped with enthusiasm, I call both Roger and Basil and tell them the idea. Rog very enthusiastic – for Bas, I guess, it's a blow on the head for the Buddha trail we've been talking about for so long, yet it incorporates many of the areas that Bas has researched.

December 8th to 13th: Sahara publicity in the USA

Tuesday, December 17th

In the car on the way to record an appearance on Graham Norton I feel re-laxed but ominously weary, as though the normal pre-interview adrenaline was not kicking in. Am I just getting used to all this front of camera stuff?

For second time in three days find myself at the ITV fun factory on the

South Bank. The show, which will be for Christmas Eve transmission, is recorded at 8.30. Norton, lean and satirical, with a mouth that seems to dominate his head, is pretty quick and energetic. The audience is young and my first few minutes are not comfortable.

He tries the 'nice Michael' tack which I still have no way of dealing with either wittily or anecdotally. They show me a series of places in the world to identify, which, true to the spirit of the show are landscape formations that look like pudenda. It's all in good spirit and he is more like a mischievous elf than a determined muckraker, but sex and bodily functions are the stock in trade of the show and I never really found the energy to get on their wavelength. A show too far, I think.

Wednesday, December 18th: London–Glasgow

Meet up with T and Al, and all three of us take the BM flight to Glasgow [for funeral of Ian MacNaughton, director of nearly all Monty Python TV shows]. Meet TG at Glasgow and Terry and Al have arranged a hire car to take us up to the cemetery in Faslane.

As we reach Ian's birthplace at Helensburgh the sun is obscured by thick mist, cool and clinging. The lane that leads to the cemetery is only a few yards from the perimeter wire of the Faslane nuclear submarine base; a few hundred yards from the caravans and colourful tents of the peace camp with its anti-Trident slogans. But once out of sight of the razor wire, there is a peaceful tranquillity about the little cemetery itself, which rises up the slope of a hill, on either side of a ruined stone church, covered in ivy.

When Eke [Ian's partner] arrives, she's supported by Francesca, her niece and Max her brother, both teenagers when I last met them during our German filming in the '70s. Now both are big and broad.

Eke moves stiffly, her eyes seem frozen and unfocused. She hugs us all and I feel her heaving with tears as I hold her. To add to the poignancy, a piper starts to play at that moment. The cortège arrives and we follow up the hill in the enveloping mist, which seems, literally and figuratively, to be freezing this moment in time. We move quite quickly out of the bitter cold, into our cars and back to the Commodore Hotel beside the Clyde in Helensburgh.

Oddly I've felt much closer to tears at this funeral than many other, grander affairs. I think it's because I'm so fond of Eke, and I know how she changed Ian's life and made him happy instead of bitter. The toll of his illness in the last year had affected her though and perhaps it was, as they say, a deliverance. He was 76.

Friday, December 20th

London is cold, an easterly grip on the city, as I hurry through St Paul's Church-yard. Is it just today that I've noticed how much chewing gum there is on the pavements? An extensive rash, like sidewalk measles, which I've never really taken in before. Are Paris or New York like this? Or is this just another dirty British habit?

Meet with Nigel and John P and J-P and Roger to update them on my thoughts about 'Himalaya'. Discussion seems to strengthen the case for the route I suggested. Kashgar instead of Kabul takes J-P's fancy, but Roger is not so sure, arguing that Kabul would play well to a British audience, though his main reason is that there would be British soldier boys out there to interview.

Everyone is keen. Mid-May is suggested by J-P as a better start time to aim for – to avoid beginnings of monsoon up in Kashmir in July.

Tuesday, December 31st

Out to shops in the morning – a few Himalayan additions to the library. Home and potter and read and make some notes ahead of meetings.

Just H and myself this New Year's Eve. At midnight H toasts the New Year with a mug of chocolate, me with a glass of Harrods' champagne which has begun to lose its sparkle.

With these suggestions of lost sparkle, and with a sky low and lowering and the familiar sound of spitting rain on the windows, I could easily succumb to New Year gloom. But no question of easing up – a new series is demanded and since my Himalayan brainstorm at the end of November, it looks increasingly possible that it can be supplied.

Where we can go and how we can go there will, I guess, be heavily depend-ent on what Bush, Rumsfeld and Cheney do to the world in the next two or three months. What's certain at the moment is that the warriors are in the as-cendant – those of us who would rather find an alternative to killing innocents will doubtless be shouted down.

Interesting times. All the more important for us to go out and meet the world.

2003

Thursday, January 2nd

Walk round to the Denselows' for dinner. Robin seems one of the most equable people I know. He loves his music and his 'Newsnight' travels and takes both seriously without ever seeming to take himself seriously.

He's encouraging about the 'Himalaya' project. He was in Kashmir a year ago, confirms that it's stunningly beautiful, and accessible – 'you just fly in'. Few tourists, lots of troops, but he was left alone to make his reports.

Clearly has a fondness for Pakistan, with its mixture of cricket and al-Qaeda, and the more he talks about the possibilities the more enthusiastic I become, and my only worry at the end of it all, is whether we're not trying to cover too much ground too fast. Pakistan itself sounds like a series.

He gives me a list of contacts, including the man who is the current ruler of Afghanistan – 'He's a good bloke.'

Friday, January 3rd

Forecast floods in South and Midlands may just be averted as the winds swing round to the East and a spell of cold, dry weather is on the cards.

To the office for a meeting with Owen Bennett-Jones, lanky Anglepoise of a body, prominent beaky features. OB-J works across the road at Bush House. He's lived in Pakistan and endorses it in much the same way as Robin last night. Full of wonderful landscape, rich and diverse cultural life, entertaining and extraordinary people. Underlying what he and Robin seem to be saying, is that you are either a Pakistan or an India man – there is serious loathing between the two, which was almost the only negative he communicated.

Go straight to the top is his advice. Musharraf is the man to talk to. Or better still the prime minister, who 'has nothing to do'. If he gives official blessing, then we will have no problems of access to the difficult tribal areas and the North-West Frontier generally.

Saturday, January 4th

A bright and beautiful morning as I drive down to see Chris Orr. Through the park, and down through Albertopolis and Chelsea; across the King's Road and over the Albert Bridge – always the most festive, decorative and camp of the Thames Bridges and the sight of it puts a skip in the step.

Chris has a studio in a small, cottagey, gabled house just across the bridge and opposite Battersea Park. Tall apartment blocks of no architectural distinction loom above him, grabbing the river view and his light at the same time. I've been asked to write 600 words about him for the Royal Academy magazine.

He's always busy, and three or four days a week teaches at the Royal College of Art where he's a professor. But he doesn't seem to have become at all stuffy or institutionalised and his work is still full of childhood influences and perspective.

Spend the afternoon trying to write the article whilst details still in my head. It's an odd, amorphous thing and I'm not quite sure how to say what I want to say and how to order and 'frame' it. So just write a lot and feel rather clumsy, as I generally do when writing about artists.

Monday, January 6th

A dazzling morning. Attempt a run. Wind brings discomforts that balance out the comforts of having sun on my face. Sheets of ice where the leakings of the Heath have frozen across the paths, so tricky going.

To lunch at the Garrick, courtesy of Ion Trewin, to meet [Orion Chief Executive] Anthony Cheetham. Michael Dover (over a whisky in the bar) assures me that the only agenda is 'for you and Anthony to get to know each other'. I've met Anthony on many occasions so I can't believe that's all it is.

Sure enough, we're only halfway through the briskly served starters when Anthony Cheetham, who is considerably more talker than listener, brushes aside the small talk and sets out his own agenda. One, he would like my help to get my travel book backlist off the BBC, so that Weidenfeld can republish them all as standalone work, which doesn't need the TV shows to sell itself. Second (and this seems to be Anthony's own obsession), do I know of an artist, living, who I might like to illustrate the covers of the new editions? This would attract considerable interest in the trade, he thinks. Third, because they would like to avoid having to fight an undignified free-for-all, he has authorised a 'substantial' offer to be made to Anne for the next book.

Michael D probes me on the diaries. I do my best to be modest but tantalising at the same time. Yes, they exist. Yes, they're copious. Yes, they go back to 1969. Cheetham doesn't bite (or appear to), Ion (editor of Alan Clark's diaries) nods with interest and gives a self-deprecating shrug when Michael playfully offers Ion's services, 'best diary editor in the business'.

Purely by coincidence, George Weidenfeld [co-founder of Weidenfeld &

Nicolson] is sitting at a table with another white-haired elderly man (come to think of it, the room is full of white-haired elderly men). This is the first time we've actually met. He's a trim 86-year-old, in an elegant suit and pink shirt and tie; confident but with a liveliness in his manner and a quick, warm, curious glance.

Cheetham, who I'm sure never says anything without meaning to, chuckles as he tells me how he fought for 'Sahara' against the pessimism of the 'money boys' at Orion – who had clearly been quite hurt by the 'Hemingway' experience. What I'm just not sure about is how much Cheetham really likes my work. He certainly values it.

Tuesday, January 7th

Some obits of Ian MacN have come in. Call Eke [his wife] to see if she has seen them. She hasn't so send them off. Quite substantial reports in NY Times and LA Times, both, of course, emphasising the Python significance. Eke says she misses someone to say 'Good morning' to. Ian's reply to her 'Good morning' – 'We'll see about that' – was equally ritualised. Very Scots. I can hear him saying it, so clearly.

Complete the Chris Orr piece for RA magazine – try to avoid taking on endless demands for interviews. Latest is for a commentary on the 'Private Function' DVD. A man named Carl Daft [producer] is trying to co-ordinate me, Alan [Bennett, writer of the film] and Malcolm [Mowbray, the director]. Alan rings me, confused. 'Oh, I . . . well, I, to be honest, I don't really know what DVD is.' I seem to reassure him and he agrees to take part and will tell Carl Daft so – 'if there is such a person'.

Wednesday, January 8th

This morning it snows quite heavily. As I don't have to be anywhere until lunchtime, I enjoy the luxury of sitting upstairs and watching fat flakes swirl slowly down, turning the roofs and trees and bushes into rounded white outlines. The hush of a snowfall, the intimacy created by the covering, is comforting and I feel very happy. Two or three inches, or six and a half centimetres as they're trying to make us say now, of snow spread over the village. Can't remember such amounts for a while and order a cab early to get to Assaggi.

Though my taxi sped through the polar conditions to get me here, the minicab to the BBC is not so lucky. A long jam behind minor roadworks in Wood Lane gives me time to marvel at the almost hysterical wonder of returning schoolchildren as they come upon the snow, and for long chats with a Pakistani driver, friendly but quite fascist. Perhaps the mix of snow and Pakistan is suitable for I'm on my way to sell 'Himalaya' to the BBC.

Meet Anne, at the BBC, to pitch 'Himalaya' to Nicola. She turns the pages of the synopsis I completed last weekend with approval. No selling is really needed this time. She doesn't gush or over-enthuse, just expresses her envy at the route planned, endorses the beauty of Kashmir (to which her parents took her as a teenager) and makes an intelligent enquiry about the need to start in Kashgar. Apart from that, the new journey is accepted, at five programmes, and she will talk to Lorraine about it in the morning.

Friday, January 10th

Have taken time off this morning to sit for preliminary drawings for a Python group portrait, something TG has pushed for on behalf of one of his young admirers, [portrait artist] Stuart Pearson Wright. I was very impressed by Wright's portrait of the Royal Society with a dead chicken on the floor in front of them that won the BP portrait prize, so I'm happy and quite intrigued by his interest.

He arrives at 10.30. My first impression is of a Victorian at the door. So resembles something out of 'American Friends', lean, pale, lanky straight hair, rimless glasses, supporting himself on an elegant cane – apologising for the fact that he has one knee in plaster after a fall whilst walking in Ayrshire. Difficult to tell age, but not much more than 30 I would think. Soft-spoken, rather correct, but articulate and quietly funny. A gentleman.

He's just done the Duke of Edinburgh and tells the story of the process so well (excellent Duke impersonation) that he has me almost crying with laughter at one point. The Duke sounds a disagreeable man, who never offered a word of praise. After the first sitting he cried 'Gadzooks!' after the result and walked out. When asked after the third and final session whether he felt the artist had caught a likeness, he took a last look at the painting, said 'I jolly well hope not' and that was that. Stuart, who is not bashful, tried to engage him in conversation only to be rebuffed with 'You're a very inquisitive fellow.' Stuart admired him for one thing: 'What a nose!'

He works on a charcoal sketch and finishes in gouache. I sense there's someone here who likes tradition, who relishes the old techniques. At the Slade, he says, he was virtually ostracised for wanting to do figurative work. His teachers sniffed at it as old-fashioned, reactionary. He should be doing installations and videos.

We've got on well, but I still feel used rather than elevated, and don't much like the result. Skilful and very well done but it seems that all 'artists', be they photographers or painters, who take trouble, are generally doing it for themselves. If I want to look good I have to rely on the likes of [photographer] John Swannell.

Saturday, January 11th

This post-Christmas period rolls on, rather relaxingly, without desperate dead-lines to chase or obligations to fulfil. 'Himalaya' could have been much more of a burden, but it seems to have effortlessly fallen into place – and here I am, with two years' work laid out ahead of me, and a period of calm before the storm.

To the National – quick tour of the Madame de Pompadour exhibition. How matter-of-fact they were in eighteenth-century France about wives and mistresses. Born Jeanne-Antoinette Poisson, J.A. Fish. She married at 22, then left her husband 'to become Louis XV's mistress' (as if being moved up some promotional ladder). We're reliably informed that their 'sexual relationship' ended in 1750. Her canny ability to not only survive but sting the monarch for enormous amounts of money (she was a consummate luxury goods shopper) is quite admirable.

January 23rd to February 14th: Sahara publicity in Australia and New Zealand

Saturday, February 15th

The newspapers and airwaves full of rumours of war. There is to be a big demonstration in London. By the look of the TV pictures it's attracting huge crowds, all mercifully peaceful, which makes it all the more impressive. H toyed with going but doesn't like crowds. I never even thought of going – partly because I'm still in some odd time tunnel somewhere, but also because I never have been comfortable in crowds either – always feeling that subtleties and nuances and the complications of issues are all surrendered in the mass.

But seeing the pictures I can only conclude that the turnout is encouraging and may well make the world a safer place than the unleashing of American missiles against the Iraqis. At the same time, if Hussein is as horrible and brutal as he by all accounts is, are we right to just leave him to it?

Final estimates of numbers at the Peace Rally exceed one million, making it the biggest of all today's worldwide rallies. Not a bad thing to beat the world at.

Sunday, February 16th

I'm not fully awake until a quarter to nine, and it's cold and grey and I don't feel motivated enough to drag myself up Parliament Hill. Helen can't yet play tennis so we breakfast together, and both of us, I think, miss the Sunday morning shot of exercise.

Our new French neighbours round for a drink later. Bernard is in charge of procurement for the company that will supply rails and overhead wiring for Stage 2 of the High Speed Link, from Ebbsfleet to within 800 metres of St Pancras itself. He has lived in Baghdad, and was one of the engineers who helped build Saddam Hussein's nuclear reactor in 1982, later bombed by the Israelis and destroyed.

Currently they're casting and designing the rail scheme; construction will begin next year. Then, he shrugs, the London–Edinburgh High Speed Line, due for completion in 2016 . . . 'just in time for my retirement'.

Monday, February 17th

Wake to a different London – London post-congestion charging, which began at seven. Reports are of light traffic, no serious jams around the perimeter as forecast. It's a clear, bright morning, and school half-term, so quite a skilful choice of starting date. Will we all just get used to it?

News via Alison that 'Sahara' has won Best Documentary at the TRIC [Television and Radio Industries Club] Awards (where I met Margaret Thatcher four years ago).

Tuesday, February 18th

I walk up to Belsize Park and to Leicester Square where I pick up a macchiato (I love these simple, satisfying, familiar rituals which seem to be all the more necessary after I've been away) and head through the largely empty arcades of Covent Garden to 34 Tavistock.

J-P updates me on progress with the route and the planning. He's most worried about altitude acclimatisation and making sure that we allow ourselves enough time to prepare for quite a long period – effectively a two-programme shoot – at 15,000 feet and beyond. Further discussions at Loch Fyne restaurant.

Jeremy Paxman looms over us on his way out. 'Plotting?' he enquires, with an almost self-parodying narrowing of the eyes. We play up to this, huddling protectively over the map.

'Secret?' he asks. When we tell him it's Himalaya, there's a gratifyingly uncalculated excitement in his response.

Wednesday, February 19th

Another fine, clear, cold morning. The war talk buzzes around, and though the government is now playing down the imminence of a terrorist attack and has moved the tanks from Heathrow, we're all supposed to be vulnerable, threat-ened, waiting for the inevitable outrage.

And yet, the sun shines, the city lumbers into action again, even the ghastly forecasts of urban chaos following the congestion charging have not materi-alised. And I'm in a taxi, on generally quiet roads riding through a benevolent city on my way to secure the deal which will keep me well-paid and well-occupied for the next two and a half years. Phoney war?

Nicola is moving to run BBC Four for a while, then going on maternity leave, and will return to her role as our exec in 2004. She wants us to meet Tom Archer, who will take over as our BBC supervisory producer for the next 18 months or so. He is a slim, intelligent, undemonstrative man – around 40 I should think – and like Nicola exudes an empathy for our project which is, I feel, well-informed and respectful of our previous experience.

J-P explains the route and the breakdown of programmes. It's a good pres-entation and at the end of it both Tom and Nicola, clearly impressed and a little envious, query whether or not it might need more time. Maybe better as six, Tom suggests. Well, of course, we can only agree. And I do feel that having gone all that way and reached (we hope) difficult and extraordinary destinations, we might as well make the most of it.

But would six be available? Nicola leaves the room to make some calls and returns within ten minutes. Yes, six hours would be quite acceptable; if we can let them know the new breakdown, then there'll be no problem over commis-sioning. Oh, how times change.

Downstairs, over a coffee in the BBC canteen, we talk through where the extra programme might fit. My instinct is to leave the first three alone, Pakistan, N. India, Nepal and Everest. J-P agrees and suggests we make Lhasa and Tibet a separate programme, with Bhutan to the Brahmaputra, 5, and Nagaland–Ban-gladesh 6.

Thursday, February 20th

One clear casualty is the Hammershoi programme next March. I had to make an uncomfortable call to Mhairi of the six-episode schedule. Made more diffi-cult by the fact that she greeted me with 'Oh, Michael, I've just been talking to Eleanor. She's in Copenhagen and getting very excited.' Only course I can see is to put it off by a year to March 2005.

So, 'Himalaya' rolls remorselessly forward. J-P expands the synopsis. Anne seems generally bullish about the budget, Roger prepares for Pakistan recce on March 9th.

Friday, February 21st

To supper with Astrid and [composer and musical maestro] Denis King. Their two other guests are [playwright] Alan Ayckbourn and his wife Heather Stoney. Up various steep flights of stairs, walls decorated with playbills, to a cosy, candlelit room in the eaves.

Sir Alan, who I've not met before, is affable and, well, very big. He seems squeezed into the little student-like room, his great slab of a forehead shining out like a helmet. He mutters some apology which makes me aware that, in jacket, crisp shirt and dark trousers I'm probably a bit smart, whereas Ayckbourn is dressed for the rehearsal room.

We're all of similar ages and everyone's cultural memories seem in sync and it's an easy and very agreeable evening, with much laughter. Sir Alan is not at all intimidating or in the slightest bit self-congratulatory. He rarely mentions his own work, listens to people and goes with the conversation rather than pushing it. He's 'been in the bar' of the new Hampstead Theatre which he thinks is a very good space – almost as if it had been designed by an actor – which is very rare, he says.

Saturday, February 22nd

Michael and Delia have invited myself and Helen to join them for the Norwich–Sheffield United match at Bramall Lane. We have to be at Stansted Airport by 11.30, to catch their private plane to Sheffield City. We park the car and are ushered through to a waiting room at Metro Air, which from the logo and cabinet displays I assume to be one of Mohammed Fayed's Harrods' operations.

The room is decorated in chintzy repro-style. Carpets, heavy curtains, classic-styled armchairs and tables with chessboards set out on them. Mike and I play a desultory game of chess as we wait for the plane to arrive from Norwich.

Then onto a very comfortably appointed twin-prop Beechcraft. Michael and Delia are accompanied by their driver Trevor (a Yorkshireman). Almost as soon as we're up in the air, he's opening up a bottle of wine and Michael, cigarette permanently on the go, is reaching for some glasses.

'We've investigated helicopters,' says Mike, 'but you can't smoke on them.' Delia seems quite oblivious to the fumes filling the cabin. A Montrachet is poured as we soar over the Fens and across the misty flatlands of Lincolnshire. Travel time is estimated at 35 minutes.

There is a thrill in descending over the city of my birth. I've never seen it from the air, and I find myself in the position of eager observer as I am so often when I fly in over London; yet below me today is endearingly unglamorous

Tinsley and Attercliffe. Struck by how much industry I can see – huge sheds, smokestacks, a heavy industrial panorama still.

One of the airport staff says, sadly, that Sheffield City has been downgraded as an airport after decision to serve South Yorkshire region via the old air base at Finningley (I remember RAF open days there!). A bit of money has been spent and, I fear, wasted, on the approaches, which take us onto the main road and into the centre.

Bramall Lane, I'm reminded, is home to the poorer of the two clubs playing today. Set in a run-down landscape of brick terraces, unkempt and litter-strewn streets. I have the feeling that the two clubs get on well and that Delia is learning a lot from United's extra-football activities. The warm, Yorkshire accents, the jokes, the formal informality make me feel very welcome.

However, the game is a disaster for United. Despite having much of the game in the first half, it's a sprightly, chasing, tails-up Norwich who take the only goal of the game, and, to make matters worse, two United players are sent off. At least this brings a hitherto docile United crowd to life – with screams of 'Cheat! Cheat!' passionately delivered at anyone they don't like.

Monday, February 24th

Mellow day, warm autumn or early spring; definitely not winter. Run in the morning and feel much lighter, easier and generally more sprightly than on Friday. Heath quiet, the ground firming, a warm chill in the air.

Collected by Mike G at 5.40. London's roads still much quieter post-Congestion Charge and I'm at the Grosvenor soon after six for the 2003 Book Awards. The meal, which is fine, is served and cleared by nine. We're then subjected to a barrage of book covers flashed up on the screens to the accompaniment of hugely amplified Manfred Mann tracks. This rather pointless and violent assault subsides and Tony Hawks bounces on, all perky-like, to subject us to another 15 minutes of jokes and banter, none of it inspired. At last the awards begin but the pace with which they're delivered is leaden. Fanfare follows fanfare, panegyrics are delivered with the usual convictionless enthusiasm.

The Best Illustrated Book Award comes around 10.45 and is announced by Alexei Sayle. The winner is . . . 'Michael Palin, "Sahara".' I must admit to a rush of pride and excitement as I make my way through the tables (not easy) with lights flashing and applause resounding. I realise I haven't prepared a speech and stumble through some thank-yous.

Michael Moore collects his Book of the Year Award for 'Stupid White Men' and goes on a bit. For me the only worthwhile thing I have to do is to deliver a five-minute intro to and appreciation of Alan Bennett.

It's now edging towards midnight – they've been drinking since six and subtlety, timing and understatement is not what they want. Throughout the speech there is, in the background, a dull, but rising chatter from the fringes of the room – distracting and infuriating. Finish my piece – Alan arrives and gives a quick acceptance, then I'm back to my table boiling with anger.

Thursday, February 27th

Newspapers full of reports of yesterday's war debate in Parliament. Clear and strong signs that without a second UN resolution there is substantial, all-party and well-informed opposition to any war against Iraq. Meanwhile Afghanistan, Osama bin Laden and those of his ilk who would find no quarter from American wrath, have been sidelined. Iraq is the new enemy. Well, at least if they can find it.

A milestone for H as she plays her first game of tennis since the shoulder op. Successfully too and she's delighted.

Tuesday, March 4th

Up to Hampstead Town Hall to check it out as possible venue for my 60th. It's been given a tatty bureaucratic gloss – desks, reception areas, council pamphlets, plastic brochure holders, quite out of keeping with the rest of the building, but it remains largely intact, with some tall windows and good-sized rooms and a rather grand staircase. Very helpful man, Phil Davies, shows me around.

Back home and after lunch out to see the War Poets exhibition at the Imperial War Museum. Rather weird film footage playing of a sports day for disabled troops at a hospital in Liverpool. In a wheelchair race, one chair tilts and tips out its occupant. It all happens rather slowly and is somehow desperately poignant. Other sequences v. Pythonic, like the boy 'over the moon with his new leg'.

Thursday, March 6th

Received a nice postcard from Alan B written the day after the Award but only just arrived. He had just been to see the new David Hare pay 'Breath of Life' with Maggie Smith. 'How was it?' Knowing I could expect an entertaining answer. 'Purgatory.'

Out in the evening with the Russians. Jo Durden-Smith [filmmaker] and Yelena [his wife] have asked us on behalf of top Russian pop/music star Boris

Grebenshchikov to an oddly and pleasantly old-fashioned Italian restaurant called Arena in Greek Street.

Boris is an enormous star in Russia – he's just finished a tour of the Urals. His wife Irina, wide face, high-cheekboned Slav, is warm, open and, like Yelena, appears to be in near ecstasy at having us there at all. 'Your wife,' whispers Yelena, 'she is *so* beautiful. She is like a French painting – you know, maybe a Renoir.'

'Renoir? They were rather round-faced weren't they?'

'Modigliani, then.'

So their warmth spills over us. That lovely Russian inability to operate on any middle level. Times are either the best or the worst. Friends are saints and lapsed friends are worthless.

Long wait for others to arrive. A Russian jazz musician with slim, shaven-headed black girlfriend. A Georgian lady with terrific breasts peeping out, and, eventually, Terry Gilliam. Haven't seen him since the day in the airport when I was off East and he was off West to LA. He's off yet again to the US, 'To see my saviour,' he says grimly, 'Harvey Weinstein.' He is bankrolling 'The Grimms' film – TG's producer friend Chuck Roven having been edged out.

All the Russians smoke constantly – not good news for H or myself, both of whom are nursing colds at various stages. But there is such palpable warmth around and it's so good to be amongst people who talk about different things that we ignore the smoke and the OK food and have an excellent time.

Friday, March 7th

Need to talk to Roger and J-P away from the office, before they both leave for long recces. Have set up lunch with J-P at St John in Clerkenwell. General discussion over general principles – plenty of women to interview, not too much empty mountain scenery, the appeal of everyday life. J-P orders braised squirrel (which, we learn from the chef, is fresh in from Shropshire) and I choose chitterlings – pig's smaller intestine. A rehearsal, I feel, for things to come.

Monday, March 10th

Taxi at 8.30 to Euston Station. It's remarkably quiet considering it's rush hour. Where are the hordes pouring into the metropolis? An odd sensation that, because of the growing certainty that we shall be at war with Iraq any time soon, combined with the growing uncertainty as to whether we shall be at war with Iraq any time soon, everyone is confused. Life as we know it can't quite go on in the same way. A holding of breath. The stock exchange fell every day last week, the bubble of the late '90s has burst and no one knows what lies ahead.

I try not to think of my decimated pension savings or the warnings of terror groups, and instead enjoy the cheery, laddish atmosphere of Virgin Trains which whisk me up to Birmingham perfectly efficiently, though the mess at the lineside, the way in which railway embankments have become dumping grounds, is terribly depressing.

Met by Stephen Cox and whisked out to Cox and Whitehouse's [leather makers] new works on an industrial estate four miles from the picturesque red-brick canal-side buildings they used to occupy. We talk about the design of two new bags – one for when I'm on camera, the other, a larger travel bag, a sort of feeder for the other. He runs me back in time to catch the 2.15 train.

Almost empty first class. Choice of menu enlivened by a beautiful black waitress with long braided hair who finds herself unable to pronounce 'Wensleydale'. She laughs heartily. Once she's got it right there's a pause to recover herself. 'And in the *other* sandwich is cheese.'

Tuesday, March 11th

TRIC Awards, back at the Great Room of the Grosvenor – scene of the British Book Awards two weeks earlier. TRIC is, as you'd expect from people who are basically high street traders and white goods manufacturers, a more homely, less pretentious nonsense than the Book Awards. I'm at the Electrolux Table next to some boisterous ladies from the office in Slough.

Angela Rippon, in scarlet dress, is an excellent host – brisk, funny and lively. She introduces Trevor Eve as the star of 'Walking the Dead', instead of '*Waking* the Dead'. She admits her mistake but Trevor Eve, who could surely have had an Angela Crippen riposte, just looks surly.

The Special Award is presented by Ronnie Corbett to Bob Monkhouse, who shakes me by the hand in the toilets. He remembered standing in line to have his 'Missionary' book signed. 'I loved that film,' he remembers as people push past us, hands reaching for their cocks. Ian Hislop, who's just buttoned himself, asks after Will. It's all very friendly.

Monkhouse's acceptance speech is gracious, modest, extremely well-delivered and *very* funny. He talks and jokes about his cancer, but seems ruddy-faced and well enough. J-P has cleared off and the autograph hunters are gathering. Almost impossible for me to get out without being constantly stopped by a pen and programme – which, I notice, has a blank page marked 'autographs'. They hop along beside me. It's like the Healed Leper sketch. 'Cliff Richard's good,' someone tells me, 'he signs but never stops walking.' So I take a leaf out of Cliff's book; but it's still an ordeal.

Thursday, March 13th

Reading Dilip Hiro's book on Iraq, a pretty concise, well substantiated account of how the country came into being, how it was used and manipulated by its creators like a sort of Frankenstein, and, more ominously, how cleverly Saddam read the Middle East compared to the Americans. The less, for instance, we did to stop Israel's breach of UN resolutions, the more he aligned himself with the Palestinians.

Whatever the rights and wrongs, 800 Cruise missiles are not going to solve anything. America is behaving like a bull in a china shop. What they have in weapons, and the Defence Budget was upped by 13.5 per cent last year (Education by 1 per cent) they lack in tact, moderation, empathy and understanding.

Friday, March 14th

Out in the evening to the Polish Hearth Club for dinner with TJ. Bison vodkas set us off happily whilst TJ fulminates about cab driver with no sense of direction. Then he settles down and fulminates against Andrew Neil who chaired a programme he was on last night about current affairs i.e. Iraq. TJ was not, in his view, allowed to make the points he wanted to make. Odd argument, as the programme itself was themed around TJ's work for the Guardian – in which he accused Bush of hijacking the English language – attacks on 'Saddam' sound very different from the reality of attacks on mosques, hospitals and innocent Iraqis.

The big, anachronistic East European grandeur of the Hearth Club was, I felt, good neutral ground – neither too American nor too British – in which to discuss the war that comes ever closer. All of us I think against it – on the simple basis that Saddam's power is declining, not rising, the UN is not responding to American threats and bribery, and the point of killing possibly thousands of people who we are going to war to save is yet to be made clear.

Monday, March 17th

Across Aldwych to Somerset House – elegantly floodlit and its silver-white walls impressive, for a Courtauld 'Meet a Painting' evening. An Evening Standard billboard leans against the wall outside. It reads 'Bush Will Declare War Tonight'.

Up on the top floor 35–40 people are being served champagne and canapés surrounded by one of the greatest collections of late nineteenth- to early twentieth-century classics. Degas' 'Woman at Window' shows why Sickert

painted the way he did, Gauguins, Whistlers and magnificent Cézanne paintings of trees in Normandy.

Then we gather in front of Manet's 'A Bar at the Folies Bergère 1882' and
Jim Cuno, the new curator, talks us through it. His style is like that of a keen
school art master – asking us questions all the time. 'What's going on here?'
'What d'you notice about her face?'

It's a good technique and breaks down the reserve of the large contingent
of lawyers and investment bankers, and has some stimulating side effects. A
woman disputing Cuno's explanation of the girl's pink cheeks. Not rouged, she
says. She's blushing.

Soon after eight I'm leaving the moonlit and floodlit courtyard and stepping
back onto the Strand. The billboard has gone.

Not more than a mile away Robin Cook has spoken against the war with such
power that he was applauded by the chamber as he announced his resignation.

Diplomacy is over, we are told. War will begin (as someone was suggesting
weeks ago) on Thursday.

Tuesday, March 18th

Overcast morning. Bush has addressed 'The American People' (he can hardly
pronounce America, let alone Iraq) and given an ultimatum to Saddam Hussein to get out of his country in the next 48 hours or face military action 'at a
time of our own choosing'.

This is a man who seems lost, almost frozen in the headlights of oncoming
events. Throughout the last 18 months he has managed to lose almost all of the
great well of international sympathy that surged up for America after September 11th.

But at least the boil of American aggression is now lanced and we shall
all see how quickly the pain caused by their overweening arrogance can be
soothed. A quick collapse with few casualties, an Iraqi people at last being able
to stand up to their tyrannical leader and defeat him by refusing to fight and
there is undoubtedly a chance that America's standing may be grudgingly increased. But there are so many things that could go wrong.

Later down to meet Goldstone and discuss Thursday's 'Meaning of Life'
shoot [filming for a documentary about the making of the movie]. He shows
me what he shot with John C in LA, at the ranch. It saddens me. I feel the man
is lost. Holed up in luxury by the Pacific Ocean, surrounded by lapdogs.

Whereas I'm in Soho, with Oxford Street cordoned off because of a suspect
package left on a bus; as I leave the office a man is being held down by police
on the pavement outside – he's moaning and groaning. It's a far cry from Santa
Barbara, but I think I know where I'd rather be.

Thursday, March 20th

My country is at war again. With Iraq. Well, no, they are at great pains to point out that it's not the Iraqi people that are the enemy, or even the Iraqi army. We're at war with Saddam Hussein. To assemble 300,000 men, aircraft carriers, missiles, bombers and huge amounts of ammo of all kinds is a lot to go after one man – he must surely feel as much flattered as frightened.

So, it's all a little unreal. Like a game, or a movie. Apparently, acting on very good intelligence in the night, 36 Cruise missiles were fired at where he was supposed to be in pursuit of a 'decapitation' (of the leadership) which is the war policy, now, apparently. So that's 36 million dollars. Did it work? Well . . . er . . . no. Saddam popped up at a news conference wearing a pair of very large spectacles and went on with the sort of hammy nationalistic rhetoric that only Bush can rival.

Tony Blair addresses the nation. His hair is short and his face coming increasingly to resemble that of Peter Tatchell, thin and drawn as a zealot. Power has made him old.

Friday, March 21st

'Shock and awe' in Iraq overnight. Simple words, presumably chosen because George Dubya could pronounce them, but their brazen bellicosity so shamelessly paraded makes it pretty clear what kind of foreign policy the US is currently planning. Good for the Daily Mirror who make their point just by adding a couple of syllables – 'Shocking and Awful' is the headline.

Monday, March 24th

War and breakfast. More general evidence that the swagger of Shock and Awe is rebounding on 'the Coalition', as they keep calling what is essentially a US–British army. Not only are they having to fight at all the towns on the way north, but they're losing the propaganda initiative as well. Early times yet, but it's beginning to look as if Rumsfeld, Wolfowitz and the architects of applied American might could at last get their comeuppance. At the cost of many lives.

Thursday, March 27th

A well-filled Virgin train to Manchester. On the way I look through the proofs of the Python anthology. None of us, apart from TG, who worked on a

Chevrolet production line and was quite possibly a Vietnam draft-dodger, had very exciting childhoods and the Cambridge Footlights stuff is interminably dull, but once Python has begun it's rivetingly readable and it's with great reluctance that I set it aside after Stoke-on-Trent and try and marshal my thoughts for the task in hand; to tout for Stanford's new Manchester store. This is its official opening day and I'm Guest of Honour.

Doug Schatz of Stanford's map shop in London is also on the train and he and I walk together out of the glittering glass-and-steel prow of the restored and expanded Piccadilly Station, down immaculately paved streets, past a huge redevelopment of the square that used to be opposite the Portland Hotel, over the tramlines, down streets in which every building seems to have been cleaned up, to Stanford's, which has been fashioned from the bones of an old bank. I sign books for an hour, then there's a series of interviews in tiny hot back rooms (the air-con isn't working and, as we're in the middle of a long, settled warm spell, the temperatures are well above 60°) then a few photos and a launch party.

The Evening News interviewer asks me about the war – the first of many such questions over next couple of weeks. Must be prepared. War is last resort, I pontificate. Shouldn't have got to this stage, but now it has, let it be quick.

And breaking news that Richard Perle, one of the leading hawks and proponents of war, is resigning – but, wait for it, not for misleading his employers and his nation to embark on a war but because of some dodgy business deal. Saddam may show no signs of cracking, but the Bush administration is clearly not as solid. Watch this space.

March 28th to April 13th 2003: Sahara publicity – New York; Chicago; Montreal; Toronto; SF/LA

Monday, April 14th

Whilst I've been away the war turned into the rout it seemed might not happen after all. I watched the symbolic moment of defeat whilst I was live on air on a radio station in San Francisco last Wednesday. Saddam slumped on a plinth in Baghdad – his likeness tugged over his feet.

Though no WMDs discovered, a clearly thoroughly unpleasant and cruel regime has crumbled to dust and Bush and Blair are vindicated nevertheless. Blair perhaps even more so – a headline in a US paper read 'Blair is not Bush's poodle. He's his guide dog'.

But also on the news, horrific reports of anarchy on the Baghdad streets – the museum which contains treasures from the earliest civilisations of Mesopotamia has been looted. American troops stood by – though they prevented looters from entering the oil ministry buildings.

Thursday, April 17th

Listen to the 'Today' show. The war seems over, though its ending seems as unsatisfactory as its beginning. US appear to have no idea what to do with the effects of a swift victory. And yet swift victory was what the neo-conservatives of the Bush Administration had promised us all along. I have the deeply uncomfortable feeling that they are only too happy to see Arabs looting other Arabs' shops or destroying Arab culture. Arab discomfiture is meat and drink to these people. Proof that they are an inferior people, or at least a hopelessly chaotic, therefore 'uncivilised' people.

The degree of criticism and analysis on 'Today' is bracing after two weeks in North America. The US reports of the war were confined largely to positive reporting of US troops in battle; criticism of war aims, objectives or consequences was so limited that I only realise now, quite forcibly, that there are different ways of looking at this war.

Friday, April 18th

To the [Brazilian photographer Sebastião] Salgado exhibition. Exhaustive examples of his work amongst the poor, neglected and war-torn of the world. Some of it very moving and I had a clear vision of myself, after 'Himalaya', trying to use my public profile in a much more targeted series, a sort of televisual version of Salgado. But then I can't do earnestness very well. Not sure how long I could sustain outrage and indignation.

Easter Sunday, April 20th

I still find it hard to wake up these mornings. A mixture of readjusting my circadian rhythms, restoring my sleep balance after the North American promotion, and a quiet, comparatively undemanding Easter break reducing early morning angst. It's also very quiet in the village.

We go and see Edith [Helen's old housekeeper], and, though we get lost and circle the ring-road in Huntingdon like souls in torment, we eventually pitch up at Risinghill Care Home. Much excitement amongst the staff and a great and successful surprise for Edith. She's in the corner of her room, useless leg supported on a stool in front of her, but she looks strong. Her hair a mass of well-trimmed curls and her smooth alabaster skin glowing and healthy. Her smile and almost tearful disbelief at our visit makes it worthwhile. She wants to be home though – 'I hate it here,' she says in the same breath as praising the garrulous girls who look after her.

Beside her, she has a copy of the Sunday Express magazine from last week with my face peering out of the cover. She's on the ball, asks about future journeys and loves to exchange memories with Helen and Cathy about the past – and how they tied knots in her pinafore and made ice-runs underneath the washing line.

Wednesday, April 23rd

Rather optimistically, dress for exercise. Peter Hislop, who is due to bring my new iMac this afternoon, arrives mid-morning with it and I spend the rest of the day either sitting in a chair beside him configuring the new, rather beautiful, smoothly adjustable 17" screen, set on its white pod, that resembles the top half of a skull, or pacing around while the slow and tedious process of trying to install a server goes on.

Out in the evening to a farewell meal for Roger Saunders and Maria before he shifts north from Hackney to a nine-bedroom pile near Beverly in Yorkshire. At one stage I ask Terry how things are going with his series, and after a minute or two of reasonably sober explanation the engine of Terry's wrath suddenly cranks into life and he's F-ing and blinding and his hands take up the strangling position as he cavils against everyone apart from Alan Ereira [director who collaborated with Terry on the documentary series 'Medieval Lives'], who 'for some reason,' TJ spits out, 'everybody hates'.

It's vintage stuff and, to be fair, Terry is aware of his tendencies, but a part of me is so relieved that Rachel didn't get the job of directing any of the series.

Friday, April 25th

Lunch appointment with Jim Cuno of the Courtauld Gallery. It occurs to me that my enjoyment of art is perhaps because painting combines a number of my natural inclinations – a sense of history, a relishing of life in all its shapes and forms, a chance to travel in the imagination and, one which I hadn't identified before, a tendency to neatness, order and a love of continuity (cf. keeping a diary). There is something of the trainspotter in my appreciation of art.

Jim Cuno is the least intimidating of art academics. He has the reassuring shape of an American backwoodsman as opposed to the aristocratic angularity of an Anthony Blunt. Endomorph more than ectomorph. Not an elitist by nature. I must say that I have the same difficulty connecting him physically and intellectually with my image of a Courtauld director, as I have connecting Paul Anderson with my image of a major film director. Which is why I instinctively like them and feel drawn to them.

Saturday, April 26th

In the afternoon H decides that we can no longer postpone one of the great avoidable tasks – clearing the attic at No. 2 – a storeroom of last resort for so much of our accumulations. Thirteen suitcases deemed useless alone – though some bear stickers from Cartagena, the Palace Hotel Madrid and points on the 'Pole to Pole' trips. Can't be sentimental.

Dusty bundles of Private Eye, one or two of the treasured Punch war editions which I thought had gone for ever. Newspapers announcing the murder of Bobby Kennedy (and a later copy of the Mirror in which Kennedy's killer Sirhan Sirhan claims in an interview that he was the only one in his jail who understands Monty Python).

Sunday, April 27th

To recycling before breakfast. I have eleven suitcases to throw away. I hurl them into 'Household Waste' with little regret and much relief. And to think what relief the sight of those bags brought on a carousel at the end of a bouncing journey across Ethiopia, or in a hotel storeroom at Punta Arenas on return from the South Pole.

Up to the Gilliams' for lunch. Terry is tootling away at the piano in the Cromwell Room. He looks older, smaller; a little less bounce in the step. A preoccupied air. He's good company as always – I've never known TG moody – but I feel that kickstarting a new movie is taking a much greater effort than perhaps it used to.

Matt Damon, at 10 million dollars, has taken most of the budget. Heath Ledger has agreed to work for one-third his usual, but that's because he thought he might be working with Robin Williams! (This could be modesty on TG's part.) Samantha Morton is TG's preference for female lead. Apparently she was very down-to-earth at the screen test, confessing to a problem with wind.

Maggie has cooked a fine leg of lamb; Holly, finishing a three-year course at Leeds, is there, an easily smiling, comfortable presence. Harry, perhaps a little subdued by the ladies and by TG and myself is tall, rangy, quiet, with striking looks, if he ever decided to become an actor.

The table, in the bow window, surrounded by the immaculate (but not fussy) garden is a perfect place for Sunday lunch and I envy them such a spot. Our kitchen table always seems a squeeze.

By chance, a message, heralded by 'You never bloody answer your phone', from [actor] Jon Pryce, who wants to drop by, with Kate. JP has been offered a part by Terry, but I detect there is the usual tension. JP complaining they're not offering enough money. TG revealing that the Weinsteins' choice is Ben Kingsley.

Friday, May 2nd

Raining steadily as I scuttle out to my waiting car. 'I'm glad I've got you,' says the driver, morosely without turning, 'You can cheer me up.' Turns out to be something of a character, a glumly funny, self-flagellating Jewish boy who began Majestic Warehouses all those years ago. 'Then I lost it. I could buy and sell, but that's all I could do. I never paid any attention to detail.' Replying to a squawky voice from HQ enquiring what he's doing, he responds with majestic lack of urgency, 'Driving Michael Palin very slowly towards the Tate Modern.'

I'm there by 9.15 – on time as it happens. Have agreed to launch a new online, interactive tour of the collection called 'Explore Tate Modern', and been asked to wear some of my travelling gear. So here I am, in Gap blue shirt and Craghoppers and irreplaceable Rockport boots sitting on some old multi-labelled cases with a Jackson Pollock behind me.

At the office I welcome J-P back from eight weeks away – in Nepal, Tibet, Eastern China, Eastern India. He seems quieter than usual, less effervescent. His shoulder is bad, his children, who came out to see him in Kathmandu, have all returned with upsets of some sort.

He and I and Rog pore over a map and try to work out what J-P's information means for the series. J-P wants to go in April or even May next year to get some of the green pastures, flowers and festivals without which the Tibet section will look rather grim.

Then back to the office. Two separate TV departments want to do a 'Life of Palin' show – an hour's tribute to 'show off your incredible talents as comedian, actor, writer, presenter and generally all-round Great Briton'. Well, I'm afraid I still see the pitfalls in this sort of thing. Invent a reputation then hit the victim over the head with it. Plus, I'm having to bring down the shutters now as two years' hard labour in the Himalaya looms. So, no to both.

Then with Roger and Vanessa to the Pakistan High Commission in Lowndes Square. The stucco terraced house is in the middle of being redecorated and we wait in a dusty room with plastic chairs and assorted debris in one corner. Then pick our way up winding passages and across bare boards to the high commissioner's office.

He is a handsome, fleshy man. A businessman, confident and lounging far back in his chair, welcoming us with smiles and jokes and green tea. Charming; his assistants are also helpful and very friendly and down-to-earth and seem highly delighted that we are going to their country. I leave with an invitation to an evening of Pakistan music and fashion at the Albert Hall on June 18th and a signed copy of a biography of Ahmed E. H. Jaffer – one of the founders of Pakistan and father of the high commissioner. He resembles Oswald Mosley.

Monday, May 5th

A significant day – depending on how much numbers mean. From today I'm 60 years old. As work commitments spread ahead for at least two years, and I'm demanded by dozens of people and causes every week, I don't sense any great turning point here. My eyesight began to deteriorate twelve years ago but my hearing would probably benefit from nothing more than a cleaning out of the ears and I can still haul myself over Parliament Hill and the Heath without walking.

I drive up to Hampstead Town Hall (described by Pevsner as 'a disgrace to such an artistic and prosperous community') to deliver the sound system [for my 60th birthday party]. Phil Daniels (the personification of a Centre Manager – the new administrocrat) lets me in. 'Would you like the door open now?' he asks, in a tone suggesting many years' practice at putting in official requests. As there's no other way of getting into the building that I can see I indicate this might be a good thing.

The Victorian tiled floor and hallway looks very fine and Phil's staff (all on time and a half today) are sweeping it and one of the women is titivating the skirting board with a feather duster.

Already had some ingenious and very different presents – Bernard Heyes [editor on the 'Hemingway Adventure' series] mocked up a National Geographic cover – with my face replacing Sir Ed Hillary's above the title '50 Years of Everest'. Helen has given me a chunky Guy Taplin boat with fish hanging from a line and two pipe-smoking male figures looking out to sea.

Complete speech, change, and drive back up to the Town Hall by midday. Balloons in place, and soon Miriam the violinist arrives. She was an unknown quantity to me, a recommendation of Tom's, and again I'd been occasionally fearful of how she'd work. No problems here – with her curly black locks of gypsy-like hair, upfront, American (I guess) personality and great playing skill, she helps bring the oddly clumpy Grand Staircase to life.

Miriam fiddles on the stairs, Monica's team pop open the champagne (Taittinger from Majestic) and the white wine (Domaine St Hilaire from Anne and Jonathan).

Party Party's banner has clearly been created by a dyslexic. Michael is spelt 'Micheal', and only moments before the party begins Will notices that 'Happy Birthday' reads 'Happy Birtday'. Will improvises an H.

A wonderful cake, covered with souvenirs of my life – school scarves, Cloudy Bay bottles, miniature Patrick O'Brian novels, Sheffield United badge, the three cats, etc. Sits on the piano and is much admired.

Helen MC's the speeches on the theme of reminiscence at various stages of life. Then Terry J, determined to lay my reputation for niceness, takes my life through the seven deadly sins and checks me off against each one – finding me guilty of all of them.

Then the children. Rachel is funny and quite straightforward, then, almost at the end, chokes back an attack of emotion and can't really finish. Of course, this finds a response in other parts of the room and is really quite endearing. She's followed by Will who is, by now, a confident speaker and very funny too, in a generously subversive way. I finish off the 'entertainment', and avoid anything too emotional, or any gushy tributes. In a sense the party itself is my tribute to all these good friends.

Share some happy but insistent tears with [my niece] Camilla over Angela, and how much we both wished she were here.

Graham in his recollections of me in our Sheffield youth, 'Whenever there was trouble, Michael was nowhere to be seen!'

The children's gift to me is a series of photos, taken at the One O'Clock Club on the Heath in the same location as the famous ones that Stuart Robertson took nearly 25 years ago. Shots of them 25 years on, up against the same fence, playing on the same swings and clambering over the same obstacle course. It shows time can't stand still, but that families can make it seem that way.

The children's gesture means as much to me as any of the presents. I think partly because it's a recognition of the fact that they had a childhood happy enough to remember and celebrate (I can't imagine Angela and myself doing the same for our parents) and partly because, though different, they all support, nurture, advise, tease, irritate and seem generally fond of – each other!

As a final treat we watch 'East of Ipswich' on BBC Four. Just H and myself. Both sexagenarians now. And still up at midnight!

Wednesday, May 7th

I feel the 'Himalaya' adventure really starts for me this morning as I pop the first of my Avloclor and Paludrine cocktails at breakfast. Prowl the shops for travel gear then home and refine my Farm Africa speech.

To South Africa House by six. The dark, varnished wood panels, the names engraved in English and Afrikaans, the lovingly painted panels which show green valleys with a 'Sound of Music'-like innocence, and romantic views of gold mines, with the spoil heaps drawn in as part of a geometric orderliness, an ideal land in fact, with not a Black face in sight. Is this relic of apartheid protected?

My second high commissioner in a week is a woman. We assemble in a small auditorium, called 'Ikinama' decorated with embossed bronze panels. She starts the evening off by inviting us to stand and remember in silence Walter Sisulu, father of the ANC, mentor of Mandela, who died yesterday.

I deliver my part-improvised, part recycled Telegraph article, speech for ten minutes or so. Pleased that I read it and speak it well and afterwards many compliments. I always find it easy to talk about something for which I really care.

Friday, May 9th

To the Bull and Last for a lunch meeting with Malcolm Mowbray. The weather continues in a state of almost perfect spring. Some cloud, a cool breeze, but mainly sunny and dry. We drink a couple of pints of Greene King IPA and eat Italian sausage sandwiches in toasted ciabatta, whilst looking out to the chestnut trees, suddenly making their presence felt, swelling green and white flowers slowly rising and falling on the branches. Behind them William Ellis and Parliament Hill schools, founts of my children's education!

I think Malcolm wants to know if I'm available for an acting role, but he doesn't push it. We talk about films we've liked; he's a big fan of [Jack] Nicholson's 'About Schmidt'. Recollections of 'Private Function' – he smiles as he recalls Maggie Smith's sobriquet for him 'our fearless leader'.

Sunday, May 11th

Prepare for Basil's arrival with dim sum. He flew in this morning from Washington. Tom, Rachel W and Rachel P squeeze around the kitchen table with the three of us and eat very well, courtesy of the generous Mr Pao.

Photos of the celebration last Monday passed around. One of Tristram's black-and-whites has the family sitting in various attitudes of apparent boredom behind me as I'm in full oratorical flow. All the children want copies.

After the house has emptied, I pack my bags for the trip. Spent lots of time yesterday preparing and still have to take some difficult decisions. Will I need rain gear? How cold in the mountains? Roger rings and sets some of my anxieties to rest.

At ten to six H and I are picked up by BAFTA to take us to the Craft Award ceremony, with Nige and John nominated. Another long evening, mitigated by the fact that Nigel wins the first award, for Best Photography (this is neat, after our long battle with the BBC to allow us to shoot on film. Nige is pretty convinced that this will be the last such documentary of its kind made on film). John was pipped at the post for Best Sound by the Queen's Jubilee team.

[Journalist] Donal McIntyre, who, like me, has been pressed into service to present an award pays me a compliment when we chat. 'You're known in the business for treating your crew well.' That's good to hear.

May 13th to June 10th: Himalaya *filming*

Thursday, June 12th

Maintenance day. Service and repairs. Sun shining complacently. Cool bright-ness. London looking clean as a whistle, orderly and inviting. I know this perception is more intense than it might have been had I not just come back from the noisy, lively, frenetic and often filthy streets of Peshawar, Rawalpindi and Lahore. That's one of the most pleasurable side effects of travel. The inten-sity of contrasts.

For now, I'm very content. The most difficult part of any series – the opening episode – is almost behind me, and I've survived the pressures of a hard-travelling first shoot. I've even started the book, in my hotel room in Islamabad.

To supper at Tom and Rachel's. Prawn risotto, made by Tom, is terrific. See their new cat, Barney, which was acquired in unusual circumstances. Not long ago, H heard a cat mewing pitifully for over an hour – traced it to the flats in Lamble Street. Neighbours confirmed that it had been thrown out of the house that morning by a woman in a foul temper. This had happened quite frequently for a week before. No sign of the neighbour in question and everyone round her flat seemed to think the cat would just get more mistreatment. H mean-while had quite fallen in love with it. Long and short of it is that she took it in, fed it, and thought of [my daughter-in-law] Rachel W's love of any furry creature as a possible solution.

Which is how H became a catnapper, and Barney ended up, blissfully happy, in 11 Charlton King's Road.

Friday, June 13th

After a morning at the desk I walk up to Belsize Park and take the Northern Line to Old Street, then zigzag my way through Shoreditch, across Hoxton Square and out onto Kingsland Road. Beneath a wide railway line, on the wall of a dark bridge, graffiti reading 'War is so twentieth century' offers a strange consolation.

A little further on is Flowers' East Gallery where there is an exhibition of giant photos of the destruction of towns and cities on the Yangtze, in prepa-ration for the flooding. They're by a Canadian, Edward Burtynsky, and are striking and powerful, their sheer size matching the apocalyptic scale of this project. An unsettling portrait of a government destroying its own country – for the greater good.

Wednesday, June 18th

A third day on the 'Himalaya' book and, beginning around 9.30, I sift through my notes, order them and eventually commit them to type.

I'm not far off 5,000 words when I leave it for the day and go for a run. As I run I start thinking about Pakistan and what I've seen and read in the papers recently. Partly provoked into a mood of gloom by the head of MI5 stating the obvious (but still something we'd rather not hear) that some form of chemical, nuclear or radiological attack on a Western city is inevitable, given that the technological know-how is available and that the anger that might provoke it is still there.

The potent mix of frustrated, resentful, repressed Islamic youth, guided and manipulated by those in whose interest it is to keep them repressed and ill-informed, plus a boorish, triumphalist, messianic America which simply doesn't seem to want to understand any point of view that contradicts its own right-eousness, is depressing and it *is* a reality.

Thursday, June 19th

Disturbing news from Mirabel [Brook, our production manager]. The mystery of our two Chinese applications, both of which have been turned down, is still not resolved. At the moment Tibet and indeed the rest of China looks to be off the agenda.

Wednesday, June 25th

Fine morning. By Northern Line to Leicester Square. The coffee cart man at Belsize Park very pleased about life as he's just become a father. 'Change my life. Completely,' he says with a seraphic smile.

Walk down Charing Cross Road to the National Gallery. 'Madonna of the Pinks', a very beautiful painting, is on display to drum up money for an appeal to keep it in the country. It's a small, perfectly painted work, with her expres-sion and relationship to the chubby child eloquent and moving and yes, I'd love to be able to see it half an hour away from my home – but many millions are involved. Put some money into the box and take a quick look at the other marvellous works of Raphael, Perugino and others before walking through to the main entrance.

The reclaiming of Trafalgar Square from the girdle of traffic is almost complete. It's been done well, with a sense of historical continuity in the stonework and balustrades. It's of an impressive scale and makes the good buildings around the square – particularly St Martin's, to a certain extent South Africa House and the National Gallery – look better and the shoddy look worse.

Out to an evening at Iradj [Bagherzade] and Shany's. I don't know who the other guests are, but many turn out to be writers (Bags is in charge of I. B. Tauris, a publishing company which he claims is making no money at all), academics, doctors – lots of professionals.

One is a lively comedian presenter of BBC World progs – whose face I must have seen in my hotel room over the last few weeks. Afghanistan her real love. She makes the whole thing sound very cosy. Mohammed Karzai – 'a very good friend, lovely guy', 'I was talking to Musharraf the other day' and so on. She seems to know all the movers and shakers and be telling them what to do. Her feeling is that it is all 'unravelling' and she's most concerned about Iraq. Later, speak to British ex-ambassador to Pakistan who is furious about the Iraq war, which should never have been fought he thinks.

Very good to have re-established contact with Bags. We tell our story on several occasions and always dissolve into private laughter.[1]

Thursday, June 26th

Mirabel comes round and, a little later, 'Shu', our main adviser on the China filming, and an author too. She's a child of the Cultural Revolution, speaks good English, but sees pitfalls and problems which we don't. Our approach is usually that honesty is the best policy. Well, not so in China. Not that she counsels *dis*honesty, but there are many things *not* to mention. Like the fact that we've spoken to her at all, or the fact that J-P is in China at this very moment with a lady from the BBC in Beijing. In fact, don't mention the BBC if at all possible, they are very unpopular in China. All in all, some minefields ahead in our visit to the embassy tomorrow.

---

1 In the summer of 1964 he and I made a spectacularly unsuccessful attempt to make some vacation money at Oxford by selling encyclopedias to American servicemen in Germany.

Friday, June 27th

Meet up with Mirabel for a coffee then across the road to the Chinese Embassy. The Falun Gong demonstrators are already in position kneeling on the pavement opposite.

A flak-jacketed policeman grins as we pass him on our way to the door. Even before I've pressed the button on the intercom a voice booms out of it. 'Yes, hello.' Once inside, the transformation from the light, classical elegances of Portland Place to the dark, dusty, heavily furnished, shrouded gloom is instantaneous. I feel I've leapt continents. No reception rooms, areas, welcoming material of any kind. A thickly carpeted space with heavily cushioned armchairs to which we're shown by a short, amiable man who then disappears.

Just getting used to these oppressive soft furnishings when Mr Lu – Lu Wenxiang – appears. He's a youngish man, looks relaxed and indicates us to step through into a room with chunky dark furniture richly inlaid with mother of pearl and roped off with a red cord in case anyone should touch it. The premises say so much about China.

I explain the project and why it will be so good for China and how very much we look forward to going there. Lu is soft-spoken and curious about how we produce the shows and talks a bit about our relationship with the BBC. At the end of it all I suddenly realise that, like many others I meet, he thinks I'm a lucky, jammy bastard, and I have the feeling he would love to be doing what I'm doing. He explains a little about China – how it's changing fast, but deliberately not as fast as Russia.

He pours water at regular intervals and hears us out and suggests November is not the ideal time to visit Tibet, because of weather and impassable roads. He asks if we'd like any background material, which I take as a very encouraging sign.

Some shopping then home and write a short personal piece about the style and attitude of the programmes to go with our application.

Saturday, June 28th

Out for a run, then quite quickly sucked into the street party. I take out a bucket of beers and Sancerre rosé on ice, then chairs for people to sit on. H makes food for lunch. It's a warm, largely sunny day and I get quite burnt. The usual embarrassments as I ask people I haven't seen before how long they've been here and get the weary reply 'Eight years.' Lunch merges into games which merge into tea – which Helen supplies. Lots of children in the village these days – which is a good sign I always think – regeneration.

Sunday, June 29th

The streets are being swept and cleaned. The sun is up again and Oak Village glowing with health. I can hardly remember such a prolonged period of comfort, for all the senses, than the two and a half weeks since my return from Lahore. London life at its best.

June 30th to July 11th: Shandur Pass, Pakistan

Sunday, July 13th

Another day of unblinking sunshine. Don't feel weary as much as disrupted by the recent trip – the time taken to get out to Pakistan (longish waits at Dubai) and then up to the mountains. The camping on the Shandur Pass was uncomfortable; thin, unlined, inadequate tents and one or two nights of bitter, numbing cold. My indignation at the continued government advice against travel to Pakistan has, via a very rushed interview with a Reuters man at Peshawar Airport, left its mark in several local papers – with stories in Dawn and Khaleej Times. As it is an issue I feel needs to be aired, I, for once, don't mind appearing in the paper.

Our visit to the Chinese embassy seems to have paid off and a trip to the Yushu horse fair next week now seems almost certain.

Monday, July 14th

At nine o'clock the doorbell rings – one of the girls and two or three boys from the house next to Bernard and Mina [our neighbours] are outside. They're just going to watch 'The Holy Grail' video and wonder if I'd like to come and watch it with them.

Thursday, July 17th

Start the day with an interview with a bright, efficient young girl from the National Centre for Social Research. I've been selected to contribute to the Social Trends Survey which involves quite rigorous combination of interrogation and multiple choice questions on all sorts of moral issues like race relations, GM food, gene therapy and genetic engineering, role of the state in education, health, etc. Has a New Labour spin, I feel.

Friday, July 18th

Out in the evening to [actor and producer] Michael Medwin's 80th at the Ivy. Take a bottle of my 1982 Lalande as a present. Michael is in great shape. The charming, cheeky smile, the golden hair and a very smart suit, all contribute to his youthfulness.

Richard Wilson is there, knackered from directing all day at the Royal Court, and [actor] Marcia Warren too. So almost a 'Weekend' reunion.

Cricketers – legends like Ted Dexter and the slightly jollier and more bumbling Colin Ingleby-Mackenzie – who are now fellow golfers at the same frightfully smart Home Counties course. Michael introduces me to the president of the club. I ask Michael if he'll one day take over the mantle. He leans in and whispers 'Not me. Not presidential material, old boy.'

Albert Finney (almost exactly same shape, walk and clothing as Terry J) reads a very funny poem written by Julian Holloway and the toast to Michael is wonderfully warm and unanimously heartfelt.

Stay on chatting to Michael White [producer, 'The Holy Grail'], Ronnie and Mrs Corbett and others, all in expansive mood in a good place with a good man.

July 20th to July 29th: filming Yushu Horse Fair, Tibet

Wednesday, July 30th: Beijing–London

The day, elongated by travelling through seven time zones, began in overcast Beijing with drizzle turning to rain.

Into the hands of Lufthansa for ten hours. Well-served by the black-and-yellow-trimmed Rheinmaidens of uncertain age, read more of Patrick French's biog of Younghusband, which made me nostalgic for the 'Ripping Yarns', slept an hour and caught up on editing of my notes for the Yushu filming. Like Shandur, a powerful visual treat, and different enough to make it a cert for inclusion. Around 29 rolls shot, which, at our 12:1 ratio means 24–25 minutes of cut film.

Which, in turn, means that even before the long adventures of September to November begin, we've already nearly two hours of the six.

Sunday, August 10th

Dense morning heat, but H up and off to tennis. Very high temps forecast and not much else to do but pull on shorts and T-shirt, open all doors and windows and surrender to the not altogether unpleasant, limpid weight of warmth.

Last episode of '24' enthrals – and sets up yet another series with the president keeling over after a nasty handshake.

And on the news the magic number 100 flashes up, confirming today as setting a new record – the hottest recorded since . . . oh, something like 1659 – 37.9 at Heathrow and 38.1 (100.6) at Gravesend. The weatherman said it was 'an honour to be working on a day like this'.

Monday, August 11th

Tom has decided that it's time for him to get out of the music business. His various projects have not succeeded the way he'd hoped. He doesn't fancy going back to working in partnership, and the business itself is going through a bad time as a result of video piracy.

At first I'm quite distressed. I've always had faith in his ability to produce good music and eventually show the world. I hate to see him defeated. Then I think of the high rent and the tricky, devious people, and the good projects which foundered because he's not a hustler and I begin to see his decision as a positive step – an awakening, perhaps even a very late awakening from a dream that never really touched reality.

His thoughts are towards mountain climbing work – maybe in partnership with Simon. Two shops may be up for sale. This sounds more positive than the music biz, but I still feel anxiety that he's cut loose in a boat without a paddle. Then, maybe, I think this whole process has shown that he is capable of being businesslike and practical and pragmatic after all. We'll see.

Wednesday, August 13th

Weather cooling at last – only 88 yesterday. To supper at Ranji's [Ranji Veling, fellow teacher and friend of Helen]. Ray Cooper the other guest. He's been in Prague with TG. Says he's never seen anyone speak to Terry the way the Weinstein Brothers do. The film's 'The Brothers Grimm' and they are affectionately known as The Brothers Grimmer.

Thursday, August 14th

Doorbell rings at eight and man from the Post Office delivers a copy of the Python autobiography, hot off the presses. It's a heavy object but fascinating and insidiously distracting. Unpickupable and unputdownable.

Slightly guilty feeling of self-indulgence as I turn the pages seeing my own photos of myself as a schoolboy staring back at me and quotes from my diaries becoming part of historical public record for the first time. We were just having a good time – now this!

Saturday, August 16th

We've been invited to dinner by Jim Cuno, at the Courtauld, who's recently moved into a house in Hampstead (once painted by Constable). It's in a quiet, attractive street of early nineteenth-century houses called Lower Terrace, and the Cunos' house, though long and narrow, has the delicate, dolls house proportions of those Hampstead Regency houses, complete with weatherboarding at the back and fretted wooden canopies.

A number of people already there; a man called Tony Lewis who has recently returned as NY Times correspondent in London – an unrepentant anti-Iraq war man, his wife sits on the Supreme Court of Massachusetts; Norman Kurland, a waggish Jewish American who was once a Hollywood agent and who now works for the Getty Foundation, his wife Deborah, a slim lawyer of indeterminate age who has travelled a bit, and two academics – she Bengali from Calcutta called Gurpa, he an English Quaker, very bright and amusing after a glass or two.

Jim, who is hosting, as well as cooking two moist and fleshy chickens, seems in his element, and his wife Sarah, thin and friendly and unintimidating, is very easy company. The chicken and sausages are beautifully cooked and Norman and Deborah have brought a magnum of Laffite-Rothschild '79 direct from their friend Jacob . . . Rothschild.

Norman was involved with 'Cheers' and I tell him of a report I read recently from some young man in one of the poorest towns in Palestine where anti-Israeli and anti-American feelings are strong, but where a recent run of 'Cheers' was greeted with great acclaim.

Now all this accords with my view expressed when I picked up my Lifetime Award recently – drop comedy, not bombs, America.

Tuesday, August 19th

The very model of a good writing day. A few phone calls scattered through the morning, some dates and details of work ahead on email from Alison. Otherwise relative calm and I push on to the Shandur Pass with something approaching enthusiasm.

Unfortunately the news is full of wretched images of our inability to live on this planet without killing each other. The UN HQ in Baghdad reduced to rubble, and, as this is happening, a bus is suicide-bombed in Israel.

Thursday, August 21st

Leave for the Artangel Imber Village evening – a happening I suppose we'd have called it – which Jeremy [my nephew] is designing and co-ordinating. We reach the Artangel car park just outside Warminster where the roads turns military and we transfer to buses which take us up to Imber Village – three or four miles away. A light drizzle is falling.

De-bussed, we join the 300 or so other strollers and having passed through a big cyclorama of old Imber – all pretty cottages with thatched roofs – we find ourselves in its depressing modern incarnation as a training ground for street-fighting.

Jeremy's surreal hand is seen in one of the houses which moves backwards and forwards, a car that appears to drive itself round the central square. He's there directing the moving house through a radio. Wafer-thin as usual, but in his element.

After walking round the breeze-block army village, we all gather at an original red-brick barn where water, wine and bread, cheese and ham are served and a video of old newsreel images of Imber is projected.

As the light fades a choir of Georgian singers appears from the gloriously untended wild undergrowth beside the barn and sing stirring and melancholy stuff.

We process through the village with a house leading us, as if we're following behind the relics on a Saint's Day procession. We walk up to the still-existing old church and squeeze inside, standing, as the musical point of the evening – an evocative lament for lost villages by Georgian composer Giya Kancheli – is performed. It's unusual, lots of short, attenuated harmonic sections, tiny sounds you can barely pick up. The Georgian choir rarely get a chance to let loose the way they'd clearly like to. All rather subdued, but quite intriguing and it feels absolutely right for this melancholy, haunted place.

Wednesday, August 27th

Slight trepidation as this is the Day of the Implants – a quantum leap in the great adventures of my mouth, and one which Bernie K was always reluctant to take. But that old upper left pre-molar has not behaved itself and it has to go.

The first part is always the worst. The knife going in, the awareness of the cutting, cutting, without the sensation. It's also quite hard physical work – with much heaving and grunts of effort – especially as the tooth is removed. My tenacious little jaw is getting a battering. I can't feel it, but I know it. After that, things settle down and everything seems easier. The three titanium plugs are screwed into place – 'Wrench, Kylie, please!' – and X-rays taken to see if they're aligned right. Then they're screw-capped and finally the tissue is stitched back over them. Painkillers and wads of blood-stemming lint in hand I take a taxi home.

To aid recovery, or rather, make me chuckle with disbelief, there's a fax from Paul Bird with a Radio Times request for me to do a photoshoot for the cover of their 80th anniversary issue. Apparently Nigella Lawson and I have topped an 'RT' poll of Britain's sexiest people!

At the moment it's all I can do to stem the bleeding.

Thursday, August 28th

Disturbing, and pretty speedy effects of one day's steroid course. Wakeful at night, but not with the sort of drowsy, semi-anxious wakefulness which always fights sleep unsuccessfully, this is purposeful wakefulness – lots of thoughts, ideas and conclusions reached as the brain races.

As a result I mull over the RT cover suggestion and smell lots of rats – it's so late, it's so casual, for a cover, it doesn't feel right my standing there and being stuck on to a photo of Nigella, etc, etc. So first thing I do, after calling the dentist to see if I should continue the course as no swelling has appeared (he says yes) is to ask Paul to cancel my cover shoot.

During the morning other symptoms – slight ache in the eyes, flushed red face, hiccups and unbidden erections! Helen jokes that my lunch with Jonathan [Clyde] could be quite eventful.

Underground to Leicester Square. Jonathan already at lunch at the spacious window table. A whole source of 'Let It Be' material, recording chat, etc, has come to Apple after tapes were bootlegged and sold by an engineer. Legal proceedings against him and a distributor in Holland (centre of bootlegged recordings) have now delivered them to Apple and the contents are, J says, an absolutely engrossing insight into the life and death of the Beatles.

Friday, August 29th

Woken at ten to seven (from my hyper-active steroidal sleep!) by a neighbour on way to a morning swim at the Lido who says water is coming up through the pavement outside the house. Call Thames Water at seven, immediately answered by an efficient, sympathetic female who promises someone on site by eleven.

No one on site by eleven. Continue on a book-writing sprint, but still no one on site when I close and save my contribution for the day and head for the gym.

No one on site when I return from the gym at seven. Water is flooding down Elaine Grove from a burst main outside Rose's old house.

Home by twelve. No one on site – or in sight. Elaine Grove remains a river. Another nice lady at Thames Water promises that it is down as an emergency and that a crew will be there in about an hour. She apologises that the work might keep us awake!

Saturday, August 30th

Kept awake, if anything, by the work not being done. Wake feeling much aggrieved, ring again, told they will be contacting us within two hours. Try to prise names out of them, or even the slightest practical estimate of when the work might be done. All I get, pathetically, but rather significantly is the admission that 'a lot of people think we have technicians all over London, but we don't, and with so many bursts, they just have to wait till they're ready'. Only she didn't mean it to be an admission.

Sunday, August 31st

Paul Anderson is in town and comes round for supper. He's been writing on an island off the Croatian coast, and is returning there tomorrow. He's not been to the house before so I show him round and he scans my books and asks what I'm reading. He's deep into big adventures, the search for the monster as he calls it, and is reading Steinbeck, 'Moby-Dick' (which he says is wonderful), the 'Odyssey'. 'These are the books in my bag,' he tells me, almost apologetically.

We have pasta and some good wine, he smokes out in the garden and finally we end up round the table and in the usual, elliptical way, he talks about me being an Ed Ricketts character (the man who accompanied Steinbeck on 'Sea of Cortez') and of his great desire to work with Daniel Day Lewis. 'I'd love to see the two of you together.' This sounds wonderfully daring and, as I tell him, terrifying.

We're both serious and silly together. I think he likes that mix. We drive him up to where he's staying in Platt's Lane; he has with him 'Hem's Chair' in paperback, a video of 'American Friends' and one of my Alwych All-Weather notebooks. Whatever may happen to us, I love his fresh ideas, lack of cliché, determination to try something different each time.

Helen is very easy and comfortable with him – rather motherly – but as she says, he's the same age as William. 'I could be your mother,' she warns him! Nor shall I forget Helen applying one of her miracle stain removers to Paul's outstretched palms. Echoes of some religious ritual as she attempts, successfully, to remove blue stains he'd acquired after he'd tried to mop up spilt water on the blue leather-covered desks of the British Museum reading room!

Tuesday, September 2nd

The day I go on to Broadband. Except that, as with anything to do with the computer, there is always a hitch. Peter arrives at 9.30 to help connect me up and fill in the online paperwork required, but BT have not connected me. They connect at 6 a.m. or 6 p.m., so their message is basically, come back later.

To the office to meet with Roger J-P and Mirabel over the next section of filming.

No Broadband by 6 p.m. Up to see 'Être et Avoir' at the Everyman. One of the most happy and enchanting evenings in a cinema. A modest but profound film, beautifully shot and observed.

To Gospel Oak School where I am to open a new 'Outdoor Classroom'. It's a strip of waste ground behind the school and below the walls of the station that has been quite imaginatively turned into a wildlife garden by Camden Groundwork. Children seem engaged and very happy in it. Photos taken by local press. Usual thing, 'Michael can you just squat down. And bring the children round – no, not there!'

Saturday, September 6th

To the book again, another set of revisions before end of weekend when I must set it to one side and concentrate on the heavy months of travel ahead.

In the afternoon H and I to Westminster Abbey for Carrie Alison's [daughter of our neighbours Rodney and Anne Alison] wedding. Rod A, because he is a CB (Companion of the Bath) has the privilege of using Henry VII's Lady Chapel for the marriage of his children, and in this splendid setting we all gather, around four o'clock.

An efficient little service with rather mournful hymns. Then we make our way out of the Abbey to the sound of the 'Wedding March' past the tombs of ancient kings – Richard II, Edward III. The founder of my school, Edward VI, is buried beneath the Lady Chapel.

Meal and reception opposite the Abbey in a room where Parliament used to meet during the early years of the Second World War – many of Churchill's great orations, including 'fighting on the beaches' were first heard here (none,

I'm told, were ever recorded live. He would go down to the BBC and re-record them).

Shared some more up-to-date gossip with John Sergeant [Carrie's uncle]. He's writing a book on the Thatcher/Major years. Early conclusions are that Thatcher was less of an ideologue and more of a pragmatist. John Major, surprisingly, he didn't like at all. He's just come back from Vietnam, filming something about 'Catch-22' with my ex-cameraman Steve Robinson. They made lots of jokes about what Michael Palin would have been doing if he were there. 'He'd be opening a hospital – talking to those poor, sick children' etc, etc.

After the meal and good, economical speeches, we wander about, look out from the balcony over the now dark quadrangle. Talk to someone who finds the new, cleaned-up exterior makes Westminster Abbey look like Disneyland. Certainly the effect of the pale floodlighting on the white stone makes it look bleached, and a touch spectral.

Monday, September 8th

Talked with Jonathan Miller who wanted to send me an invitation to his next exhibition. He works a lot with serious Germans on operas and the like and in some discussion they used their love of Monty P to prove they had a sense of humour. One of them said to J – 'Take the "Parrot Sketch". It's so *true*.' J, and I, thought this very funny.

Friday, September 12th

As always before filming begins, the pace gets frenetic. One of the planes that drones above me as I try to grab a last half-hour of sleep may well be Basil's flight from Washington.

To shops for last-minute extras, then I'm at the dental surgery by midday. He inspects. The wounds are healing, but slowly. An implant might pop through the repaired gum, but nothing to worry about. Gives me a course of antibiotics, always useful.

Saturday, September 13th

To Daunt Books. Is it my imagination or are there far more books about the Sahara than I ever remember? No, it's not my imagination says the Daunt Books lady, they have proliferated in the last year. Despite kidnappings it's still an upcoming destination.

I start to pack. I don't know why, but there's always a lot of detail which makes each departure more complicated than it should be. Medical, throat sweets, tissues, clean-wipes, etc, all demand a lot of forward thinking.

I heard on Friday that when at Simla I shall do a sequence at the Gaiety Theatre which is putting on a Michael Frayn play called 'Chinamen'. I've been in touch with Michael to ask if he can email a message for the cast and crew. I shall be given a short walk-on part, I'm told! Despite opening of his new play 'Democracy' this week (to v. good reviews), he finds time to send a message.

Now I must put my mind to all those emails which hang unanswered in my inbox. From Monday a different life begins!

September 15th to October 22nd: Himalaya *filming*

Thursday, October 23rd

Slept reasonably well in the coffin-like flat beds of Club World. Served a good, hearty breakfast as we cross the North Sea. Our late arrival, after tiresome hold-up in Bangkok over a spare part for the air-con system brings us into the crowded airspace of the south-east at its busiest time.

Pristine white Concorde being prepared to leave London for the last time on regular service. An announcement warns any who might be travelling to-morrow to leave an extra hour earlier as congestion around the airport for Concorde's last landing is expected to be serious. A lot of people, like me, who will be sad to see the noisy beauty sent into retirement. It has been a part of my life, and for sheer excitement, there's been no transport experience to beat it.

Thanks to the schedule, which will return us to the mountains in less than two weeks' time, Nigel, Peter, John P, J-P and myself are travelling light and we clear the baggage hall with unusual speed. I'm home by 10.30.

H out. Elsie very friendly. Garden strewn with fresh fallen red leaves. A note from Kirsty Dunseath [editor at Weidenfeld] confirms 'Sahara' as No. 2 on Sunday Times Non-Fiction Paperback – between Patricia Cornwell and Michael Moore!

In the afternoon to see Dr Shannon to have my chest and throat checked after the meltdown on the Annapurna Trail just over a week ago. Everything clearing up, she confirms, but adds that it may well happen again if we return to altitude. She's a jolly, straightforward, redhead who, by some weird coincidence, did part of her training at Kathmandu General!

It is a treat to be home – as usual. The BT broadband drama, which has taken Peter almost seven weeks to sort out, seems to be almost at its conclusion and I enjoy being able to click straight into my email and online.

Sunday, October 26th

Determined not to hurry this weekend through, I take as much sleep as I want and am out of bed at a quarter to nine for Alastair Cooke in the bathroom. A. Cooke – even more of a constant in my life than Concorde!

At lunchtime [South African musician and ex-neighbour] Jonas Gwang-wa, with various members of family and friends, arrives to collect the bags of clothes which H has set aside for Violet [his wife] over the last couple of years. Jonas looks trim and well. Last night he played at the QE Conference Hall for a party to celebrate last night of an ANC Conference, and ten years of independent South Africa. He settles back and has a beer or two. He sounds to be still the unofficial minister of music in the new South Africa.

Tuesday, October 28th

Kirsty Dunseath emails with news of another reprint of the paperback. Do my bit for publicity of same with a couple of phone interviews for USA, then to the Renoir, with Rachel, to see a film called 'Waiting for Happiness', set in Mauritania.

Full of memories – the constant wind, the salt-white expanse of sand, the wrecked freighters beached on the sand and a sequence of trying to catch the iron ore train which is a re-run of our antics up at Zouérat. Slow-moving, beautifully shot piece. Sissako, the director, seems to revel in the colours of the desert – especially the fabrics and the vivid patterns of black African dress and design. Rich textures and intriguing performances.

Thursday, October 30th

Snatch an hour at the gym then off to do 'Parkinson'. Originally a Python combo of myself and Terry J but it's boiled down to just me.

A full show – Emma Thompson, Pavarotti and Rod Stewart, as well. Pavarotti is wheeled on – literally, I'm told, as he's almost unable to walk, so huge is his upper body and so short and weak his legs. In face he resembles a sort of Pavarotti kit, an assemblage of the constituent parts of Pavarotti – the big white South American-style trilby, with a poncho slung over the shoulder, the implausible eyebrows, the smooth unreal skin texture, the immobility as of paralysis of some sort. He sings and it is a very fine and a beautiful sound; during it his eyes moisten and glow.

Mike does an interview then the great man is shifted away like a piece of scenery and the full orchestra reassembles. I'm told that 37 of them will be playing the Python theme; and, indeed it must rank as one of my grandest entrances.

Michael does look more ashen than when I last saw him – a little of the sparkle, the puckish liveliness has gone and he looks a bit like Pavarotti in that way. An ageing man fighting to give the audience what used to come so easily. They are both 68, but Pavarotti's face is clear as a baby's.

The chat goes comfortably. Python reminiscences. At the end Emma leans over. 'You're really good at this!' she mutters. Both she and I, however, note how quiet the audience is. 'If this had been America, they'd be roaring.' Well, perhaps.

Rod sings 'As Time Goes By'. Like Pavarotti, he looks as if he's just been unpacked from the box. In his case, marked 'Jack the Lad, Sixties Rocker'. When he talks, it's as if we've entered a time warp. He's been in America most of the time, but has no American affectations or trace of an accent. He barely seems to have been touched by the passing of time. His spiky hair remains carefully spiked, *his* face (he's 58) is smooth. Very weird.

I almost cling to Emma for sanity. She remembers sending me a fan letter during Python – saying how all the girls at Camden spent their breaktimes reciting Python sketches. Apparently I wrote back saying that we'd sue.

Saturday, November 1st

Gathering things together for Tibet/China.

This has been a very welcome break. My fears about the brevity of the return home unfounded. After the privations of Annapurna I was in the perfect state of mind to enjoy home comforts. I slept well, though most nights marked by a succession of semi-conscious mountain travelling flashbacks, ate well, spent time with friends I wanted to see, didn't feel guilty about not writing the book (too little time), was able to stand back and prepare myself, physically and mentally for the month to come. Saw all the children and two good movies, and caught the last sunny days of autumn.

Small pleasures, like driving through Regent's Park this morning – seeing the intense variety of colours on each tree; rounding Hyde Park Corner as a platoon of horse guards, red and gleaming silver, passed through the Victory Arch on their way towards the Palace; a last-minute Sheffield United equaliser against Stoke keeps them hanging on at the top of Division One; the unlikely news of Henman beating Roddick (quite soundly) to progress to tennis final in Paris.

November 2nd to December 2nd: Himalaya filming

Thursday, December 4th

After a morning's work take a run. Not cold but wind makes it seem so. Lovely to be on the Heath again. Weigh myself on return and find that the Himalayan crossing has reduced me to lowest weight for 20 years – 11-4, 160lbs.

Out in the evening to Hatchards Christmas party – at which authors are expected to attend and be prepared to sign. In one corner the neat, oval face of [travel writer] Eric Newby (who, for a moment, I thought, had already passed on – but not at all – 84 and, though frail, quite perky). He seeks me out later and, with the faithful Mrs Wanda N at his side, enquires after me, though we've never met before. Sad to see him shuffle and I detect that quick look of impatience on Wanda's face as he attempts to communicate something. I ask if he's still travelling and he nods emphatically. 'I'm going to Guildford tonight.'

Saturday, December 6th

A piece in the Telegraph gossip columns today which sprang from a joke I made to one of their young, earnest scavengers at the Hatchards signing that for all I know John [Cleese] might be running for mayor of Santa Barbara (what with Schwarzenegger the new governor). Of course it comes out, misreported and humourless, as fact. John apparently told me he was running for mayor.

Only in a gossip column but still prominent (and, I have to say, plausible) enough to require some explanation. No sooner have I punched JC's address up on my screen than the phone rings. 'Hell-lo Mickey, how are you?'

JC's contacts had already flashed the news across to him. We talk amiably. He's had flu for seven weeks, he says. 'Nothing to do but lie down.' It obviously depressed him but he's soon off to recuperate in Mexico. He's writing a film with a young man – 'Rather odd, you know, writing with someone so young. It feels rather intimate, almost sexual.' He laughs; this develops into a cough and I hear him lean away from the phone and rack his lungs for phlegm – a deep scouring expectoration. Anyway there's a part for me, he says. Someone who runs a pet shop.

Tuesday, December 9th

Bright, cold start. Up to the grandly huge St Dominic's Priory for the funeral of Alice Cane [a neighbour]. She died of a heart attack, 83 years old. Her death affected me more than I'd have expected. Not just a loss for the village, a break in the continuity, but loss of someone who always struck me as having a fire inside, a sparkle in the eyes, a vitality that was infectious.

A requiem mass, so not much change out of an hour and a half. The hymns are largely unknown to me but a confident black lady behind knows them all and guides us through, though she has an irritating way of punching final consonants!

Out into the wispy foggy sunshine at eleven.

Anne takes me to Claridge's for lunch at the latest Gordon Ramsey spot. I've never been inside Claridge's and rather like it – the black-and-white marble floor and the elegant Caprice-like interior. Such a joy to be in a hotel which doesn't mess around with vast atriums. The modern Asian hotels seem to think it obligatory to create huge, intimidating, fuel-guzzling hallways stretching up many storeys sometimes. Claridge's is on a human scale, even if you have to be a pretty rich human to feel comfortable here.

I'm not well-disposed to these posh Michelin-starred eateries. They all too often lack warmth and friendliness. The staff treat the diners with immaculately polite contempt and as we're supposed to be having the *best* meal in the world, one is automatically super critical. And so it is today.

Wednesday, December 10th

To Long Acre for the Stanford's refurbishment party. Meet Bill Bryson for the first time – seems a decent, low-key, unsensational man. [Travel writer] Redmond O'Hanlon by contrast, grasps me in a bear hug. Eric and Wanda Newby potter by. Eric a little vague – starts thoughts then loses the thread. Sad to see such an elegant dresser and elegant writer so flawed, but he doesn't seem in the slightest bit self-pitying. They ask me to come and see them in the country and I'm quite touched (his 'Slowly Down the Ganges' remains one of my favourite travel books).

Friday, December 12th

Picked up at nine by a heavy-set, crop-headed driver from VIP Cars, who, disconcertingly, has a stubby grey protuberance attached to his left ear – some sort of radio/telephone I guess. Using the weird route worked out on a computer screen we make our way to a studio in Park Royal [for a shoot for Vanity Fair].

Around 25 personnel to take the photographs of, dress, make up, watch and provide for Terry G, Terry J and myself. JC, already this week, shot in LA, Eric I in San Francisco; then we'll all be composited together.

The idea is that all the Pythons are shot in coffins, lid open (of course) and engaged in some activity. The not quite dead idea. JC is looking cross and reading the paper, Eric chirpy and playing a guitar. I'm a lumberjack reading a map, Terry J is in drag with a bikini-clad model and Gilliam is hoovering up GC's ashes.

Then a series of snaps, in black and white, suits with a discreet Python give-away. Eric has a tin of Spam, I'm holding a parrot.

All quite satisfactory and it's good to see Terry G for first time since April last when he went out to Prague. He looks tight, his face honed and weathered by the experience, like a battle-hardened general. I know now what Terry's going to look like for the rest of his life. He claims not to have spoken to the Weinsteins for several weeks. TJ looks a little lost, wistful and vaguely melan-choly, and I suppose I'm the perky one.

Saturday, December 13th

Out of the house at a quarter to ten and down to Marylebone High Street for first assault on the shops.

Park round the corner from the Ed VII Hospital as the stretch of Beaumont Street in front of the hospital has been cleared. The Queen is in for a knee op-eration and removal of 'lesions' on the face. I walk up the street. Behind barriers the news teams are gathered, lenses pointed at the front door. I see Nicholas Witchell arriving – he's in a long, thick coat, and nods at the crews as if aware of his exalted status.

Sunday, December 14th

Up at my desk around ten. Hoping to organise myself as next week is set aside in my schedule for 'Himalaya' writing.

Ranji rings around eleven. Have I been listening to the news? Saddam Hus-sein has been captured. I'm afraid none of the news from Iraq, good or bad, makes me jump any more. It's a mess; lots of Iraqis are still dying and the filter of US and 'Coalition' information is a way of concealing the truth. One thing travel has done, is to make me realise how different realities on the ground are from media efforts.

Up to see the Gilliams for tea. Maggie tells us more about the ghastly injury she sustained in France earlier this year – when a horse kicked a hole in her knee and shattered the kneecap. She had to have regular blood transfusions as the wound bled for four days.

After much ringing of phones Terry appears from his eyrie, Harry having shouted at him to 'Turn down that music!' He looks a bit like Saddam Hussein without the beard. Blinking and bleary, as if he's been up all his life.

To bed after twelve. The image that will not go away for a long time is of

the ex-Iraqi dictator, bearded, dishevelled, disoriented, shagged out and reduced to the level of a wretched victim. Real justice, I suppose.

Tuesday, December 16th

My scheduled book-writing days slip away unfulfilled, but there's not much I
can do about it. It's hard to be reclusive at this time of year, and only two weeks
back from crossing the Himalaya on film, I find I still have a thirsty appetite
for diversion, good company and a little luxury. All this is promised by a free-
loader's Christmas lunch at the River Café, to which I repair after another few
hours on the Christmas cards.

Jonathan C, the two Terrys, Ray and myself assemble at the bar. Alan Yentob
is at a nearby table. He waves enthusiastically and I chat for a while. 'What's the
occasion?' he asks, almost breathlessly, and I realise that three Pythons entering
a restaurant – especially one as conscious of charisma as Ruth and Rosie's – is
considered quite something. 'Just a lot of old guys having lunch.'

It's an enormously jolly lunch. Terry J sighs and hums happily. I hear him
point out something to the auburn-haired waitress who's finding our table
much to her amusement. 'Isn't the light wonderful in here?'

A little later he becomes wonderfully, irrationally fixated on Alan Yentob.
'What *is* he doing here?' Terry hisses. 'It's *four* o'clock!'

Home. H has been to see her knee man today. News not good. Apparently
it's a mess in there. No tennis for at least three months.

Friday, December 26th: Boxing Day

Low cloud, drizzle, wet pavements, gusts of wind creating a suggestion of cold.
Out for a run. Oak Village quiet as the grave. Across the Fields and over the top
of Parliament Hill.

A few runners, maybe a dozen in an hour, even dog walkers seem fewer than
usual. Do dogs have hangovers? Meet Michele Hanson coming onto the Heath
from Millfield Lane. We exchange good lines heard over Christmas. Like Aunt
Ros's 'You know Arthur Lewis?' 'No,' says Granny abstractedly, busy on her
own train of thought. 'Dropped dead. In the kitchen.'

Michele's friend overheard this from two ladies talking on the bus, 'And then
he tore my skirt off. You know, the Gor-Ray one.'

H and I up till one again. 'The Office' Christmas special the culprit. Lovely
stuff, though shot through with a valedictory feel that marks it out from the
series. One can see an end in sight – and somehow ends don't suit 'The Office'.

Saturday December 27th

I take Granny G to the National Portrait Gallery. We do the Tudor room very thoroughly (so much intricate detail, like the ring in Shakespeare's ear) then up to the restaurant for a cappuccino and a back view of Nelson.

On the way out of the NPG, as I lead off through the revolving glass doors, there is a loud bang. It's GG's head making contact with the glass surround of the doors. Battered, but not bruised, she walks with me to inspect the new extended pedestrian area of Trafalgar Square. The plinth on the north-west corner remains empty as no one can decide on who or what should be put there. I think it should perhaps remain empty, a monument to British indecision.

Have heard a lot more detail of the family over these last few days. Uncle Leonard, one of GG's uncles, who fondled young girls. 'I expect he fondled me,' says GG briskly. 'We didn't worry about that sort of thing.' Another dimly remembered relative had one eye and one leg.

'She was a shepherd.' Another double-take from H and myself. 'A shepherd? With one eye and one leg?' 'No a Sheppard, dear.'

Sunday, December 28th

Another 'pulse' (as they like to describe passing weather fronts these days) of rain passes through overnight and the skies are clear for drive up to Abbotsley with Granny.

I never like the moment of waving goodbye to Church Farm, with Granny holding the back door ajar. It feels worse today, as she's so obviously enjoyed her Christmas, and been able to forget for a while that this was the year she turned 90.

Jeremy has been offered more money than ever before to design a Broadway musical called 'Masada'. He thought a Zionist musical may be good for his bank balance, but that was before he read the script.

Around ten H and I are left on our own for the first time in six days of Christmas. Slowly put the house together again. Good days though. Though the children have all gone, it's still a family house.

Wednesday, December 31st

An end of year listlessness prevails. Shops open but not busy, Post Office closing earlier than usual, shelves waiting to be restocked in the New Year. Wrap presents for our guests tonight, and manage some work on the book before it gets dark.

I feel my life on a reasonably even keel. Much more content with life as it is and circumstances as they are, than I used to be.

The 'Himalaya' series, which has underpinned the whole year, has not only become reality, but looks as if it will be something special. The worst discomforts are, I think, now over and they have produced some exciting results and a ton of material. So the pressure to prove myself has eased a little.

My health (touching wood as I write) has held up well despite a few torments (such as the powerful Annapurna Trail attack of cold and cough combined) and, with '80 Days' and 'Pole to Pole' both playing over Christmas and New Year on BBC Two, and, most unexpectedly, 'Sahara' becoming one of the top ten bestselling non-fiction paperbacks, I feel that the travel shows are beginning to have the longevity of Python.

The children's lives may all be undergoing change next year. Hopefully Urban Rock, Tom's mountain gear company, will give Tom money, motivation and an escape from the malaise of the music biz. Rachel could seal her reputation as a safe pair of hands in network TV if she can be as effective with 'Changing Rooms' as she has been with smaller fry. Will has consolidated a reputation as a witty speaker and may move on from the Soane before the year's out. I end the year much more interested in my children's progress than my own.

What the hell, I'm 60 now, anything I can do is a bonus!

2004

Thursday, January 1st

At dinner last night I was jokingly describing late-night life in the street outside and particularly the violent oaths, the streaming abuse, the 'you fucking, fucking fucker, what the fuck are you doing' and everyone laughed and that was that.

Within a couple of hours of falling asleep, when both H and myself were deeply unconscious, we're woken by someone thumping a car and, sure enough, a woman's voice screaming 'You can't fucking *do* this to me!' Bang! Bang! A man replies 'Leave that fucking car alone, that's my mate's fucking car.' The little drama plays itself out over a half-hour or so and all is quiet again. Funnily enough, it's only then that Helen and I start to chuckle.

H can relax today, no cooking or caring or shopping. She puts her knee up on an icebag and watches 'The Sound of Music'. I read Alan Bennett's diary in London Review of Books. His precise, elegantly expressed observation of the mess we all make of our lives is unequalled. He picks over human behaviour like a geologist collecting specimens.

Sunday, January 4th

Monk-like existence since the turn of the New Year. Driven by the imperative to complete the North West India section of the book before we go out on the road again, I've spent most of the days up in my workroom.

'Sahara' paperback seems to have finished its comforting autumn run on the bestseller lists, but 'Himalaya' is taking shape. Frustrating thing is that I can't seem to improve my style, or even find quite the right voice; it's very much like more of the same. But, thank God, the material is plentiful.

Monday, January 5th

The end of the holiday. Phones start to ring, emails ping and I have the impression of the lights going on again, the current being reapplied.

Drop in at the Hospital for Tropical Diseases' Health Clinic and pick up some malaria pills, then on to Green Park. Lunch at the newly opened Wolseley with Tristram P. The tall, vaulted space once a car showroom, bank and Chinese restaurant, has a hint of the Islamic about it. Black-and-white tiles and a black lacquer-ish finish hint at something more exotic than banking. TP joins me – led to the table clutching bags, one of which contains a book of postcards for me from the French colonial period in Africa. Independence, in many countries, meant the disappearance of decent postcards. In a sense I suppose they were showing off; cultural trophies, subconscious symbols of possession.

Home then down to T2000 for the New Year party. Word on the railways goes from apocalyptically awful to cautiously hopeful. At least there were more people using the railways last year than for 40 years, say the half-fulls. But at a current subsidy of £3.80 per traveller say the half-empties (£1.20 under nationalised BR).

To the NFT to meet Rachel and H and see, at R's suggestion, Chris Guest's 'Waiting for Guffman'. Usual brand of sweet and cruel parodies. But the acting is excellent, observations painfully realistic but cheerfully over the top as well, so, in the end, laughter and gags carry it rather than deep social comment, messaging, or anything uncomfortable like that.

Thursday, January 8th

Wake to heavy rain and wind. Find it rather comforting. Have slept well, on and off, and my health seems restored. Rise a little gingerly, but after breakfast feel able to do battle with the book again – unfortunately, have lost an important day, and many interruptions this morning mean I don't have time to get into a flow.

Katy Hepburn [Terry's sister-in-law, artist and designer] comes round at lunchtime to collect a copy of the original Python 'Bok' [the second book we published, 1973] for some exhibition. She's lovely, Katy, slim and frail and deceptively laid-back, but always working, currently on a book of U2 photos. 'Of course all the band want to vet all their pictures, so none of them with their mouths open.' We both think it might be time for a book of photos the celebs didn't want you to see.

Friday, January 9th

Off to lunch with J-P, clutching hot off the press schedules for the next leg. J-P very good company, whether it's talking about Sting's ability to absorb very strong drugs (ayahuasca) and come out the other side or agonising about whether his son Callum really wants to go to Westminster, or would be happier at a state school, he's full of bright ideas and good gossip. Likes his image as a bit of a rascal, but deep down his values are solid and quite conservative.

We talk about the insurers, who, since having to fork out for J. Pritchard's AMS scare,[1] are now demanding health and safety regs be applied to the letter. So helmet for me when on elephants and horses, and preferably no railway journey, as I might be a target for separatist guerrillas in Assam.

Tuesday, January 13th

To Worldwide Studios at ten to record a DVD commentary for four of the 'Ripping Yarns'. Despite the BBC having got rid of video and DVD rights in a clear-out twelve years ago – and never having repeated the series whilst Jane Root was at 2 – they insist on having two women along to make sure we say nothing that might be libellous or rude about the BBC. What cheek.

It goes well, despite having to cover some of the awkward personal areas of Terry's relationship to the 'Yarns' and the adjustments we went through which virtually led to the end of our writing relationship. TJ on very good, benign form – generous about my perfing too.

January 14th to February 19th: Himalaya filming in Bhutan and Bangladesh

Sunday, February 22nd

Mike picks me up at two to go down to BBC Showcase in Brighton. Find myself taking tea in a chintzy suite with the director [of our interview] and Michael Aspel and David [Attenborough]. 'I've been reading Treasure Island,' says David with enthusiasm. 'Just got to Blind Pew, tap-tapping along the street. Wonderful.' He has taken down one of the books that line the shelves of an alcove open in front of him. Indeed an 1895 edition of 'TI'.

The meeting is, as I'd expected, long on waffle and short on focus. 'The emphasis should be on entertainment,' flaps the director. David, Michael A and myself nod obediently.

Monday, February 23rd

My first run since the New Year. Chilly north wind but dry and sunny intervals which suddenly illuminate dull corners and make the whole run more

---

1 John Pritchard, our sound recordist, had been diagnosed with Acute Mountain Sickness after working at high altitude in Tibet.

interesting. I'm feeling on good form – physically well and quite an appetite for the writing too.

Join Basil for a meal at 'The Canteen', as he calls Royal China. Get there around eight to find TG, Jeremy Thomas [film producer], Ray (Cooper) and Basil already there. I'm told there are three others coming 'who you don't know' adds Ray.

They turn out to be a lively couple – he, Serge, is an Italian commercials producer with good stories of how he produced Fellini's ads for the Banco Roma. Fellini turned in two-and-a-half minute spots instead of the required 30 seconds and in the end the Banco Roma accepted and paid for them as they were!

They have a daughter, who's obviously fathered, or mothered by someone other than them, as she's half Nepalese. A disconcerting conversational companion. Her reply to every attempt I made to engage her attention was a brisk toss of the head and 'I'm sorry?'

The other side of the table soon requisitioned by Terry G who F'd and blinded about the Weinsteins. Jeremy enjoyed this, I think.

Ray and I had some good laughs. 'Sit on My Face' has been cut out by the company who are showing the George H film in San Francisco. America, what *is* happening to you?

Tuesday, February 24th

Talk to Amir, Mr Dry Cleaner, about the Iranian elections – resoundingly won by the conservative Islamic parties. He has all sorts of gossip including a report from a friend that a picture of him and his father casting their vote had been shown to counter any doubts about non-voting. Unfortunately the picture was from the last election and the man's father couldn't have voted this time as he was dead.

Wednesday, February 25th

At around three I leave the house for an interview to help publicise the Amnesty concerts on DVD. London seems very beautiful today. Clean, moderately crowded, its irregularities picked out and celebrated by the vivid winter sunshine. The nightmare of Dhaka, which I left less than a week ago, may help to make everything look and feel better, but most of it is to do with being back on my own patch, in a city I understand and know my way around.

Walk through Soho Square, to NATS Recording Studios. Roger Graef greets me with a big hug. He seems a little smaller and greyer than I remember, but he always gives off a wry energy and appetite for life – as befits one of the pioneer fly-on-wall directors.

Downstairs we look at the shows and I'm interviewed for about 40 minutes. Thanks to my diary I've been able to recall more than I expected of those riotous late-night shows, 28 and 24 years ago respectively. Terrific 'Dead Parrot' and 'Cheese Shops' – John on powerful, high velocity form and the audiences seemed to be listening as well as celebrating.

Read myself to sleep with Richard Eyre's diaries. I've always thought of Richard as being someone of incomparably higher intellect and energy, but it's comforting to read of his doubts and sleepless nights. Above all else, I see him as sane and sensible as well as gifted.

Sunday, February 29th

Can't summon up the energy for an early morning run. It's dour cold weather out there. Instead I get up to my workroom early enough to take full advantage of the extra writing day afforded by this Leap Year.

In the afternoon Rachel drops by on her way back from an Elvis party in Banbury. She's very relieved that the BBC liked her opening 'Changing Rooms' prog so much. 'I think I'm quite good at the editing,' she says, in a rare display of immodesty.

Wednesday, March 3rd

Little to report. Bad diary days, but good writing days. We now get up around 7.30 and I'm up at my desk by nine having taken in lots of fruit and the day's news (more slaughter in Iraq, 220 Shias murdered during Ashura festival. The day before yesterday, as part of a festival commemorating death, young men were beating themselves senseless. Yesterday the real thing). Am ready to write by nine, if no complicated arrangements to be made.

Relive the start of the Annapurna trek. Interrupt the afternoon's flow to look at the latest cull of photos sent by Basil for the second half of Pakistan. Standard very high, I'm pleased to see. Call Basil – 'Well, it ought to be, I took so many.' Finish the day's work by half past six. Very satisfied with progress so far. Well, in quantity certainly.

Thursday, March 4th

To the RA for the Vuillard exhibition. Buttonholed by a 'You don't remember me' (YDRM) on Mansfield Road. Battered face, must have been attractive once. Claims George Harrison asked to marry her nine times.

The RA seems to have been invaded by a rather upper-class Saga crowd, mainly women of a certain look, perfectly harmless except for their numbers and overwhelming presence which tend to upstage the paintings. Try not to be sidetracked into looking at faces in real life and concentrate on the figures on canvas. Unfortunately, they seem to be the same sort of women in the paintings as there are in the gallery.

Some of his smaller canvases give me all the satisfaction that I once discovered on first acquaintance with Vuillard and which made him (along with Bonnard) one of my favourites – I treasure the portrait of his dentist – can't be many of those around in the world of art.

Friday, March 5th

Hard to get restarted on the book. Partly foot off the pedal yesterday, partly small niggly things on my email that need sorting out. Just distilling the number of things people want from me takes time and concentration, and as, in very many cases, these are things I would never want to be involved in otherwise, I feel put upon too.

H and I walk up to [our local bistro] Ravel's for a good supper. Ravioli and lamb chops and plenty to talk about. Back home and end up by chance catching the last three-quarters of 'Kissing Jessica Stein' which I loved when I saw it on a plane and H quite enchanted by it tonight. New York wit, but the observation is clever and charming and true and not preachy. A movie I should like to have made.

Tuesday, March 9th

Read 'Road to Oxiana', having met the man who is writing a biog of Byron at the Courtauld today. We chatted about the debt owed to Byron by the Chatwins and the Thubrons – and how much of travel writing should be re-christened fiction.

Thursday, March 11th

News of train bombings in Madrid. Atocha Station – 'Hemingway' filming and Toledo trip. Happy associations. Deaths too, put at around 15 people. ETA [Basque separatist group] suspected.

To Moving Picture Co in Wardour Street to see work in progress on TG's 'Brothers Grimm'. Excited. I know it won't be like anything else I've seen for a while. Excitement dulled a little by long wait downstairs – without tea, coffee, lunch or anything – whilst Terry and the projectionists work on some synch sound problem.

A one o'clock start becomes a two o'clock start and being a Gilliam this is not a succinct movie. Disappointing script, the lines stick firmly on the page and TG's way of dealing with it is to encourage his actors, or allow his actors to mug horribly. So in come outrageous accents (all poor imitations of JC on the battlements in 'Holy Grail') and grotesque and unfunny mugging.

Ray C and Charles McKeown [actor and writer] confirm my own feelings about lack of tension, drama and depth in the story. Both wonder just what market it'll go for. I feel a pang of regret for the days on 'Time Bandits'.

The numbers killed in Madrid have risen from 15 suspected this morning to 198 confirmed by midnight. Dull ache of doom. And inevitability, and disbelief that the 'war on terrorism' can ever result in victory.

Tuesday, March 16th

To lunch with J-P at the Connaught. A perfect confluence of good food, good wine and celebration of a kind after my first sight of the third episode [of *Himalaya*] last night. Nigel's work is consistently excellent, Alex has edited sequences (especially Lekhani, the Annapurna Trek and Everest Base Camp) fluently. Only occasional worries are my looking a chump and not asking the right questions – but generally speaking it is hugely encouraging to be pretty sure now that we have three very solid episodes, which can only get better.

J-P was talking to his friend Gore Vidal in LA. He's convinced the Madrid bombings have been motivated, even arranged by the Bush admin to keep up the mandate for war against terror. I almost wish he were right. My gut feeling is that they were the work of an increasingly confident al-Qaeda-inspired splinter group, as one way of combating the American and British failure to address any of the issues that make the Arab world so angry. The killings in Palestine and Israel, the special forces hunting bin Laden in the Tribal Areas, the refusal to admit that any of the killings of civilians caused by our bombing in Iraq is of the same order of the killings of civilians in terror attacks.

We are in a fortress mentality now, backs against the wall. Initiatives have run out, they're landing blows and we have to think of some way of calming, rather than inflaming the situation. What we need is a statesman, or statesmen to emerge who are prepared to listen, discuss, and by talking defuse some of the anger that the Arabs fall into so easily. Neither Bush, nor Blair seem to be the men to do it.

Wednesday, March 17th

Back to the book. Have to push myself to want to do it. By telling myself I have to do it. Take a break for a run. Warm, swift going.

Work on until time to go to Travel Bookshop's 25th anniversary party. It's at a place in Westbourne Grove called Twentieth Century Theatre. An equivalent of a local theatre auditorium in a provincial town. Probably 1920s, approached up stairs and into a big, open area, high and functional.

Have a good chat with Benedict Allen [writer and explorer]. He's got a batty programme idea of being lowered from a Zeppelin into parts of the earth surface that have, literally, never been trod before. Abseiling into Venezuelan craters, etc. Says they can't afford a Zeppelin and are having to rethink.

Sunday, March 21st

Life ruled at the moment by my determination to get the book to Lhasa, and have revised copy ready for Bas next week. Work through the morning on a hasty (too hasty) edit but by midday I've reached the goal and theoretically have won myself ten days on my writing schedule – and completed 25,000 words, near enough, in last month.

Watch 'Panorama' on al-Qaeda. All gloom, Sword of Damocles sort of stuff. Not giving an inch, or giving an inch, this seems where the debate is at the moment. Meanwhile al-Qaeda sets the agenda and we, the West, seem to be making fools of ourselves.

March 24th to April 6th: Himalaya *filming*

Thursday, April 8th

Spotty sort of night. The loosening of my bowels, which broke up my night on the flight from Bangkok, seems to still be unresolved, but sleep deepens just as it's time to get up.

A year ago I was selling 'Sahara' in the States as the war in Iraq looked to be coming close to a short and satisfactory end; as I shave this morning, the news is of a war which should have ended, flaring up again. Forty US troops killed and hundreds more Iraqis dead these last two or three days.

Good Friday, April 9th

On an Easter note, R has brought me a cutting from the Observer which suggests that when polled about their preferences for Biblical films, 10 per cent chose Mel Gibson's 'Passion' and 90 per cent 'The Life of Brian'.

Easter Monday, April 12th

A day to ourselves. I write, Helen goes to gym and shops. Largely overcast, introvert day. Village quiet.

H and I to early evening performance of 'Station Agent' at the Renoir. An absolute delight. Some of the most convincing, natural, understated performances add a touching and appealing quality to a quietly gritty little movie. Oh, and it's about trains!

Drive home past St Pancras which has now closed for three years' work on the main station and train shed. All for the best, I think, but I hear rumours that it will never be called St Pancras again, for fear this might confuse international travellers. I'll keep my ink dry, but I feel letters to the editor coming on!

Wednesday, April 14th

Slowly reorient myself to 'Himalaya', but haven't got far across the Tibetan plateau when Judy G rings. Nigel [Greenwood, my cousin] died an hour ago at Trinity Hospice. That I hadn't been in touch with him since I got back makes me a little uncomfortable. I know I'd kept putting off calling for fear of how he might be. We didn't know each other that well, but I always enjoyed seeing him. He was provocative, a good left-winger, a man of ideas and great love of life.

At the end of day's writing, I take H, Mary and Mary's good friend Rosie to the Duchess Theatre to see a one-man show about the life and work of George Gershwin by a man called Hershey Felder. A very pleasant surprise, marred only by protracted and noisy unwrapping of and sucking of sweets behind us. After the last one had been consumed there was a short pause followed by heavy snoring!

Up on stage a rather lame book was saved by Gershwin's incomparable music culminating in a great rendition of 'Rhapsody in Blue' – which Hershey's commentary revealed, Gershwin's Russian Jewish father had misheard as 'Rhapsody for Jews'.

Thursday, April 15th

Thank Eric for sending me (as an advance birthday present) a sheet music collection of Lumberjack Songs by one Elmore Vincent – The North-Western Shanty Boy.

Duck out of an offer from Nic Kent for me to present a new 'landmark' series on the Art of Drawing. I think I shall adopt a policy of rejecting any proposal that mentions the word 'landmark'.

Tuesday, April 20th

I walk up to Mexico Gallery to help celebrate their first anniversary in Fleet Road. Space in the studio now fully opened up. Mexican stuff on first floor and down below where Sangria is served, an exhibition of what they call Outsider Art. Not quite sure what this means other than access for artists who cannot get shown through conventional channels – homeless and helpless, but with a talent for art. I quite like what I see and buy a pic.

By this time a Mariachi band has arrived and reminded me how much I dislike Mariachi bands. Not so much the live music but their fixed grins, silly old macho poses and generally intrusive presence. I remember how sick of them we became in Mexico when we could hardly have a meal without them strutting up and blasting away at us. However, it all brightens up a damp Gospel Oak evening.

Wednesday, April 21st

In pouring rain down to British Museum for a Patrons of the Art Fund reception in the drawings and painting room.

A tall, geeky-looking man spoke wisely and wittily about the serious problem of funding new acquisitions. The Prints and Drawings department – one of three most prestigious of its kind in the world – is down to £5,000 a year for new work. Ludicrous, embarrassing and the sort of thing that future generations will have to have explained to them, because they won't believe it.

Thursday, April 22nd

It's a fine day, a little fresh but sunny skies and friendly clouds, so take off for a run at midday, then back for a quick lunch and change for Nigel Greenwood's funeral. Tom is the only one of our children who accompanies us (Will is giving a talk at Exeter College and Rachel is filming 'Changing Rooms').

Given our embarrassing record of late arrivals at any event involving death (Nigel Jones's funeral, George H's memorial at Henley, even Peter Cook's memorial service, which was only up in Hampstead), I organise cab early and we're outside Holy Trinity in Sloane Street with 25 minutes to spare.

Clearly a big crowd, and as I hover, waiting to be briefed about my pall-bearing duties, I have time to marvel at the mix of people Nigel knew. Hockney is in a group of three with the formidable Maggie Hambling who gives off a smouldering wariness, a complete absence of any hint of approachability, which I always respect, as she does good work.

Eventually they're all inside and like a group of nervous schoolboys the coffin party are briefed beside the bus-stop. An impatient, sergeant-major-like chief undertaker drills us as though we're complete incompetents who should never have been entrusted with such a task in the first place. He's probably right, and as we hoist Nigel aloft and try to juggle our feet to the right step I have the distinct feeling that I can hear Nigel's trademark laugh coming from inside the coffin.

It's a long way down the aisle until we reach the two trestles on which the coffin will rest. 'Don't kick the trestles!' hisses our instructor, in a stage whisper that could be heard at Peter Jones's.

For someone who was brought up in the church but, at the very least, rarely worshipped, this is a full-blown affair with choir, hymns, thundering organ, anthems, prayers, holy water sprinkled on the coffin, as well as a rather incongruous sixties' guitar-accompanied song which has [Nigel's daughter] Phoebe hiding a smile.

At the end of this hour-long solemnity, we have to raise the coffin, turn it so as not to knock over any of the tall candle stands, and carry Nigel out. Maybe it's the way the weight's distributed but it seems much harder work this time.

Once out of the church we're suddenly into real life again. Six red-faced men carrying a dead man in a box to a hearse parked at the bus-stop. The pavement's busy, chattering schoolboys are brought to a halt, and all I hope is that no one recognises me from Monty Python (where I first learnt to carry coffins).

It's here, though, beside this mundane, busy main road, that I see Phoebe and Judy and Sarah [Nigel's elder sister] and the girls shed tears for the first time. The tight, Greenwood-Palin control breaks down. Thank God.

Tuesday, April 27th

Phone interview with Good Housekeeping (a magazine I've always gone out of my way to help out – no political agenda, quite middlebrow, probably middle-aged and women; my audience, in fact). What books will I be reading this summer and why? 'Star of the Sea' by Joseph O'Connor, is my lead. Then 'Trawler' by Redmond O'H and 'Short History of God' by Karen Armstrong.

Lunch at Sheekey's. TG joins us for coffee. He is not happy with 'Brothers Grimm'. Has shown it in New York and though friends all loved it, the cards were not good and he had to endure being taken through it the next day by Bob Weinstein – frame by frame. He just wants out now – but has to provide a third cut (nine minutes have come out) before his contract is up in July. He's already talking fondly of next project – a low-budget four-hander produced by Jeremy Thomas.

TJ is writing a sequel to 'Knight and the Squire', and was asked to take part in a new musical of 'A Woman in White'. He turned it down and has since been very pleased to see that it's gone to Michael Crawford instead.

Talk tonight at the Highgate Literary and Scientific Institution. On general subject of my travels; only 100 allowed into the intimate, square lecture room, but an 'overflow' listen to it through an old speaker in the Reading Room.

Then some book-signing, and photos in the old library built in 1839 and a gossipy meal with Trevor and Valerie Grove at an Italian restaurant just along the road.

Valerie, Trevor and I have all met and talked with Blair at various times and unanimously agree that he has lost some of the style, enthusiasm and apparent decency that we all once admired. Valerie was pleased that she'd made him laugh! Otherwise, they seem to be obsessed with litter, and speak highly of the precision of the latest litter prods issued to the Highgate Society!

Walk home. After the heavy rain the air is full of good smells. Down Merton Lane and cut across the Heath. A gusting wind makes the trees look lively. No one about but lots of dark paths and bushes and I hold my umbrella ready in truncheon mode. In the wet, dripping darkness the Heath has a formidable presence. Dramatic, atmospheric. Wonderful. Find myself thinking that I would feel lost without the Heath and that perhaps I shall live beside it till I die.

Wednesday, April 28th

In the evening to the Albery Theatre to see Lee Evans and Michael Gambon in 'Endgame', with Dan and Laura Patterson. I've always resisted Lee Evans's Norman Wisdom-ish tendencies, but here, from the moment he comes in with his funny walk (and it is funny – and not spastic, which is the easy thing to do) he uses the stage superbly. His physical movements are precisely awkward and eloquent.

Gambon, who only moves when pushed in the chair by Evans, is still phys-ically powerful. He uses his hands as expressively as Evans uses his body and the pair of them held my attention completely. Loss, humour, dignity compromised, it was all wonderfully tight and also entertaining.

And I could see the Beckett in Python – which is probably why I responded so well.

[Cartoonist] Tony Husband rang on the scrounge for 'favourite jokes'. I said I didn't know any, but on the phone to Bleasdale this a.m. I heard a nice one – about the dyslexic, insomniac agnostic who lay awake all night wondering if there was a Dog.

Thursday, April 29th

Long dream in which I'm about to go to prison. I'm with the film crew, not the family, and they all seem to accept that I shall have to serve at least 18 months. I never know what for, but the feeling of what I shall lose, and the panic over how I shall go to the loo are vivid.

I manage to carve out a decent, if distracted morning's writing, then off to Ace to watch Progs 3 and 4 with J-P and Roger.

To the Sad Pub (aka the Grand Junction Arms) for a beer. Rog goes into hospital tomorrow morning to have a skin graft on his nose. 'So when do you think the big bomb will go off in London?' he asks, but no one's particularly interested in pursuing this one.

Friday, April 30th

Complete a look through and selection of Bhutan photos. I'm developing disturbing signs of Himalaya sickness – symptoms include inability to look at pictures of monks or mountains or men with very long horns without feeling deeply uninterested.

Sunday, May 2nd

Suffering a crisis of physical confidence after reading in Trevor Grove's book 'One Dog and His Man' – a witty, urbane paean to the Heath – that my 'flat-footed' style of running resembles 'a long-legged penguin being chased by a polar bear'. Like a pilot grounded after an accident, I feel I have to get back in the air again, so off I go this morning, taking care to use the toes and generally be a lot less penguin-like.

Thursday, May 6th

Down to World Wide in St Anne's Court to record more 'Ripping Yarn' commentaries. Terry has his fan club organiser there. A lanky girl from Nottingham.

We look at (and talk through) 'Whinfrey' (good jokes, no story), 'Curse of the Claw' (strangely satisfying) and 'Stalag Luft' (somewhere in between). I suppose it sticks out a mile that TJ should have had more involvement as actor and director. Unfortunately director was never on and of course the one thing I couldn't say as we burbled on was that I needed some space of my own, away from Terry, to develop my own way of doing things. Unfortunately I made a muddle of it. Still, there is some very good material and very funny ideas. Just a little difficult to sit through them all with the friend you elbowed out!

Monday, May 10th

To Abbott and Holder in Museum Street to have a look at Stuart Pearson Wright's Duke of Edinburgh portrait recently published in one of the papers. It is wonderful, the Duke made to look slightly, but whimsically absurd. Wright has stripped him of rank and authority and painted him with bare torso, covered with wispy greying hair and with a bluebottle perched on his shoulder. It's crisp, clear and beautifully effective. Unfortunately it was sold, almost immediately after it appeared in the paper, to a man in San Francisco for £25,000. I'd have paid that and more.

Up to dinner at the Doganises'. A middle-aged man in expensive dark trousers is halfway up the steps talking into a mobile phone (how long must he have had to make those calls in the chauffeured Merc?). It's a man referred to throughout the evening as Penrose, and he's the husband of Anne Robinson. Anne has had a second dose of cosmetic surgery and the skin is drawn tight as a lampshade across her little face. She looks like a hairless chipmunk.

Talk generally light and on the naughty side – Rigas [Doganis] remembers helping research one of his wife Sally's TV programmes by testing the services of local saunas. The sign: 'Requests of a sexual nature will be reported to the police' made him laugh a lot.

Tuesday, May 11th

A glum blanket of low cloud, nurtured by a north-easterly breeze, mirrors a glum time to be British. Continuing evidence of torture and mistreatment by the Coalition forces are just the shit on the cake of a dreadfully mismanaged

display of 'Western Strength' which now seems like arrogance and incompetence of the most dangerous kind.

The appalling Rumsfeld continues to draw a salary, the bumbling Geoff
Hoon equivocates for a living. Blair grins, Bush apologises, but these are masks,
surely, for some much deeper and more basic emotion. Panic. The trouble is
that when there's panic around, the leaders' fantasies and paranoias are only
intensified. The second casualty of war is sanity.

Thursday, May 13th

JC rings; do I have any more memories of the Fawlty Towers Hotel. He's addressing some conference in Toronto.

By coincidence I've been sent a clipping from a Toronto newspaper: 'I read
that Michael Palin of Monty Python fame died last year. Is this true?' I ask John
what he thinks. 'Not to my knowledge,' he answers, after some consideration.

Friday, May 14th

Warmth in the air. Dry, settled temperature rising to 70s. Almost a year ago to
the day the first shots of 'Himalaya' went in the can in Pakistan.

Up to Markos to have my hair cut. Danny the Lebanese man who does my
hair for £8.50 talks about life in the country and how it only really got back
to normal once it was free of foreign interference. Iraq seems to be in the same
boat.

Nice letter from Bleasdale thanking me for sending him 'Football Days'. He
talks of a boy telling his friend that Alan's really famous. 'He's been a question
on "Who Wants to be a Millionaire" *and* "University Challenge".'

'He's been a question,' muses Alan, adding, 'As no doubt I have been to many
people and few have found the answer. Least of all me.'

Saturday, May 15th

Whilst raiding 'American Friends' box I'm surprised by the generally rave reviews the film received here – all expressing delight and pleasure. Then I pick
up the Canby 'New York Times' review and realise that not only did it destroy
us in the USA, it left me feeling, in my memory's eye, that the film had been
something to apologise for – which it clearly hadn't.

Clear a lot of emails. No doubt about it – emailing doesn't save time, it eats
it up, voraciously, insidiously.

H and I watch Eurovision, on and off. It is like one long sketch about bad taste, saved by Wogan, and by a very good documentary on another channel analysing the importance of Picasso's 'Demoiselles d'Avignon' – a title he never gave it; he always called it 'The Brothel'.

Sunday, May 16th

Various errands including taking some of H's garden clearings to the recycling centre. As I tip my bags into an enormous skip a man next to me says 'You could make a garden out of all this.' One of the staff comes up to ask me to move my car and seeing it's me softens his approach. 'Do you know Ken Loach?' he asks. I mutter something about having met him a few times. 'Well, he's over there.' And there indeed is Ken, heading for the garden waste.

'A great leveller, this place,' he says as we mount the platform and talk about the Cannes Film Festival – he's got to go for a day next week – and the difficulty he's having making a party political broadcast for the Stop the War Party. It's not just that no one will give them any airtime, but that getting it right is so difficult – everyone has their own ideas of what should be said and how it should be said.

We're deep in conversation when he looks up anxiously. 'I've got my grandson in the car,' he says and rushes – well, Ken doesn't rush, he disappears – in a hurry. Britain's best, most honest, most prolific director drives off in what looks like a Ford Fiesta.

Monday, May 17th

Temperatures up to 80° today. Enervating combination of fatigue and heat makes concentration difficult. Prepare thoughts for my appearance tonight before the Player/Playwrights group.

Meet at the Horse and Groom pub in Great Portland Street. It is hot, but I enjoy my time with them. On my feet for an hour or more. Thoughts about writing – why I write, what I've learned, what are my weaknesses. A good focus for thinking about such things, which I rarely talk about. My conclusions about myself? Sketch-writing ruined my life. Made me lack confidence in longer work and lazy about structure and plot.

Thursday, May 20th

A note from Ken Livingstone lies on my desk asking if I would write something about his transport policies ahead of the election on June 10th. Another, longer letter from Neil at Camden Bereavement Service asking me to write to Jane Roberts and John Carrier in protest at the withdrawal of funding. But first an obligatory visit to a local school, Carlton, for discussions about doing some shows/presentations to raise money for them.

The school looks clean and bright, but the problem is falling rolls. Now down to 353, from 500 twelve years ago. No one wants to live in Queen's Crescent, she says. The old spirit of the place has been fractured, the white working-class supplanted by people from all over the world (which is what draws me to the school, I must say).

I feel sorry for them, they work so hard, yet I feel this hard, unforgiving, Chris Woodhead-inspired education-as-a-business approach is now coming to roost in all its ruthlessness. Carlton is a highly successful school that is going to the wall without anyone doing anything to help.

Friday, May 21st

No 'Himalaya' writing. Spend the morning composing a letter of protest to Jane Roberts, leader of Camden Council, and John Carrier of the Health Group responsible on behalf of the Camden Bereavement Centre. It's well-run, successful and filling an ever-increasing demand. Could there be a worse time than this to cut money?

This slog of a day much brightened by the news that within a couple of hours of my letter being faxed through a meeting has been arranged to discuss the matter and it looks as if the future of the service will be assured for two more years. I'll believe this when I see it, but it does raise the usual questions of celebrity being listened to more than common sense.

Wednesday, May 26th

To Wyndhams for [Michael] Frayn's 'Democracy'. I like the Wyndhams – a proper theatre, well, a proper West End theatre, good-looking and not brutal to the legs. Terrific first half and oddly disappointing second.

[Director] Michael Blakemore, his cream suit and white face making him seem like some boat under sail, drifts into the bar for a mineral water. He says he's writing a book of memoirs called 'Arguing with England'. I ask if he and Frayn are doing anything else together. He looks a little pained. 'I just want to stop,' he says, and then in that hopeless way that I understand so well adds, 'but you know, if there's something you can do'.

Sunday May 30th

Last night on the late news I heard that [playwright] Jack Rosenthal had died, so first I wrote a letter to Maureen [Lipman, his wife], then rang up Denis and Astrid [King] to find out more. Astrid very tearful, apparently they were both with Jack a few nights back. It was difficult and he was in much pain. At one point he'd leaned over to Astrid and with some difficulty got out the words 'I'm sorry I've not been good . . .' Astrid, thinking this was a reference to his whole life, broke in with reassurances, only for Jack to grab her arm and finish the sentence . . . 'company'.

Monday, May 31st

With H up to Jack Rosenthal's funeral at Golders Green Crem. We're on the side I don't know, which is the Jewish cemetery. A nice, friendly man offers me a yarmulke as we go in. Seems rude not to wear it, especially as it's a rather good shade of deep blue. Helen whispers that I don't need to wear it. Feel rather hapless, damned if I do and damned if I don't, but the sight of both [John] Alderton and [Tom] Conti their great manes of hair unencumbered, makes me think I would be better with it off.

Maureen is dealing well with everybody and I join a queue and give her a hug. She rather sweetly says that Jack and I had things in common. 'You were both shy people, well not "were" in your case, who everyone wanted to talk to.'

[Jack's daughter] Amy made a sweet and eloquent speech, full of humour and admiration and regret, and brother Greg (who earlier told me 'you're something of a legend in the travel industry') a short and unsentimental piece.

But what material Jack offered. A universally loved man with an extraordinary track record. A man who was fascinated by people rather than polemics, street life rather than systems. A rare talent he had for bringing forward the people in the background – and I identify with that.

Tuesday, June 1st

With H to a Courtauld Patrons' function. A small group of us. Nick Ferguson who I assume must be chairman of the Patrons is a jolly man. He talks very jokily about contributions. Yes, if you have a collection to bequeath to the Courtauld, you could have a room named after you. 'Give us 50 million and you can have the whole bloody building named after you.' I suggest something smaller. How about a door? How much would that cost? 'The Palin Doorway,' he muses, 'that's got a certain ring to it.'

Wednesday, June 2nd

At the desk by nine. Begin an edit of Bangladesh. First couple of pages depress me. I'm trying to say something big and meaningful, but as I'm always worse on the general than the specific, it reads clumsily. Take a knife to it, then some intricate stitching and it feels better.

At half past seven I have completed the revision. Watch Yentob on Hopper. They seem to suit each other in some way. Alan cannot but cut a vaguely sinister figure, the dark rider of the art world, and Hopper, in most of his appearances, looked pretty unhappy. Someone tried to make a case for his 'dry, ironic humour', but this wasn't a show for laughs.

Thursday, June 3rd

To tea with Alan B. I've been wanting to ask him about diaries – and diary publication; whether he's ever regretted going public, how he controls what goes out, etc. Also I just like to catch up with him every now and then.

He answers the door looking very dapper – in what look like moleskin trousers, some newish light-grey handmade shoes (though of course he'd never buy anything with the name Handmade attached) and of course his tie and sweater. The rooms seem even darker and more Moley than I remember. The patina of soft yellow-ish brown that seems to cover everything has deepened with the years.

We talk around things over a cup of tea. He's always got a good book-signing story. Today it's of a lady who comes close to the table and leans into him confidingly. 'I want to be buried in a little plot right next to yours,' she says. Alan replies with jocular reassurance, 'Well, that won't be for a long time yet,' and she replies with some indignation 'I don't know about that, I'm the same age as you!'

The 'History Boys' gave Alan pleasure. Such fun to do, he says, though he thinks the boys are pretty free and easy with him. 'I can't imagine them talking to David Hare like that,' he says with more relish than criticism.

He says that he and Rupert might be moving. Alan concerned about where he'll write. 'The place set aside for my writing room in the new house looks out onto a back wall. I mean, I don't think I can write without watching people go by.'

On the diaries he's positive. He thinks I should publish, bearing in mind that, as he says sagely, 'people will want you to be the way they like you'. A good editor is important, of course. Mary-Kay Wilmers at the LRB seems to do much of Alan's editing, but, he cautions, 'she wants to make sure I conform to how she wants me to be, so she takes out things.'

Before I leave, he mentions his illness and I ask him what actually happened. It was bowel cancer. He had a 50–50 chance of survival but when he came through it, they revealed that that had been on the optimistic side. It should have been diagnosed earlier. 'I didn't talk much about it because I didn't want to be a celebrity cancer victim,' he says.

Sunday, June 6th

Sixtieth anniversary of D-Day landings and a veritable orgy of remembrances – largely the result of a combination of our love of round-number anniversaries and the realisation that the men who stormed ashore in 1944 are now in their 80s and dying off at an accelerating rate.

But there's something potent about this particular event – it was a significant military and intelligence success and the psychological turning point of the late war – the earlier war being dominated by the German defeat at Stalingrad.

A service from Caen cathedral brings tears to my eyes before I'm even dressed, and its calm, un-triumphant tone moved me more than anything else I heard or saw.

Sunday, June 13th

Noisy night in the street. Shouts of 'Oi Michael!' wake me up at one point. The football supporting classes are getting very excited about tomorrow. The thing this year is flags of St George on little plastic poles stuck on to car windows, from which they flutter ungracefully. I don't mind the flags themselves but writing England on them is a shame and writing 'The Sun' on them is just plain horrible.

The evening is warm and pleasant and TG and Maggie and Jim Cuno come round for supper and I feel quite relaxed about the football. In fact, as England and France kick off in Lisbon I don't even bother to watch.

We eat in the garden and judge the state of the game from soundings. We hear the shout of joy from around the area which, when I check with the TV, confirms that England have scored. From then on, long silence and when I switch on again it's 90 minutes and England have at last conceded a goal. Moments later it's two. A turnaround of disastrous proportions for England. Rachel rings later, seriously upset.

There is complete silence in the neighbourhood.

Monday, June 14th

Off to Ace to watch the rough cut of programme six. The heat and the defeat by the French last night seem to contribute to a general lowness and the viewing does little to lift the mood. It's quite a shock to find a programme that just doesn't work and probably a good corrective after our general assumption of success each time we've put the previous shows together.

Bhutan is slow and flat. Surprisingly it's Bangladesh that lifts the programme. The colours are brighter, the people more interesting, the issues more relevant, and the presence of a city – Dhaka – is invaluable.

Surgery will be carried out over the next few days. This is a bit like England's next game. Heads must be raised, morale boosted, etc, etc.

An email from Michael Dover. 'I spoke to Ion [Trewin]. He'd be honoured and delighted to work with you on the diaries.' I'm honoured and delighted myself because I've huge respect for Ion. But I shall have to make a big decision – otherwise I shall be wasting his time.

Monday, June 28th

To Blacks. Terry tells me about Anna [Soderstrom, his Swedish fan]. She sounds formidable. 'She beats me in every argument.' She's learning French at Oxford, having mastered English in a couple of years. He would like me to meet her and we tentatively discuss a date later in the week.

Thursday, July 1st

To Carlton School at half past nine to talk to two assemblies about 'Himalaya'. As always, impressed and invigorated by the light and colour, the various things made by the pupils that decorate what could be gloomy corridors, and the enthusiasm they all show. Hands are up and straining skywards well before I've asked for questions.

I've brought props along including, very successfully, my Karamojong wooden stool from Uganda. It's made to be portable, so is light, but quite small for British bottoms. The children all manage it, but the teachers sprawl all over the place. Much laughter.

Friday, July 2nd

Another Basil evening at The Canteen. Bernardo Bertolucci is the star guest of the night. He is late. Word has just come through of the death of Marlon Brando and Bernardo has had to write an appreciation.

So it's just Bas and me and, eventually, a rather battered and bruised Terry G who seems to think he will have to come back to work on 'Grimm' in December, as the Ws are not happy.

Bernardo appears; smaller, less physically impressive than I'd somehow expected. His back is bad and he walks with a stick. As he sits down, I notice a wince of pain and his complexion is unhealthily pale.

His wife, Clare Peploe, is sat next to me and proves to be excellent company. 'I'm interested in just about everything,' she says, displaying eagerness rather than intellectual control. So we talk about all sorts of things – India, the success of Michael Moore's film in the US.

On my other side is Magda, Bernardo's one-time costume designer now amanuensis, and Nicolo, the Italian cinematographer who was sacked from 'Brothers Grimm'. He's like a wild, curly-headed boy – with loud laugh and unselfconscious enthusiasms.

Bernardo thinks that Brando's 'decline' began after 'Last Tango' (well, I suppose he would say that). He could never really match up to the power and freshness of his early work and celebrity depressed him. In other words, a trapped genius, who unlike Elvis and James Dean and John Lennon, had to live to grow old.

Monday, July 5th

Rested after weekend and ready now to take on the new discipline of writing and recording commentaries. On my otherwise relaxed journey out to Ace, a stationary car suddenly pulls away from side of the road right beside me, pushing its way into the traffic quite dangerously. I give it a blast on the horn. Instantly a rage-contorted face on the front of a short-cropped head appears from the window, snarling and screaming. 'Wanker!' it roars several times, louder and louder each time.

I'm clearly dealing with serious manic behaviour, so I keep well out of any argument and on we go. For at least a mile I get masturbatory gestures out of the window, sudden inexplicable brakings and general symptoms of powerful aggression. I ignore it as much as I can, but it leaves me shaken.

The sheer intensity of his belligerence suggests psychopathic tendencies, but I wonder if someone like that shouldn't be reported, not for his bad driving, but as a clear danger to the public. It's a bit like seeing a bomb with a sparking fuse attached. And it could have gone off in anyone's face. And maybe will, later today.

Tuesday, July 6th

Slowly, infinitely slowly, work my way through prog one. Trying to keep commentary tight, precise, light, informative, digestible, funny and harmonious. Leave off at six with less than half the ground covered.

Taxi to Frost's party in Carlyle Square. Usual mad jumble of well-known faces, almost a caricature of the celebrity event. This is Frost's world, Frost's technique embodied in a social event. Nothing too deep, nothing too close, nothing too critical, nothing too intimate – just lots and lots of encounters, like names on the fast-rolling caption at the end of 'The Frost Report'.

Having said that there are moments of enjoyment. Denis Healey, thin and old, but bright-eyed still, prowling through taking photographs of people he likes. One of which is me. 'I just love your programmes,' he twinkles, before moving on. I tell this to Ronnie Barker, who's looking a little pale and pasty, and he replies bleakly 'He said that to me too.'

I was quite happy to get away. Never even saw David [Frost] or Carina [his wife], but the wraith-like Thatcher passed close by me, like a ghost.

Tuesday, July 13th

Another shortish night. H has to be up early to make breakfast for Granny, who's not allowed to eat anything after seven. I know both are anxious – H more than she lets on, as it was she who suggested Granny should have the op.

She does her hair and then I see them both off to the Princess Grace Hospital at 9.30. Granny looking like a little uncertain girl going off to her first day at a new school.

Hear, about four, that Granny has had the op, and they've replaced the entire kneecap – the option that was always on the cards when they went in and saw the damage. Longer stay in hospital, more trauma, but it's done.

Helen goes in to see her in the evening – with Mary. She's on a morphine drip and they're a little worried that when she drifts off to sleep, her breathing slows alarmingly. Very woozy too. H quite concerned when she gets back and when Mary rings at 11.30 is thrown into momentary panic that it's the hospital calling to say something dreadful has happened.

Wednesday, July 14th

Wake early again. A surfeit of worries, none serious enough to deserve to keep me awake, which only adds to my irritation.

There's commentary recording for 'Himalaya'. Always an intense scrutiny for myself here. Voice under the microscope as it were, and I've never been able to approach the process without some trepidation.

Rog's evilly projecting nose, with its sarcophagus of plaster gradually getting filthier, makes him look like a cross between Hannibal Lecter and Worzel Gummidge. He's extraordinarily tolerant and good-natured about it.

Lunch/interview for Sainsbury's Magazine with Brian Viner at Vasco and Piero's in Poland Street. When I get there, the restaurant is packed and noisy but Paul [Vasco's son] allays my anxiety as I notice a table at the back all set up with a lamp on a stand and a photographer and assistant squeezed in by the door to the kitchen. 'They're all media people in here anyway, no one'll bat an eyelid.' And he's right of course.

The photographer treats me a bit like one might treat cattle: 'Let your eyes just wander up to me.' 'Now talk, just talk, using your hands.'

Wednesday, July 21st

Lunch with J-P at Blacks. We discuss our futures. He wants to do something with Gore Vidal before and during the November election. 'Probably the last thing he'll be able to do like that.' Gore is on a bottle of whisky a day and has difficulty walking.

I muse about a Middle East programme of some sort. I do want to travel more, but I'm less, indeed not at all, interested in building up the Palin personality – the least happy part of the process for me – and would rather use my abilities as observer and communicator to put more focus on others and less on myself. The Middle East *does* beckon.

Home and work on Commentary 2 as Helen goes down to visit her mother – who is improving (and talking more) by the day. The staff love her.

Listen to a Radio 4 half-hour in which Joan Bakewell chairs a conversation on lust. Faintly arousing, but Radio 4 doesn't really do erotic.

Tuesday, July 27th

Up to Belsize Park Station clutching a selection of the diaries for Ion T. He's a little late and I settle myself at a table at Mon Plaisir in Monmouth Street and read 'Prospect' and order a pastis and feel frightfully sophisticated.

A good, reasonable lunch. Carrot soup and pavé of haddock, a half-bottle of Pouilly Fumé and coffees. Ion has been asked by J. Julius Norwich to read Duff Cooper's diary. It's over a million words long and begins in 1918 and goes on till the '40s. Apparently JJN quite taken aback by the amount of philandering old Duff got into, not to mention his habit of writing them down in detail.

So I hand over my baby to Ion, three Sellotaped folders in a Daunt Books bag, and tell him to be ruthless. Not something that comes easily to Ion, I should think.

Friday, July 30th: Bath and London

Complete the book, well, the remains of the book, by 2.15 and I'm on the 2.52 back to London. Something called the 'Adelante' service. Smooth and quick, despite several stops. Railways so changed now. The service much less formal. Tall blonde girls are the new porters on Great Western. Much less strictness, or less *obvious* strictness about rail travel. And trains bustling everywhere, most of them full.

Saturday, July 31st

We've been invited out to a picnic by Jonathan and Pauline [Clyde]. Drive down around three; it's an hour and 20 minutes to the village of Bramley. An attractive, unpretentious red-brick farmhouse, eighteenth century − dog rose round the door sort of thing. Tiled floors, overgrown corners of the garden.

Olivia arrives. Though she is direct and down-to-earth, her vicarious celebrity life is complicated. She's been driven here in a black car and will be picked up later by another black car to take her to Dhani's birthday party at a club in Cavendish Square.

Much preparation, then drive up to Silchester, about two or three miles away. Important Roman settlement once upon a time and the enclosing walls still standing. We look in the church, walk round the walls; about two miles in all, then break out a picnic. Tuna cooked on a portable barbecue − delicious marinade. Olivia tells the story of how she and George met. Denis O'Brien [George's business manager] had hired Olivia to meet George and take him to the house they'd found in LA (in the same neighbourhood as Elvis P). She said she was a fan, but also rather sorry for George. He'd lost Patti, he seemed to have few friends with him.

She got him to the house after a drive from the airport in a car full of guitars (he was about to go out on the road). G didn't say much but when he got to the door of the house, or the courtyard anyway, he says to Olivia, 'So what d'you want me to do now, carry you over the threshold?' Olivia, still recounting the story as if she were the blushing groupie of 25 years ago, said, 'OK. Yes.' That, apparently, was that.

Olivia is picked up and whisked off, we trail back to the house, have some tea then hit the road. Dumbly, we take a wrong turn and find ourselves heading for the M3. After negotiating the same roundabout twice, I notice a big white van irritatingly close on my tail. Turns out to be a police van. He flashes me to a halt, then approaching rather as if he'd cornered Osama bin Laden, warns me that I have only one brake light working ('but we can't prosecute you for that') and was driving erratically. I explain I was looking for the M4. He solemnly takes my name, asks if I've had a drink and summons up a breathalyser from Basingstoke. I'm under the limit, but we're well out of our way and don't get home till nearly 12.30.

Tuesday, August 3rd

I've accepted an invitation to a Romaine [Hart] event at the Screen on The Hill at 6.30. A terrific downpour around 5.45. Not for long, but powerful and with the muggy heat, feeling tropical. Somehow this energises me and I set off up to Belsize Park, picking my way through the puddles.

The movie, 'My Architect', is utterly enchanting. The 'young man' is both director and star. He's Nathaniel Kahn, illegit son of Louis, as a result of one of Louis' three close relationships with vigorous, talented, highly intelligent women. Put together as a journey round my father, it works on so many levels. Architecture and emotion, humour and insight, all weave a beautifully told tale.

Saturday, August 7th

Hot, stuffy night; azure skies this morning. Some shopping, prepare house for visitors. Simon, Nancy and Tim here for lunch.

Tim very big. Still greets me with a hug and his lovely warm smile and Simon and Nancy always give the impression of being carefree, though I'm sure there are complications hidden beneath. Simon's acting career must be one of them.

I gather he was to audition for 'Spamalot', but something went wrong at the producers' end and he was never called back. Nancy shows her fiery side when defending him. I suggest that we're all too old to play Pythons these days. 'Tim Curry's not too old,' she returns, quite tartly. She's right and this reminder of his casting in 'Spamalot' stirs vaguely disquieting misgivings about the project as a whole. But still, Python can survive 'Spamalot' and if it's a big hit, we'll only benefit, so what's to lose?

They leave around six. H goes to look after Shirley's demanding cat (which has to have its milk warmed to a certain temperature). She's also looking after Jonathan and Bernie's goldfish and Sarah's garden [all neighbours].

New Statesman carries a risky piece about terrorists not targeting London because London is full of terrorists planning attacks on other countries. It is the most hospitable Western capital to all shades of opinion. Something to be proud of, or ashamed of. Answers on a postcard.

Monday, August 9th

Wake up, hot and uncomfortable, system clogged and dehydrated by too much wine, heat and dampness in the air. Back to sleep, but fitfully, short staccato dreams and not feeling much rested by morning.

Watch Rachel's 'Changing Rooms' after supper. Awful, over-decorated, fiddly rooms, but once again, R delivers a show full of bounce and good nature – an escapist half-hour very well realised and shot through, I think, with R's personality. Ring her up – Proud Dad.

Tuesday, August 10th

Cooling off as the rain comes down, in varying strengths, for most of the morning. Slow progress on the commentary. A lot of small interruptions and quite a lot of detail rather than narrative to write as we move through Tibet.

In evening Helen goes out and, as I'm going to present prizes at Gospel Oak gardens evening, Cathy G and Michael have come round to Granny-sit and cook supper. Michael runs me down to Clarence Hall, the residents' meeting place on the Clarence Way Estate in Hawley Road. First time I've actually ridden in the great red motorcycle sidecar that he lovingly created for Cathy G. Squeezed in my nacelle we roar down over the Grafton Road humps, my head sticking up and back at an angle, as if I'm in some flying dentist's chair. Heads turn. A dramatic arrival, but few to witness it as Michael drops me a little beyond the hall.

Fifty people have turned out for the awards, all of which are for gardens on the council's estates. After the presentations – silverware, cheques, etc – there is a ten-minute section for questions to Michael Palin on 'his life and work'. They're mostly written. The first is 'What's your phone number?' A blonde woman with heavily vamped eyes and a big nose winks at me as that's read out.

One of the winners, I'm glad to see, is a Muslim man. Unfortunately he disappears just before the presentation, leaving his young children to collect the award, and, in a very self-possessed way, assure me that he's just had to go out and pray.

Friday, August 13th

Take The Times up to Granny to read with her breakfast in bed. I point out the cheerful front-page story which suggests that 40,000 a year either die or suffer illness from the incompetence of doctors and nurses. We laugh. A hollow laugh as it turns out later.

I've had a heavy humming in my left ear for a few days and as it's persisted I've tried to get an appointment to see the doctor. For two days I can't even get through, but today I'm lucky.

The doctor sees some inflammation in my 'bad' ear, but an awful lot of wax in my 'good' ear, for which she prescribes bicarbonate of soda – 'We don't syringe any more,' she says briskly.

Take the first set of drops and continue typing up the commentary. About 5.30 take the bicarb drops for the other ear. An hour later I'm feeling a little dizzy and slightly nauseous. For a couple of hours I'm unable to move without lurching dizziness, causing me to grab at walls and banisters like a drunk. Worse, though, is a feeling of profound and ever-present nausea, which any movement only exacerbates. It's quite a relief when I actually do throw up.

After that all I can do is sit or lie still and hope whatever it is will pass. It doesn't. It gets worse. H rings NHS Direct and then the Camidoc Service. They tell me that it's caused by the treatment to my ears which has affected my balance, and he would, he says, not have prescribed two treatments at the same time. He thinks it should be gone by morning, which is all I want to hear.

One last retch brings up all the water I've drunk, plus the paracetamol he'd prescribed, with dam-breaking force. H leaves me to sleep it off. It's a very nasty turn indeed. Thank you, Doctor.

Tuesday, August 17th

Working day starts with an interview for a Polish newspaper to publicise the 'Sahara' book out there. A keen Python fan who sees and is highly intrigued by links between my 'defence' of the old British Empire, my education at Oxford and my part in the creation of Monty Python. I talk about the history of subversive opinions over the last few hundred years and that I regard their existence as an example of what's good about Britain. Thus talking myself neatly round to his theory.

A low-key day brightened by the arrival of the finished 'Himalaya' book, almost 14 months after I started writing it. Immensely satisfying to see a year's worth of paperwork, drafts, corrections, slide selections, design arguments, debates, schedule squeezes and the like all condensed between these two covers.

Thursday, August 19th

With the finished 'Himalaya' book nestling beside me as I write, and two-thirds of the TV series complete, I find myself with the unfamiliar sensation of time on hands.

Tube to London Bridge, walk through Borough Market (is it all getting *too* tidy?) and on to Tate Modern. A second and longer look at the Hopper. Very rewarding. I admire and enjoy the look of his paintings, and then there's the extra level of psychological intensity. The blowing curtains, the lurking presence of dark woods, the scouring, almost scorching light. Much to think about.

I walk along to the Hayward. South Bank freshly washed by a heavy shower, now the sun's out and the walk feels inviting. A brass band plays – not the old school of brass band but a sort of jazz brass band; lots of mostly black boys on trombones, etc. Lively.

To Lartigue exhibition [Jacques Henri, photographer] and his nonchalant, almost flippant visual observations of growing up a rich boy in France. Avedon was a big fan, and I can see why. Both society photographers with a highly original twist.

No word yet from Ion on the diaries – well, there were 200,000 words there, and he's only had them for three weeks.

Sunday, August 22nd

A fairly relaxed Sunday. Marcus [my nephew], Morag [his wife], Louisa [his daughter] and Camilla [my niece] all round in the afternoon. Marcus and Morag preoccupied with the lively, attention-seeking Louisa, now one and a bit. A head of blonde curls, and a definite propensity for male company. Usual talk about who she resembles. Camilla, as she stood at the front door, was breathstoppingly like Angela for a moment.

I must say it is bewildering to think that Marcus, Camilla and Jeremy were all raised, with great success, by a woman who had no self-confidence and felt she was a failure. How much I would love her to be here now – but then Louisa, who is a lovely, bonny child, is part of her and part of her legacy.

Wednesday, August 25th

To BUPA at Battlebridge House for a check-up. Everything is familiar and reassuring – to start with anyway. Sight, hearing, blood pressure, pulse, all normal. In the cycle test I feel positively Olympian – though it does only last eight minutes – and am deemed to be amongst the super-fit for my age.

Then down to earth. 'We have an issue here,' says Dr Musgrove – a worldly, well-dressed, genial middle-aged man – as he looks at my blood test results. 'You're anaemic.' The figures for haemoglobin and red blood cells and platelets all marked 'L' for low. They show a 10 per cent drop on two years ago. The figures mystify him – 'normally what might be caused by blood loss' – he can find no evidence of anything to indicate I'm losing blood.

He gives me a thorough examination, squeezes stomach and can find nothing to suggest a blockage. We discuss symptoms. Increased tiredness, low energy levels the most obvious. Of course I've felt tired recently, but have done whenever I've been working hard.

Home to ponder on these disquieting findings. I've never, in 24 years of BUPA tests, had such an anomaly. Immediately feel very tired. But there's work to do and letters to write and bills to send off and emails to answer so I shall need all the chi I have today.

Angela [Martin] says that BBC publicity are proposing doing a set of 'Himalaya' ads on 900 hoardings up and down the country. Will I be able to squeeze in another photo session next week?

Thursday, August 26th

Mike arrives to take me to a Radio Times cover photoshoot at Whipsnade. Two years ago it was camels, today it's elephants – Indian, I have checked.

The photographer Mark, who's done other covers, is sharp-tongued and nervously restless as he shoots. This isn't an easy one as, unlike me, the elephants are not going to do as he tells them. I work with one three-and-three-quarter-tonne female, who is brought in behind me, so I can't see much of what she's doing, but I feel the weight of her trunk coiling around my neck and occasionally tightening pressure around the shoulder – which I take as a reassuring sign of friendship, but is more likely to be a tightening wariness as the camera comes closer.

'That's it! That's the cover!' shouts a triumphant Mark on at least three occasions.

Thursday, September 2nd

A long morning's recording – the commentary goes smoothly, but various other bits and pieces to do for international versions, DVD, etc.

Lunch with J-P at Blacks. Talk more specifically than ever before about future plans. My most likely agenda is a clear year off in 2005 to let a bit of fresh air in and give me time to sample other areas beyond the travel documentaries. If nothing better comes up, I'd like to begin prep work on a new series in 2006, for delivery at end of 2007. Quite like the idea of Brazil.

Friday, September 3rd

Take advantage of a beautiful day to set out on my 25th anniversary run.

On September 3rd 1979, after some regular jogging at Sag Harbor and with the encouragement of Jim Fixx's book [1977 bestseller 'The Complete Book of Running'], I began regular running over the Heath, which, apart from breaks for travelling, I've continued for 25 years. It's helped me physically; more importantly, it's helped me mentally. The inner strength and relaxation that always follows such an intense physical effort – the endorphin-supplemented calm – has helped me deal with various degrees of anxiety, especially before big acting, speaking, public appearance days.

At one time I couldn't take on something like that *until* I'd run. This created a dangerous dependence, and I've weaned myself off any direct association between running and general performance. It's still a significant part of my life, though, and I take as much delight from my sylvan surroundings today as I did 25 years ago. I've never varied the course much. It is shorter than it once was, but it's basically about 50 minutes' hard work.[1]

Nicola Moody has suggested lunch. She's back from maternity leave and has seen the first three shows. She's very happy and thinks the BBC will be 'very proud' of the series. Quite swiftly off small talk and into her business which is to find out when I'll do another series, what it might be, and to reassure herself and her keepers that I'm not about to do a Michael Parkinson [who had just left the BBC for a brief spell on ITV]. On all counts I'm able to be reassuring. The 25th anniversary run has put me in a most benign mood.

Stella McCartney is at the next-door table with two older men in suits. We chat as I leave. She wants to do a job swap with me.

---

1 Jim Fixx died aged 52. Of a heart attack, whilst running.

Tuesday, September 7th

To work on commentary. Early cloud breaks up. Good-looking day. So much to write, sequences seem to soak up the words.

To see [dermatologist] Jeremy Gilkes about my back and the itchy spots that haven't responded to treatment. Yes, quite seriously worse, he says, peering and fingering. It's eczema (I can't even spell it) and needs a thorough assault of regular treatment. Tell him I'm not so happy rubbing steroid cream on my back and he prescribes a different preparation. Steroid free, but expensive, tube cost £36.

Have been given a tape of finished Show 4 and watch it before supper. I'm enchanted by it. Drawn in to the world of Tibet which has a unity and harmony of visual scale (Nigel's crisp, clear colours are work of someone at peak of confidence). It's exotic and engaging – the Sonam, yak-herding sequence at Yushu has a lovely intimate quality. Tibet works because it puts me in with a rarely seen, but eye-catching and intriguing group of people, and makes them accessible – brings them out. I think, though I may be overreacting, that this episode is one of the classics.

Friday, September 10th

Today I have the irksome task of signing books at [Orion's warehouse] Littlehampton. As usual, the best part of a tediously laborious day is the gossip about others. Susannah [Constantine] swears like a trooper, neither she or Trinny [Woodall] sign their full names – the latter just T and a kiss. Ian Rankin they like, but he's a bit of a wild boy. At the last signing he consumed an entire bottle of Scotch, with Cokes, as he signed. Yann Martel ('Life of Pi') is 'intense' and his visit next week is not much looked forward to.

By 5.45 I've completed about 2,100 signatures. Then there are posters to sign and at last I'm free.

Tuesday, September 14th

Try to buy tickets for 'History Boys' but almost totally booked out for foreseeable future so call Alan who promises he'll get me six for two weeks' time. I ask how his new house is going. He says the builders have become so popular in the neighbourhood that he sees little likelihood of them ever moving out. 'And one of them's a playwright,' he says.

Monday, September 20th

To lunch with David A at Assaggi. A fierce squally shower hits and we both arrive looking as if we'd completed pieces to camera on Tierra del Fuego.

I feel I've rather forced D to the lunch, but I needed to see him before our on-stage performance at the RTS [Royal Television Society] tomorrow. He's clearly rushing about – just back from Kentucky and off to Ecuador next on his latest bug series. His enthusiasm is tempered by doubts about how best to hold an audience for five hours with only insects to look at. He also seems aware of the competition. He maintains I don't have any but he does, which is hard to believe. I think it's the technology which he feels might be copied.

Tuesday, September 21st

Very uplifting email from Christine Walker at the Sunday Times about my 'Mountains' piece. More than grateful, she seemed to discern something special, particularly in the opening descriptions of Sheffield childhood. Maybe I should buckle down to a memoir. Still no word on diaries from Ion.

A run at four. On the way back I meet Alastair Campbell. He is training for the Great North Run, an up and down half-marathon in Newcastle. He took part in the Ethiopian Marathon – 15,000 official entries, 20,000 unofficial, all squeezed through potholed streets of Addis. He loved it.

Apart from a tendency to stand a little too close when talking to you, I have a sneaking liking for the man. There's interest and vitality and a lack of pretension and pomposity. He thinks perhaps he should start a support group for people who've changed career in middle age. Says he finds it hard to start the day without a list of things to do and jobs to tackle.

To the RTS. David and Susan (David's daughter) already there. I have taken the gamble of playing the humour potential as much as possible and David goes along with it as well. He's a great storyteller. He's relaxed, it's the end of the day. He's not going to be given a severe grilling. This is a celebration and that tone carries us through what seems a highly satisfactory 45 minutes – then questions.

Afterwards we sign some autographs and I suggest a meal which seems exactly what David's up for. We go to L'Étoile. Elena greets us with great joy. She tells me that all the reservation books she ever kept at Bianchi's have been, on Melvyn Bragg's advice, sent to the Museum of London.

Friday, September 24th

To a studio in Gosfield Street to record my links for a four-part BBC Four series of Peter Cook's work – trawled from the archives. It should be much more
satisfying than the recent TV biog of Peter in which, as each clip was getting
into its stride, we cut to someone telling us why he was so funny.

Thursday, September 30th

Train to Leicester Square and walk through to Rules. A young man stops me
on the way with a brisk 'Excuse me?' When I turn to him, perhaps ever so
slightly irritated, his jaw drops and he seems lost for words. 'You're Michael
Palin.' I nod. 'What can I do for you?' 'Well, I just wondered if you knew where
the nearest Abbey National branch is?'

Friday, October 1st

To LBC in Marylebone for a half-hour on the Danny Baker morning show. It's
a fresh, original approach. The studio is hung with trails of faux autumn leaves.
Danny conducts much of the interview standing up and, though it's not strong
on formal information, it's bright and literate and once I pick up the pace, it's
a joy after the plodding story-recounting that's my usual lot.

I pick up a copy of the Independent to read over breakfast at RIBA [the
Royal Institute of British Architects in Portland Place had, for a while, one of
the best restaurants in some of the finest rooms in London]. The Sue Gaisford
piece is good, addressing the book carefully and enjoying my 'Autolycus' side
– 'a snapper up of unconsidered trifles'. It makes warming reading, alongside
an excellent mixed grill in a room half of which has display of entries for the
Stirling Prize. An experience like this is probably as close to any of the fantasies
which filled my mind in those cold mountain lodges of Tibet with only mo-
mos and dahl for breakfast. And lunch. And . . .

Down to the South Bank to see 'The History Boys' at the Lyttelton. Full
house and it deserves it. A long play – three hours (though Richard Griffiths
who is in the central role says Alan first delivered five hours) but delightfully well-played. Teaching – the old ways of making the boys recite poetry by
standing on the table – is an angry cry from Alan against modern, unfeeling,
target-led education. Education not for life but for passing exams.

Go back to see Richard afterwards. He is very big and his dressing room is
very small – as are the wages, he says, rather ruefully.

Saturday, October 2nd

At BH by 9.30. Sandi Toksvig, dressed down as if she'd just come in from the garden, but I suppose that's the joy of radio. She's organising a birthday party for her 14-year-old this afternoon. Apparently under instructions to 'get everything ready, but stay in the kitchen'. Easy to talk to. She knows about travelling, presenting and comedy and the half-hour goes very swiftly by.

Helen reads me almost the perfect preview – this one in The Times, which Will alerted her to. 'It would be impossible to recommend this series too highly.' All adds to the general glow, but I can still hear ominous chords reverberating somewhere.

Sunday, October 3rd

Exercise has been a casualty of the last feverish week and so set off this morning in calm and autumnal conditions. Meet the 'We Love You, Michaels' head on in the Lime Avenue. [A class of middle-aged ladies who exercised on the Heath on Sunday mornings. One of them spotted me as I toiled, sweatily, towards them and shouted 'I love you Michael!' Now they all do it.]

We watch the first of the 'Himalaya' series go out at Roger's. It's pouring with rain when we set out for Acton – reminding me very much of conditions when we went round there two and a half years ago to watch the first Sahara show on the night the Americans bombed Afghanistan.

Have to go round the Shepherd's Bush roundabout to give H her first sight of one of the hoardings with the Great Leader's visage thereon. I still can't quite distil the essence of my feelings on seeing my face, lit up, 10-foot-high at major road-junctions. I want to laugh. Laugh at the huge, rich, silly absurdity of it all.

Monday, October 4th

First exposure to the critics – as opposed to the previewers – over breakfast. The Guardian ironic. Very Guardian, very irritating. The Independent seems equally disappointing, and that worries me more because I like Thomas Sutcliffe's stuff. From all the people, scenery, culture on show in the first episode, he picks up on alliteration in the commentary. Neither review is thoroughly or consistently bad – it's as if they want to be, but can't. But they're intellectuals and there's nothing intellectuals mistrust more than popular success.

Still, my mood is verging on the gloomy as I take the first of two calls from Australia and give half-hour interviews to Sydney and Melbourne.

The fax rattles into life and a handwritten page emerges. I reach over and pick it up. 'Michael – 8.6 million! Brilliant, love Nicola Moody.'

8.6 is the overnight; she is certain it will hit 9 when all the VCRs are count-ed. Whatever, she is jumping for joy. Bobbing about on the waters of relief and realisation (oh no, alliteration strikes again!) that we have successfully scaled the top of a *very* high mountain today.

Tuesday, October 5th

After lunch, on the Underground to Covent Garden and the office. It's buzz-ing with people. A film crew setting up in the conference room to shoot an interview for a documentary on Spike. The interviewer is Jane Milligan, Spike's daughter. A down-to-earth girl, lives in Highgate, does some acting and sing-ing. She doesn't seem complicated and has a refreshingly unneurotic view of her father. A man she loved who could be difficult – and (like Peter Cook and John Cleese now I come to think of it) liked to pick on someone and pursue them – the objects of their humour (and scorn?). Jane was touching. She said she always felt I was the closest to the spirit of her father's humour.

At four this is over and I'm rushed downstairs where there is something in the air. Some heightened, near-hysterical pitch in an otherwise merely frazzled office. The news is that the book of 'Himalaya' has gone straight to the No. 1 spot, ahead of Robbie Williams's biog – with sales of 11,000 plus. Never before have any of my books reached No. 1 ahead of the series starting so this is very thrilling for all concerned – and for me, frankly unbelievable.

Wednesday, October 6th

To the first public signing of the campaign. Organised by Condé Nast Traveller at WHSmith in Kensington High Street. Angela is downbeat about it but, when Mike and I arrive, there's a queue squeezed up against the temporary wall of the shop next door, running down to the corner of Phillimore Gardens and still half an hour to go. Three bouncers stand guard around me, shaven-headed and arms crossed identically in front of them. They exude menace, but are soft as putty, fetching me coffees, advising punters on which page the book is to be signed and generally being powerfully obliging. I think of the Dalai Lama dealing with his line of 700 pilgrims in McLeod Ganj and know that scribbling a name without looking up isn't an option.

Friday, October 8th

Tom is 36 today. Seems scarcely possible.

J-P calls and quotes a rave review in Broadcast. '"Palin is wise",' he reads. 'When have you ever had that written about you?'

Saturday, October 9th

To Broadcasting House by 10.30 for the Jonathan Ross show. I know I'm not really going to shine this morning. The last weeks and days leading up to and beyond transmission have been demanding, and I feel calm but uninspired. Don't feel up to comedy sparring.

As it is, JR, effusive in purple suit (for radio?), is not lost for words, loves me and the show and I'm happy to let him chatter on. He also plugs the 'Ripping Yarns' and says he's going to play it to his young son tonight 'because he ought to know about these things'.

Monday, October 11th

Out in the evening to Daily Telegraph Travel Awards. Enormous throng of people. Graham Boynton, travel editor, seems rather anxiously jolly as if he's organised something out of his control. And he has. They seem to have tried to inject a touch of Las Vegas razzmatazz – quite unnecessarily.

I'm given a 'serious' award. Voted for by 'the editors' of the newspapers and Graham B gives a flattering citation. As soon as it's in my hand I squeeze out of the crowd, find Paul and we make off to the Neal Street Restaurant where Michael D, Helen and Ruth [Michael's wife] are waiting.

In addition to my award on the table – later stuck under a chair – Michael has brought a long panegyric from, of all people, A.A. Gill in the Sunday Times, who, in a rather potty, but gratefully received review, calls me a cross between Katherine Hepburn and Candide. I'm also 'a great good thing'.

Tuesday, October 12th

Late afternoon hour at the gym. An evening to myself. These solitary moments are rapidly diminishing and I clutch at them gratefully, like a swimmer coming up for air.

Saturday, October 16th

J-P rings to draw my attention to a front-page story in the Independent about plans to dam the Tiger Leaping Gorge, which will displace 100,000 Naxi and destroy much of their land and villages. It's seen as a chance for the revived Chinese environmental movement to try and influence big planning decisions. Extraordinary timing. Yunnan means nothing much here, but in two weeks it will get a major boost from the series.

Friday, October 22nd: Baslow–London, end of Himalaya book-signing tour

Hear more wind and rain in the night. Sleep well and up soon after eight. Greyness over green grass and drystone walls as I peer out of my curtain.

The Cavendish Hotel, familiar to me as The Peacock, underwent rebranding in the mid-'70s when the Devonshires, I suspect under 'Debo's' influence, took firm control of the tourist potential of Chatsworth estate, and of the Mitford connections as well. I'm in Jessica – one of a series of rooms named after the girls. Angela is in Unity – whose second name, I note, was Valkyrie.

Yesterday, in a storm in Chesterfield, with buyers coming in soaked and windblown, I signed – and sold – 847 copies at the Peak Bookshop – a proud, now ecstatic independent. Not since '80 Days' have I experienced quite such an intense and rather thrillingly unquantifiable reaction to anything I've done.

Thursday, October 28th

Alyce Faye's 60th birthday party at Bibendum, which, with impressive generosity, JC has hired for the evening. John is having to organise the entertainment – which will take the form of eight speeches, all ordered to be short and irreverent where possible. 'You're Number 8' says John with a touch of fond malice.

Michael Winner's lady is good company. Michael is quite happy to talk of his disastrous book-signings – he has an autobiography out at the moment and goes from bookshop to bookshop by helicopter. It's not only expensive but unlikely ever to be recouped. 'I found one place where all my books were in the back passage – the whole of the front of the store was filled with your stuff.'

John is relishing his role as ringmaster and the more confident he is about the ability of the speaker the ruder he is about them. [Broadcaster] David Hatch is before me, and I get the 'never stop talking' intro. 'Do order your taxis now because Michael Palin will be the last speaker.'

Monday, November 1st

Out to supper with Dan Patterson. Meet up with Clive Anderson on the door-step and later joined by Angus Deayton and Lise, Steve Abbott [my manager] and Nicola [his wife] and Stephen Fry.

Dan leaps around like a frisky, overexcited puppy. He loves stories and jokes and humour so much that there are few other pickings to be had. Mind you we start with our own embarrassment as the chocolates that Helen grabbed for us to take to our hosts, turn out to have written on them (and not visible until the box is opened) 'Thank you, Michael x'. They must be out of the 'Parkinson' goody bag. Anyway, great mirth and, at the end of the evening, quite a good anagram game as the letters on the chocs are eaten one by one!

Friday, November 5th: Amsterdam–London

Reading 'A Sunday at the Pool in Kigali' [novel by Gil Courtemanche] at half past one after a day of nine long interviews, three photoshoots, a one and three-quarter hour slide talk and a book-signing.

This morning I have only to get myself back home. The morning paper has Bush triumphant and trying not to squint. Is it my imagination or is he becoming a touch more fluent – less nervous with words? Anyway, I'm over the anxiety I felt on Tuesday night and the ratty gloom I felt on Wednesday morning. I just avoided listening or reading too much. I didn't want to hear any more of the primal roar of the Christian right. God help us all if they run America these next four years.

Uncomplicated flight home. Michael Heseltine sits next to me. He doesn't seem keen to chat, so we remain in our separate worlds. He reads the Daily Mail from cover to cover and as soon as we've landed in London snaps open his mobile and begins to make calls. As the plane has arrived early and there are no 'stair-drivers' to help us disembark, we're all in limbo. He keeps asking to be put through to 'the Planning Department'. 'I want to know about a decision taken last night by the Planning Department?' He doesn't seem to be having much luck.

Mountains of mail at the office. Many from those who couldn't get to see me at signings – including a heartrending letter from a child who was reduced to tears when not allowed in at Lincoln.

Fireworks night and the explosions – crackles, thuds, thumps, whirs and shrieks fill the smoky air for several hours. H and I walk up to Ravel – very happily – past a group of lads from the council estate flinging fire at each other and grunting hoarsely.

Eat tagine, drink soup and a half-bottle of Rhone and sleep very deeply through almost the entire 'Ten O'Clock News'.

Saturday, November 6th

A good gathering of the clan before I leave for the Antipodes tomorrow. Rachel very tired after her last 'Changing Rooms' shoot in Boscastle, but happy with the way it went. Tom and Rachel never seem to change much, the more volatile Will in extremely good mood after a week away from the museum. He takes his work very seriously, is conscientious – but I think doesn't leave himself much time for all the other life-enjoying experiences in which he wants time to indulge.

November 7th to November 27th: NZ/Australia book publicity

Sunday, November 28th

A long night's journey into day. After 14 hours in the sky, chasing the darkness all the way from Singapore, my NZ–Australia 'Himalaya' tour comes to an end as our 747 settles onto the Heathrow tarmac at a quarter to seven. It's dark outside and the rain is coming down, but after a 24-hour journey from sunny, hot Brisbane I'm desperately glad to be home.

Tuesday, November 30th

Some anniversaries. Two years ago I first came up with the idea of 'Himalaya'. A year ago I was completing my last day's filming in Yunnan, and the end of the fourth episode and the most gruelling five weeks of filming I've ever undertaken. Today, I'm on the phone to Angela M to bring her up to date on my antipodean adventures when an email from Michael D – in big, red, festive numbers – reports a sale of over 53,000 copies of the book in the last week. The overwhelming scale of 'Himalaya's' appeal is wonderful, but I feel strangely bloated – as if in the not altogether healthy throes of surfeit.

It certainly sets me in good mood for my only appointment on this recovery day, which is a delightful one – lunch with Sarah Miller at the Wolseley.

Of course, what lunch in one of London's most fashionable watering holes would be complete without a sighting of A. Yentob. Such is my current status that he is soon over to our table; as it happens he's accompanied by Peter B-J [Peter Bennett-Jones, top talent agent]. PBJ, ruddy-faced and very English, contrasts with the dark, bearded features of Yentob in a way which should surely have delighted a renaissance painter. Alan purrs amusingly and digs away to try and uncover my future intentions. Talk of Brazil – well, it's worth flying a kite – and Alan goes away nodding approvingly.

To the Royal Academy to see the William Nicholson exhibition. Just my sort of thing – skilful use of paint, portraits and landscapes of various eye-catching styles and the great canvas depicting the Canadian generals in the First World War. He comes across as an undogmatic eye – full of interesting nuances and love of light – and, I suppose, of British subjects.

Am beginning to fade as I eat my fishcakes (H being out with her friends) and look forward to an early bed when Terry J rings, tells me he's now living in Highgate, and could he drop in. He's on his way back from a Roger Graef premiere of the Amnesty 25th anniversary film and says it was so crowded he left almost immediately.

Al asked Terry to give up Anna or leave the house. He chose to leave. He says he knows the whole situation makes him look rather foolish, but he's spent his life making sure everyone around him is happy and now he's going to do something for himself.

Tuesday, December 7th

Weather low, grey and dreary. No air movement and London smells like an old rubbish bin. And we have the appealing prospect of our least looked forward to signing venue – Lakeside Retail City in Essex. And as we head into the unwelcoming, slightly menacing gloom of the Thames gateway redevelopment, cheering news comes in from Michael Dover. In the last reporting week 'Himalaya' has continued to outsell any other book in the country. I watch as Angela writes down the numbers on the margin of her newspaper: 67,000 weekly sale.

The Lakeside complex at West Thurrock is a car park surrounding domes and gallerias – but all done on the cheap. We park up at a loading bay around which blows the remains of packaging – paper, cardboard, plastic, gently stirred by the breeze. On the way back I get Mike to drop me off at the Courtauld where I climb the stairs to look at the Manet 'Face to Face' exhibit – two enigmatic but fine Manet canvases opposite each other compared and contrasted in detail. I walk through the courtyard to Somerset House. White tents along one side offer tables and refreshment and behind them a line of flambeaux on tall poles, a Christmas tree and, at the heart of it all, the skating rink.

Seen from the windows of the Courtauld, up amongst the Fauves paintings, the scene looks like another canvas. Down on the ground it's like being backstage at the theatre. Noise, sparkling light, activity, but all of it somehow restrained, like a private house party given by hosts of immaculate taste.

Walk out onto Waterloo Bridge, the Thames at high tide; I like the fact that in the heart of the capital is a huge area of real estate, composed entirely of dark and murky water. Turn back from the bridge – aware that I'm the only one standing staring into the water below and worried that they may mistake me for a suicide.

Wednesday, December 8th

To Daunt's talk and signing. The shop with its Edwardian green glass lamp-shades looks inviting and they have squeezed 120 people around the staircase and in the galleries at the back. Heads peep over the gallery rail reminding me of Sickert's paintings of the Music Hall.

On stage for over an hour. A relaxed talk to an audience who've already taken glasses of wine and seem very appreciative. The shop, to its credit, is not particularly geared to bestsellers and you never see stacks of one book around. The ethos is about all books and all authors, rather than a few high-flyers.

Saturday, December 11th

To the Owl [Bookshop in Kentish Town] where I sign books down in the basement, talking to Gary the shop manager about our various literary pref-erences. He's just started on Dickens – feels as a bookshop manager he ought to – and is reading 'Pickwick Papers'. His son enjoys the stories too. Must make an effort that way myself.

Having completed this subterranean signing, I walk up to Kentish Town and down on the Tube to Green Park to repeat the process at Hatchards. Drop a contribution into the Salvation Army box as a small band plays carols outside Fortnum's. A tuba player recognises me and grins.

Tuesday, December 14th

Dental start to another crowded day. Martin Gough at 9.30 to investigate cause of pain. He finds that the bridge on my lower right side is loose and in re-moving it half the supporting tooth breaks off. He cleans out the root and it looks as if I shall have to invest in some more implants. As it is I'm three teeth short now, and a Weidenfeld & Nicolson meal at Rules in about three hours' time.

A reward for us all this meal, though I'm given the additional bonus of a magnum of 1996 Chateau Latour. Michael says they consulted with no less than Hugh Johnson over this choice! However, the book sales last week are, according to provisional figures, down by a few thousand, but still over 60k.

The old problem of expectations. If you sell three books one week, you hope to sell five the next, and are delighted if you do. If you sell 67,000 you're eying 70k+, and are disappointed if you don't.

Home, and set to completion of my appeal for the Farm Africa carol service. Only ten minutes, they said, but getting it right is crucial. Not too many figures, keep some humour, find an emotional note which is convincing and not shrill.

Taxi to Chelsea. The event is at St Luke's Church, an enormous, neo-Gothic place – a bit severe on the outside, and inside a tall, groined ceiling and a scale that reminds me of King's College or some of the great Dutch interiors. Apparently it's full – 'Sold Out' reads the sign on the door. Pevsner says the place holds 2,500!

I'm shown to the front row and sat next to Christie [Peacock] of Farm Africa. In the pew on the other side is Michael Portillo, who's reading a lesson, and Tony Britton, the actor – another reader. Portillo comes across, shakes hands in a chummy way. I get the impression he still thinks of himself – and indeed behaves – as a natural prime minister.

It's all rather grand and overwhelming as the lights dim and the solo verse of 'Once in Royal David's' soars up to the rooftops. I feel a peculiar mixture of intense nostalgia and cultural dislocation. And aware that I haven't a tie!

Think back to one of my first public appearances, as a reader, at age nine or ten, at the carol service in Ranmoor Church [in Sheffield] – and what torture it was and how my knees wobbled. Here I am, about to address thousands – in Chelsea – for at least ten minutes. George Alagiah reads a Churchill piece, 'God Rest You Merry' begins and ends and I walk up to the lectern, rest my notes on the great brass eagle and begin my message – which is that small solutions have more lasting effect than grand initiatives. I'm rewarded with the first round of applause of the evening.

Wednesday, December 15th

It's a fine morning and I take one of the short, sharp bouts of exercise that have been so infrequent these past six breathless weeks.

Back in time for a BBC Radio Wales interview, and arrival of Ion T at 2.30 to discuss the diaries. Settle him down on the sofa upstairs (having hoovered it dry of cat hairs). Edith takes quite a fancy to Ion and settles herself down on his papers.

He notes all the descriptions of meals and remarks: 'you did drink a lot' – but he says it in quite a merry way, but also in a way which suggests much of my dietary information would be the first to go! He's sensible on the publication schedule – it couldn't, in his opinion, be ready before 2006. We talk for a couple of hours. I really do my best to test Ion's keenness to take this on, but he is happy, indeed, looking forward to the task. We agree on a chronological approach (1969-81 being suggested parameter for first volume).

He makes the point that, although he's edited diaries for years, every one is different as every one reflects the character of the diarist. An obvious point maybe, but I think what he's trying to say is that there are no rules for the presentation of a diary.

So he walks off down the village, and I feel as I did the day Will Wyatt left the house having delivered the invitation to do 'Around the World in Eighty Days', that this might be the start of something.

To the Stammering Centre Christmas party. All well – the Centre thriving. Lena [Rustin, speech and language therapist] is there – the heart and soul of what it's all about, but she's thin and fragile and it's sad to see a fighter fading. I have a good talk with her and hold her hand – her skin feels fragile and papery like my mother's did as she grew older, and I feel that I'm holding her hand for the last time.

Thursday, December 16th

Things have been oddly quiet after our lunch on Tuesday and it was Steve [Abbott] who revealed last night that not only are sales of 'Himalaya' down but we've been knocked off the No. 1 spot by 'Da Vinci Code' and Sheila Hancock's memoir of John Thaw. Rumbles in the jungle.

Prepare the evening's entertainment at Carlton School – a 'Himalaya' talk with slides in aid of school funds. Feel I have to push myself on to make one last effort, even though physical and mental faculties feel to be desperately flagging. As it turns out, it's one of the very best occasions of all the 'Himalaya' events. The school shines and sparkles and the corridors and passageways are full of posters, collages, photo-displays (there's a board dedicated to me!) – all the work of the children. A stage upstairs and a full take-up of the 220 tickets available. All this atmosphere brings out one of my happiest performances.

Friday, December 17th

The three months of concentrated publicity and book-signing are over and I can face today without having to think of getting somewhere, scribbling on something, or gauging the length of yet another talk.

It's raining heavily, for the first time this month, which I take as divine indication that it's all right to stay at home. Cards to deal with, emails too, no peace at Christmas up in my room. But it is comforting to be at home and not have to go anywhere.

H goes to see her surgeon. He thinks her right knee is in quite a serious mess and may decide on a completely new knee. He also feels that an arthroscopy would help remove the fragments of cartilage which are on the move inside it.

Sunday, December 19th

Out to meet Rachel for one of her film outings. This time to BAFTA to 'The Sea Inside' – a Spanish film about euthanasia, based on real events and set in wild and rather seductive Galicia. Well-played, a little long, and a score which definitely places it as a popular film rather than an intellectual teaser or mood piece. Rach goes off to Putney with various Christmas presents, I return home, feeling pleased that my daughter and I get on so well.

It's been a cold, bright, lovely winter day and the night is clear and the sky starlit as I set out to walk across the Heath to the Pryces' party. I love the walk. Not only the physical exercise, but the silence in which to let the imagination roam. A half moon makes the ponds I pass less threatening and I'm passing Highgate School in less than half an hour from home.

Terry and Maggie are there and I haven't seen TG since he left for Canada. He's done the film – 'on time, on budget, and I've just seen it and it's a piece of crap!' – and now has two movies to finish editing. I tell him I'm taking a year's breather. 'Well, now you can write the "Water Music" screenplay' – from small acorns mighty trees do grow I think to myself as I head back across the Heath, in the freezing air.

Tuesday, December 21st

Chilly, grey but dry. Must do some running before Christmas and this morning seems the right time. Am padding along towards the Ladies' Pond when I notice the doors of the mysterious Water House opening and a car emerging. I've watched the creation of this house as I've run by over the years and eagerly seize any opportunity to peer in when the doors open.

Then I realise that the figure by the car is Terry J. The Water House is Simon Moore's house and this is where Terry is now living since he left Camberwell. He's off to counselling. 'What's going to happen?' I ask him. 'I don't know,' he says, 'maybe the counsellor will tell us.'

He shows me the house, with a large, secluded lawn in front of it – modern, but not too modern; looks rather good. We agree to meet for a drink. Terry goes off to South London and I carry on to Kenwood.

The West Meadow is particularly striking today. Silent as a graveyard with mist forming a wall as it clings to the leafless trees. Wintry and atmospheric. How can people fly away from quiet beauty like this?

Christmas Day

All the children come round during the morning to unpack their Christmas bags. Will, after his ten-day holiday in Spain is on very good form, and everyone seems less worn out than usual. Fill the cars and drive round to Albert Street.

Twelve of us with Eve and Esther [daughters of Helen's niece Catherine] in attendance – Esther asleep when we arrive, a small, white-wrapped bundle down by the coat rack, looking like yet another present.

Michael Stratton [H's sister Cathy Gibbins' partner] arrives on his way back from looking after the down-and-outs of Cricklewood. 'They've had their Christmas dinners and now they're regurgitating them on the pavement,' he'd told me cheerfully on the phone.

Back at Julia Street by quarter past nine. I get sidetracked, just before bed, by a lovely Radio 4 prog called 'The House'. Sounds of life in a long barn in Suffolk: Roger Deakin communicating it well. And on the answerphone, news that Lena died on Christmas Day.

Sunday, December 26th

Granny G at the breakfast table – sitting, hunched forward she looks like a dormouse. Her cough still troubling her. 'It's only my trachea, dear,' she reassures us.

A policeman comes to the door whilst we're sitting around after breakfast. Apparently a car was violently smashed up in Lamble Street last night; did we hear anything? Both H and I did wake after a couple of loud bangs, but had gone back to sleep when there was no further noise. The genial, red-haired PC is pretty sure who did it, an aggrieved husband who he describes as 'a bit of an oik', taking it out on his wife's car. He sounds reassuringly zealous about catching the man, but worried that he has no witnesses.

Later in the morning Rachel rings. One of the wheels has been stolen from her car and a side window smashed. The police, who are there when we go to pick her up before moving on to Will's, reckon it was someone deliberately targeting her alloy wheels. The spirit of Christmas.

Monday, December 27th

To the Jewish cemetery at Bushey for Lena Rustin's funeral. A cold, exposed place. Eighty or 90 mourners. I'm given a yarmulke and we all move into a tall chamber in the middle of which is Lena's coffin, with Ronnie [Lena's husband], looking suddenly small, shrunk and vulnerable standing beside it.

It was less than two weeks ago that I talked with Lena at the Christmas party.

The chief rabbi, Jonathan Sacks, comes up to me, takes my hand, says, with feeling, how pleased he is to see me there, as I meant so much to Lena. He and the family's rabbi take the service. Mourners stand, men on one side, women on the other. Those nearest the coffin show real grief, those behind them bewilderment and sadness.

I'm asked to go back to the house, which is quite a compliment I guess. Follow one of the family – Clive the RAF fighter hero, who'd ejected out at 200 feet! – through the traffic to a modern, suburban house in Kingsbury, within sight of the towering new Wembley Arch. All the mirrors in the house are covered for the seven days of mourning and Ronnie shows me a cut in his shirt which symbolises the tearing of garments.

The extraordinary scale of the earthquake and consequent tidal wave damage in the Indian Ocean is quite shocking. Thousands believed dead or missing – and still in the middle of all this natural horror, the suicide bombers in Iraq are showing how destructive we can be without nature's help – blowing themselves up and sending another 20 innocent people in Baghdad to their deaths. It's hot by the fire and I feel tired and oddly dispirited by the time I turn off the news and head for bed.

Tuesday, December 28th

The phone rings. It's [author] Jill Dawson. She's been talking with Mark Thompson about a BBC Emergency Appeal for the tsunami victims and my name was top of the list. I have to be true to my immediate reaction, which is not me please, and she apologises for having put me on the spot.

After I put the phone down I feel troubled about my response. Lazy? Cowardly? I think it's such an epic and enormous and continually darkening tragedy that I couldn't and haven't the time, energy and commitment to offer. Also, I prefer the smaller causes that really need my help. There is no question in my mind that I made the right decision.

Earlier we watched Rachel's name appear at the end of the last 'Changing Rooms'. Moment of quiet pride – though for Rachel, with another of her wheels stolen last night, and a further night of holiday inertia before anyone will help her, this is a less than totally happy Christmas.

Wednesday, December 29th

The saga of Rachel's Ford Focus continues. No wheels taken last night but she opened it up this morning to find a duvet inside. Believing it had been dumped there (the rear lock being broken) she pulled at it and revealed a man beneath it. A tramp who had obviously taken refuge in the car on a cold night. Rachel shocked and angry, yelled at him to get out. The 'tramp' apologised. He thought the car was abandoned because two wheels were missing. Rachel insisted he leave and he came back, memorably, with the line – 'All right, all right, just give me time to clear up.'

An interesting development in spam on my email – an invitation to join a Sikh and Punjabi matrimonial website!

Friday, December 31st

Two of our phone lines have gone down including the line that feeds my computer. A genial, loping, engineer who looks like an American comedian, spends an hour or more on the faults. He has to climb up the telegraph pole outside to fix my computer connection. I like the thought that this worldwide miracle of communication all depends on a sturdy wooden post trailing wires out across the street like the spokes of an umbrella.

I need this connection as the last creative task of 2004 is to write some copy about Finland for the 'Spamalot' theatre programme. As soon as I let go the nonsense flows as freely as it used to, and I'm quite reluctant to leave this rich seam of silliness to go up to South End Green for last-minute shopping. Work away through the afternoon and tie it all up and send it off to Eric in early evening.

Where do I go from here? There is an appetite for my travel shows which doesn't seem to have been sated. My age doesn't seem to worry an audience normally preoccupied with younger role models. I clearly have a future if I want it. I feel, though, that I desperately need 2005 as, at the very least, a gap year. I want to enjoy the pleasure of taking things in as well as giving them out.

Looking into the crystal ball I see Palin's Diaries Vol 1 for autumn of 2006, and Palin in Brazil for the autumn of 2007. When I'm 64.

Later, woken briefly by the New Year street cries of Gospel Oak. 'Fucking take me fucking home!'

2005

Saturday, January 1st

In the evening Channel 4 run a long 'countdown' compilation in which 300 comedy writers, producers and practitioners choose their Top 50 comedians. Mel Brooks at 50, Eric Idle at 21, John Cleese second only to Peter C. I came in at No. 30, very touchingly endorsed by Vic and Bob, and just below Spike.

Sunday, January 2nd

The tsunami disaster has filled the news this past week. Could we have sent warning? Should people have been told that when the sea goes right out, it's surely the sign of an impending surge of water? Once again – man's infinite belief in himself has been tested. Next time there will be a tsunami warning system in place in the Indian Ocean which will potentially make such loss of life a thing of the past. Like so many 'disasters' in my lifetime, Hillsborough, the King's Cross fire, the worst has to happen before the best.

Monday, January 3rd

Buoyed by three wildly enthusiastic emails from America, one from Eric, one each from 'Spamalot's' producer and publicist, responding to the silly Finnish programme notes I wrote on New Year's Eve. I am just as keen, I realise, to be appreciated for being silly as I am for being serious. Which is perhaps why I've never held any position of responsibility.

Tuesday, January 4th

It's nearly midday by the time I'm washed, tidied and at my desk. The phone rings almost immediately. Sarah Miller trying to get together a mega-Tsunami Fundraiser at the Four Seasons Hotel. I much more readily agreed to the vicar of St Martin's Gospel Oak for a tsunami fundraiser.

Saturday, January 8th

Strong winds during the night. Occasional gust feels powerful enough to pull the house off its foundations and send a message of fragility. Then later there's rain, flung across the window like some physical attack. By morning it's calmer, the rain has gone. Ragged white clouds and wind still pugnacious. I have to take some exercise, so off up and running up Parliament Hill, defying the bluster. The grass is an intense emerald green after the scouring of rain and wind and Kenwood House shines like the Grail does in pictures.

Jeremy, Melanie and the children come round for tea. Hard to believe Eugene was once silent – he now chatters on. He's very keen on chins – he described mine as looking like a stone on a beach; apparently he recently saw one that looked like a bottom (he likes bottoms). The owner of a particularly spectacular cleft chin was not, at first, amused.

Esmé wants to watch me working in my room, so I have to go to my desk and address an envelope or two. She soon gets bored.

Monday, January 10th

In the evening to Mosimann's in Belgravia at the behest of Lin Cook who told H on the phone yesterday that ten years on from Peter's death she felt it was time to draw a line and begin living her own life. To mark this rite of passage she has invited us to have dinner with her, her brother and his wife and two of the team who made 'Not Only But Always' – the film of the life of Peter – Rhys Ifans and the producer Charlie Pattinson. It's Helen's last night before her big knee op but she decided it would make a very good diversion.

Rhys Ifans arrives quite late, having had to return to his flat in Camden to collect a jacket and tie. He's a soft-spoken, genial man with a quiet sense of humour. He's much exercised by the tsunami disaster and reports that orphaned children are being exploited by sex traffickers. He's initiated one of the many tsunami appeals – this time with rock bands, etc. He asks if I'll take part. Put on the spot at the table I stand my ground and apologise for not being able to appear but agree to do a filmed insert.

Despite Lin's intentions it is Peter, rather than her, who dominates the evening. I notice she still talks about him in the present tense. Also learnt for the first time tonight that Peter spoke French and Spanish and German fluently.

Tuesday, January 11th

Taxi into the Princess Grace at ten. Helen quite swiftly taken up to her room and given various pre-op examinations. I have to leave her at 11.35 to get to Simpsons-in-the-Strand where I am one of three speakers at the Oldie lunch.

Simpsons' faded gentility suits the Oldie very well. Richard Ingrams, looking like the slightly absent-minded housemaster, in clothes which look suspiciously as if they haven't been changed since he left Shrewsbury, welcomes me, as does Barry Cryer who has come along as a guest and apparently loves these events.

Both Richard and Barry heartily disliked the Peter Cook film (though both admired Rhys's performance). Barry thought it made Peter seem ambitious, cruel and vindictive. 'Not the Peter *I* knew.'

My speech is the last of the three. Peter Ramsbotham (upper-class, ex-army) speaks passionately about the ethos of our prison system which, while costing £3 billion a year, goes out of its way to encourage reoffending that costs the economy £30 billion a year. [War reporter] Janine di Giovanni speaks about Chechnya and Bosnia and other war zones she's visited.

So I'm the 15 minutes of fun. 'Himalaya' stories, then besieged by middle-aged women on the way out. Quite elderly mothers volunteering to come on my next trip – 'I'm a qualified secretary' – whilst their embarrassed 40-year-old daughters raise their eyebrows in the background.

At seven I call the hospital. Put through to Helen herself. Operation took two hours. New right knee, left knee arthroscopy to tidy up loose bits. She's drowsy and her voice very soft and faint. Call long list of relatives and friends then drive down to the hospital. Helen doesn't look bad considering and though she's always on the edge of sleep we talk for a while. She's anxious to comb her hair, put on her jewellery and generally look like her normal self. Almost obsessively so. Around nine the anaesthetist and the surgeon come round. He hadn't wanted to give her a totally new knee, but had to once he saw the damage – quite a serious deterioration since he last saw her.

Friday, January 14th

To the hospital. Helen's back is uncomfortable now. She's thin and her skin very light resulting in a tenderness which prevents her from lying comfortably in bed. She sits awkwardly on the edge of her chair. I don't like to see her like this and in these unconvivial surroundings.

I'm tired too. Tired from all the comings and goings. When I do get back home, there's a queue of calls on the answerphone which have to be dealt with. And once more, exercise has been limited to walking London.

Saturday, January 15th

To John Lewis to look for a fleece which will take the rub off H's back. Take it into the hospital. H had a better night thanks to a tab of Temazepam. Rachel is there with her. The noisy lady next door – who apparently complains in a loud upper-class voice about everything – is in full swing. The place feels quite cramped. Boxes and pieces of equipment stacked in the carpeted corridor. Rachel and I walk up and down this cluttered passageway with H, who only feels better after she's done some walking.

Home. Forget how time-consuming it is to have to answer all the phone calls. H and I usually share it. Lin Cook comes round, pouring thanks, compliments and general gratefulness all over me and bringing six 'Himalaya' books for me to sign. She's also got me to agree to an Evening With for the P. C. Foundation, in November.

Back to see H in the early evening. She says she's now feeling very bored at the hospital – this surely a sign of recovery.

Supper with Terry J who seems careworn. Transpires that the Daily Mail have been poking about and plan to run the story. I ask when and Terry mumbles, 'It's today I think.' There's a Daily Mail on the bar right in front of us. Terry doesn't want to look, but when he goes for a pee I pick it up. The issue of what's laughingly called a newspaper has story after story of famous people with what they sees as problems. Rod Stewart's unhappy at 60, Noel Edmonds keeps his wife under electronic surveillance and Terry Jones, Python star, has left his wife for a 21-year-old Swede. Unflattering pictures of all the participants, but an embarrassing page all round with Terry being quoted from somewhere as saying that 'fidelity isn't important'.

Tuesday, January 18th

To L'Étoile for lunch with Barry C and Alan B. Alan is quiet – more listening than talking – Barry's anecdotes roll out and provoke reactions from him occasionally. 'I'm a recluse,' Alan maintains unconvincingly. We talk about 'Not Only But Always'. Alan, I feel, thinks much of Rhys Ifans' portrayal of Peter was good – possibly even justified – but, as he says, 'it never showed things when they were working'.

Alan remembers too how unlikely it was that Dudley's club foot would be mentioned so openly. 'It was a long time before Dudley would talk about it and then only with a little embarrassment.' Then he added, 'No one ever mentioned the fact that I was gay, either.' It's quite remarkable that this self-effacing, gentle man in jacket, sweater and tie – 'I always wear a tie' – is the most successful playwright in London. Reassuring too. He has one concern, neither he nor anyone else can contact the woman who's typing up his diaries. She has them all and he doesn't know where she is.

With the sonorous chimes of Big Ben sounding a quarter to four I step into the revolving door of Portcullis House; everyone at security seems to recognise me and are complimentary about the series. A few Tibetans from the Dalai Lama's office are already there. Clearly this meeting will not, as I presumed, be just for MPs.

I'm led upstairs to a big room laid out as if for Committee Hearings. I'm told it's the Grimond Room. Like Portcullis House itself it's an attempt to mix gravity and modernity. The weight of history and the lightness of technology.

A number of people are gathering round the crescent-shaped table at the head of which sits John Wilkinson, a Tory MP who seems decent, correct and full of gratitude for my agreeing to come along. He makes introductory re- marks (like most MPs I've met, they're totally absorbed in their own world and he seems to know nothing about Python and the rest).

I haven't prepared a speech and rely on recall – then find I can't remember the difference between Shigatse and Gyantse. Otherwise I say what I want to say – holding this slightly intimidating floor for some 15 minutes. Various MPs ask questions. One of them wonders if I worry about missing the 'complexities' of places. I have to admit I do.

Then the various pressure groups had their time. One of them was the Free Tibet group who had a quiet go at me for giving the impression that all was well in Tibet and that the Chinese were accepted. The Dalai Lama's office, Tibetan rather than English, were much less aggressive. Finish on the hour. Wilkinson offers me tea and we adjourn to a café in the mighty atrium. Lord Weatherill, an ex-Speaker, had been at the meeting. He regaled me with his experiences in India, and shows me eventually to the passageway down to the Underground. 'Where do I get your book?' he asked, as though he'd never heard of bookshops.

Thursday, January 20th

The tsunami concert at St Martin's. Big turnout, wine served at the back, ap- plause after each item. I read from my diary and an edited version of the Tagore poem 'Earth'. Lesley Garrett sings after me. Never been too comfortable with the operatic, but it does send shivers down the spine to hear the long, power- fully sustained high notes fill the church.

Pevsner described Lamb's original interior as 'both striking and harrow- ing'. I can't quite understand where the 'harrowing' comes from – but there is a touch of the exotic, fanciful and faintly oriental in this little corner of old Gospel Oak.

Sunday, January 23rd

Hamish MacInnes rings from Glencoe to ask me up there. He's thinking of writing a book called 'The Sadist's Guide to the Highlands', strong on all the dark legends and of course full of statistics of death and destruction which he rather likes.

The Observer carries news that the Pope's autobiography has been secured for Weidenfeld and Nicolson by his friend George W [Weidenfeld]. So me, Trinny, Susannah and the Pope!

Monday, January 24th

Will has brokered a meeting between myself and [broadcaster and local historian] Dan Cruickshank. Take the Underground to Liverpool Street. A Northern couple can't wait to have a chat with me. Try to keep nose firmly in book. They haven't been to London for a while. 'It's all very different, isn't it?' I'm drawn in, which is perhaps a mistake. 'What are the differences you see?' 'Oh, well, the immigration, for a start.' As we're the only Caucasians in the carriage, I go back to my book.

The glittery modern city seems big, bold, brash and confident around Liverpool Street and I make my way past the great glass walls of the new bank HQs and turn up a narrow, incongruous cobbled street to what looks like a Dickensian film set, and turning to the right I'm faced with a fine run of tall, narrow Huguenot houses.

Into a panelled passage, much like 24 Hanbury, but narrower, and through to a room about the size of a snug in a pub, lit by one electric lamp and many candles – several of them sprouting from a glass candelabra; a flickering log fire burns in a decorative iron grate. Dan seems a giant in these little rooms, and early on he comments on the lowness of the ceiling and I realise he must be John's height.

In this pre-industrial atmosphere, we sit and talk about making television programmes. He's like Terry J – very critical of the whole process on his recent 'Great Treasures' series. He had to work at a ridiculous speed – 'six minutes for each treasure' – to get the series done and producers come in and do their edits without consulting him.

We repair to The Light for supper. On the way Dan shouts excitedly – 'Look! A deep hole!' – and points out some roadworks. The prospect of the pile of rubble beside it is just too much and pushing aside the red and white plastic barrier he walks round it, chatting away, turning over the mud and prodding it with his finger. 'Clay pipe,' he announces and hands a small fragment to Will who hands it to me.

We drink a couple of bottles of Fleurie and talk about some of the many things which interest all of us. The encroachment of the City – and the venality of the City's politicians – the pleasures of Calcutta – a place over which he rhapsodises – and whets my already aroused appetite. I'm glad Will brought us together like this. A magical glimpse of old London and a very contemporary conversation.

Tuesday, January 25th

To the Neal Street Restaurant. Have been invited, with H, to a meal with Antonio [Carluccio] and Priscilla [his wife] and others including Anthony Minghella. We talk briefly about TG and he tells me the saga of how he was asked by the Weinsteins to come and look at the 'Brothers Grimm' film and in effect re-cut it. He refused. But he makes it quite clear that the more money you take the more interference you can expect from the studios. I like him, but I don't think there's much mischief there. A good head boy.

Wednesday, January 26th

Collected at 11.30 and driven down to Upper Ground to appear with Terry G on the Des and Mel show – Des O'Connor and Melanie Sykes – in order to promote Rémy Renoux's Monty Python in French show which opens at the Riverside.

Terry talks of Minghella – 'very ambitious' – and says that he may have refused to re-edit 'Grimms' 'but only after I called him and told him not to'. He gurgles with laughter.

Apparently the Mail have run the Terry J story again – this time on their front page – probably with a bit of new info from Anna's family. This is why Terry J is not coming out to do publicity for MP in French. He daren't put his head above the parapet any more.

Friday, January 28th

To the Riverside to see 'Monty Python's Flying Circus – At Last in French', on press night. Some terrific clowning. Python's timing and underplaying finds very little echo amongst these joyful Frenchmen (and woman), and clothes are taken off at the drop of an underpant. But at times I find it glorious and rather liberating. The laughs come from Gallic freedom rather than Anglo-Saxon restraint.

Wednesday, February 2nd

Lydia, the French girl from next door, comes round at two with the twins to ask me some questions about 'Himalaya'. One of them is quite difficult – 'What's the lowest part of the Himalaya?'

To a new club/viewing theatre part-financed by Dave Stewart, called The Hospital, to see 'Tideland' – TG's latest and by far his cheapest movie, shot last autumn in Canada (standing in for Texas). I watch, entranced as ever by TG's pictures, and frustrated at his failure to rein in the actors, but am full of admiration at the performance of the girl who holds it all together.

After two hours (and yes, it did seem like two hours), the film ended. Silence in the room. Terry gets up, grinning and muttering and calling for reactions. I find it impossible to sum up what I'm feeling. Need time. So better get out fast.

Thursday, February 3rd

Lie awake for a half-hour before I have to get up, with images from 'Tideland' flooding into my mind. I realise how much of a grip it has on me. The more I sift through the memories, recall the images, the more I'm confused about my initial response. This could be a small masterpiece, or it could be a large indulgence, but I'm beginning to edge towards the former.

Monday, February 7th

My new printer arrives. It is an advance on the old clattering ink-jet Epson, but much heavier. When I get it out of the box it seems much bigger too. It looms up over the desk. Helen, much to her mirth, sees what the problem is. I've got it the wrong way up.

Monday, February 14th

Less than five weeks from Helen's surgery, the old routine of our life is almost restored. More recovering than suffering now and this morning H is out of bed before me for the first time since the op.

Off to a private view at the Royal Academy. It's a fine morning. The sun shines and there's a bite in the air. Arrive at Burlington House at half past eight. Sukie Hemming – very good value, with authority and humour – is in charge of shepherding through our group of BM patrons who have a little more than an hour to take in 1,000 years of Turkish history, art and culture. Some exquisite work – especially the graphic art and painting attributed to Muhammad Siyah Kalem – Muhammad of the Black Pen. Work done in the fourteenth century shows a wonderful grasp of line and movement in the figures of men and, especially, horses; this influenced by Chinese art I wonder. Makes the work of contemporary Europe seem stiff and formal.

I walk briskly down Piccadilly to the Wolseley – order a coffee and a croissant and look through the playbook of 'The Weekend' in preparation for next meeting.[1] Steve A and I meet up with [theatre producer] Jeremy Meadow who seems quite sincere and sensible about his proposed revival of 'The Weekend'. Initially for a tour, but always with the West End in his sights. He has a good, straightforward manner. Realistic about the play. Thinks that the casting of RW [Richard Wilson], in his Meldrew heyday, skewed the production. He'll also keep it lower key and would never go into a theatre the size of the Strand. We part with hope.

Tuesday, February 15th

Tonight to the Commonwealth Club in Northumberland Avenue to speak to the Pakistan Society. Talk for half an hour then questions. I try to do without notes these days. Danger is I occasionally lose the thread, or labour a point or two, but beside the benefits of being able to perform rather than just read, it's so much more enjoyable for me – and ergo, hopefully, for them.

Wednesday, February 16th: London–Oxford

Drive up to Oxford to get on my hind legs again tonight – this time at Brasenose graduates' dinner. Am taken to the principal's lodging. Professor Roger Cashmore, a heavy-set, bearded physicist who used to run the CERN accelerator programme in Geneva, can't wait to show me some papers he's discovered. They're copies of the will of George Palyn, dated 1610, and confirming his four exhibitions to educate poor men, preferably from Cheshire, at Brasenose. Notice that on the document, James I calls himself King of England, Scotland, France and Ireland.

---

1 My play *The Weekend* was first produced at the Strand Theatre in 1994 with Richard Wilson in the lead. It received mediocre notices.

Friday, February 18th

The moment has come. My bluff has been called and a day's filming to talk about the Fish Slapping Dance for a Python DVD has become a reality. Collected at ten and driven to Teddington Lock where this masterpiece was originally shot. Walk across the steel footbridge and along the lock. A crew is assembling. A man called Albert is unpacking the fish. Rather touchingly, the local fishmonger who supplied him says he knew exactly what was wanted as he'd provided the fish for the original shoot 33 years ago. I climb into my slapping-outfit in the lock-keeper's hut.

Quite a long, concentrated, set of speeches, but the cold wind adds urgency and I keep my cool too. All done in three hours and across the river and a quick lunch at the Angler's Arms. The time at Teddington Lock, like Brasenose yesterday, feels like beating the bounds. As if time's going backwards. Is this healthy?

Friday, February 25th

Cold, snow drifting about as we get up. Have to try and help the Hammershoi team get hold of David Hockney. Call Alan B. He had a bit of a falling out with the other great Yorkshireman some two years ago — all to do with Hockney letting Rupert [Thomas, Alan's partner and editor of Interiors Magazine] down on a promise to contribute to Interiors — but he puts me on to [art dealer] Annely Juda and I'm quite swiftly given a contact number in LA.

Alan tells me that yesterday there was an auction in support of the National Theatre in which one of the prizes was lunch with Alan and the boys from the now multi-award-winning show 'The History Boys'. The lot went to a man from Yorkshire for £19,000. Alan thinks he must want more than lunch for that. 'He probably wants to eat it off the bare bottoms of the cast.'

Monday, February 28th

Talk on the phone to Eleanor about Hammershoi. I spent the weekend boning up on him and feel that I still don't have a clear idea of how we shall tell our story. What is the search for Hammershoi? Where does it begin and what will be its conclusions?

A good half-hour later I'm much clearer in my mind and spend the next hour refining what we've discussed. Hammershoi is a man who assiduously covered his tracks, leaving us only with the precision and still beauty of the work. Celebrity, place in history, etc, seemed not to bother him. So our search is paradoxically one in which the lack of evidence leads us to the truth.

Wednesday, March 2nd

Up to have my hair cut by Danny who I always mistakenly call Jimmy. He's Lebanese and we talk about what's going on in his country following the bomb blast two weeks ago that killed their most popular politician. Now crowds in the square forced the pro-Syrian government to resign and he thinks that maybe the Syrians will withdraw their army. So long as the Syrians are in Lebanon, says Danny, their own economy will be saddled with the corrupt skimming off of money to the occupiers.

Walk home in bitter wind and rain. Write material for the C. N. Traveller Tsunami appeal dinner tonight.

I'm the first of the two guest speakers – Rory Bremner being the other. Sarah Miller introduces me – 300 guests, all nice and quite spoilt. It goes fairly well. There's not much excitement among the audience. They expect celebrities – and many of them are celebrities; David Gilmour of Floyd, Stelios of easyJet, Sting, I think is there too – but I battle on. The Tagore poem is received in respectful silence – and many, like [restaurateur] Jeremy King, who's at our table and Deyan Sudjic, Sarah's architect journo hubby, make special complimentary mention of it.

The evening is all about surfeit – surfeit for a good cause, I suppose, but still surfeit and there's nothing very edifying in seeing a lot of very rich people part with tiny proportions of their livelihood to the accompaniment of cheers and whoops. Rory goes off and works tables. Always seems on the go. Loves being loved and would make a good PM.

Tuesday, March 22nd

Another very busy day Hammershoi filming with long interview/encounters and pieces to camera as well. Centred in and around the British Museum. Wonderful Ann Widdecombe-like lady guide. Refers to the hot dog dealers outside as 'the Salmonella Brothers'. Almost alone with matchless Greek sculptures for two hours before public are let in.

Wednesday, March 23rd

To the Tate and film up in the restoration room – lots of light and wonderful space to work except the roof leaks. Aware from my interview with Rachel, one of the conservators, that the Tate empire is authoritarian and quite frighteningly controlled. Pleasant amenable ladies tell you what you can and can't say.

Friday, April 8th: Copenhagen–London

Goodbye to the gang at Heathrow after completion of Hammershoi filming, Mike picks me up and we drive back in light swirling snow showers. Last weekend, he says, it was spring, now winter has returned. But it's a different winter to the one I've left behind in Denmark. Here in London, the unforgivingly numbing cold wind is absent and the leafless trees of Copenhagen are in marked contrast to the blooming, blossoming verdance of London.

Hammershoi leaves me puzzled. I'm not quite sure what the story will appear to be – how best we can turn my interest into a journey which is tight and watchable. How we unify all the undoubtedly striking shots and intriguing interviews into a coherent whole makes me feel a touch vulnerable on this one.

Tuesday, April 12th

Interview requests are just coming in as T2000 have called for the removal of Jeremy Clarkson's 'Top Gear' from TV schedules. Avoid getting involved. I never watch the programme anyway.

In the post I have been sent a play by David Pugh [producer of 'The Weekend']. Another 'ART'-like job. Tom Stoppard translation of smooth, effortlessly funny French comedy, currently called 'Wind in the Poplars' by Gérald Sibleyras. Pleasant, funny, light. A three-hander, limited West End run. Richard Griffiths – best actor winner last year for 'History Boys' – has said yes and wants to work with me. Tempted.

Irritating cough persists, spoiling the end of the day.

Wednesday, April 13th

Take a cab to the office. In the main room a Swedish TV crew is setting up for my in-depth interview with [journalist] Christine Ockrent.

Christine O very efficient, professional and altogether agreeable. We talk for almost an hour, then the Swedish camera crew insist on some shots of me walking outside. 'Try to forget we're here,' they shout whilst pointing the camera into my face from point-blank range. I nip across Catherine Street in the face of an oncoming vehicle, but it misses them.

I've arranged to meet my errant little friend Terry up at the Flask for a drink. Simon Moore, back from a longish sojourn in the US, has reclaimed the Water House. Terry has moved into a smaller house nearby which he is renting for a year. Any suggestion that his ardour for Anna has eased and some accommodation with Al will be made, has proved false. Last weekend Terry moved all his books and personal effects out of Grove Park.

Terry sighs a lot, occasionally looks almost imploringly towards me and asks 'How are *you*, Mikey?' as if demanding some sort of admission that yes, I might change my life if I were honest with myself. Truth is, the more I see of the process of destroying one life and setting up another, the more it confirms me in my own ways, and makes me feel ten times more fortunate to have what I have.

Perhaps he is just living the fantasy that he has always seemed to favour – a world of no possessions, no possessiveness, a world where everything is shared and enjoyed together. Terry the leveller. Finally brave enough to live what he believes in. If others can't deal with it, too bad.

As my instincts are almost the opposite, I feel, in a way, one of the rejected. One of the too bads. He's lovely, friendly, warm company as ever, but as I leave the house and head back across the Heath, I feel that I'm making the journey from fantasy to reality.

Friday, April 15th

Morning of letters, diaries, emails. Paul sends up a 'goodie box' which, as a BAFTA nominee, I'm entitled to. Perfect example of the rich being rewarded. Supposedly worth £2,000! It contains women's make-up, a lacy black poncho, tiny pair of wraparound black sunglasses. They've clearly sent me the wrong box.

Saturday, April 16th

Bas brings dim sum round for what also happens to be our 39th wedding anniversary lunch. Rachel joins us. She starts ten night shifts on 'Hell's Kitchen' at 11.00 tonight.

Take Bas to Baker Street to meet up with his parents. 'None of our family likes China,' said Bas earlier, with a tinge of regret.

Back home I succumb to this stealthy cold which has stalked me on and off since the Hammershoi filming. Tonight it feels more active – I'm sneezing fiercely. So H and I spend our 39th anniversary in separate beds.

Sunday, April 17th

The spectre of BAFTA looms over the day, so I can't really relax. I shall have to give an acceptance speech for my Special Award, though, since I let them know

I would ad-lib, I'm told that my time has been cut to one minute 30 seconds.

Arrival at Theatre Royal quite smooth and we're well on time. Red carpet laid out across Catherine Street. On either side barriers hold back fans with autograph books and photographers shrieking atavistically. I'm photographed with Fiona Bruce for some reason – she's tall, slim, giraffe-like and friendly.

Slowly move in, talking, greeting, chatting on the way. Events like these move at an almost snail-like pace, paralysed by the general gushing intercourse of luvvies who haven't seen each other for days, possibly weeks.

Griff Rhys Jones is an exception to this and sits in the row behind us, head buried in the programme. Good for him.

To my surprise my own award comes quite early on. Eddie Izzard, who called me last night to say he'd just come in from LA, mainly to present the award, and wanted to check if it was all right with me to avoid the conventional praise, is terrific. A funny, silly, very Pythonic bit involving me and Che Guevara, ending up with something like 'Michael Palin is well-known for being nice and he says that anyone who doesn't believe that can fuck off.'

I keep my speech reasonably tight, say all the things I want to say – a few tributes then backstage, obligatory photograph, and eventually back to my seat on the aisle to await the Factual Series nomination.

The Factual series award is a bit of an anti climax, rushed through without any of the entries being shown to the audience and won by the powerful 'The Power of Nightmares', something in every way different from 'Himalaya'. Urgent, heavily opinionated, didactic – but also very watchable. Adam Curtis the producer strides up with a little team. Like all winners of 'serious issue' awards, he's eschewed the requested Black Tie and wears a big messy shirt outside his trousers and berates the world for continuing not to listen to what he's saying.

H and I, clutching my silver BAFTA, back home just before one.

Monday, April 18th

Maria Aitken [theatre director and fellow actor in 'A Fish Called Wanda'] has sent a copy of Simon Gray's 'Quartermaine's Terms' which she wants to revive in West End with me in the lead for a short run.

Wednesday, April 20th

Begin reading 'Quartermaine's Terms'. It seems a touch passé at first – jokes about people forgetting names, light banter, no one listening to anyone else, but the writing is always easy to read and listen to. It's intelligent and funny. And the end is very moving, done with an unsentimental and deceptively light touch.

Yes, I can see myself making a good St John Quartermaine. Much more tempting than the Sibleyras plays. I suppose because 'QT' is so essentially English. I enjoy all the nuances that make it more than just wit.

Picked up at 5.20 by Mike G and Steve [Abbott] and by six we're outside the Grosvenor. Meet the grave-faced Frenchman who owns Orion, through Hachette and Lagardère (weapons, I think). He says he has a copy of 'Himalaya' 'always in front of me in my office'. Why there's no French edition is discussed, but not resolved.

'Himalaya', up for Book of the Year, picks up an early win, for the less than illustrious TV and Film Book of the Year, sponsored by Channel 4. Much joy around the clump of Orion tables and I'm up on the podium for the second time in a week, to collect my Nibbie from Carol Vorderman and Richard Whiteley. Book of the Year goes to 'The Da Vinci Code', which has sold zillions and, though no one seems to have a good word for it, has been read on a massive scale.

A manly hug with Ewan McGregor and Charley Boorman, whose motorbike diary was also in the film, TV category. They are both good, down-to-earth enthusiasts. Ewan seems to have resisted all the blandishments of stardom and approaches everything with a positive delight in the hand life's dealt him – or so it seems.

Ion T, who is at our table, joins me in the car home. The Diaries and their publication sort of hang in the air. Ion being discreet but, I hope, enthusiastic.

Thursday, April 21st

To lunch with Maria A at Two Brydges. I've decided that, although I like the play and the prospect of working with her, to agree to even the most limited of runs would jeopardise the 'free time' I feel I need this year. Maria then catches me on the wrong foot by countering that she herself wasn't thinking of doing it this year anyway and would favour spring 2006. I'm a little confused by this and she presses home the advantage. All sorts of nice things said about my acting – and although she herself has decided not to act again, she sort of feels I owe it to myself and to the punters to return to the theatre.

I suppose what may decide this issue is that we love discussing the play and its potential. We laugh a lot and both bring things out that the other hasn't seen. So by the time she tells me that Simon Gray is so enormously excited about the prospect of my doing it that he's demanded she ring him immediately after the lunch, I find myself wriggling on, rather than off the hook.

Next spring – say February to June – could be possible. Everyone is keen. The sun floods in and across the linen tablecloths; the world seems a very good place at half past three this afternoon as Maria completes her seduction. We agree to be in touch at the end of the weekend, when she will be back in New York.

Home via a book launch at the Fine Art Society for Jack Rosenthal's auto-biography. The long, narrow room is absolutely packed. The third event this week when I've experienced moments of Hillsborough-like panic.

If I were a believer in fate I would note that on the day I've become closest to being talked into doing a theatre play, I should bump into Braham Murray (director of my only other serious West End production ['Hang Down Your Head and Die' at the Comedy Theatre] 41 years ago) and Nic Kent from the Tricycle, a director I admire enormously, who takes me quite startlingly aback by saying 'I hear you might be doing something with Maria?'

Friday, April 22nd

A beautiful, bright morning. Lie in bed trying to think of all the reasons I should not do 'Quartermaine'.

Read 'QT' again, then some of Simon Gray's early diaries – 'The Uncommon Pursuit'. I sense a kindred spirit there – grumpier and more intellectual than me, but I feel we both like the same things about life, and notice the same things. This heartens me.

Read some reviews of 'QT' – the LA Times irritable 'but where's the play?' – and wonder if it might not be too light, too middle-class, too undemanding. So I'm confused. To the gym for some hard physical work and to give the brain a rest.

Monday, April 25th

Wake with vague disquiet about how to deal with the 'QT' offer. Having been bullish most of the weekend, doubt swept in last night. If anything the feeling has hardened this morning – it's concentrated around commitment. This year's long breather is in its infancy and yet I'm seriously thinking of tying myself up for five months immediately it's over. This gives me precious little room to move, and makes something of a mockery of a year to think, consider, reflect and open myself to all sorts of influences. The sad truth is that, after all my elation, I'm going to have to be the pourer of cold water.

Then it suddenly becomes more complicated. I'm on the lavatory listening to Radio 4's review of the papers at twenty to eight when suddenly I hear my name mentioned. 'And finally . . . the Independent carries news that Michael Palin's travel days are finally over.' The report is read out, quite amusingly, and John Humphreys comes out of the item with a pleasant . . . 'Ah, there we are.'

I feel as if I've died. For a moment I wander round in T-shirt and underpants, like some confused old pensioner. Twice I pick up the phone and dial the BBC to protest and twice I put it down. It's all come from a rushed conversation with [journalist] Richard Brooks (posing as a good friend) who intercepted me at the Fine Art Society as I was desperate to get away and find a cab after the J. Rosenthal launch. I dare say I'd used a bit of exaggeration, irony and probably most dangerously, humour. None of which was reflected in the stories.

Take a run over the silent, soggy Heath and by the time I return the phone is ringing almost continuously. The Independent even has me as third leader on the editorial page: 'Bon Voyage to Michael Palin', welcoming my 'retirement' as good for the environment. The run has done me good – sharpened up my reactions. Make coffee and set to work reassuring the world that I've no intention of giving up travel or travel programmes.

Then off to a lunch and awards ceremony at the Voice of the Viewer and Listener. Nice, low-key affair. The place, Hamilton House, near Euston, smells a little like an old folks' home, and many of the core members attending are considerably older than me.

Jocelyn Hay, who started the group as a way of rallying support for TV against Mary Whitehouse and her like, is good news. Bright, pleasant, sharp and humorous. Michael Grade had been addressing them this morning. 'He came on his own,' she notes approvingly. 'When John Birt came to talk to us he brought 12 people.'

After sandwiches and a glass of wine, an admirably short awards ceremony, in which I'm given the final prize for being voted (by the members) the year's outstanding contributor to television. It gives me a chance to rebut the rumours of retirement, and there are a number of journos sniffing about who I hope will carry the rebuttal away with them.

Home, lie down and recover for 20 minutes, then set to writing what was to be the main business of the day, my email turning down the 'Quartermaine' part.

Tuesday, April 26th

Paul has emailed me a rather sour note from Richard Brooks complaining that our denial of 'his' story has impugned his integrity as a journalist, etc, etc. Talk of legal action even.

The Independent has published my letter, but only in the 'Briefly' section with any mentions of the newspaper's own shortcomings in not checking the story excised!

To the office. The Times Travel section call, asking if I will write 500 words about my decision to quit. I tell them I'm not quitting, so they ask if I'll do 500 words on why I'm not quitting.

Finally track down Angela M who gives me good advice – basically not to bother with R Brooks' threat. She says he's behaving like an eight-year-old who's been caught doing something wrong and won't admit it. Nevertheless, I shall email a reply – not taking up the issue, but just pacifying him.

Home. Reply from Maria A, who understands my situation, and suggests we do 'QT' as a radio play. Three days instead of five months. Not a bad compromise.

Thursday, April 28th

A new acting offer, this time via Charlie Pattinson of Company Pics (who made the Pete/Dud film). Would I be interested in playing George Gently, a detective created by Alan Hunter, whose books Peter Flannery ('Our Friends in the North') is about to adapt?

Playing a pipe-smoking detective, shades of Maigret, feels, however intriguing, to be almost a cliché of the actor reaching the mellow, declining years of his career! But I *am* curious enough to ask to read the book.

Friday, April 29th

Paul sends up the George Gently novel and I read it in the garden after lunch. Homage to Maigret and Simenon's unglamorous, unflinching view of the world, but none the worse for that as I was once a very big fan of Simenon's short stories. He liked railways too. There's definitely something here and if Peter Flannery is adapting, it will be brought out. Specially like the early '60s detail. But will I not just get myself back into the hole which I've only this week climbed out of – committing myself a long way ahead. And would it be the best use of my time and talents?

Wednesday, May 4th: Trento–London

After breakfast I walk into the old town [of Trento, where I'd been for their annual Mountain Film Festival] for the last time.

Last night they showed 'Life of Brian' (with subtitles) to an appreciative audience of 200 or so. I feel the atmosphere chill occasionally. The plan to chop up Pilate's wife – 'cut all her bits off, send 'em back on the hour, every hour' – sounds uncomfortably reminiscent of what the Red Brigade used to get up to. Once again, I'm struck by, and rather proud of, the boldness of the film and how British it is. It's a film from a country that really does care for free speech, and I can't imagine this attack by humour could be brought off as successfully anywhere other than Britain. A definite heir to a long tradition.

Thursday, May 5th

Start day, as I often do on my birthday, feeling vaguely unhappy. Oppressed by all the things I still have to do – the inability to move without being pointed at or written about.

Ion T comes round at half past ten. He has made an edit of Diaries '69–72 and as we go through it I feel a welcome resurgence of commitment. Feel glad I put 'QT' aside and will probably do same with Gently. (I received a wobbly-written card from Simon Gray saying he'd thought of me for 'Quartermaine' after seeing 'Our American Friends' (sic). He sounded disappointed about my decision. The radio version was fine, 'but I really rather feel that Quartermaine, who is heard so little, needs to be *seen*'.)

Thursday, May 12th

Walk around to the Avenue – a smart restaurant in St James's – to collect a cheque from a broking company called IPAC on behalf of Farm Africa. Dickie Attenborough, who lost daughter and granddaughter in the tsunami, is also there to collect an award. 'Are you going to do lots of jokes?' he asks anxiously. He is remarkable and though I've felt before that he tends to turn on the emotion at the slightest excuse, now, when he has every excuse for it, he seems dignified and restrained. A trouper. 'Seen much of my younger brother recently?' he asks. I tell him I saw a photo of him in the paper, rather cruelly taken as he slipped into a hole whilst planting a tree at Kew. This seemed to visibly brighten Dickie.

Saturday, May 14th

Catch the 10.07 from Paddington, with H, and we're met at Bath by Will and [architect] Ptolemy Dean, for this is the day I've agreed to open the 1830 Gardener's Cottage at the Holburne Museum, by another of Will's friends in architecture, Chris Woodward (whose job Will took over at the Soane).

Squeezed in W's car, H and I are treated to a lightning tour of Bath ending up at a wonderful Gothic pile called Midford Castle. said to have been designed to resemble the Ace of Clubs – after the owner had won money on that card at the gambling table.

Catch the 4.42 back. Diverted along the Kennet/Avon Canal. Very beautiful ride through Bradford-on-Avon, then brutal reality intrudes at Newbury Racecourse Station, where we stop to pick up people at end of race day. A great, heavy, noisy, well-oiled throng fills up the first class coach and reduces rest of train to standing room only. I'm pointed out, talked about as if I wasn't there. Still as one of them gets up to leave the train at Reading, he nods at Helen and grabs my hand, 'She's gorgeous. Why d'you keep buggering off?' A good question.

Sunday, May 15th

After lunch prepare a few thoughts for the Roundhouse show tonight.

Sign books in dressing room at the Prince of Wales, then on to the stage for sound check with the star – Alan B. He says he's just had a birthday and later, totting up the years, I realise it's 20 years since we celebrated his 50th at the Box Tree in Ilkley [whilst filming 'A Private Function'] so Alan is now 70.

He still seems boyish. Photocall with the exotically tall Torquil Norman – a philanthropist to stand alongside Ondaatje – another tall, thin man – and Marcus Davey, the beaming, egregious director of the Roundhouse. 'I'm the only one with a tie,' Alan points out, 'as usual.' 'It's a generational thing, Alan,' I mutter, as the camera flashes relentlessly. Alan nods. 'My mother used to say that wearing a tie stopped you getting TB.'

Tuesday, May 17th

Out with Terry J and Bill [Jones, his son] in the evening. Terry looking generally sad, apologetic and downcast. Bill is not only the most genial and good-natured person I know, but also eminently sensible. If Terry is to go through with it, then, advises Bill, he can't keep telling Al he still loves her, or that she's the most wonderful friend; however much he might mean it, it begs the question for her, as it does for us all.

On the way back to Terry's for a nightcap, we find ourselves in the middle of an elaborate night-shoot, being filmed just down the road from Terry Gilliam's. Pond Square bathed in light from a Wendy grid raised high above the trees on a crane. A number of the lighting boys recognise us. 'You in this, Mike?' they ask with some incredulity. It turns out to be 'Basic Instinct 2'.

Thursday, May 26th

Up a little earlier than usual and tackling various tasks. Call Alan [Bleasdale] – his husky deep voice is as reassuring as it is articulate – can't understand why he isn't a radio star. He could be the British equivalent of the great Chicagoan, Studs Terkel. The answer lies perhaps in the fact that Alan is the great Provincial Hero. He's never cracked the metropolis, he remains first and foremost a stern Liverpudlian. He's steeped in its language, culture, politics. Alan doesn't need London – and indeed I think his best work has always had a strong element of home ground in it.

He says he's been writing 'non-stop' for the last five years. Laughs – 'The Wilderness Years', he calls them. Now working on v. interesting project of the sinking of the Laconia. He's also hoping to adapt 'Treasure Island', and rumbles a hint about a part.

Friday, May 27th

Jeremy Meadow, who seems the straightest man in showbiz, calls to say that Pru and Tim West have turned down 'The Weekend' ('not unpleasantly') as has his first choice as director. We discuss options on his list. I wonder why he hasn't got Ken Cranham down there. 'Audiences don't really know him,' but he takes my point and adds his name. He will next check availability of [Pauline] Collins and [her husband John] Alderton.

Friday, June 3rd

Sleep, though it's another short night, and wake, largely untroubled by doubts today of my decision over Diaries and by implication, the shape of the next ten years of my life. Next ten years! Can't believe I wrote that so blithely.

No one in the family has raised an objection. Close friends I talk to can't wait for me to publish. Kath [James], who, as transcriber, knows them better than anyone, wants me to go ahead. So the die, I think, is cast.

Walk up to Belsize Park. Macchiato in hand, crisp NY Herald-Trib in bag, I cannot be much happier. Rattle down to Leicester Square and walk to the office. Michael, Ion, Steve and myself get round the glass-topped table at eleven and pretty soon I can see that this will not be a contentious meeting. Ion quite happy to accept my role as primary editor with Kath J as my assistant. I reiterate the point that I would like the Diaries to be treated in a more low-key market-ing style than 'Himalaya'. I want them out there as a record, and an entertaining record, and not sold as sensational or revelatory or 'the *real* MP', sort of thing.

Sunday, June 19th

A Python meeting – well, a business meal – which I've organised up at San Carlo. TG, JC and TJ and myself assemble and it's quite an agreeable, enjoyable session. TJ jokes from the beginning that he'll agree to anything as he's so desperate for the money. JC exhibits pathological dislike of any lawyers of Eric's and wants to find out who we can trust to deal with the rights for 'Spamalot'.

All of us wary of Eric's most recent suggestion – inevitable though it is – that he and John Du Prez [composer and Python collaborator] be allowed to work their magic on 'Brian'. General feeling that this is a different kettle than 'Grail'. John, on the other hand, is not against a stage version provided he can work on the script. TG couldn't care less (he has two new films coming out in the next three months).

Sunday, June 26th: Melrose–London

Wake in guiltless comfort at the restrained and well-appointed Eildon House in Melrose, after a night at the Borders Festival [promoting the *Himalaya* book]. Even with the curtains drawn my spacious room is filled with sunlight.

A man called Alan is the only other guest at breakfast. Intellectual friend of Alastair Moffat's. We talk about travel – how we go too far, too fast, too easily and don't take in the detail. Encounters like this all help me shape the next journey – the next move.

Fly back. An unexpected call from Eric, who has not had what he considers a satisfactory response to his email about starting work on 'Brian the Musical' – which we discussed a week ago at San Carlo – other than to hear that JC considers there will not be time for a group meeting until April next year.

Eric sees only the damage that can be done to 'the team' that made 'Spamalot' such a hit (for us all) by such delay. Talking to Eric is a bit like flying into enemy territory. Flak all around, most of it slightly off target but quite bright and noisy. I bat back what I can. Agree that no meeting till April is ridiculous, quite take to Eric's proposal of working on a few songs and some script for us to judge the work before deciding, but really I'm in the middle of a possibly unresolvable feud between him and John about what is to be done with 'LoB'. JC wants to be involved in the writing and structure, Eric wants to do it himself.

Monday, July 4th

A weekend of big events – for all of which I was grateful to be a home spectator. The Live 8 concert filled Hyde Park. Rock stars played at ruling the world.

Pink Floyd reformed. Madonna shrieked 'Are You Fucking Ready London' and apart from the music it was all a bit embarrassing.

Venus Williams pulls back to beat [Lindsay] Davenport. Grunting and glamour defeating modesty and concentration.

Cleese rings. He's going to email Eric and everyone else about 'Brian' as musical. He doesn't want any work done without him – and anyone else who's interested – being involved. We'll see.

Tuesday, July 5th

The weather has turned quite surly. Cooler and grey skies with threat of rain. Try to get my fitness back on track with a mid-morning run, then drive over to meet Jonathan Clyde and George Martin for lunch at L'Aventure. Buy Radio Times on the way. Good as their word, they have given monster coverage to the Hammershoi film, including a cover with me on board the three-master in Copenhagen and the big, bold heading 'Palin's Passion'.

Pleasant, quiet lunch with Jonathan C, George Martin and Giles, his son. George is a big man. Tall, slim with eyes that pin you down. He's also getting quite deaf and to begin with, his voice is several decibels too loud and fills the restaurant. 'We're working with these Cirque du Soleil people in Montreal. And you know, the French accent is *so* funny.' Maybe Giles gives him some subtle signal that we're eating in a French restaurant, and he readjusts.

I must remember that this tall, long-faced, handsome Englishman across the table from me – talking like a liberal headmaster – has been close to much of the entertainment that accompanied my adolescent and early life. Sellers, Spike, the Beatles – all made to sound good by George.

Apart from a huge project with Cirque du Soleil – 'Their sense of humour is very different from ours,' he says. 'Clowns,' Jonathan adds, wincing – he's also agreed to front a series on the History of Sound Recording for PBS. I sense a very proud man, very English too, determined not to let deafness reduce a life dedicated to hearing things better than anyone else.

Wednesday July 6th

The Guardian runs my Hammershoi piece today. I'm up there on the masthead looking weirdly like [film critic] Alexander Walker (how I wish Graham were around – he had an obsession with Walker and would have adored the picture!) and two pages of 'G2', one of which is entirely taken up by a Hammershoi interior. Bold and striking.

By the time I get home from my run, suitably panting and sweaty, I hear the most outrageously unexpected bit of news from Singapore. London has been chosen, by four votes, ahead of Paris, Madrid, New York and Moscow to host the 2012 Olympic games.

It's the best moment, better for being a surprise, but good because I feel London is ready to do the games and do them well. The glumness of the '70s and '80s has been replaced by a growing sense of being *the* world city of the early twenty-first century. An acknowledgement that Livingstone and Blair and others avoided the anti-foreign bias of America and the complacent self-regard of Paris.

I set off for the BBC Four Mark Lawson interview with optimism that I can deal with whatever comes at me.

Though the interview has been arranged to publicise 'Himalaya', Mark Lawson makes hardly any mention of the book and goes into a long – one-hour – interview to try and prove his thesis that behind the sunny exterior of MP lurks an unadmitted depressive.

All I feel is that Mark Lawson managed to avoid any areas which might have shown off natural vitality, humour and inventiveness. The whole interview felt like – well it felt like being forced into clothes that don't fit, whilst standing in front of a mirror.

Thursday, July 7th

At the desk, preparing for Kath's arrival when Rachel rings. Around 9.45. 'Dad, what's happening?' The first indications that something is wrong in the Host City 2012. She's on her way to work, has experienced Tube disruption and now passes on the news that a bus, possibly several buses, have been blown up. The very best day followed by the very worst.

Dizzyingly awful drama. Screaming sirens, flashing lights, police barriers, yellow jackets, urgent voices. Immediate worries – the family. All well. Rachel at Shepherd's Bush on way to Acton to edit. Will working from home. John Du Prez rings. Kath's train stopped at Reading. I'm mightily relieved. John is going to pick her up and take her home.

So, my most immediate anxieties set aside, I sit, for far too long, taking in the Breaking News on the TV and Radio 5. Fascinated and repelled. Work is almost impossible. Gradually the truth emerges from all sorts of rumours. Four explosions. Three in the Underground, one on the bus, right opposite the square in which stands the kneeling statue of Gandhi – apostle of non-violence. There are 'fatalities' and soon 'fatalities' become 'those killed'. I take it all in, distracted, with a slight tightening in the pit of the stomach. The smile is wiped off London's face.

Figures of 37 dead as we go to bed.

Friday, July 8th

In good and bad times this week London's spirit has been intensely scrutinised and defined in articles, letters, broadcasts. The very multiculturalism, diversity, tolerance that was celebrated on Wednesday, was seen as the reason why we were attacked on Thursday (almost universal feeling is that this is al-Qaeda work).

I'm to lunch with Peter Fincham, head of BBC One and the managing director of Television, Jana Bennett, and fully expect this to be cancelled in view of the crisis. But it isn't.

First time I've met Lorraine's successor. He's fresh, bright-eyed, interested. Ex-Footlights, of the Griff Rhys Jones, John Lloyd Cambridge intake. Speaks reverently of Python. 'There was nothing we could do that you hadn't done.' Whether he'll survive or not with this relaxed, accessible manner, I don't know. Jana is less open, I feel. Perfectly nice, but her instincts are much more political. A certain wariness, a sense of judgement being made.

Fincham's first question is whether I'm still opposed to letting them do a TV tribute to me. I tell him I am. Then the question of a future travel series occupies most of the discussion. They appreciate I'm giving no hard answers and making no decisions until the end of the year, but were I minded to do another, they would love to be able to give it a tentative slot, earmark it for budget and promotion.

As I can think of no good reason for not doing another series (especially as Middle East is materialising nicely in my mind) it's a question only of which autumn. So they suggest setting it all in place for transmission in autumn 2007.

Drive home, listening to the radio. Death toll from yesterday up to 49, and that doesn't include those killed on the Piccadilly deep tunnel between King's Cross and Russell Square, who have still to be brought out. It's odd how close to home these attacks have been. Next to the white screens erected outside Russell Square Station is the spot where I often park to go to the Renoir. The bus was blown up half a mile from Rachel's flat, the Aldgate attack little more than a mile from Will's house. Because so much of the damage is underground and can't be seen, it sort of reduces the outward and visible impact. No iconic and terrifying images like the attack on the Towers or the hole bursting from the side of the Madrid train.

To the gym then out to supper with Simon Gray. I wanted to meet him, because I felt I'd come close to him as a result of 'Quartermaine' and 'Smoking Diaries'. I'm dropped off at the Belvedere in Holland Park. He's already at a table upstairs, smoking away and working on what looks like a Coke.

He's a big man, wearing what looks like two shirts one on top of the other, an unruly thatch of greying hair, big, slightly moist eyes which he sometimes fixes on me and I wonder why. Is he trying to size me up intellectually, or assess me as a Quartermaine?

Once we get talking I feel, because I've read his diaries, that we don't have to make small talk. His voice, low register and breathy from all the fags, is sometimes difficult to hear. He's read my Guardian article on Hammershøi and is looking forward to the programme – but the way he picks on certain loose phraseology in the article makes me aware that he's intellectually much more rigorous than me and may well be disappointed.

Walk back with him down towards Holland Park Avenue. I hail a taxi and we shake hands. I still feel him holding something back, whilst being extraordinarily easy to talk to at the same time. I don't sense that a follow-up meeting is on the cards. Quite honestly he doesn't seem that healthy and I have the feeling he's no longer interested in making too many new friends.

Saturday, July 9th

To Bernard and Mina's new house opposite the synagogue in Dunston Road. A good crowd to talk about the recent triumphs and travails. Bernard's French, his boss is an Iraqi, who's lived in London for 27 years; also there was a French banker, disillusioned with his work and looking for a change of life, his Polish wife, and two pretty daughters who are about to start at the Lycée, a French restaurateur who has a bistro in Baker Street and his Anglo-French wife, who once worked at Buckingham Palace.

I felt quite reassured, being amongst this polyglot mix. They were fiercely fond of London, and if there was any united criticism at all it was directed towards the French. Arrogance and aloofness had cost them the Olympics. Chirac was a political dinosaur, a left-over from another age, out of touch with the people. Patrice the restaurateur, almost triumphantly, made the point that in a recent poll in Europe, the French were voted 'the most hated people'.

Then why is this sample of French people such funny, generous, agreeable company? Are they just making us feel better about what's happened? Or is it just that none of them lives in France?

Tuesday, July 12th

To the NPG for a Patrons' breakfast and special preview. The exhibition – 'The World's Most Photographed' – is good in the small details, most memorably a set of studio shots, by Hoffman, of Hitler trying out the pugnacious hand and arm gestures he was to use so theatrically at rallies. All carefully worked out beforehand.

A certain heightened awareness of my surroundings, but otherwise I feel less anxious than I'd expected. Maybe to do with the fact that this isn't rush hour. Bombs seem to go off around quarter to nine. The train is very hot and the streets of Belsize Park offer little relief. Unblinking sun, barely a breeze.

Apparently the identities of the bombers are now known. They are all Pakistani Yorkshire boys – born and brought up in my home county – who blew themselves up along with 50 or so others. This sounds like a nightmare scenario, a very minor civil war. When they bombed, the IRA always issued communiqués, declared their political intentions; these boys belonged to no known organisation, nor seemed to want to make any other point than that they were willing to die – and because they left documents at the scene, wanted people to know they were willing to die. Chilling revelations.

Wednesday, July 13th

Quiet supper with H. Long, grim news report on the bombings. One day of exultation, since then a week of corrosive bad news. The day before the bombings, one week ago today, feels more and more like an innocent, prelapsarian age, when we all knew how to be happy.

Thursday, July 14th

Brave the heat after lunch – walk to Belsize Park and on the Underground to Leicester Square. Walk through crowded streets full of young, lightly clad Londoners. What a young city London is, I think to myself, then pause as I remember that from the perspective of a 62-year-old most places would seem that way. Except perhaps Frinton.

Home, train grinds to a halt in tunnel outside Camden Town. I know that this often happens but for any foreigners whose minds have been focused on those who died in three Tube bombs a week ago the lack of reassuring information can't have helped.

Monday, July 18th

Tom round after lunch. He had an accident on his bike on Friday. Speeding along Hamilton Place when a car door was opened right in front of him. No time to stop, crashed into the door, smashed the window and skidded along the road on his side, embedding fragments of glass in quite deeply. The owner of the car, a brand new Mercedes, was more shocked than Tom and v. apologetic.

A butler emerged from house opposite to offer Tom a place to clean himself out. Turned out to be state-of-the-art opulence, the occasional residence in London of one of the Gucci family.

Manage to draw up a schedule for the Diaries. In the few pages I'm able to read today I come across details of a trip with the boys up to the playground at the end of which 'Tom fell off his bike and had to be brought home'.

Thursday, July 21st

To Carlton School to hand out certificates and say a word or two to the Year 6 leavers. Am having a coffee with Dalu, the head teacher, in the reception room when Michael, the caretaker, brings news of more incidents in London. 'Flashes of smoke', bangs, at three or four stations on the Underground including Warren Street – through which I passed little more than three hours ago. A bus has been hit as well. I feel that tightening of the stomach, and a momentary surge of panic caused by not knowing the details. Where is this going? What more is there? How many deaths? How bad is it?

We know little more when the time comes to begin assembly. Dalu, rightly, decides not to tell the children – we don't know enough, and there is such an unreserved excitement and anticipation about this day that we all feel must be allowed to play itself out. The school is restless, but they listen politely. I end on multiculturalism – what this school represents is surely the way forward – the face of the future. Though I wish I felt as confident as I looked. Fortunately, we're told in the office afterwards that no one has died in any of the attacks. Nor has there been any damage. But stations are closed and people are scared again.

Friday, July 22nd

Have taken up Mike Parkinson's offer of a ticket to Lord's for the first Test against the Aussies – apparently this is the hottest sporting event since Wimbledon – and all seats booked throughout the Tests.

At the Bicentenary Gate, as I check, for the umpteenth time, for the ticket, I hear a drawled greeting and a chuckle of laughter and look up to see Peter O'Toole, surely the most elegant of Britain's senior citizens, leaning up against the wall. He glances down at my white shoes, trousers, shirt and jacket and then up at the greyish skies. 'Bit optimistic,' he suggests.

Eager sense of anticipation as 10.30 comes around. Seventeen wickets fell yesterday in a frenetic day's play. England looked down and out but the lower order digs in and we're up and down applauding Kevin Pietersen's disdainful series of boundaries off Glenn McGrath.

Then, after lunch, it settles in to predictability as Clarke and Martyn pile on the runs for Australia. By now the wines have made their rounds several times.

Peter Salmon is networking round the boxes. He asks me if there's any kind of sports-related programme I'd like to do. So I tell him about 'Stenhousemuir' – my idea of looking at how a lowly club like that survives. A study, I suppose, of how failure is dealt with, lived with and sometimes celebrated. 'I'm a Burnley supporter' says Peter, 'I know what you're talking about'. He's intrigued I think and promises to get back to me.

I've been spotted on camera, and this is accompanied by a visit from one of the TV production team with an earpiece in, eyeing me as I remember being eyed by a master at school, to be selected for some unwanted but inevitable task. Round to the press box at tea interval to talk to Atherton and Mark Nicholas. I like them both very much – Atherton especially, a straightforward, well-balanced, intelligent man – we talk Hemingway. Athers remembers EH's only reference to cricket – 'over in England the cricket players will be sharpening their wickets'. And I got to shake the hand of Geoffrey Boycott – who, his girlfriend assures me, is 'a god' in India. Stay to the bitter end – just as well, as Warne is caught out off the last ball of the day.

Arrive home, soon after seven, to yet more depressing news. Police have pumped at least eight bullets in the head of a suspected bomber at Stockwell Station. He was revealed not to be carrying a bomb, and this sounds a desperately bad call for the police.

Monday, July 25th

The second bombing incidents, though failed, seem to have affected morale as much, if not more than the first wave on the seventh. The 7/7 attacks were monstrous and shocking, but the bombers themselves are dead, their details known, and London rallied and was getting into its stride again.

With the abortive attacks two weeks later, from which all the participants escaped and are on the loose, and in response to which our Met police force pumps eight bullets into the head of an innocent Brazilian, we're entering a troubled, nightmarish world of suspicion, misinformation and confusion.

Against all this, the surge of pride, pleasure and emotion when on Saturday afternoon, Tom, fresh back from Friedrichshafen mountain equipment fair, let me know that his wife Rachel is pregnant. Very early stages, so controlled euphoria, but I experienced that swell of positive, heart-bursting sense of achievement, which I experienced when Tom was conceived.

Own flesh and blood, stage two!

Thursday, July 28th

A week on from the last, failed attacks, three or four police stand at the entrance to Belsize Park Station. They've clearly been told to be amiable, friendly and unthreatening.

London quieter perhaps than usual, but not by much and no air of menace. Even, for once, the chorus of wailing police sirens, that has characterised the city these past three weeks, is stilled.

To the office, a copy of the Guardian 'G2' is on the desk. I'd alerted Steve to have a look at it when I saw that the lead article featured a new book by one Jeff Connor, who has spent the last year seeing what life is like for a club at the very bottom of the Scottish League. It's actually East Sterling rather than Stenhousemuir, but he has done, in effect, exactly what I wanted to do.

Friday, July 29th

Hear from Paul that the Met have somewhat redeemed their PR disaster at Stockwell, by picking up two more of the four July 21st suspects, and picking them up alive. Later news comes in that the fourth suspect has been arrested in Rome. Breathe a sigh of relief. This surely won't be the end of 'martyr' bombings, but at least there is a trail which can now be investigated.

Jeremy Meadow calls. John Alderton has turned down 'The Weekend', but irrepressible Jeremy, who always rings from the side of a road somewhere, has sent it (and an offer!) to David Suchet.

Sunday August 7th

Helen has a minor coughing fit at six and I don't sleep much after that. I keep turning over in my mind the shape of things to come.

I see-saw over the Diaries. Torn between fear of opening myself up and all the unnecessary and unwonted hassle that might arrive from publication. I feel that I'm at a crossroads and what I decide in these next few weeks will shape and, in a sense, pin down the next ten years for me. So I wake, feeling cheated of the slumber of the content, and rise a little jarred and confused.

Tuesday, August 9th

Out at Warren Street. A fine morning, warm sunshine. London clean and quiet. Am virtually resigned to extricating myself from the Stenhousemuir project, mainly on grounds of time. However, by the end of an hour's chat with Peter Salmon and two of his cohorts, I find myself in much deeper than when we all sat down.

Peter's boys have done some interesting research: Stenhousemuir's nickname is The Warriors, and the main industry in the area is a toffee factory. I worry about appearing patronising or condescending, but this could be overcome by spending time in the town, rather than arriving by limousine from Edinburgh every morning. I'm drawn to the idea of looking more closely at a community, seeing it from the inside; fine detail and all that.

By the end of the extremely positive meeting, I've talked myself into an equally positive next step. To extend my trip up to Glasgow for the Hammershoi cast and crew viewing on Friday to include a visit to S'muir. Research reveals they have a home game against Elgin.

I'm picked up by Bernard and taken out to East London for my tour of the CTRL (Channel Tunnel Rail Link) works that Bernard is involved with. Portakabins in dusty Dagenham. A shunting loco has been secured, on which we travel through 10k's of tunnel to the eerily empty, but more than half-finished Stratford International station. Escalators rise from the platforms. Light grey canopies, half-fitted, with plastic covering still flapping from them, are clamped to the 30-foot-high walls of this enormous man-made hole, a kilometre long. There are some 5k's of tunnels on the French network. They are constructing 40k's on the 67 miles from Folkestone to St Pancras alone.

I'm allowed, indeed encouraged, to drive the 1400hp engine back through the tunnel to Dagenham. On the opposite line, one of the last of the long concrete trains sets off into the tunnels to deliver its load to the last few hundred yards of track into St Pancras. Epic stuff. Dust blows everywhere. This is backstage at the biggest rail project in Europe.

Friday, August 12th

Up in Glasgow and collected by BBC car. It's been almost impossible to find hotel rooms tonight; the explanation being the International Piping Championships which take place tomorrow with 40,000 bagpipers and their fans filling the city.

The Hammershoi crew screening is at midday. Generally cordial. I see the faults bigger on the big screen, but it remains largely satisfying. Hear the word 'pretentious' bandied by the crew – in jest of course, but I suspect the joke conceals their true feelings.

Arrange to meet Marcus [my nephew who lives with his family in Glasgow] for supper. He'd told me a couple of weeks ago that there were gaps in his knowledge of Angela's life that he wanted to fill, and we end up talking about my sister. Marcus wanted to know if she was a good actress and might have made it had she persevered. I said I thought not. He remembers her as 'quite a snob'. I said that given our background of declining gentry, I too had a quite constricted and conventional attitude to the social hierarchy, but that I lost it as soon as I met Helen.

These and many other things were mulled over without rush and am glad we've established a way to talk about Angela. I never want her to be ignored.

Saturday, August 13th: Stenhousemuir–London

Call from Steve Anderson of Mentorn who was going to hire a car and pick me up, to say that he'd been stuck in a tunnel for half an hour after a security alert; he'd meet me at the ground – and meantime was sending a car to take me to Stenhousemuir. It's a white leather seat number complete with capped chauffeur – not exactly what I wanted for a discreet visit to a run-down Scottish working-class town.

The weather perks up as we near. My polite, deferential driver takes me up and down the few roads of the town, past the toffee factory (which looks deserted) and the football ground – almost hidden by the factory; beyond it the cricket pitch and golf course. The houses are generally two storey – quite basic, not run down or in any way tragic. A few sullen youngsters hang around the car park, but otherwise all seems disappointingly tidy – and visually very dull.

Send the car back to Glasgow and make for the only place of refreshment, the white-walled Plough Hotel. The bar is full; noisy, smoky and, to my surprise, a predominantly elderly clientele. There are two hours to kill before I have to be at Ochilview so there's no option but to grin and bear it. I'm 'looked after' by a heavy-bellied man and another wiry middle-aged Scot with a darting glance; both friendly. By the time I leave the Plough I've had 3 pints of heavy, and none of the men seem to be going to the game with me. They refer to the club as 'Stenhousemuir – Nil'.

At the ground I'm met by blazered chairman and entertained, along with Steve, fresh up from London, to a very good lunch. The entire crowd (403 people) fits in this stand, so very little atmosphere for the players. The teams seem strangely uninvolved, as if there's little connection with their supporters. I learn that they're mostly boys from Glasgow rather than round Stenhousemuir. Half-time drinks and pies with the directors of Elgin City and S'muir, all in blazers, with trophies in cabinets – feels very much like a Masonic event.

Stenhousemuir win a bloodless game by 3 goals to 1.

There is nothing romantic about what's happening up there – it's more like routine. The club hangs on, the glory days of the mid '90s when they won a cup, slowly fade and yet no one seems to be offering much resistance.

Quite frankly, there's no magic about the club for me to spend two weeks of my life here. Maybe I did it all in Golden Gordon.

Monday, August 15th

Lunch with Paul Smith. Organised through Will, who persuaded Paul to come and talk at the museum. Am at the Soane by half past twelve to meet up with Will.

We walk into Covent Garden and Paul Smith's HQ at Kean Street. There's something playful and formal about the Paul Smith approach. No one wears uniforms, or goes around with headsets, hi-tech is carefully camouflaged beneath a Boy's Own kind of jolliness.

We're taken upstairs to Paul's floor. Like Will, I can see Paul dressed in Regency. They're both tall, quite angular. His hair flares out, his eyes are smiley but keen. He has been in Italy for five weeks and looks well. His desk is covered in books, magazines, photos, toys. He's a collector in the Soane mould, though more ephemeral than antiquarian.

Paul deserves his knighthood – he has managed to combine personal enthusiasms for the unusual, but always individual and crafted, with pretty sharp business sense (77 stores in Japan alone). He has a non-stop enthusiasm for everything around him and loves transmitting it. Fabrics he's found, leathers – he's into a cowboy phase at the moment – and tho' there's something very British about his enthusiasms, he looks abroad for inspiration. Much of his work is done in Italy.

His spirit, and his combination of entrepreneur and eternal schoolboy, dominates and defines the operation. He's like a Willy Wonka – proudly showing us round, introducing us to the various components of the Paul Smith world. 'This group here,' he holds out his arms at an angle to mark the corner of one room, '16 million a year, they turn over, just that group.'

In response to my question as to how he recruits – does he keep a sharp eye on the emerging talent of fashion colleges? he chuckles. 'Oh no, I'm much more interested in someone who knows about architecture, or painting.'

Twenty Kean Street is a wonderland. An apparently happy, devoted, well-treated workforce, (some 160) in bright and lively surroundings producing a constant stream of innovative clothes, shoes, hats, and making money all round the world.

Wednesday, August 31st

A hot and humid end to August. I tackle a cupboard in my room which is stuffed full of all manner of things – the filleting of all this takes up most of the day. Letters written from me to Helen in the two years before we were married are evidence of my dog-like devotion, love and general dottiness over her. With our 40th anniversary only a half-year away I feel quite pleased, not so much with the illiteracy of my hopeless devotion, but with the fact that it wasn't all wasted!

Thursday, September 1st

September offers cool objectivity after the restlessness of high summer. Soon children will be going back to school, traffic jams will get worse, Parliament will rumble back into action. Already the leaves are turning on the creeper, and though it's very warm, the air is a little fresher.

Letters to be dealt with. Proposals include my idea for 'great sewers of the world' for Radio 4. They want me to present, and of course, I'd be very tempted. But I fear it will have to go down as one of those many things I wanted to do, but needed another life to do them in.

The 'Himalaya' paperback is performing very poorly, and Steve has figures which I think I should discuss with W&N/Orion. For once, their sales knack has deserted them. I feel I must make a decision on the next series very soon. If possible by the end of September – this will give us more preparation time than we had for 'Himalaya', and a potentially less stressful schedule.

Monday, September 5th

Grizzled TG lining up with his 'Grimm' stars at the Venice festival, in photo in the Independent. Terry taking on the critics 'people have their opinions, and some of them are wrong'. He's putting his faith in the children whose minds are open much wider than the critics, he says. Good fighting stuff, but it seems like a rearguard action.

Tuesday September 6th

To lunch at Rules with Rog. Oysters, steak and kidney pie and a talk over the new series. I push forward the idea of following the Silk Road, and Roger, who after all suggested it before 'Himalaya', is pleased and excited.

By the time I get home, I've begun to put my finger on the reason for my continuing reservations about the Silk Road. It's predictable; doesn't leave us as much freedom to create our own route and our own journey – an important element of our success. Audiences could trace our route before we'd even started. The idea of going from Istanbul to the coast of China and calling it ASIA forms in my mind and I scribble down a suggested route – including the 'Stans' – and send it off in a breathlessly enthusiastic email to Rog.

Asia – now that has magic and scale and a nice touch of mystery.

Wednesday, September 7th

Sober early hours thinking made me recant over Asia. Rog not ready until January, Basil hard at work on his book. Just too ambitious. And more mountains – some as tough as the Himalaya.

Tuesday, September 13th

Rachel rings in a sunny mood as she's just heard that, despite what she reckoned to be her poor performance at interview, she has been asked to go out and work on 'I'm a Celebrity' for a month in Australia in Nov.

To a beak-dip with Roger and Alex [Richardson, travel show editor] at the Sun in Splendour. Roger has invited Nigel [Meakin], which turns out to be a clever move. We discuss the latest twists and turns of another series. I tell them I'm swinging back to Brazil – and this starts a ball rolling quite productively. Nigel has filmed in Brazil and is certain we'll not get six programmes from that one country. Roger is keen to start in the Panama Canal. Uruguay, Argentina and Venezuela are interesting because none of us knows much about them, so a necklace of countries to the East of the Andes begins to emerge as a possible route. Nigel forcibly reiterating the point that my audience loves to see me cross borders.

Thursday, September 15th

To lunch with Steve. Progress towards defining my future plans is beginning to accelerate. Last negotiations on the Diary deal have been completed, so within a week this will have reached point of no return, with Weidenfeld's official public announcement that they have secured world rights for my scribbles.

We talk about South America. I've had no serious withdrawal symptoms since Tuesday night's chat at the Sun in Splendour and it feels a good prospect.

I need a day away from diary editing to think it over but I expect by the weekend to have taken the plunge.

Letters at the office and a press cutting from Front magazine in which an aggrieved correspondent protests at my inclusion on the Biggest Cunts page. 'Palin is a credit to the nation and the cunt who wrote this letter isn't fit to lace his hiking boots.' 'Palin was a mistake,' they reply, which leaves me oddly disappointed.

Monday, September 19th

A potential South America schedule makes striking reading at first, but there is something which worries me. I think it's that this is going to involve a lot of landscape travel – big distances, majestic waterfalls, and a limited number of occasional encounters – many of which seem to likely to be with ex-pats on colonial verandas. It worries me that East of the Andes will not be the equal of 'Himalaya', and yet will look as though it is trying to ape it.

I set out for a run as dusk is falling and turn things over in my mind as I go. The more I contemplate E of the Andes, the more uncertain I become and by the time I get home I'm pretty sure the die is cast against it.

Tuesday, September 20th

Despite irresolution and indecision sweeping over me again I sleep well and have not much changed my mind over the South America idea. If anything I've hardened my attitude. Have called a meeting of Steve, J-P and Rog at No 34.

J-P arrives, full of beans. 'A good omen,' he enthuses, producing the Footprint guides to Venezuela, Argentina and Brazil, '3 for 2 at the local Waterstones!' I explain my doubts straight away and there is little or no attempt on anyone's part to try and change my mind. Rog agrees that South America could be seen as escapist after 'Himalaya', and tho' J-P puts up an alternative argument, I think the point is taken that there are fewer opportunities for human contacts, and a Latin-American homogeneity which could wear thin after six shows.

Then, out of a good discussion, comes a shaft of light. Roger, I think, mentions Europe and this leads me on to suggesting not the well-trodden territory of Western Europe, but the less well-known, but newly liberated East. New Europe – now there's an idea. Closer to home both physically and politically. New countries, old religions and traditions. Dense and complex and full of people to talk to.

The clouds have moved on, the sun's out, home – via Stanfords once again, this time to collect maps with Moldova and Bosnia Herzegovina on.

Friday, September 23rd

An email from Roger, ahead of our meeting later today, pushing his preference for South America and expressing concern that New Europe, so easily
accessible now by cut-price airlines, may be an unglamorous disappointment.
This makes me sit down and put to paper my arguments – not *against* South
America, I expressed those on Tuesday – but in favour of New Europe. The
reasons are not hard to collate. I feel convinced that this offers a way out of the
clichéd Palin 'Britain's Favourite Traveller' format. It's one step ahead of what
people will expect, and to be one step ahead is, and has, always been important
to me.

Rain is puttering down steadily as I make my way to the Tube, and more
persistently when I emerge from Leicester Square station a half-hour later. A
half-hearted last attempt to consider the South American option, but by the
end of a two-hour meeting I've persuaded J-P and Roger of the virtues of the
European option and Steve opens a bottle of Sainsbury's champagne and we
drink a toast to the next series.

West End heaving as we walk up St Martin's Lane to the Ivy. Alan Bleasdale,
the Thompsons and another of his partners in Diplomat Films are throwing
a party upstairs (for which the guests have to stump up later!). Alan delivers a funny speech of welcome. He recalls that one of the local papers did a
poll to find out 'The Best Scousers, Alive or Dead'. Alan came 14th. 'If you
want to know who came 13th,' he bellows, 'open the envelope in front of
you.' Laughter, syncopated according to opening skills and condition of eyesight, crackles round the room as we all read that Red Rum, the horse, was
number 13.

Most astounding news of the evening: Robert Lindsay telling me that Simon Russell Beale is to take over as the king in 'Spamalot'. Rather like Alec
Guinness taking the part.

Friday, September 30th

I call Peter Fincham's office. He's out but returns my call twenty minutes later
and I tell him of my plan to do Eastern Europe as the 2007 journey. He engag-
es easily on the subject, accepts that I've moved on from sand and deserts, but
expresses a caution that audiences look to me to take them somewhere exotic. I
explain my reasons and as I talk them through, he adds his own reactions – he's
been to Bosnia, I haven't – and by the end of a five-minute ramble round the
subject he sounds convinced by my conviction.

Thursday, October 6th

At the office, Steve has a grave face. Apparently a Telegraph journalist has been investigating the affairs of the Peter Cook Foundation and found things to be quite seriously wrong. In five years it has never made money, and no centre has been opened and, it appears, not a single child helped. In a month's time I'm giving my Evening With in aid of the Foundation – and apparently some tickets are being sold for £150.

Steve has been given figures and accounts for Companies House to back up this gloomy story, which the Telegraph are running on Monday next week.

Friday, October 7th

Steve rings with confirmation of the Peter Cook Foundation story. The journalist is in Hampstead this morning and is clearly aiming to make this big. We agree on a statement from me. A moment later Ian Hislop rings – which is very rare. Did I know that enquiries were going on into the affairs of the Foundation (which is taking out ads in Private Eye to advertise my concert?). 'We'll be blamed,' he says ruefully, if the affairs of Lin Cook are revealed to the world.

Monday, October 10th

A weekend of guests and visitors. Tom, Rachel W and Will over to celebrate Tom's 37th. He'll be a dad for his 38th, hopefully. Walk up to get the Telegraph, which, sure enough, has an article on the Foundation. Illustrated with photo of me and the ticket for my concert and Peter and Lin, written by one Dan Fenton, it says nothing more than we expected. But it's brought out into the open the stark reality that the Foundation has been a failure.

On the previous page an interview with the headmaster of Shrewsbury, trying to limit the damage caused by yesterday's serialisation of John Peel's posthumously published autobiography, in which he tells of being raped by an older boy at the cemetery outside Shrewsbury. 'Raped at Shrewsbury' was the headline in yesterday's Sunday Tel., which might cut the school's waiting list quite considerably.

Wednesday, October 12th

To Pimlico on the Tube and walk through to the Tate. The current exhibition – Degas, Sickert and Toulouse Lautrec – is well-attended but not impossible.

Avoid the bottleneck which always gathers at the start of the exhibition and have time close to most of the pictures.

As A. Bennett says in his new 'Untold Stories' collection, looking at art is tiring – and looking at paintings of quality, whose detail it's worth taking in, even more tiring. The Degas repay concentration, but best of all is a selection of Sickerts – which underline what an original talent he had – he's taken the uncelebrated, ordinary man and woman as his subject, and with nods to Degas, composed his paintings voyeuristically. He loves the female body but doesn't idealise it. His are big, used, bodies.

Private Eye has a quarter page ad for the P. Cook evening so we should soon find out if the Telegraph piece has affected sales. The Roundhouse confirm they are in talks with Lin and the Foundation. I need, though, positive confirmation that this is where my money will go.

Home with TG in a cab. 'Brothers Grimm' has, he admits, not performed well in the States and tho' he has hopes for Japan next week, it's the US.grosses that solely determine his future bankability. 'Tideland' has been reviled by critics (especially the trades) and Jeremy Thomas wants to cut it to make it more commercial. TG feels that the subject is the subject – there's no way of disguising it by a few cuts. I know he's ahead of his time and that 'Tideland', and all the rest, will be lauded as 'brave' in TG Festivals years from now. Not that that is any consolation to him at the moment.

Thursday, October 13th

Awake by 6. Can hear the soft tinkling of rainwater in the drains outside. I wish I could lie and think of what lies ahead with unequivocal satisfaction, but generally it's the opposite that intrudes – doubts, vague resentments at freedom curtailed, friends waiting to be contacted.

To see the Making of the Concert for Bangladesh documentary that has been put together at the behest of Olivia. This was a first, a pioneer mega-celebrity concert. Once the screening began and we were confronted with George – at little more than Dhani's age – breaking nervously into 'Something', I found myself unexpectedly affected and had to wait until the song was finished and we went to some more clinical present-day interview before I could properly dry my eyes.

It was almost George's first public appearance without the Beatles. The '60s dream had passed, Clapton was there and not there, so drugged he had trouble standing still, but none in playing.

All the problems temporarily overcome by the unity of the audience who witnessed rare and wonderful performances. Dhani said later that Dylan had never done a better version of 'Just Like a Woman'. Watching it made me aware too of how smooth, well-ordered and controlled are our Good Cause concerts now. Technologically smooth and efficient but mostly lacking the magic of the Concert for Bangladesh, the improvisation, the uncertainty which makes it so moving to look at – and made me feel George's absence most poignantly. This was George at his best – and I almost reached out to grasp Dhani's hand as the concert went on. It would have been the next best thing.

It moved me to a determination not to just be content with the average, the easy, the purely conventional and acceptable. I must be true to George's legacy and make something of my own – make it special and different and well, take risks, keep taking risks. Resist the BAFTAs and the pathways of the stars. In a most unexpected way tonight's screening of the Concert for Bangladesh was inspirational.

Thursday, October 20th

A meeting with the BBC to try and pin down the next big series. After a breakfast at the café/bar of the Electric in Portobello Rd, we troop next door to the Cinema Club to meet Fincham and his head of documentaries – Richard Klein.

Klein arrives first. My initial impression is cautious, when I see his long, unbuttoned shirt cuffs – a fashion statement I associate with Laurence Llewellyn-B. He's lean, sharp-eyed, and looks rigorous. Peter F, jolly, engaged, interested and easily amused, is the most unthreatening sort of executive, and as we all sit round a big low table, Richard Klein proves to be equally interested and enthusiastic. He is German, educated in England, living now in Bristol, who knows more about the territory we're expecting to cover than the rest of us put together. The resulting harmony – after an unrushed discussion – is all the more valuable as we're dealing with people who know exactly what they're talking about.

'Well, see you in two years then,' says Peter, as he gets up, leaving Steve to fold up the maps of Europe. We part on optimistic terms, and New Europe (or whatever) is from today, in safe hands, barring any palace revolutions at the Beeb. I must say Peter F seems almost too good to be true.

Monday, October 24th

I didn't sleep very well. Partly anxiety I suppose, as 'Quartermaine' becomes a reality this week. Partly because, unbelievably, my throat is playing up again. Not the cough I was inflicted with in August and September – but in this case a niggly soreness, which could preface a fully fledged streamer of a cold or even loss of voice. Oh God, doesn't bear thinking about.

Up to Parliament Hill for a run between the long periods of forecast rain. Heath slippery after last night's downpour and, almost at the end of the run, as I'm running through the glade of trees to the east of Parliament Hill, I slip, upending myself spectacularly and landing on my right hip with considerable force. Nothing broken, and I continue the run, if a little gingerly, for a few hundred yards, before I notice that my right forearm is covered in blood. I'm not quite sure where from. A slightly mad-looking man on a seat calls after me 'go home and have a bath!' Wash off the blood to reveal a series of superficial scratches, long and fierce enough to look impressive.

The jarring of my hip hasn't immobilised me but I'm unable to hurry along the Underground platforms as I make my way to the 'Quartermaine' read-through at the Bloomsbury Baptist Chapel. The cast – James Fleet, Francesca Faridany, Harriet Walter, David Yelland, Clive Francis and Andrew Lincoln – all polite in that first-meeting sort of way. A good read-through. I feel comfortable in the part from the start and hit most of the funny lines. Heartily encouraged by Clive F, playing Eddie Loomis, and who's done the play twice before, who gives me a friendly and appraising clasp of the shoulder.

Out into a swirling wet windy London. Umbrellas being turned inside out. Stagger to Tottenham Court Road station and home.

Tuesday, October 25th

Sleep on and off between coughs and taking of Strepsils etc. So, hardly rested for first day of 'Quartermaine' recording.

To Shepherds Bush to the Sound House studio. Maria [Aitken] already has given orders for me to be regularly topped up with a ginger and honey hot drink and real chunks of ginger root too, no sachets for her.

I find the first hour or so difficult – difficult because the opening scene between Anita and myself is very much in at the deep end – and what with having to get used to holding the script, turning the pages soundlessly and working round a microphone with someone making creaking noises behind me as I sit down, it seems to lose the lightness of yesterday's read-through, and I feel quite frustrated by the end of the first morning – because I know that lightness – albeit concentrated – is the essence of Quartermaine.

Simon Gray arrives as we're finishing lunch. He's very nice, but his presence makes me even tighter and I find I get quite simple lines completely wrong.

In the afternoon I was more relaxed and did quite a long, revealing speech well. Maybe that's what I needed – something to get my teeth into. Anyway, it saved the day. We're sent home at 5. My sore throat seems to be morphing into a cough but, so far, my voice is unaffected. Take Sudafed and settled into the spare bedroom for a night of throaty trials.

Thursday, October 27th

A night broken by coughs and sneezes – sometimes in such a combination that I feel my body's being turned inside out. To Shepherds Bush for our last day's recording. The weather does its best to improve my mood – the sun shines from an unbroken blue sky and the forecast is for records to be broken as the temps nudge 70°.

Fed by wonderful infusions of ginger and honey, and Maria's boundless enthusiasm, my thick head seems no obstacle to a good last day's work.

A photocall at lunchtime. The Radio Times picks off the 'stars' – Andrew Lincoln, Harriet and myself – before assembling the rest of the cast around us. An unwelcome awkwardness this, for I feel the play itself is an ensemble piece, with not a single junior role in it.

We're finished soon after three. The last scene, with Quartermaine's sudden realisation that his comfortable, accepted way of life is changed for ever, is very similar to the last scene of 'The Dresser'. More understated perhaps, but more effective for that.

Then we all say goodbye and go our separate ways. I linger. Maria, who took me on one side at lunchtime to urge me to reconsider my decision over 'Quartermaine' on stage, realises, I think, that I shan't be able to go back on that decision – now the travel series is firming up. She says she's going to ask Simon to write a play for me to do in two and a half years' time.

I drive home, car roof open, visor down against the warm and powerful sun, feeling quite sad. The fact that I enjoyed these last four days on 'Quartermaine' so much, despite feeling so physically uncomfortable, says a lot for the actor's life. I feel close to our little group, and the playing of good lines and the creation of interesting, well-explored characters leaves a potent buzz of pleasure and achievement.

Friday, October 28th

A reply to my message to Simon G makes email almost worthwhile. He suggested we meet up – with wives, after we've seen [the revival of] 'Otherwise Engaged' – 'or, a little after that so that you don't feel obliged to spend the evening talking about the play. I suspect it'll have a rough time in the West End,' he goes on, 'all that good grammar from people with bad manners. It really is dated, but then so am I, in my soul.' Emails being so essentially functional, it's a pleasure to read something that rambles so intriguingly.

Terry and friend Stefan Kitov (a Bulgarian cinema owner and now the Sofia Film Festival organiser) drop by. Stefan tenaciously works on me to go to Bulgaria for next year's Film Fest. He could be a very good contact for the New

Europe series. TJ likes our title – 'very good, it's got a political significance too.' Terry is on good form until we drift onto the state of the world, and his delivery and general behaviour goes up an octave. At one point he delivers a fierce denunciation of capitalism; all rambling, unfocused stuff, but what he lacks in precision he makes up for in intensity. It's as if he's fighting some unseen assailant who's about to drag him off.

Saturday, October 29th

Enough energy returned to my healing system for me to quite relish the task of putting together a present for Nigel Meakin's belated 60th party tonight. Have decided to buy him a New Europe goody bag, with something from each country we might visit. Already have some juniper sausage from Poland (bought at a new and welcome delicatessen in Fleet Road), and by ten I'm at Stanfords filling up with Czech phrasebooks, glossy guides to Croatia, a map of Transylvania. Drive across to Selfridges, where I add Turkish delight, more Polish vodka, and pack them all in a rucksack from Muji.

Drive to Brentford where Nige and Rhian now live, a ghostly quiet new development between the High St and the Grand Union Canal ('You can go up to Llangollen on that!' Nigel tells me, quite proudly). Nigel hasn't quite reconciled himself with Europe, but is, as he says, 30 per cent enthusiastic. A warm, friendly, comfortable, easy evening.

Thursday, November 3rd

To a launch party at the Fine Art Society for Gerald Scarfe's latest collection. Gerald calls me over as I wander down the stairs. He's standing in a stellar trio – with Tom Stoppard on one side and Mike Nichols on the other.

Mike winces as he talks about the prospect of 'Spamalot' going to Las Vegas. He would prefer it to go into a conventional theatre but Steve Wynne [casino owner who was keen to stage 'Spamalot'] has other ideas. 'The problem with Wynne is that he's almost blind, which doesn't help in discussions of how the show should look.' Mike pauses; I see a similarity to Gilbert and George in his trim, slight, suited tidiness; 'he's surrounded by all these guys who keep referring to him as a man of vision.' Mike lets the lightest of smiles cross his face, 'which he manifestly isn't.'

Sunday, November 6th

Marcus Davey at the Roundhouse talks about a recent TG appearance on the Culture Show in glowing terms. They took him to the Dennis Severs house and he was, of course, animated, irreverent and thoroughly good value. I urge Marcus to try and get TG to appear again talking about something that excites him – a painter, a building. He really could become the new Robert Hughes.

After lunch the rain sets in, pattering on the dome-cover at the top of my spiral staircase as I try to think myself into the two-hour performance I have to give at the Peter Cook charity show tonight.

Eric has sent a somewhat testy email telling us all that he and John Du Prez have songs and a draft book for a 'Brian' musical but they can do nothing until they have 'a deal' with us. Resent the pressure with no attempt on the other hand to understand our divided feelings on the project. But in Python setting the pace is all important, and Eric now firmly has the initiative over those of us who are still arguing over when we can make a meeting. Send my reply into cyberspace, firmly stating that from March next year onwards I'm not available.

Picked up by Mike at 5.30. H comes with me. On the other side of Leicester Square the crowds are gathering for the premiere of the new Harry Potter film. Quietly, less glamorously, the Prince of Wales is filling with Palin fans – I'm told that over 1,000 seats are sold and the rest will go at the door.

Curtain up at ten past seven. Feel quite comfortable out there on stage, but aware that it was to be a long evening, half-carried by ad-libs and improv, half by readings. Some things worked, others fizzled out. But when I first sneaked a look at my watch I saw that I'd done an hour without noticing. Wound up the first half at about 75 minutes. The second half was shorter. H said I was much more relaxed. Then to the Q&A, which gave me a chance to tell stories I'd not already told and we went happily along until about 9.45 when I brought the show to a close.

As Mike took us back, H was telling me about the audience and how complimentary they had been. As H never goes out of the way to offer flattery unless it's due, I felt a certain pride creep in alongside the predominantly bursting sensation of deep relief it was over and done with.

Thursday, November 10th

Another diary editing opportunity slips away as I'm drawn back to the transport speech – tidying, refining, incorporating new info. Hear, via the office, that Alistair Darling [secretary of state for transport] won't be able to make it. And at midday he rings me personally to apologise.

Rachel rings from Coolangatta, Queensland. She's happy. A bit woozy still from jet lag but installed in an apartment and has already been down to see the stretch of jungle where the contestants will be put. Shown funnel-web spiders and snakes and leeches – in bottles only!

Friday, November 11th

A message from JC. He's at the Crowne Plaza Hotel in Christchurch (which I know well) and leaves his number. But when I ring and ask to be put through to John Cleese I'm told there's no one of that name staying there. The receptionist straight bats so well that all I can do in the end is go through the charade of leaving a message for Mr Cleese, who isn't there, asking for him to call me back. Which he does. His assistant Gary has booked him into the hotel under the name of Volestrangler, without informing anyone who might need to ring him.

Monday, November 14th

After a quiet weekend writing and reading diaries, I have a break this morning, as have been asked to meet David Puttnam on UNICEF business.

To Queen's Gate Place Mews, where David and Patsy have lived for 35 years. They have immaculate good taste and the wide, low-ceilinged spaces have a design unity which has been zealously observed. He seems to have settled now for the wise, benign, grey-bearded guru, hands in pockets, shoulders a little hunched, handmade white linen shirt, eyes sparkling with an interesting mixture of compassion and opportunity, makes me some coffee himself – a small, perfect espresso – then we settle down in his small side office.

He and Sarah from UNICEF outline their hopes that they might be able to 'piggy-back' on my new series. I'm a little defensive (David is a master of the art of persuasion) and tell them that we don't deliberately set out to cover issues – just the country and its people. But we have to start somewhere. I suggest that we should meet up in the New Year to talk over where UNICEF's work is concentrated and if it can lead us to some good stories.

After Sarah's gone, David asks if I will take over from him in two and a half years' time as president of UNICEF. 'They're wonderful people, and I've managed to extricate myself completely from the bureaucracy, and that's important.' He thinks I have the right credentials for communicating and enthusing.

He's just come back from Mozambique and talks of small townships about to be wiped out by AIDS. He has awful stories from Sarajevo of villages where Christians protected Muslims and were then killed by other Muslims. But David has no rage – some bitterness, but basically, like me, he's an optimist.

'Being a film producer is a perfect preparation for all this,' he reckons. 'You learn never to give up.'

Tuesday, November 15th

Rachel calls from Australia. She's having, or has had, a day off – one in every three, but then when she works it's on 15-hour shifts. She's bathed in the sea and run along the beach and sounds as if she's dealing with it all. Bemoans the fact that this part of Australia (or the restaurant clientele anyway) are in bed by half past nine.

H and I out to the British Museum to a Patrons' view of the 'Persia – Forgotten Empire' exhibition. The curator John Curtis has a strong raison d'être for the exhibition and that seems to be that Alexander the Great was a complete and vindictive bastard who not only destroyed the beauty and civility of the Persian empire, but set light to the temples of Persepolis quite carefully and deliberately and destroyed local records so that it's only through the Greeks that we know about the Persian empire – history being written by the winners. In short this exhibition is correcting historical misinformation.

Friday, November 25th

Good chat with J-P D who is going on another recce next week. So far, he says, the prevailing feeling he gets in E. Europe is that people don't want to dwell on the past, the recent wars and upheavals; they want to talk about now and tomorrow.

Back home. Wonderful email from JC taking great exception to Eric's use of the word 'doolally' in describing his recent behaviour.

Sunday, November 27th

Look through the 'Himalaya' slideshow ahead of this evening's performance at the Palace Theatre. I'm enjoying having the time to revisit my travels. Feel that the reflection time required has usually been snatched away as new projects come rolling along, obscuring the traces of what's gone before. I have done so much travelling in the last 16 years and looking back is as important as looking forward.

At the Palace by a quarter to five. Lovely, well-restored theatre, outside and in; thank you, Andrew Lloyd Webber. Eric tells me, via one of his more placatory recent emails, that it looks as if this is the favoured theatre to host 'Spamalot'

– from October next year. It would be a perfect home for the show – 1,400 seats, and a highly visible and extensive frontage on Cambridge Circus, and right on the cusp of Soho and Covent Garden.

Tuesday, November 29th

Phone interview with Dagbladet, the Norwegian popular newspaper re 'Himalaya' (which I first dreamt up at this desk three years ago). Interviewer is a travel journalist with the unforgettable name of Odd Roar.

Wednesday, November 30th

I'm at the London Clinic by 9.30 to see the ENT man. Young, very public school charmer who introduces himself as 'Johnny Harcourt'. He could be one of Rachel's friends. He examines me quite thoroughly, with a camera probe up the nose and into the sinus cavities. 'Well, absolutely no sign of sinusitis or throat cancer – none at all,' he reassures me. I must admit that the possibility of throat cancer, or some nastiness down in the oesophagus had crossed my mind, but it's still a shock to hear the word, even accompanied by a disclaimer.

He wonders if I've ever 'knowingly' broken my nose. No. For some reason, he clearly thinks I'm lying. 'Are you sure?' Well I'd remember if I had, wouldn't I? 'It is a little twisted to the left'. I come away touching it much more gingerly.

Sunday, December 4th

Have begun acquainting myself with the history of the Balkans – today finished Mark Mazower's pithy history lesson. Realise that there will be less of the glamorous and exotic to this exploration of Europe – or if there is, it will always be balanced by the amount of cruelty, brutality and violence, especially in the twentieth century, which it is quite shocking to accept as it was so close to home. Added to that, I'm reminded by Timothy Garton Ash on the 'Today' programme that 'Eastern Europe' is not considered a catch-all for every country that was the other side of the Iron Curtain. The Czechs, Slovaks, Hungarians and Poles regard themselves as Central European at the very least – countries that have always been at the heart of the great European movements – the Renaissance, the Enlightenment, Modernism. They would regard 'Eastern Europe' as Ukraine, Moldova, Belarus, he says. So, we must be careful with the glib labels.

Watch Rachel's name go up on penultimate 'I'm a Celebrity'.

Monday, December 5th

In some ways life seems as difficult and unsatisfactory when there's not much work to shape the day, as it does under the pressure of the fiercest deadlines. I find myself curiously agitated about what to do with myself. I think I've never been that good at driving myself. I've more often than not needed some outside force to start the ball rolling.

Tuesday, December 13th

To Pine Street for the Stammering Centre Christmas Party. Travers [Reid] is honoured with a short speech from Diana and myself. I think he's been overshadowed by Lena in the past. He then presents an award for work in stammering therapy to a lovely girl from Sheffield who has come down specially with her father. We talk later. Her studies show how important the psychological background is for stammerers – the theory which underlies all the treatment here, and which is why the therapists here are so unhappy with quick-cure treatments.

Wednesday, December 14th

To Tavistock Street for a pre-Christmas gathering of the Europe team. Nige is now '88 per cent' converted to the Europe journey.

In the evening, up to the Heath library, next to Keats's well-preserved villa. A cluster of people around the gate. They're the disaffected who haven't been able to get tickets; generally good-natured but subtly conveying that it's all my fault for being so popular. I feel suitably guilty.

Inside the organiser's flapping about in excitement and apprehension. Officially limit is 80, and they have around 150 squeezed among the racks. I've decided to take the line of least preparation and do a speeded up 45-minute version of 'Himalaya'. A few questions, then a few books to be signed.

Walk home, trailed (at suitable distance) by two Russian women who live locally, from Grafton Road. One asks me, looking tragic as only the Russians can, 'Mr Palin, you know many of the spiritual leaders.' I jump in rather swiftly to hang her up, suspecting a long philosophical agenda here. 'Well, Mr Palin, will you write to them and help save the swimming baths in Grafton Road from closure.'

Thursday, December 15th

Rachel arrives back from Australia at lunchtime, suntanned and freckled and looking well. Her bag was deemed so overweight that she had to unpack at check-in. We watched the very dramatic, high-quality DVD of her free-fall jump. I had to hang on to her for dear life as we watched her being thrust out of the aircraft over Botany Bay. She loved it and would happily do it again – though things like that always seem more tempting in Australia!

Tuesday, December 20th

Meeting with J-P, Roger and Steve A to bring us all up to date on the Europe series. I find the hardest thing is finding a title to describe what it is. We settle on Palin's Europe as a working title. I do feel the geographical destination should be in the title, but we all agree that Europe doesn't resonate like Himalaya or Sahara. After a couple of hours we have the six shows theoretically blocked out, and it's by and large agreed in principle that we should try and complete five of the six episodes before end of 2006.

Roger confirms that he would rather only do two of the six programmes. 'I *shall* be 70 next year,' he says, and the reality of this, the 17th year of our collaboration together, strikes me forcibly and poignantly. Whatever we've said before, this is our last outing together. Whether we should have embarked on it, time will tell.

Thursday, December 22nd

Lunch with Steve. Just as the year is beginning to run down, demands and requests come tumbling in. Travel Channel, who have acquired rights to all my shows in the US for the next few years now want to begin shooting some trailers. UKTV, who are interested in picking up all sorts of Palin-iana for their various digital channels want to do three long interviews. I'm going to have to tread carefully in the New Year. Time will be so easily eaten up.

Thursday, December 29th

Another day on or below freezing mark. After lunch I feel increasingly flu-ish. Hot-headed, heart thumping – rather alarming really, as I'm not quite sure what's going on – cold, cough, then fever. Fortunately I have energy enough to read – complete V. Woolf's 'A Room of One's Own' and whilst constantly dabbing a runny nose, I feel up to listening to 'Quartermaine's Terms'. Not bad, but I think I know what Simon means – a play is meant to be seen, and Quartermaine doesn't have the presence on radio as he would on stage.

Saturday, December 31st

The year ends in atmosphere of resounding anti climax. H is still enfeebled by the collapse of her system on Christmas night. She coughed and felt nauseous during the night and tho' she gets up and comes down, it's rather like living with a ghost.

I feel better and come out earlyish to M&S to buy supplies. Tissues and cough-mixture probably highest on the list. (Funny how handkerchiefs have virtually disappeared from our lives. Ever since going to Japan for the first time I've been aware of the insanitariness of what we lovingly knew at school as the 'snot-rag'. The role of pocket handkerchief and toilet paper (as opposed to washing), both quite severely questioned as result of my travels.)

So to end of year report. Where has all the time gone? Lots and lots of people who I'd like to have seen and haven't. Many talks and appearances but my diary for the new year now gratifyingly free of public appearances. Pluses for 2005. Have met Dervla Murphy, and Simon Gray and worked with Maria Aitken. Have seen more of my ow country than for a while. Eden Project visit. Walk with Will and Dan Cruickshank.

As so often happens, the years between the very hard work can be much less satisfactory than one hopes and expects. Not travelling, not fighting a book deadline does not necessarily make me a happy man. All through this last year I've had niggly health problems – usually around the head and throat. The message is clear, is it not. I'm not comfortable sitting at home for too long. Bad news for 2005 maybe, but better for 2006.

2006

Sunday, January 1st

Another post-Christmas day trails away. I watch the final 45 minutes of Channel 4's 50 best comedy films ever. 'Grail' at No 6, but 'Brian' the winner over 'Airplane'. I'm, as always, amazed how time seems to heal all those imperfections, the shooting, playing and writing which once used to worry me so much.

The movie-fest – of necessity lots of very short clips – comes to an end at midnight with various contributors being forced to sing 'Always Look on the Bright Side' – mostly hopelessly. Why 'Shaun of the Dead' should be No. 3, and seven places above the unforgettable 'This Is Spinal Tap', I fail to understand.

Monday, January 2nd

Out in the morning to collect an antibiotics prescription for H. Have to drive up to Hampstead to find a chemist open. What a sad decline in the look and feel of what was once one of the area's great attractions. Now Hampstead High Street is a mess of shops which seem to share no local pride, nor in many cases, local function. It's 75 per cent an outpost shopping mall, with predictable, well-known brands aiming at visitors more than locals. I think that it's pretty much an aesthetic disaster now, with few, if any, premises reflecting the way Hampstead High Street used to look, or was intended to look.

Tuesday, January 3rd

Business opens at 9.30, with an interview for the Observer about outstanding and memorable places in one's travelling life. I choose the rapids of the Urubamba and the Pongo de Mainique. Become very eloquent on the subject.

A day of gloom, low cloud and drizzle; I come across P. Leigh Fermor's 'Time of Gifts' which unlocks the bottleneck in my mind as to where to start on E. Europe reading. Settle down with his rich, swirling prose and lots of maps.

Thursday, January 5th

To London Bridge and walk through Borough Market towards the Tate Mod. The smell of coffee from the Monmouth Coffee House is a wonderful treat as I pass by.

The Rachel Whiteread boxes, squashed up one end of the Turbine Hall – which must be one of the most daunting artistic spaces to fill – look initially rather powerful, but once amongst them, with their cold, reflective white poly-ethylene surfaces seeming to bleach out any interest, I feel unconnected, and rather bored by the whole thing. I'm not interested really in what the 'space inside a box' looks like or represents. That's an intellectual idea which I feel she's explored thoroughly enough already. I'm interested in things, objects, that directly reflect human experience in all its flightiness and diversity and ingen-uity and pathos.

Up to see Jeff Wall's lightboxes, which are striking, but again, oddly alienat-ing. They're of a size which is, I gather, supposed to pull you into the world he's depicting, but the world of urban Vancouver doesn't really pull me in. Long for a refreshing draught of Henri Rousseau, but there is such a crowd of school-children lined up on their way in, that I decide to cut and run.

Saturday, January 7th

Soon after breakfast down to recycling with a car-boot full of household droppings. Very sharp temperatures – hands numb as I heave the paper and cardboard, books and plastics into their various bins. In these Siberian con-ditions, I could have done with a quick return home but the man in charge today comes over to me with outstretched mobile and asks if I'll talk to his wife.

Bas comes by, long black coat, black hat, sublimely cool. Brings me the 'Hands' book to read – contract signed yesterday, so MP foreword will have to be written.[1] We sit and talk and drink tea and whisky by the fire, then up to TJ's in the evening.

Good food – lots of little starters – and as my appetite is beginning to return, I appreciate Terry's titbits of smoked eel and homemade rillettes and salmon mousse ('I've discovered the wonders of gelatine' enthuses TJ).

General good buzz of conversation, everyone talking about what they do punctuated by Terry's outbursts, which seem to come from nowhere, like fire-works. One such is an impassioned, blazing defence of George Galloway, who's

1 *Hands: A Journey Around the World* was a book of photographs Basil published with Thames and Hudson in November 2006.

just agreed to go on 'Celebrity Big Brother' – a decision which Terry heartily defends, less from anything he knows about Galloway and more from a violently indignant response to the news that he has been banned from talking politics in the BB house.

Later, a lightish chat about my experiences with the strangely attired healer/ witch doctor who I filmed with in Mpulungu, Zambia on *Pole to Pole* has Terry exploding again. 'Why should we laugh at people like that when our legal system is run by people in silly wigs!'

After a main course, Terry asks if any of us would like to see the house he's bought up the road. He admits it's an 'awful' house. 'I'd love to go and see an awful house' says Basil drily, which makes me laugh.

Monday, January 9th

A cab to the Admiralty restaurant and as I'm early for lunch, take a glass of white wine and open up my [Orhan] Pamuk book. Very chatty fellow diner at the bar next to me. 'What are you reading?' 'Oh, very highbrow.' Turkey? 'Yes, gone a bit off the radar recently' – and so on. Quite irritating. He's a headhunter from Epsom – looks younger than any of my children.

Then TG arrives, grizzled face enclosed in the high sheepskin collar of a flying jacket, making him resemble a Frans Hals portrait. He's followed by Bas and we sit down to a very convivial lunch, the first of 2006. Terry G claims his career is over. Despite these apocalyptic tendencies we laugh a lot – TG is his usual energetic self. On Thursday he will renounce his American citizenship and give up his US passport.

Basil reappears in his long black cashmere coat and hat and inveigles, without much resistance, I have to say, most of the office staff out to PJ's bar for a drink before he flies off to Hong Kong. It is very good time to be pub crawling in London – the post-Christmas calm creating ideal conditions for the flaneur.

Tuesday, January 10th

To the office – letters, including one from an 18-year-old called Lucy Harvey who has taken some trouble to avoid the usual fan clichés but what comes across instead is a rather over-elaborate school debater style. She does note at one point that I 'remain a gracious, noble and unassuming man'. Quote this to H later as she's flossing her teeth and she raises eyes heavenwards.

Thursday, January 12th

Meet up with J-P to talk through progress so far on the Europe project. We roll out the map and go over the route. George Carey, who is producing a Russia series with David Dimbleby (which J-P is directing) has, through Richard Klein, made it clear that he feels we should not do Kaliningrad, because David will be starting his series there. This makes me see a very deep red, and there can be absolutely no question of doing any deal on this. In fact, it's so ludicrous that I can't believe J-P, Klein or Carey should even think it worth mentioning.

Friday, January 13th

To the background of thudding hammers and drills as [builder] Dave and his boys break a hole out of the kitchen to take the new extractor fan I try and conduct an interview with a man from the East Anglian about my appearance, in March, to raise funds for Ion Trewin's local church. I'm afraid all East Anglian journalists now have to pass the Alan Partridge test, and very few do. They all sound just like him – the inflexions, the laboured jokiness, the occasional serious foray – everything signalled like directions in a department store.

Saturday, January 14th

Another heartfelt plea from Maria A for me to reconsider playing Quartermaine on stage. Simon has given her the rights for another year. 'He agrees with me I must go back to you. It's not a play you can do with the wrong person and almost everyone else seems wrong to me now.'

Less joy at seeing myself leaning out of a train window on the front page of The Times, beneath the headline – End of the Line for Palin? Page three is entirely devoted to an article which leads with the news that senior members of T2000 have expressed their unhappiness at having a president who travels so frequently on aeroplanes. This is followed by a long and not all unfriendly, indeed rather tantalising account of my travels, and a very brief suggestion from T2000 elder Mayer Hillman that I might reconsider my position. Feel relieved that I didn't get sucked into the 'story'. An editorial which picks up the story writes, very much in my favour, that the 'greens' are being overreactive here. Mind you, it manages to get the name wrong and Transport 2000 comes out as Travel 2000.

One other paper picks up the story – the Independent on Sunday – and wonder if I want to reply. Decide, in this case, that silence is golden.

Monday, January 16th

The Palin's Europe office opens officially today. As I write the realisation of this seventh outing seems still a long way off, which may account for why I feel gloriously insouciant about it at the moment. Well, no, that's not quite true. I have to admit, I feel very excited about it.

Tuesday, January 17th

First we have, I feel, to decide on a working title. Palin's Europe didn't stick. J-P sends me schedules headed 'Palin's Wild East', Roger's slightly more prosey little programme and series descriptions headed 'Palin's New Europe', or 'Polonaise'. J-P, Steve, Sue Grant [production manager] and I unilaterally decide on 'Palin's New Europe' as the least worst title and this will go on visiting cards for the recces etc.

Journalists wanting to know if I'm trading my carbon emissions, and letters from fans – one asking which is my favourite cheese and another (from Germany, I think) wondering 'what is it that you have with the word "lavatory"?'

Monday, January 23rd

Roger Saunders has managed to find a copy of JC's biography of me for 'Life of Brian' [we all wrote biographies of each other for the film publicity], which goes on about my talking all the time – and then going home 'when everyone else is in bed' and writing it down in a diary. JC's humour at his most sustained, and I ring him to ask if I can use it at the front of the Diaries, as a sort of Mission Statement. He's in LA rehearsing with Camilla [his daughter] and Garry [Scott-Irvine, who worked for John] for some one-night shows on campus. He offers me another line if I want it – 'I'm using it in the show at the moment, Mickey. Many people like conversation, Michael likes talking.' 'Now that's cruel,' I reply. He laughs.

Thursday, January 26th

'Another Limp-Dem Admits' is a headline in the Sun – and shows how Neanderthal are their attitudes, or rather the attitudes they claim to represent, when a man (in this case MP Simon Hughes) declares himself to have had homosexual affairs. Jokily intended I'm sure, but insidious and nasty and homophobic. I assume the 'limp' references is to limp wrists, the old theatrical gay image, it certainly doesn't ring true to my knowledge of gay men – who seem anything but limp.

Work through the last 100 pages of the diary with Ion – quite a lot of extra footnotes to do, plus some text inserts. Paul shows me a copy of the Reader's Digest – which carries the results of a poll to find the Top 20 Most Trusted Britons, accompanied by a letter complimenting me on coming sixth! We have much laughter at the list's expense. Attenborough (David) is No 1, which I thoroughly agree with, and I come below Bill Oddie and Cliff Richard! But I am seven places above the Queen and one above the highest placed woman – Judi Dench. Tony Blair is down in the 80s and at No 100, Peter Mandelson.

Sunday, January 29th

Jeremy Meadows called to say that, after much disappointment, we do have someone interested in [a revival of my 1994 play, 'The Weekend'] and that's from [Scottish actor] Tom Conti. I talk to Tom today. He is very complimentary about the writing, finds it funny but is worried about the structure – and especially the information given to the audience – how and when it's delivered. 'I'm very keen on this sort of thing.'

He will read it again and then, I suppose, we shall have to meet up and discuss the possibility of changes, not something that I have much stomach for at the moment. Sometimes regret that Jeremy is so keen on prodding 'The Weekend' back to life. I feel that the reaction of so many, from Alderton to Rik Mayall, is evidence that there is something innately wrong.

Tuesday, January 31st

Have been invited to lunch at the Old Bailey by Mr Alderman and Sheriff John Stuttard [who, like me, was at Shrewsbury School] 'to meet Her Majesty's Judges'.

Stuttard is keen to talk about his Peking to Paris car trip in which he drove a Rolls-Royce across the Himalaya, but his dogged, earnest enthusiasm is no match for the wackiness of another judge, His Honour Paul Folke. He is very mischievous.

It turns out he is in the habit of sending postcards to various colleagues, signed 'your camel boy', or 'do you remember me Sahib? When can I wash you again?' He grins with a certain quiet pride as his naughtiness is catalogued.

Later take the opportunity to see a court at work and slip into the back of the court where a tall, lanky young black man is being cross-questioned about an incident in which he stabbed a man three times.

At one point the prosecutor, bristling with impatience, asks for someone *'anyone'* to provide the defendant with a pen. Much scrabbling around in the well of the court, a clicking of biros. 'No, not to *write* with!' he cries. When a pen is found, he instructs the defendant to imagine it's the weapon he used. 'Hold it as you held the knife on that afternoon . . .'

Today, the Bailey looks like any provincial town hall. Ornate marble floors and tiled ceilings give the impression of the stern, grand timelessness of the authority of the land. They disguise the reality of what's really going on here, where behind glassed and panelled doors are 'some very nasty people', as the security chief put it to me. On both sides of the law, I've no doubt.

Emerge into Newgate Street, quiet but for an assortment of camera crews on the opposite pavement. Walk away round the corner into Ludgate Hill and there ahead of me, catching the brightness of a clearing afternoon, is the restored West Front of St Paul's. Buy a ticket (for £9.00) and walk around inside.

Down in the crypt where the remains of so many great British worthies lie – Florence Nightingale, Nelson, Wellington, Singer Sargent, Arthur Sullivan, Turner. Two women are sitting at a table over a cup of tea at one end of the undercroft. 'I don't know,' says one to the other, 'I lose all my feeling of spirituality down here. I mean it's just a café, isn't it.' They spot me and request an autograph, 'You're not going to do anything silly in here today are you?'

Wednesday, February 1st

Call TJ and wish him a happy 64th. He says he's been in the papers again. The Daily Mail were tipped off that Anna is taking belly-dancing classes in Oxford, and spread the story about yesterday. TJ sounds rueful, and a little dazed. No anger though. Much more anxious to tell me how much he's enjoying working with [his son] Bill on the director's cut of Erik the Viking. Most directors expand their work, but Terry and Bill have taken the scissors to Erik, quite ruthlessly, and it's now down from 140 minutes to 75.

Roger rings, he had seen the Mail piece (of course he would) and goes straight to the reference in it to myself and Helen, who are reported to be the most vehemently upset of all the Pythons at Terry's new relationship. Rog relishes my discomfiture at this, but then he does have more than a little sadism in his mischievousness.

In the evening over to the Ledbury – a made-over pub with very chic and sophisticated style. A little too much telling you what's what. Clever food but interesting, indeed.

At the table Richard Klein, Roger and J-P. It's at Richard's instigation that we get together and talk over the series. He keeps apologising for not knowing how we work, but is clearly anxious to put across some of his thoughts on the content and emphasis. Peasant and rural side of life very important in E. Europe he says, and he hopes we will make the scenery look as beautiful as it is. I feel in total agreement with him on this. Eastern Europe in Colour wouldn't be a bad title.

Thursday, February 2nd

Weather at a standstill. To the Adventure Travel Show at Earl's Court to collect an award from the good readers of Wanderlust magazine.

I'm taken there by an Algerian, a qualified engineer and architect reduced to driving minicabs. He's pale, slim, middle-aged and given to outbursts of bitter, angry intensity which usually end in self-disgust.

Says Bouteflika is a good president. He was a foreign minister, has experience and has been able to deal with the corruption of the recent administrations. Then off he'd go. 'Oh, the corruption! The corruption! Some of those people were criminals! Criminals!' and so on, reminding me of the kind of characters John used to play so well in Python.

Watch other awards being dished out, Luang Prabang in Laos voted best city (Cuzco second), Namibia best country, then an award for safest country, won, almost inevitably, by New Zealand.

Friday, February 3rd

Monotonous run of sunless days continues. This weather vacuum is becoming less attractive as the days go by and I try not to think of the muck in this cool trapped air.

To lunch at Moro with Mhairi. Hammershoi to be shown as official entry at Montreal Arts Docs festival. Discuss future ideas. I push Antonello da Messina as a possible subject for our fifth collaboration, or Artemisia Gentileschi or the American industrial painters of the '20s – Sheeler etc?

In the pattern of our favourite Friday evenings, H and I walk up to [our local, Polish-run bistro] Ravel's and then back early enough to take in some TV. Tonight an excellent episode of the rude, cheeky and fresh 'Shameless'.

Wednesday, February 8th

As I trot past Kenwood pond I keep an eye on the slow unfolding saga of the swans and their cygnet. Have watched him, or her, from birth almost, then into a dark grey shadow of its parents and now, a year or more later, into a swan in its own right, still smaller, still moving in the company of its mother and father, but white instead of grey. Gives me pleasure to watch this little family developing.

With Jonathan and Pauline [Clyde] to see 'Who's Afraid of Virginia Woolf' at the Apollo. Packed house and rightly so. It's a tremendous production. Kathleen Turner, sounding throaty and breathless (acted or real?) is perfectly pitched. Her emotional journey through the play is complex and must require enormous concentration, but you never see her doing it or thinking about it – it just is there, she plays it as if this is happening for the first and only time. Bill Irwin, a touch camp in his body movements, is otherwise immaculate – a weak man who turns out to be strong, just as she appears to be the strong woman, who turns out to be weak. He choreographs the evening, and his quiet but cutting attacks (in defence) are superbly done. The guests are both strong too. This is great theatre. It plays with the audience, drawing us in with humour and clever verbal fencing into a deep well of private pain and keeping us there, unable to look away.

Tuesday, February 14th

Two Valentine cards – one from the cats and one from Helen. These are just about the parameters of my life at the moment.

To the office at ten to work through my latest batch of changes, additions etc with Ion. We break for lunch at the Loch Fyne – very full, see Paul Merton and Jessica at another table. Merton has moved into Macklin Street just up the road. Says he's done some research on Macklin. He was an actor who lived to be 100, was accused of murdering a fellow actor with a poisoned wig, conducted his own defence and was acquitted.

Roger [Mills] is back from Poland. 'Very, very cold,' he says. 'I *loved* it.'

Wednesday, February 15th

Lunch with Steve at the Loch Fyne. Michael Codron [theatre producer] immaculate – white trimmed beard making him look like some Mediterranean admiral. I tell him that he was being discussed yesterday as Ion and I debated which of his many stage credits should grace our footnote. 'Which were you most proud of?' I ask. 'Hang Down Your Head and Die,' he returns, without a pause.[1]

---

1 The Oxford University anti-capital-punishment show, which he brought into the West End in 1964. I was 21 and one of the cast.

The BBC finance man, Godfrey something or other, is continuing to make life difficult, so this morning Steve, regretfully, put in a call to Peter Fincham asking him, basically, do the BBC want me or not? Awaiting reply.

To 34 Tav to continue combing the text with Ion – who has been lunching at the Garrick with Alan Strachan. Strachan was once approached by Michael Codron with a view to writing his biography. Strachan agreed but insisted that Michael would have to be completely open and candid with him about his life. Nothing could be hidden. He never heard from him again.

Thursday, February 16th

Roger round here mid-morning to talk to me about Polish recce. He is quite certain there is a complete programme in Poland. As usual, more men than women to talk to. 'This is going to be a very different sort of series, Mike,' he keeps saying.

Friday, February 17th

At quite short notice, and to capitalise on Tom Conti's interest in 'The Weekend', a reading has been laid on up at Conti's house in Hampstead.

The run-through, at an enormous round table, with the sun pouring in, is enjoyable. Tom doesn't seem to sell himself very well; mumbling, mistiming jokes, pausing before lines that demand a split-second response. But he is good at the serious end of the play. Really quite moving. His is a realistic performance – perhaps he's deliberately trying to play down the comedy.

Tom gives little away afterwards; Jeremy will let me know. But it was good to see the play brought to life again. I see faults that need to be corrected, but it isn't beyond redemption, and Tom's downbeat mumbling would I hope be nothing more than the way stars use to keep something back from us mere mortals until the vital moment (viz Kevin Kline's excruciatingly hesitant early reads of 'A Fish Called Wanda').

Thursday, February 23rd

Finished 'Dead Souls' soon after 5.[1] Last day was the best. I felt nicely relaxed, on top of it. I have to feel comfortable and at ease with those I'm working

1 *Dead Souls* was Dan Reballato's two-part BBC radio adaptation of Nikolai Gogol's novel of the same name. I took the part of the narrator.

around in order to give my best. I can't operate well when there's tension around. I've no real idea how it will all sound – but working with Mark Heap was close to playing comedy with Cleese.

Friday, March 3rd

Resign from the Groucho Club, which I've been meaning to do for the last five years. This decisiveness possibly prompted by the fact that this morning I'm in a suit and tie and soon off to Westminster Abbey for Ronnie Barker's memorial, but most likely the result of my having, as from last Monday, been elected a member of the Athenaeum.[1] What with grandfather-hood beckoning and establishment status endorsed by the Athenaeum, this month could mark a new chapter in my life. Part 307: Respectability.

An email from Maria headed NO PRESSURE – which reported [playwright] Simon Gray's praise of Quartermaine: 'You and Michael make him telling and poignant and therefore more visible than I would have believed possible. Michael really ought to do it on the stage . . . and one day he might rather regret the missed chance.'

Taxi to the Abbey, wearing my heavy Donegal tweed overcoat against the silent, still coldness. Photographers and TV crews flanking the west door and demanding soundbites. Then led in and escorted past the serried ranks assembled in the nave and up to a place amongst the select few in the choir stalls.

Next to me two stalls were reserved for [director] Sir Peter and Lady Hall, neither of whom showed up. It was an odd occasion. Ribald, once lusty Ronnie, who avoided the spotlight unless forced into it, is given a full Lord Nelson, Francis Drake, Winston Churchill-style homage. Terrific organ chords, soaring voices of the choir, hugely stirring hymns, interspersed with tributes – from Michael Grade, Peter Kay and Ronnie Corbett (who had to stand on a box to be seen above the chancel pulpit) and, as is fashionable now, recordings of Ronnie himself doing a racy monologue, a clever but overstretched sermon in rhyming slang.

It shouldn't have worked but it did. The Abbey was the perfect foil for Ronnie – or perhaps it should be the other way round. The functionaries in the Abbey itself played the ceremony with faultless confidence, the music was powerful and immaculately executed and of course the great Gothic walls put human pretension firmly in its place.

It wasn't a tearful affair – Ronnie himself rarely became emotional. He was cool and clever; but what this was was a celebration more of the BBC as the

1 The Athenaeum is a members' club on Pall Mall, established in 1824.

central pillar in British cultural life. Witness the turnout of the D-G, the chairman and all the top brass.

At the end I walked down the aisle alongside Stephen Fry and confessed to him that when we had prayers and responses for all those who write and perform comedy I felt on shaky ground. All those who have done funny vicar monologues? All those who wrote and performed 'Life of Brian'? But as Stephen said reassuringly, 'This is the Church of England, it's all OK.'

Saturday, March 4th

Local shopping. Drop in to the chemists run by Pakistanis, the deli run by Italians, the dry cleaners run by Iranians and a new speciality food shop run by a Pole. By the time I've talked to them all about life and the state of the world it's almost lunchtime.

Up to Hampstead for supper with Romaine Hart [film executive], Harry Shearer [the American actor who co-created and starred in 'This Is Spinal Tap'] and his wife, the singer Judith Owen. Almost a year ago Harry introduced me at the Film & TV Academy in Los Angeles and it's good to be able to thank him again for what was a perfectly pitched, not at all daunting evening.

Harry has a house in New Orleans. He's just come back from Mardi Gras – the first since the flood.[1] When I ask him how much he was affected by the floodwater, he approvingly notes that I didn't ask, like everyone else does in America, how he was affected by the hurricane. It wasn't the hurricane that did the damage, it was the water that spilled over inadequate defences.

Their house was fine, and Mardi Gras had been wonderful. Harry dressed up as a chocolate bar – everyone wears fancy dress, he says, no one's self-conscious about it. But over half the city remains completely broken and empty.

Talk about his Polish Jewish ancestry. He makes the point, as I'm rhapsodising somewhat about the plucky Poles, that virulent antisemitism existed in Poland before the Nazis 'honed it' down. So Harry isn't so keen to go back there. His grandparents all perished in the camps.

Later, as we're discussing 'Saturday Night Live', he again opens my eyes a little wider as he talks of his stormy relationship with the programme. Harry thought them slack and institutionally lazy. Harry was appalled that the SNL team relied on cue-cards, on the show itself.

Good, lively evening. He says there exists a piece of paper on which all the possible names for the group that became Spinal Tap were written (shades of Python). It was almost Spynal Tap.

1 Hurricane Katrina, which devasted New Orleans in August 2005.

Tuesday, March 7th

Rain set in for the day as I walk across Trafalgar Square to the Athenaeum for my first visit as a member. The elegant square building is under wraps at the moment whilst painting work is done.

Up the shallow, broad steps, beneath the heroic portico and into the hallway. The doorman looks over his glasses at me and I introduce myself, a little shyly. Am shown where to hang my coat and where to leave my bag. Quite like having to put my bag aside. It means I can wander the rooms unencumbered. Walk into the Drawing Room; the magnificent sweep of the room and its books and magazines liberally spread about strikes me yet again. And there, sitting with a lady close by the door is Eddie Mirzoeff. The woman is [producer] Jenny Barraclough. She seems delighted to see me and anxious to tell me that she was one of my many supporters. She sounds wonderfully enthusiastic about the place. 'It's not stuffy at all. You should see us at Christmas all gathered round the piano, thumping out carols.'

I test the library straight away asking if they have a book highly praised by Robert Kaplan, whose 'Balkan Ghosts' I'm reading at the moment. It's Rebecca West's 1934 Balkan journey called 'Black Lamb and Grey Falcon'. Promptly, two hardbacked volumes are brought to me as I sit in one of the armchairs of the Drawing Room looking out over the sodden junction of Waterloo Place and Regent Street.

Wednesday, March 8th

To 34 Tavistock Street to go through the near 600 pages of the diary text one by one, yet again, with Ion. This time to go through the words of warning from Alan Williams the lawyer. There isn't much that I hadn't expected him to flag up, though he has homed in on quite innocent entries, concerning Eric mostly, e.g. 'Eric returned from a naughty week in Tenerife with Barry Cryer', he queries 'Should I know something about this relationship?', 'Eric has been gallivanting round Europe with Ron Wood' which he also queries.

Thursday, March 9th

Sidetracked, willingly if time consumingly, by Will's request for some message of support for the opposition to Camden Leisure Department's plans to hijack a large area of Lincoln's Inn Fields to build corporate entertainment facilities during the summer.

It makes me very angry that the principle (hard-won) of public access to these old-established garden squares for rest and quiet should be so errantly ignored by a borough wanting to make a fast buck. Let corporate entertainment take place in the corporation's buildings not in our public space.

Mike G picks me up at 6 and drives me to the Isle of Dogs (now the very heart of corporate London) to the anonymous hotel where I am to open the Excellence Awards for [Helen's sister] Mary's Mental Health Trust. Arrive early, so much time spent hanging around shaking hands. As so often, a worthy organisation is friendly but chaotic. I'm supposed to be the mystery guest, yet I'm left standing in full view at the top of the stairs with the guests pointing me out and asking 'Are you the Mystery Guest?' 'Yes, I'm the Mystery Guest.' 'Sheila, come and meet the Mystery Guest.'

Friday, March 10th

To Kew Gardens, where I am to cut the ribbon at the opening of a new Alpine House. I'm met by Stewart Henchie, the splendidly titled Head of Hardy Display, and we go through a staged approach to the new Alpine House.

He introduces me to Eddie Davies, a short, solid, white-haired man who has given so much money to the project that the House is to be named after him. He's a tough, determined northerner with a very wide range of interests, especially of a scientific bent; we talk about molecular structures and the potato crops in Europe which were introduced from South America, and reached a stage where further improvement was impossible without going back to the South American parent and examining its cell structure and reintroducing it. He's rather like the Bill Fraser scrap-merchant character in ['Ripping Yarns'] 'Golden Gordon'. When I ask him what his relationship with Bolton Wanderers is, he snaps back 'I own the club.'

The new House is small, and built in a fan-shape – a beautiful, graceful piece of design by the architects of one of the most impressive modern structures, the Millennium Bridge at Newcastle. I give a short speech, then after the opening, a chance to meet the architects Wilkinson & Eyre. They're currently working in Liverpool on a City of Culture project. Not quite the same as Glasgow, says Chris Wilkinson, the administration is much less organised and the political situation 'chaotic'. But he's optimistic that the Liverpool City of Culture year will produce some good new building. I'm reminded of Bleasdale's maxim 'You can't polish a turd'.

Monday, March 13th

Agreed to talk to young offenders at a prison called Warren Hill near Shingle Street this afternoon, so decide to make it a Suffolk day, and alleviate some of my guilt at so rarely visiting my parents' grave [in Southwold churchyard].

Long delay on the narrowest part of the A12 means I don't reach South-wold until 1. Walk to the main square, buy a deep yellow, almost ochre potted primula and take it to the grave. A hard old wind catches me as I walk around the base of the tower and find the small area of stones – I must say, en masse, they do make a graveyard about as interesting as a car park. A moment's quiet contemplation of the qualities of those two people who brought me into the world, and are now ashes in a Suffolk churchyard.

Drive down the coast to the prison. HMP Warren Hill rises amongst the low windswept trees of this empty, marshy expanse of coastline. In red-brick, mod-ern but somehow reminiscent of a medieval fortress. Except that it's designed to stop people getting out, rather than getting in. Into a pair of doors like an airlock. One slides open and you stand in limbo waiting for the door to slide shut before the other opens. The whole place looks more like a mausoleum than a place for living people. Windows are tiny apertures and the walls are designed to block out any view of the sea or the coast or any land around. The occupants could be anywhere.

I'm led through, across an open area to one of the education centres. A big room, two snooker tables, lots of space around it. In a corner, gathered in a semi circle of deep blue upholstered chairs are the lads I'm to speak to; 15 to 18 years old. Never an easy audience at the best of times. The group of women who are running this educational centre seem to have little structure to the afternoon. 'We thought you could sit there,' one said, indicating a single chair facing the rest. And that, by way of introduction, was it. So I sat there and started. Tried to roam the faces evenly, make some eye contact. This seemed at first to make the majority of them uncomfortable. Was it that to be open and friendly with me would be like consorting with the enemy? Or was it that they just didn't know how to respond to someone who didn't play authority games?

I could soon see the dynamics of the group. One or two spoke confidently, heads held high – almost with a swagger – they were the bullies, I guess, for they made little sneaky remarks at anyone who appeared to be enjoying them-selves. One or two were so withdrawn they could never raise their eyes from the floor. What was going on in there? Could this self-imposed straitjacket be loosened?

I must have talked – rambled rather – for over an hour. They had some ques-tions. One boy very keen to know if I'd smoked anything interesting. Applause was generous and one of the male warders shook his head in amazement. 'You can have a job here any time. I've never heard them so quiet.'

I tried to mix with the boys rather than staff afterwards. One asked, aggressively, how much I got for doing this. I said I got nothing. 'How many of these are your people?' he asked, nodding at the large group of staff who'd snuck in the back. When I told him I'd come alone, driven myself, he weighed this up and nodded with interest.

When it was time to go I shook hands with them all. They responded with much broader smiles than they had when I first sat down in front of them.

Drove to Shingle Street – the end of the road and as bleak a piece of coast as you can imagine. Cold wind, a great expanse of pebbles, a black dog and me the only two creatures on the beach. Cleansing, and a little disturbing at the same time.

Thursday, March 16th

Phone goes just after 8. It's Tom. Rachel has had contractions since 5.30 and her waters have broken. It's all happening. We collect them from Charlton King's Road at ten to nine and take them down to UCH.

A cold, grey, lowering sky. Back home and wait for news. And wait and wait. Rachel having constant contractions but the baby not willing to enter the world just yet.

Friday, March 17th

I'm sleeping in the back bedroom, or rather trying to grab some sleep in between bouts of coughing. At half past six I hear Helen's voice outside. 'Dad, you've got a grandson'. Rachel eventually gave birth at 5.30 this morning, after almost 24 hours in labour. The baby's hand was up on the top of his head, making his elbow stick out; but this was only discovered much later in the labour and meant that Rachel had been wasting a lot of energy pushing.

The surge of emotion, the complete collapse of my tear ducts that I feared and hoped for had been stunted by 24 hours of false alarms and phone calls. But it is wonderful news and, I suppose, the fact that it's a grandson and ensures the Palin name continues, makes it the best of all results.

Frustratingly, I am expected up in Oxford to be shown around the Pitt-Rivers Museum extension prior to the Waynflete Dinner at Magdalen.[1] Drive to Oxford at lunchtime, eating a hurriedly made sandwich as I go. Arrive at the Old Parsonage [Hotel] by 2.30.

Later, after a break at the hotel, in which I've donned black tie and dinner

1 An annual celebration of the foundation of the college by William Waynflete in 1448.

jacket and pulled my long Donegal tweed coat around me, I'm walking along St Giles' talking to Helen who has Archie (the name they toyed with is now the one they've chosen) on her knee, and it seems appropriate that as she describes him on his first day on earth, I'm passing the gates of St John's College – the home for so long of Archie's great-great-great-grandfather Edward, of whom he is now a direct heir.

Saturday, March 18th: Oxford–London

On the road by a quarter to ten. First stop, a letterbox where I post a card to Archie. A photo of camels descending a sand dune, by Wilfred Thesiger, with a message wishing him a happy life.

Home by 11, and drive over to Tom and Rachel's. See Archie for the first time. He's being held by his grandmother. First impression is of a ruddy little face, flushed dark against his white baby-suit. On closer inspection of this warm, myopic little bundle, I notice his long slender fingers, ears with a tiny peak at the edge, and a patch of dark hair. His nose, mouth and eyes are working hard, as if he has just woken from a timeless sleep – which in a way he has. Hold him and feel very proud and happy. Rachel looks a bit dazed and tired but her trademark wide eyes are full of relief and pleasure. Tom handles the baby skilfully – drawing much praise from his mother.

H and I have been invited to Bernard and Mina's for her special Moroccan 'couscous'. They entertain in numbers and there must be 15 or 16 there when we arrive. Physically I feel quite reduced by this long and debilitating cough, but they're a good bunch and champagne flows, as do toasts to the new-born Archie.

Not much time to talk to the French contingent, but as usual, they're awfully polite. I ask if Chirac and the French are not now feeling rather smug about not joining Tony's intervention in Iraq, but they take the view that the French, though they may have been critical of the intervention, should now be lending a helping hand.

Thursday, March 23rd

To see my grandson. Have now seen him with both eyes wide and kicking his legs – well, stretching them straight out in front of him. I talk to him. His eyes rove about. Take him to the window and he blinks against the light. Adorable.

Tuesday, March 28th

To the office conference room to talk through the Europe itinerary with J-P.

J-P feels that Turkey should be given a longer slot than we have for it at the moment. He, like me, is drawn to the far-eastern border with Iraq and Iran, with wonderful scenery like Cappadocia on the way. I think we both feel we might need Turkish exoticism to leaven the homogeneity of much of East Europe. He's on recce again tomorrow and we shall not meet until after Easter.

To the freshly painted Athenaeum, sparkling like a jewel-box with Pallas Athena dripping gold above the door. I bump into [the writer] Victoria Glendinning and thank her for being the first to endorse my membership. She's bright, friendly and still a little intimidated by the place. 'I've not had the courage yet to sit at the Members' table,' she says. I feel a certain common ground with her.

The Drawing Room is almost empty and I pick out a copy of Foreign Affairs magazine, settle in an armchair and read, with a sense of dreadful gloom, the history of the British occupation of Iraq after the First World War. A mirror of what is happening now. So clear that it will take some extraordinary turn of events to break the pattern of history. Meanwhile our money and our international goodwill trickle away.

Home just in time to pick up a call from Will telling me that the Lords' Committee has blocked the insertion of a new clause which would have enabled Camden to close off part of Lincoln's Inn Fields for corporate entertaining. As Will has led the fight for the Soane this is something of a personal triumph and I'm hugely pleased for him.

Write five minutes about the importance of Geography and take a cab to the Serpentine Gallery. Walk around the Ellsworth Kelly exhibition. Quite clean and refreshing, demands looking at art in a quite different way, but pays off. I like the bold simplicity. More flaneur-ing – down to the Serpentine, as big black clouds gather I sit by the water and read through my speech.

Then on to the RGS [Royal Geographical Society]. Everything goes well. Lots of geog teachers and pupils and administrators and the government minister, Lord Adonis – very nice, but so slight that the name might have been some Private Eye joke. I can say not a word against him or his commitment to launch the Action Plan by sending a free 'Himalaya' hardback to every secondary school in the country.

Monday, April 3rd

I have an interview with BBC publicity about 'Quartermaine's Terms'. A pleasant lady who I don't think has an instinctive grasp of what it's all about. After

I've described the plot as pithily I can, I end up explaining that St John Q is a decent man at the centre of all manner of deceit and selfishness who eventually pays the price of inertia. There's a short pause and then she says 'oh, dear!'

To the Ivy to meet the woman who is organising our 40th anniv to go through all the details. Our marriage nearly ended the other night as H and I argued over menus. I wanted morel risotto, she certainly didn't. Then I reminded her that we had paid a £600 non-returnable deposit, so we couldn't really afford a marriage break-up before the 16th.

Tuesday, April 4th

To Wardour Street to record commentary for a DVD of 'GBH' [Alan Bleasdale's 1991 TV drama series]. Robert Lindsay [my co-star] and Peter Ansorge [Channel 4 commissioner] are in the booth with me as they show us the opening episode. Unlike the equivocation that TJ and I felt when judging the 'Yarns', it was a fine piece of work on everyone's part. Probably the best thing I've done, outside of comedy, and our confrontation in the school is powerful and quite chilling.

Robert L is very complimentary and afterwards, as we sit having tea in the Groucho (from which I've just resigned), I tell him that I'd like to do Beckett. 'It's a great part,' he confirms. 'No, I mean Samuel Beckett.' Robert, with eyes ablaze, jabs a finger 'That's it! That's what we must do next. "Waiting For Godot"!' I must say I feel a few volts of real excitement go through the system.

To bed and chortle with pleasure at Wanderlust magazine's feature on World's Ten Greatest Explorers in which I feature as the only one still alive, at No. 9, ahead of Aphra Behn and behind Yuri Gagarin! Still I am in the company of Cook, Burton, Columbus and Darwin. My nomination, Xuanzang, in at No. 2. To sleep, feeling slightly embarrassed.

Wednesday, April 5th

In the evening meet up with Sherrie [Levy] at V&P's [Vasco & Piero's Italian restaurant]. At the table next to us Ken Livingstone, in cream suit and sporting a confident tan, is entertaining Bob Kiley [American, London's first Traffic Commissioner] and his wife. Ken springs up and grasps my hand. Introductions all round. I ask why we haven't seen him in here for a few years and he pleads fatherhood rather than mayorship.

Sherrie in good form; quite impressed that she's sat next to the mayor of London, but not nearly as impressed as when she hears that Hugh Laurie is a friend of ours. '*Really?*' She's mad about him – or rather his character in

'House'.'And my mother is too. He can put his slippers under my bed any day, was what she told me.'

Thursday, April 6th

Walk round to Tom and Rachel's. Archie is lying in his pram. Whilst slumbering his expressions run the range of emotions from serene peacefulness to sudden fierce frowning followed by a rush of blood which turns his little head into a tortured turnip for a few seconds before suddenly clearing and settling and every now and then letting a flicker of a smile stretch his wide mouth and dimple his cheek.

Sunday, April 9th

An hysterically jolly Sunday lunch with Archie as the centrepiece. He's awake enough to be passed around and we all have our photo opportunities. His dark eyes are quite striking and he's beginning to focus on faces and straining to look about him.

I'm afraid I'm besotted, indeed it could well be that I have some compulsive disorder where Archie is concerned. I'm photographing like a lunatic, and have his image stuck up on walls and the board in my workroom. I guess I shall settle down eventually, but right now I find myself counting the hours until I see him again. A month from today we shall be on the road again, and it will be a question of counting weeks rather than hours.

Tuesday, April 11th

To David Attenborough's 80th (he's actually not 80 until May 8th, but UK TV want to mark the completion of a special called 'David A's Best TV Moments'). Earlier in the day I'd been to Sotheran's [rare book dealer off Piccadilly] and found a small book of animal poems from the 1930s with scraperboard illustrations which took my fancy and I've wrapped it up for him. Gathering of those who have contributed to the programme, so I feel rather the odd one out, tho' I suppose I'm included as I made 'Life on Air' with D.

David, a little less straight than he used to be, as his weak knee gives him an odd rolling gait, a bit like an over-played pirate in a musical. His face still unlined and his eyes piercing. He makes a short speech explaining how little he likes celebrating his birthday (except of course for tonight) and will be off in the Galapagos on the day itself, which seems appropriate.

He carries out his social duties very well, coming round to us all. He has the book I gave him and is delighted with it. 'Just some sort of nice doggerel poems, nothing serious,' I say. 'No, not the poems! The illustrations! This man,' he taps the cover, 'is one of the finest illustrators there ever was.' I'm ashamed to say the name that means so much to David, means nothing to me, but I've clearly, by chance, found just the right present.

He has work for the next two years, he says, and has begun a new series on amphibians and reptiles. 'Then, that's it,' he says. 'Well, it should be, anyway.' 'Slow down, David, please – until you stop, none of us can.'

Saturday, April 15th

On the road at half past ten to collect Granny G from Abbotsley. The driveway at Church Farm is carpeted with primroses and primulas and dwarf hyacinth. The colours are later this year, but seem more intense and plentiful than ever.

In the afternoon I introduce Granny to Archie for the first time. At a quarter to five the football results show that Sheffield United are now assured of promotion to the Premiership, whence they departed in 1994. No one but me is terribly excited, but I like to think Archie might absorb a little of my joy.

I'm upstairs toying with final draft (which constantly eludes me) of a speech tomorrow when Granny arrives back and moments later I hear a thud and a cry from downstairs. Granny fell off the step in the hall when trying to hang her coat up and swinging round caught her head a cracking blow on the kitchen door.

She's already apologising at a rate of knots, but the bump grows, and, as she is 93, we all think it best to have her checked by doctors. Luckily all is well, no serious damage and Granny arrives back about 12.30 carrying a pamphlet on 'Head Injuries'.

Sunday, April 16th

Fortieth wedding anniversary. So much to do there's barely time for personal celebrations, but we're still happy to be in the same bed together, and the implications of the day are subsumed by the weight of things to worry about.

First of all the anxieties in Granny's health, and that's dispelled quickly when she arrives at breakfast apparently none the worse for wear for a cropper that would have laid many a younger woman low.

We go down to the Ivy in a taxi, arriving about half past twelve. Table-placings have preoccupied us for a couple of evenings, but I think they're now right.

The Ivy service is impeccable, so H and I heave a sigh of relief. One waiter per table, and a maître d', so once we're seated all goes like clockwork. I'm pleased the way those who have little in common but us, seem to get on, Margot [my childhood friend Graham Stuart-Harris's wife] and Dick [Air Chief Marshal Johns] and Graham [S-H] and Barry Cryer; all sorts of unlikely couplings.

Food is very good – navarin of lamb tender and flavoursome. I make my speech after the main course and expect that to be that, but Graham springs to his feet and makes a boisterous, touching reply.

Archie is star guest. By now he's being passed around as people queue for photo ops with him. I proudly lug him around to the various tables and his eyes are open and flicking around. Then he's fed and in later photos he's a bundle clasped against many capacious bosoms.

Robert [Hewison] then drills various people into what sound like very lightly prepared speeches. Ian [Davidson, scriptwriter and university friend] is very funny describing how I lost my temper and as suddenly regained it, whilst throwing a chair. Others are less fluent though Terry J, who has looked a little down at heel throughout, manfully rises to the occasion and praises Helen. 'I can't think of a single bad thing about Helen' which in view of her reaction to his activities over the last couple of years, is generous.

Tuesday, April 18th

After yesterday's gentle bank holiday, catch-up day, I'm at work early on the first of the 'Diaries' publicity interviews. Down the line at BH to a cheerful, not very demanding fellow called Ryan. Stock Python questions, not much evidence of his having read the Diaries.

A short break during which I take a coffee in Nero's nearby. Have forsaken my reflux-teasing macchiatos for one cappuccino a day. A lady sitting at the table next to me points out a moustache of white foam on my upper lip. 'I thought you'd like to be told,' she says with quite unselfconscious maternalism. A trim, middle-aged woman with a suntan looks a bit cheeky.

Back to BH to spend an hour with Mark Lawson, pre-recording an extended interview for 'Front Row'. Mark is never too academic and intellectual with me, he goes for the popular areas – Pythons; the endless descriptions of food and drink. The 'n' word. 'Those expecting to find Michael Palin revealed as anything other than we know him will be disappointed.'

Thursday, April 20th

H and I down to the British Museum at nine o'clock for a private view of the Michelangelo drawings.

Neil MacGregor [Museum director] was in ebullient form, shaking my hand warmly, looking a little pink around the face, he spent several minutes talking to H and myself about the exhibition. Pointed out that what made MA so revolutionary was that he, for the first time, used the human body, its movements and poses and shapes, to express inner truths or emotions or values, which until then had only been shown on the face.

H asks about MA's models. The men, Neil says, would have been those who worked around the studio, but there was no such thing as a female model. If they had posed naked they would straightaway have been considered prostitutes. 'Which is why Rubens always used his wife!'

Saturday, April 22nd

Have been asked, at the last minute, to appear on 'Loose Ends' to talk about 'Dead Souls' which starts the first of two parts on Radio 4's Classic Serial tomorrow afternoon. There has been almost no pre-publicity, apart from a piece by Mark Heap in Radio Times and, having listened to episode one, I feel it deserves a boost. The sound design, by Steve Brooke, is clever, and very effective.

Into the studio where the twitchy, lanky, Dickensian figure of [poet and comedian] John Hegley rises to meet us. He looks worried. Victoria Mather, next to me, is interviewing the wife of Marilyn Manson (whose real name is Brian) who looks dark and sexy in a porcelain sort of way. She takes two hours to dress every day and is a Michigan girl who now goes under the splendid name of Dita Von Teese. Victoria keeps brandishing photos of her, stark naked, in the book she's written. Quite off-putting.

Wednesday, April 26th

Write some remarks to flesh out the Voice of the Viewer & Listener awards script which I've been sent. Then a run and cab down to Carlton House Terrace – the Royal Society HQ, where I am to present the awards for excellence in broadcasting. Quite grand surroundings, but the enigmatic VLV continues to puzzle me. Their supporters are such an odd mixture – half old-folk's home geriatrics with a sprinkling of producers about to retire and one or two young ones as well. I still don't know exactly why they exist and from where they draw their strength, but they clearly have enough respect to bring together, in a half-empty room, Jeremy Paxman, Jon Snow, Charles Wheeler, Kate Adie and the producer of 'Bleak House' to collect their prizes.

It's all low-key, which is a charitable way of saying amateur, and yet avoids much of the pomposity and cant of the big, burbly sponsored award ceremonies.

It could do with tightening up a little, whilst not losing its good taste and charm.

I talk a little to Charles Wheeler afterwards. I have always seen him in the same mould as James Cameron – a fluent, compassionate, unsensational, accurate reporter. To hear him say how much he envied me my access to people in Nepal makes me reassess my general attitude to our journeys – that we're not quite in the big league as far as journalism is concerned. Wheeler says quite matter-of-factly that as far as he's concerned I've made the transition from entertainer to reporter.

Bubbling quietly with this accolade I cross the road to the Athenaeum. Find a free armchair in a busy Drawing Room, order a coffee and a glass of Mercurey and sit and read Arthur Schlesinger Jnr on history and the impossibility of objectivity. He has a quote from President Kennedy which I scribble down: 'we must face the fact that the United States is neither omnipotent or omniscient – that we are only 6 per cent of the world's population . . . and that therefore there cannot be an American solution to every world problem'. This should be nailed to the foreheads of a few of those in the White House now.

Out again soon afterwards for the Hatchards 40th Author of the Year party. End up giving my email address to Princess Michael of Kent, a big girl with big hair who is interested in all my travels but when she hears we're off to Europe is even more thrilled – she's half Bohemian, half-Hungarian(?) and says she knows some wonderfully well-read, art-collecting aristo with several castles who I should speak to. I try and state our policy of speaking, wherever possible, to the ordinary folk, but she brushes that off: 'the ordinary people are one thing,' she lectures me amiably, 'but this man is remarkable.'

Monday, May 1st

May Day. Another holiday, and one I accept quite gratefully. Continue my reading on Europe – today in the doughty company of Dervla Murphy, whose energy puts me to shame. On her bicycle through Bosnia she sees some awful sights, and occasionally brings me up with a start, as when she comes across three plaintive puppies sucking on the teats of a dead mother. Dervla, judging that they will not survive, puts them into a bag, weighs it down with stones and drops it into the nearest river.

In the evening H and I go down to Spitalfields to see Will. We drink Prosecco and wander the house. It's local election day on Thursday and Will is much entertained by the number of parties including apparently the Nigerian Parking party.

We walk round the corner to Strada (yes, the chains are now moving into an area they previously wouldn't touch with a bargepole) and the first person we see is the celebrated local MP himself – George Galloway. Without the mid-rhetorical bluster Galloway looked small, almost furtive as he made his way with one or two followers trailing behind, up towards Brick Lane. And his skin was olive-green and looking shiny and polished. He reminded me of a little, finely crafted jade Buddha.

I smiled and said hello, as one does when taken by surprise by celebrities, and his eyes narrowed and he nodded and muttered an acknowledgement.

Wednesday, May 3rd

To the office. Added another patronship to my collection with £1,500 donation to the British Library – which makes me a 'Woolf' patron, as opposed to Austen (5k) or a Shakespeare (10k). In view of my well-publicised admiration for Virginia's diaries it seems appropriate. I think I've covered nearly all the major cultural institutions of the capital. I'm happy to be able to help and don't really need all the signs and symbols of giving other than the invaluable bonus of out of hours visits.

J-P and I walk across the Aldwych to Caffè Nero on the corner of Waterloo Bridge and discuss, in appropriate Central European café surroundings, the first shoot, now less than two weeks away. A predictable problem, he says, is that few of the countries we shall visit see themselves as Eastern Europe, and others baulk at New Europe. I suggest we just call our project Europe, and postpone a title until we're back and have put it all together.

Charles Clarke and the missing foreign criminals supposed to have been deported,[1] John Prescott made to look a careless old lecher in the Sunday papers and Patricia Hewitt raising the ire of the NHS by trying to improve it, all make Labour's chances in the local gov. elections tomorrow seem poor or even non-existent.

[Neighbour and Labour stalwart] Sally Gimson thinks the Conservatives could take Gospel Oak. They've been promising everybody everything and sadly, she says, there is a strong racist undercurrent which they are only too happy to swim with. I hope any political shift will be an adjustment rather than a reversal.

1 A Home Office blunder – for which Clarke, as Home Secretary, was blamed – allowed more than 1,000 foreign prisoners to escape possible deportation after their release.

Friday, May 5th

Labour has lost overall control of Camden for the first time since 1971. All through the very bad years, they were unoustable, now, as the borough has become a distinctly more pleasant, more efficient place to live, they lose out. Probably a reaction (of the 36 per cent who voted) against Clarke (un-deported criminals), Prescott (figure of fun), Hewitt (nurses flak) and Tony Blair (Iraq mess), but if it is just about parking and unreplaced heating in tower blocks then the baby is being thrown out with the bathwater. All three Gospel Oak councillors have been defeated and replaced by three Conservatives. This hurts.

Saturday, May 6th

A moody sort of day. The unabashed heat of the last two days has gone. It's dry, cooler and clouds are building up. Rain is forecast for the afternoon, which we should be very grateful for, so leave earlier than usual for Abbotsley. Stop on the way at the nurseries at Everton where H fills the car with boxes of plants and I stand around feeling helpless. I never really felt a gut instinct for gardening. I love the end result but so much of the process bores me and still does.

The old man who started the nursery is called Percy. He's weathered like one of his plants and has a broad country accent. I wonder if there is a new generation of Percys growing up, or are they a dying breed. Quite unselfconsciously he comes up with old saws like 'no gladness without sadness'.

If Archie puts me in touch with the future, I feel that people like Percy – and indeed Helen's mother – keep me in touch with the past.

Tuesday, May 9th

Cab late, as they always seem to be in the morning rush hour. Oak Village, like much of the area, barricaded in by the pipe-laying work. To see Paul Ettlinger, for my BBC programme medical. (Apparently if things go wrong with my health and I haven't had the medical then my highest claim could be £1,000,000. With the medical it would be £2,000,000.) He's brisk to the point of bewildering – turn round here, look in there, head to the left, head to the right, sit down, stand up, lie here. The good news is that everything seems to be in working order.

Mimi [Robinson, in the office] sends a wonderful piece from a women's mag called Grazia in which the issue of power being an aphrodisiac is debated. The woman writing against this writes 'what rings my bell is quiet confidence, the reason I'm beguiled by the craggy-faced intellectual Jonathan Miller. And

Michael Palin's laid-backness is so enchanting I'd go from pole to pole to have dinner with him'. That's what you like to read four days after your 63rd birthday. Thank you, Jan Masters!

May 16th to July 22nd: Filming in Slovenia, Croatia, Bosnia, Albania, Hungary and Ukraine

Wednesday, July 26th

Pleased that I seem to have bounced back from the last shoot, and feel very little residual tiredness. Maybe going round Europe just isn't as physically demanding – and the absence of jet lag means no days sabotaged by readjustment of circadian rhythms.

Lunch with Steve at the Engineer. A catch-up, really. Nothing to spoil the party. The money's coming in, and now Diaries is about to become a reality – we await, with bated breath, the punters' reaction.

In the evening we take Gordon and Clarice [Tom's in-laws] to V&P's. Quite superb food and little additions arrive unbidden. Gorgeous slivers of melt-in-the-mouth Umbrian ham and Vasco's sister's legendary lasagne, light and intense. 'I shall never be able to eat lasagne again,' worries Clarice. They're great company. Gordon, a Taurean like me, occasionally flies off the handle, according to Clarice. We agree this might be a Taurean thing – both of us driven to point of explosive frustration by the failures of those of other star signs to sit back and enjoy life the way we do.

They love Tom and notice how much children – they have six grandchildren besides Archie – respond to him. He should have been a teacher.

Friday, July 28th

Another hot, sticky one-sheet night. Little respite from the heat down here in the south-east. Addison Lee [cab company] people-mover to Liverpool Street. Good driver, an Ethiopian who has lived here 16 years and before that 5 years in Bulgaria. Complimentary about the travel shows in the best possible way. 'You are an ordinary man,' he compliments me, and I take that as a perfectly desirable endorsement.

Meet Paul B, Michael Dover and David Rowley [the book's designer] who are accompanying me to Bungay to see the first copies of the Diaries come off the press at Richard Clays.

We're collected at Diss and driven to Bungay. Clays, who also printed Harry Potter and most paperback bestsellers, lies behind a discreet modern doorway in a side-street south of the town centre. And there, on a table in the board-room, is a pile of the Diaries, fresh off the production line.

A tour of the factory. See the books being bound – as usual I'm dazzled by the intricacy and delicacy of the machinery for turning dust-jacket flaps, apply-ing hard covers, cutting, trimming and all that goes into confecting the book.

We're given lunch in a pretty, well-kept English country garden (for whose upkeep a German is apparently responsible). Vichyssoise, cod and Chablis and fresh fruit, and a feeling of good fortune.

Tuesday, August 1st

To where Alex is editing. Find him and Roger up on the 2nd floor – and shots of Budapest riverfront on the screens behind them. They locate various sequences (more or less instantly now it's all digital) like the train wheel change at Chop, the Unicum tasting with Péter Zwack, the flirty fittings of my jacket with Katti Zoob, the rain pouring down in Lviv and the rotating fairground ride in Yalta. Quality of photography is marvellous – can't see anything lost by going to High Def Tape – and it all seems jolly and energetic, so leave feeling reassured that we haven't lost our touch.

Helen goes out in the evening and I watch two of Terry's 'Barbarians' shows. Good stuff. Terry has plenty of good meat to chew on here. I learnt a lot, but I do resent having theories shoved down my throat as relentlessly as this. Oddly Terry (and I suspect Ereira) employ a sort of intellectual aggression which seeks to lay waste all interpretations it doesn't like, with the same degree of ferocity it so condemns in the Romans!

Realise that what separated me from Terry was my inability to deal with this sense of urgent intensity, of smouldering grievance. I liked him most when he was just being funny.

Wednesday, August 2nd

To Daunt's for some books on Bulgaria; very few, and Moldova none at all. The discrepancy in their shelves between books on Western Europe and those on Eastern Europe gave me an idea for the 'New Europe' introduction.

Once home I try to put in an hour on the NE book but a chorus of inter-ruptions including the visit of the organic farmer from the Forest of Dean who supplied our Christmas turkey. His great love is plums and he quite seriously asks me if I would be available to open a Plum Museum.

Friday, August 4th

At midday Mike G is here and takes me to BH to record an interview with Steve Wright about the Diaries, to be used in two months' time. Terry Gilliam has just been in – our paths missing each other by a couple of minutes. Coincidentally, I'd been reading a Guardian article about 'Tideland' on my way to the interview. TG quotes me in it as having left the screening without a word, but been unable to forget the images. He seems to like telling people that I thought it either his best, or his worst film.

A photo session for Saga magazine goes on a bit. Photographers desperately trying to find a new way of looking at old goods. End up in the intimate little garden of a block of flats further along Tavistock St. Lots of elderly ladies come by, which I suppose is suitable.

Supper with Simon and Phillida [Albury] at a Lebanese restaurant in the Edgware Road. The news broadcasts have been full of awful pictures of Lebanese towns, villages and cities laid waste by the latest Israeli offensive, yet here in little Lebanon all seems energetic, good-humoured and generally positive. It is like being transported to a different country; the few indications that we're in London, like a red bus, or a black cab, being swamped by the sheer weight of Middle Easterners meeting, greeting, eating.

Saturday, August 5th

I get out my bike (for the first time this summer), pump up the tyres and cycle, or attempt to cycle, up to Highgate to give Terry G a copy of the Diaries.

TG and I sit around the table on his terrace and chinwag very happily. He's had quite a bruising time with 'Tideland', which opens at the Curzon this week. He believes it needs time to sink in. Most people have my initial reaction then like me can't forget it. He hopes to get Johnny Depp for the new, revived Quixote for which Jeremy Thomas seems close to assembling a budget. TG grins as he says that a chatty email to Depp went unanswered for so long that Terry, exasperated, eventually sent a follow-up email: 'A simple fuck-off would do,' and received a fulsome and apologetic reply from Depp within 15 minutes.

Somehow, battered and bashed about as he is, Terry has this indomitable Black Knight-like resilience which makes talking about all his disasters and setbacks just as pleasurable as talking about his 'successes'.

And cycling back down Highgate Hill is the bonus for me.

Sunday, August 6th

Attend to a lot of emails and letters which I should have dealt with a week ago, then sit in the garden after lunch to read Bulgakov's 'The White Guard' and think back to Kiev. I enjoy the way that places we've seen stay in the mind – not all of them of course – and to relive my time there and to reignite memories is a great enjoyment.

In the evening up to Terry and Anna's new house for supper. Take a bottle of wine as a house-warming present and a copy of the Diaries. My relationship with Terry through the 1970s is one of the big themes of the book and his response will be interesting.

Jenny Lewis [poet and Oxford friend] is there and Heidi, the bubbly, eager widow of Rick the architect who persuaded Terry to buy 2 The Hexagon. Helen admits she thought it an awful place and couldn't understand T's decision, but it has been simply and cleanly converted and looks good. Why it looks particularly wide, airy and spacious is that there is no clutter. I don't know where Terry and Anna keep all their stuff, but they've managed to achieve the feeling of starting with a very clean slate. Apart from a brief rumble about privatisation when we're talking about prison conditions, Terry is quiet, and spends most of his time preparing a meal of all sorts of delights culled from a recently discovered Farmer's Market in Muswell Hill. Then at the end of the evening he shows us how he can suddenly move his left hip without pain (something about a 'bursa' bursting) and skips around like the ex-leper. A lovely evening – largely I think because the women outnumbered the men!

Monday, August 7th

I set out for the barbers. First time I've seen Danny since the war was inflicted on his country. Almost 1,000 of his fellow countrymen, women and children killed in the last month and any ceasefire seems stymied by the Arab league and the Lebanese who don't believe Israel has been restrained sufficiently.

His family live north of Beirut, but even there two bridges have been bombed preventing people from getting around. Aimed at Hezbollah, but proving that Israelis believe in collective punishment. As Danny says, he is no friend of Hezbollah, but the heavy-handed interference of American-backed Israel, is making them into heroes.

May 2003. Greeting Roger Mills, friend and mentor, at my 60th birthday party.

Helen's brilliant idea for my birthday cake – dotted with icing sugar mementoes
of my life so far.

April 2004. With my great-niece Louisa.

Top Dharamshala, 2004. Meeting the Dalai Lama. *l-r*: Roger Mills, MP, His Holiness, Nigel Meakin, Peter Meakin (Nigel's son and assistant camera), Vanessa Courtney, Basil Pao, John Pritchard.

Above Wearing my khata, the white Buddhist scarf, a symbol of blessing and respect. The Dalai Lama asked if he could travel with me.

Left Another famous Himalayan. With Imran Khan in Islamabad.

2004. BBC splashes out on a billboard campaign. It never quite happened again.

2005. The children of our French neighbours show me their school project.

Top Christmas 2005. Family crowd round Michael Stratton (in visor) and his festive motorcycle sidecar.

Left 2005. In my workroom, Edith and Elsie guard the equipment.

Below 2006. Enjoying a joke. Helen and her mother, who had just turned 93. She lived to 104.

April 2006. Ecstatic grandpa with my first grandson, Archie.

Archie's first sight of Barry Cryer.

Above May 2007. Court jester. With the then Prince of Wales at the 80th birthday celebrations of the Royal Television Society.

Left December 2007. What's my name again? *New Europe* book-signing in Tewkesbury.

Below 2008. With my nephew Marcus, his wife Morag and next to me my niece Camilla at the Union Club.

Left 2009. With TJ. What have we seen?

Middle 2009. Lean on me. Helen and TG at his Highgate hideaway.

Below Summer 2009. With family at the local street party. *l-r.* Archie (with signpost), Gordon Winder, Helen, Tom, Clarice Winder and their daughter Rachel, with Wilbur (my second grandson, coming along nicely).

Thursday, August 10th

Breaking news this morning (how the media love their 'Breaking' news) of a dastardly plot to down airliners over the Atlantic which has been 'disrupted' by the security forces. Around 20 arrests in the London and Birmingham area. Chaos at the airports (which of course is nothing new, especially in August) as implications of new, improvised security measures feed into the system. Reports that a co-ordinated series of attacks were to be made using material smuggled on in hand luggage. One result of these scares is that information slips out that one either didn't know, or didn't know you had to know. In this case it is that hand-baggage checks are not as thorough as we think. The country's level of threat has been raised to 'critical' which means an attack is imminent. Are they still out there? Even without their ringleaders.

Sign and send accompanying cards out with another lot of Diaries. The first Python reaction came from Terry J this morning in an email saying how much he was loving them.

Late news before bed – alert still 'critical' but no physical damage done yet. Bush has given one of his uninspiring mealy-mouthed little reactions, notable only for his use of the description 'Islamic Fascists'. His mouth is as tight as his mean little eyes. I honestly think he is one of the scariest world leaders in my lifetime.

Sunday, August 13th

Late lunch with Tom, Rachel, Rachel P and Archie at Pizza Express. We always enjoy these weekend lunches – the place is so efficient, uncrowded and the pizzas of consistently good quality – and I get to play with Big Archie and hold him up in the air above my head.

TG rings – he's 'just got to the end of 1979'. This the first reaction of his to the Diaries – which, thank heavens, he seems to like. He says that it's clear throughout how keen John was to work more closely with me – something that hadn't quite registered very significantly with me.

Eric is in France so won't have received the book yet and John, according to Roger Saunders, is 'between retreats' in France and Arizona, so he won't have received his either. Somehow this echoes the pattern of Python that comes through in the Diaries. Terry J, Terry G and myself in one place, Eric and John, increasingly, somewhere else.

'Tideland' has had generally poor reviews, but Rachel, who went to a Q&A screening last Thursday, was impressed by how well Terry talks about the work – usually better than the work itself.

'In one way,' bemoans TG, 'reading the Diaries was quite depressing. I'm still in the same situation I was then, looking for money to make movies.' He said he'd hoped to get a deal for his next one in place before the 'Tideland' reviews came out, but had failed. But he's so chipper in adversity that I almost long to hear of more disaster.

Tuesday, August 15th

Begin some concentrated reading on Bulgaria. Run late in the afternoon. Becoming more of an effort these outings up to the top of Parliament Hill and through the cathedral of beeches to Kenwood and back. Feel myself slowing down. Harder work. But so long as I pace myself generously the body is able to cope and I'm loath to give up this test of the system. Ideally would like to keep running regularly until I'm 65.

Wednesday, August 16th

Arrive at Archie's at 10.30. He's in Helen's arms – she having come on from the gym. He likes his granny, gurgles, laughs and spreading both arms out pushes forward and clamps them on any hair he can find.

Tom and Rachel go out to the gym themselves and we take the Arch out for a walk along the backstreets. Such gentle, agreeable strolls given an added touch of poignancy for me as I know I shan't see his absorbed, increasingly aware looks-around for another three weeks.

Lunch at Loch Fyne with Michael D and Basil. We discuss the 'New Europe' books. Bas has shown MD the latest photo cull and I've sent him 4,000 words on Estonia, and he sounds happy and will now be able to put something together for the Frankfurt Book Fair.

Michael Codron, wider than I remember, but well-tanned and as usual, looking a little cross, settles himself at a nearby table. Gives me a nod. A few minutes later one of the waiters delivers a note on which Codron has written 'Has anyone ever asked you to do "Quartermaine" in the West End?'

I can't be writing notes all lunch so I walk across and bring him up to date with the situation. He hadn't heard the TV play but says he'd read a very good review by Valerie Grove. 'In the Spectator? or possibly the Oldie.' He sort of spits those last two words out. He reminds me that he put on the original production. 'It wasn't a very happy show,' he reflects. 'Harold [Pinter] and Simon [Gray] didn't get on that well and well, Edward Fox was Edward Fox.'

August 18th to September 5th: filming in Bulgaria, Macedonia, Moldova

Wednesday, September 6th

Reorganise myself this morning. Catch up with the world I've left behind. I have had enough reaction now to enable me to breathe sigh of relief on one score – the edit works; the decision to make the diaries public works too. Or at least, enough people have appreciated it the way I hoped they would.

Of course, I can't wait to catch up with Archie. I walk him through to Montpellier Gardens, the first time I've pushed him on my own. Towards the end of our walk, throughout most of which he's been happily preoccupied with trees, children at the playground and whatever's going on in his own little head, his bottom lip trembles, curls down at the sides and he starts minor bawling. I end up racing him home. A man on a mobile in Torriano Avenue stops briefly to shout 'Push that pram, Michael!'

Take the Northern Line to the office. I find a seat, plonk myself down and reach for Orhan Pamuk's 'Snow' which is beginning to reward my early perseverance, when, squeezing next to me, a symphony in white, is Michael Frayn. 'What are you doing now?' I ask, vaguely expecting a translation of Racine or a Broadway Musical of 'Noises Off'. But he taps his Hackett plastic bag. 'I'm taking this jacket back, it's still got the security label on it.'

Talk of Eastern Europe – of Dennis Marks, who produced Michael's single-city docs that I liked so much back in the '60s. 'My problem was, I couldn't do interviews. Just couldn't do them.'

Tuesday, September 12th

Since we started 'New Europe' on May 16th I estimate we have spent 80 days on the road. By this time on my first travel series we had seven shows in the can; currently I think we may have three and a half. Getting there is proving to be a major timewaster and yet we are only flying and driving round our own continent.

Talk with Roger through the Poland shoot, which is down, mercifully, to two weeks and two days. It looks tight and varied with some good 'headline' stuff, like an interview with Lech Wałęsa,[1] an on-stage appearance with Poland's Python-obsessed, favourite comedy group. Auschwitz and Salt Mines and rafts into Slovakia.

---

1 Lech Wałęsa served as the president of Poland between 1990 and 1995. He was the first democratically elected president since 1926 and the first-ever Polish president elected by popular vote.

Wednesday, September 13th

Call Alan B to ask him where I should deliver his advance copy of the Diaries now he has a house in Chalcot Crescent. He says he's still at Gloucester Cres. 'What we do is – and I'm quite surprised no one's got hold of the story – we eat here and sleep there.'

So happy am I to hear his voice and bubbly chuckle that I decide to take the tome round personally. He's off to M&S. He slips the book into his bag, commenting on my photo on the front, 'You look quite mischievous.'

Helen is working late at the CBS [the Camden Bereavement Service], so we meet up at the Pizza Express just as the rain's starting. Pestered by the sort of fan who says the last thing they want to do is disturb you and then disturbs us for three or four minutes. 'It's nice to meet a celebrity who's also . . . good, you know. Sat next to that Lamarr (Mark, I assume) the other day; never bothered to speak to him.'

Thursday, September 14th

Meet Rachel at the Donmar for the new play 'Frost/Nixon'. A lovely, intimate space, the Donmar; nowhere quite like it where you can get so close to such good actors doing the best new plays. Stephen Merchant and friend next to Rachel and myself. The new series of 'Extras' opens tonight. He hates watching himself and his work, he claims. He's big; as tall as Cleese, with a face as odd and animated as John's is cool and clipped.

The play is good. Very well staged, and there are issues, about television and how David understood it instinctively and Nixon didn't. No interval, thank goodness, so tension well sustained.

Friday, September 15th

Lunch at Soho House. Arranged by John Goldstone [producer] to get as many Pythons as possible – which means only TJ and myself – together to talk about future plans for release of the TV shows on DVD outside US etc.

Terry J is subdued. Exhausted he says by his holiday. I'd always thought it sounded a tall order to visit and stay with all those people he'd ever known with houses in France. A sort of mass reply to invitations. And so it has apparently proved and Terry looks mournful, like a sad old dog. Anna, apparently, doesn't want to eat French food ever again.

JG benign but persistent as usual, trying to pin us down to publicity commitments. He confirms what I've heard, that JC is selling the ranch in Montecito, and his New York apartment, in an attempt to simplify his life. Significant news really. First time I've heard John seriously contemplating economic contraction.

Sunday, September 17th

I lie awake at first light, listening to the rumble of the big intercontinental jets coming in. A kaleidoscope of desperate but interconnected images forms and reforms in my mind – a book waiting to be written, questions for a meeting with Lech Wałęsa, a DVD on Mauthausen concentration camp only half-viewed, cases, sleeping bags, letters unwritten, back-gate locks that need replacing. Where the Second World War began and what to say about it. Books still to be read. The usual pre-filming turmoil. Is the fact that I still suffer this anxious confusion a good thing? I have to tell myself that it is – it's the only alternative to complacency. Still, let no one ever say it gets easier.

September 19th to October 5th: Filming in Poland

Friday October 6th

Walk to Charlton King's Road for a morning with Archie. His head seems to have thinned out. His eyes lock on to yours. He shows caution as he weighs me up, then a half-smile, addressed as much to Tom and Helen, before looking again at me, less quizzically. End up throwing a ball about as if it's too hot to hold and reducing him to hysterics. Another milestone.

Go through schedule at the office and talk to J-P about Romania/Serbia, as the last filming trip of the year is to be. Send him by fax some good material from the Brit ambassador in Warsaw who was once at Belgrade. He talks of the Serbs, with some awe, as 'people who really love to party'.

Sunday, October 8th

In the evening watch the 'Culture Show' special on me. Pretty excruciating, especially the praise – Mark Kermode, a very bright man, calling me one of the most underrated film actors (all based on my perf in 'Brazil' as far as I could see), Vic Reeves talking about how he enjoyed just watching my face. 'I just want to kiss it sometimes.'

Monday, October 9th

Listen to my 'Book of the Week' reading of the Diaries and feel quite pleased. I think I've learnt over the years how to read and, more importantly, how to prepare for a reading. It's so not easy.

Evening Standard has a review by Pete Clark which I find a little disturbing. He says the diary reveals me to be ambitious and energetic. Funny how I never thought of myself as ambitious. Which I suppose I was. Oh dear, this is an odd time.

Nice settled, unambitious supper with Helen and her mother. Ham, mushroom sauce, leeks, peas, mash and a glass of Beaumes de Venise.

Tuesday, October 10th

The post brings cheer in the shape of a postcard from Alan B. Enthusiastic, gossipy praise for the Diaries: 'practically saved my life in Glasgow.' Helen tells me that Terry J has rung. 'He's got cancer.' Some malignant polyps in the colon – should be possible to isolate them. I gulp for air.

Later, meet up with TJ and Anna at the Gatehouse. He confirms the news and the prognosis. There is a small danger that the lymph glands might be infected, but his surgeon has caught the cancer at an early stage and is hopeful.

A happy evening, considering the circumstances, Terry determined not to be got down by it.

Terry had seen Eric last week. He confirmed that Eric was hurt by the Diaries (or it sounded more likely he'd been hurt by the Telegraph's crude serialisation), but had decided not to let it get in the way of our friendship. Which leaves me sad and only a little relieved.

Thursday, October 12th

Pat W, who's painting the outside of the house, has read something in the Daily Mail about the Diaries. 'I never realised you didn't get on together.'

A combination of tiredness and Diary gloom is only dispelled by a late run across the Heath. A fine, clear evening. The exercise seems to shake the system up a bit, and the spirits too. I feel things tilt into perspective.

H and I watch Stephen Fry's accessible and quietly powerful documentary on bipolar disorder and then, when we should have gone to bed, Elaine Shepherd's 1999 documentary on the Pythons, with Eddie Izzard presenting very wackily. Well-chosen clips which were given time to run. And we all spoke well about the same differences which the Daily Mail tried to sensationalise yesterday, all there and expressed six years ago.

Sunday, October 15th

Though we're heading for late October, the days are still warm and comfortable. Front page story in the Observer that this has been the warmest summer since 1659. Global warming is moving fast.

Monday, October 16th

Helen and I watch the South Bank Show on 'Spamalot'. Eric on good form – much happier and more relaxed than with the Pythons breathing down his neck. The stuff with John Du Prez particularly touching. They work well together. No pretension, good clips and altogether a superb plug for the show.

Have my Romanian schedule now – looks neat and busy and a colossal amount of travelling on the first day – in the middle of which an interview with Ilie Năstase [the former World No. 1 tennis player] is sandwiched. No let-up yet.

Tuesday, October 17th

A demanding day ahead culminating in the 'Spamalot' opening. Last night was press night and though the Guardian was sniffy, professing a greater liking for Lerner & Loewe's 'Camelot' than Eric Idle's 'smart-arsed' Spamalot, the Independent is a complete rave.

Made some progress on Romanian history, before a car arrived to take us to the Palace (Theatre). Terry G arrives preceded by his son Harry, who is now of almost Cleesian proportions, and a male model. Then Eric. Much the suavest of us, in what I should think might be a John Pearse suit. Unusual long, tapered jacket which makes him look a bit like a heron.

A glass of champagne unfreezes the situation (how we could have done with something similar on the opening night in New York) and very soon we are making jokes and Eric is becoming very warm and grateful to us all for coming and hugs are exchanged. We're then led out to the front of the theatre where press and photographers are crammed together. 'It's Do Not Adjust Your Set,' beams Eric 'that's what it is.' But for visual impact we do miss Cleese. He's in Australia. There were plans for a cut-out but Eric was against it. 'If he can't fucking be bothered to make it,' he says, charitably.

The volley of flashes breaks on us like a military assault. Jeremy Irons is talking to the press and has to be hustled out of the way and into the theatre. 'Fuck off, Jeremy' and lots of generally well-meant banter as we bundle him through the door.

The 'Spamalot' package, acting, dancing, music, sets, costumes is pretty irresistible – well certainly to Helen and me, but in row in front of us is Michael Frayn and Claire [Tomalin] – she watches the entire proceedings with a look of bewilderment bordering on horror. I'm quite relieved she's not there in the second half, tho' Michael stays on.

A successful, very silly first half, then some more champagne and Eric suggests we all come to Las Vegas for the opening in March next year, combining it with his 64th birthday. All agree to make it if we can, such is the bonhomie amongst us.

19th October to 4th November: filming in Romania and Serbia

Tuesday, November 7th

Put off writing for another day. Peripheral stuff crowds in and I leave the house at 11.15 and walk up to Belsize Park, where I buy a Herald Tribune to help gauge the mood of America on mid-term elections day. The editorial firmly of the opinion that George W and the Republican Administration has been a disaster for America.

At two o'clock Mike G arrives, J-P hovers, and it's time to go and discharge our obligations to the Nepal Tourist Board [I had promised to give them a plug at a travel exhibition]. Drive through the Limehouse Tunnel and out beyond Canary Wharf. A truly dreadful architectural and cultural wasteland. A landscape of packing cases.

Eventually locate the redoubtable Wongchu Sherpa, driver of this particular event, in a neat suit and looking every inch the businessman he's become since giving up summitting. Bit of a disappointment really – where are the dreamers, where are the poets?

Nearest we get is Brian Blessed, whose bulk, beard and bonhomie are irresistible. 'I hate *bloody* microphones!' he roars, stomping away from the podium and trying desperately to rally an audience who sit politely and professionally – trying to concentrate whilst the racket and babble of the rest of the trade fair goes on around them.

I make my remarks, can't hear if there are any laughs; then we're all presented with awards for helping Nepal – prayer scarves are thrown around our necks, goddesses thrust into our hands, T-shirts stuffed into our bags. Photos flash – all quite manic. I talk to a Nepal travel expert who says that his business went up by 300 per cent after 'Himalaya'.

Thursday, November 9th

Meet Terry up at the Wrestlers. It's less than three weeks since he had what his surgeons call 'the second biggest op of its kind after open heart surgery', and he seems quite comfortable downing a couple of pints. It's a nice pub with a roaring fire and mostly blokes around the bar. Terry looks thinner, smaller. There's less of him but that's understandable as he was fed intravenously for over a week. But his eyes seem less bright, as if the voltage has been turned down, and occasionally I catch a look, halfway between pensive and puzzled, which alarms me.

He talks of Anna's newest acquisition – a puppy, called he says, with rueful humour, 'Nancy'. The father was apparently called Frank.

Monday, November 13th

An evening at the Travellers Club with Will, who became a member earlier this year. Will on good form, much buoyed by a meeting of the Spitalfields Society earlier in the evening at which confirmation was given of their successful rescue of a row of fine Georgian (or earlier?) houses at Sheerness. They will restore them and sell them. He's also recently been asked to take an Austrian-American with a lot of money to spend in the London art world on a tour of parts of the capital. The man arrived and Will devised a tour of the City which apparently was so successful they've asked him to do another in Westminster. He may not be earning a lot at the Soane, but he does enjoy the status that being associated with the place gives him, and opportunities like the tours give him huge pleasure. Sitting back on the sofa before the fireplace, looking out at the lights of Pall Mall and sipping a Glenmorangie, with Helen and Will talking and smiling opposite me, I feel as content as I could ever wish to be.

Tuesday, November 14th

To ABC (Australian Broadcasting Commission) by 8.45. It's close to Broadcasting House, but much more domestic. Reminds me of how offices used to look. Slightly scruffy, rooms with handwritten instructions taped to the door. A straggly walled garden outside. I like the company of Aussies; never feel judged by them.

A down-the-line interview to help sell the Diaries in Oz. Not entirely satisfactory. The interviewer is clearly a seasoned and respected TV journalist who probably has better things to do than talk up my Diaries. The focus of questioning is all on Python – an unfortunate consequence of 'The Python Years' subtitle for the Diaries. Once again I have to go back over old ground – about the characters, about how sketches were written etc. Do my best to be fresh, sunny and brimful of enthusiasm.

Diaries (always reviewed by men, always homing in on Python) seen as too long, not enough detail of Python. Judged by one or two to be too nice to be a great diarist, or in one case 'too content'. Marcus Berkmann in The Spectator an exception to the rule. He says pleasure is in the background detail. But I generally have the feeling that more savagery and less observations on the weather would have been preferred.

Thursday, November 16th

Now I can begin the 'New Europe' book from the top. A lot of preparation of the ground and don't put finger to keyboard until late morning. Can't shake off residual tiredness, which is tiresome as I have to shine on 'Parkinson' tonight – one of the few high-profile TV interviews about the Diaries.

Down to ITV Studios on the South Bank for 6.30 recording. Tiny dressing room but full of accessories – including white and red wine, flasks of coffee and tea. Newspapers, Hello! and OK! magazines (read the latter from cover to cover, riveted and appalled!), biscuits – for 'Parkinson' is now sponsored by a biscuit company, Bahlsen.

A well-balanced show without spectacular celebrities. Patrick Kielty, a clever, quick comedian/presenter from N. Ireland, then no-nonsense soap legend Wendy Richard – also the dolly-bird of many '60s and '70s sitcoms. Endearingly straightforward, has had two ops for breast cancer, and finally myself. Michael intrigued most by size of the diary. 'This is like a brick'.

It all goes very quickly, and afterwards there's a new element – a guestbook for Michael – I notice that both Wendy and Patrick Kielty have put 'you're the best', or 'still the best', and rack my brains to be grateful but not unoriginal.

Friday, November 17th

I am interviewed for BBC World Service children's week by a 12-year-old from Scotland called Max Tollan. I got on well with him. He's sharp without being precocious and admiring without being sycophantic. One of the most enjoyable interviews I've done – with anyone.

This week London's Al Jazeera studio opened. Apparently Frostie has already struck, getting Blair to agree with him that the intervention in Iraq had been a disaster. What with this first-time public admission and the caning of George W in the mid-term elections last week the pendulum has begun to swing back. As the ship sinks the hawks are becoming the rats.

Saturday, November 18th

Terry and Anna round here in the evening. Terry looks stronger than he did ten days ago. Anna is straight and upright and reminds me of some of the women painted by Hammershoi. Tomorrow Terry is seeing Cleese, who's briefly over here; John rang me and apologised that he hadn't time to meet up, but was very worried about Terry. Terry looks a little wary. 'I'm slightly worried about this amelioration in our relationship.'

Sunday, November 19th

To St Bride's in Fleet Street for a PEN Writers in Prison event.[1] As I approach up a narrow side lane, the thrilling sound of a choir at full blast emanates, and then is quickly doused. They're in rehearsal for the service at 6.30. Canon Meara is the priest in charge. Said, approvingly, that he'd seen me on 'Parkinson'. Am I happy with the piece I'm to read? I am, but it is quite gritty. No punches pulled. I ask if the phrase 'Horny man for fucking' will be a problem. He shakes his head firmly. In context it is part of the whole paraphernalia of torture and they are Farooq Sarqui's words and he was the man tortured.

Antonia Fraser is to read the other piece and [journalist and broadcaster] Bel Mooney will give the address. Antonia arrives with Harold [Pinter]. She blooming, like a ship in full sail, her magnificent prow cleaving through the greeters. Harold, by contrast, is like an old warship that's fought its last battle. He doesn't look happy, but then he never did. He gives a flicker of a smile in response to someone's laboured 'We met a couple of times . . . I think it was at the so-and-so,' 'I'm afraid, since I've had cancer, I can't remember anything,' he replies.

The service is a proper one – with prayers, mighty hymns ('He Who Would Valiant Be'), an anthem and psalms and Nunc Dimittis. I read my horrifying text, conscious of speaking clearly, not melodramatically, and above all without

---

1 PEN International was founded in 1921 to fight for writers freedom. I had agreed to read a piece for them by a writer tortured in prison.

rushing. I don't think I could have read it much better and by the end you could hear a pin drop.

A drink afterwards at the back of the church. 'We could hear every *word,*' said one lady, as if this were a rare thing at a public event. Later, watch 'Parkinson', with H. 'I was a bit . . . ?' 'Cocky?' suggests H.

Sunday, November 26th

Downpours through the morning, with thunder and lightning accompaniment. Very cosy in bed as the storms come through. Terry J can come to the supper I've organised (on Gilliam's suggestion) with JC at Odin's. He writes, 'I'm giving a sperm donation in the afternoon, so I'll need a square meal.' Finish watching 'The Last Emperor' – gorgeous, costumes and photography, the script becomes a bit perfunctory. Tom helps me with computer problems. Later he sends me a video clip of Archie in the laundry basket which causes me severe emotional collapse.

Tuesday, November 28th

In Glasgow. Write in the morning. Email being not deemed enough for such important news, Michael D rings me personally to convey that the Diaries have leapt up the charts and will be in the Top 10 – at Number 5 – in the Sunday Times list this weekend. Puts a spring in the step.

I'm on stage at the Logan Hall tonight. All seats taken, and in the front row, along with Steve and Michael Dover, is John C; he rang yesterday to ask where it was and though I have momentary qualms about talking about the Diaries with him so close by, I needn't have worried. Francine Stock is my interviewer, so my work is already reduced, and she deals with it all well, giving me time to elaborate, illustrate, remonstrate and generally give a performance – her questions are always to the point, but never too aggressive. Time goes fast and we have some good questions – 'Was Python your peak?' An enormous queue keeps me at the signing table until after 11.

Wednesday, December 6th

As I attack Parliament Hill for the second time this week with a blustery north-west wind pushing me back, I can't help entertaining thoughts of retirement from all this running; immediately I do so I feel like a surrender monkey. Two ways of looking at it. 'I *am* 63!', or 'I'm *only* 63'; by the end of the run, coasting comfortably across the fields, I feel the spirit of the latter take over.

Friday, December 8th

Onto the Underground and to Hatchards to sign a further 200 books. Back across Piccadilly and through the streets of art dealers to St James's Square and the Athenaeum. Very empty. Talk to Jonathan the secretary and leave a copy of the Diaries for the library.

Up into the Drawing Room and enjoy a coffee and glorious few minutes to myself in one of the finest rooms in London. Take down a book from one of the generously stocked shelves. Seneca the Elder, in translation. 'Nothing is so fatal to talent as luxury' I read. Echoes my penultimate entry in the Diaries about our recently acquired resources of freedom, respect and comfort – 'not always the bedfellows of creativity'.

Wednesday, December 13th

Drive to the BBC to record a Christmas appeal for Farm Africa. I'm afraid my enthusiasm for their cause has been affected a bit by the goat-controversy.[1] It's all too Python for words, but keeping goats or not keeping goats is debated passionately in the media, and the central issue of keeping Africans out of poverty has been sidelined. So I can't fulfil this particular obligation with my usual bounce, but manage to act with enthusiasm, I hope.

Thursday, December 14th

A good writing day, then to Carlton School in early evening for the Aladdin panto. It's the first big production on the stage that I raised money for. The new head, Jacqui, says the year's been hard but rolls are good and the school survives. For how long I wonder – the handsome building it's in is big for the numbers and the newly planned custom-built schools like Haverstock have many advantages over this fine relic of Edwardian civic pride. I make a short speech, talk about my Christmas carol experience as a five-year-old school child then declare the stage open. Curtains swing back to reveal the words 'Michael Palin Theatre' across the front of the stage. Feel quite proud.

1 Farm Africa is a charitable organisation that works with farmers in Eastern Africa. Their encouragement to make goats a priority was attacked by some (notably the journalist Matthew Parris) on the grounds that goat herding degraded the soil needed for growing precious crops.

The cast are almost all first-generation immigrants and there's something enormously pleasing in seeing how they all work together.

Friday, December 15th

Watch Al Gore's 'An Inconvenient Truth' documentary about the environment as one of my Academy tapes and am very impressed. There's something accessible but also a touch heroic about the man who introduces himself as 'the man who was once the next president'. The issue needs something like this to set people talking, and the revelations of the speed of ice lost in the Arctic and Antarctic is well, chilling.

Tuesday, December 19th

Confirmation that the Diaries registered 20,000 plus sales last week and their predictions based, as Michael writes, 'on algorithms and entrails or whatever' are for 200,000 or so, in all markets, by April next year, so no embarrassing piles awaiting the great shredder.

TJ has made me sensitive on the Eric issue though, and I can't think of the Diaries clearly any more. They seem to have hurt more than I ever expected.

Wednesday, December 20th

Assemble for a beak-dip at the Dover Castle in Weymouth Mews with Alex, Roger and John Pritchard. A table and plenty of space for the first half-hour but by seven o'clock the place is packed.

Alex [Richardson, our editor] is far from bouncy about the series. I think episode one is taking so long to fashion that he's feeling oppressed by the weight of work, and, more worryingly, I don't hear much about compensating virtues – like good material and great sequences. He doesn't see an extra episode in the material so far. A downbeat assessment and certainly a contrast to the optimism of the 'Himalaya' editing.

Thursday, December 21st

Cold night; below freezing again. Reports of 40,000 affected by fog at Heathrow. BA cancel all internal flights, the marquees up again outside the terminals.

Off to the Stammering Centre. What was to be a quick drop-in to meet Jane

Fraser of the American Stuttering Foundation has grown into a reception with an agenda and request to make a speech. The very good news is that Jane Fraser is a lively, charming, smart, intelligent and rich lady, the best kind of American, well-travelled, well-dressed, well-read. In the speeches she reveals that she, like me, had to live with a father who stammered – or stuttered as they would say in America – and she spoke unsentimentally of the feelings only children of stammerers know. She is the perfect saviour, I think.

Jane F has been a long-time admirer of the Centre, and her remarks make us all swell with pride. The local MP Emily Thornberry has taken up our case, and she also spoke at the reception. A short, well-built lady who impressed with her grasp of the situation.

Monday, December 25th: Christmas Day

Age gap now 93 years, between Granny, born before the First World War, and her great-grandson Archie P, just over nine months in this world. Lovely to see them together.

Tuesday, December 26th

Watch 'The Queen', with Granny. Helen Mirren is quite staggeringly assured these days. One feels she could play Spartacus and get away with it.

Sunday, December 31st

Looking back on 2006, it is of course dominated by our first grandchild. The arrival of Archie was one of the most exciting and profoundly felt experiences of my life, let alone 2006, and his presence has made us both quietly delighted and deeply happy. I dare say this might sound over the top in future but that's the way it feels now. The publication of the Diaries occupied more mental than physical time in 2006, and I've learned a lesson or two from the experience.

The work dynamic has been stoked by 'New Europe', with four and a half months spent on the road. I'd written often enough in the Himalaya diary that we couldn't carry on indefinitely with all the stresses and strains, but 'Himalaya' was so successful that expectations were raised and I felt I had to see the advantages of our team, our unit, our control, our status, rather than possible pitfalls.

Results so far and word from the editing room suggest that we'll have to wait a while longer to know just how good the series will be, whereas with 'Himalaya' we sort of knew at this stage. First marriage amongst our children. And Helen and I, forty years on, are still happy.

2007

Monday, January 1st

Still, clear, cloudless morning after the weekend storms that saw the old year out. Gruesome, intrusive, depressing photo footage of Saddam's execution. Editors obviously not wanting to be left out, choose instead to be with the voyeurs, filling their front pages with indistinct images that we could well have done without. Interesting that later, on a documentary clip from the 'Life of Brian' shown at 8.30, the nation was not allowed to see Graham Chapman's willy. Unlike Saddam's roped neck, it was tastefully blotted out!

Can't really wait to get stuck in to 2007. New Europe a challenge, but a challenge I'm absolutely sure I was right to take on. Just hope what we've done already will have the right tone and balance; but have nine months from now to shape it.

Wednesday, January 3rd

Up to see Danny and have my mane of Christmas hair trimmed. Talk Lebanon as ever. A year ago optimistic, now after the ill-judged Israeli invasion of last year his mood is of deep gloom. Hezbollah the only winners and they don't represent his views.

Friday, January 5th

Enjoy a clear run on the NE book and get stuck into Albania. To the gym for a quick, vigorous and exhausting workout. Archie here late afternoon, now in full crawling mode, he sets off for the fire, repeatedly.

Saturday, January 6th

Out in the evening to dinner at Ranji's. Simon and Phillida there, an added liveliness to the evening. Simon suffers from serious inability to remember names and faces. The proper name for it, says Simon, is prosopagnosia. Ranji looks this up in the dictionary and finds that it has a more specific meaning, which is the inability to remember names and faces 'of those well-known to the sufferer'.

Wednesday, January 10th

A flurry of activity in last 24 hours over my Comic Relief recording today. I've agreed to do an introduction and appeal on the Darfur issue[1] – though it's to be somewhat tenuously based on the fact that I visited Sudan in 1991. I'm uneasy about this process of strapping a celebrity to an issue, and uneasy that Comic Relief are moving into political areas in a dangerously simplistic way. But I've also a great regard for Richard Curtis [founder of Comic Relief] and Emma [Freud, his wife and collaborator] and I've a book deadline to meet. So I try and make it as uncomplicated as possible. Then late yesterday I get a few of the 'while you're doing that . . .' requests and am sent a suggestion in which I play against the nice MP image by swearing a lot. Doesn't take me long to dismiss this. Playing with one's own 'image' is what there's too much of these days. It's not real comedy, it's comedy of celebrity.

Thursday, January 11th

Very strong gusting winds, clouds screaming past, and eventually rain. To lunch with TG at the Engineer – prompted by a phone call from enthusiastic Eric to TG to try and pull together some kind of post-'Spamalot' animated movie. As I park my car, a gust of wind takes my ticket and it blows across the road. Short comedy sequence involving me, the wind and the ticket which ends up with me finally cornering the ticket in someone's basement stairwell. How well could I have explained myself if the door had opened and found me crouching there?

Monday, January 15th

I must now focus on preparation for Turkey, so read up on their history, as complex and unfamiliar as most of the countries we've been through. This is the bit that feels like mugging up before exams. It's only background tho'. I learn more from a couple of hours in the country itself than from a couple of days on the books.

1 The armed conflict in the Darfur region of Sudan where rebel groups were fighting against the government which they accused of oppressing Darfur's non-Arab population.

Out in the evening with H to a Krug-sponsored 'New Year's Party' organised by Sarah Miller. 'It'll be fun,' she assured me, repeatedly. Not quite our sort of thing, but we enjoy the unexpected – every now and then.

It's held at William Kent House, which is tacked on to the back of the Ritz Hotel. It's been bought by the Barclay Brothers (mysterious pair who own the Telegraph) as their entertaining place in London (they live most of the year on a tiny Channel Island). It's been decorated with restrained sumptuousness at clearly unsparing expense. Walk through carpeted rooms to a sort of drawing room.

Terence Conran is sitting down talking to Deyan Sudjic – new head of the Design Museum. Stand about being plied with Krug Vintage '95, which after the first glass ceases to be quite as sensational as it ought to be.

Eventually, after far too long in the drawing room, the tall polished wood doors of the dining room are pushed open and there is a long table surrounded by crimson walls and a fussy coffered ceiling. Various jokes about it being Sir Terence's worst nightmare. Sarah whispers that it's only been used once since it was completed, and that was for the Queen's 80th birthday.

I'm sat between Sarah Miller, bubbly, lively, and Sarah Spankie, her art editor, a little more low-key, but nice, bright, unassuming company. Helen is across the table next to James Dyson the carpet sweeper man. He's tall, thin with close-cropped grey hair, the antithesis of the inventor, he could be a good-looking monk.

Not many words with Sir Terence, he seems very frail and reduced in stature. Still he does love to talk about anything vaguely rude and is most interested in the implications of being called Spankie.

A good adventure, and H, surprisingly, really enjoyed herself. Perhaps a closet socialite in there somewhere.

Tuesday, January 16th

Overnight rain. Read piece in the Independent about man with testicle problem, immediately feel an ache in that area. Train to Leicester Square and up to Orion for various meetings. Michael greets me with the news that the Diaries are at their highest point yet in the Sunday Times list – No. 5 this week. This does not mean huge sales – he says the figures are between three and four thousand, but it is an encouraging sign that, contrary to the experience with all the TV tie-ins, the Diaries have a life after Christmas.

Thursday, January 18th

Wake with unpleasant realisation that I shall have to get my attitude to 'Spamalot – the Animated Movie' – sorted before I leave for Turkey. Eric is pushing us into what looks like our new Python movie. Everyone resisting being pushed, but TG, like me, is approving of Eric's energy and persuaded by his tenacious enthusiasm that something can be done.

Played with Archie and made him laugh a lot – mostly by the simple method of showing him something, hiding it, then slowly revealing it again. Works every time.

January 19th to January 31st: Filming in Turkey

Thursday, February 1st

A busy day back. Terry's 65 today so I give him a call, rustle up some gifts and agree to meet him at the Spaniards for a lunchtime drink. There is a funeral party there, taking up most of the car park and the bar space but I see Terry in a corner, on his own, studying a book by the light spilling in from a small-paned window. A Vermeer moment. Terry looking scholarly and seems fine after three of six of his chemo sessions.

He is determined to carry on with life as before, and thinks this positive attitude is what keeps him well. We talk over his musical for Lisbon,[1] his current absorption in Richard II for a learned journal, and his need for money to pay off his mortgage.

We drink some Harveys and part affectionately. I sense a shadow of something as we leave. Maybe just a slowing of his movement, quite understandable in the circumstances, but also something more – an inkling of a light fading – and that makes me feel sad for a moment – then I think that it's not just Terry who should be thinking positively, but his friends as well.

Friday, February 2nd

To Molinare by ten o'clock to see the Baltics rough cut. It's running at 1 hour 06, which seems over-indulgent knowing it has to fit into an episode which also contains Hungary and the Ukraine. But once I've sat through it, I appreciate exactly why they've kept it at this length. It works, and it works as a single episode. There is no point squeezing this in with Hungary and Ukraine

---

1 *Evil Machines* was a musical play based on Terry's book, due to be staged in Lisbon.

or Poland. It works entirely on its own. Alex's well-paced editing gives it an unrushed feel, Nigel's camera is solid, fluent and assured – moving beautifully over the action and capturing faces and giving a presence to what seemed quite ordinary people at the time.

To the office at 3 to record two pieces for Orion conventions or conferences on tape. Always find this spontaneous 'be funny' approach quite difficult. I don't feel easy before a camera the way I do before a live audience.

Monday, February 5th

Out with Terry J to see the Bedford Hours [the French medieval manuscript] and other rare and rarely seen jewels of the British Library's collection. Terry is captivated straight away by a Chaucer edition. He's never seen this work, open at the page with a picture of Chaucer in blue smock – which TJ says is generally accepted to be the most accurate likeness of him. Sir Colin Lucas, new Chairman of the BL, welcomes us, but his speech rambles on saying little that we didn't know already – the British Library is a wonderful place, wonderful collection, priceless archive etc., all of which we know otherwise we wouldn't be here.

The works are very fine. The Master of Bedford a careful, delicate illustrator with faces modelled in some detail, the colours deep and intense, and the huge illuminated initial letters given enormous thought and care.

Terry mutters a little about the hypocrisy that these pious works represented for the rich and famous of the early fifteenth century, but, as works of art, they are glorious.

Anna professes complete exhaustion at TJ's unstoppable socialising. They've either cooked for or been cooked for for the last ten nights. As Terry drops four of his chemo tablets, Anna pleads for a quiet night in.

Wednesday, February 7th

George Andraos [Lebanese computer genius, who has saved Helen and myself from many a panic attack] here to do some computer maintenance for me. He doesn't waste time, I'll say that. He sits at the desk and like a man playing all the fast bits in a piano concerto works away, con brio, for an hour, checking this, removing that, sighing with momentary frustration. I'm like the page turner beside him – occasionally being called in to provide my password. Not a great writing day as must prepare for the Loncraines this evening.

Richard L checks my computer and, moving as deftly as George, pulls out all sorts of programs, including setting up Google Earth. For the second time today I feel envious of someone's technical confidence, and frustrated at my own lack of the same. George A, and to a lesser extent Richard, believe that everything can now be done on the computer screen – which prompts me to look around at all my books, writing pads, mugfuls of pens for reassurance.

Helen cooks a superb lamb roast and I bring out a bottle of the Pichon-Longueville '82, to celebrate the year we last worked together. It's sensational, and now only four left.

Richard is hoping to do a film with Jack Nicholson. Nicholson has been offered 10 million dollars. The film itself will cost 8 million.

Thursday, February 8th

Wake to the silence of snow. The usual repertoire of noises which heralds a new day – footsteps, voices, deliveries, cars being started – is absent. Up at 7.30 and looking round the landing blind I see a respectable covering, 2 inches, I should think and still snow swirling down. The village, and our back garden, remain picturesquely unviolated for about half an hour.

At 5 I take a taxi down to Alie Street near Aldgate; I've agreed to give a talk on my travels to raise funds for the Historic Chapels Trust who've restored the German church there. The church is a delightfully quirky place. Built in 1763 to serve the growing community of Germans involved in the smelly, dirty sugar-baking business. The ten commandments are above the altar, written in German and there's a board with the names of benefactors including that of Frederick, King of Prussia. I draw some comfort from the fact that it has survived two wars against the Germans without being vandalised by locals, or bombed.

I address the congregation (350 tickets sold) from a fine carved wood pulpit, some 15 feet high. Audience largely preservationists, but talk for 50 minutes or so on my travels and then take Q&A. An Asian gentleman asks me if 'there is hope for civilisation'. I say yes.

Sunday, February 11th

I have to get myself together for a fundraiser at the Phoenix Cinema. They've shown the 'Holy Grail' and afterwards I'm to be interviewed by Mark Steel. Arrive a little early so stand in the foyer and talk to Mark – a consistent, unreformed London working-class critic – with a neat, unspectacular comic style. Easy to get on with and a Python fan 'because my parents weren't'.

Thursday, February 15th

Archie comes over and I'm helplessly sucked into the world of repeated opening and shutting of doors, fast crawling and so on.

To the V&A for Orion's author party. Hugh Johnson [the wine writer] seems keen to chat. Tells good story of some Soviet bloc country which was persuaded to send all its wine to Moscow in return for a fleet of tractors to help in the vineyards. When the tractors eventually arrived, they were all a foot too wide to go between the vines, so the whole stock ended up having to be replanted.

Helen Mirren, toast of the Western world since winning BAFTA for 'The Queen' and the Oscars soon to come up, is there. I'm asked to come and say hello. Trouble with such situations is that you cannot help, no matter how hard you try, to have a normal, natural conversation. You become one of the courtiers and cameras are there to inhibit, and agents to control, any ordinariness – which is a pity because Helen is, at heart, rude good fun. With her is Edna O'Brien. Kiss HM on both cheeks, but Edna proffers only the mouth.

Monday, February 19th: London–Sheffield

Prepare myself for an intense Sheffield visit, including receiving a 'legend of Sheffield' recognition and a talk with Sam West on stage at the Crucible.

To St Pancras by midday. The old station now dazzlingly transformed. The brickwork, warm terracotta, looks as fresh as if it had just been built. The ironwork painted an unexpected shade of sky blue – which is apparently what was found underneath when later accretions chipped away. Barlow's roof has been thoroughly renovated, but transparent strips between the panels bathe the place in daylight. Other surprises, a frieze of decorative tiling running along the sidewalls – quite a subtle touch. The whole effect is light and bright and expansive and well, almost fabulous.

At Sheffield there are changes too, the station has been cleaned up and where the car park was there are now fountains and a long, reflecting stainless steel installation – a bit like a giant slug in shape – which follows the road and provides a barrier for walkers.

I give my name at the hotel reception and am met by a trace of irritation and a 'Mr *Who*?' Not a good start for a Sheffield legend.

The ceremony involves short speeches. My joke about the Arctic Monkeys [the band, also from Sheffield] which I thought up in the bathroom this morning – 'wherever I am in the world, in the snows of the Arctic, or with monkeys in the jungle, my heart swells when I hear any fellow-Sheffielder being recognised' – is lost by a loony shouter at the back of the crowd.

The crowd is small – a number of young and a number who seem slightly mad. TV interviews, radio interviews and a walkabout. Now, embedded on the pavement beside the town hall is a star marked 'Michael Palin, Actor, Writer, Traveller, Comedian' or some such. I'm in select company with Gordon Banks, Helen Sharman, David Mellor and Def Leppard!

Thursday, March 8th

Out with H to John Hemming [writer, explorer, ex-director of the Royal Geographical Society] and [his wife] Sukie's. David Attenborough standing with a bow-legged roll – like an old sea captain. Susan accompanies him. Upstairs John introduces us to Prince Sidi Hassan and his wife. He's a short, portly, balding man, the son I guess of King Hussein of Jordan, who does much travelling round the world in the cause of conflict resolution. In a gap in the conversation, he catches my eye, leans across the table and says slowly, clearly and quite loudly, 'My wife and I want to say how very, very much we enjoyed your series on the Crusades.' I promise him, as tactfully as I can, that I shall pass this on to Terry J.

David has been in Madagascar filming reptiles and amphibians. The only thing he really seems to hate is writing the book.

Raining as we leave – find a cab. Back at Julia Street the driver seems to spend forever on my receipt – when he passes it to me, it's with another receipt on which he's scrawled 'I write screenplays of East End gangsters. Help me. Henry' and his phone number.

Monday, March 12th

In the evening, H and I go to see the Dennis Severs house in Folgate Street. The old house which offers to take one back three hundred years is virtually on the fault line between ancient and modern. The City office towers rise all around, and another great wall is going up on Bishopsgate – a looming bulk over the remains of the old city. Meet one of Severs's acolytes outside the big Queen Anne pedimented front door. Slight feeling of being about to enter some religious establishment, a hushed lowering of voices.

Inside it is a remarkable atmosphere that's maintained. Smells and soundtrack of muffled conversation, a thunderstorm, clocks chiming in the City, glasses being clinked, all help to enclose you in the past. The rooms are all packed with period furniture, crockery, pictures. One has to remember that maybe 30 members of the family, and their servants, would live here. Even the cleanest of them would only bathe once every fortnight, hence the aromatic smells used to cover up for lack of personal hygiene. An evening of wooden floors and wax candles.

Sunday, March 18th

The afternoon spent in Oxford. Mike picks me up at a quarter to two; easy journey; to the Playhouse and then meet up with Tish Beeby, who's run the place for years, and Libby Purves who's linking the evening. Libby doesn't really do small talk; but we sit and have a coffee together and it transpires that we have something in common, both of us have close family who committed suicide – in her case her son, and less than a year ago. She talks capably and without obvious emotion about it, but she's clearly upset that she can't understand it. He suffered from schizophrenia, knew his madness, wrote about it, tried everything to defeat it, was positive and hard-working, but it got him in the end. We both talk about family responsibility and guilt. She feels that he would have done what he'd done however hard anyone had tried to help and understand him. I feel the same with Angela.

Various other members of the cast arrive – Jon Snow, who's one of the most assiduous do-gooders (and I use that entirely as a compliment) that I know. Both he and Libby are broadcasters in the big sense – dealing with big thoughts and ideas and sadly, I'm far too interested in the inconsequential, in what's happening here and now amongst the people I'm with. For a traveller I've very little interest in 'the worldview'.

The evening is to raise money for a Parkinson's charity. Barbara Thompson, a Parkinson's sufferer herself, can't stand or sit still as she waits in the wings, but once on, plays jazz saxophone enchantingly well. One of the highlights of the evening for me.

I've assembled the concentrated version of my dad's illness from various diary entries, and it reads quite movingly – as a tribute to him, to my mother and also as an account of the progress of the disease.

A man with a bow tie, big moustache and slightly surprised eyes looks almost like someone dressed for a comedy sketch, but turns out to be one of the doctors who pioneered the newest treatment which is the implanting of an electrode 6 centimetres into the brain. It has transformed people's lives.

The show begins at 5 and we're all still on stage at 7.30. There's a party afterwards, but it's too late for me, Libby leaves for home too. 'I have to write a piece for The Times tomorrow,' she bustles, 'A political opinion. Can you think of a political opinion for me?'

Tuesday, March 20th

At midday a car arrives to take me to the new University College Hospital for the Service Commitment Awards and lunch. Met by the chief executive, plus various others. Quite informal – taken to meet the staff in the café. Meet a lady who saw me in Timbuktu – not on TV but actually in Timbuktu – a big, soft-handed lady with a soothing voice and sleepy eyes. Meet another from Southern Sudan and two very excited waitresses from the Philippines, After much chatting taken to the stage which has been erected in one corner of the atrium. 'Ask them about the lifts!' H had instructed me as I left – they are apparently legendarily full and slow. I didn't have time to. They were so busy explaining why one of the revolving doors was broken, why the celebratory cake, made at another hospital in the group, had been dropped and written off, and why at the last minute the power failed so the PA system wasn't working. Home, manage some writing, then out with H to a party given by the Archbishop of Canterbury.

A long, cold wait on some draughty stairs to sign our names in a book, then down a long corridor with some good portraits of former archbishops flanking the walls. At the end of the corridor the archbishop and his wife stand on the threshold of a big beamed hall, welcoming us all. He's a soft-spoken man, with a straggly grey beard; quite short and inoffensive and well-decent. He has a son called Pip, who must be ten or eleven, and talks enthusiastically, unselfconsciously and a touch precociously. The room is not too full and the guest list quite eclectic.

[Scientist and broadcaster] Adam Hart-Davis, the world's least self-conscious man, is dressed like a pearly king – making some quick series about the cosmos. I talk to Seb Coe about the Olympics. I, the optimist, venture that whatever happens, it'll be all right on the night. He looks at me rather wryly. 'In *this* country, are you sure?'

Richard Dawkins, the arch-atheist, is there. Looking a little uncomfortable as well as the author of 'The God Delusion' might in an archbishop's presence. Dawkins encouraged by a good reception for the book in the US: 'the atheists are coming out of the woodwork'.

Terry J a little put out at being lionised, indeed raved over by the sculptor Antony Gormley, only to realise that Gormley had got the wrong Terry. TJ doesn't like Dawkins much, he says. Lots of good stuff in the book, but 'he shouts too much'.

Thursday, March 29th

To BH where I've agreed to take part in an interview about radio with Alan Yentob. Except that Alan rang me yesterday to assure me that it wouldn't be all about radio, but all about me and my career generally – a variation on '40 Years Without'.[1] I find out now that my appearance has been billed as a Masterclass.

---

1 *Forty Years Without a Proper Job* was the title of my stage show.

Alan, his usual chatty, charming, concerned self, clutches a copy of the Diaries and expresses his pleasure in them. We talk about the redevelopment of Langham Place; Yentob thinks it may take years to complete. Mark Thompson [BBC director-general], looms up to say hello as we have pre-class coffee in what was once John Birt's office. 'This is where you came for the bollocking,' says Thompson, affectionately. No, not affectionately.

The audience is BBC employees – around 250 of them, and it's a spirited and enjoyable hour for which I feel quite well-prepared by having prepared nothing. Good reaction and at the end a couple of people say how refreshingly open and candid I was. One of the benefits of old age is that you are more and more able to say what you want and not care.

Monday, April 2nd

By Northern Line to Waterloo and walk through to the National to take part in a reading to launch the compilation of PEN letters and pieces called 'Another Sky'.

Ronnie Harwood greets me genially, paternally and warmly. '*Young* Palin,' he beams, and once again tells the tale of my being 'the best Dresser' ever.[1] This time he adds a little relish to the story. 'We wanted him to do it in the West End, but, oh-no, he had to go to the other side of the world. Couldn't *poss*-ibly do it!' I don't remember being asked to play it on stage, still, maybe the diary will help.

Will Boyd is one of the readers. He's a diarist. Has been since 1982. It's proved very useful, he says, in various legal spats, providing him with details of meetings, dates etc. that have enabled him to fight various tussles successfully. He says he couldn't envisage it being published though. Too bad, I say. I think it would be one of the great literary journals.

Monday, April 9th

This morning I have the bright idea of taking Granny G to the Wallace Collection. Beautiful day with a cool edge to it, but spring has firmly taken hold and blossom on the trees and the wisteria bursting out in the garden. GG loves the ornate prettiness of the collection, though we have an interesting moment together before Xanto's 'Head of Penises', a portrait of a man made up entirely of dicks – apparently as a protest against the prevailing fashion (in the late

---

1 Ronnie Harwood was a playwright who won an Oscar for his adaptation of *The Diving Bell and the Butterfly*. I starred in the BBC Radio 4 adaptation of his play *The Dresser* in 1983.

fifteenth century) for rich women to have their portraits painted. Xanto sounds a good man, as we used to say at Shrewsbury.

Friday, April 13th

A very important day for the New Europe project. The Baltics, now down to transmission length and with Roger's sometimes rather sententious commentary on it, is first rate. Poland will not disappoint either. So we have an extra show. All agree that we should put them together as seven and approach the BBC with seven. Cutting them into six will I think be very difficult.

Saturday, April 14th

Tomorrow the last journey of the last series of journeys begins. Honestly. I promise.

April 15th to May 4th: filming in Czech Republic and Germany

Saturday, May 5th: Dresden—London

Alarm wakes me at 6.25 in my room at the Radisson in Dresden, formerly the Gewandhaus, the Cloth Hall, bombed and burnt out during the massive Allied air raid on February 13th 1945. Final packing. Down to breakfast by 7 o'clock.

The Meakins wish me a happy birthday, John Pritchard hands me a book in brown paper wrapping. 'Oh dear, something of an explicitly sexual nature?' I joke. 'Well, it is in a way,' says John, and he's right. It's Terence Blacker's biography of Willie Donaldson [the British satirist who published under the name Henry Root], and as we coast north to Berlin, along smooth, under-filled autobahns, between the woods and the rapeseed fields and the slowly twirling windfarms, I slip back into the past. For a while Willie's urbane banter came back to me. His light, softly upper-class accent, languorous manner, and I smile to myself all over again. His life went in a completely different direction from mine, and yet, I felt I needed people like Willie to prevent me becoming too dull and conventional, and for a while, I, a new boy in London, greatly appreciated his assurance and his good subversive instincts.

The crew of flight 283 from Berlin produce a card, signed by all including the captain, and four miniatures of champagne, and in his car in the car park at Heathrow, Mike turns and presents me with a cake and a single lighted candle.

Home soon after three o'clock and there to welcome me in is Helen and standing beside her, Archie P, only recently woken from his sleep. He chuckles and smiles and shows me that he has really learnt to walk since I last saw him. But he reserves his greatest pleasure for the opening of my pile of birthday cards. For some reason watching me slide a paperknife into the envelope and extract the card sends him into fits of laughter.

Thursday, May 10th

Yesterday's newspapers had front-page pictures of Paisley and McGuinness laughing together as the new Northern Ireland Assembly opened.[1] Why, for fuck's sake, couldn't they have laughed earlier? A horrible image, mocking the 3,000 or more who died because both these men were better at fanning hatred than making jokes.

The reception at the Leathersellers [one of the ancient livery companies in the City, who had given money to the Stammering Centre – I was a guest speaker] is pleasant enough, but as happens at things like this, I have nowhere to hide. From the moment I arrive, to the moment I leave, I am questioned and cajoled. Apparently there are now 153 livery companies, including one for IT people and one for firemen. Very masculine and very strong on ritual. Rose water is passed around in which we dab napkins and apply them to brows. We rise for the National Anthem twice.

When cigars were passed round there was a certain regret in the Master's voice as he observed that this would be the last time they could do this. From July smoking in circumstances like this will be illegal. Attitudes to smoking have seen one of the most drastic changes of my lifetime. As I was growing up, it was non-smokers that were thought odd.

Tuesday, May 15th

About midday Peter Fincham calls; amiable, bantering but clearly he's just woken up to the series title – or more likely, been woken up to it by someone else. Fincham thinks it was going to be called Palin's Wild East. This, as far as I remember, was a J-P idea which he must have used at some point of negotiations. I explain why it's gimmicky and meaningless as far as I'm concerned, and quite out of keeping with the other clean, clear geographical descriptions. Europe must be there somewhere, I feel. We agree to differ for the moment. He will try and come up with something that suits us both. Good luck. At one point

---

1 This was a key moment for the confirmation of power-sharing. Paisley and McGuiness had been sworn enemies through most of their lives.

he says, 'I know you won't like this but we do have a viewers' panel which can give an opinion on titles, almost overnight.' I think he senses my lack of instant enthusiasm for this one. 'I shouldn't think you'd like that would you?' 'No, I'm afraid I wouldn't.'

The title is a niggler. Always has been. I feel New Europe has passed our tests and that we should now go firmly ahead with it. His point is that it sounds dull and worthy, 'like something that might get 1.5 million on BBC Two'.

Thursday, May 17th

Out with H to see 'The Entertainer' at the Old Vic, with Olivia H (for whom it's a birthday present) and Ray Cooper. Ray stuck in traffic and misses the first act.

A cracking performance by Robert Lindsay. He is the most marvellous entertainer – has the old music hall act so perfectly that I could sit and see him do that all night. Sadly, there's a lot of rather tedious and tediously played domestic stuff without him – which fails to light me up. Meal afterwards with Olivia and Ray. Olivia talks with her usual delightful openness about how she's rather keen on luxury spas, and how much she likes the company of musical widows – Barbara Orbison, Mrs Peter Capaldi, Yoko.

By the time we finish our meal and step outside, it's after midnight, and Olivia is now sixty years old. We all sing Happy Birthday to her on Coin Street. And dance it as well.

Saturday, May 19th

To Olivia's birthday party at Friar Park. Weather good and we're outside Henley in just over an hour. Remenham Hill is chock-a-block and it's another half-hour before we squeeze over the bridge into Henley – past the church where Mary Ovey married Ted Palin, up the hill to Peppard and in through the gates of Friar Park. The gardens impeccable, and after two weeks of rain and drizzle, the colours are deep and rich in the crisp sunlight.

Ringo, lean as a whippet, with three silver rings in the earlobe nearest to me, stabs out very funny barbed shafts about everybody. He talks of how hard the Beatles worked in their prime. 'We'd have one day off in two weeks, and Paul would go and judge a beauty competition.'

The meal is beautifully served. Three all-vegetarian courses; tho' even these seem too much for Ringo, who sends back everything touched with any suspicion of dairy product. They bring him rocket and shaved parmesan. He just eats the rocket.

Olivia has the knack of being herself in circumstances that might well overawe others. The table is immensely long – over 70 people at it I would guess, and yet she replies to Dhani's toast with a laugh and ends by imagining what George would say were he here. 'I remember what he said when I turned fifty,' she says, and after a neatly judged pause goes on, 'I've never shagged someone over 50 before!' Paul catches Ringo's eye. 'Not quite true,' he mutters. 'There was that one in Mansfield.' But this is lost in the applause and the singing.

Back home. Leafing through [theatre critic] Kenneth Tynan's diaries hoping for some insight into the genesis of 'The Entertainer', come across an entry in which Tynan recalls having gone to review Frank Ifield at the Palladium, under the impression that he was blind (he says he got muddled with a singer of similar name) and gave him an admiring review just for being able to get about the stage with such ease.

Tuesday, May 22nd

Day's work broken by the Royal Television Society 80th birthday celebration at Clarence House, courtesy of the Prince of Wales. Have already received a whole list of instructions about the event – from special passes, to instructions to bring two kinds of photo ID, to how to greet Their Highnesses – Ma'am, as in 'Jam', not 'Farm'.

Charles seems slighter than I remember. He must be an inch and a half shorter than my memory of last meeting. Either he's shrunk or I've grown. We talk about Romania and quick as a flash he's on to the Eminescu Trust and his love of Transylvania. 'I'm trying to get a Transylvanian brand going,' he says, not entirely ironically I feel. He clearly feels that the traditional agricultural methods out there are worth encouraging. Apparently one phone call from him scuppered the Dracula Theme Park.

Lots of newsreaders there for some reason. Natasha Kaplinsky receives me as if she might be the hostess, proffering a cheek. Fiona Bruce's gangliness rather attracts and I joke about the erotic appeal of newsreaders with George Fenton [the composer]. 'Perhaps she'll give you a private sign as she reads the news.' Ooh yes.

Friday, June 1st

Despite celebrating completion of the book with an office lunch on Wednesday, it is still running my life, as I begin the laborious process of the final revision – reading as carefully and thoroughly as possible, feeding in notes from both Michael D and Steve A, and reminding myself that this is just about the last chance to make it something I shall be happy with, if not proud of, in the months ahead – and, I suppose, long after that.

To the Barbican to meet up with Judy G [my cousin] to see Amira, the singer from Sarajevo who we filmed almost a year ago, in London for her first concert here. She'd contacted me by email and I'm afraid this evening was more of an obligation than an inclination. But it turned out to be one of the best nights out. Amira and her cool, unflashy but effective and highly listenable group, play a captivating first hour after which a gypsy band called Taraf de Haïdouks take over. Pretty undisciplined except when playing, they wander about the stage in large numbers, upstaging each other, but convey a terrific sense of high spirits and spontaneity and turn the Barbican into a bar-room in the Balkans. A little too long but joyful and quite brilliant playing.

Sunday, June 3rd

Watch the first of the 'Great British Village Shows' at 6.45.[1] It's bouncy, a little too relentlessly jolly with not much detail about, but chipper and cheerful and we call Rachel (who has a party of 11 watching with her) to congratulate her.

Then the last two episodes of '24', run together. Very satisfying and at last, real up-to-the-wire excitement. All left hanging on Jack's love-life – which is never, to be honest, either convincing or at all involving. Get your gun out, Jack, and shoot a few people.

Tuesday, June 5th

I'm at work on the proofs when Peter Fincham rings. He's still beefing on about the title and wants to urge me once more to put my name above the title. 'Palin's New Europe' rears its head again, and I'm afraid I'm not for turning. There is no perfect title, and never has been for this series, but I think it important not to change my title style after six series. He's worried about the Sky menu – will people be put off by 'New Europe'?

Eventually Peter, sounding a little irritated, yields to my stubbornness. I could be wrong but I have the feeling that he is as irritated with his own marketing people for putting him in this spot, as he is with me.

---

1 A BBC programme, co-hosted by Alan Titchmarsh, in search of Britain's best village shows, which Rachel directed.

Wednesday, June 13th

A good start to the day. Lots to do, but I'm feeling quietly on top of things. Then the phone rings. It's J-P. 'This'll amuse you,' he starts, but it's irony in his tone that worries me. Last night at some BBC bash Peter Fincham had approached him, still worrying about the title. On the way to the office I think it all through. Two things shift my position. One, that I think this is a detail that's threatening to derail the fragile confidence on which TV series are based at a time when we should all be united, and at a time when we need the BBC to give us a good strong slot.

Another niggling anxiety is that 'New' Europe makes the title more of a construct, more subjective than either Himalaya or Sahara, and that maybe it would be clearer to make it my view. My New Europe. So, somewhere between Camden Town and Leicester Square I made up my mind to retract my New Europe insistence and live with 'Michael Palin's New Europe'.

Steve makes a good point that Palin's New Europe is a very male-oriented, school-register name and 'Michael Palin's New Europe', less assumptive and more acceptable to the female audience.

Friday, June 15th

To the Royal Academy to meet Mary Anne Stevens for a talk about how I can be helpful in the planning, publicity and general success of the Hammershoi show which they're putting on next summer. For once, I don't feel intimidated by talking to exhibition gurus – for I do know quite a lot about a very specialised area. A good talk and an hour of Hammershoi worship later I make for the Green Park Tube and home by 4.30.

Granny, who's staying with us for the weekend, is discomfited. She tells me that on Wednesday morning her foot slipped from clutch to accelerator and she drove her car quite hard through a brick wall, writing off both car and wall.

Monday, June 18th

To a café/restaurant called Bbar, opposite the Queen's Gallery, to judge the Paul Morrison Award [given by Wanderlust magazine] for best travel guide. Rest of the judges already there, sat around a glass-topped table with coffees and water. Bill Bryson, Mark Ellingham of Rough Guides and the third man, Mark Carwardine, who's a writer and co-authored books with Douglas Adams of the 'How to Save' variety and Lyn, the Wanderlust editor and a secretary.

Bill greets me with some pleasing statistic about a recent list of top-selling non-fiction titles, in which there were only two authors who'd written the books entirely by themselves – that was Bill and myself. I protest, saying that I copy most of mine from the Rough Guides. Mark E looks suitably cheered.

Joined by John Brown, who I assume is now the publisher of Wanderlust. Used to publish – indeed still does – the great Viz magazine. I tell him that it was the one thing which both my boys and myself could laugh at together, much more so than Monty Python.

June 26th to June 28th: In Trento, North Italy where the New Europe book is being printed

Friday, June 29th: Trento–London

Farewells – the book now safely in the hands of Dario and his team at the printers. For me, a much-appreciated lull between writing the book and writing about the book, which will begin in August.

The news caption 'Allarma a Londra' which we saw (without illustration or lacking footage) in the lounge at Verona, refers to a bombing attempt last night, outside a nightclub at the top of the Haymarket. A Mercedes packed with petrol, gas canisters, nails and ready to be detonated caught in the nick of time. On the radio we hear that another Mercedes full of explosive material was found nearby. Traffic warden had slapped a ticket on it and it had been hauled off to the car pound in Park Lane!

Monday, July 9th

Phone calls and emails and then to Molinare to look at prog seven with J-P and Alex. I'm disappointed by the first viewing, which is not a good sign. Good chat afterwards. I suggest replacing one or two cut scenes and trimming others. It could be that I'm just tired of it all, but I suddenly felt constricted by Europe – by the introversion of it all – and found myself longing to get away from dark shadows of pasts and into the superficial sunlight of somewhere like the sub continent.

Walk to the office. A man from Brazil stops me and is complimentary about the work. 'We love you there.' (Interesting timing, as Brazil was dropped in favour of New Europe.)

An interview at the office with Mary Riddell for Good Housekeeping. An astute, experienced journalist (Observer, New Statesman). She has a habit of raising an issue – my appeal to women, my polymathic tendencies, then showing only a limited interest in my replies – as tho' she expected them and has written the piece in her mind already. I feel awfully inadequate in these situations. I'm not going into the confessional, so I have to keep this polite barrier up – and it's quite an effort for an hour or so.

Wednesday, July 11th

At last the commentary process has started to gain momentum. After a clogged start to the week and a slightly negative post-holiday reluctance to get down to anything, I managed a good day, back in the groove, as they say, remembering the pleasure that can come from working out how to tie up sequences or images and complement their immediacy with information, attractively delivered.

Out to supper at Sheekey's with Terry G and Eric. Eric in town after a few days on his own in Provence and at the Royal Crescent in Bath. He looked well – tanned, and after a slight formality between us at the beginning, relaxed. He blames a poor management link-up for the 'Spamalot' disappointment in Las Vegas, where it will come to an end in February. The New York production is still booming, as is the tour.

We laugh at the memory of the centurion and jailer sketch which only this afternoon I had to describe to a young reporter at the Observer as my favourite scene in 'Life of Brian' – voted top comedy in the newspaper's latest poll. Not really a cloud on the horizon – and Eric getting much pleasure from trying to trap me into playing Arthur in 'Spamalot'.

Wednesday, July 18th

To Molinare for the first commentary recording. [Sound mixer] George Foulgham's assistant pops his head into the studio to say that Richard Briers is recording next door and has asked if I might drop in. We take a short Briers break and it's well worth it. He's a warm, friendly man – so genial and affable that just this brief meeting lifts the spirits. His grandson, aged 13, is going to the Stammering Centre in two weeks.

Lots of smiles, reminiscences about Brian Blessed. Briers, with mock anguish, recalls Blessed's visits to a film set they were working on together. 'You know, you had your aunt and some friends and your grandparents perhaps and Brian would bellow across. "Briers, you old pouf!" at the top of his voice.' He's like a more extrovert Alan Bennett – without the malice.

Friday, July 20th

Steve is the first to tell me that there is a serious typo in the book which has come to light when the book was being prepared for the website. A question mark has been inserted at the end of the very last line of the book, making a nonsense of my conclusion.

I feel very angry. I know some collective editorial madness took hold of everyone at W&N in the days before Trento – text disappeared or reappeared in the wrong place. Perfectly proofed material suddenly appeared with mistakes where none had ever been. Almost like a virus taking hold of the book. The trouble is that this is not a mid-text mistake that can largely be concealed.

To supper at the Davidsons', which is just the distraction I need. They've a new house and new haircuts. The house smaller than before and the haircuts shorter. Their [Hampstead Garden] Suburb houses – and the way that Ian and Anthea furnish them, always make me feel I've stepped back to the '30s or '40s. I expect Just William to come slouching in, socks round his ankles, accompanied by the Rowntree boy with his rosy cheeks.

Good food – lovely, relaxed chat and it's midnight before we get home. I've not forgotten the question mark though. It gives me a sharp stab of, at best, disappointment, to think about it.

Sunday, July 22nd

Put some thought into what I'm going to say tonight at the Dick Vosburgh memorial concert (Dick died whilst we were filming in Prague).[1] It's held at Finsbury Town Hall, a richly decorated Art Nouveau interior with classical ladies holding stucco electric light clusters out from each bay as if they were expelling serpents.

Beryl [Dick's wife], slow and now very round, with all her children surrounding her. Denis Norden [the comedy writer and presenter] is there, a head and shoulders above us all, immaculate, but he's gone blind. 'I'm sorry, I can't see you. Tell me again who it is?'

The 'show' is very long, but well sprinkled with music and songs. Ronnie Corbett on tape, David Vincent's very funny piece read out by Barry Cryer. 'He was the sort of person who'd go through a door, and *then* open it.'

---

1 Dick Vosburgh was an American comedy writer and lyricist. He appeared as a Russian spy in one episode of *Flying Circus*.

Tuesday, July 24th

A day of tasks put off because of the commentary treadmill. Take my old office chair, amongst other things, to recycling and hurl into the huge 'metal only' container without the expected sense of sadness. My new one is wonderful.

Meet Alastair Campbell outside the Post Office (which since the 'improvement in services', is no longer a Post Office). Talk of diaries. He's a little upset that people have picked him up on small inaccuracies. 'It's a diary, for God's sake.'[1] He'd thought long and hard about publishing it, but felt that it had insights into how government worked which could be instructive and counter the prevailing mood by showing that politicians have feelings. He sounds like me worrying about Pythons when he says that Tony initially was very apprehensive but now it's out has apparently accepted that it's honest – 'that's what happened and maybe it's a good thing people know about it.' When it comes to sales, he's doing well, but has been swept away from the top by the Harry Potter tsunami – a million sold in 24 hours, that sort of thing.

Up to have my hair snipped. Danny whispers in my ear that he's leaving, but he can't be seen telling me this as the others will accuse him of touting for business. Alastair Campbell comes into the barber's. A waiting customer can't believe what he's seeing and asks us for an autograph. 'I'm afraid it's a prayer book, but it's all I've got,' he says turning to a small blank page at the back.

In early afternoon Michael Dover rings to say that 164,000 32-page sheets will be destroyed and reprinted and the 47,000 copies already bound will be treated with a special 'disappearing' chemical which should take out the curve of the question mark and turn it into a full stop.

To Orion House to meet Michael and Ion for our lunch visit to George Weidenfeld. On our way to the mansion block just west of Tite Street on the Embankment where Sir George – sorry Lord W – lives, I have my first sight of a bound copy of 'New Europe'. The treatment for the removal of most of the question mark has worked perfectly. Michael says they've got large numbers of Albanians working their way, by hand, through 47,000 copies.

Up the steps to the 2nd floor, I think. Welcomed by a Filipino maid in black into a modestly sized hallway with a number of sexy pencil sketches by Klimt on the walls (all bought for a song just after the war and now, I should imagine, immensely valuable). Women naked except for string of pearls, that sort of thing. I'm shown into a high, square room full of books and oil paintings of various popes. Lord W, who likes to be called George, clearly has a thing about the papacy – in fact Michael tells me that George, if he were able to be anything he wanted, would be a pope.

He sits, in a perfectly fitting pale-brown suit, with collar, tie and matching

1 *The Blair Years*, Campbell's diaries, had just been published that month.

handkerchief discreetly peeping out of the top pocket, on the padded leather top of a brass fender. I have a quick glance round. Everything in immaculate good taste, but gathered with care not to look showy or ostentatious. A lot of small timepieces. Books in small stacks on the tables. One by Gordon Brown on top of the pile. No sign of Alastair Campbell's diaries. George claims to have read my own Diaries. He tells me he looked through the index and found 206 people he knew.

A glass of white wine, then we're shown through to a breathtakingly fine room, very long, with room for huge paintings on the wall – again they all look like Old Masters – I see little modern work. Black wood bookcases fifteen feet high, and tables of various sizes, including a small round one laid for lunch in the bay window. George seats me solicitously so I have a view of the grubby Thames at low tide, with a battered steel barge moored up.

We talk about Eastern Europe – and George takes centre stage; like his flat, he is impressive but never ostentatious. His opinions are well backed up, and he's clearly a man who enjoys talking, and is happier, it seems, dealing with the Big Issues – Middle East, Iran etc. etc. rather than publishing tittle-tattle. He's 88 this year, recovering from a knee operation but travels extensively.

He was one of the wise men whom the Polish pope invited to Castel Gandolfo every summer. Groups of eight at a time had lunch and supper with the pope and gave him the benefit of their wise views. 'He wasn't an intellectual. He wasn't a particularly bright man, but . . . He listened I think.' I like George. He's well-connected and thoughtful and energetic.

He entertained Wilson and Jim Callaghan here one evening – deliberately so that Wilson could confirm Jim Callaghan rather than Denis Healey as his successor. 'They decided that in the car home.'

H and I out at 7 to meet Sam West at Sheekey's. More clogged traffic and diversions and we don't get there until ten to eight. Sam has his girlfriend – Sheffield-bred Laura Wade, a pale, pre-Raphaelite face. We both enjoy mushy peas.

Sam collects stamps, watches birds, loves trains – he's also just acted in Pinter's 'Betrayal'. The run, at the Donmar, wasn't long enough to get under the skin of the character, and it isn't transferring. 'Deceit, betrayal and broken marriage? Not the ideal recipe for a night out,' he says. Which is a bit of a condemnation of the West End theatre and what it has conditioned its audience to expect – musicals, mainly.

Thursday, July 26th

Into town at lunchtime to meet Tristram P at the Union [Club in Greek Street]. TP comes from editing 'Foyle's War'. We talk. Stephen Frears drifts in, dressed

like a vagrant and in good, mischievous form. He's been on a film panel in Is‐
chia. 'Nothing to do with film,' he says, 'It's all about promoting Ischia.' TG had
been on the panel. 'Now there's an angry man,' says Stephen, admiringly. 'He's
very, *very* angry.' His companion is Tim Bevan, looking younger than I remem‐
ber and tanned and trim as Stephen looks pale and crumpled. They make an
odd pair. Good food. Sardines and pea risotto. Wish I'd joined *this* club. That's
the thing about clubs, you always want to join the one over there.

Walk from Belsize Park in a healthy downpour. They're saying that over
UK as a whole the summer has been wettest since 1789. That's a statistic with
a rather fine ring to it.

Monday, July 30th

To V&P's where John Goldstone has booked a table for lunch to discuss the
plans for selling Python Live to some new operator (I read this prospectus on
the train this morning and it's full of ghastly merchandising jargon, with not a
whiff of humanity or empathy for Python's basic subversive instincts; a sense of
humour, quite important for anyone dealing with Python, completely absent).

JG has been 'entertaining' all the Pythons over the last six weeks, gauging
reactions. I'm wary of what we're getting into – and about how much advertis‐
ing will be allowed on the site, and how much control we'll have over content.
JG talks of 'mashing' – this new process much evident on YouTube of content
being made available to punters to mess around with.

Thursday, August 2nd

Work in the morning. A harder commentary this week and the first of Roger's.
In Hungary and Ukraine. Archie in the afternoon.

Working on after he's gone, it's dusk and I hear an angry raised voice,
screaming abuse. Not common round here, but it does happen. Look out of
my window, and there, sitting on Jonathan and Bernie's wall, is a young woman
in a yellow summer dress. She's bent over, shaking with sobs, and on either side
of her are two young boys, presumably her children. Both their bikes are laid
on the pavement and they sit either side of her, not visibly upset, but quiet.
Then one of them, who can't be more than seven or eight reaches out and
touches her face. She can't be comforted. She shakes her head and I think I hear
something like 'if he loved me, he'd be here.' A few moments later she's on her
mobile, screaming and shouting at somebody – really out of control. The two
little boys wait, as I'm sure they've done before, for it all to pass.

I go back to my desk and a split-second later, hear a wild shriek from the woman. 'Cunnnt!' she yells. They move away, perhaps even through her anger, she can see she's gone too far. Later I see the three of them trailing down Oak Village after a man. She's taunting him, continually. He tries to walk on, every now and then, goaded beyond control, he swings around and bellows back at her with incoherent venom. What should I do? Stop watching? Keep out of sight, like the rest of the village? Call the police?

I watch in case he tries to strike her, then I'd have to go out. To my relief and consternation, they disappear round the corner. The big angry man, the slim, attractive angry woman and the two quiet boys following along, pushing their bicycles. Of course I think of Archie.

Saturday, August 11th

Lie in bed thinking about what's expected of me, in the next month especially. The extra programme will require me to be writing and recording commentary during series launch week. The BBC's decision to bring forward our transmission date to Sept 16th, when we had hoped for early October has increased the squeeze on time. What could go, I wonder to myself, is the long week reading the audiobook in Bath. If I read only the abridged version (as originally planned) and not the full-length version I could give myself an extra day and a half.

Saturday, August 18th

Death of Bill Deedes at 94.[1] I should like to one day be 94, but only if I can be like him, still filing copy, full of anger and indignation, after his visit to Darfur.

Monday, August 20th

Roger tells me of his visit to the BBC last week; he had to be present at a media/marketing conference for the series. 'All about people watching on mobile phones,' he said gloomily.

The whizz kids there think that if the series can reach Griff Rhys Jones 'Mountain' figures we'll have done well.[2] As these are just over 4 million, it looks as if they'd be quite happy with a 50 per cent drop in our audience from our last series. I would so like to prove them wrong.

1 Bill Deedes was a journalist who at one point was both a Conservative MP and editor of the *Daily Telegraph*.
2 The BBC series in which Gryff Rhys Jones explored the mountains of Great Britain.

Thursday, August 23rd

A cab to Charlotte Street for a gathering for [the Ukrainian writer] Andrey Kurkov – to which I've been invited by Harvill Secker. He's one of the great finds of the last year for me. His economically written, apparently light, bright style covers many levels of complexity – sex, food, politics, above all wonderfully deft and delicate touches of humour – mostly black.

He's easy company – so like his hero – a basically decent man with appetites. He looks hot and almost flushed with the excitement of what's happening to him. He's a good talker and listener – but, like his writing, he doesn't go in for anything long, heavy or earnest. He explains something that's mystified me. Misha the Penguin [who features in Kurkov's bestselling book 'Death and the Penguin'] was there to represent the Soviet man – left behind, bewildered and out of place, after the collapse of the revolution. He chose a penguin because penguins only feel comfortable amongst large groups of other penguins. The Misha character's isolation suddenly becomes poignantly clear.

An average meal. Andrey tells jokes and I think would like to sing. He also loves jazz. All round good company.

Friday, August 31st

'Nation Mourns Again' is Private Eye's cover beneath a picture of Diana. Ten years ago today the almost unbelievable, barely comprehensible news came in, and ever since then the nation's relationship with Diana has hovered between a slobbery, showy sentimentality and a tireless attempt to sanctify her into a sort of young, blonde Nelson Mandela. Neither has worked, and from what I've seen of her in action in her life she would not have wanted either. She seemed instinctively down-to-earth, straightforward and oddly enough, for someone with a thousand ball gowns, modest.

Meet TJ in the Gatehouse for a couple of pints. He says he's exhausted – been to Paris with Anna, and some of Anna's friends. Mainly vegetarian, who led Terry to some very bad restaurants. Walk to the Bull along the Old North Road. Terry's limping and says that he'll probably need a second new hip. Very pleasant meal at the Bull; a re-run of the last time I saw TJ and Anna, five and a half weeks ago. Anna seems to have a determinedly sunny temperament which must help her deal with Terry's tortuous life. We part happily with TJ consoling me over some review of the Diaries in the LA Times. 'He just completely missed the point!'

Monday, September 10th

Pleasant, settled, sunny morning. Trawl through various emails; read the Good Housekeeping piece which seems to be fine, if a little on the irritating 'I know Michael better than he does' side.

Paul, in response to my query, drops, almost casually, the news that the Radio Times will not be doing a cover for 'New Europe'. For someone who likes each series to follow familiar patterns of build-up, this is an ominous sign – further evidence perhaps that Eastern Europe just isn't sexy.

Tuesday, September 11th

Osama bin Laden in his 'anniversary' address to the world promises further destruction. To be honest, I'm more interested in getting through the next week; I'm on the front of the Guardian, sitting in my garden yesterday with the umbrella up, looking old and miserable. The piece reads well though. It should really have been the introduction to the book.

Thursday, September 13th

Thanks in part to Angela's judicious scheduling of publicity interviews, I don't feel as hot and bothered as I expected to by this time. Last night's cast and crew screening at BAFTA went very well. Sequences from all 7 shows, well-chosen to fill the big screen in the Princess Anne Theatre. At last Nigel has what he's always wanted – the very best projection – and the high-definition stock which blows up much better than film. The midsummer night in Latvia is as good as Sven Nyqvist. Afterwards Clem V [Vallance, co-director of '80 Days' and the two following series] who doesn't gush and therefore more weight attaches to his judgements, pleased me by saying that he thought Eastern Europe was exactly the right place to go after Himalaya.

Sunday, September 16th

Another series is launched today – and it may be a sign of the times that I slept well, despite the anxious days ahead – and the amplified sounds of Archie breathing and turning, coming from the little speaker beside us. He talks and potters and gurgles away from seven until around a quarter to eight when we get him up. He radiates his morning cheerfulness amongst us.

The sun's up and shining from a clear sky. The Observer TV and Radio section has me sitting in the Julian Alps on its front cover, and a lively preview, generally positive, but worrying about the amount I drink on the shows, and suggesting I see a liver specialist.

In the evening to Steve and Nicola's in Primrose Hill for a T/X party. The three children are wonderful hosts – showing where the loo is before we've even shut the front door behind us. Feel strangely nervous as nine o'clock comes round – and I've given Helen the collywobbles about the opening episode, so both of us are wary; it's fine, of course, and zips along and apart from a sluggish centre in Serbia and Dubrovnik, I'm well pleased. Mind you, I did have a shot of Stolly to start the evening.

Monday, September 17th

The odd sense of opening the papers, as if opening a box with a very bad smell coming from it persists this morning. This is probably the most important day of the series, the day on which we first hear the reaction – the day, I suppose, on which judgement is passed.

The Guardian review by Lucy Mangan is very nice about the show. Thomas Sutcliffe isn't bad in the Independent, tho' ties himself up with a long opening paragraph about the BBC's cosy relationship with me – as if constant returns of 8 million plus aren't enough to explain it, then praises with faint damnation.

A call from Paul just after ten o'clock that overnights were 7.5 million. Quiet delight as Peter Fincham calls, in a welter of congratulations – how long ago was it that he called me to say that New Europe was a turn-off title worthy of a late-night documentary on BBC Two? From this moment on everything becomes easier. No flop to deal with, no recriminations over whether or not we should have done Europe, or whether we should have started with the Yugoslav episode. Vindicated.

Wednesday, September 19th

Roger rings early. Reads me a piece in the Daily Telegraph Diary – I usually dread Diary mentions, but this, by one Liz Hunt, is complimentary, comparing me with other travel presenters, saying that with most it's all about them, but I let the people I meet speak for themselves. Also, this both satisfying and unsettling sexual frisson which I sense quite frequently – 'he still looks like the good-looking sixth-former you always had your eye on'. Welcome as this sort of thing is, I only wish I'd taken more advantage of it when I *was* a sixth-former.

Thursday, September 20th

Try and beat out a shape and content for my Goldman Sachs speech, but end up answering a clamour of emails, reacting to the show. My ad-lib whilst moving about the sailing boat in Belgrade – 'old arthritis playing up' – has already attracted interest from the Arthritis Society wanting me to be their spokesman.

At five o'clock up at the top of Goldman Sachs's Fleet Street offices, where the Daily Telegraph used to be, admiring the view of St Paul's and preparing to busk a talk on diversity of world cultures. Into a smart, wood-lined lecture theatre – with a console at every desk with screen and microphone. Stephen Lewis, a nice man, who looks and dresses rather like a teacher at a public school (he was at Shrewsbury) introduces me saying that this has been the hottest tickets of any of their events. 'I can safely say that 15 per cent of all Goldman Sachs employees in Europe will be watching this afternoon.'

I've trimmed down the talk, leaving out the more philosophical side and concentrating on the funnier areas – this is a good call, as they all seem to want to laugh, and expect me to make them do so. Afterwards a drink and am struck by how unhierarchical it seems to be – as many women as men, and the staff look relaxed, not cowed.

Friday September 21st

To ITV on the South Bank for the Morning show. On the way in meet Ed Balls; he's very interested in the Stammering Centre. Turns out he himself stammered when young, and I can still hear the traces of it. 'If there's anything I can do to help?' he says. So I ring Diana [de Grunwald] who is, of course, hugely pleased to hear this from a member of the Cabinet. 'Oh, there is, there is!' she says.

Saturday, September 22nd

To 'Excess Baggage' at Broadcasting House. The other guest is Bruce Parry, whose 'Tribe' series I've come to rather late, but with great enthusiasm. He gets on with people with engaging ease, and conveys uncomplex enjoyment of what he's doing. In fact, a presenter after my own heart. We get on well; he's an ex-Marine, taut and obviously but not ostentatiously in good trim. We share similar views too, especially about the limitations of our programmes – impossible to find the truth, impossible to merge with another people completely, but he's clearly fond of people who live on the edge.

Across to do Jonathan Ross's radio show. In his introductory riff he talks about how well preserved I am and likens me to [the British film actor] Stewart

Granger. He rather likes this and I become Stewart Granger for the next few questions.

Monday, September 24th

A day I approach with trepidation. My first BUPA medical for over three years – since the blood test fiasco of August 2004. I've done all the preparations, scoured my 'business' for pea-sized samples and attached them to the bowel cancer test cards. A messy business. And I'm at the centre just around the time the second overnights should be coming through. Switch the phone off and decide not to worry. Que sera. My pulse rate remarkably low considering.

Doctor Musgrove is officiating, as he's the same doctor I saw last time; he knows about the blood test mess-up and he's old school enough to admit to me that it was their mistake. He's also embarrassed about having to refer to me as a customer. 'I don't know why, but we can't call you patients any more.' He's even more sheepish as at the start of our one-to-one consultation he has to offer me the option of having a 'chaperone' in the room during the examination. It's bad enough having Dr Musgrove's fingers up my arse without somebody watching (though I don't tell him that).

I'm relieved to be told by Philippa – my nurse for the morning – that I'm in the Top 15 per cent of fitness for people of my age.

In the changing room I switch on my phone and pick up Paul's text message that we were down a million to 6.4 last night. On the way home I call him and am reassured. 'Himalaya' dropped 1.2 million after the first episode.

Friday, September 28th

Collected by Terry J, on the way to a meal with John C and TG. Terry's affairs seem, as ever, needlessly complicated. He's off to Boulder, Colorado, tomorrow morning on a lecture tour to publicise his book on Richard II. 'I don't think anyone'll know who he is.' He mutters something about 'New Europe', but claims never to watch television. John is already at the corner table at Odin's, deep in a book which looks like a novel, but turns out to be a how to live better and understand the world manual. Champagne has been brought to us by the management. Terry doesn't like champagne very much, and it's far too warm anyway. He orders a bottle of rosé. John asks him how he is and Terry, for once, doesn't give his usually breezy reply. 'Well, things aren't altogether good,' he says, and I worry he might have had a relapse or a return of the cancer. But it's graver than that.

'It's my libido,' says Terry mournfully. 'It's not normal.' We all take this in light-hearted amusement. John reports, with cheerful surprise, that he 'gets an outing every now and then'.

As ever, there's a feeling that we could, if we wanted to, do something together that would be good. 'Monty Python Speaks', suggests John. An 'anonymous friend' sends over a bottle of Dom Perignon. John composes a note of thanks on the back of the menu, referring to our benefactor as 'a fucking crawler', and we all sign.

Monday, October 8th

Ratings slip, last night's programme down to 6.0 overnight. BBC Two, with a fresh 'Top Gear' series picking up 6.0 at eight o'clock, and ITV showed Scotland's World Cup game. I just hope we don't slide below 6.

Run later, and in the afternoon various bits of deskwork. Try to find a contact for Peter Fincham, who has resigned as head of BBC One after a Will Wyatt report fingered him for not dealing more speedily and openly over the 'Crowngate' affair.[1] General feeling is that BBC One has lost one of its better controllers. He was impetuous with me over the 'New Europe' title, but otherwise looked after us well.

Wednesday, October 10th

In the evening out to Daunt Books for a 'New Europe' talk. Maan Barua [an Indian environmentalist], who's filled out a little bit since we shared a boat on the Bramahputra four years ago, is now at Oxford (helped by some money from me and Mark Shand and others) and he's at the talk. With him an older man called Sushrut who is full of good information. Did I know that cows on the Bangladesh border in Assam now carry photo identity tags, so that if they stray across the border they can be returned. Also he knows of a Museum of Miserliness in Bulgaria – which is devoted to ideas and inventions to avoid spending money. Would have been perfect for the series.

Friday, October 12th

An award from Psychologies magazine and a letter congratulating me on being voted the fourth 'sexiest brain' by their readers. After Louis Theroux, Jeremy

---

1 The Will Wyatt report was commissioned by the director general of the BBC to investigate potentially misleading footage of the Queen via clips of *Monarchy: The Royal Family at Work* that were shown to journalists.

Paxman and Alan Rickman; and three ahead of Gordon Brown.

October 15th to October 19th: Himalaya book tour, Glasgow–Leicester

Saturday, October 20th

Last night I was congratulating myself on a successful first signing week. Arrived home at 5.15 yesterday afternoon – laden with gifts, many for Archie, most from Liverpool.

Attacked my correspondence and email immediately, but by the time I was ready for bed, the undiagnosed eczema-like rash on my back had returned with such sudden virulence that I decided to take a tab of anti-inflammatory.

Wake this morning as if felled by fatigue. Everything seems an enormous effort. The slightest upset makes me almost rigid with anger. And my back, anointed with Protopic by H, adds its own irritation to my irritation.

H thinks my back rash may have been aggravated by many hours in the back of the car. She may be right, but as many more hours in the back of Orion's driver Bob's new Mercedes beckon next week, it only augments my gloom.

Sunday, October 21st

Feeling much better. Sort out emails and things to do before Australia. Think I shall take on the 'Timewatch' Last Day of World War One documentary – in some shape or form.[1]

In the evening to Roger and Susie's – they've laid on a special evening for the transmission of Roger's Poland episode – there's a marquee on the lawn, chairs, tables, a screen – the Acton Odeon, Roger calls it. The show is well-received and such wise and nodding heads as those of George Carey and Will Wyatt confirm my feelings that this might be one of our most popular. There's no strong opposition on ITV – *and* there are 600,000 Poles working and living in the UK.

Friday, October 26th: Cambridge–London

A leaden sky over the flat fields of Cambridgeshire. To the 15th and final signing of the UK tour, at Milton Keynes.

---

1 I had received a proposal to present an episode of BBC's *Timewatch* dealing with the killings that happened after the Armistice had been officially signed.

After much talk of the changing face of television, it's the changing face of bookselling which has struck me most. Even in the three years since Himalaya, the supermarkets have taken a much bigger slice of the market, and made popular books even more popular. Personalities, celebrity trials and tribulations, trauma and cookery have carved out a huge market along with the yoghurts and the paint and the underwear. Traditional bookshop sales are no longer the mainstay of the bestseller market.

Disappointed a little too by the TV figures. Poland kept the last week's audience, 5.8 million, winning the time slot for the sixth week running, but the fact that it didn't improve on numbers reflects a sense of audience reluctance to be carried away – as they were by 'Himalaya'. 'New Europe' seems to be more cerebral, more demanding, less exotic and escapist. So, big figures still but I think the days of sweeping the board are over. I shouldn't mind, but having once experienced the heady delights of book and series supremacy, I'm a little ashamed to admit that I do.

Grey skies, heavy lorries hemming us in as we head through a no-man's land of vast warehouses – Amazon, Asda, the big names that have built their cathedrals here on the old gravelly soil of Bedfordshire. In keeping with time-honoured tradition, we get lost in Milton Keynes, but once sorted, the signing, our last at a WHSmith, is good and busy and 90 minutes solid.

October 29th to November 14th: Himalaya Publicity in Australia/NZ

Thursday, November 15th

Qantas flight one from Sydney. We turn and wheel over the city and drop down eventually to land from the west. It's been nearly twenty-seven hours since I began my journey home in the freshly cleared skies of wet and windy Wellington. London lies beneath clear skies, its various satellite towns picked out in clusters of orange light, like tacky jewellery; the temperature is below freezing; the car headlights follow one another in an unbroken line, homing in on the waking city. A great machine cranking up for another day.

The surge of energy which I always feel on return from some long flight, especially first thing in the morning, serves me well, and I attack unpacking, reordering, and stacks of letters and emails with all the purposeful joy of being back home.

Archie is brought round about a quarter to four. 'To keep you awake,' as Tom puts it. And he succeeds admirably – we climb the stairs together up to my room and I have to spin him round on my chair for ever.

Stretch my eyes apart until half past nine. A very cold night, and, gratifyingly, I sleep through most of it.

Friday, November 16th

Up at 7.30 and embark on the day. Shining brightly, the low sun helps keep my mood optimistic, tho' my brain feels sluggish. Work on high volume of letters and emails – many offering ideas for my next series. 'The History of the Oat-cake' is one.

Monday, November 19th

In the afternoon H and I go to the Cigala restaurant in Lamb's Conduit Street where Michael Henshaw's memorial service is being held.[1] A rather melan-choly occasion. Those who I remember from the heydays of Michael and Anne's parties – Mercer, Fay Weldon, Wesker are either dead or not present, and I don't recognise many of the greybeards.

I'm asked to speak and a rush of memories floods back. Michael, generous with his time and his wine to young upstarts like TJ and myself – gradually los-ing interest the more successful we became. An unorthodox man who seemed to understand our own unorthodoxy, and was a critical if sometimes contrary help to us during the early years of our professional lives. I find myself missing him quite intensely.

Back home a note from Tom Dunne. Whilst in New York I'd told him about my first unpublished novel and he sounded keen to see it. Well I sent it out and apparently he likes it enough to suggest doing some sort of deal for publication, subject to my re-working the second half of the book. 'This material can form the core of a superior novel. I love the first third or so.'

Tuesday, November 20th

To lunch with Michael Katakis and Kris at the Naval and Military – the In & Out Club, a fine 1720s building in St James's Square, in a corner directly opposite the London Library. Michael looking comfortable leads us into the bar – another fine room with classical frieze and comfortable clubby chairs. Kris looks frail. Her hair is growing again after the operation to remove her tumour and she looks rather good with a punky cut, it goes well with her strong cheekbones.

A lovely lunch, quiet and civilised, looking at the cabs circling a grey, wet St James's Square. Kris, though frail, becomes quite animated later in the meal, as

---

1 Michael was Terry's and my first accountant and a fierce advocate for the rights of creatives and writers. His wife Anne became Python's manager.

she and Helen exchange experiences of surgery. She's a tough, doughty girl and a really decent person. I *do* hope we see her again.

November 22nd, 23rd and 24th: Book tour, Oxford, Belfast and Dublin

Monday, November 26th

Distinctly jaded this morning. Feel I need more sleep, more rest, more peace and quiet at home, instead of which I shall be dragged out on display again today. Repeatedly.

Car at 9.15 to take me to the Stammering Centre for the Ed Balls ministerial visit. He's accompanied by John Bercow, an MP who's compiling a review of facilities like this within the Health Service. Emily Thornberry, Islington's MP, is there and there must be a dozen private secretaries, health officials and press in tow.

I go with Ed Balls to see a couple of children and their parents who are here for therapy. He tells a little boy of six that he himself had difficulties when he was young, but this is the minister's only mention of his own experience. His private secretary, a thin woman with mousy short hair and a persistent sense of time, is trying to move him on, but he stays a good half-hour beyond the allotted time, and he talks well with some of the teenagers, relaxing them despite their sometimes crippling stammers.

Photos together outside the Centre and much optimism all round as the party sweeps off. I was also impressed by Bercow's grasp of our funding problems and Emily Thornberry's on our side, impressively tough!

From there back home for moments before being picked up by a car with Alastair Campbell in the back. He lounges, sprawls, groin thrust forward, wearing a tracksuit and Leukaemia Research Insignia. He's persuaded me to turn out for an hour to publicise my own charity appearance on Wednesday. We have to trek out to one of the least convenient radio stations – LBC out near Latimer Road. He's on his mobile for much of the way, but amiable enough and we arrive early and sit in the LBC canteen together. He's intrigued by me, I think, and how I operate. I protest that I'm prone to laziness, blown by the wind in whatever direction but he has none of this, 'You've got it sussed,' he says with a trace of envy, but qualifies this with a fine Campbell-ism '*I'm* telling you. You've got it sussed.'

The interviewer seems a little flushed around the cheeks as she introduces us – 'Well, this afternoon I'm in a ménage à trois with Michael Palin and Alastair Campbell.' We overrun. Alastair by now is a little impatient. He's revealed he doesn't like chat shows 'especially phone-ins – urgh!', as casually as he admitted to me that he removed all the Brown–Blair spats from his diary. 'I just took the whole lot out.' The publishers, Random House, are of course anxious to get at the seven-eighths of the diary he didn't publish. Alastair shakes his head 'Not until Gordon's gone.'

We talk to Classic FM then he goes off to a meeting in Victoria – from which, he says, he'll run home to Gospel Oak. I rather like the rogue, well, not a rogue, buccaneer might be a better word. Clearly he misses being at the centre of things – the manipulator, the enforcer; he seems like a man to whom these titles are worth the effort. But he's a loyal Labour man, and will not say a word against Tony's successor.

At 6.30 to Elena's Etoile where a party for Elena [Salvoni, one of the great maître d's, formerly of Bianchi's and L'Escargot], her loyal customers and her book, is laid on in the upstairs room where I last came for the Kurkov event.

Beryl Bainbridge touches Elena's cheek in wonderment. 'Your skin . . . absolutely smooth.' 'Soap and water,' says Elena, crisply.

Not many celebs there, despite the title of her book, 'A Life in Soho'. Meet the very gentle, friendly Bert Kwouk, who bemoans the passing of nearly all his co-stars with the exception of Herbert Lom, who's 90 and still holding out for the big parts, though none come. Bert has settled happily as a regular in 'Last of the Summer Wine'. 'Not a bad place for an old actor.'

Tuesday, November 27th

Work on my speech for the geography event this evening. Tube to Charing Cross then walk along the Embankment, enjoying the sense of bustle – traffic speeding one way and the other, commuter trains clattering across the bridge out of Charing Cross and the enormous circle of the London Eye, at the other end of the speed spectrum, barely moving, somewhere from which to watch London at work.

Coats and jackets off with bags through scanner, then body search (obligatory). Led through to the Speaker's House. A tall, intricately decorated room hung with portraits, tucked up by Westminster Bridge overlooking the river. The Speaker, Michael Martin, is a warm, genial Scot, face almost permanently on the edge of a smile. Physically a little reminiscent of Samuel Johnson or Rembrandt. A large man, full of humanity. He has to have these quarters (quaintly mis-named a 'house') for he's expected to be instantly on call whenever the House is sitting. So he's a Master of the house, and a servant at the same time.

Ordnance Survey have organised the evening to put pressure on the government to keep supporting and funding geography. Various speeches and my 'rant' goes down extremely well. Audience of around 100 people, several MPs, teachers, education officials. Given the august surroundings, the carved panels and painted coffered roof, I think I do quite well not to be intimidated.

As I walk out into Palace Yard, with floodlit Big Ben surprising me with its looming presence just above me, groups are being shown around and I do have a sense of the majesty of it all – OK, not always reflected in the goings-on within, but necessary to stir the soul. A very romantic building.

Walk up Whitehall. Reflect as I go past the succession of barriers that now stretch across the mouth of Downing Street, that I remember a time when, like any other citizen, I could walk into Downing Street unimpeded. No great wars in most of my lifetime, but perhaps a much greater sense of the ever-present threat of violence.

Wednesday, November 28th

Helen and I picked up at a quarter to seven to go down to the Criterion for my 'Audience With' in aid of Leukemia Research. Met at the stage door and led into a labyrinth of corridors until eventually our greeters admit that they're lost. Lots of 'oh, it's *this* way'. We keep passing two stagehands whose grins broaden every time we go by. 'Remember Spinal Tap,' says one of them.

Eventually into the foyer. Alastair C looks agitated. Alan Yentob has disappeared. [Literary agent] Ed Victor fetches me a glass of warm champagne. No one seems to be in control.

Eventually Alan is located. He's just come back from Marrakech where he's been meeting people so famous and distinguished that I've forgotten who they are. He has a disordered sheaf of notes and jottings which he juggles around during our interview. Various clips are shown – including my rarely seen impersonation of David Attenborough which is rather good. I'm on stage for about an hour and a half. The Criterion, from what I can see, is an attractive little theatre – 650 capacity and full, I'm told.

Afterwards we're lost once again in backstage passageways – and couldn't find Helen, or Alastair C or anyone else. So we walked down Piccadilly to rendezvous at the Wolseley.

Alan was soon off networking a table at which Nick Mason [of Pink Floyd] and Joan Collins were sitting. Ed Victor (as he put it, living proof that you can beat leukaemia) was trying to organise a table for us. All standing around looking at each other. Eventually, after much choreography, we all get sat down – the four men together at one end, the four women at the other.

Alan and Alastair get into boys' talk about Brown and the latest Labour party donations scandal [over recently discovered third-party donations]. If Alan will not hear a word against the BBC, Alastair will not hear a word against the Labour Party. But he is pleased with the evening and especially the auction of two books. His diary 'The Blair Years' signed by both of us, and my diary 'The

Python Years' signed by both of us, went for nine thousand pounds. Seventy-five thousand pounds raised for the evening.

Not to bed until after midnight. Last thing I have to do is set the alarm for 5.45. Amsterdam, the final lap on my international 'New Europe'-flogging tour, beckons.

Monday, December 3rd

Rare and pleasing prospect of a weekday with no appointments at all. A work-day without work. And the sun is shining. To the V&A to buy cards, look at a couple of Buddhas and some Chinese Emperor's robes, then decide to walk into Mayfair. Walk around the Wellington Arch, surrounded by a mismatching clash of war memorials. None finer than Jagger's superb Artillery Monument (impossible to contemplate it in stillness owing to the relentless thunderous rumble of Hyde Park Corner traffic), but the figures and the way they stand – unapologetic, non-triumphal, soldiers at work – are very strong.

In the evening out to see 'The Band's Visit' at the Screen on the Hill – a thoughtful comedy, which, in a short time, created complex, beautifully played performances. An Israeli film about an Egyptian military band which gets lost overnight in Israel, and how they interact with the locals. Egyptians portrayed with some dignity, the Israelis, like their land, awkward and defensive at first.

Tuesday, December 4th

Up to Tewkesbury to a singular, independent bookshop called Alison's to do a signing in aid of the flood fund. Half of all their profits from my book sales will go to flood relief. On the way into the town we pass houses still being cleaned up, their owners living in caravans in the driveways. Some will not be back in their homes until next summer, a year after the floods. Usually it's because of insurance wrangles.

I sign stock and 130 pre-orders up at the top of the old shop whilst in the street below a Town Crier, in scarlet jacket and tricorn hat, announces to the people of Tewkesbury that I'm here.

Wednesday, December 5th

To the office to meet [BBC documentary maker] John Hayes Fisher, for whom I've agreed to work on 'The Last Day of World War One'. He loves First World

War battlefields and cemeteries, has a twinkle of humour beneath a hang-dog exterior, and I think we shall have an interesting time.

Thursday, December 6th

Taxi at half past eight; takes me to Charlton King's Road to pick up Tom and Archie, for this is our long-discussed visit to show Archie the Terracotta Warriors at the British Museum. Archie cries out appreciatively as soon as he sees the two Chinese figures on the posters outside. To be honest, that would probably have been enough for him, but we are on the list of 'VIPs and patrons' for the nine o'clock showing and there is a warm welcome for us – 'so *this* is Archie? He's the one we've been waiting for.'

Archie loves the ramp that runs up past the shuttered, neglected bookcases of the Reading Room on which the Terracotta Warriors exhibition has been built, and he gurgles with delight at the figures of the warriors. Of course he wants to touch them, and is a little frustrated at being restrained. Introduce him to Jane Portal [the curator], who stands, a discreetly elegant figure eyeing the throng with the slightly disbelieving smile of a Broadway producer who has the hit of the season on their hands. I still feel the whole thing is hugely overrated, and a sort of hysteria has gripped the nation.

On the way out bump into Neil MacGregor. He sees the hysteria as proof of the innate cultural interest and awareness of the British people. 'It shows they *are* interested in other countries,' he says. 'I mean you must know that.'

Archie marks his first visit to the British Museum with a pair of powerfully scented poos, which enables the three of us, father, son and grandfather, to test out the nappy-changing facilities, which prove to be excellent; wholly satisfactory in a way that the Terracotta Warriors exhibition never quite achieved.

Out to the Dover Castle to meet up with Roger, Alex and John P. I've just received the BBC report on the series performance. Very strong on every indicator but the audience profile confirms we're tapping the oldies – 39 per cent of our audience is older than me (over 65) and more women than men.

When I come out, it's raining again and wind threatening to whip the umbrella out of my hands. Have written one Christmas card so far. And today I received a circular letter from Paul McCartney urging me to consider the moral benefits of becoming a vegetarian – life's rich pattern.

Friday, December 7th

Last day of the signing campaign – and the elements are friendly. In the heart of the slightly unreal Canary Wharf complex well ahead of schedule. Feeling of having been transported to another city altogether. The towers now most-ly complete and the Isle of Dogs is effectively transformed into a clone of Manhattan. The buildings are bland and undistinguished but they harmonise well and the detail at ground level is well done. Signing in an atrium outside Borders, below-ground with Lehman Brothers bank rising above us. A very ef-ficient and successful final signing. People buy books, the way they do business, in brisk and uncomplicated fashion. Few babies to be displayed or dealers to deal with. Nearly 400 dealt with.

Sunday, December 9th

A pile of letters to be answered and requests evaluated lies beside me, piled up and put aside as I completed the book publicity campaign. Now I can delay it no longer, so set to the little stack of demands which includes a request from Oliver Brind, Prince Charles's man, to make some kind of film about the charity in Transylvania, as well as book publicity visits to Budapest and a Palin presence at a film festival in Bologna in June.

I look from the letters and emails to the calendar for next year; I've marked busy days with yellow highlights, and I must now try hard to make sure those dots don't join up to become the big pre-ordained chunks of commitment that marked 2006 and 2007.

Archie, Tom and Rachel visit in the afternoon. I buy the Mail on Sunday (a paper whose investigative methods have more than once made me vow never to have anything to do with it again) because they're giving away a CD of 'The Missionary' and the names and faces of 1982 are blazoned across the top of the front page.

Dearbhla [Molloy, who played my wife in 'GBH'], who I can't have seen for half-a-dozen years, comes round in the evening with her partner Michael. He's immediately warm, soft-spoken, humorous and easily friendly. The sort of person you'd like to have as your doctor, bank manager or judge. Turns out he's an acu-puncturist and homeopathic doctor who lives and practises in a small village near Chipping Norton, close to where Sam Mendes and Kate Winslet live. Dearbhla is godmother to one of their children and Michael approves of them both, speaking especially warmly of Kate, and her dedication to convincing the young women growing up today that they shouldn't be coerced into looking thin.

Helen cooks a chicken casserole and we all talk as if we'd known each other for years. Dearbhla's play at the Tricycle – 'Doubt' by John Patrick Shanley – raises all sorts of debate about child abuse, paedophilia – definitions, implica-tions. Three of the four of us, Helen being the only exception, had experienced in our childhood behaviour which today would have been condemned, but then was just accepted.

Tuesday, December 11th

Have a 'celebrate London' day planned out. First to see the inside of the new St Pancras International for the first time since it became the Eurostar terminal less than a month ago. The whole place virtually unrecognisable from the grimy, poor cousin of London stations that I stepped out of in 1955 for the first view of what's now my home city.

Everything clean and sparkling – where the Burton beer was stored is now an arcade of cafés and coffee shops. Light pours in through the central glassed area, transforming the look and feel of the station, and the painted steel supports are revealed in all their delicate, sinewy power. The inscription on the base of the arches 'Butterley Company, Derby, 1867' lifts the spirits. And it's not much disturbed by trains, you have to go beyond the arch to find the Midlands and the Sheffield trains. A certain, almost unreal, calm, serenity and silence reigns, as though no one can quite believe what's happened to St Pancras – now talked of as one of the World's Great Stations.

To Sotheby's to look at a Frederick Gore painting of Charlotte Street just after the War. Not a well-covered period in painting and there's a charm and life to what was then a pretty dismal post-war scene.

Meet Ronnie and Anne Corbett, rolling in very jolly fashion out of the chairman's lunch. I'm sitting in the foyer, writing in my diary some details of the afternoon when Ronnie appears before me – 'You're writing up your diary, just like you used to in "Fierce Creatures"!' We fall to talking about the extraordinary Evening Standard poster 'Comedian Bites Homeless Man'.

Wednesday, December 12th

At 5.30 picked up to go to the Parkinson's Disease Society Christmas Concert at Westminster Cathedral. Last year they filled St George's Hanover Square with 500 people, this year they've sold 1,500 tickets to fill the Cathedral. And what a strange place it is. A huge arch – tiled and mosaicked – dominates the eastern end, and the ceiling, unlit, seems to disappear into the night sky. I'm sat beside Phyllida Law and Richard Briers, who are both doing readings.

The whole event matches the grandiosity of the building with a brass band – the Crystal Palace band – and two choirs, and a thundering organ. Also the extraordinarily beautiful Barbara Thompson playing a powerful, jazzy version of 'Greensleeves'; with exquisite control of the instrument but less control of her own movements. There's also a choir of Parkinson's sufferers who sing Negro spirituals and other lively songs whilst many of them try to control their trembling.

The Cathedral is almost too big, too enveloping, even for an evening of this complexity, it seems to swallow up the intensity and purpose of the event – and the brass band can't even be seen, all in their bright uniforms stuck away behind the male-voice choir dressed identically in dull evening dress.

Richard Briers mutters subversively and Phyllida Law seems pleasantly whacko. I ask how Emma [Thompson, her daughter] is – 'Oh she's at some sort of vigil tonight, probably sex-trafficking or something of that kind.'

I read from 'Pickwick Papers' – a well-described, very visual piece about Mrs Pickwick being kissed under the mistletoe. Jane Asher, slim as a stick, in a tight black dress, dwarfed by the scale of this mighty religious emporium, MCs with great authority and charm. A national treasuress, if ever there was one. And not *just* because she introduced me as 'The Magnificent Michael Palin'!

Thursday, December 13th

Gordon Brown is just arriving in Lisbon to sign the new EU Treaty. So significant was it that he couldn't get to Lisbon until after the final lunch, and signed privately after many others had gone home. At least he's presenting the British reputation for diplomatic eccentricity, but his early days as a 'new broom' after Blair are now long past and I must say, his touch seems erratic and at times plain embarrassing.

Friday, December 14th

To the Steve Wright studio for a pre-record and out by 12.30. The very last event of the 'New Europe' publicity campaign.

Take a copy of Pepys's Diaries to bed. Quite encouraged by reading. It's not full of wall-to-wall aperçus, and a lot of time spent going out, or getting from A to B.

Saturday, December 15th

Gilliam calls. His film is underway [what would become 'The Imaginarium of Doctor Parnassus']. He's been filming for a week – night shoots – last night Heath Ledger hanging beneath Blackfriars Bridge. Terry absolutely exhausted, 'I just can't *do* it any more' (i.e. he's happy at last).

Monday, December 17th

Shopping in the morning. Managed to get into Amell's the art dealers and have a look at their Hammershoi. It's a beauty. In marvellous condition, shining with good health, the portrayal of light falling into the room and onto the various objects – pewter plate, Ida's neck, varnished table, piano, is textbook stuff. They're asking £1.2 million, and have a Japanese buyer interested. At half the price, I'd be interested. Potter around Piccadilly and Mayfair. Buy a cricket book by Prince Ranjitsinhji circa 1897, for Steve, dominoes in a leather bag for Paul.

To Le Gavroche for a Diaries lunch with Michael D and Ion. It feels cramped today – maybe the effect of Christmas decorations – it's also full and the basement, with its low ceiling and haute cuisine, feels like a luxury crypt. The sort of place you might go for the last meal before a particularly expensive form of euthanasia.

The latest sales figures on the Diaries show sales more than respectable. We agree to have the next Diaries volume prepared by the end of next year if possible. I shall make the first cull and pass it on to Ion. Michael, in his usual, well-concealed, critical mode, suggests perhaps that the last volume 'might have been a little "heavy" for bedtime reading'.

With H, to meet Basil at the Canteen. PB-J [Peter Bennett-Jones, agent] is the only other one at the table. He is that rare thing, a very straight, very decent, very clever businessman. Reveals that he has just taken on (at the urging of his brother Owen) the lovely lady – Mishal Husain – who reads the BBC evening news at the weekend, and who I've been enthusing about (much to Helen's bemusement) for a long time.

Tuesday, December 18th

Gather together all my office presents and down to 34 Tavistock Street. My driver, a young man in a crumpled donkey jacket, looks exhausted, and at the traffic lights on Kingsway falls asleep and I have to prod him awake. For the rest of the journey he is slow and surly and even asks me 'Did you often prod your driver?' He turns half-profile to me – a strong, good-looking face – probably Pakistani. Can't wait to get out.

Work at the office then walk to Orion House to sign 'New Europe' books for the staff. Orion is riding high – selling a much bigger volume of books this Christmas than its rivals (largely because of Richard Hammond, I have to say, who's selling nearly 70k a week – as opposed to my 20k), but Michael is not particularly happy. 'No one's making much money,' he says gloomily, 'once the deals and the discounts are taken into account.' But in a sun-filled office

everyone seems very happy to see me, and at a full hour, it's a last, very satisfactory signing.

Thursday, December 20th

At the NPG, I concentrate my attention on a room hung with the work of an
etcher and printmaker called John Kay, who portrayed the Edinburgh of the
Enlightenment, with good, inventive, satirical irreverence. Self-confessed owner of the biggest cat in Scotland, Kay seemed fascinated by size. The etchings
here show the tallest man in Scotland, and possibly the world, at 8 foot, and a
Polish Count called Boruwlaski, who was only 3 foot 3 – his name bastardised
in Scots to Count Barrel O'Whisky. He's also a great admirer of sizeable noses.
In short, a real find – a Pythonic face of the serious Scottish Enlightenment.

Wednesday, December 26th: Boxing Day

Slow, unhurried start to the day. Sunshine and settled skies as I walk up to
South End Green after breakfast to collect a Times for Granny (Independent
for ourselves).

GG sits by the fire. She can't move much, but so much wants to. The three
Rs in her life are reassurance (that she's really done rather well to get this far),
repetition (of stories about those who have reassured her recently) and regret
(her mind is sharp and clear, and she hates the physical decline).

We walk up to Lismore Circus before lunch. Down below us the cutting
that carries the Midland line to the new St Pancras International resounds with
the noise of track maintenance. No one is travelling by train today. They can't.
It seems that however much maintenance they do, it's never enough to prevent
the Christmas close-down, which further dents the railway's case for a 24-hour,
seven-day a week alternative to roads.

Thursday, December 27th

Archie and I clean up the garden, 'Dada', and 'Mama' and 'brush' are three of his
clearest words now. He's very good company, observant, anxious to try things
out for himself, stopping and listening at the various Gospel Oak noises – the
ambulance's alarm as it speeds down Mansfield Rd, the airliner emerging from
the clouds on its way into Heathrow. Each is greeted by a finger pointing upwards, quizzical 'awerreh?', followed by a 'goodbye' if it's a plane.

I drive down to have lunch with Will and Elspeth at Hanbury Street. Edward

Burd [my architect brother-in-law] arrives about 2, and then the imposing figure of Dan Cruickshank and with him, a well-bred girl – well, lady – called Katherine Goodison, another of the Spitalfields Trust set.

We set off for the second of our Dan–Will–MP East London walks, numbers this time swelled to seven. We've only reached the corner of Brick Lane when Dan grasps a bollard. 'Eighteen-ninety'! he exclaims with delight – original scheme.' Then across by various back-routes to Mile End Road; the streets almost entirely Bengali-occupied. Young men drive flash cars fast and dangerously at full throttle (reminds me of the gypsy drivers in Plovdiv). There's a lot of bling and external glitter. Dan worries about how they make their money to buy these cars and is, 'on my darker days', quite worried about the gangland ethos of these Bangladeshi streets – where once the Krays held sway. The smells of food and the restaurants look good tho'.

Friday, December 28th

H and Mary take Granny back. Quiet day for me. Read Geert Mak's 'In Europe' and watch the DVD Rachel gave me – '12.08 East of Bucharest' – a little gem. Says so much about the change in E. Europe these past 20 years, yet endearingly and often very funnily.

Watch 'Atonement' after supper. Tries to be true to the book, but Ian McEwan's descriptions are so tight, controlled and literary that there really isn't much a visual director can do. Spends far too much time on the Dunkirk beaches, playing with big casts, big effects and generous CGI, but in the end the most effective few minutes of the film are Vanessa Redgrave, speaking straight to camera. Words win in the end.

Monday, December 31st

See the old year out with a run – somewhat laborious after a month of indulgence. Heath beginning to fill up with middle-class families; fathers trying to look interested, mothers loudly teaching their families 'That's a pergola, darling', 'A city is the centre, the conurbation is the bit around it.'

Home by mid-morning and have time to complete a last task of 2007: reading the ten shortlisted entries for the British Airways High Life Travel Comp. One clear winner, one worthy runner-up, the rest are too often wordy; self-conscious parodies of travel writing.

John C rings from Montecito. He's sitting outside his house with a dazzling sunlight reflecting off the Pacific. I encourage him not to go on in this vein, as here it's flat, cloudy, dull, damp weather of no great interest. He's ringing to see if we (i.e. Python) should give public support to Barack Obama's candidacy. He backs off quite quickly when I profess to not knowing enough about the man and his policies. 'Just a thought, Mickey. I want to try you out before approaching the others.'

I ask him what he's reading. He tells me he's become very interested in life after death. I can't resist an inward chuckle. John having devoted himself to the perfect life is now turning his attention to the perfect life after death. He recommends a book on reincarnation by a man called Ian Stephenson. 'He died a year ago,' says John. With no information as to a forwarding address.

The year when a big new travel series comes out follows a reasonably predictable pattern, but 'New Europe' never proceeded as smoothly as 'Himalaya'.

The book did not have the shelves to itself. Richard Hammond, Ewan [McGregor] and Charley [Boorman], and Jeremy Clarkson, all proved that a more rugged, aggressive laddishness was what the public wanted. But a last-minute push put us at No. 6 in the bestsellers.

I feel I've got away with it, but not much more than that. The route, the laborious winding route, didn't help. We tackled too many countries, and failed to guide our audiences properly through the maze.

Archie has been a counterpoint to all the work and his presence, rather than creating *more* pressure, has been relaxing. Paul and Steve and the office have handled everything with marvellous, apparently effortless, efficiency with the result that I enjoyed the process of commentary, publicity and book-signing perhaps more than I ever have. This may partly be due to the tacit acceptance that this really was the last long journey (H had been against my doing it, for the first time ever) and, having completed it, and despite the obstacles, come out with the highest-rated documentary of the year, added the warmth of relief to the buzz of success.

But heck, I'm nearly 65. I have lots I want to do – body and brain have had a good outing this year, and need stimulation.

2008

Friday, January 4th

A dull day, no sunshine to bring out the colours, but I carry Archie out onto Waterloo Bridge and we watch the boats sliding beneath. At the end of the day, Rachel P has rooted us out to see 'In the Shadow of the Moon' [the documentary about the Apollo missions] at the NFT. It looks, and sounds, very powerful, and reminds me how important and how inspirational America's heroic efforts felt at the time. Now, of course, it's seen as an historical event, a technological over-achievement in a way, as stunning to watch as Concorde, and about as useful. We thought it would be the pathway to the stars, but somehow it didn't happen like that. The Moon programme, which roughly spanned Python's TV life, is trapped in history.

The pictures of the earth from the moon are still very moving. Michael Collins, of all the astronauts, brings a wonderful touch of humanity to his extraordinary account. Neil Armstrong didn't say much.

Monday, January 7th

Picked up at 11.30 and driven to Old Street to be photographed by Rankin for the cover of the new uniform edition of the travel books. Squeeze through cars parked tight up against a grimly industrial door, and led into what seems at first like a sweatshop. Paltry light through unwashed windows, bare floors, bare walls. Full of young men and women at computer screens. This, it turns out, is, appropriately, the production centre for Dazed & Confused, a fashion magazine started by Rankin himself.

He's short and well-built with a thatch of shortish hair which he perpetually musses around. 'I don't know if you know my work,' he says, and hands me a heavy book full of pictures of cleverly lit bodies doing strange things with very little on. A penis with a tape measure alongside it, a face covered in strips of uncooked bacon, a map of Tasmania decorated with a mass of coloured pins – the usual sort of thing.

First we do my close-ups, in black and white. Each shot appears on a screen and focus, colour balance, indeed every little detail can instantly be checked electronically. Then why does it take quite so long? I start at midday and it's nearly two o'clock before they find one they're happy with. There are four people from Orion here, and four working with Rankin, so it's quite a crowd for a single close-up.

After some sandwiches we go for the full-length shots. Rankin squats on the ground. I've changed into my travel 'uniform' of baggy Craghoppers and old blue shirt. Increasing air of desperation about what should surely be a doddle. A re-think of the lighting and more posing. There's a dog barking in the background by now, and barking completely out of time with some booming country music which has been switched on somewhere for some reason. Rankin, who I sense is getting rather bored with Orion's pedestrian demands and would probably prefer me to be baring my bottom or doing something zany, pronounces 'that's the one' and we all nod. Hands are shaken and three and a half hours after I got here, my likeness is satisfactorily captured.

But he has a certain dramatic lighting style which makes the pictures quite special. He consoles me as I leave '*no one* likes having their photo taken, Michael. Except possibly Kylie. And Robbie Williams.' 'Kate Moss *must* enjoy it?' 'Kate? Hates it.'

Thursday, January 10th

Roger asks if I've seen the Telegraph. He always does this and apart from Saturdays, I never have. Apparently a front-page story that John and Alyce Faye are to separate. A year ago I'd have been less surprised, but I'd spoken to John a week ago and he'd given no hint of it. I even asked him how A-F was. 'Mad as a hatter, as usual,' he'd responded, not unaffectionately.

Friday, January 11th

To Carlton School at 11 to entertain the children. Perform for almost an hour, leaping about imitating enraged elephants and showing them how different Cossack dancing is. Have taken a variety of hats from my travels which I tell a story about then ask the children to come out and try them on.

There are one or two over-confident swaggerers in the making, but by and large the children are delightful, and the international mix makes for some strikingly good-looking faces. Jacquie [Phelan, the head teacher] tells me that 89 per cent of the nursery intake doesn't have English as a first language, and I talk to children from Albania, the Congo, Bangladesh, from all sorts of difficult places with multiple problems – and they smile and show interest and enthusiasm and what looks to me like real pleasure. Jacquie says it's the parents that are the most difficult to deal with. They are often the ones who are threatened by their children's openness, and anxious about their ability to mix with so many children from so many backgrounds. What would seem to be an extraordinary opportunity is too often seen as a threat.

Tuesday, January 15th

Awake to the sound of hissing tyres and water trickling away down the drains. The almost monotonously, Welsh-wet, winter weather persists. I look at footage of 'Extras' and 'The Office' in preparation for an interview about Ricky Gervais this p.m. Assured work, meticulous observation, good taste in comedy and excellent pacing. Why then, should it leave me so depressed? Its assumptions about human condition, I suppose.

The interviewer has an agenda which somehow prevents me from saying exactly what I wanted to say, so I'm not totally happy as I sit before the hot lights for half an hour. And the crucial question is, how does Ricky, who demolished the celebrity cult so spectacularly in the last episode of 'Extras', feel about having a tribute programme made about him?

It's even more Blade Runner-ish outside as I walk south. The rain lashing the umbrella, lights smudgily reflected off wet tarmac. Through Soho and down Haymarket to the Athenaeum where I dry out, read the Bookseller, and sip a Scotch and ice before the last lap of my journey – to Downing Street.

'Oh, we know who you are,' the weapon-wielding policemen grin and point me to the hut where I have to put my bags through a scanner, before walking the seventy yards or so to the open door of the prime minister's house.

I've been invited by the Grandparents' Association, whose 21st anniversary this is. The core of the charity's work is to try and help those grandparents, often among the least well-off, who are bringing up their grandchildren because their parents won't (family splits, re-marriages) or can't (in prison). They have little protection in law or recourse to national funds to help with all the caring they have to do. Sobering stuff.

Sarah Brown makes a very good impression. No make-up, very matter-of-fact and friendly without being fussy. 'We have a favourite restaurant in common,' is her opening line to me. It's V&Ps of course. Then Ed Balls bounces up. He repeats his interest in and support for the Stammering Centre and what a good day he'd had there and is generally very amiable. He makes a short, but agreeable speech to the gathering. He's quite a sense of humour, tho' the remnants of his stammer have by no means gone away. Watching him in front of the fireplace talking to us all I thought he looked very much at home.

I do sometimes feel that my life is, as Shakespeare noted, played out on stage. Today, I've enjoyed being on stage – the London set was very well done, and the other actors a constant surprise and stimulation.

Tuesday, January 22nd

Markets in free fall around the world.

To the office. Antonio Carluccio has taken up one of the spare rooms up-stairs, which adds a touch of life to the place. He's been out recceing the area for a good espresso. Hasn't found one yet but he's promised to let me know. He no longer owns the Carluccio chain and is concentrating on a TV series about mushrooms. With his close-cropped crinkly hair, dark sun-scarred features, deep blue cotton shirt and exotic smell, he certainly adds a touch of class to 34 Tav.

Despite economic troubles, Steve gives a very upbeat assessment of Urban Rock, one of the great successes of the last three years. All the money they paid for the business will be paid back by March.[1]

Bad news on the News at Ten. Heath Ledger, the star of TG's latest film, has been found dead at his apartment in New York. He was 28.

Wednesday, January 23rd

A half-hour phone interview with a Croatian journalist re 'New Europe'; after which a sombre call from Ray Cooper. He tells me that all was set up for the Vancouver filming next week – even Ray himself was about to earn some acting money, playing a scene with Ledger next Tuesday. Terry's on his way home – Amy [Terry's daughter who worked on the production] is distraught. Fortune has dealt Terry another blow.

January 24th to January 28th: Holiday with Rachel and H in Morocco

Tuesday, January 29th: Marrakech–London

Home, with all connections working smoothly, through an empty North Terminal at Gatwick, to the Gatwick Express, and into a friendly cab who recognised me. Embarrassingly enough, I'd packed two Braun alarm clocks and both have gone off in my case – one still ringing as we get in the cab. This, of course, echoes the Python customs sketch: 'Have you any clocks and watches in there?' Man [banging case as four clocks go off at once], 'No! No!' – Rachel gets some satisfaction out of observing that Python experience is repeating on me.

---

1 Urban Rock is a climbing equipment business bought by Tom and his business partner, with a little help from bank of Dad.

2008

Thursday, January 31st

A short, sharp depression moving through. Very strong winds, rain scattered across the window. Shock news in the paper of the death of [columnist and broadcaster] Miles Kington. Another constant in one's life, or so I thought, but the fickle finger of fate took him out early. Funny, dry, charming, life-enhancing man.

A screening of Nick Broomfield's 'Battle for Haditha', at the Curzon Soho, and a motley gathering is assembled already – Sabrina [Guinness] my contact, George Fenton, Brian Eno and Tony Benn – a little stooped now, with a shock of silver hair, but a quick and lively glance and a joke too, as we shake hands, about seeing each other everywhere, but never meeting.

Stop the War Coalition lady speaks before the film. Nick B says the film speaks for itself – which indeed it does – from the very first powerful image of an American armed convoy raising the desert dust as they drive out on patrol, music thumping at full volume in an echo of the napalm scene in 'Apocalypse Now'. Brings the war in Iraq home, in all its horrors, in a way which 'embedded' news reports never seem to do. Shows, unsparingly, that it isn't a game out there. No applause at the end, but great praise.

I slipped on a banana skin left on the steps of Tottenham Court Road station. Stayed balletically upright, but gashed my shin quite dramatically. 'Python slips on banana skin'. Who would have any sympathy?

Friday, February 1st

To the Ivy for an Alan Bleasdale/Diplomat Films evening. An eclectic mix of TV execs, actors and directors. Alan looks the same as ever, but leans on a stick and claims that his knee has deteriorated to the point where it causes him 'excruciating pain'. But he manages to stay upright at the podium for a long, very Alan-ish monologue. He thinks that Liverpool's year as European City of Culture is fatally flawed. 'Liverpool was always corrupt,' he growls. 'Now with all this money coming in it's just going to get much worse. If Derek Hatton were still around he'd be laughing.'

Sit next to Julie Walters, who is a real treat. Very unassuming and down-to-earth and presently writing her autobiography. I feel she's one of those rare people you could talk to about almost anything.

Helen encourages Alan to have his knee done asap. He says he'll do it if she'll hold his hand whilst they give him the anaesthetic.

Tristram [Powell] and I were talking about Alan Bennett and honours, and how he's turned down everything. I'm of course compromised, already a commander – what would I do if a knighthood were proposed? I always liked

445

Michael Frayn's reason for declining, simply that he wanted just to be Michael Frayn for the rest of his life. Tristram tells me Francis Bacon's reservation about a knighthood being that it was 'so ageing'.

Thursday, February 7th

In the evening, H and I and Terry and Anna set off for Basil's Chinese New Year party. Terry G, with a fine grey beard, is also with us. He says that Heath Ledger's death was like losing a member of the family – Maggie very cut up – and Amy saw him like a brother. TG is trying to use what there is of Ledger [in the film that became 'The Brothers Grimm'] to graphically create a performance, and is hoping to get Depp, Colin Farrell and Tom Cruise to each work for a week playing the different mirror images of Ledger. With his mixture of computer wizardry, rewriting and celebrity casting, he thinks he can save the film.

Friday, February 8th

Deal with business at the office then cab up to Stephenson Way by Euston Station. Tucked away in a cobbled back street is the Royal Asiatic Society, which I'm visiting in order to see the latest stage in the work of Ramesh Dhungel – the Nepali scholar who is, with my help, unlocking the Hodgson Archive.[1] All a bit stiff and formal to start with – people standing by their work stations as if being inspected at school speech day. I try and defuse the officialness – which is, for me, only an obstacle.

Ramesh is very voluble and the letters of Hodgson and others that he's revealed are fascinating – hints of the Great Game, requests to be included in a visit to Tibet to collect zoological specimens, for instance. A surreal touch to a letter from the French government withdrawing the Légion d'Honneur which they had given to Hodgson three years earlier as it should have gone to another Hodgson – the US ambassador in Algiers!

I'm very much drawn to institutions like this – not too big, proud of their collection and possessing some beautiful work offering a glimpse into another world.

---

1 Brian Hodgson was the British Resident in Nepal, between 1820 and 1843. He wrote the first history of Nepal and codified the country's flora and fauna.

Tuesday, February 19th

A double dose of royalty today. I've been invited to Clarence House for a reception for the Cinema and TV Benevolent Fund, for whom I appeared in a video. They've also asked me to give the 'Loyal Address' at the Royal Film Premiere tonight – it shouldn't be long and words have been sent which allow little room for improv.

Into a suit and down to the Mall. As I step down from the car a marching band emerges from Buckingham Palace. The sun catches polished helmets and cuirasses as they march down the Mall beside me.

Simon A is there and Sir Paul Fox quite matey. He tells me that he'd been asked to talk about his memories of the Python days. 'But I said no,' he confirms, eyeing me combatively. 'I know what that's all about. I'm not being caught out,' he chuckles, a touch manically. 'It's all about how there was no comedy before Python and it was all changed afterwards. Well, what about "Dad's Army" . . .'

As before, guests are urged to organise themselves into manageable groups as the Royals progress around the room and Simon organises Sir Paul, myself and two others into a meetable unit. No sooner has he done that than I'm asked if I will come and meet the Royal couple before they start to work the room – probably my bonus for doing the Loyal Address. So I'm led to a sort of no-man's land between the VVIP room and the drawing room, and have my own time with first Camilla, then pink-faced Charles. I defy anyone not to get on with Camilla – she's easy to talk to, affable, direct, curious and unstuffy. She asks what I'm doing and I talk about the *Timewatch* First World War doc – also bang on to Charles about this – telling him about my great-uncle Lance-Corporal Harry Palin and how his body was never recovered. 'Well, of course, I lost a relative at Loos,' he counters. Try to rack my brains which member of the Royal Family died in the First World War.[1]

Later, as people are assembling for speeches, I bump into Dickie Attenborough and Peter O'Toole, sitting together. Wonderful double act. Dickie rather affectionate and accommodating, Peter a little more dangerous. He offers his knee to a young lady interviewer and claims he's doing nothing these days – lying in bed. 'Wonderful mattress' – he gives me the name – 'No bed sores.'

Friday, February 22nd

More Timewatch filming today. To Queen Mary University of London in Mile End Road where I'm to interview John Oxford, one of the country's leading

---

1 It was Fergus Bowes-Lyon, brother of the Queen Mother.

epidemiologists. He's a natty figure who wears an Afghan scarf carefully arranged around his shoulders, throughout the interview. His tiny office is a mess, but an exuberant mess, like a student flat. Odd clocks, a piece of broken chair, a cocktail stick and cluttered pieces of 1940s furniture. He's one of the government's closest advisers on SARS, HIV and particularly, the bird flu threat. He thinks that some kind of bird flu outbreak is unavoidable, and wherever it starts it will spread all over the world. The more reassuring news is that the government is taking the threat very seriously – and currently has vaccine supplies for half the population. He talks to me about Spanish Flu in 1917–1919 – history's worst epidemic – and that only one place was untouched – the island of Samoa.

After lunch down to Sidcup to interview Andrew Bamji – a more conventional medic I thought from his appearance – but even he had a wacky side: he can instantly improvise poetry on any subject, and frequently wins the competition for poetry pastiche in the Oldie. From him I learn about how horrifying facial injuries were dealt with during WWI. Bamji feels that that anyone who has seen the injuries would never send men out to fight. And that it was always the Glorious Dead but never the Glorious Wounded.

Monday, March 3rd: Bradford and London

Another short night, after 'American Friends' showing (soundtrack seriously soft) last night and a late curry.

Lunch in the Midland Hotel – 'Restaurant & Toilets' (is the sign for the restaurant) and lots of 'CAUTION, RAISED AREA' signs, wherever there's the slightest incline (Health & Safety? Lawyers?), but it has been a comfortable, friendly base for the three nights of the International Film Festival. A city-centre hotel that's very much part of the city itself – at various times I saw a Pakistani wedding, the Optometrist's Ball and the Grimethorpe Colliery Band on their way to a competition, and that was whilst sitting in the bar.

The weather is mercurial. Dark clouds, snow swirls, then broad sunshine. It's been a hectic weekend, with all sorts of demands. I approached the whole thing with dread, I leave with satisfaction and already, a nostalgic regret.

Friday, March 7th

Archie, now a very solid miniature person, does the rounds of all his favourite things in my study. Up the staircase, onto the roof, throw some of the gravel around, come down, fiddle with copier, fax machine, shredder and video – and then, if time, my mobile phone. He has a lovely way of putting his finger up to his ear as we wait for a machine to warm up.

Run through Camden Group names and details one last time then driven down to Tate Britain to a Late at the Tate talk with Tim Marlow. I'd originally agreed to take part because Alan Bennett was to be my co-conversationalist, but he dropped out and Tim substituted. He admits he doesn't know very much about the Camden Group. He runs White Cube and is preoccupied with the modern British art scene. When a questioner asked us both what was the first painting we'd bought – his was a 1997 Tracey Emin of Tracey mutilating herself – mine was a large cow beside a fence.

His rapid delivery and lines like 'Tracey is an accident waiting to happen' seem a little incongruous when we're talking about the rather placid Camdeners, but the hour passed very smoothly. I banged on about my disapproval of big art exhibitions sucking the lifeblood out of museums, and my plea for the individual rather than collective appreciation of art. In fact I was over-opinionated.

Tuesday, March 11th

To the Royal Academy where Eleanor and Mhairi have agreed to meet me. They try to pin me down to something we might do together. El has an idea for doing Hopper's journeys in America, with two actors and me as omniscient presence experiencing it at the same time. I come up with an idea of taking one of my paintings – like the Inshaw, and using David Hockney to tell me how it is being a painter (he's my age), learning about craft, execution, commissions etc. etc. I quite like this as I explain it. Then there are the women – why are there so few recognised female painters like Berthe Morisot and Artemisia Gentileschi? We leave it unresolved.

Wednesday, March 12th

Work on a few words for the BBC World Service Awards tonight and then leave the house at 3.30 for BAFTA where the evening's show is being rehearsed.

Awfully friendly and ebullient Lyse Doucet is my co-presenter. She's disarmingly friendly and quite happy to tell me that, as soon as the foreign secretary turned them down, I was first choice – later she whispers, 'that was my idea!' Lyse is Canadian, but her special field is the Middle East, particularly Afghanistan. She urges me to go there. 'You can go to the north without the military.'

Attend the pre-show reception, briefly, as I can feel my voice getting more and more strained, then wait for the seven o'clock start in the BAFTA bar. Graham, the barman, recommends me a brandy and Benedictine for the throat.

It soothes and relaxes, and I'm reminded of Neil Innes's advice to me when I lost my voice before going on stage in New York – drink whisky, 'won't restore the voice but you won't care!'

Only ten awards. Good strong stories – awards for bravery in bringing stories out of Burma, or covering the devastating floods in Bangladesh, or child prostitution in Africa. Things that matter, for God's sake. And *no* goodie bags!

The last award, which has everyone on their feet, goes to Alan Johnston, the correspondent who was held hostage in Gaza for six months. A standing ovation as he walks to the stage. It was on this day, March 12, last year, at almost exactly this time, that he was abducted and began the half-year of imprisonment. I like him and everyone warms to his modesty – and his eloquence. Unlike the Oscars, that's what these World Service Awards were about. Eloquence.

Thursday, March 13th

To the Bluebird Restaurant in Chelsea for a meeting with the Eagle Rock team who are behind the big Python documentary to end all Python documentaries which Bill Jones [Terry's son] and Ben Timlett [his working partner] have been pushing for a year or so. Recently the Pythons generally expressed the view that it was too much of the same and we didn't need another Python documentary, but, with Terry, I've agreed to at least go and see the people behind the offer. They envisage six hours for DVD and TV with a theatrical compilation of it all for cinema – Beatles Anthology style.

Share a cab home with TJ. Both of us feeling more positive about the idea and the better for having met and talked with the instigators. TJ agrees to summarise our thoughts and let me see what he's come up with.

To the Dover Castle for a drink with Roger, John Pritchard and Alex. Much jollity. We talk of global warming. John presents a powerful case for a tax on farts.

Wednesday, March 19th

Out at midday to an RNIB fundraisers'/trustees' lunch given by the Duke of Westminster. I've been asked not just to attend the meal but to speak 'after the cheese and biscuits'. All attendees to be given a signed copy of 'New Europe'. The Duke runs the Grosvenor Estate from a newish building in Grosvenor Street. Up on the eighth floor he can look out over properties that make him the richest man in England.

The place is modern, efficient, purposeful and his grace tries to match this mood. He's immediately recognisable from the dark circles around his eyes, so well-defined that they look like something David Attenborough should be here to explain. He's bulkier than I'd expected – well-built and shaking hands energetically, greeting people a little too like subjects.

I'm sat between a lady who knows all about the new school project they're wanting money for and on the other side a bright, funny lady magistrate who regales me with details of the cases she has to deal with. A professor caught pee-ing in a public place – near Colchester as it happens, who, strictly by law should have been punished – 'but what's the point, he wasn't causing any trouble, he wasn't flashing it around. So we let him off.' Another man caught wanking while driving. She seemed to take great pleasure in telling me these tales.

Walk to the Savile Club, location for yet another interview about Python, this time about 'The Holy Grail' for a series called 'Movie Connections'. Carol Cleveland has just been interviewed and we have a coffee together in the ante-room of the bar (women aren't allowed in the bar until 5). Carol talks most of the time; a short, but poignant recital of her latest lost opportunity. A new TV series, for which she had virtually been offered the lead by the director, only to miss out after the producers plumped for someone else. 'I don't know, Michael, but this has made me more depressed than anything.' What can I do, but listen, sympathise as usual, and in the interview, to reiterate how damn good she was in 'Holy Grail'. And everything she did in Python.

Thursday, March 20th

Spend forty minutes on the phone to an ex-journalist called Kerry Blackburn who has been asked to make a report and recommendation to a BBC com-plaints panel following criticisms by one C. J. Lincoln of E17 that the Yugoslav episode of 'New Europe' was heavily politicised, with a very strong pro-Serb agenda. As I have beside me, as we talk, a copy of a letter from a Serb suggesting quite the opposite, I'm not too worried. He can't accept that anyone was to blame for anything in the Balkans, except the Serbs. As this flies against almost every accepted, well-researched view, it must make him even more vituperative. Kerry admits that over 60 per cent of the people the BBC Trust has to deal with are serial complainers – like, although she can't of course say it, one C. J. Lincoln of E17.

A TV crew here to interview me for the two new DVDs which will be part of the add-ons for a release of all the Python TV shows. Archie enjoys the setting up of lights and camera etc. in my workroom. He shows one of them how the fax machine copies – complete with his finger up, listening gesture, and shout of joy as the two sheets emerge.

Out to supper at Odin's with John. Connie Booth [John's ex-wife] and [American theatre critic] John Lahr arrive. Of course it's a delight to see

Connie again – so soon after watching her beautifully pitched performance in 'American Friends' – and John Lahr exudes good sense and good humour. We talk about diaries. John Lahr rather fascinated by when and how I write. JC says if he had to keep a diary, he'd have to make it all up. John L suggests that all diaries are a fiction. Direct speech is the most difficult area, he feels. Unless you write the exact words down at the time, or have a phenomenal memory, it's very hard to do justice to the speaker. A single word missed here or there is effectively misquoting them. 'I suppose you'll go home and write all this down.'

On the whole a very happy group. At one point John says something (I've forgotten exactly what and *certainly* can't make it up) which has Connie hooting with laughter, just like she did in Python audiences – a little glimpse of how 'Fawlty Towers' must have been written. 'Hello ex-wife,' says John at one point, with considerable affection.

Tuesday, March 25th

Run, for the first time in nearly three weeks – work, weather, visitors, a ten-day mini-cold all having prevented me. At the start I wonder quite seriously how long I can keep doing this, but I complete the circuit; the Heath is very empty and I feel wonderfully better. Maybe I can complete thirty years of running after all. Only two years to go!

Thursday, March 27th

Out in the evening to the Savile Club – Simon and Nancy host a convivial dinner, with Maureen Lipman, Al Jones now Telfer, Michael Blakemore [theatre director] and Mark Shivas [television producer]. Michael Blakemore looking very elegant. He tells me of the joys and pleasures of being with Hoares Bank. Established about the same year as Coutts, it remains a family-owned, private bank with no connection to any other big group. Michael makes it sound so tempting.

Nancy asks me to encourage Simon to take up his diary-writing again. He looks pained. 'I know! I know,' he says. 'It's so difficult to say everything I want to say.' I advise him not to aim too high. Think of it just as a record of the day – if it's great literature as well, so much the better. But that's not what diaries are for.

Friday, March 28th

Steve gives me the news that China has banned the 'Himalaya' series. Despite extolling the beauties of Yunnan and Szechuan, I have spoken to the Dalai Lama and that is incompatible with a showing in China. Evidently.

Wednesday, April 2nd

As I walk down Devonshire Street I find Frank Gardner, the BBC correspondent shot in Saudi Arabia by al-Qaeda, in his wheelchair beside a stack of crash-barriers next to the Chinese embassy. He looks young, his face bears not a hint of any trauma; vaguely saintly glow to it. He extends his hand. 'Fellow travellers!' I admire him enormously. He's onto a story about Tibetan protest groups disrupting the progress of the Olympic flame through London this Sunday. His mobile goes and he reaches inside his jacket. 'Hopefully, this'll be some news from the Chinese embassy.' I leave him to negotiate his story.

Aching and coughing, I seek solace in John Huston's film 'The Dead', which I bought from Amazon at the weekend. A delight. Such terrific performances. The only disappointment is when the cast and audience have to leave the wonderful house and the party's over.

Monday, April 7th

Still not feeling right, but decide to begin the week boldly – so onto the train at Belsize Park and make my way to Pimlico and thence to Tate Britain to draw up a list of paintings I'd like to talk about with Tim Marlow later this month.

A lady from Channel 4, who clearly can't believe her luck, asks if I'll say a word or two to their news programme about David Hockney's gift of his monumental Yorkshire landscape 'Bigger Trees Near Warter' to the Tate. A section of it has been hung this morning. Then Nick Serota [Tate director], gaunt as a monk with a sticking plaster on his cheek, emerges, smiling broadly, and the next thing I know the artist himself is before me. David, like his blond Yorkshire twin, Alan Bennett, seems eternally cherubic. He'll be 71 next year and his complexion is fresh and clear and his face barely lined. Even now you could put a cap on Hockney and Bennett and they'd still make convincing schoolboys.

We talk about Saltaire Mill. David remembers the Mill when it was working and the tremendous noise it made that reverberated through the whole of Saltaire. I end up being interviewed, whilst David, completely unruffled, is being photographed yet again. He's certainly much easier with the press than is Alan.

I retrace my steps to Pimlico Station and getting out at Green Park walk through the crowds to Sotheran's to look for a birthday present for David [Frost] tonight. As they so often do, Sotheran's comes up with the goods – a book published by themselves of a collection of all the best cartoons of Winston Churchill.

H and I duly set off to the Lanesborough, hoping that this will not be an overwhelmingly crowded affair. And it isn't. As we stand waiting in the lobby for the receptionists to find out whether Sir David is here or not, one other couple, bearing a present of similar size and shape, stand tentatively nearby – it's Joanna Lumley and Stephen Barlow, and, apart from family, they're the only other guests. The unexpected intimacy of the group of us was a relief and made for a comfortable meal, despite the surroundings. An atmosphere of international high-class escort liaisons.

Jo has very straightforward views about things she believes in – that in others might sound either phoney or even calculating. She believes that life is short, and we should never let anyone we care about slip away without telling them we care. She'd written to Harold Pinter – 'I'd heard he was very ill' – just to tell him how wonderful she thought he was and how marvellous was his work. Apparently, she'd received a very 'nice, uncharacteristically Harold' letter back. Hearing over the weekend that the Duke of Edinburgh, 86 now, had been admitted to hospital to monitor a chest problem, she'd picked a few flowers from her Stockwell garden and taken them in to him. She snaps into an impersonation of lascivious photographers as she left asking her if she'd stood by the bedside etc. 'Of course, I hadn't. I just left the flowers in the reception and went home.' She thinks the Duke has been greatly misrepresented, he has collections of Aboriginal and Inuit art – did I know that?

Stephen B is very amiable and easy-going and seems to deal with his powerhouse (albeit a gentle, caring, thoughtful, well-intentioned powerhouse) of a wife without any fuss. They make a very good couple – married for 22 years she tells David, 'though of course that's nothing compared to the Palins.' She's right. Our 42nd anniversary is now only nine days away.

Monday, April 14th

Antonio Carluccio has carved me a very beautiful ash walking stick with cloven head for a grip. A mushroom caps one of the forks. Thank him. He's been in hospital, 'a bit of plumbing,' he says dismissively.

Home, then out with H to the British Museum for a Patrons' view of an exhibition of American Prints in the collection – 1900–1953. Some revelations, including a rather dainty pastoral print (from 1930) by Jackson Pollock, and evidence of how Hopper's style was influenced by an Australian-born printmaker called Martin Lewis. Also Ashcan work by Sloan – not dissimilar in its scope to the way Camden Group looked at London. Scenes of families lying out in the open on the top of tenement buildings in New York, before air-conditioning.

Wednesday, April 16th

Fine, cold morning. Nice to be together just with H on this our 42nd anniversary. Unfortunately I'm still dogged by the aftermath of the cold, and coughed at various intervals in the night. Begin to worry about my throat – it does bear the brunt of these periodic attacks.

Friday, April 18th: Liverpool–London

Breakfast, and a walk along into the centre of the city then divert down past the Liver Building onto the waterfront where the Isle of Man Ferry is berthing. It's a bleak place, not a tree or a garden or a blade of grass; hotels and expensive housing blocks. Accessed by car. Pedestrians very much the second class here, like the worst American city centres. Cut off from the real life of Liverpool by a highway.

Home and still feeling the benefits of a very successful opening of 'Art in the Age of Steam' at the Walker Gallery.

To Tate Britain to talk about some of my chosen pics with Tim Marlow. Like me, I think, he'd rather not rehearse too much, and we only have three hours at the Tate. Tim's team have obviously worked a lot together before. Phil Grabsky, who's done six programmes with TJ, is director and also on one of the two cameras. I find the concentration required to justify my choice of paintings – a Turner, a Stubbs, a Marcus Gheeraerts, a Wright of Derby, a Sickert, a Bacon, a Whistler quite tiring. We dash from one part of the gallery to another and I try not to talk bollocks.

Home just after midnight. The front door had been kicked earlier in the evening, with such violence that the lock was broken, but the door, augmented and strengthened after the last incident like this, was undamaged. Poor H – both these attacks have happened when she's been on her own. Why? Class hatred? Drugs and anger most likely. But apparently the noise was terrifying – and H is not easily given to hyperbole.

Sunday, April 20th

We're woken when Archie wakes. Can hear him happily ruminating, reflecting, talking away to himself. It's a drab morning; the east wind has dropped, but it's chilly and grey. Doesn't stop him and me doing the ritual walk to the bridge. 'Woo-woo!' He now says 'railway' beautifully and I'm afraid he's, even at the age of two, as avid a trainspotter as I ever was.

Tuesday, April 22nd

Steve A and Paul let me know that Channel 7 in Australia have pulled the 'New Europe' series after only three episodes. No more news, as yet. I'm puzzled, rather than angry; well, not puzzled, just rather unsurprised. From beginning (when BBC Worldwide sold the show away from ABC [Australia's public broadcaster] without consulting me) to end, Channel 7 have been unhelpful and unreceptive. But they did give us a lot of money!

Sunday, April 27th

'The Andrew Marr Show' may be one of the BBC Factual's success stories, but I still have a plaintive driver's voice on the phone at eight o'clock telling me that he can't find my street.

I'm met at stage door reception and taken up to an office beside Studio TC8. On grubby sofas at one end of the room Mariella Frostrup sits cutting bits out for her newspaper review. On the stairs I meet Andrew M, a slight, unimposing figure belying his authority as interviewer of great skill. Martin Bell, in the white suit that I want to ask him about, but thinking it might be so predictable I don't (I mean him and Tom Wolfe, why?), prowls the newsroom like a bull on Valium, before getting a handful of papers and retiring to a desk to make his choice. Young men seem to staff this outer room and perhaps that's why it is such a mess – no quarter given to comfort or aesthetics of any kind. A student pad after a long night.

Just across the passage the leader of the Conservative Party is in the hot seat, and I'm on after him. Cameron extends a hand. 'Fellow Brasenose man,' he begins, but any further matiness is brought swiftly to a halt by the floor manager – 'no time for that I'm afraid.'

Andrew M very easy, intelligent interviewer, then I'm removed as David Miliband (who unless he does something very foolish, will probably be next leader of the Labour Party) is inserted in my place. His interview is fluent and assured and helps to bolster the government after a week of U-turns and fresh awkwardness from G. Brown. At the end of the show myself and Martin Bell and Miliband are lined up on the sofa for last thoughts. I suggest that there's nothing wrong in U-turns, if a genuine mistake has been made, and announce that I'm going to start the 'U-Turn Party' which gets a laugh.

Off to breakfast. Miliband, who looks to have been assembled from a kit — the regular hair, the unblemished face, the suit, the red tie, clearly ambitious, fiercely bright but trying to be as chummy as possible — asks me to sit beside him, and tell him what my favourite Python sketch is.

Monday, May 5th

Sixty-five today. Like eighteen or twenty-one, sixty-five was always an important milestone when I was growing up. Sixty-five meant it was over — working life that is. Almost every managerial professional had to take retirement at sixty-five. My father welcomed it, spent most of his sixty-sixth year preparing to move away from Sheffield. I don't contemplate moving, nor do I contemplate retiring — though being sixty-five has coincided with certain feelings that may change how, when and why I work. The prospect of another travel series to match the seven I've done over the last twenty years, is now, I think, almost negligible. I've done enough; others have moved into the market; I'm interested in so much else — art, writing a new novel, possibility of some acting.

Our two-day break in Norfolk and Suffolk made H and I realise quite how long ago it was we first met and fell in love. Nearly fifty years. We revisited Southwold on Saturday, scrubbed the moss and lichens off Mum and Dad's gravestone, and ended up watching 'East of Ipswich' — my recreation of our first meeting — with a packed house at the High Tide Festival in Halesworth. Must move on, was my conclusion. You can look back but you can't go back.

Friday, May 16th

Take Bas to the Athenaeum. He hasn't a tie on but his black jacket buttons up so elegantly to the collar that you couldn't tell, and of course in any sartorial contest Basil at his most informal would show a clean pair of heels to most of the members here. We sit in leather armchairs worn smooth by generations of influential bottoms and sip the house white — a good New Zealand Sauvignon — and Bas explores an interesting new idea. His Dutch publishers suggested he do a photographic book about water. PB-J (now representing Basil) apparently suggested it might be a good subject for an MP series. And here, in the fading light, beneath the mighty chandelier, with Londoners rushing for buses and tubes in Pall Mall and Regent Street, we discuss what strikes me as a possible breakthrough idea. Immediately I think of Lake Baikal and the Aral Sea as one programme. The great canals and irrigation schemes of China another. The short, hopeful, period when canals in England seemed to be an essential part of the Industrial Revolution. The temples in Japan, built close to running water to help the monks concentrate and contemplate. Water as destructive force, water as empire-builder (Venice). Another glass of Sauvignon and the potential seems all the more seductive.

I need to go home and think. We pick up taxis in Pall Mall and bid farewell until the next time Bas comes through town.

Monday, May 19th

Olivia H has requested that we visit George's Garden at the Chelsea Flower Show. Arrive around eleven into the midst of a gigantic press-call for the Show, which the Queen visits tonight and which opens to the public tomorrow. There's a little table marked 'Celebrities' tickets', and as I collect ours I notice a sheet of paper headed 'Celebrity Spotting', which is swiftly secreted.

Fortunately, we meet Neil [Innes, Python collaborator] and Yvonne (who designed the garden) and they show us to the little patch of the show which is dedicated to George. Rather sweet it is too. A red-brick wall with the street name 'Arnold Grove' attached and a bicycle leaning beside it and some long grass, from Friar Park, then across a multi-coloured tiled pathway are lupins, delphiniums – to represent the sixties and all lead up to a circular pavilion with a stone (or plaster) couch which represents the next life. The mics and lenses are never far away and I'm interviewed pretty relentlessly as I walk. Trouble is I keep losing Helen, who makes off as soon as she sees a press group about to pounce.

Friday, May 23rd

A good, refreshing run before lunch blows away a morning of rather negative thoughts and inability to find much strength of purpose. Preparation for my 'Evening With' at Carlton School. The event has been dogged by a disabled access problem. There is none, and this was made clear on the adverts. A disabled man wrote to the CNJ [Camden New Journal] and made it all sound as tho' he were being victimised by the school, by Camden – even by me. The school responded with a good letter pointing out the age and design of the school, and together with Camden, made sure that my talk would be relayed to a room on the ground floor, and that the man would be most welcome and everything would be done to make him comfortable. I make a point of talking to him myself before the talk. No quarrel with me, he says, or the school but, and here he goes a little unfocused, if we can find money to go to war, we should find money to allow disabled people full access everywhere, every time. I bite my tongue – wanting to say just how well cared for are the disabled here compared to almost any other country I've been to, but he makes his point, and all I can say is that I hope he will enjoy the talk and hope to see him afterwards.

Two bits of bad news dampen my spirits. The disabled man left without watching any of the talk, and the SATs figures for Carlton put the school right at the bottom of the borough's results. So sad, because I feel it's schools like this which show an example for the future of integration of local and immigrant families.

Wednesday, May 28th

Car pick up at 7.30. Drops me off to talk on the 'Today' programme about the launch of a campaign to raise funds for Oxford University. At TV Centre there is no one to meet or greet me. Eventually, as the clock clicks on past 8, I have to ask a PA working on a quite different show if she would mind telling someone I'm here. A girl wanders down eventually from the 'Today' show. Young, amused. Not an iota of apology. I'm shown in to the 'green' room and indicated a messy trolley of mouldering food.

The interview (Chris Patten is in a radio car) is with Jim Naughtie. Patten is smooth, I'm enthusiastic. We seem to get away with it. Afterwards a quick word of thanks from Jim N, and a note asking if I can get to the launch – at the British Academy at 10 Carlton Terrace.

I have time to talk a little with Ian Hislop and Richard Dawkins – the other two high-profile alumni who've been rounded up. We look at treasures from the Bodleian Library together (photographers snapping as we do); one book has a hugely magnified, precisely detailed drawing of a housefly. Wonderfully rich and complex. 'Now who could deny a divine hand in that?' ribs Hislop as Dawkins peers at it. 'No, the Great Man was certainly on form that day,' replies the Great Doubter.

Friday, May 30th

Today, a fishmonger from the North-East banged on the door and asked me if I'd sign an autograph 'To the Vermin Family'.

Tuesday, June 3rd

Receive a letter from Dervla Murphy, in which she thanks me for sending her a copy of 'New Europe', bemoans the fact that John Murray, her publisher, has been swallowed up by Hodder Headline, who like Orion, are now part of Hachette/Lagadere. 'The book industry' is a phrase that clearly appals her. 'I refuse to operate any longer as an industrial worker and have found myself a congenial new publisher, the Eland Press.' Good for her. And I hope for the estimable Eland.

Most joyful communication of the day was the following, a clipping from another pensioner, cut out of Monday's Sun!

The Dalai Lama jokes he would like to be reincarnated as Michael Palin's assistant. The Whip's source spoke to the Tibetan spiritual leader, who has met Palin, and it transpires he's addicted to the former Python's travel shows, watching them in his hotel wherever he is in the world.

H and I out to see 'Jules et Jim' (again) on re-release. Had forgotten just how dark a film it is. The jolly music and the bicycle rides are both from the happy first fifth of the film – from then on it's all downhill in a different sort of way.

To Pizza Express at Kentish Town which, contrary to rumour and expectation, still survives. First opened in London four years after 'Jules et Jim' was made, Pizza Express is our adult life.

Tuesday, June 17th

At 6 I put on black tie and Bob drives me down to the Carlton Towers Hotel – now known, in this post-colonial age, as the Jumeirah Carlton Towers Hotel, for another Lady Taverner's evening. At least I know what I'm in for this time, which is an evening of generally benign, but ruthless exploitation.

I parade into the dining room with Judith Chalmers [presenter of 'Wish You Were Here'] to the sound of 'Around the World in Eighty Days' and from then on I must flaunt myself and indeed be flaunted as if I were expensive jewellery. For this is all about rich people putting their hands into their pockets – not of course to pay higher taxes which might in the end provide much more money for the children they're trying to help, but to make themselves all feel better.

Plusses, as ever, include the great dry wit of [cricketer] Rachael Heyhoe Flint, who's a wonderful companion at the table; Roger [Mills], who runs a geography quiz in gentle, serious schoolmasterly vein (I'm out on the second question – the Amazon is the longest river, true or false? I say true, but it's the Nile! Much amusement all round). All in all, a rather good evening, once you've got used to the milking. A woman in long white ballgown offers £1,000 for a photograph with me.

Sunday, June 22nd: Dorset–London

A wild inhospitable night at the Chapel House near Plush, after a successful day at a wedding. Rain throwing itself against the windows, a strong wind buffeting our B and B and we slept very content in our narrow double bed.

By morning the front had passed on to the north and a cheerful bright day of alternating sun and cloud had me itching to get out and have a walk. Short stroll up towards Buckland Newton. Fields green and sparkling after yesterday's rain. Village and church nestling in a hollow ahead of me. Almost impossible, I'm afraid, to describe the beauty of the countryside without falling into cliché, but I felt, as strongly as I've ever done, that I must spend more time in places like this; the countryside stirs some deeper need to be away from crowds and noise and the clamorous demands of London – or perhaps to be able to combine the best of both.

More relevantly, I felt quite certain as I walked along the rise that I no longer feel any desire to make another travel series, which is all to do, I think, with a desire to spend longer at home, and in my homeland. It's as if any remaining shreds of indecision had been cleansed, finally, from my mind. The big travels are over.

Wednesday, June 25th

Pleasant day so I take a second run of the week. Normally the loveliest part of my run is emerging from the South Wood onto the rolling green lawns of Kenwood. Today, the Pasture Ground is littered with vehicles, generators, technicians, assembling the vast stage for the Kenwood concerts. A reminder that English Heritage are not above destroying the quiet and beauty of the places they are there to protect. I was offered a pair of free tickets by the organisers of the first concert – Brian Wilson on Saturday, and without thinking, gratefully accepted them. When I stopped to think, I turned them down – as I realised they just wanted celebrity endorsement for bringing corporate entertainment to my lovely, quiet Heath.

To Miles Kington's memorial service at St Martin's in the Fields. Long, but quite acceptable. The church is lovely and light and the blue sky could be glimpsed through the intricate thick glass windows like a cubist painting. The tributes were generally good and literate. Adrian Hamilton, his Independent editor, exceptional. Noted that Miles never came into the office, ever.

Sunday, June 29th

A roast lamb lunch – it's quite cool and cloudy outside so no one tempted into the garden, then Clarice, Gordon [Tom's in-laws] and myself take our grandson up onto the Heath. By now the sun's out and all sorts of activities under way. A jazz band is playing on the bandstand by the café (in contrast to the massive, dominating stage at Kenwood they fit in easily with all the other goings-on), a cricket match is being played, all in whites, on the William Ellis pitch.

We then dance with Archie – 'Tequila' our favourite, and Gordon and I do lots of falls and roll-overs for him. Unfortunately, as we get home, his mum rushes out to welcome him and trips and falls for real, with Archie in her arms. Short tearful moment, then he's back on his irresistible, energetic form again.

Wednesday, July 2nd

Twenty-four-hour heatwave has ended. Back to clouds and occasional blue sky. Better, it has to be said, for getting about. Call JC, who's at the Chewton Glen Hotel.

He's busy, has sold the ranch, so no more complaints about shortage of money, wants to write a stage musical of 'Wanda' with Camilla and thinks that Python should move its representation to a big American agency. 'I have ten Agents at CAA, Mickey,' he steamrollers on, 'and eight of them are really good.' I guess all this post-Alyce hyper-activity will melt, thaw and resolve itself into a dew, but at the moment he sounds like a bull that's been let out of a darkened room.

To meet Richard Klein at the Beeb. Shepherd's Bush under siege. A column of trucks has closed the eastbound Westway. A fuel protest – oil prices today reached 140 dollars a barrel, up from 70 this time last year – patrolled by and in collaboration with the police.

Richard sounds excited by our latest proposal [for a 'Return to 80 Days' special].

Sunday, July 6th

Wonderfully, and at last, no reason for me to leave the house today.

Rachel P drops in in the afternoon. About to start a very tough week's filming at a school in Essex for a Sky fly-on-the-wall documentary. The Wimbledon men's final begins while Archie's here, but he's long gone by the time it finishes, a few minutes after 9. Of course we get sucked in; the tennis quite sublime most of the time. Nadal, looking like he was working, grunts and sweats and picks his shorts out of his arse – the steam locomotive to Federer's smoothly purring diesel. But it's Nadal who finally prevails. Apparently the longest ever Wimbledon Men's Final. Technically the best I should think.

Tuesday, July 8th

I've been asked if I'm interested in a documentary about Pepys for an anniversary in 2010. Have shown interest – details have been sent (another Scots connection) and must now mull them over.

To lunch at the Connaught with J-P. The hotel has been refurbished and now looks much like any other plonky modern interior – full of silly big vases and long stems of what might be plants of some kind. I miss the wood-panelled old-school elegance, and resent its replacement by design of the bland spa-centre, international school. A good meal though. J-P will finish the Fry series in September. Rather pleased to hear that they have had exactly the same dose of problems as ourselves, including tussle over the title. BBC wanted Stephen Fry in America. J-P preferred Stephen Fry's America. BBC worried about why America rather than US – offence to Canadians, Mexicans?

Thursday, July 10th

A playwright called Steve Thompson rings. He's read the Diaries and would like to write a play about Python versus ABC.[1] He's been commissioned by Hampstead Theatre. Talk for quite a while and I help him out with information and also enthusiasm, for I think it would lend itself to a stage production. At four o'clock he comes round to collect bits and pieces. I like him and trust him, and having seen how well 'Frost/Nixon' did I think there could be real potential in a dramatisation of the case.

Friday, July 11th

To the office. Steve tells me that on both the big 'New Europe' posters – at Chalk Farm and Camden Town stations – a little Hitler moustache has appeared on my Rankin photo.

1 In 1976, we brought a case against American Broadcasting Company for drastically editing down the Python shows for broadcast without our permission. We lost the initial case, but won on appeal.

Monday, July 14th

Rachel P rings after the first day of her filming at the school in Enfield to say that she has been offered the job of series producer. This is a level she's never reached before and I think it's an acknowledgement of her talents and attributes that after the current producer resigned (because of a family crisis) Rachel should be the one they turned to. We discuss it and I can only echo her own voice which is that it might mean more responsibility but it'll also mean more control – and I think she's ready for that. She's a good communicator.

Tuesday, July 15th

Talk to Archie on the phone – very voluble these days. He's moved on from heavy breathing.

I finish initial edit of another tranche of Diaries – up to and including Angela's death. I can't read without tears the entry describing the funeral at Chilton – which I couldn't write about without tears.

Wednesday, July 16th

After some more Diary work and a run over the Heath – Parliament Hill full of school sports days – I meet JC for lunch at Wiltons. Unlike most previous visits the tables are full today. Fatty Soames at a booth nearby is joined by Simon Heffer [the historian]. Soames's voice initially raucous but he calms down. John arrives. He's a little tense to start with, and the tension spreads to me who was feeling most relaxed.

After John's established all the things he can't have, 'is there cow's milk in this?' etc. etc. he softens, forgets what he's not meant to have and orders it anyway. John's full of beans, rejuvenated, with an apparently inexhaustible appetite for work. His collaboration with Lisa Hogan [who was in 'Fierce Creatures'] about a man fleeing California for tax reasons should, he thinks, be made next year, by which time he and Camilla will have finished their 'Wanda' libretto, and he may have time for a documentary series on the paranormal. He's had work done to pad out the lines and troughs and remove any gauntness of ageing: 'I want to look sixty, Mickey, for a bit longer. It's the only way to find work.'

He will be on 'Richard & Judy' later this afternoon signalling the start of a charm offensive aimed at 'countering some of the things Alyce is saying about me' and preparing the Great British Media for his return here for most of the summer months.

So by the time John has to go, I'm left feeling quite old, worn and dull. The shining new vision (he's also discarded, along with Alyce, about 20lbs in weight) is away to prepare for Richard and Judy. Actually once he's gone I feel a sense of great peace descend. The soft womb of Wiltons seems a most attractive place and how better to emphasise that I don't have to race around like a mad thing than to stay and read a little and to this end I open my Simon Gray diaries, order a fine Calvados and for ten minutes I'm as happy as it's possible to be.

JC is very good on 'Richard & Judy' later, big, chortling, outrageous, charming, praising lemurs and being very rude about me. 'Have you *seen* his travel series?' "Oh that's a nice hat!" 'I mean.' Very funny, I have to admit.

Saturday, July 19th

Leave at 12.15 for lunch party at Shreela's [Shreela Flather, later Baroness Flather, first Asian woman to enter the House of Lords].

Meet Liam, architect of the commemorative gateposts at the top of Constitution Hill, marking the commonwealth countries' war dead, which I admire. Turns out that Shreela was the chief mover and instigator of the posts that flank the road. Liam has just completed a memorial in Staffordshire to those Commonwealth soldiers who've died since the end of the Second World War. A pair of concentric walls with a slit in them through which the sun shines directly on the 11th hour of the 11th day of the 11th month.

Gary [Flather, Shreela's husband] holds court in his wheelchair. For someone with MS he's reasonably healthy. He's reached the age of seventy and been given two and a half more years as a barrister in Reading. He works largely with mental health cases and maintains that in all the cases he's been involved in he's never come across a bad person – whatever their crime they're worth the cost of possible redemption – indeed it's our duty to do all we can to achieve it.

Simon A and Phil arrive late bringing Ben Okri and Rosemary Clunie [artist and collaborator]. Ben grasps me as if we were very old friends – which in a sense we are, thanks to Shreela. He's bringing out a book – a novella, or series of novellas. 'No one'll like it,' he says confidently. When I ask him what he's doing now, he says he's reading a lot. My ears prick up. Reading what? Proust – 'nearly finished, it's taken me ten years.'

Home and get my copy of Proust down and read the first few pages yet again. They do strike a chord, draw me in, but am I really prepared to put in the time to surrender to the rest of the memories before I die? Probably not. But I shall keep trying.

Monday, July 21st

H and I leave after lunch for SOAS – School of Oriental and African Studies –, from which I'm to receive an Honorary Fellowship. Helena Kennedy, president of SOAS, arrives straight from the Old Bailey trial of a group of terrorists accused of plotting to blow up airliners across the Atlantic last year. 'You know,' she says with her cheerful energy, 'the people who've made getting on a plane take so much longer.' Helena gave her summing up speech this morning. Finished at one o'clock and has made her way to SOAS by a complicated combination of public transport and taxis. She's quite unfazed by such a rush. Changes out of her trainers into black high heels, dons her gown and hat and is ready for the ceremony, at which she gives a fifteen-minute address that is perfectly pitched.

I, like Helena and other luminaries, am also robed up and be-hatted and when the time comes a nondescript blue upholstered chair is placed in front of the lectern in the Logan Hall and at right angles to the audience. Here I sit, like Whistler's Mother, whilst Professor Michael Hutt reads his tribute.

Good music throughout. A gamelan orchestra plays, with almost painful intensity, in the tent afterwards, through which I walk to mingle with the graduates, who are a largely impressive group from all over the world.

Tuesday, July 22nd

To the office for a meeting with Seona Robertson of Caledonia Films who wants me to do a Pepys documentary for 2010. She's intelligent, well-read, experienced and has all the right instincts. Documentaries should be about people, she says. Should tell their stories. Less interested in dramatisations and gimmicky special effects. I like her attitude. She's around mid-50s I think and has made enough good shows to make me, by the end, less keen to slam the door.

To the British Museum for a private view of the Hadrian exhibition. Interested to learn that Hadrian banned circumcision as part of his unbelievably vicious reaction to a Jewish rebellion, and that there was no word for homosexual in Latin and to have lovers of both sexes was quite acceptable. Otherwise, lots of Roman might and big busts of the emperor reminding me of 'Life of Brian'.

Wednesday, July 23rd

Up early and to the Foreign Office by eight o'clock at request of David Miliband. I expected some particular proposal, request to get involved or at least an angle of some kind, but it's nothing of the kind.

I'm shown into 'the Ambassador's Waiting Room' at the top of the mighty staircase and Miliband, after only a minute or two, wanders in to collect me, hand extended. I feel I should call him foreign secretary, but it doesn't feel right. His eager boyishness, air of casual informality demands a 'David!' – as though we were old friends. I'm 22 years his senior.

Then through an outer office into a huge room in which he seems almost lost – everything around is big, imperial and consequential (except the plate of biscuits) and reduces David to something slim and almost insubstantial. These offices seem built for a Palmerston.

He asks me about what buzz I pick up from my travels – what people abroad think of Britain. He's putting a lot of thought into our national identity. What defines us as a people. The 'narrative'. He sees his job as partly dealing with what he calls 'instrumental' foreign policy – trade alliances, legal and political relationships, security etc. – but wants to talk to me about the other side of it, which is how we are seen, how we want to be seen, if you like, the philosophical or even emotional side of things. He seems troubled, aware that the public is disillusioned with power, politics. I suggest that we are still admired for our tolerant, open system, our international broadcaster, the BBC, is trusted more than its rivals, our education system is attractive to many outsiders. I tell him that our involvement as America's ally in the Iraq invasion has done us enormous harm and has slipped the moral rug out from under us like nothing else. He nods as if I'm only confirming what he knows.

I feel sorry for him. I had expected the Foreign & Commonwealth Office to be inspiring, but instead it's overwhelming; every wall, every stone moulding, every inscription is almost devoutly Imperial, and of course devoutly out of date.

After nearly an hour spent chatting very easily together – tho' he can't conceal a yawn or two – he shows me gently out. I'm given a tour of the bowels of the place on my way. The grand Locarno Room is splendidly restored and yet the chairs drawn up in rows for some conference jar completely. Modern blue and chrome. Ghastly.

Up to see Hammershoi [at the Royal Academy] for a half-hour just as it opened. Lovely work. I look very carefully at how he achieves so much with so little – the direct stylistic antithesis of the Foreign & Commonwealth Office.

In the afternoon to the London Clinic for an MRI scan. The first time I've ever undergone something like this. Not a great problem – no claustrophobia – but I'm given no choice but to listen to James Blunt through the headset.

Friday, July 25th

To Harley Street just before 9. Very warm, close atmosphere. Harcourt [my ENT doctor] has something to tell me; I can sense from the way he sits me down and takes up his place very close and directly in front of me. There was no ear problem revealed by the scan. However, the doctor who analyses these things, detected an enlargement of one of the main blood vessels leading up to my brain. Nothing that could be caused by ill-health, it's something that's been there for 65 years. However, it might need treatment as abnormally large blood vessels, or aneurisms, could lead to haemorrhage. Another scan has been requested by one Dr Colquhoun to ascertain how serious it is.

Well. I take all this in. The good and the bad. And wonder how often I can survive these little scares. Out of the window in a house opposite, an elderly, large, half-naked man is shaving conspicuously, his belly bulging.

Steve calls to say that the BBC Trust has upheld the complaint against our 'New Europe' opening episode from the ranting man who accused me of not being anti-Serb enough. Depressing news. It will encourage professional complainers like my accuser, and make producers more cautious about editorial freedom.

Monday, August 4th

To lunch at RIBA with Peter Luff who's off to India this evening to help bring various experts on the environment together. His take on it all is pretty gloomy. The high-powered international people he's dealing with think that we have only eight years left before the deterioration in our climate conditions becomes irreversible and things like methane gas escape become unavoidable. Clouds of burning methane gas swirling across the heavens is one of the images they're using to try desperately to wake us all up. There *could* be a sea-level rise of 20 metres before the end of the century. Oh dear, it's pretty dreadful, indeed so dreadful that we eventually grin at our gloom and get on with the Pinot Grigio.

Call Paul who says that only the PA and a quite dogged reporter from The Times have rung about the BBC Trust report, but later, when we meet Nancy and Simon at V&P's they tell me it was a small item on the six o'clock news.

Nancy and Simon are a little late for our rendezvous, but preceding them into the restaurant come Ray Cooper and Terry G. TG looks well as he always seems to when he has a film that's spiralling out of control. Meanwhile Johnny Depp has made optimistic noises over a new Don Quixote. So Terry is quite pumped up.

Tuesday, August 5th

An email from Francine Bates, Ed Balls's special adviser, has come through, saying how much he's looking forward to seeing me at the event at 10 Downing

St in September and rather significantly noting that the minister is now talking (for this read 'prepared to talk') openly about his own stammer. I think this is something that he's felt much more moved to do since visiting the Centre, and which accounts for why he's such a valuable ally.

Wednesday, August 6th

Most difficult task of the day is to write to Seona at Caledonia Films and explain why I'm not interested in pursuing the Pepys documentary. I fear that my heart wouldn't really be in a traditional documentary – especially one that might be padded with historical reconstruction. If I decide to do another documentary, I want it to be quirky and odd and different and probably my own invention. I email my feelings and Seona sends a very sympathetic response. No Pepys.

Run – for the weather is cooler – but it's still quite hard work. Then to the London Clinic for another MRI, this time to look more closely at the blood vessels in my neck and head. Only ten minutes and no James Blunt. Instead, 'Band of Gold' – whose lyric is much darker than I'd thought – but then I've never listened quite as intently as I do inside the tube.

August 7th to August 12th: Holiday with H in France

Tuesday, August 12th

Left Bergerac in the pouring rain, but on time at 1.30. Good, refreshing break, with two hot days and the rest intermittent sun and cloud.

Whilst I've been away Simon Gray has died and so has Bill Cotton; and the Olympics have begun in Beijing and the Russians have invaded Georgia. See what happens when your back's turned. A happier piece of news in an email from [American novelist] Chuck Alverson, now living in Serbia, telling me that, following the BBC Trust criticisms of our opening 'New Europe' programme, I'm now a hero in Belgrade!

Sunday, August 17th

Middling sort of day. Occasional reminders of the long hot summer days three or four years ago, but they're tantalisingly few. Olympic news makes up a little for this lost summer. The British seem to be winning medals regularly. I notice that medal is now used as a verb as well as a noun. 'All being well we expect him to medal in this event.' As we already have the verb to meddle it's a little confusing.

Monday, August 18th

Not a glimpse of sun through the sheets of surly black cloud that follow a night's rain. I respond to Eric's rejection of any involvement in the Eagle Rock documentary. Feel that it's time to prick this particular bubble.

No one, apart from Terry, who only wants to do it for financial and nepotistic reasons, is that keen. I don't think we can, or should, take on something of this scale unless we're all committed. I see the inevitable scenario being a Mike and Terry-favoured documentary with us left to do all the sweeping up. All this I try to put, unambiguously, but fairly, in an email, and feel much better after I've sent it out.

To meet Ian Gordon, ex-Frost producer and occasional fellow dinner party guest. Recently he's become more friendly, asking me for a contact with Eric and word of John, both old friends of his. He's suggested we meet at White's in St James's Street, London's oldest club, I think.

I'm there 15 minutes early, up the steps of the white stuccoed building with a bay window that I've never really taken in before. Am sat in a leather armchair in the bar and offered a drink and a newspaper. Accept the latter.

A group behind me sit and talk, in the sort of plummy upper-crust accents that everyone in authority used in the 1950s, but which rarely get much of a hearing over the airwaves these days, except in comedy shows.

Bruce Anderson, whose largely belligerent right-wing opinions are healthily expressed in the Independent every now and then, is the centrepiece of the group and it's not until he stands up to pay his share of the bar bill that the sheer bulk of the man can really be fully appreciated. He makes Nicholas Soames look like Victoria Beckham.

They talk of the recent Russian invasion of Georgia; as all of them seem to have been close to the reins of power at some time, the discussion, or what I can hear of it, is informed. Anderson thinks that the Georgians should never have been offered membership of NATO, and most subscribe to the view that Russia, though overreacting at the weekend, was goaded by the West, particularly America and Britain, in a heavy-handed and clumsy way.

A line of members, all male here, sit silently watching the Olympics on a TV screen. The only women to be found at White's are the waitresses in old-style black dresses. They're from the Philippines and one from the Seychelles and love meeting me. Once again, I marvel at this paradigm of Empire. The powerful being served by the powerless.

Tuesday, August 19th

After a recommendation from Terry Gilliam I get into the office early enough to meet Susannah Corbett, daughter of Harry H [Steptoe in 'Steptoe and Son'], who's writing a book about her father. I remember him rather fondly [working together in the film 'Jabberwocky'] – a very careful, powerful, serious actor who could be very funny and very moving. Susannah, who has his great big eyes, confirms he was a very shy man, and a perfectionist. She didn't recollect the experiences of Maggie Gilliam who, as make-up artist on the film, had to put a toupee on top of his existing toupee for fear of exposing the fact that he wore a toupee.

I enjoy talking to her and am quite surprised by how emotional I become in recalling the scenes we did together. I never really kept up with him after 'Jabberwocky'. He died, of a heart attack, at 57.

Friday, August 22nd

Drive to Regent's Park and walk through to Marylebone High St. Buy a teapot at Divertimenti then, feeling for the first time a chill of apprehension at what might be the possible outcome, make my way to the London Clinic to see Mr Bullock the neurologist, for further news on my aneurism.

Mr Bullock is a neat, tidy man at an old-fashioned wooden desk in a surgery that could have been a coffee room in some tasteful boutique hotel. He mostly apologises. Apologises for the way treatment of one thing has led to revelation of another. It isn't serious, but it is there – up in the brain, above the Willis Circle where blood vessels gather, there is a very small nodule, or bulge, visible on one of the veins. He says that improvements in and popularity of scans are revealing many of these little bulges. They're generally stable and don't grow or start to leak. He checks my family history, which along with my non-smoking and my general fitness, suggests I'm in the least likely category for any worsening. Likelihood problems probably 0.05 per cent.

Upshot is that he would like to check my blood pressure and lipids etc. and then give me another scan in a couple of months. If no development at all, then he will be reassured that it's as unlikely to cause trouble as he thinks it is.

Thursday, August 28th

Have organised an Archie tour, culminating in a close-up visit to the epitome of his current 'towers and tick-tocks' fascination, Big Ben itself. We cross Westminster Bridge and are standing right below Big Ben as eleven o'clock strikes.

From this climax of the expedition, to St James's Park where Archie chases squirrels, and is at one point photographed by a young Japanese woman – after a polite request of course. 'He's so cute!'

He's with us most of the afternoon so not much gets done. I feel almost guilty at surrendering myself to adventures with Archie but perhaps I shouldn't.

Friday, August 29th

Broken night's sleep – car doors, voices, noise in the street and high humidity. Once I've lost my confidence in sleeping then the dominoes start to fall and one after the other worries proliferate pushing their way into the gap of sleeplessness. Find myself turning over in my mind what I should do next – what I want the rest of my life to be; how great or little appetite I have for something new, how difficult it is, having done so much, and received so much in return, to feel that anything is new any more. Do I want to be more private, less public? Will I miss the recognition? And so on and so on until I hear Helen get up and into the bathroom around 7.

Heave myself up, glad as always to exchange the theoretical for the practical. Have breakfast, get to the desk and deal with emails. This takes up most of the day, which is enlivened by emails from the States. Eric Idle, showing what I take to be a joke emblem with McCain's white head joined by a smiling bespectacled, much younger woman and beneath the words McCain/Palin. Turns out McCain has chosen a gun-loving pro-lifer called Sarah Palin – governor of Alaska – to be his running mate.

Saturday, August 30th

My namesake on the front pages: 'Palin to Shake Up Election Fight in US', the FT proclaims. On the news she's referred to as Mrs Palin, and it is disconcerting to hear that 'Mrs Palin has been strongly attacked by the Democrats.' Mrs Palin's weaknesses are discussed as we go about making our pots of breakfast tea.

Sunday, August 31st

Wet end to a pretty dismal month. To Abbotsley, arriving soon after 11. Granny has slowed down quite considerably. Her movement much more stiff and laborious. I notice she can't move out of the way easily. Her temple is still tender after her fall, but it's the sharply reduced mobility which worries me most. Church Farm is a long house, on two floors, with a lot of ground to cover, and for a 95-year-old with restricted movement it suddenly looks more like an enemy than a friend.

Thursday, September 4th

Acceleration of life in September continues with invitation to drinks at the Frosts ('just to sort of celebrate everyone's return, you know'). A stellar collection of 50 or so, including Jemima Goldsmith, Paul McC, Tim Rice, Greg Dyke, Geldof, Seb Coe, Parkinson and so on. A nice enough group. Paul is off to Tel Aviv to do first appearance since banned there with the Beatles. We talk about the problems of playing in Israel. I ask if he'll be doing anything reciprocal, say in Ramallah. Paul confirms that he will, but without a lot of publicity. Parky's written his autobiog – in four months, according to Mary. Geldof is scarecrow-like as ever, but I do like his liveliness, energy and general sense of absurdity (whilst being probably one of the best businessmen present). Joanna L is smoking rather dramatically and we talk travel. She wants to go to Yemen – says we must do something together.

Tuesday, September 9th

Rain and more rain forecast. Not against the rain but the prevailing gloom that goes with it is beginning to get me down. Day after sunless day – apparently the least sun in August for 130 years.

Terry's asked me to lunch at Black's with Sanjeev Bhaskar, who's now playing Arthur in 'Spamalot' – and whose style of dead-pan seriousness Terry likes much more than what he felt was Tim Curry's knowingness.

Sanjeev is a bright, soft-spoken, funny companion. He can also run Terry head to head on intellectual conversations about religion – the pre-Christian era religions were all about how you lived your life, about personal behaviour and personal enlightenment. Only after Christ did the aggressive, proselytising, political religions like Islam and Catholicism come along. We talk on as the rain sprinkles Dean St. He's a TV traveller as well and accords me most undeserved respect!

Wednesday, September 10th

A man stops me in the street and thanks me profusely for the help he and his children received at the Stammering Centre. This makes up for a furious, hysterical letter from America accusing me of antisemitism in the Diaries. The vehemence of people's feelings, over something they've completely misunderstood, is frightening. I would hate to be physically close to someone who harboured such anger.

Thursday, September 11th

Clearing the desk after the several days' concentration on the Diary edit. An interview with the Sun about the Stammering Centre, then much of the afternoon putting together thoughts for a speech tonight at 10 Downing Street on the same subject.

The whole area around the central government offices in Whitehall is clad in scaffolding and plastic sheeting. The image of somewhere shrouded and wrapped in itself seems to suit the predicament of the Labour government at the moment. The fine interiors look a little tired, lacking sparkle, or maybe I'm just letting my imagination loose. Sarah Brown emerges and she too seems less lively than when we last met. Never an extravagant extrovert, she nevertheless had a glow that impressed me on our last meeting; tonight she seemed weighed down, as if some inner light had dimmed.

She suggested we could do the speeches and then leave everyone to enjoy themselves. So, then and there, we're moved up toward the fireplace, in front of which first Lord Egremont, an ex-stammerer, then myself, and finally Ed Balls, an ex-stammerer, make our speeches. Egremont powerfully and movingly describes the plight of a childhood stammerer. The agonising wait as the teacher went round the class asking everyone for their name and so on. His delivery, in clear Oxford English with an upper-class twist *most* effective. As H said later, we're lucky to have trustees like that.

I'm the only one who speaks without notes, but with my strong feelings about stammering, my father, the Centre and Ed Balls's advocacy of our case, I'd rather let my emotions through unfiltered. Ed B speaks and it's music to our ears. He sees this only as a beginning and hopes that he and the Department will be able to extend the influence of the Centre across the country, saving families the cost of a trip to London each time.

Monday, September 15th

Rather like the collapse of the Twin Towers, the victims of the credit crunch continue to fall, this morning the staggering news that Lehman Brothers and Merrill Lynch are finished – Lehmans left to stew in their own juice, Merrill Lynch to be tucked under the skirts of Bank of America.

Life seems to go on, the newspapers are fat with supplements, a small forest of cranes covers the London skyline, and, as I arrive at Western House for a lunchtime appearance on the Jeremy Vine show, I see the huge concrete service towers of the new Broadcasting House looming above me. Where is all the money to pay for all this?

If Lehmans, Merrill Lynch and Northern Rock and now, quite possibly, AIG – America's biggest insurance company – haven't got it, and Fannie Mae and Freddie Mac haven't got it, who has?

In the evening out to Fleming Collection for a Joan Eardley private view. Very strong stuff and a great talent for using oil paint in a vigorous and powerful way, lashing herself and her canvas to storm-swept Scottish beaches. She died at 42. They say she burned herself out – caring only about painting and never about herself.

Wednesday, September 17th

Is it my imagination or do more traumatic world events happen in September? This morning HBOS, 5,480 of whose shares I hold, and a year ago each one worth over a tenner, is near collapse. Another run. General panic. Nothing much I can do but get my head down with immediate problems. Speech to write for Henley Festival. Nancy alerts me to a Michael Palin for President website in America which advertises buttons and indeed thongs bearing my likeness!

Thursday, September 18th

With the media in full apocalypse mode – banks, Gordon Brown, both doomed – it seems appropriate for H and I to go down to Shipleys in Orange Street to finalise our wills. Interesting areas come up with how my notebooks and original manuscripts will be dealt with – I want them to stay in England. Also the question of Python income and copyright. It's confirmed that Python executors have no power to make or effect any deals so long as there is a Python still alive – the last man standing principle.

Saturday, September 20th

Have been sent a proposal to present a BBC One two-parter on Death. Helen thoroughly recommends.

Tuesday, September 23rd

To lunch with Tristram. He's in a corner of the bright and dim Madmen-style 1950s interior of St Alban. The Corbin & King stamp of excellent service and good food – poached duck egg on morcilla and thin strips of perfectly cooked liver – without the hysteria and hustle of the Wolseley. TP is putting together a stage version of 'King & Country'. He talks wryly of his 'slide through the disciplines' – from film to TV to theatre. 'What's radio like?' he asks and we both laugh. Both agree, for some reason, that Germaine Greer has become irritating and I recommend him Craig Brown's wonderful parody in Private Eye. Craig Brown we like, though I remember he did me in Travel book style and I was rather hurt! 'Yes, he did my father too,' remembers TP. So I don't feel so bad.

Can't decide about Death. The documentary, that is.

Friday, September 26th

The Damoclean Sword hanging over the world economy seems almost palpable, and I check newspaper billboards and Evening Standard headlines as I make my way to the office, for the latest news. But Central London seems busy enough and street behaviour reflects the harmony of the weather.

Meetings with Sandy Lieberson [American film producer] and quiet, rather nervous man called Sam Buckman, about the Gilliam 'Tribute' evening in November. Useful, because I'm able to tell Sam B, in particular, that we mustn't be too solemn, that they mustn't overload the evening with clips at the expense of hearing Gilliam speak and others talking about him. And Sandy and I both agree that we shouldn't end the round-up of his work with Tideland – but put something in afterwards to remind people that Terry's best when he's being funny.

Lunch later with TG. We agree on so many things – both of us wary of charities. More particularly the big, sophisticated fundraisers; TG and I both feel that the constant evocation of 'Africa' as a target for good causes is just too loose, too unspecific and very often too patronising. There may be a lot of money going into Africa now, but as TG says, much of this goes into propping up corrupt ruling regimes. The inventiveness and traditional skills of the people need supporting, not the palaces of the powerful.

Greatly refreshed by bracing chat with Terry, I take the Tube home, glad of any free time to push on with the increasingly absorbing and wonderful 'Palace Walk' [novel by the Egyptian writer Naguib Mahfouz].

Lovely conditions for evening run. As I come back over Parliament Hill, the skyscrapers of the city are tinged red with the reflections of the sunset. 'Embarrassment of Riches' I'd call that, if I were doing a cartoon.

Monday, September 29th

More strong autumn sunshine. I'm heaving bags of discarded summer garden down to recycling, and all's well, except of course for the world's financial system which is once again close to collapse after a few rogue Republicans voted against the Bush/Paulson bail-out plan. Here, the last of the famous old building societies that I'd grown up with disappeared, paying the price of their own hubris at thinking themselves banks.

No one seems to be throwing themselves out of windows as I'm driven through London to meet M Dover and Kirsty Dunseath. We discuss a possible new novel. Kirsty tries to steer my inclinations and enthusiasms, but I reiterate that I'm still keeping all my options open for next year. But I told them about 'Scottish Waste' and the body in the sewer and that excited some good responses.

Tuesday, September 30th

At last, I've cleared enough debris away to be able to find time for '80 Days Revisited' preparation – looking at the places, making notes on Dubai and Bollywood and scanning the Bombay-Mumbai debate. I tend toward Bombay having seen that the Mumbai name-change was orchestrated by a rather unpleasant-sounding Hindu fundamentalist administration called Shiv Sena.

Run later in the afternoon and then, a little reluctantly as I'd have loved an evening in, over to The Belvedere in Holland Park for the launch party of Michael Parkinson's autobiog 'Parky'. Am given a glass of champagne and listen to the odd, halting, low-key speech from the publisher. Apologising that copies of the book aren't available (clearly a boob) and apologising, almost for Michael himself, 'he's a pretty good chap', 'few enemies', that sort of thing. Michael stands listening to this with considerable dignity and barely a muscle moves through the entire speech. He then gets up and has them laughing with tales of early signings at bookshops: 'Daylight doesn't do him any favours' – a fan's remark overheard, and he ends up rather touchingly referring to the shovel episode in 'Ripping Yarns' and my giving him the title of the 'Second Most Boring Man in Yorkshire', which he says was his preferred title for the autobiog.

The camera pack see me talking to Michael Winner and the shouts go up 'The Three Michaels! Please.' And it takes a long time to find a cab home.

Wednesday, October 1st

Meet the producer, Claire Davies, and the exec, an older woman, of the Death programmes. They're enthusiastic and committed without being pushy. We find ourselves talking about the subject for over an hour without any difficulty. All sorts of ideas, thoughts, stories come spilling out in what's more like a production meeting than a job interview. We part with much agreement. I've been reassured that this whole rich subject can be confined to two one-hour docs, but I feel I need time to think about it.

Friday, October 3rd

To the office. Talk to Steve about 'Death'. He's a little wary. I think he had the concern that I was going to go off into a series of 'Palin on . . .' documentaries over which we'd have less control – this one being BBC and Open University backed. I've decided not to make a decision until after the weekend.

Monday, October 6th

A lot of rain and wind over the weekend has cleared and it's a beautiful bright morning, cold and clear. Successful in my quest for a hat at Bates's tiny old-fashioned hat shop and workshop in Jermyn Street. London looks alive, smart, trim and open for business, but the stock-markets are on their way down again and everyone's clinging on to the sides as the roller-coaster ride goes on.

Have decided to accept the Death job, in principle. I lay awake this morning turning the whole thing over in my mind. Part of me is worried that, with '80 Days Revisited' just about to unfold, this is not the best time to be making my mind up about future commitments. Then in comes all the accumulated doubt and confusion in my mind over what it is I really want to do next – how do I best enjoy my life? I'm not anxious about maintaining my fame and celebrity. To be honest it would be quite a relief to not have people thinking I can change the world for them.

News of another 'Black Monday'. There seem to be so many of them these days.

October 8th to October 26th: Filming 80 Days Revisited *in Dubai and India*

Tuesday, October 28th

For some reason I feel bright and buoyant about future plans. As a result of our generally happy, constructive and successful film shoot, I'm tempted to reform for another travelling special. I've considered Iran to be a good destination for our sort of treatment. I think it has the right kind of edge, and the right kind of novelty to make a significant destination. So, as I sip my macchiato and make my way up past the Garrick, a plan for the next two years begins to take shape. Diaries and Death for 2009, and research for an Iran mini-series, two or three programmes, which would be shot in the spring of 2010.

Thursday, October 30th

On the train to Sheffield at 11.25. Slowish progress beyond Derby. Gives me time to immerse myself in Simon Gray's latest book 'Coda'. It's in the style of all the Cigarette Diaries, rambling, discursive, joyfully on the button in his little observations, but this last volume is stripped down to an account of his deal- ings with cancer, and his realisation that mortality is almost all that concerns him now. What makes it so difficult to read is, ironically, the easy, confident style – honed now in so many of his autobiographical writings, characterised by curiosity, fear, humour, and at its best here as the Grim Reaper approaches (he uses a frightening image at the beginning of the book of seeing a creature crouched in the corner of a room, as if waiting for him). So we readers who have got to know and love his style so much are faced with the end of our relationship with him. I rush through, unable to stop reading, but not wanting to get to the end.

Met at the station by a slim, pale, busy lady with a wild thatch of red curls, wearing only a Helen's Trust polo-shirt, on what is a very cold day. This is Lou- ise Jordan, GP to the Duke and Duchess of Devonshire, guiding light in this campaign to help those with incurable diseases to die at home, on whose behalf David Blunkett sought me out. My involvement has grown into a two-and-a- half-hour show at the City Hall, with all the attendant marketing, promotion and publicity. She thinks they've sold 1,500 tickets and some sponsors have covered all the costs of the evening.

To the City Hall first. A mammoth building, with all sorts of rooms and chambers. The stage has been decorated with flags and bags and some film lights – huge brutes the like of which I haven't seen for twenty years or more. A difficult few minutes spent trying to explain that we must have as little light as possible on stage for the first half. There are two small screens high above all the stage distractions which will need all the help they can get. The lighting man is stubborn and unhelpful but we reach some compromise.

I know as soon as I start on the slides that something isn't right. There are no gasps, not even any murmurs of appreciation when the pictures come up. I have to work hard on the stories which go down well, but I know I'm not getting much help from the projection. There's obviously goodwill from the audience so I'm determined to give them the best I can in the shorter second half. The Fegg readings work marvellously, and the laughter is often near hysterical. I finish soon after ten, feeling elated. The Duchess of Devonshire is brought on stage and presents me with some silverware and later meet the Duke and of course David Blunkett, who was one of the very few who didn't care what the projection looked like. He's keen, humorous, and like most politicians, a little keener to talk than to listen, but I liked him. Could see he might, as he was, be vulnerable to admiration.

Friday, October 31st

Halloween. At least a dozen visits from trick or treaters. All quite jolly, noisy and friendly apart from the last lot – a gang-group, quite out of control – looking for trouble. Helen gives them chocolates, but we still get an egg pushed through the letterbox. Like an idiot I instinctively tear out of the door and chase them, which they love.

Monday, November 3rd

It's a week since I completed the '80 Days Revisited' shoot and returned to London from Bombay. Maybe because of all the demands on me at the moment – not just charity shows, but publicity for said charity shows, and the urgency of material for the book – I don't feel I've had the pleasure of relaxing after work done. So I'm still a little scrambled. Sleeping patchily, feeling not quite as sharp as I should be.

Mark Thompson was full of chat yesterday on and off the screen at the Marr Show – and what stuck in my mind was his incredulity that BBC Scotland had never once interviewed the now notorious Fred Goodwin, the big wheel at RBS, who was also one of the most ambitious, greedy and ultimately dangerous figures of the boom years. Also the sense that on the Ross/Brand issue[1] Thompson felt that for once, after being pushed around by Ross and Brand's agents, the boot was now on the other foot and he could hear the sound of renegotiations on the BBC's terms next time.

See some extracts from Roger Deakin's new book in the paper, and remember how much I like and admire his writing. Reading Roger Deakin is the next best thing to living in the country.[2]

---

1 The comedian and chat show host made lewd prank calls on BBC Radio 2, to *Fawlty Towers* actor Andrew Sachs, and were suspended for it.
2 Roger Deakin, environmentalist, author of *Waterlog*, *Wildwood* and others.

Wednesday, November 5th

I hear, with huge relief, that Obama has won the American election. Conclusively. No hanging chads this time, no mean Florida scandals. He's given McCain and Palin a walloping. Just heard he's taken Indiana which has been Republican for the last 44 years.

It's a drab day, and not one which encourages celebration. I'm not popping champagne but it's just good to know that what one commentator described as 'our better angels' have won the day and the dreadful darkness of Cheney, Bush and the neo-cons is over.

Out in the afternoon to appear on Alan Titchmarsh's show. An ITV show recorded in TC4 at Television Centre. How television has changed. ITV, once the sworn enemy, in the bosom of public service broadcasting. The same studios where we recorded Python back in the 1960s. Titchmarsh is a cool customer and listens as well as he talks. David A is on, supporting the release of a boxed-set. He rather takes me aback with a greeting about 'not having to worry about your sister any more' until I realise he's talking about Sarah Palin.

End up doing a most superior wine-tasting. The expert pops a bottle of Dom Perignon and gives it a sniff. 'Sugar Puffs,' he says with satisfaction. And he's *exactly* right. Dom Perignon *does* smell exactly like Sugar Puffs!

Out to supper with Terry and Anna at the Hexagon. Terry a little weak on the hip that's just been re-serviced, but he provides an elaborate meal of which, for me, a green olive tapenade was the star. Oddly enough, there's not much talk about Obama. Did we all expect it? Or maybe it's just that we all know these are difficult times and he's not going to have a magic wand.

Thursday, November 6th: Sheffield–London

Fairly chaotic day at the Documentary Festival, but at least there's a dining car on the way back. I try to tip the very Sheffield waitress on the train, 'Oh don't worry, love, they pay me all right. And I only do it to get away from my husband.'

Monday, November 10th

To Devonshire Place, an outpost of the London Clinic, to see neat, white-haired Professor Monson. Monson is a part of the aneurysm alert instigated by Mr Bullock – 'who is a very good neurologist, and a very conservative one,' says Monson. Monson pronounces my blood pressure very satisfactory and seems generally happy – 'You're certainly the fittest person I've seen today.' Which would have meant more if it hadn't been a mid-morning appointment.

Tuesday, November 11th

I've a meeting with Dinah and Clare from the Death show this morning and I'm worried that, despite my best efforts, I can't get to like the project more. The material they sent me adds up to a lot of interesting areas, but too many – combined together the feeling is of something curious but superficial. And I can't feel my own way into it. The personal angle remains elusive.

I suppose I'm expressing more negatives than positives, but this is an essential part of the process, and I feel I have to air all my doubts. We talk for an hour and a half and by the end I think I've made my decision. Their brief is nebulous; rather than have a clear plan, Dinah insists that they'll do anything I want to do. But she's missing the point. I didn't want to do a programme about Death in the first place. But I was intrigued enough to meet further.

Friday, November 14th

To the office, where Antonio C has laid on dim sum from his favourite Chinese restaurant – the New World – as a thank-you to everyone at 34 Tav. He's working from home now after his life took a turn for the melodramatic. Splitting from Priscilla Conran, he took up with a 40-year-old with young children. He didn't want to take on the children as well as the mother. He stabs himself accidentally on purpose in the chest. On recovery he's booked in for a month of psychological repair work at the Priory. Which is where he met the new girlfriend to whom he introduces us today ('We both met in the Nuttery'). She's called Annabel. The man still looks wonderful (over 70) but I can see he's been quite bruised.

Bas arrives and the two of us go to Tate Britain to see the Francis Bacon exhibition. I'm dazzled by Bacon's skill, the astonishingly original mix of composition, technique and subject, but it seems the work of a bitter man, full of anger. The public, in the form of a big crowd of quiet spectators, seems to intrude on this private world, and yet be unaffected. Art can be so fierce and provocative and powerful, yet its audience must be the most well-behaved and docile in the world. I *do* like Martin Creed's runners though, still unselfconsciously sprinting up and down the central hall. Shall miss them when they're gone.

Monday, November 17th

On the Overground to Acton Central to see our '80 Days Revisited' being edited. Dubai is bland, with an awful lot of time spent on very run-of-the-mill
helicopter views. Once we get to India everything's more immediate, and visually
richer and more complex and the end, as I share with the captain and crew [of
the dhow 'Al Sharma'] the leave-takings of 20 years ago, brings a tear to the eye.

I set out on a circuitous route from Acton to Westbourne Park, where I
leave three books for restoration with a lady called Kathy Abbott who works
from a small, friendly little studio in a Maida Vale mews. She says she'll give the
books to the restorers at Bernard Quaritch. I feel a sense of embarrassment at
the mundane books that mean something to me – our decaying old Visitors'
Book, my mother's Bible, and my 1955 Ian Allan Combined Volume. Quite
what Quaritch will make of these I can't imagine – but Kathy sees no problem.
'They're *books*,' she assures me, not unreasonably.

Tuesday, November 18th

Out in the evening for another visit to Downing Street – this time as one of
the Soane patrons. A cool clear night in Whitehall and a long slow line at the
security shed. I'm told there are two events on tonight – one at No. 11 and one
at No. 10. At the end of the evening I have a chat with Sarah Brown.

Despite the gloom and doom of the economic crisis Gordon's reputation
has grown as people forget that he might have seen this coming and failed to
do anything about it, and give him the benefit of the doubt. Now he can be
statesmanlike and he even won a by-election a couple of weeks back. On the
way out a group from the No. 11 event (who Sarah had referred to as 'the
rowdies') are lined up having their photo taken outside the shiny black door
of No. 10. When I emerge, the men shout at me to join them. Shout being the
operative word. No acknowledgement of where we were, just oafish loudness.

As I stood in Whitehall, in conversation with one of the Soane patrons, I'm
interrupted again by this bellicose bunch, roaring at me and quite oblivious to
the fact I'm talking to someone. Rude night at No. 10 – could be the title of
a Hogarth painting.

Wednesday, November 19th

Walk up to Pilgrim's Lane for the oft-postponed Tea with Alan Bennett and
Michael Palin, won at a fundraising auction at the Roundhouse (for £7,000
someone told me).

The door opened by a bubbly lady with a loud laugh, who introduces me to her friend, then her friend's mother, Pamela – rather dashing; eighties, I should think, a character. Both families are Jewish and consequently quite easy to get on with. Minimum amount of awkwardness. Alan arrives, apologising for being three minutes late. 'I was stopped by the vicar.' Turns out to be the vicar of St John's Downshire Hill. 'He wanted me to come to a service.' 'Do you know him?' 'No, never met him before.'

Then we're led to a table and served a substantial tea – smoked salmon, egg and anchovy rolls, four wonderful cakes, including one which Pamela, who has some style, assures me is Gateau Réglisse. The loud laughing lady tells me how a friend of hers was cured of post-natal depression by seeing me sing 'Poly-ushko Pole' with the Russian Pacific Fleet Choir.

John Sergeant's resignation from 'Strictly Come Dancing' a big topic of conversation. John Fortune apparently rang Alan and said of Sergeant's work, 'Dance? He can hardly walk!' Everyone of course very sympathetic towards him. A new folk hero!

We chatter on quite happily – Alan telling tales I've heard before – like he and his brother being born on exactly the same day, May 9: 'Both conceived on August Bank Holiday.' We break up after a couple of hours, Alan given a lift home by the loud laugher and I walk up to Rosslyn Deli to buy cheese for Will's 38th birthday party tonight.

Cab to Hanbury Street. Lovely atmosphere there – we eat up on the first floor by candlelight. About 20 altogether.

Thursday, November 20th

No rush of appointments today, so time to organise myself, to have a run and to hone my pieces for the TG Tribute evening. To the Curzon just before 7. A little preoccupied by all the things I have to do, and daren't risk more than a glass of wine due to MC'ing duties; all of which cramps the social style a little.

Terry has made sure that the workers on the films are well represented – and far from being a glittery, red-carpet evening, it's an intimate reunion for those who made the films. Jonathan Pryce and Roger Pratt both there to make 'remarks', as it says in the programme. Sandy L, of course, and Jeremy Thomas. And Terry J, of course – though I detect a certain lack from him of wholesale support for this TG tribute. Must rankle in some ways.

Jeremy Thomas draws a gasp from the audience as he announces plans to remake the Quixote film, and later, TG talks on stage with the excellent Mark Kermode about the delays on Imaginarium – still months from completion owing to insurance problems. As MC I was being as rude as I felt necessary but Terry quite missed all that – 'you're so *nice*'.

Friday, November 21st

Into the office. Fortify myself with some positive decisions – not to go to a Python celebration at the Munich Film Festival next June, not to do 'The Real Inspector Hound' at Chiswick in January, not to be the voice of Noah in an animated film for a friend of Terry J's, and a clutch of other resistible offers.

To lunch at the Wolseley with Sarah Miller [to discuss work for Condé Nast Traveller magazine]. Sarah is always good to have lunch with. She knows everybody, but never behaves as if she does. I've been thinking about what I might do to satisfy her unquenchable enthusiasm for my work, without becoming part of the high-end, playboy, spa and spoil-yourself aspect of the magazine. I suggest doing a city. She's interested. Calcutta? She's very interested.

Ring Alan B, who'd enjoyed the tea, after initially fearing that it 'might get rather noisy'. Said I'd promised to try and revive the Three Yorkshiremen and we talk some dates and I ring Barry Cryer – who's on some kind of exercise machine that's rotating his hips. Not only does he not mind having a chat on the phone, he also tries out jokes from his show with Colin Sell including a convoluted Princess Di story which ends up with a confused mother, on hearing the news of Diana's death, telling her children 'she was chased by Pavarotti on a motorbike'.

After some to-ing and fro-ing we agree to meet up at L'Etoile on January 5th. Alan quite busy up till the New Year. Barry says he gets snowblindness looking at his diary after Christmas.

Wednesday, November 26th: Turin–London

Travelled back from Turin Film Festival with Bill Forsyth [Director of *Local Hero, Comfort and Joy, Gregory's Girl*, etc.]. Bill remembered I'd sent him a fan letter all those years ago. 'And, knowing me, I probably never thanked you for it.' True, but knowing him I wouldn't have put that down to discourtesy, just total involvement in his work.

'Being Human' clearly didn't work and was difficult to make and he felt that there was no one there to whom he could talk about his problems with the film. Puttnam [David, producer] virtually told him to pull himself together and get on with it, which was not what he needed. From then on he seems to have withdrawn and still talks as if he'd given up for a while. But he's an idea now for a new film and has some Arts Council money to develop the script, though I sense that despite his successes, he still lacks confidence. He's very Scots in his self-deprecating pride.

Thursday, November 27th

I scan the morning paper with more than usual interest, for details are coming through of armed terrorist raids on Southern Mumbai, and there are pictures of rooms ablaze in the Taj Hotel, which has been occupied by gunmen, and reports of machine-gun fire mowing down people in Leopold's Bar.

The Taj, which only a few weeks ago was our haven of peace and comfort away from the hurly-burly of Mumbai, is now a murder scene, and there are reports of bodies lying beside the pool – where we had many meetings – and of grenades destroying rooms. Unbelievable. Except for the fact that the Taj had tightened security in the wake of threats even when we were there, with the main entrance blocked off to vehicles and two security scanners and a bag search on the way in. They must have known something was coming.

Friday, November 28th

Catch the train to Acton. Richard Klein is already there, slim and dapper in his dark jacket. I congratulate him on being promoted to controller of BBC Four. He claims to be terrified of the work involved, especially in the current breast-beating climate at the Beeb, following the Ross/Brand affair. (Latest rumours are that Ross will be forbidden from swearing when he returns. I hear the sound of stable doors banging.)

The grim scenes of the attack in Mumbai continue to fill the screens. People lying dead where we felt so comfortable and secure a month ago.

Tuesday, December 2nd

This morning I work on commentary and continue for most of the day. Not far from completion when I have to break off and go to Buckingham Palace for the 60th anniversary of Contemporary Applied Arts, of which the Duke of Edinburgh is patron.

After identification at the outer gates, 'We know who you are sir, oh and by the way my son's just discovered Monty Python and "Ripping Yarns" – and it's made him much more interesting!' I'm swept across the gravelly forecourt and through into the internal courtyard.

No other guests seem to be about and as I'm guided from footman to foot-man, through rooms made for giants, I begin to wonder if I'm either terribly early or embarrassingly late. Turns out I'm neither – it's a very small gathering, assembled in a reception room off to the left at the end of the long Picture Gallery. Quite a long wait before the Duke himself appears. Quite a bit shorter than me, complexion a little sallow, eyes lively, amused, darting about as if keen to be mischievous.

He seems puzzled at why I'm here. 'You jump around a bit. What're you doing with this lot?' There are two Americans alongside me. He gives them a quick glance and nods at me, 'This chap flagellates himself in all sorts of remote places.'

He makes a short welcoming speech. He didn't say much, but rather wonderfully remarked how pleased he was that we should all be here together tonight celebrating the sixtieth anniversary of 'of . . . of . . . of . . . whatever the organisation is that we're celebrating.' He laughed, then everyone joined in. In his defence, I'd say he had no notes – and that for myself I've never found the name Contemporary Applied Arts has tripped off the tongue.

Friday, December 5th

Morning at the office. A wave of Python-related plays and other adaptations. On the way home in a cab I start to read 'Pythonesque', a script for the theatre by Ray Smiles, and find myself bursting out with laughter so frequently that the driver looks at me in his mirror. 'You seem to be enjoying yourself.' And I am. A shrewd view of Python and the Pythons in a series of vignettes inspired by our own material. He's captured the rhythms of Python very well. Another idea is a TV comedy-drama-doc based on John and myself appearing on the show with Muggeridge and the Bishop of London. Can't work out why so many should come along at the same time and put it down, possibly, to the success on stage and film of the Frost–Nixon interviews. Feel, in an odd way, that I really should be dead before they do all these things.

Monday, December 8th

Meet up with Terry and Sanjeev Bhaskar for supper. TJ has suggested the Beaujolais Club – off Charing Cross Road. Terry doesn't like his skate and they get him another portion which he doesn't like either. Once he's comfortable, Terry is the most perfect companion, but there's always an edge of anxiety about a meal, food, wine and its presentation, which can be counterproductive conversationally. And I fear it won't get any better. But a mellow evening and we all get on well and the place is quite a gem. Their annual membership charge is whatever you paid the year you joined. So for Terry it's £5. He joined back in the 1960s and the patron produces his original application, signed by Nigel Walmsley and Delia Smith!

Friday, December 12th

A busy day ahead. First to Al Jazeera, in a comfortable, clean and modern basement at 1 Hyde Park, for an interview re the '80 Days' book with David F. His stock is a little higher today with five Golden Globe nominations for the 'Frost/Nixon' film.

After the interview, which is comfortable enough, I'm driven over to the office for an interview for a BBC documentary about Bill Cotton. For some reason I find myself recounting Python's dread of the BBC Light Entertainment party and what to wear. Apparently, Michael Parkinson, interviewed recently, had remembered Graham Chapman turning up in ballgown. Quite likely.

Saturday, December 13th

To the Danish church in Regent's Park, which I've passed many times in the last 40 years and never been inside. Sadly, the reason for being there today is the funeral of Gerd Andresen, our neighbour for almost 20 years, who died, unexpectedly, from pneumonia, though he was apparently suffering from various cancers.

He was a tall, strikingly good-looking man, and involved in some of the more important modern structures in London. He was vividly brought to life by a family friend and by Jacob and Anna, his children, who spoke impressively and boldly and affectionately.

His love of very strong gin and tonics and the image of he and his daughter Anna having a cigarette each after a night out in London, conjured up a man who lived life to the full. In the simple, white-walled, tall, rather austere church, following hymns I couldn't quite understand in the original Danish, I found myself feeling the loss of this amusing, opinionated, creative, knowledgeable and companionable Dane much more keenly than I expected.

On the way out, the green grass and the hedgerows of Regent's Park were good to see. A large puddle had formed at the entrance to the church which people had to step across. Now Gerd would surely have seen this as a problem to be solved.

Thursday, December 18th

Terry J picks me up at a quarter to eight for our much-postponed trip to Aardman [the animation team who made Wallace and Gromit] in Bristol. The train starts, then stops and a series of impenetrable announcements direct some passengers to other trains before the classic announcement, 'this train is now considered a failure'.

At Bristol we're met and driven to Aardman – a long, low, inconspicuous modern shed at an American-style light-industrial park called Aztec West. We meet Nick Park, the god figure, and the other diminutive bearded genius Pete Lord.

They're all very unstarry and anxious to return to how much Python has meant to them and how much it's influenced their humour. When they eventually come to the Fegg project [inspired by our book 'Dr Fegg's Encyclopaedia of All World Knowledge'], ostensibly the reason why we're here, their interest is unfeigned. They've even made a plasticine model of Fegg, which is brought out and stood on the table.

Both sides promise to take it to the next stage which is the creation of a Fegg world, a clearer definition of who or what Fegg is, or represents. 'The anger in all of us,' suggests Terry.

Tuesday, December 23rd

Carol singers come round early in the evening. Two boys, around ten. They immediately parrot 'We Wish You a Merry Christmas'. H and I now ask them if they'll sing another carol. They look blank 'Is there another one?' one says. The brighter, more outgoing of the pair does the first two lines of 'Silent Night' – rather well. I join him for the rest of the verse, and we sing rather tunefully together. We could have made a fortune down Oak Village. The other lad just looks awkward, uncomfortable and resentful. And firmly keeps his trap shut.

Saturday, December 27th

Woken from deep sleep by noise of what sounds like a case being run down the pavement. So complete has been the silence in the village these past few nights that this is a considerable intrusion. It's H who figures it out first – the recycling truck which normally trundles down on Thursday is here two days late. No mention of this on the public notice so I race about the house, unlocking back and front doors, four locks in all, neutralising the overnight alarm – grabbing the bins and getting them out onto the street just in time. When I finally get back to bed, H's only comment on my burst of energy is to ask if I had my pyjama bottoms on.

Sunday, December 28th

Out with H to Loncraines' party. Talk to Ian McKellen about acting – he had to learn how to do it, he says, and where do actors get apprenticeships nowadays? He remembers GBH. 'You were awfully good in that.' I confess that the thought of doing theatre worries me, 'the same thing night after night.' 'Well make sure you don't do the same thing every night,' suggests McK, adding, 'but let the rest of the cast know that!'

Monday, December 29th

Having suggested to Will last week that it might be good to do one of our London walks, I find myself on the Northern Line to Old Street. We head south today. Down Brick Lane and across Whitechapel Road, zigzagging round the back and down to Tower Hill where the most dreadful '70s and '80s office blocks squeeze haphazardly around a prodigious traffic system, across which the ancient walls of the Tower rise. Of course there are gems to be found – Trinity House, beautifully and carefully restored after the war, for instance.

We retrace our steps east, along Cable Street, stopping at Ensign Street where Dan points out some historical bollards which date from the 1830s and bear the insignia of the Royal Brunswick Theatre, which is no more, having collapsed almost as soon as it was built. Through into Well Close Square where many of the older dwellings were condemned by the church, who wanted the old 'vice-ridden slums' removed. Thus disappeared houses which had stood since the 1690s, had survived the bombs of the Second World War; they didn't survive the church's indignation.

Across towards Wapping and Dan's enthusiasm peaks as he describes to us the size and scale of the London Docks ahead of us. Built between 1801 and 1805, at a time when the country was at war, its control of the seas in the balance, this was a huge risk for the businessmen who put up the money. But it succeeded until it was closed in 1968. Much of the rest of this great fortress of trade has been taken down. The final death knell was the wholesale presence of Murdoch's News International.

Some angry graffiti from the battle of Wapping still survives, but there is still something infinitely hostile, dehumanising and sinister about the great sheds which mark Murdoch and Thatcher's victory over the unions.

Wednesday, December 31st

Goodbye to 2008. A recovery year after the seventh and probably last long travel series was completed in 2007, I feel as if I've been very busy, but haven't achieved much. The first cull of the '80s Diaries took time, I made two documentaries – 'The Last Day of World War One', well-received, and 'Around the World in 20 Years', which early returns suggest was less well-received.

I've given a lot of talks, mostly for charities – Helen's Trust, the Stammering Centre, CBT, and given up time to front a fundraising film for Oxford University. Have kept my eye in with the Arts World – making a half-hour film with Tim Marlow, talking about the Camden Group and Hammershoi at the RA, as well as opening one of the most praised exhibitions of the year – the Age of Steam at the Walker in Liverpool.

I end the year still unclear as to exactly what I want to do next. The Diaries will take up time, both editing and in publicity, and I've a proposed Calcutta trip for Condé Nast; but in the last months of 2008 I batted away the Death series and the Pepys series.

I mooted Iran as a documentary for 2010 and still feel that's the closest I shall get to a new travel project. I must say I feel much happier to take life at a slower pace. I want to see more, read more, think more, even.

2009

Friday, January 2nd

After a pre-theatre supper, taxi down with Terry and Anna to see the penultimate night of 'Spamalot'. The 'House Full' sign is outside the Palace and all 1,350 seats are taken. A good atmosphere inside and I find myself easily seduced by the music, colour, energy of performance, inventiveness of staging and choreography – or as Terry puts it, the suspension of my critical faculties. Backstage to have some champagne with Sanjeev [who plays King Arthur] – in a remarkably Spartan dressing room – and others in the cast, including the Swedish rock star who won a TV show competition to play the Lady of the Lake. She says she can't really believe she'll be back in Stockholm on Sunday with no more Excalibur to wield.

What I miss from our original performances is the edginess (dreadful fashionable word) – the odd and yet revealing portrayals of English stereotypes of the time – the militarism, the fear of predatory women, the little dark areas of the lives we were brought up with. For this jolly, happy, well-performed show the edges have been rubbed off, any psychological complexities lost.

TJ doesn't like it much. I like it on its own terms. Both of us agree the Lancelot gay musical sequence is our least favourite. Herbert wasn't *gay*, Terry insists. But apparently Eric and John (who played Lancelot) thought he was. TJ and I, as writers, disagree. So we're right.

Monday, January 5th

Continuing very cold. Light snow in Oak Village. Murky morning light. Philip Hensher begins his Independent column 'Michael Palin is a kindly and intelligent soul'. What more could one want for encouragement on a grey, freezing morning. Then he goes on 'but one thing I doubt he would ever claim to be is a pillar of English literature.' It's all to do with 'Pole to Pole', along with 'Fever Pitch' and others, being used on the GCSE syllabus as an introduction to English literature.

It does puzzle me, I must admit, but I've taken considerable pleasure in the agitation it causes others and the delight that such headaches as 'Shakespeare, Dickens and Palin. Discuss' in today's Indie, bring me. And there are encouraging signs that I'm regaining the name Palin after a year in which it was in danger of being subsumed by Sarah.

This was to have been the day of a Three Yorkshireman reunion – but Alan B can't make it. He's having some 'tests' this week and, as he said to Barry 'I won't be at my best.' Barry C keen to meet up anyway. Barry arrives at L'Etoile and we tuck ourselves into one of the glassed-in booths by the window and toast our absent friend. We happily reminisce and catch up on news of our contemporaries – Frost, Cleese, Corbett et al. Barry smiles as he remarks on how Ronnie C's voice is getting deeper and deeper as the years go by, and he muses, with a touch of unmalicious regret, that he and Terry [his wife] 'never get asked to the Frost parties.' We're a little like Shallow and Silence, but we laugh a lot more.

At three we're out on Charlotte Street, one of my enduringly favourite London streets, and the wind whips cruelly cold air down past us as Barry shields his lighter and pulls on a Consulate. Like the old days.

Thursday, January 8th

Lots of emails. Ominous signs from the Bill and Ben documentary. Ben anxiously asking if we'll (that is TG, TJ and myself) sign a letter assuring contributors that this is a bona fide documentary with full support of well . . . us. Except Eric, of course. Then there's an email from [producer] Margarita Doyle asking me if I'll help them sort out John Cleese, who's proving very difficult to pin down for interview.

Friday, January 9th

This prolonged and intense cold spell, which has lasted since Boxing Day, is due to break over the weekend. I'll miss it. I quite like the frozen certainty of the days. The lack of rush and hustle in the weather transmit to my working arrangements. I feel equally unrushed and unhustled as I hunker down in my room, looking out over ice-glazed roofs and puffs of steam from heating outlets rising visibly into the cold air. The heavy lumbering pigeons which flap and struggle in the creeper during the autumn have moved on and the garden is visited by smaller, more delicate birds – robins, tits, a wren or two. It's all very reassuring in a world in which little else is. The unemployment figures rise, the national debt grows. The Israelis, with their hard single-minded anger, are smashing Gaza – and somehow making themselves believe that three Israeli deaths are worth six hundred Palestinian deaths.

To see Tracy the physio for the first time in over five years. She rapidly diagnoses my left knee problem and begins her un-tender ministrations aimed at relieving tightness of the tissue around the knee. I try to make chatty conversation but at times only a gasp of pain will do. At least it's not cartilage or anything necessitating an op. If I do my exercises she thinks one more torture, sorry *therapy*, session will deal with it. And I can run again.

Monday, January 19th

This, they say – whoever *they* are – is officially the worst day of the year. Post-Christmas, mid-winter, bills to be paid for end of year excesses etc. It runs to type this morning. Steady rain as H clambers out of bed to go to the gym. Still too dark to make out the time on the clock beside the bed. Hunker down until growing guilt at wasting a day hauls me up at half past seven.

The news is suitably unpleasant. Bank of Scotland group, which includes my bank Coutts, is about to reveal the biggest yearly loss in British history, the result of bad decisions taken by such as *Sir* Fred Goodwin, which have colossal and far-reaching consequences yet to be fully revealed. Apocalyptic amounts of money lost.

Watch a timely, quite simple but very powerful film called 'Private' – about a Palestinian's house in the Occupied Territories which is commandeered by the Israeli army. Speaks very effectively to us Westerners for whom space, a room of our own is a basic necessity. There are no rockets, bombs or surgical strikes here, just the slow erosion of privacy – occupation of the body – and the mind.

Thursday, January 22nd

Rather enjoyable interview for what I thought was a genial Scandinavian press agency, but turns out to be for a Norwegian women's magazine. I'm aware of the need to be upbeat in interviews after my disastrous if honest attempt to convey worldweariness in the Telegraph's Nigel Farndale interview. Editorialised down to an essay in self-doubt, it's prompted seriously concerned calls from Michael Katakis and a letter from an ex-Salopian teacher counselling me not to despair and quoting from the Bible!

Later, to the British Museum to follow up some of the leads from my Herodotus reading. They've led me to the Assyrian galleries and the Parthenon gallery – absolutely superb sculptures – such grace and style and vigour – and this when we were putting up Stonehenge?

Tuesday, January 27th

Rita Gardner has rung and asked if I will consider being next president of the RGS [the Royal Geographical Society, of which Rita was the director].

To the Natural History Museum – a rich, ornate but never pompous building, which has benefited from £110 million refurb. (Another example of money spent well in the fat Heritage lottery years.) Mike Dixon [director of the museum] is hosting a gathering to raise funds for a gallery which will be dedicated to the enormous, half-million-strong collection of illustrations that the museum has and is rarely seen by the public. Including the first ever visual depiction of a kangaroo to be seen in the West.

Thursday, January 29th

Two days of potentially heavy feasting ahead – well, three, if you include last night, and on Tracy's advice, no running until the Achilles is less sore. I began, a little dubiously, to take statins from Monday. Only 10g a night but I'm still quite self-conscious about it – and what it might do.

To lunch at the Travellers with Frank Gardner – a thank-you, I suppose, for writing a foreword to his book [a memoir of his travelling life called 'Far Horizons']. By chance, and in very clubbish fashion, I've bumped into Lord Conway, who's the current president of the RGS. 'We want to talk to you,' he says – but I tell him Rita already has. 'And . . . are you interested?' Of course, but need time to think it through. His parting words don't altogether convince me. 'I've done it whilst doing a full-time job at the same time.' I've got several full-time jobs, I tell him, which isn't quite the joke I think he thinks it is.

Frank Gardner says the Travellers Club attracted him 'because it's full of spooks', and he casts his eye round just to check. The assault on Gaza has given a serious boost to jihadists, he feels, just as the hardliners were beginning to lose their influence. He shakes his head in frustration at the BBC – and Sky News – decision not to run the DEC [Disasters Emergency Committee] appeal. He can understand the theory, but the subtleties and nuances of the BBC's decision will not be appreciated in the wider world where it will be seen as yet more evidence of Western bias towards Israel. The recent thwarted attempt to bring down a series of airliners over the Atlantic was much more well-advanced and deadly than most people were aware of.

At the Union Terry and I meet up again with Barry Booth [musician, with whom myself and Terry J had collaborated on an album of songs called 'Diversions']. He has been with a wonderful woman called Liz for twenty-five years or so. She's the head of a primary school in Lewisham and when Terry gets worked up over Tony Blair's 'despicable' failure in education (for instance) she stoutly corrects him and says that she has only praise for the resources given to schools as a result of Blair's commitment. Terry, who tends to only see things in black and white, good and evil, Terry or not Terry, is chastened and the debate then becomes much more reasonable and less of a rant.

Sunday, February 8th

As part of my Calcutta prep [I'd been commissioned to write a travel piece for Condé Nast Traveller]' I go with Rachel to see Satyajit Ray's 'Days and Nights in the Forest' at the Barbican. Rachel spotted it was on, of course. On the way to pick her up, I and my driver, who is either Indian or Pakistani, fall to discussing 'Slumdog Millionaire', the Danny Boyle film which is the favourite for BAFTA honours tonight. He hadn't liked it – nor had the ten friends he'd gone with. 'This is not an Indian film,' he feels, 'it's a Westerner's view of India.' He didn't even find it very exciting.

Monday, February 9th

To the RGS to meet up with Rita Gardner and Andrew Linnell, who want to pitch the presidency to me. A certain feeling of urgency as Rita has her bags packed awaiting her departure for Australia tonight. Andrew is head teacher of a comprehensive in Maidenhead, I think, an impressive man, quietly authoritative and competent. It would be a big commitment . . . three years, three General Councils to chair annually and expectation of my chairing dozens of evening lectures. I need some time to think it over. Before I leave I wander the tall, draughty rooms of Lowther Lodge, purchased for the Society in 1912 by Lord Curzon. His portrait, by Singer Sargent, hangs over the fireplace. He looks magnificent in all his finery – 'President of the Society 1911–1913'. Various members of staff hurry by, purposefully, behind me. I wonder what they think of me, gazing up at Lord Curzon like the little boy looking up at the train driver.

To RIBA [Royal Institute of British Architects] for lunch. They always seem to have a table free and because it's not just a public restaurant, there's a sense of style and purpose to the building which adds a touch of gravitas. A suitable place, I feel, to think hard about the commitment that the RGS Presidency demands. I order fish pie and a glass of wine and make a list of PROS and CONS. The PROS outweigh the CONS quite considerably. Have to remind myself to think through all the negatives and not just surrender to the euphoria I feel about being asked and being here, in one of my favourite London interiors, with a glass of white wine before me.

Wednesday, February 11th

Morning of decision. Although I'm inclined to accept the RGS role, I have last-minute collywobbles about time it will take up and the greyness of the geographical world – after all, these are scientists and schoolmasters, not my usual parish.

Sun pours in as I raise the blinds in my workroom and before anything else I sit down and make some last-minute checks – look at the RGS website and its latest programme and also scan a list of the 66 previous presidents since the Society was founded in 1830. Among a lot of multi-titled grandees, legendary names like Fuchs and Shackleton have held the presidency. The fact that I'm being given a chance to join them is both thrilling and intimidating – and it's the status of the Society that finally pushes me into composing my email of acceptance to Rita in Australia. Tap the 'send' button and confirm one of the more significant decisions of my life.

Andrew Linnell calls later. He's very pleased. He reassures me that I have wide support. Ten years ago my nomination might have been contentious, on the grounds of my not having the right background, but things have changed, the Society's changed and become much more inclusive. Still, this is a promotion and I shall be forced to raise my game! Helen a strong advocate of my accepting.

I walk briskly up to Highgate. Meet TJ and TG and a friend of Terry's in the Prince of Wales. Apparently a recent survey showed 'Brazil' among the top 25 films of the hard right in America. TG reminds us that Timothy McVeigh, the Oklahoma bomber, used 'Tuttle' and 'Buttle' [from 'Brazil'] as aliases. And I remind us that Sirhan Sirhan, the man who shot Bobby Kennedy, was a Python fan.

Sunday, February 15th

Anxieties about my RGS decision come and go, but my immediate anxiety is to think of something to say at Jonathan Benson's 70th birthday party which Milly is organising this afternoon.[1]

Jonathan beams, Buddha-like, and makes an odd, distracted speech which involves lots of jokes about famous people who've sent telegrams. Corin Redgrave, Jonathan's oldest friend, is there. He's had some sort of stroke. He's either out in the garden smoking, or asking people very loudly for a cigarette. I have a perfectly sensible conversation with him – he's been playing his one-man show – Oscar Wilde's 'De Profundis' in Paris. Later I hear that he has a Tourette-like

---

1 Jonathan was first assistant director on *Life of Brian*, and *A Fish Called Wanda*, and Milly art director on *Jabberwocky* and other TG films.

propensity to proposition women in the most lewd way, and later does so to one of the guests. Completely out of nowhere – 'C' word and all. He used to be an elegant, good-looking man, but his head seems to have thickened and his complexion reddened and he looks like some dyspeptic Prussian general. Very sad.

My few words of tribute seem to be appreciated, but unfortunately as soon as I start talking, so does a yellow cockatoo.

February 21st to March 1st: Calcutta for Condé Nast Traveller

Monday, March 2nd

Halfway through last night I woke with a sore stomach, and spent some of the early hours nursing it, carefully, clutching a hot-water bottle and looking through the well-illustrated book on [the American painter] Andrew Wyeth which was sent to me before I left by the ever-eager Mhairi McNeill. I'm taken with his work. A very fine draughtsman and a very strong sense of place – the fields and farms of Maine and Connecticut – which I can see making a strong impact on screen. Also aware of the similarities with Hammershoi. Bare, stripped-back canvases – never crowded, never fussy. That same sense of stillness. By the time my stomach has calmed and I make my way to a cold bed for the last two hours of this broken night, I'm excited by the prospect of a film on Wyeth.

Wednesday, March 4th

Meet [my photographer friend] Peter Robinson for lunch at the Frontline Club, in a fairly nondescript neighbourhood beside St Mary's Hospital in Paddington. The club was founded in 2003 for journalists and photographers, and copies of books by various correspondents – like Jeremy Bowen – are on display. Peter sits in the corner reading a small yellow hardback called 'Against Happiness'. I ask him about it. 'It's about the joys of melancholy,' he says, rather cheerfully, adding, 'I love melancholy.'

He lives out of London now, up in Rutland. 'It's very white,' he says, and I envisage snowy fields stretching into the distance until he adds, 'after Bermondsey.'

The fatigue that has settled on me since returning from Calcutta begins to weigh down and I head back home. My taxi driver chatters away. 'I had that feeling this morning – you know the feeling of the sun, warm against my face, for the first time this year. There's a word for that isn't there,' he goes on. 'That feeling of the sun on your face for the first time after the winter.' Neither of us can think of the word.

March 7th to March 8th: Sofia Film Festival

Monday, March 9th: Sofia–London

I'd anticipated the trip to Bulgaria [for the film festival] with some dread – being a duty rather than a pleasure; coming at such a busy time, last straw sort of negative thinking. As it happens it's been a wonderfully restorative weekend. I was very well-quartered, well-looked-after, well-fed, constantly praised and had two of the best nights' sleep in a fortnight.

Woke to sunshine then a leisurely breakfast and a walk round the compact and accessible main centre of the Bulgarian capital, including a happy half-hour in the small Archaeological Museum which I discovered on 'New Europe' filming – dazzling technical and artistic skills of the Thracians (who Herodotus rated very highly).

The news of two soldiers shot by Republicans in Belfast soured the day. Something I'd hoped had been consigned to the past, but in truth, never really believing that the peace process had eradicated the idea of a united Ireland.

Thursday, March 12th

In the evening I have been asked to address the Fountain Club at Barts Hospital. The audience – which is, I'm told, a near record 111 – all seem to be of a certain age – consultants, surgeons. Sit near a very chatty lady whose speciality is young boys' penises. Apparently one in every hundred has the hole slightly off centre which can have problems and requires sitting down to pee. She's very much against circumcision; in almost every case unnecessary; she admires the skill of the Jewish circumciser but says there are Muslims who will chop the foreskin off at six years old – 'on the kitchen table'. Only at a gathering of medics could one start a conversation with a woman about foreskins – and then, when you know each other better – go on to the weather.

Saturday, March 21st

Rumblings of trouble at the RGS. The Financial Times Weekend section leads with a piece by Justin Marozzi asking why the Society was no longer sending out big 'signature' expeditions under the RGS banner – to explore the world.

His small group of what look to be quite privileged, articulate, desert travellers, are pushing hard against what sounds like a reluctant RGS, to make some change to policy. They've succeeded in forcing an SGM – Special General Meeting. I groan inwardly, but am a little reassured by Rita's email which suggests that all this will be sorted out in the dying months of Gordon Conway's presidency. I slightly resent the fact that this was not flagged up at the meeting with her and Andrew when I specifically enquired about problems and issues.

Monday, March 23rd

A good talk on the phone with Rita. The 'Desert Mafia' (my phrase, not hers) are in a considerable minority and most of the Society seems happy with the way that the present policy works. Rita says she's heard from Ranulph Fiennes, for instance, to reassure her that whichever way the vote goes in May, won't affect his commitment to the RGS. He, she says, is aware that the RGS can no longer spend its limited funds on 'adventure'.

Thursday, March 26th

Down to the British Museum for a Patrons' view of an exhibition in the Print Gallery (rapidly becoming one of my favourite places to visit – good material, well lit and displayed). All work done on paper either in pastel/crayon or graphite, much of it Scots – Thomas Lawrence, Ramsay and Skirving – eighteenth and nineteenth century. The attraction being that they were done quite quickly and the subjects are relaxed and natural and informal. An ink sketch of Turner (in the 1820s) looking at work in the BM's Print Room is a delight. I've never seen the great man caught like this, so absorbed in appreciation of someone else's work. Also a surprise self-portrait of Sir Joshua Reynolds when young – he looks like one of the Bee Gees.

Tuesday, March 31st

Woken by recurring music jingle from Archie's 'Bob the Builder' book. At half past seven I go in to find him standing leaning on his bed reading a book. 'Hello, Grandpa. *I'm* all right.' Wants his book read to him and selects a step for us to sit on together.

Much activity in the sky this evening. Barack Obama is arriving in London for the G20 talks, and unfamiliar helicopters are buzzing about. Marine One should be crossing quite close to us on the way from Stansted to the

American ambassador's residence in Regent's Park. About eight o'clock a big black '24'-style helicopter duly rumbles overhead, moving swiftly south-west. President or decoy? Later, I watch the most recent episode of '24' – just to know what's *really* happening.

Tuesday, April 7th

At midday I leave to go down to South Kensington for lunch and a pitch from Mike Dixon of the Natural History Museum to try and enlist my help in fundraising.

They have a volume of Audubon's Birds, a hefty book over a metre high. Consummately beautiful work, and Judith, the efficient, humorous, authoritative curator, has to don gloves to look at it. A first edition of Darwin with accompanying letter to a friend. Confirms what a normal, thoughtful, friendly, agreeable almost ordinary sort of Victorian Darwin was. Also fine wildlife illustrations from Captain Cook's voyages.

In the evening to Frost's 70th at the Lanesborough. We're separated for the meal and I'm on David's table between [philanthropist] Helen Hamlyn and Prince Constantine of Greece's regal Danish wife, Queen Anne-Marie. Others at the table include John Scarlett, the head of MI5, and [ex-MP] David Owen.

The odd Mr Scarlett has a thick neck and close-cropped balding pate. His eyes flick about and he doesn't seem to be particularly relaxed. Not long into the meal, a heavy comes in, whispers something and they both leave. Of course, we're left assuming the worst – al-Qaeda attack? Pakistan nuclear secrets found in North Korea? He comes back an hour later, giving little away. Of course.

Speeches by Ronnie Corbett – who gamely sings his way through a song he's written, 'Frostie!'. Then wise old bird Tim Rice whose quotes from Spandau Ballet are witty but lose most of the guests. Alastair Campbell, who makes the mistake of reading summaries of all the mentions of Frost in 'The Blair Years', giving the impression that it was his party rather than David's. Wilf Frost is an excellent MC. David cuts the cake, does jokes as if he were at a Rotary lunch and we all mingle before being led by Julie Felix turning the clock back and singing 'Forever Young' to David.

Late night and almost too many well-known faces. Does David know anyone ordinary?

Thursday, April 9th

To the RGS to meet the outgoing pres – Gordon Conway – and be shown around by Rita. Gordon and I talk at the huge table in the council chamber. He's an academic – an expert on climate change who was vice-chancellor of Sussex and ran the Rockefeller Foundation in New York for seven years, deciding on the whereabouts of millions of pounds of grant money. He's operated at the highest levels of government.

I'm not exactly put at my ease, but he's encouraging about things like the Monday lectures, assuring me that minimum preparation is required and that the vote of thanks doesn't need to be formal. 'They're good fun!' he says.

Rita takes me to meet various heads of department (they have a full-time staff of 50) and I'm impressed by the new reading room for the Archives – and glimpses of the collection of maps, atlases, photos and artefacts that are the legacy of 180 years of RGS expeditions and research.

Wednesday, April 15th

Walk to the office, enjoy picking my way through the back streets. And as I walk I sort out my thoughts and come to the conclusion that the next big thing I should do is write a second novel. Have an idea – 'The Truth' – story of writer nearing retirement age who's asked to write a new biography – or a newspaper piece about a blameless and successful and respected man, who the editor/publisher feels needs 'reappraising'. All about the misuse of the word truth.

Thursday, April 16th

Forty-three years since we married – fifty years since we first met and we're still content, perhaps more so than at many times during the hurly-burly years of Python and beyond. In an odd way I think the travel series – with the combination of personal confidence and long periods away from each other – helped us both become aware of the strength of the relationship.

After a busy morning at the Diaries, I tidy everything up and take them to the office where, in a mad rush of papers, printings and last-minute corrections, the final text is prepared and handed over to Michael Dover. A process of elimination that began over a year ago is, for now, complete.

Michael asks me what I'm going to do now – not, I think, quite expecting such an explicit answer. I'm going to write a novel. I've told Helen and Steve earlier today and now I tell him, seeing as he's asked. I even tell him the rough idea of 'The Truth'. So the afternoon ends on a heady note. A book delivered, my tenth in the last 20 years, and a new one born at the same time.

Celebrate at V&P in the evening, with Mary B. Lovely meal. Gilliam arrives later. Paul [maître d'] talks of Clement Freud, a great V&P stalwart who died this morning aged 84. Paul tells us that Freud had organised a party here for his 85th – due in nine days time. He had apparently put off a triple heart by pass op until after the party.

Sunday, April 19th

Gilliam comes round for lunch – on his own, full of enthusiasm. He's hoping that 'The Imaginarium' will open in Cannes. The French want it in competition.

Everyone – well Amy Gilliam mostly – trying hard to get the stars. TG speaks in some awe of the Depp machine. Fifty people work for him, he's able to commission a screenplay of every book that takes his fancy and word is he's been offered 65 million dollars, plus royalty points, for the next Pirates of the Caribbean movie. TG doesn't think any of this is doing Johnny much good.

Monday, April 20th

On my way into town on the underground a youngish man who walks with a stick settles down opposite me. 'Do I remind you of someone?' he asks, smiling. 'Someone you've worked with?' He presents a profile but I still don't get the clue. 'Bryan Pringle!' Ah, *now* I see it – the scout in 'American Friends', the guard at the gates in 'Jabberwocky'. A lovely, warm man and unfussy actor. His son, my companion, is called Craster Pringle and has a sad story to tell. He was himself an actor, but has had to give all that up as he has some muscular, or bone condition which keeps him in almost permanent pain. He's on morphine much of the time. He's got a good strong face and he's soft-spoken and seems most considerate. No hint of bitterness. I feel helpless but our conversation, which ends when he hobbles off at Euston, seems to have a resonance which I can't put out of my mind as I join the crowds in the Piazza and make my own, fortunate way to my comfortable fresh-painted office, to discuss my next two books which are to be given the publisher's full support and attention. Craster is writing. He says it's about the only thing he can do now. In some odd way I envy him being able to live with pain. As though he's achieved some victory that makes him a better man than me.

Wednesday, April 29th

At Tavistock Street I spend an hour being interviewed by the two Freeman brothers for an OUP [Oxford University Press] short guide to Anxiety. I enjoy their company a lot. Glad to be able to express myself, and they're encouraging and easy to talk to. Such a relief to be able to talk about such intimate things as one's own sense of anxiety, without fearing how one's remarks will come out in a newspaper. Anxiety exists, it's part of the process of doing what I do – and never goes away altogether, however much experience one has, though experience does help you to manage and recognise how anxiety affects you.

Felt rather good at the end of the hour. I needed to be opened up – normal anti-press defences were unnecessary. 'We didn't choose you because we thought you might suffer from serious anxiety,' Daniel reassured me. I suggested that he should read my diary if he wanted an insight into the strains and stresses of the creative process. Whereupon one of these eminent clinical psychologists reached in his bag and produced a well-thumbed copy of 'The Python Years'!

After this intense but liberating hour, another equally intense, but oddly more disturbing hour spent on an interview and photoshoot with a Somali man, who after five years as an asylum seeker in this country has at last been given refugee status. Musa speaks English well, has a quick sense of humour. He is quietly, but firmly critical of the system here – whilst at the same time telling me that the Somalis who were given asylum in Scandinavia came over to the UK because they can set up businesses much more easily here.

We talk about the pace of life here, the compartmentalisation of the British, their un-African love of privacy. What I want to say, but can't, is that the reason he's here is because it's better than where he was. But I think, at heart, he knows that. An impressive young man.

Saturday, May 2nd

The sun shines, beneath the burgeoning wisteria outside my room a pigeon settles on its nest. All calm and quiet. The phone rings, it's Gordon Conway. The first time he's ever rung me at home. 'Your name's on the ballot papers now, so you may well get a few calls.' He's referring to the adventurers v the Society issue, which will be voted on at an SGM on 18th May. 'It's beginning to get quite nasty,' he warns. But most of all he wants to make sure that I'm 'on-side', and not going to spoil the last month of his presidency by encouraging the rebels. Feel half thrilled, half appalled at what I've got myself into.

Sunday, May 3rd

John Hemming, the man who was for me the face of the RGS, writes in support of the 'explorers' in the Observer this morning – ahead of the May 18 vote. Since Gordon's call I see the whole thing more clearly now, and later I read the 'Beagle' Campaign's website and it confirms my feelings. They feel that the emphasis of the RGS and its work has been slanted towards academics, theory and education, and away from action. There is much more lurking beneath the surface of RGS politics than will ever be dealt with on the 18th. This will run and run and I'm in the firing line for the next three years. (Sorry about the ragout of metaphors.)

Tuesday, May 5th

Sixty-six today. I have scheduled some work at Broadcasting House – reading my introduction to the Children in Need 'Around the World in 80 Days' enterprise,[1] which starts next week, and then to another studio where Mariella Frostrup is to talk about my five favourite books for 'Open Book'. Though I'm there at the appointed time neither Mariella, nor her producer, has arrived. I contact Paul to find out what's going on, and he eventually gets back to me to say that they're looking for a birthday card for me.

Mariella is brisk and efficient and bright without flaunting it. We get on well. 'Arabian Nights', 'Down With Skool', 'Zen and the Art of Motorcycle Maintenance', 'Raj Quartet', Virginia Woolf's Diaries all get time – though not much. Then back down to BH reception where Colm Tóibín awaits – he's the rest of the programme. A big man with a pugilist's face – I want to go up and congratulate him on the wonderful book of his I read recently, but can't remember the title, so slip away, feeling rather cowardly. (It was 'The Master'.)

TJ and Anna round. Their impending child (outline recently revealed to the world by a Daily Mail snapper) is a girl. To be called Siri.

Wednesday, May 6th

To SOAS to see two films at the Palestinian Film Festival. (A bit of preparation for my visit, now just about two weeks away.) Short films made cheaply, both deal with eyewitness accounts of the loss of Palestinian land, first in 1948, but more particularly after 1967. Lots of undercurrents – some

---

1 A series made to support the Children in Need charity, where twelve celebrities attempted to follow in the footsteps of Phileas Fogg (and me).

Israelis blatantly triumphal, some argue cogently against what their government has done.

Wednesday, May 13th

PalFest trip advice suggests I update my inoculations – typhoid and diphtheria particularly – so I call up the Hospital for Tropical Diseases' Travel Clinic. It's 9.30 and a brusque recorded voice tells me 'the Travel Clinic is closed. We are open from 9 o'clock in the morning until 5.30'. I call again, at 10 o'clock only to be told they're closed and open at 9 o'clock. Eventually I get through and a recorded voice tells me that 'all our receptionists are busy, please leave your name and number and we'll call you back.' They never do. It takes a fourth call to actually fix anything up.

Spend some time talking to Rita G. She sounds weary and quite upset about some of the things that have been said in the press about her and Gordon's stewardship by the Beagle campaign.

Friday, May 15th

Could have done with another quiet day to consolidate all the clearing and sorting, but eager emails from Rémy Renoux[1] who is in London and Alexander Gorkow, the Munich journalist who interviewed me a year ago, who's also briefly in London (for the Eric Clapton Albert Hall concert) have forced me to re-plan. So I'm at the office by a quarter to eleven and meet and have a coffee with the ebullient Rémy – a sort of French Terry J, with less indignation.

Then the two tall Germans – Alexander and Julia – appear from up the stairs and we move together across to 2 Brydges where we talk rather earnestly about politics. The week-long revelations of some of our MPs fiddling their expenses is all everyone's talking about. 'Cleaning moats', 'Trouser presses'. As I say to Alexander, 'We don't even do corruption very well.' Michele the waiter heartily agrees, 'you should learn from Italy,' he grins.

Monday, May 18th

As I'm walking back from the Red Lion & Sun, after a pint and supper with TJ and Anna, we're intercepted just before turning off Grove Lane by a black-clad security guard. He hails Terry familiarly but then, more sotto voce, warns

1 Rémy was the producer behind the French stage version of Monty Python's Flying Circus.

him that there's a man with a camera in a grey Mercedes parked a little way up Grove Lane. Terry doesn't seem too worried; it had happened recently to him and Anna after they'd had a meal at a pub in Lavenham.

Tuesday, May 19th

I'm doing my exercises when I hear H sounding very wrathful. When I return to the bathroom she's full of indignation because an Evening Standard reporter has just rung the doorbell and asked if he can speak to me about the RGS. It's only twenty to eight. We're not dressed and so H sent him off with a flea in his ear. The bell goes a half-hour later. At least I've had a cup of tea by then, and I've also seen a piece in the Independent which is how I know that the Beagle group lost the vote by 63 per cent to 38 per cent at last night's Special General Meeting. I assume that's what his visit is all about, but he assures me that he just wants my general thoughts on the subject. I give him my views and tell him I'm not making any longer statements until I'm officially president and can find out a little more about the job.

He seems happy – young man with a reporter's notebook, I see – and goes off. Ten minutes later the phone rings and it's his editor at the Evening Standard who registers quite unconvincing mock disapproval of the door-stepper's tactics and then tries to get an interview himself. The outcome of all this hassle is a feature in the Standard later in the morning. Under the headline 'Palin ventures into uncharted waters as head of warring geographers' is a reasonably straightforward account of the situation, quoting what I'd said earlier, illustrated with a photograph of Terry, Anna and myself in Grove Lane, Highgate late last night.

So I've been door-stepped and 'papped' in 12 hours. I never thought geography would be this exciting.

Wednesday, May 20th

Meeting with Rita and Gordon at the RGS. We digest the vote, the possible knock-on effects. Rita says the group is driven by a small core of younger members, but Robin Hanbury-Tenison may have been fanning the flames. The Times and The Spectator have been particularly unpleasant – with Charles Moore writing the most vindictive piece about Rita. Very bitter, but unfortunately very eloquent.

Thursday, May 21st

To early evening showing of 'Encounters at the End of the World' – Werner Herzog's view of Antarctica. Concentrates largely on people like himself – eccentric, poetic, odd and singular – and he searches out animal behaviour to match. Memorable image of the single penguin heading off to the mountains. Choosing, apparently quite willingly, not to stay with the flock or head for the water as a group of others do. The lone penguin stops, looks around and goes off in a completely different direction – and it won't survive.

May 22nd to May 27th: Palestine Literary Festival

Wednesday, May 27th: Bethlehem–Tel Aviv–London

Alarm wakes me at five past two. I've been asleep for an hour and a half. Leave by far the most comfortable room I've had on this short trip – in the splendid one-time home of the Jacir family, kicked out in what they call the Nakba (The Catastrophe) – which followed the creation of the state of Israel in 1948 – and into a taxi waiting to take me to Tel Aviv airport.

The physical appearance of Bethlehem is not at all what I'd expected. This is not the little town of Bethlehem I sing about at Christmas; it's big – as big as say Henley or Evesham – with plenty of the bland modern concrete blocks that have risen all over the Holy Land in the last ten or fifteen years. At the end of the street the great dividing wall shoulders the Palestinians aside. Rachel's tomb, a centre of pilgrimage, can no longer be reached because it is behind the wall. Only three minutes' walk from the hotel is Aida refugee camp where nearly 5,000 Palestinians who lost their land and homes to Israeli expansion now live with the help of the UN.

We speed through the empty streets of Bethlehem and out into the countryside where, for the first time, I feel a sense of the Biblical Bethlehem. Then, at the bottom of the hill, a security checkpoint. I'm peered at by a very young man who doesn't smile. My driver advises me that if I'm stopped at airport security, I shouldn't mention that I've been anywhere in the West Bank. 'Tell them you're a tourist and you've been staying in Jerusalem. And if they ask how you know me, tell them I am the driver sent by the hotel.' In the event, I'm not questioned, just stared at and waved on again, so I've over two and a half hours to kill.

A violent British film – 'The Football Factory' – is playing on the screens in the un-smart, rather Soviet-style business lounge. Men kicking the shit out of each other as mothers in the lounge change their baby's nappy.

Thursday, June 4th

Out of the house soon after half past eight. To Martin G [my dentist] to have impressions, colour matches etc. taken before installation of my six implant teeth later in the month. A rather uncomfortable 75 minutes, with much stretching and squelching about in the mouth.

Round the corner to the Wallace Collection and restored my mental equilibrium in the company of Dutch foodscapes, English grandees and voluptuous French nudes. Then lunch with Steve, Mhairi and Elinor to discuss the possibility of making a programme about Andrew Wyeth independently of the BBC. By the end of the meal, all of us having agreed in principle to filming dates in late March, early April, my mind is beginning to race towards the afternoon at the RGS – my first visit there since becoming president.

As it turns out, it's much less demanding than I'd feared. I spend two hours with Rita, sitting at Livingstone's table, going through business ahead. No direct approaches to me from the Beaglers yet, tho' Justin Marozzi reportedly criticised Gordon's last speech on Monday for completely ignoring the SGM result. Marozzi spluttering on about a 'Stalinist' state.

The party that I've laid on for the staff is popular and pretty well-attended. I've given quite a lot of thought to what I should say to them all but the gist is in the opening, when I tell them I think it appropriate that my first Presidential Address should be to the most important people in the Society – without whom it wouldn't be what it is etc. Talk to a lot of people, try and project an easy and relaxed style. I've decided that I'm not going to change to accommodate the presidency – rather the other way round.

We vote – for who is going to represent us in the European Parliament Elections. Enormous list. Twenty-two names on the ballot paper. The electoral officer is having to push down the ballot papers into the big tin box with a long white plastic spatula.

Sunday, June 7th

Tom rings and rather sheepishly confesses that he's twisted, sprained or maybe even broken his ankle whilst kiting on the Heath last night. A gust caught his mighty 7-metre canopy and lifted him some 20 feet in the air. He asks if we've got any crutches. Rachel, eight months pregnant, was not impressed by Tom's feat – or indeed Tom's feet.

Monday, June 8th

Am rhapsodising about the paperback of 'Hemingway Adventure', first copies of which I've only seen today, when my jaw drops, eyes stare and a familiar feeling – that of printing chaos – comes over me like a physical blow. This time it's not a typo or even a feast of typos. Thirty-one pages *of a completely different book* have been bound into the text. On page 88 we're coasting through Spain, then page 87 of a book on the Housing Crisis in Britain appears, followed by twenty pages on Slum Clearance Renewal.

On the other hand there is a fulsome email awaiting me from my French publisher, Hoëbeke, desperately keen to publish another of my travel books in French. So, for every cloud . . .

Wednesday, June 10th

Helen takes an Ad Lee to the St John & St Eliz at a quarter to seven. She's operated on in the morning and when I call at 12.15 she's in recovery. But the op has gone well and she has an artificial ball and socket joint in her right thumb.

Thursday, June 11th

Have been asked to write another foreword – this time for a Barry Cryer biography. Barry himself asked apparently. So, as I'm in a limbo before the RGS Council papers come through and as I wait to hear word from H at the hospital, I set to. It writes itself – swiftly and, I think, with the right edge of humour and silliness leavening the praise.

Saturday, June 13th

At half past three I leave for BBC Radio 2 interview. A band called the Maniacs have been on live and Jarvis Cocker and friend wander in – tho' he's not performing until after me. I've not met him before, but he is a Sheffield boy and we talk about the city, and our fondness for it despite its habit of getting things wrong. He remembers the Olympic-style pool which was 6' too short. Talk about Park Hill Flats, now gutted, as Urban Splash developers have run out of money – Jarvis and his fellow musicians' eyes light up – 'yeah, they're like a great pigeon coop.' Jarvis, who looks like the myopic school swat, comes to life, waving his arms around in imitation of giant pigeons. We all agree that the great thing about Sheffielders is they're unimpressed.

My 40 minutes at the mike go smoothly. Apparently, Archie listened at home, and kept saying 'Hello Grandpa' to the radio.

Monday, June 15th

The first council meeting under my presidency. At three o'clock we assemble around the council table. It's a grand room, but a little dusty and shabby, its long, languid curtains drifting up to the ceiling. Mostly men around the table – all conventionally turned out, apart from Barnaby Lenon, the new Vice-President for Expeditions and Fieldwork. He is the only one, apart from myself, who seems to take in the faded splendour of the surroundings. 'Ceiling could do with a bit of work,' he notes. I think we've similar thoughts here.

The discussions on the SGM are useful – general feeling that we must communicate our strengths, blow our own trumpet and talk to our members and fellows more. I can see there's much to do. Tensions in the Society need to be resolved. Light must be let in.

Tuesday, June 16th

Wake up thinking that perhaps my best course of action in the RGS debate might be to make contact with John Hemming [director of the Society before Rita Gardner], and, on a purely private, old friend basis, find out what's really bugging the core group, how deep their disaffection goes and so on. Put this to Rita later. She doesn't react with much enthusiasm. Worried, I think, that I might be seen to give the Beaglers some hope, and myself a lot of hassle from others once they've heard. I'm more worried about being seen to be cut off from those such as John who I associate so much with the RGS that it seems almost perverse not to talk to him.

Tuesday, June 23rd

Terry tells me that all the rest of the Pythons are going to New York in October for a red carpet premiere of the Bill and Ben documentary, despite all the initial reluctance to even take part and a specific condition of our taking part being that we don't endorse it by attending a premiere. So everyone's changed their mind and I think TJ hopes I will too. Only problem is that I've a big, already advertised fundraiser in Sheffield that same night.

Weather's warming up into summer heat, finally, and there's an almost Mediterranean feel to the Heath as I walk through the long, wispy grass and down the majestic oak avenue on my way from Terry's house to meet up with Will and [his friend] Jim Bobin at the Wells Tavern in Hampstead Village. Jim a dad twice over now; he's writing and directing 'Flight of the Conchords' in LA. I hope it doesn't make Will feel he's missed out. He seems happy enough. And he is very funny. *He* should be the one writing TV comedy.

Wednesday, July 1st

Interview with Mike McCarthy of the Indie – my first specifically about my presidency of the RGS. He's a Python fan and clearly finds it a little unexpected to be talking about interdisciplinary expeditions to a man who's said 'Welease Wodewick'. A good hour's chat. I try to think of how and what I should say, but the spontaneous is much more fun.

Andy Murray coasts through to the Wimbledon semi-final. The nation prepares to celebrate.[1]

Thursday, July 2nd

The heat goes on. I complete all the various pieces for the RGS – autumn bulletins, a president's report I call President's Progress, and my thoughts on the appeal – and set off in late afternoon to see Rita before she goes on holiday. I have one or two initiatives. 'Michael Meets' [a series of interviews] looks as if it's going to work out. Musa [the Somalian refugee] is willing to give it a go. I suggest commissioning a booklet on the history, architecture and treasures of Lowther Lodge. Also want to do Geography and Art – but need to give it some thought.

Robin Hanbury-Tenison is in the hall as I'm leaving. Neat as Neil MacGregor, but his eyes bigger, casting around like an ageing bushbaby.

To Brown's Hotel in Albemarle Street for a remarkable anniversary. It was here in 1949 that George Weidenfeld and Nigel Nicolson held the launch party of their new publishing company. Sixty years later it's still in business and, thanks to Michael Dover, I have a page to myself in the official celebratory booklet. Most remarkable of all is that George W himself is still in business. He'll be 90 next year.

Antonia Fraser (who began her career in books as his head of publicity) introduces him with wit and warmth, and George, after complaining briefly that the light isn't good enough to see his notes, delivers an impeccably graceful speech without once looking at them.

1 He loses to Andy Roddick 6–4, 4–6, 7–6, 7–6.

Monday, July 6th

Over a busy weekend the Michael McCarthy piece came out in the Independent, harmlessly, but sending out the clearest signal so far to the Beaglers that I'm not going to change the present course of the Society. We shall see.

Tuesday, July 7th

Feeling like staying in bed a few hours longer but the up at 7.30 routine now well-established and it means I'm processed and ready for work at 9. I read a calculation of Benjamin Hayden in 1810 that he who 'began to study' at 6 in the morning had, by the age of fifty, an extra eight years of time in his studying life, over he who started at 8 o'clock. So, I've lost many years to somebody.

Wednesday, July 8th

My writing week is broken up with various unwanted appointments; this morning being my promise to [foreign correspondent] Richard Lindley to go along to the 150th anniversary of the St Pancras Almshouses, just round the corner in Maitland Park. Prince Charles is officially marking the occasion with a visit.

When I arrive parked cars unfortunate enough to be in the direct line of royal approach are being hoisted out of the way. As we queue up to show our invitations 'and two current photographs', a noisy road-brushing vehicle is sweeping the gutter as clean as it's probably ever been.

The houses are quite charming with neat brickwork and pointy gables, but what's best is a wide courtyard garden, in which, today, there is a string quartet playing in a tent and tables set with cups and bits and pieces of food. Talk to Frank Dobson, who is the most modest and unpompous of politicians. The prince and his retinue arrive at 10.15 and I'm required to stand in the rather gloomy interior of the communal hall, with portraits on the wall and maps and plans on the table to await His Highness.

Next to me is Mary Pellegrinetti, the oldest resident, and Charles spends quite a time with her. When he sees me his eyes widen: 'What on *earth* are you doing here?' We have a jocular chat in the course of which I mention my elevation to the RGS presidency. He takes this in and then, with a frown of recall adds, 'Do get them to organise some more of those expeditions.' Oh, dear.

Thursday, July 9th

Putting aside all distractions, I began work on my second novel (well third, if you count the unpublished one). I'm a little disappointed to find that my working title – 'The Truth' – is not unlike Al Franken's book 'The Truth (with Jokes)' – a great title. Still I don't let titles take over and I just launch into the story and feel the dialogue flow and the whole situation comes to life and I really enjoy myself. I have to break for lunch as I've arranged to meet Nick Crane [writer, traveller and television presenter] at the Engineer to continue the conversation about geography and the RGS.

Nick is an excellent companion. He's enthusiastic about my initiatives to bring in new and young members through 'Michael Meets', and I ad-lib the idea of a themed evening which might get public attention. Anything to raise the profile, fly the flag. He thinks I'm in a good position to unite the Society, provided I don't change what I am.

Home and push the novel to nearly 1,000 words on opening day.

Friday, July 10th

Norma Farnes arrives to interview me for a book on Spike Milligan.[1] She's boldly and smartly dressed and has an unflappable Teesside temperament which must have ensured her survival in a job few others could have taken on. Not only Spike, but Galton and Simpson, Johnny Speight and Eric Sykes were her clients during heydays and stormy times. She says that she's doing the interviews with those people she knew Spike respected – like Jonathan Miller and Richard Ingrams. She even uses Spike's old tape recorder, a brick-sized black cassette player with a handle for carrying. Spike, she says, always regretted that he never had a university education. He could be very cruel, and was, she admitted, 'a shit' about a third of the time, but she vigorously defends him against biographer Humphrey Carpenter's charge that he was a shit most of the time.

Spike's depression interests both me and her. In making the 1972 'Other Side of Spike' – a Granada documentary about his return to the psychiatric hospital he'd been in, which I remember for its brutally honest insights – he was driven to another breakdown. Fondly she talks of Eric Sykes, who never complains, and of Ray and Alan[2] – and the day Ray Galton took the unilateral decision not to write again. The pair of them – still friends – go off on gourmet wine tours of France.

1 Norma acted as agent to several comedians and was Spike's agent and manager for more than 35 years.
2 Ray Galton and Alan Simpson wrote, among other things, two of the greatest ever comedy series – *Hancock's Half Hour* and *Steptoe and Son*.

Saturday, July 11th

I go with Rachel to the Renoir to see '35 Rhums', a very touching little story about a father and daughter who live together after their mother's death and look after one another rather like man and wife. Then the time comes for her to leave. Claire Denis (who made the strikingly memorable 'Beau Travail') creates with unrushed care a very telling, emotionally intelligent tale. It has a theme of moving on – of time never standing still – but it's elegiac at the same time.

We eat afterwards at Strada – father and daughter – and then hurry to the car parked in Handel Street as the rain comes down, and Rachel hooks her arm in mine.

Monday, July 13th

I hone my speech for Robin Hanbury-Tenison's book launch at the RGS. Have decided not to write anything and not to be afraid of what will undoubtedly be a gathering of the Beagle stalwarts. I shall be myself – and unapologetically so. It's not going to be so difficult – reading some more material sent to me by Alistair Carr [one of the Beagle group organisers] I find myself quite in sympathy with their spirit, if not the practicality of what they're suggesting. Far from destroying the Society, they are, if anything, overprotective of its good name and reputation.

It all went off well. I restricted myself to water, so as to be clear-headed if challenged about my thoughts on exploration and RGS expeditions, but no challenges came – indeed my hand was shaken warmly by many elderly members who professed themselves supporters of the Resolution but who saw in me their ideal president! We even had royalty dropping in, in the shape of Prince and Princess Michael of Kent. She very attractive, he looking just like a Tsarist prince who'd somehow escaped the Bolshevik firing squad. He was soft-spoken, courteous, very complimentary about my travels and, predictably, a great supporter of the old-style expeditions.

As I left, Alistair Carr came up to introduce himself. He shook my hand and in the short time we had reiterated that he and his group wanted no harm to the Society. I in turn said I didn't feel the issue was one which should polarise the Society as it was in danger of doing. He agreed emphatically and it was all very cordial. John Hemming, who I was talking to at the time, said approving things of Carr – 'they're good people', but he too seemed pained by the potential rift, and we agreed to meet and have lunch together.

I left feeling quite encouraged – almost indeed a little buoyant. I suppose it's a good thing for a conciliator to like both sides so much.

Saturday, July 18th

The papers are full of swine flu headlines. They seem to reflect the confusion of opinions and of course, our desire, in these days of artificial intelligence, for calculated certainties. It was supposed to go quiet during the summer and revive in the autumn but it's clearly not behaving the way it should and people are dying and so on. Today's scare story involves dangers to pregnant women whose immune systems are reduced – and children under five. So Rachel and Archie, round here, and both looking extremely well, are, for now anyway, both in the 'at risk' category. Nobody really seems to know. I'm sure we'll all be very scared at regular intervals.

In the evening to the Bat Mitzvah party of Lilly Glucksmann, Steve's stepdaughter. Steve's rabbi, a tall well-built man who dances rather well, introduces himself to me. Referring, I assume, to my West Bank experiences, he says 'I want to apologise to you on behalf of the Jewish people for what you went through.' Of course I wave this away, but it does lead us to talk, briefly, about the good and the bad on both sides, but my worry that the bad had too much political influence and the good were kept apart by this insidious apartheid. But he thought my letter in the Independent 'a model of restraint'.

Monday, July 20th

Lunch with John Hemming at the Tate. The impression I have, at the end of an absorbing hour and a half is that John loves expeditions. He makes the arguments that they're good for the Society and don't cost too much if properly organised, but the bottom line (as they say) is that he loves larking about in the rainforest. He does have excellent contacts in Brazil where he's most highly regarded and he has brought back much information – not all of it directly relevant to geographers. What I don't sense is any great common purpose with Alistair Carr and the Beagle campaign. John is speaking for John. We part most cordially.

Thursday, July 23rd

To Clerkenwell for my second day of diary recording. Not the easiest bit this, with Angela's death to be described. Oddly I'm fine, until I read about picking up the bedside book at Croft Cottage the night she died. As I read the inscription I feel my voice faltering and I have to stop as a huge well of tears and sadness catches me. Quite unexpectedly. It lasts no longer than five seconds and I carry on and read all the rest without a break. Actually, I'm relieved and surprised rather than embarrassed. It's something spontaneous and unbidden and reminds me how I felt about her loss, as if it were yesterday.

The day that I have marked on my diary as 'Archie 2 expected'. No signs of any new arrival.

Tuesday, July 28th

To the Stammering Centre for a long overdue visit to see the place at work. Starts with minimum of fuss as I sit at the back and observe as the seventeen or so teenagers, only two of whom are women, are patiently taken through various strategies for coping by the therapists – all of whom are women.

They learn to slow down their speech as a way of reducing the pressure – a slow steady rhythm to avoid the pitfalls of staccato. Another strategy is to get them to create an artificial stammer. Most of these young stammerers are in the second week of an intensive summer course and in a group they all sound remarkably fluent. One boy makes the interesting observation that after they go back amongst their friends the lack of stammer is noticed, and not always approved of, 'it's like putting on a funny accent.'

Friday, July 31st

After an edgy sort of night – noises outside, the half-expected call from Tom and Rachel and anticipation of the Vanity Fair shoot [to accompany an article on Python], with all of us physically together since, unless I've forgotten something, the 'Spamalot' premiere in New York.

But no baby is born, the sun's out, and a Mercedes is ready to whisk me away from our half-painted front door (I like the grey undercoat so much I'd like it to be the main colour, but H can't be swayed) to a studio in Curtain Road in Shoreditch – a little strip of cleverly converted light-industrial buildings, which reminds me of Soho in New York.

Five hours have been allotted to the shoot. Annie Liebowitz, who was to have done it, put in a bill for £80,000 for transport of her equipment alone so she was deemed too expensive and instead they're using a man called Tim Walker, who is, I feel, much less likely to use this as an ego-trip for himself and his ideas, and has a Python feeling that we all like. He wanders about, a slight slim figure, trying to galvanise the cast of fashion editors, assistants, make-up and hair to get us ready. Difficult, as the woman in charge of clothing us doesn't know who we are and has never seen Python. 'So you *are*?' she says to Eric. 'I'm Michael,' says Eric helpfully.

John C is, however, not feeling sunny. Though he tries his best to be cheerful, he has, among other things, pain from a frozen shoulder. Terry J, by contrast, looks very good in the Savile Row outfits which we all wear for the first shot. It transforms him into the sort of person who he'd normally rail against – he's become a hedge-fund manager, or a very plausible Harley Street surgeon.

It takes for ever to get us dressed. 'I'm sorry, you've got John's trousers on' etc. etc., but eventually we're gathered together, on the white strip, with brollies and bowlers – just like they once did with the Beatles. This is not Tim Walker's idea – he's much more keen on having us in straitjackets and then a rather nice idea of a narrative linking a series of individual shots of the Pythons on fire.

Wednesday, August 5th

Rachel will go into the Whittington tomorrow to be induced.

To John Swannell to have a new set of photos taken. He's very much of the fashion photography world, and must have done well as he owned one of the oldest and most sought-after homes in Highgate. He's chatty – always keen to hear my latest travel news. He did Tony and Cherie's Christmas card two years ago. He shot Tony in the garden at No. 10. When make-up decided Tony needed hairspray, Tony retreated to a far corner of the garden and had the spray applied behind a wall.

JS remembers the effect when a can of hairspray was found poking out of Arthur Scargill's holdall.

Thursday, August 6th

A grey, sluggish sort of morning after a hot and sticky night. Up at 6 and, as arranged, round to Tom and Rachel's by 7.30. Archie just waking up and very happily surprised to see us in his bedroom. He's been told what's happening, but doesn't seem to be interested and gives his mother a cursory goodbye, little knowing how different life will be when she returns.

There's general upheaval around the house and garden when Tom rings and H comes to tell me that Rachel has had a little boy, our second grandson. Then a rather awkward communications vacuum, as everyone has to be told, except Archie, who will wait until his parents can tell him themselves. I'm longing to tell him myself and feel rather frustrated.

Friday, August 7th

Archie bellows down the phone to me 'I've got a little brother Spike. He's sleeping. D'you want to come over and see him?' And with even more enthusiasm 'I've got a trampoline! D'you want to come over and bounce on it with me?'

Tom calls about midday in some alarm as they're reconsidering the name (or *he* is anyway, after some disappointed and puzzled reactions!). I quite like the name but it's less euphonious than Archie – a little harder – and to be honest, he didn't look like a Spike to me.[1]

Sunday, August 9th

Call to see how JC is in his New Forest eyrie. We exchange jokes prompted by the cricket – a Yorkshireman calling out to someone who'd scored two own goals 'about as much use as a chocolate teapot' and my own story heard today of a wit shouting to the luckless Ravi Bopara as he marched out to bat 'Ravi! Your mother's on the phone. Shall I tell her to hold?' This makes JC laugh so violently I worry that he might suffer some permanent damage.

Tuesday, August 11th

Leave at 5.30 for a meeting I've arranged with the Beagle fundamentalists – Alistair Carr and Justin Marozzi – at the Athenaeum. I feel the need to meet them face to face, to humanise rather than demonise them.

They feel, not surprisingly, that they represent a lot of deeply discontented people and that they have been denied access to the Society they claim to love. Marozzi's failure to get elected to the council, his failure to secure a lecture for his book on Herodotus – all are seen as indications of a deliberate attempt to keep them out of Society affairs. They both seem genuinely grateful that I have taken the trouble to meet them. I reiterate the need for inclusion and for trying to involve a representative of their feelings in the review process.

Saturday, August 15th

A real breather today. No one else but ourselves to get up to Abbotsley, and once at Church Farm nothing much else to do but pick damsons, plums and

---

1 After some deliberation he becomes Wilbur Spike.

apples from the groaning trees in the orchard, listen to Granny G's latest news of the village and her reflections on growing old. 'We all live far too long, I think'. Do crosswords together, eat lunch. A day of complete relaxation.

Home and H and I watch a little gem of a film about Elvis's breakthrough year of 1956 ['Elvis '56']. In the film, all in black and white, there is an image of Elvis, returning to Tupelo from New York on the bus (after recording 'Don't Be Cruel', 'Hound Dog' and other classics at RCA) and waving goodbye to his fellow travellers as he crosses a piece of waste ground and walks off up the road to his parents' house. This must have been almost the last time he could walk the streets of America alone. A poignant image.

I worked out that this time 50 years ago I would have been returning to Sheffield after the traditional August fortnight holiday on which I'd met Helen. A 50th anniversary of a sort. Poignant too.

Tuesday, August 18th

Terry picks us up at 7 and we go down to see 'Mountaintop' at the Trafalgar Studios. A tour de force for two black actors – it's an imaginative depiction of Martin Luther King's last night in Memphis. Daring stuff – taken as its basis that he spent it in the company of a black room-service waitress who turns out to be an angel.

Strong performances by David Harewood, and particularly Lorraine Burroughs, successfully tread a fine and constantly moving line between folksy black comedy and inspirational oratory. Afterwards toil up many flights of stairs to meet the actors, both from Birmingham (Warwickshire *not* Alabama). It's a tribute to their performance that they both seem hardly recognisable from what you see on stage. Here, they're two friendly people relaxing after work – which could have been in a bank – for the last 80 minutes they've been giants.

Friday, August 21st

To see Ron Marx the osteopath. Ron, a wiry, apologetic but ironic character observes that my right Achilles tendon is thicker than the left. I've one shoulder higher than the other, one leg longer than the other and my feet turn outwards quite markedly. On the other hand, he comments as he grasps my head and twists it around, 'a good neck'.

Saturday, August 22nd

Up the M4 to watch Sheffield United play Reading at the Madejski Stadium at the invitation of the owner himself, John, now Sir John Madejski.

We're shown by a succession of friendly and welcoming men and women staff, to a small room with a half-dozen tables set for lunch, and a sliding glass door which gives directly onto the chairman's/directors' box. It's all laid out on carefully honed hierarchical lines and reminds me that modern stadiums still have old social prejudices.

Apart from the United directors, the only others who are allowed into the chairman's suite are 'patrons' – individuals, or representatives of companies, who give enough money to the club to be pampered each week at the highest level. Sir John appears, a little hot, a little breathless, a little late. He's affable, and easy-going. Introduces me to two Indian-born doctors – 'without them I might well not be here,' he adds mysteriously.

Sir John tenses up as kick-off approaches. He doesn't seem to be enjoying himself, anything less than a win will be seen as a blow for the club in which he has invested so much. They score first, but the Blades come back with a graceful, controlled move to score an equaliser and after the interval they take control of the game. One goal is disallowed, then a 25-yard shot slips through their goalie's hands and United are 1–2 up. They add another ten minutes before the end and the 1,000 United fans, isolated at one end of the ground, set up a terrific noise. I too am leaping up and clapping before suddenly realising who I'm with. Try to show restraint but it's no good.

Terry and Anna come round for supper. Terry has been reading the Diaries for the past two days. His reaction very similar to the first volume. He likes some things (especially Ma in New York), has no recollection of others, and is slightly miffed by not being accorded due credit – in this case for thinking up the 'Christmas in Heaven' idea, and perhaps, for not being given enough credit for thinking up the 'Fallen Women' element of 'The Missionary'. I feel on delicate ground here, but it all passes quite agreeably between us.

Wednesday, September 9th

Last day of our Majorcan family holiday at Las Palmeras [near Pollenca]. I have a last swim. The air is cool and fresh, with that hint of herbs and leaves and hot stones which is such a delight in Mediterranean climes.

Home to 60 emails, only one of which I open, to ascertain that Terry, my old friend Terry, had become a dad again – aged 67½ – Siri born on Sunday evening. His happiness is infectious and overwhelms whatever else one might feel about suitability of such an outcome.

And, according to a press cutting sent through from the office, a recent poll voted me top of a list of BBC presenters who the public felt gave value for money. Thirty per cent voted me 'worth every penny'. J. Ross at nine per cent!

Thursday, September 10th

Gingerly, and having consulted Ron Marx, I embark on what I've missed so much these past few weeks, a run across the Heath. The heel is still tender but doesn't affect my mobility and I'm able to canter to Kenwood and back without pain. This is a significant outing and marks 30 years of regular running. Like Will and Rachel, I've become addicted to the process. It's kept my weight reasonably steady, it's helped clear my fuddled head on many occasions, and the rush that it gives my mental state has helped me confront some difficult situations in a much more positive frame of mind. In short, my thirty years on the run has kept my head above water. And been almost wholly beneficial.

To BAFTA for a screening of the Bill and Ben documentary – 'Monty P, Almost the Truth'. Terry J is the only other Python there and I congratulate him on Siri's arrival and he rather sheepishly produces photos of his new daughter as her brother Bill, thirty odd years older, looms over TJ's shoulder. The producers are glowing with pleasure after receiving a message from Eric, which gushed compliments. Considering he refused to be involved in the first place, this is seen as even more exciting. Before I see the film I know that this must mean Eric comes off very well in it – and indeed he does: comfortable, relaxed, confident, talking with that trademark scatological dogmatism, but sounding sharp and remembering well. Gilliam, always a great and energetic and colourful talker, runs him a close second, with John next most positive and TJ and myself – ironically the two who pushed the documentary in the first place – sounding milder and gentler.

Saturday, September 12th

Lots of Saturday papers thud through the letterbox but only The Times has anything substantial: Alan Frank's slightly disappointing but very positive interview notes me down as the George Harrison of the Pythons. The one who comes across as quieter than the others – this not being at all to do with how much he has to say – but that because the others in the group were so busy talking loudly themselves.

Sunday, September 13th

Think I might be going through one of those brief but disturbing reassessments of my personal appearance. I've had them before – usually triggered off by a photograph or a chance remark which sends me, warily, to the mirror, to reappraise myself. I thought, as I brushed my hair in Mallorca last week that I'd caught the sun and some bleached streaks had appeared rather attractively in the central area of my scalp. Or so I thought. H, of course, the voice of hard reality, told me these were grey hairs and had been there for quite a while.

Then a Guardian Online photo which once again emphasises the vivid contours of age. 'That's what makes you attractive,' says H in the bathroom this morning, not altogether convincingly.

Monday, September 14th

In reasonable shape for the start of the publicity season [for the second volume of Diaries]. To Maida Vale BBC studios – home of the BBC Symphony Orchestra and in a small, red-tinged studio round the back, which rather resembles a fortune teller's grotto, I submit to Jonathan Ross's questions for 'Film 2009'. It's first thing Monday morning, the sun's shining pleasantly outside and Jonathan, in his dark suit, black shirt and shoes, reminds me of a vampire caught in the dawn light.

In early afternoon, Bob drives me to TV Centre, where I'm on Simon Mayo's 'Five Live' programme for around 45 minutes. Mayo is a relaxing but sharp performer, lulling you into a false sense of security then dropping in something unexpected.

At the end Iain Banks [Scots author, 'The Wasp Factory' etc.] joins me and we have a little change-over chat. Turns out Iain was one of the students at Stirling University in 1974 who did a day's work as an extra on 'MP and the Holy Grail' – in the battle sequence. Says, rather proudly, that he was a knight – and has dined out on the story ever since. I've just talked about the slow progress of my second novel. He's written 25.

Tuesday, September 15th

News that Patrick Swayze and Keith Floyd have died today. One the personification of health and grace, the other the personification of dissolution. Death the great leveller.

Wednesday, September 16th

Continuing sense of my body failing to take seriously the demands ahead. My heel still not strong enough for the number of therapeutic runs I need and my shoulder and left arm is still not mended, causing me uncomfortable, broken nights sleep. But there is no option other than to face up to what's been arranged, try and ignore an incipient sore throat and take one step at a time.

To a publication party at the Garrick for Ion Trewin's biography of Alan Clark. Clark, MP, writer, has been dead ten years, but his much younger wife Jane is there. Her hair is turning grey but she has a quick, shrewd, and lively glance – someone I would think who doesn't find it hard to enjoy herself – maybe the attraction to Alan was similar to what attracted Helen to me. Laughter; easy laughter! Ion, quite ingenuously reads a list of 'no-shows', including Melvyn Bragg and others, who have obviously got better things to do. George Weidenfeld says a few words. We're all given a free book which happens rarely these days and Ion dutifully signs. Read some of it on the Tube; looks intriguing; a flawed man, carefully documented. So much more fun than a hero.

Thursday, September 17th

Publication day for 'Halfway to Hollywood: Diaries 1980–88'. My 11th book.

Begin with a walk down to Burleigh Road to see Ron Marx. He's vexed that my left arm and shoulder are still playing up and fills me with so many needles that I lie there feeling like a porcupine for half an hour.

To St Pancras branch of Foyles. Am down by the escalator which leads from the Midland line platforms. Above me, way above me, the reborn Barlow roof keeps out the elements, there are shops selling fresh food, fresh-baked bread, cafés exuding the smell of real coffee, and a line of adoring fans awaits. I have to close my eyes a moment and think back to this very spot 56 years ago when I stepped off the Sheffield train into a grimy, blackened station that was so clearly the poor relation of all London's terminals. The renaissance is magnificent and barely believable. Thank God all this was done before the bubble burst.

Wednesday, September 23rd

Start the day with a rather heavy plod of an interview for a Polish newspaper ahead of the publication of 'Himalaya' there. Maybe it's just her voice that makes every question seem laden with a mixture of doom and boredom – or maybe it's the familiar East European fear of optimism.

Then off towards the Fens and a quite extraordinary evening. A Robert

Topping, full-on, sign-everything stock blitz in his attractive old shop with a view right onto the majestic Ely cathedral. Then into the cathedral itself for a BAFTA-organised event in which Mark Kermode interviews me about 'A Life in Films'. It's odd enough to see my likeness looming from three screens, one at either end of the transepts and another slung in front of the choir, but to be sat beneath the lantern looking out over a thousand faces, with the soaring stone arches reducing us all to insignificant dots is overwhelming, unreal – the stuff of dreams.

Fortunately we move on from awestruck inarticulacy to one of the best, most comfortable, and I think most revealing interviews I've done. 'Every Sperm Is Sacred' fills the screens and the old walls of the cathedral and no one seems nervous of laughing or applauding. I ask the Dean how often he allows use of the cathedral for such events. 'Often as possible. We need the money.'

Monday, September 28th

Introducing first RGS lecture tonight. In the event the lecture goes well. David Coulson is a very experienced African hand with Hockney-like hair and features. He's brought a lot of friends and family over from Nairobi – where they seem to live quite comfortably. More than a whiff of Happy Valley about them – they're confident and attractive and I should imagine, not short of a bob or two. They still refer to Kenya as Keenya.

Tuesday, October 6th

To King's Place to record a podcast for the Guardian online. The Guardian operation is extremely cool, chic, hi-tech and rather daunting. No noise (the hundreds of keyboards seem to work away soundlessly) no mess, no sunshades, no bottles, no lingering smoke in the air – nothing that I remember from the newspaper offices or newsrooms I've visited before. It's all very cleverly designed, but looks more like air-traffic control than a newspaper.

To the National Theatre for an evening 'platform performance'. Meet Simon Williams backstage. It's the opening night of 'The Power of Yes' by David Hare, and Simon's in it. He's very funny, slightly anxious and confesses he doesn't understand it all. 'Someone said it could have been in Spanish.' A big night in town for TG's 'Imaginarium' is opening in Leicester Square and the Booker Prize dinner's on, which is why my interviewer – Mark Lawson – arrives in a D-J. Angela has to readjust his made-up bow tie for him. 'My son borrowed it for a Hunt Ball and it hasn't been the same since.'

Wednesday, October 7th

To the RGS, despite feeling like a good long laze at home, to meet up with Musa and Esmé [Peach, from Refugee Action] to discuss my 'Michael Meets' talk with him in November. He's much younger than I thought. Only 25 and yet I feel he's lived many lives more than me. Also a little relieved to hear that he's done some press, radio and TV interviews on behalf of Refugee Action, and doesn't seem to be intimidated by sight of the Ondaatje Theatre – in fact he and Esmé both thought it much more intimate than they'd expected. Talk through his story from leaving Kismaayo in Somalia at the age of seven to arriving in the UK, on a forged passport, from Tanzania, at 11.30 at night. He was nineteen years old.

He hasn't seen his mother and many of his surviving family since 1998 and he's been very low sometimes – watching TV all day long, living on hand-outs. Now he has refugee status and is working at Refugee Action to help those who arrive there to feel comfortable.

Friday, October 9th

Take my first run of the week, then to Wig Specialities to find a wig to go with my Betty outfit [as worn when explaining the meaning of life at the end of the Python film of same name]. I'd always thought Wig Specialities had closed long ago, but it's just the greatly unchanged façade that gives that impression – inside and up the stairs there's a wonderland of posters and photographs and bustle and the smell of powder. It's like being backstage. I'm offered a big pile of a wig which I'm told is 'the Margaret Thatch' wig. It looks very assertive and striking and a little over the top and it's chosen unanimously.

Paul rings to say that the Telegraph has picked up, from one of my answers in a Daily Mail Q&A to be published tomorrow, that I talk of having taken cocaine. I ring their newsdesk. All quite jolly. I tell them it's a non-story, truth being that I tried it twice whilst doing 'Sat Night Live' in the 1970s – 31 years ago – and haven't used it since. Probably best to have dealt with the story truthfully, but I wonder at the Telegraph, which is sounding more and more like the Sun these days.

Saturday, October 10th

The Telegraph has run the 'non-story' of my cocaine use with the headline. 'I used cocaine admits Python nice-man Palin'. The Mail interview is actually rather sweet, mostly taken up with my saying nice things about Helen. Still, nice things don't sell papers.

Tuesday, October 13th

Walk from Covent Garden across Piccadilly to Burlington House – an eighteenth-century walk with satisfying sense of continuity. Been thinking about my fondness for continuity recently. I suppose I'm an instinctive conservative but an intellectual and emotional radical.

Met at the Institute of Chemistry – one of the out-buildings flanking the courtyard at the Royal Academy. I'm entertained to a tasty lunch by the Council of ABF – the Artists' Benevolent Fund. Then we troop across the road to the Linnean Society, and in the very room in which Darwin and Wallace first made public their theories of evolution by natural selection, the AGM takes place and I speak about art – and my progress from philistine to fan. I read the Picasso cycling race from the very first Python Show, 40 years and eight days ago, and it goes wonderfully. They *love* the jokes about artists.

Sunday, October 18th

On 'The Culture Show', filmed down at BFI South Bank. Programme seems to be entirely run by young women, apart from Eddie Morgan, the producer; all perfectly lovely and friendly. 'I see your book had great reviews this weekend . . . Guardian. Independent' one chatters away, 'I can't believe I'm taking Michael Palin to the toilet,' says another.

But out on the stage things are less smooth. Two presenters, Mark Kermode and Simon Mayo, absolutely dependable on radio, but less comfortable it seems with his new role as an arts presenter. An audience half-fills the place – but Rachel is there and waves at me and gives the Palin grin.

The interview could barely be shot more stiltedly – answers cut off in full flow, 'whilst we change batteries'. It all militates against flow or spontaneity. I'm asked to cut down my replies and shorten for no other reason than they've 'very little editing time'. Your problem, not mine, I want to say, but don't. It's all a far cry from 'I can't believe I'm taking Michael Palin to the toilet.'

Monday, October 19th

By taxi to Lowther Lodge [for the Society's regular Monday night lecture, introduced, if he's around, by the president]. The long evening is quite bearable. [Mountaineer] Andy Cave is a good speaker – articulate, conversational – with a great deal of humour. He opens his talk by saying how he met some climbers on Stanage Edge in the Peak District and was telling them of the pressure on him to complete his latest book. One of them was very sympathetic as his father had just completed a book and was quite stressed about sales figures – and that climber was Tom Palin.

After the talk, I attend a dinner of the Geographers' Club – founded in 1830, and from which the RGS grew. They seem to exist still as a dining club and I have to bang a gavel (carved from the timbers of HMS *Victory*) and call for a toast to the Queen and then to the Society – as has been done for a hundred and seventy-nine years. Lord Chorley is one of their members. Talks of the Beagle campaign. 'A lot of it was very nasty, anti-Rita stuff,' he confides.

Tuesday, October 20th

To the Dover Castle to meet up with Roger and John Pritch. Roger gathering material for a talk called 'Hairy Moments' – what happens when we're in near-death situations – to be delivered at his local church.

It's while John is in the loo that Roger drops a bombshell. 'I've been diagnosed with the early stages of Parkinson's. It's what your father died of, isn't it.' It's only when I get home that Roger's news sinks in. It's not a death sentence, nor is Parkinson's as intrusive as it was in my dad's time, but the disease can't, as yet, be cured, nor the condition reversed. Roger, my mentor, friend, giver of strong, sound, unblinking good advice, whose parents lived, clear and sharp-minded into their 90s, will never be the same again. And, despite all the contrary evidence, I know it could be laying in wait for me too. Considering how much I've drunk, I go to bed very sober.

Friday, October 23rd

Suspicion of sore throat yesterday morning induced temporary wave of panic about my tendency to hoarseness on stage (something from which none of the other Pythons ever seemed to suffer – which of course made it worse), but this morning, tho' I have a niggly cough, I'm confident my voice will last the day.

A bright, breezy afternoon as I walk along Kensington Gore, to the stage door of the Albert Hall for the recording of Eric and John Du Prez's Oratorio 'Not the Messiah'. Such has been the carefully and thoroughly orchestrated hype for the event that I cannot simply walk in and start work. There's a small pack of fans squeezing around me at the door. One or two genuine fans – many more are dealers – and they are so completely single-minded that they disregard any personal appeal. I think if I had a heart attack and collapsed on the floor, one of them would be trying to get the last autograph before I died.

Backstage are Neil [Innes] and Terry G and TJ and Sanjeev B – who is enormously equable, agreeable and a generally comforting counterpoint to the rumbles of discontent from Pythons who don't really want to be here. In our shared dressing room Neil, TJ and TG are so constantly on the point of boiling over about the way they've been 'used' that I have to introduce a swear-box policy, with a pound for every criticism of 'Not the Messiah'. Neil can't stop his speechless disbelief that Eric should have inserted a Dylan-style protest song into the show. 'That's exactly what *I* do!' explodes the gentle Innes.

The performance – which begins at 8 – is also the dress rehearsal and it's quite a strain waiting for half an hour's make-up as Mrs Betty Palin and then trying the whole drag outfit on for the first time – ten minutes before doing it. Of course, it all goes well. Mrs Betty Palin – in her long turquoise dress – is greeted with prolonged applause, as is every Python appearance. We're called back time and time again.

I feel that lovely rush of relief and joy having belted out 'Lumberjack Song' with an 82-strong orchestra, 200-strong choir, to a 6,000-strong audience at the Royal Albert Hall on a Friday night!

Tom and Will there, but Tom with bad news – Barney, their cat, was run over this afternoon and killed outright. Nothing nasty or squelchy thank goodness, and Archie's dealt with it quite well. Apparently a delivery man came to the door and Archie greeted him with the words 'Barney's dead. He's in a bag over there. D'you want to see him?'

Monday, October 26th

Tonight there's another RGS lecture, but I feel more comfortable with these now. This will be my fourth introduction and it's Sara Wheeler who I'm sure will have a good tale to tell. Write out my intro and also read up on the Arab League, whose representatives – including Secretary-General Amr Moussa – will be given the red carpet treatment as they pay us a visit tonight, on which could hang a considerable amount of income, in return for partially exclusive use of Lowther Lodge at time of the Olympics.

The globes in the council room have been dusted down and the curtains swagged and silver candlesticks are on the table for the Arab League dinner. I'm impressed that the Society has so much silverware, but I'm told, confidentially, that it doesn't. The RGS sold their family silver a while ago and this all belongs to the family of Ann Morris, who is organising and co-ordinating this whole Arab League initiative. She's produced a brochure '2012 Arabian Days' – a cultural festival to be held during the 2012 Olympics – which seems to incorporate music, dance and lots of other things I'd like to see more of at Lowther Lodge.

Thursday, October 29th

To the RGS in the morning. Rita seems on very good form. 'I've got my bounce back,' she declares, admitting that she had not felt like this in the early summer – battered as she had been by the Beagles. Rita thinks my appeal letter is the best she's ever read, and I think much of her buoyancy comes from having a good relationship with me. 'I have to learn how you like to do things,' she says, 'and you have to learn how I like to do things.' After five months we seem to have achieved a certain harmony.

To the Chelsea Arts Club for lunch with Will Boyd – long promised and too often put off. Not busy in the dining room, whose walls are hung with some seductive examples of early twentieth-century British painting, and three big canvases reflecting the life of the club back at its members.

Will is very together, I feel. No dark places. He lives comfortably, nearby. He's probably more ambitious than he appears, and doesn't disguise his interest in earnings nor his enjoyment of his popularity – he's recently struck big in Germany with 'Restless', and clearly loves the associated buzz.

We talk about the way some of the glittering authors of the '80s and '90s have come down to earth. Rushdie and Amis no longer breed bestsellers. I have the feeling that Boyd sees himself as a steady hand on the tiller – eschewing fireworks for good, solid, well-crafted writing. 'Any Human Heart' is to be made into a series by the BBC next year. The film rights to 'Ordinary Thunderstorms' have been sold. By any standards, the Boyd machine is a formidable one. He's interested in my Diaries, which he's reading. He admires and is slightly shocked, I feel, that my Diary is 'so candid'. Candid about myself, we both agree. Though we agree on the importance of her diaries, he thinks Virginia Woolf a horrible piece of work. 'If she'd been called Virginia Smith would anyone have read her stuff?'

Sunday, November 1st

Martin Lewis [organiser of music events, now living in the USA] is bombarding me with messages as the sun goes down. The Republican contender for governor of New Jersey is using Python footage – the Déjà Vu sketch – to dis his Democrat opponent. A defeat for the Democrats will be seen as a blow to Obama, so Martin wants to enlist some Python support. They never asked if they could use the Python sketch and I send a message which concludes that he's made a terrible mistake and got the Palins wrong – clearly looking for Sarah's support, not mine.

Monday, November 2nd

Small victory, Martin Lewis emails to say that Chris Christie – the Republican in NJ's gubernatorial election – has removed the Python sketch very swiftly from his website!

Wednesday, November 11th

Remembrance Day, and having accepted an invitation to a special service at Westminster Abbey 'to mark the passing of the dead of World War One'. The invitation makes much of medals being worn, and after some agonising I decide to don my CBE. (My gaffe is not in wearing it, but as I find out later, on the back of the invitation, for not wearing it on the short ribbon). The car drops me off at the Athenaeum where I tidy myself up, arrange the medal, tuck my warm raincoat around me and walk down the steps, across the Mall and through St James's Park to the Abbey.

A watery sun breaks through the greyness, the ducks are noisy. Celebrities, as I've learnt in the past, are not expected to arrive on foot and as I try to make my way, as instructed, to the West Door, a policeman officiously turns me away and orders me round to the North Door. Walk through the crowds lining the route who seem to appreciate my presence "'Ello, Michael!' and indeed encourage me on. 'Don't be late now, Michael!' At the North Gate I'm welcomed, profusely, by the army staff, and led around to . . . the West Door. Welcomed by the Abbey staff, I walk down the nave flanked by men and women with medals; the place is packed and when I reach the north lantern, beside Poets' Corner, the lady on duty raises her eyes heavenwards as I present my ticket. 'Another pink A!' she calls across to a colleague, shaking her head in despair. 'There's nowhere. I just don't have anywhere left.' She pauses and shakes her head again. 'Pink A, oh dear.' Eventually she finds me a seat. As I sit down, I realise this little episode has given those already seated some considerable enjoyment.

Ten minutes later, as the prime minister, and Major and Thatcher and others appear, the same lady approaches me and asks if I'd like to move nearer the front. 'Three diplomats haven't turned up,' she explains, and I'm on the move again and ensconced by a pillar in amongst various African dignitaries. On my chair is a small reservation card. 'Government of the Cayman Islands, UK Representative', it reads.

Can't see very much but I have a good view directly ahead of me of our long-suffering prime minister. Gordon sits, jaw set firmly, brow broad and head raised defiantly. He is framed, expressively, by one of the Gothic choir stalls – the word 'Cantuar' inscribed above his head.

The Queen and the Duke arrive, almost perkily. She in jaunty purple, the

Duke laden with ribbons and medals and cords and braid and chatting in sprightly fashion to those he meets. The Bishop of London follows – a marvellous figure, bearded like an Orthodox potentate.

Jeremy Irons reads a Carol Ann Duffy poem slowly and sonorously – a little too slowly and sonorously. One hymn of the three no one knows at all and the organist thunders out flamboyant trills and fanfares, so no one but the choir seem to know where we are. Gordon looks grim throughout and and doesn't attempt to sing.

Monday, November 16th

In the evening Angie and Teddy [parents of Will's American friend Heather] come over and we walk up to Ravel's [our local bistro] which is almost empty. Teddy talks of his lunch with George W. Bush, before he became president, and how good a storyteller he was, and how friendly and generally excellent company. 'His problem was,' judges Teddy 'he had absolutely no sense of curiosity.'

Teddy has now given up on the GOP, bitterly disillusioned by their opposition to healthcare and other social legislation. Angie is worried that Obama faces a threat not just from the Republicans – whose entire policy is based on what hurts Obama most – but also from the idealistic and liberal left wing of the Democrats who, she thinks, feel Obama is not being strong and defiant enough in pushing through his legislation. Heather is in Stockholm talking to the Nobel Foundation on the Enlightenment, and they're off to join her on Wednesday. These are definitely not the 98 per cent of Americans who don't have passports.

Wednesday, November 18th

Rumbling underneath are my concerns about the 'Michael Meets Musa' event at the RGS. Pressure on me to show that this is a worthwhile initiative and not a gimmick; pressure on Musa to deliver in front of a much bigger and more formal audience than he's ever done before.

Unusually, for an RGS function, I decide against wearing a tie – want to keep this as informal as possible. When I arrive at Lowther Lodge, around half past four, almost the first person I see is Musa, wearing a suit and tie! We test the mikes and look at pictures on the PowerPoint – including some old photos of Somalia from the RGS archive, 1894 being the earliest.

Need not have worried. When we kick off at 7, the theatre is absolutely full, but Musa, who sits in the centre, with Esmé on one side and me on the other, is steady, measured and articulate. He tells his story to the audience as he had told it to me and it was moving and occasionally very funny. One woman gladdens my heart by telling me that she thought this was exactly the sort of event that would bring an interested younger generation to the RGS.

Wednesday, November 25th

To Sky at Isleworth for an appearance on Mariella F's 'Book Show'. We're all asked to talk about 'the character in literature that stole your heart'. Andrew Marr chooses Natasha from 'War and Peace', John Banville Cheetah the Chimpanzee, and I choose William Brown. Turns out that not only are all three of us avid 'Just William' fans but that Richmal Crompton was Marr's great aunt!

Monday, November 30th

To the Travellers for lunch with Lord Selborne. John Selborne, a past president of the RGS in Rita's time. He's a short man with wispy hair and a quiet, vaguely distracted air. He'd never met Rita when he was chosen as president and says he could see her look of horror that 'another Conservative peer' was about to be foisted on her. But he'd taken her to dinner and reassured her she had nothing to fear. He's a fan of his predecessor Lord Jellicoe's ability to solve all the problems over a drink or a meal. Jellicoe, a war hero, was evidently quite a naughty man. His name came up in the Lord Lambton sex scandal[1] and he was forced to resign. Apparently the name 'Jellicoe' had appeared in Lambton's diary. This was later found to refer to a pub of the same name and not to Lord Jellicoe at all.

John S thinks that Rita and Gordon Conway were unnecessarily intransigent. Jellicoe would have sorted it with conviviality, he thinks.

The meal, in fine surroundings, is, except for the wine, quite awful. The lamb noisette is like chewing your way through a car cushion.

Tuesday, December 1st

To Southport on the affluent coastal strip north of Liverpool, where I am to sign at Broadhurst's, an independent bookshop which attracted my attention with a photo of the local Orion rep, dressed in full Gumby outfit, sat in a deckchair in the window. My gut feeling that this might be worth the detour

---

1 In 1973, conservative peer Antony Lambton's liaisons with prostitutes were revealed in the *News of the World*.

is admirably justified. Broadhurst's is a well-preserved Victorian terraced shop, with a coal fire burning in the grate beside the signing table and books new and old stacked up on four floors. A Shakespeare & Company of the Lancashire Coast. The owner, who looks and dresses like an enlightened company director, has an antiquarian book business here too. William and Biggles in first editions alongside histories of Liverpool's banks in the early nineteenth century. Refreshments, courtesy of a local café, await us on polished silver cake stands.

Monday, December 7th

Worry myself from sleep at some dark and unearthly hour. A lot to do at the RGS and all the other pre-Christmas business flits in and out of my mind – presents, parties, and the feeling that I've been mugged by Christmas yet again, forced into all the usual rituals with no alternative avoidance strategy. And the bathroom is leaking water down into the sitting room.

Rita and the staff prepare the council meeting material so thoroughly and so commonsensically that all those present have had their homework done for them. I manage to keep a grip on the complex agenda and allow everyone to chip in without hijacking the meeting. Two and three-quarter hours passes quickly in the draughty old chamber, and as the 15 or so members disperse, the corridors are filling up for Gordon Conway's farewell talk.

I realise how little I know about my predecessor's background. His interest in how things grow dates back to earliest days – fieldwork at Latchmore Primary School. Like David A he continued this early spirit of curiosity, and he's now one of the top agronomists and heading the programme on Africa for the Bill and Melinda Gates Foundation. As I say in my vote of thanks to him, I rather envy the way the course of his life was set by what interested him at the age of ten. If that had been the way with me, I'd still be a trainspotter.

Heading home across Hyde Park, loosening my black tie, I feel relieved but also aware that I've enjoyed the afternoon and evening – I've enjoyed being president, and everyone seems to think I'm doing it well.

And it's stopped raining. And my weight's down below 12 stone again.

Wednesday December 9th

Work at home. Clearing the desk, and even, at the end of the afternoon having time for the novel. Excited by writing again and beat out a rather satisfying paragraph before my last 'Halfway to Hollywood' event – at Daunt's. The place is packed. I read with confidence and enjoyment. In fact as I'm reading extracts from the diary – bringing Mum momentarily back to life, I realise how much more I've enjoyed talking about these Diaries than the last one, and how happy I am doing this reading in this fine bookshop and how much I shall miss this sort of thing.

Thursday, December 10th

To the Prince of Wales in Highgate for a drink with Terry J. 'You looked tired as you came in, Mikey,' he says to me. A certain truth in that. I could do with a long holiday and a few days of sleeping late. I'm sure he could too.

Friday, December 11th

A call comes through from one Charlotte Moore, who introduces herself as the new Head of Documentaries. She sounds anything but comfortable as she unfolds a tale of some list, purportedly compiled by someone at the BBC which the Mail has got hold of. On it, various remarks are made about presenters. I'm apparently classed under 'Occasional Sparkle', 'Limited Popularity'. We both laugh. She more nervously than me. Of course, she goes on, it's completely not what they feel about their valued presenters and she's apologetic and of course very irritated by the Mail. When I ask if such a list did exist or was fabricated, she avoids the issue. 'We must meet up and discuss what you might want to do next – maybe after Christmas.'

Saturday, December 12th

A long day ahead, with the RGS Children's Lecture to be delivered and then up to Suffolk for Neil Innes's 65th.

At the RGS a monster map of the world has been laid out on the floor of the exhibition room for the children to walk on; general buzz of expectation – nearly 600 have turned up. Rattle through the photos, and needful of how difficult it is to keep children's attention, have to be lively and remember to tell plenty of funny stories. Taxi home, then swift transfer to my car and we set off for Suffolk.

Overnight we're to stay at the Swan in Southwold. In the Admiral's Room – on top floor with windows giving panoramic views over the town to the sea and to Walberswick across the Blyth.

We get a little lost trying to find the party destination in the damp darkness. It's in a collection of buildings – one of which, the Old Vicarage, is also having a party. Diana Quick, indeed, has spent quite a few minutes at the wrong party, before being redirected to Neil's.

Once we're inside, we're away from the rain, but not the cold, as the heater in the garden tent has exploded. Paul Merton is next to me at the meal. Very chatty and straightforward, but a little chippy about certain things — not what I'd call a happy, contented man. He readily admits that the difference between the two of us as travel presenters is that I seem to like travelling and he doesn't. Still, it hasn't stopped him doing a new series on Europe.

After the meal Neil and John Altman and a handful of other musicians play away. Terry Blacker gets up and sings two very good songs he's written. The evening has the character of Neil and Yvonne — warm, friendly, easy-going, thoughtful, inclusive. A real pleasure.

Sunday, December 13th: Southwold–London

It's raining again as we pull back the curtains. The Sunday Times carries a half-page on the BBC list, with large photos of myself and Delia Smith, who both appear at the bottom of the list labelled 'Occasional Sparkle, Limited Appeal', together with Robert Winston, Sophie Raworth and Giles Coren. It gets odder. The other end of the list, headed Top Ties (highly valued) is topped by the magic name of Alan Yentob, whilst such as Paul Merton and Dan Cruickshank are lumped together as Mid Range (average appeal).

Despite this I enjoy a very fine breakfast, after which H and I dodge the showers to walk to my parents' grave. (The only comment I'd made to the press about the list over the weekend is accurately reproduced in the Sunday Times – 'Occasional Sparkle? I'd like to have that on my gravestone'.)

Tuesday, December 15th

My new best friend, Charlotte Moore, rings at 9 o'clock. Concerned about the list. I thank her for alerting me to it on Friday, but confess that until I saw the Sunday Times at Southwold on Sunday morning I hadn't realised what it was. 'Occasional Sparkle' I could and did laugh off, but 'Limited Appeal' worried me more. And limited appeal compared to say, Alan Yentob worried me enough to ask for some sort of explanation. Not an apology, an explanation. If, as I suspect, it was written by someone higher up, possibly the BBC's Head of Knowledge itself – George Entwistle – then it would help to know, and would save us knocking on that particular door again. The silence from the top brass since the list came out doesn't reflect at all well on the national broadcaster.

Sunday, December 20th

As the news media try to digest the blindingly obvious result from [the UN Climate Change Conference in] Copenhagen – that 193 nations are not going to agree on a legally binding international treaty after only ten days together – the fiercely cold air from the East tightens its grip and continues to make global warming something which, for today at any rate, is devoutly to be wished.

Six Eurostar trains have been stuck in or near the Channel Tunnel, with cold outside and warmth inside the Tunnel blamed. 'Travel chaos' has reared its entirely predictable head again.

Tuesday, December 22nd

Have suggested an office Christmas outing to 'The Woman in Black', which has been playing at the Fortune Theatre since way before the office moved to Tavistock Street. I've passed it so often and feel bad at never having seen John Nettleton in the role, or the adaptation which was done by Stephen Mallatratt, who adapted 'Hemingway's Chair' so promisingly. Today I finally lay these pangs of guilt to rest and together with Andrew and Peter, Mimi, Lyn, Steve and Paul make the two-minute walk across Drury Lane and take seats in the Dress Circle of this intimate, compact little theatre. It's an intimate compact little play. Two hander, very effective. Starts on comedy and turns into Gothic horror (shadows on the wall) before ending quite grimly. Structured well. Lots of quite young children so the two actors have to ride some laughs in odd places, but it does deliver, in ungimmicky style, the equivalent of reading a really good ghost story. And there is no happy ending. In fact two very unhappy endings.

Friday, December 25th: Christmas Day

Rachel has stayed overnight. We open stockings, then Will arrives bearing gifts. Dan Cruickshank assures Will that the 'Occasional Sparkle' list had been the work of G. Entwistle, as suspected, after his petulant slamming of the door on reporters.

In a convoy with Will over to Lancaster Rd. Archie excited, but not much more so than usual, which is very excited. Tom pulls off another magnificent turkey dinner with so many extra veggies, potatoes, etc. that the word trimmings seems quite inadequate.

Home – quite shattered with the sheer effort of enjoying my Christmas Day, and a fierce, stabbing reflux which seems like some sort of divine vengeance.

Monday, December 28th

In the evening, we take GG to a pre-theatre supper then on to our Christmas family outing. We've chosen a show at the Roundhouse called 'La Clique', and I had to pull a few strings to get some seats, such is the demand.

At the beginning of the show we're ominously warned 'this is not the sort of show for people who like to sit with their arms folded'. My misgivings at having not thoroughly checked the content only grow when the first properly circus-ey act comes on. Two punky-haired women 'all the way from New York City!' do amazingly athletic things on the trapeze while smoking and appearing to be drunk. As they hop up on the trapeze only yards above Granny's head, they thrust out bottoms squeezed into hotpants. On one is written 'Yeah' and on the other 'Fuck'. I realise there's really no point in my trying to either explain or apologise. The show is rude in a robust music hall sort of way, but some of it is *very* rude – including the splendid Ursula Martinez (born in Croydon) who combines striptease and magic with brazen lustiness – so that by the end, the climax I suppose you could call it, she's stark naked and manages to find her red handkerchief in her fanny.

Granny seems unfazed by the relentlessly noisy soundtrack, the references to clitorises and the singing of Queen songs with us all waving our arms in the air. 'I missed one or two things, I think,' she says afterwards when all the mayhem has ended, 'but I am 96 and I have seen an awful lot, dear.' Not stark naked ladies fishing hankies from their vaginas, I'll bet.

Thursday, December 31st

It's cold and grey, with a light but persistent drizzle. My last run of 2009 – sliding and slipping across a waterlogged Heath. Then into preparations for the party. The usual suspects – the Davidsons, the Alburys, the Burds and Ranji. We look old, I think to myself, as we link hands and sing the old year out with Auld Lang Syne, and I'm not the only one who feels little affection for the year just past. 'Winning the Ashes was the only good thing,' Edward reminds me as he and Mary leave, just before 2 o'clock.

The temperature has slipped below freezing and a flurry of snow has dusted the cars in Oak Village, as I put down Roger Lewis's 'Seasonal Suicide Notes' and switch off the light. We have the house to ourselves. And Elsie and Edith. Two thousand and nine feels like a marking time sort of year. The second in a row indeed, except for the RGS dimension. Which has been the dominant feature of my life in 2009.

Actually, it's been quite a geographical year. My week in Calcutta/Kolkata was a highlight, a new favourite to add to the list, and my article was much admired. Few journeys have taught me more than the five days in the West Bank in May. I've been reacquainted, quite happily, with Sofia and the Bulgarians. I've spoken in support of the preservation of Captain Scott's hut and been voted Top Travel Personality 2009 by Wanderlust readers. And in the dying hours of the year, I find myself quite seriously considering another travel series. Brazil for 2011?

Index

4.48 Psychosis (Kane) 84
9/11 attacks 142, 144, 146, 147, 162
24 (TV series) 234, 410, 502
35 Rhums (2008 film) 516
50 Greatest Comedy Films (C4 special) 349

À Bout de Souffle (1960 film) 111
A Fish Called Wanda (1988 film) 5, 38, 39, 48, 170, 312, 358, 462
'A Life in Films' (BAFTA) 526
A Private Function (1984 film) 37, 207, 227, 318
A Saint She Ain't (1999 King/Vosburgh show) 17
Abbott and Holder gallery 264
Abbott, Kathy 483
Abbott, Nicola 289, 421
Abbott, Steve
    finance manager 289
    on *Himalaya* sales 294, 332
    The Weekend revival 307
    at Book Awards 313
    Diaries and 319, 333
    Stenhousemuir project 328, 330–1
    MP's South America idea 334
    MP's *New Europe* idea 335, 338
    Peter Cook Foundation and 336
    New Europe meeting 347
    lunch with MP 357, 375
    at *Diaries* interviews 390
    New Europe book 409
    New Europe title 411
    Palins' visit 421
    Urban Rock and 444
    China bans *Himalaya* series 453
    on *New Europe* 456
    New Europe posters 463
    complaint about Yugoslav episode 468
    MP discusses Death programmes with 478
    Wyeth idea 510
    Lilly's Bat Mitzvah party 517
ABC (American Broadcasting Company) 463
ABC (Australian Broadcasting Commission) 387, 456
Ableman, Sheila 126
Absolutely Fabulous (BBC) 143
Adams, Bryan 194
Adams, Douglas 176, 411
Adie, Kate 190, 371

Adonis, Andrew, Lord 366
Adventure Travel Show, Earl's Court 356
Adventures of Baron Munchausen (1988 film) 127
Afghanistan 145, 147, 149, 151, 161, 203, 209, 214
Agland, Phil 85
Aitken, Jonathan 88–9
Aitken, Maria 88–9, 312–14, 316, 339, 340, 348, 352, 359
Aitken, William 88
Al Jazeera 488
al-Qaeda 151, 161, 162, 258, 323
Alagiah, George 293
Alan (Eildon House) 320
Alan (sewer visit) 87
Albania 395
Albert (Palin cat) 100, 127
Albury, Phillida 377, 395, 465
Albury, Simon 128, 377, 395, 447, 465
Alderton, John 268, 319, 328, 354
Algeria 87, 109, 131, 143, 145, 147–8
Alison, Carrie 239
Alison, Rodney and Anne 239
Allam, Roger 158
Allen, Benedict 258
Altman, John 537
Alverson, Chuck 469
Amanda (JC's office) 6
America 69–71, 161–2, 217, 218, 220, 386, 389
    elections 97, 102, 472, 477, 481, 531–2
American Friends (1993 film) 84, 208, 265, 317, 448, 452
American Stuttering Foundation 393
Amir (Mr Dry Cleaner) 254
Amira (Sarajevan singer) 410
Amis, Martin 38, 531
Amnesty concerts 291
An Inconvenient Truth (2006 docu) 392
Anderson, Bruce 470
Anderson, Clive 39, 66, 289
Anderson, Paul Thomas (PTA) 182–3, 197–8, 222, 238–9
Anderson, Steve 330
Andraos, George 399–400
Andresen, Gerd 488
Andresen, Jacob and Anna 488
Andrew, Prince 29, 184

Index

Andrews, Michael 132
Angie and Teddy (Heather's parents) 533
Anne-Marie of Greece, Queen 502
Ansorge, Peter 367
Antonello da Messina 356
Apocalypse Now Redux (2001) 151
Arab League 530
Archer, Jeffrey 45
Archer, Tom 211
Arctic Monkeys 401
Around the World in 80 Days (1989 series) 73,
    113, 143, 146, 156, 157, 249, 292
'Around the World in 80 Days' enterprise 506
Around the World in 80 Days - 20 Years On
    (2008) 462, 477, 478, 483, 486, 488
Art Fund 198, 260
Artangel Imber Village evening 236
Arthritis Society 422
Artists' Benevolent Fund (ABF) 528
Asher, Jane 435
Aspel, Michael 253
Athenaeum Club 359, 361, 366, 372, 391, 520
Atherton, Mike 327
Atkins, Eileen 194–5
Atonement (2007 film) 438
Attenborough, David
    RTS dinner 15
    Millennium Show 49, 50
    Life on Air: ... 159–60, 180–2
    Grierson Lifetime Award 197
    on *Treasure Island* 253
    at RTS with MP 283
    Farm Africa award 317
    loss of family in Indian tsunami 317
    tops Most Trusted Britons 354
    80th birthday 368–9
    Hemmings' evening 402
    Life in Cold Blood 402
    MP's impersonation of 430
    Palin joke 481
Attenborough, Richard 'Dickie' 182, 447
Attenborough, Susan 283, 402
Australia 425, 426
Ayckbourn, Sir Alan 212

Bacall, Lauren 69
Bacon, Francis 446, 482
Baddiel, David 66, 108, 191
Badly Drawn Boy 198
BAFTA 14–16, 227, 311, 312, 526
Bagherzade, Iradj and Shany 230
Bain, George 82
Bainbridge, Beryl 177, 429
Baker, Danny 284

Bakewell, Joan 274
Balkans, the 345, 451
Balls, Ed 422, 428, 443, 468–9, 474
Baltics, the 398, 406
Bamber, Helen 118
Bamji, Andrew 448
'Banana Wars' 9
Banco Roma ads 254
Band of Brothers (2001 TV series) 166
The Band's Visit (2008 film) 431
Banks, Gordon 402
Banks, Iain 524
Banville, John 534
Barbarians (TV series) 376
Barbican, the 410, 497
Barclay Brothers 397
Barclay, Humphrey 32
Barker, Ronnie 273, 359
Barlow, Stephen 9–10, 454
Barney (Tom's cat) 228, 530
Barraclough, Jenny 361
Barrie, David 198
Barua, Maan 424
Bates, Alan 194–5
Bates, Francine 468–9
Battle for Haditha (2008 film) 445
The Battle of Algiers (1966 film) 147
BBC
    MP involvement 2
    German Python shows 12
    MP visits 18, 338
    Rachel Palin working for 18, 19, 137, 528
    White City 18
    books 26
    Sahara and 92–3, 123
    Health and Safety day 109
    TJ and 116
    Natural History Unit 160
    unpopular in China 230
    New Europe and 338, 407–8
    finance and 358
    Barker's memorial 359–60
    medicals 374
    goat-controversy 391
    Yentob and 404–5
    Light Entertainment party and 488
    interviews 511–12
    MP 'value for money' list 523
    'Occasional Sparkle, Limited Appeal' 537
BBC Books 102, 104
BBC Showcase, Brighton 253
BBC Trust 451, 468, 469
BBC Video 30
BBC World Service 388, 449–50

BBC Worldwide 157, 456
Beale, Simon Russell 335
Beatles, the 237, 321, 408, 473, 519
Beaujolais Club 487
Beckett, Samuel 262–3, 367
Beeby, Tish 403
Behn, Aphra 367
Being Human (1994 film) 485
Bell, Martin 144, 456
Bell, Robert 67
Belmondo, Jean-Paul 111
Ben (medical adviser) 185–6
Benchley, Peter and Wendy 83–4, 145–6
Benn, Tony 445
Bennett, Alan 73–4, 188–9, 213–14
    possible *Hem's Chair* adaptor 60–1
    The Lady in the Van 74, 77, 148
    Tristram Powell's party 103
    A Private Function 207, 318
    LRB diary 251
    History Boys 269, 282, 284, 308
    MP asks about Diaries 269
    tea with MP 269
    ill health 270
    on Dudley Moore 302
    MP on 302
    worried about diaries 303
    Hockney and 308
    birthday 318
    Roundhouse show with MP 318
    Untold Stories 337
    Diaries and 382
    praise for *Diaries* 384
    compared to Blessed 413
    honours and 445
    drops out of Tate talk 449
    compared to Hockney 453
    Tea with ... event 483–4
    Three Yorkshireman reunion 485, 494
Bennett, Jana 323
Bennett-Jones, Owen 205, 436
Bennett-Jones, Peter 290, 436, 457
Benson, Jonathan 163, 498
Bercow, John 428
Berkmann, Marcus 388
Bernard and Mina (Palins' neighbour) 152,
    209–10, 232, 324, 329, 365
Bernard Quaritch 483
Bertolucci, Bernardo 113, 272
Best in Show (2000 film) 115
Bevan, Tim 417
Beyond the Fatal Shore (2000 docu) 89–90
Bhaskar, Sanjeev 473, 487, 493, 529
Bin Laden, Osama 144, 151, 154, 214, 420

Bird, Paul
    MP's PA 237, 311, 315, 354, 506
    on the Met 328
    Diaries and 375
    on *New Europe* 420, 456, 468
    on viewing figures 421, 423
    warns MP about cocaine in *Telegraph* story
        527
Birt, John 68, 315, 405
Birtwistle, Sue 38
Blacker, Terence 406, 537
Blair, Cherie 118, 174
Blair, Tony 76–7, 496–7
    Clinton and 10
    Tate Modern visit 73
    MP on 83, 92, 262
    JC and 118
    re-elected 123
    Iraq War 191, 219, 257, 265
    Bush and 220
    not trusted 354
    French and 365
    local elections 374
    Frost and 389
The Blair Years (Campbell) 415, 430, 502
Blakemore, Michael 267, 452
Bleasdale, Alan
    Oliver Twist 4, 7, 27
    Grade on 152
    works 189
    Dog joke 263
    MP sends *Football Days* to 265
    'as a question' 265
    MP on 319
    14th Best Scouser 335
    'You can't polish a turd' 362
    GBH 367
    Bleasdale/Diplomat Films evening 445–6
Bleasdale, Julie 189
Blessed, Brian 94, 94–5, 386, 413
Blunkett, David 479, 480
Bobin, Jim 44, 513
Bodleian Library, Oxford 459
Bogarde, Dirk 183
Bonnington, Chris 91
Book of the Week (R4) 384
Booker Prize 526
The Book Show (Sky) 534
Boorman, Charlie 313
Booth, Barry 496
Booth, Cynthia 451–2
Borders Festival 320
Botham, Ian 130
Bourgeois, Louise 73

Index

Bouteflika, Abdelaziz 356
Bowes-Lyon, Fergus 447
Boycott, Geoffrey 327
Boycott, Rosie 29, 33
Boyd, Susan 73
Boyd, Will 37, 38, 73, 405, 531
Boynton, Graham 287
Bradford 448
Bragg, Melvyn 103, 283, 525
Branagh, Kenneth 35
Brand, Russell 480, 486
Brando, Marlon 272
Brass Eye (Ch4) 131, 132–3
Brazil 412, 517
Brazil (1985) 39, 384, 498
Breaking the Links (Camden scheme) 170
Bremner, Rory 309
Brick Lane 16, 61, 98, 438
Briers, Richard 413, 434, 435
Brind, Oliver 433
British Book Awards 213–14
British Library 373, 399
British Museum (BM) 260, 309, 344, 370, 432,
    454–5, 466, 501
Britton, Tony 293
Broadhursts of Southport 534
Brook, Mirabel 229, 230–1, 239
Brooke, Steve 371
Brooke-Taylor, Tim 29
Brooks, Mel 299
Brooks, Richard 315
Broomfield, Nick 445
Brothers Grimm (2005 film)
    TG's indecision 193
    script 200
    Weinstein bankrolling 215
    cast 223
    Weinstein brothers and 234, 262, 272, 305
    MP sees progress on 256–7
    TJ on 295
    Venice festival 332
    TG on 337
Brown, Craig 476
Brown, Gordon 46–7, 83, 416, 428–30, 435,
    475, 483, 532–3
Brown, Joe 201
Brown, John 37, 412
Brown, Mr and Mrs (Palins' neighbour) 28–9,
    48
Brown, Sarah 443, 474, 483
Brubeck, Dave 198
Bruce, Fiona 409
Bruce, Lenny 31–2
Bruno, Frank 5

Bryson, Bill 245, 411–12
Buckman, Sam 476
Buerk, Michael and Christine 9, 10
Bulgaria 380, 424, 500
Bullock, Mr (neurologist) 471, 481–2
Buñuel, Luis 108
Burd, Edward, (Helen's brother-in-law) 15,
    105, 438, 539
Burd, Mary (née Gibbins, Helen's sister) 15,
    105, 259, 273, 362, 438, 504, 539
Burgon, Geoff 117
Burn, Gordon 85
Burns, Milly 498
Burroughs, Lorraine 521
Burtynsky, Edward 228–9
Buscemi, Steve 184
Bush, George W.
    elections 97, 102, 481
    Iraq War 142, 203, 218, 219, 257, 379
    Blair and 220, 265
    mid-term elections 386, 389
    storyteller 533
Bush, Laura 162
Byron, George, Lord 256

Cadell family 75
Cadell, Francis 'Bunty' 75, 81
Cadell, Gill 75
Callaghan, Jim 416
Camden Bereavement Service (CBS) 266,
    382
Camden Town Group artists 186, 449, 455
Cameron, David 456
Cameron, Rhona 108
Camilla, Duchess of Cornwall 447
Campbell, Alastair 190, 283, 415, 428–9, 430,
    502
Cane, Alice 244–5
Carey, George 352, 425
Carlton School
    travels Q&A with MP 152
    Sahara talk 197
    improvements to 198
    raising money for 267, 391
    assemblies 271, 326
    Himalaya talks 271, 294
    Aladdin panto 391
    MP entertaining children 442–3
    Evening With . . . 458
    disabled access 458
Carlton Towers Hotel 460
Carluccio, Antonio 305, 444, 454, 482
Carpenter, Humphrey 515
Carr, Alistair 516, 517, 520

Index

Carrier, John 267
Carwardine, Mark 411
Cashmore, Prof. Roger 307
Cave, Andy 528
Cézanne, Paul 127
Chalmers, Judith 460
Chamberlain, Annie 12
Change for Good campaign (UNICEF) 94
Changing Rooms (BBC) 249, 255, 261, 277
Channel Tunnel Rail Link (CTRL) 209–10, 329
Chapman, Graham 321, 395, 488
Charles, Prince 65, 67, 184, 409, 433, 447, 514
Charlesworth, Michael 175–6
Cheers (TV series) 235
Cheetham, Anthony 206, 207
Chelsea Arts Club 531
Chelsea Flower Show 458
Cheney, Dick 203, 481
Chicago 6, 8, 9
Children in Need (BBC) 506
China 229, 230, 232, 288, 453
Chitour, Said 145
Chorley, Roger, Lord 529
Chowdhury, Dalu 152, 326
Chris (publisher) 59, 60
Christie, Chris 532
Christies 144, 152
Christy, Desmond 42
Churchill, Winston 161, 239–40
Cinema and TV Benevolent Fund 447
Cirque du Soleil 102–3, 321
Clapton, Eric 196, 201, 337
Clare (Death show) 482
Claridges 245
Clark, Alan 525
Clark, Jane 525
Clark, Pete 384
Clarke, Charles 373
Clarke, Peter 191
Classic FM 429
Clays (printers) 375–6
Cleese, Alyce Faye (née Eichelberger) 11, 32, 288, 442, 464
Cleese, Camilla 353, 462, 464
Cleese, John
    USA residency problems 6
    in Mexico 8
    suits for commercials 11
    back in London 22, 23–4
    TG rude to 24
    hip replacement 25, 26, 27
    MP visits 32
    Python script meetings 33, 34

A Fish Called Wanda 38
no to '60 Minutes' CBS 38
on *Hemingway* book 53
Human Face 53, 85–6, 115
on MP's CBE 53
Blairs and 118
Tate Britain photo 137
sends TJ fruit on sale or return basis 156
Barry Took and 165
calls TG 166
Spamalot discussions with MP 170
evening with MP 177
Meaning of Life docu 218
ill health 244
'running for mayor' 244
Vanity Fair photo shoot 245–6
Amnesty concerts 255
Holy Grail and 257
asks MP for Fawlty Towers Hotel memories 265
Alyce Faye's 60th birthday party 288
second in Top 50 comedian list 299
Brian Musical 320
Python meetings 320, 390, 423–4
Spamalot (musical) 320
books hotel as Volestrangler 343
'doolally' according to EI 344
Brian biography of MP 353
'Michael likes talking' 353
characters played 356
TG and MP on 379
compared to Merchant 382
selling US properties 382–3
in Australia 386
worried about TJ 389
at *Diaries* interviews 390
Obama and 438–9
separates from Alyce Faye 442
supper with MP 451–2
MP calls 462
wants a *Wanda* musical 462, 464
full of beans 464
lunch with MP 464
MP asked to sort out 494
Vanity Fair shoot 519
cricket jokes with MP 520
Clemons, Clarence 20
Cleveland, Carol 451
Climate Change Conference, Copenhagen (2009) 538
Clinton, Bill 10, 122
Close, Chuck 35
Clunes, Martin 15
Clunie, Rosemary 465

Clyde, Jonathan 173–4, 237, 247, 275, 321, 357
Clyde, Pauline 275, 357
Cocker, Jarvis 511
Codron, Michael 357, 380
Coe, Sebastian 124, 404, 473
Cone, Claribel and Etta 127, 139
Connaught Hotel 177, 257, 463
Connolly, Billy 183–5
Connor, Jeff 328
Conran, Priscilla 305, 482
Conran, Sir Terence 397
Constantine, Susannah 282, 304
Contemporary Applied Arts 486–7
Conti, Tom 268, 354, 358
Conway, Gordon, Lord 496, 501, 503, 505, 507, 508, 534, 535
Cook, Lin 29, 300, 302, 336, 337
Cook, Peter 29, 188, 190–1, 261, 284, 299, 300, 302
Cook, Robin 48, 218
Cooke, Alastair 8, 165, 242
Cooper, Ray
    Python meetings 34
    Radical Media fire 36, 37
    plays the spoons 99
    on Cirque de Soleil 102
    George Harrison and 133, 134–6, 150, 201
    TG on 136
    on Weinsteins 234
    River Café Christmas lunch 247
    meal with MP 254
    sees progress of Brothers Grimm 257
    watches The Entertainer 408
    Ledger's death 444
    RIBA lunch 468
Corbett, Anne 233, 434
Corbett, Harry H. 471
Corbett, Ronnie 29, 35, 216, 233, 359, 414, 434, 494, 502
Corbett, Susannah 471
Coren, Giles 537
Cotton, Bill 94–5, 124, 469, 488
Coulson, David 526
Courtauld Gallery 217, 222, 235, 256, 268, 291
Courtney, Vanessa 114, 224
Coward, Noël 69, 138, 180, 188
Cox, Stephen 216
Crane, Nick 515
Cranham, Ken and Fiona 1, 103, 319
Crawford, Michael 262
Creed, Martin 482
Crichton, Charlie 38
Criterion, The 430
'Crowngate' affair (BBC) 424

Cruickshank, Dan 304–5, 348, 438, 490, 537, 538
Cruise, Tom 446
Cryer, Barry
    A Saint She Ain't 17
    Helen chatted up by 25
    Milligan on 120
    OBE 124
    Took and 165
    Oldie lunch 301
    Three Yorkshireman 302, 485, 494
    EI and 361
    Palins 40th wedding anniversary 370
    Vosburgh memorial 414
    MP's foreword to bio 511
Cuba 24
Culture Heritage and Sport, Dept of 198
The Culture Show (BBC) 342, 383, 528
Cuno, Jim 218, 222, 235
Cuno, Sarah 235
Currie, Edwina 191
Curry, Tim 276
Curtis, Adam 312
Curtis, John 344
Curtis, Richard 52, 396
Curzon, George, Lord 497
Curzon Soho 378, 445, 484
Cusack, Sinéad 194
Czech Republic 406

Daft, Carl 207
Dagbladet 345
Daily Mail 384, 527, 536
Daily Telegraph 336, 384, 421, 527
Dalai Lama 286, 303, 453, 460
Damon, Matt 223
Dando, Jill 16
Daniel (trainer) 108
Daniels, Phil 225
Danny (MP's hairdresser) 265, 309, 378, 395, 415
Darfur, Sudan 396, 418
Darling, Alistair 342
Darwin, Charles 502
Daunt Books 88, 240, 292, 376, 424
Davey, Marcus 318, 342
Davidson, Anthea 414
Davidson, Callum 252
Davidson, Ian 370, 414
Davidson, Jean-Paul (JP) 121–2, 386
    MP meets for breakfast 111
    Sahara series 142, 164
    Burns' Night party 158
    MP's 'Himalaya' idea 203

planning *Himalaya* 210, 211, 215, 224, 239
TRIC awards 216
in China 230
Himalaya series 241, 287, 288
good company 252
lunch with MP 257
Himalaya viewings 263
discusses future with MP 274
MP's South America idea 334
MP's *New Europe* idea 335
E. Europe recce 344
New Europe meetings 347, 352, 366, 373, 383
New Europe title 353, 407–8, 411
discusses *New Europe* with MP 355–6
New Europe viewings 412
Fry and 463
Davies, Alison 137, 210
Davies, Andrew 61
Davies, Claire 477–8, 482
Davies, Eddie 362
Davies, Phil 214
Da Vinci Code, The (Brown) 294, 313
Dawkins, Richard 404, 459
Dawson, Jill 297
Day Lewis, Daniel 238
Days and Nights in the Forest (1970 film) 497
Dazed & Confused 441–2
de Grunwald, Diana 3, 422
Dead Souls (Reballato's radio adaptation) 358, 371
Dead, The (1987 film) 453
Deakin, Roger 296, 480
Dean, Ptolemy 317
Deayton, Angus 289
Deborah (dental nurse) 12
Deedes, Bill 418
Def Leppard 402
Degas, Edgar 217, 336–7
Del Toro, Benicio 118
Democracy (2004 play) 267
Demuth, Charles 69
Denby, Jonathan 72
Dench, Judi 354
Denis, Claire 516
Denselow, Robin and Jadzia 127, 205
Depp, Johnny 49, 96, 99, 123, 377, 446, 468, 504
'Desire Unbound' (2001 Surrealist exhibition) 151
Devonshire, Duke and Duchess of 479, 480
Dexter, Ted 233
Dhungel, Ramesh 446
Diamond, Neil 11–12
Diana, Princess of Wales 419, 485

Dibdin, Michael 68
Dick Vosburgh memorial concert (2007) 414
Dickens, Charles 292, 435
Dimbleby, David 352
Dinah (Death show) 482
Dixon, Mike 496, 502
Dobson, Frank 514
Doganis, Rigas and Sally 72, 264
Donaldson, Willie 111, 406
Donmar Theatre 382, 416
Doubt (2007 play) 433
Doucet, Lyse 449
Dover Castle 392, 432, 450, 528
Dover, Michael
  book titles 18
  W&N and 36, 293, 513
  MP has supper at 91
  book signings 102, 104
  Sahara book 131, 155
  Diaries and 206, 271, 319, 375, 390, 397, 503
  Daily Telegraph Travel Awards 287
  Himalaya book 290, 291, 293
  New Europe meetings 380
  at *Diaries* interviews 390
  New Europe book 409
  lunch with Weidenfeld 415–16
  typo in *New Europe* 415
  on books 436
  Diaries lunch 436
  novel meeting 477
Downing Street events 75–7, 118, 174, 443, 474, 483
Doyle, Margarita 494
'Dr Fegg's Encyclopaedia of All World Knowledge' 24–5, 479, 489
Dragon Rapide disaster (1954) 3
Du Prez, Eric 529–30
Du Prez, John 320, 322, 342, 385, 529–30
Duffy, Carol Ann 533
Duncan, Lindsay 7
Dunkley, Chris 57
Dunne, Tom 21, 63, 71, 162, 427
Dunseath, Kirsty 241, 242, 477
Durden-Smith, Jo and Yelena 214–15, 215
Dyke, Greg 68, 473
Dylan, Bob 337
Dyson, James 397

Eagle Rock 450, 470
Eardley, Joan 475
Eastern Europe 344, 345, 355–6, 416
Edinburgh, Duke of 208, 264, 454, 486–7, 532–3
Edith (HP's old housekeeper) 221–2

Index

Edith (Palin cat) 71, 100, 111, 127, 293, 539
Edmonds, Noel 302
Edward, Prince 4
Egremont, Max, Lord 474
Eland Press 460
Elizabeth II, Queen 73, 76, 246, 354, 397, 458, 532–3
Elizabeth the Queen Mother 165, 166
Ellingham, Mark 411, 412
Elliott, Nick 4, 178
Elsie (Palin cat) 15, 100, 127, 199, 241, 539
Elspeth (Will's friend) 437
Elvis '56 (1987 film) 521
Ely Cathedral 526
Emin, Tracey 449
Eminescu Trust 409, 433
Encounters at the End of the World (2007 docu) 509
Endgame (2004 play) 262–3
Enfield, Harry 36, 133
The Engineer 86–7, 96–7, 375, 396, 515
English Heritage 6, 461
Eno, Brian 445
The Entertainer (2007 play) 408
Entwistle, George 537, 538
Ereira, Alan 116, 222, 376
Erik the Viking (1989 film) 355
Estonia 380
Ethiopia 28
Être et Avoir (2002 film) 239
Ettlinger, Paul 374
European Parliament Elections 510
Euros (2000/2004) 22, 23–4, 78, 270, 271
Eurostar trains 538
Eurovision 266
Evans, Lee 262–3
Eve, Trevor 216
Evening Standard 156, 384, 508
Excess Baggage (R4) 422
Extras (TV series) 382, 443
Eyre, Richard 11, 38, 255

Fairweather Low, Andy 201
Fanshawe, Simon 35
Faridany, Francesca 339
Farm Africa 226–7, 293, 317, 391
Farndale, Nigel 495
Farnes, Norma 515
Farrell, Colin 446
Faulkner, Richard, Baron 103
Fear and Loathing in Las Vegas (1998 film) 9, 36, 118
Feaver, Bill 188
Federer, Roger 463

Felder, Hershey 259
Fellini, Federico 254
Fenton, Dan 336
Fenton, George 409, 445
Ferguson, Nick 268
Fergusson, J. D. 75, 77, 81
Festen – the Celebration (1998 film) 10
Fiennes, Ranulph 501
Fierce Creatures (1997 film) 179, 434
Film & TV Academy, LA 360
Film 2009 with Jonathan Ross (BBC) 524
financial crisis (2008) 474–5, 478, 495
Fincham, Peter 323, 335, 338, 358, 407–8, 410–11, 421, 424
Fine Art Society 314, 340
Finney, Albert 233
Fitzgerald, F. Scott 79
Five Days in May: London 1940 (Lukacs) 161
Fixx, Jim 281
Flannery, Peter 316
Flather, Gary 465
Flather, Shreela 465
Fleet, James 339
Fleming Collection 475
Fleming's Bank 75
Flowers' East Gallery 228–9
Floyd, Keith 524
Folke, Mr Justice 354
Football Factory, The (2004 film) 509
foot-and-mouth epidemic (2001) 114, 115, 116
Foreign & Commonwealth Office 467
Forsyth, Bill 485
Forsyth, Frederick 158
Fortune, John 484
Forty Years Without a Proper Job (MP stage show) 404
Fossey, Dian 194
Foulgham, George 413
Fountain Club, Barts Hospital 500
Fox, Edward 380
Fox, Sir Paul 167–8, 447
Foyles 525
France 3, 13, 91, 324, 365
Franchetti, Alberto 4
Francis, Clive 339
Frank, Alan 523
Fraser, Antonia 58, 389, 513
Fraser, Jane 393
Frayn, Michael 198, 199, 241, 267, 381, 386, 446
Frears, Stephen 416–17
Freeman, Daniel and Jason 505
Freud, Clement 504
Freud, Emma 396

Freud, Lucian 11, 188
Freud Museum 11
Friel, Anna 184
Front magazine 334
Frontline Club 499
Frost, Carina 29, 273, 473, 494
Frost/Nixon (2006 play) 382
Frost/Nixon (2008 film) 488
Frost, Sir David
  Soap Box Awards 25
  garden parties 29, 273, 494
  Peter Cook Tribute Show 191
  Blair interview 389
  birthdays 454, 502
  drinks at 473
Frost, Wilf 502
Frostrup, Mariella 456, 506, 534
Fry, Stephen 37, 66, 129, 130, 289, 360, 384, 463
fuel protest 462
Full Circle with Michael Palin (1997 series) 101, 146, 157

Gagarin, Yuri 367
Galloway, George 350–1, 373
Galton, Ray 515
Gambon, Michael 262–3
Gardner, Frank 453, 496
Gardner, Rita
  asks MP about RGS presidency 496, 498
  MP meets with 497
  talks to MP 501
  shows MP around RGS 503, 507
  'Beagle' Campaigners 508, 512, 513, 529, 531
  Selbourne on 534
  sitting room. council meeting prep 535
Garrett, Lesley 303
Garrick Club 206, 358, 525
Garton Ash, Timothy 345
Gatehouse 384, 419
Gay Pride 82
Gaza 450, 494, 496
GBH (1991 TV series) 184, 367, 433, 490
Geldof, Bob 473
general elections 123–4
Gentileschi, Artemisia 110, 356, 449
Geographer's Club 529
Georgia 470
Germany 96–7, 97, 406
Gershwin, George 259
Gervais, Ricky 190, 443
Getty, Sir Paul 128, 129, 179–80
Gibbins, Anne (HP's mother) 277–8, 472–3

family Christmases 50, 105, 248, 296, 437, 438, 539
  London visits with MP 91, 248, 405–6
  returns home 115
  Robertson and 154
  Palins visit 165, 374, 520–1
  on family 248
  kneecap surgery 271, 273, 274
  becomes a great-grandmother 369, 393
  has accident 369
  ill health 369
  supper with Helen and MP 384
  has car accident 411
Gibbins, Catherine (HP's niece) 296
Gibbins, Cathy (HP's sister) 103–4, 222, 277, 296
Gibbins, Eve and Esther (HP's great-nieces) 296
Gibraltar 121
Gibson, Mel 259
Gilkes, Jeremy 282
Gill, A. A. 287
Gilliam, Amy 444, 446, 504
Gilliam, Harry 223, 246, 385
Gilliam, Holly 223
Gilliam, Maggie 31–2, 223, 246, 295, 446, 471
Gilliam, Terry
  'Don Quixote' film 9, 49, 96, 127, 377
  Fear and Loathing in Las Vegas 9, 36, 118
  rude to JC 24
  watches *Lenny* 31–2
  Python script meetings 33, 34
  commercials 36, 37
  Radical Media fire 36, 37
  on Europeans 80
  lunch with MP 80, 159, 166
  60th birthday 98, 99, 118
  evening with TJ and MP 117–18, 175
  Cannes Film Festival 121–2
  on Depp 123
  Python meeting 123
  'On the Ropes' 127–8
  Adventures of Baron Munchausen (1988 film) 127
  on Cooper 136
  and 9/11 attacks 142
  JC calls 166
  off to 'fix the swimming pool' 166
  Spamalot discussions with MP 170
  Time Bandits 179
  Brothers Grimm 193, 200, 223, 234, 256–7, 262, 272, 295, 305, 332, 337, 446
  lunch with TJ, EI and MP 193
  tribute evening for George Harrison 200

Index

Gilliam, Terry—*contd*
  MacNaughton funeral 202
  group portrait 208
  Weinstein bankrolling *Brothers Grimm* 215
  background 219–20
  Pryce and 223–4
  MP to lunch 223
  Weinsteins and 224, 234, 246, 254, 262, 272
  Vanity Fair photo shoot 245–6
  tea with MP 246
  River Café Christmas lunch 247
  meal with MP 254, 504
  visits MP 295
  Tideland 306, 337, 377, 379–80, 476
  Python meetings 320, 423–4, 498
  Culture Show 342
  lunch with MP and Basil 351
  renounces American citizenship 351
  MP gives *Diaries* to 377
  on *Diaries* 379
  on JC 379
  Brazil 384, 498
  Spamalot West End opening 385
  Spamalot animated movie 396, 398
  Spamalot in America 413
  supper with EI and MP 413
  Frears on 417
  The Imaginarium of Doctor Parnassus 435, 484, 504, 526
  death of Ledger and 444, 446
  MP on 468
  Spamalot (musical) 473
  discusses Africa and charities with MP 476
  'Tribute' evening 476, 484
  Monty Python: Almost the Truth and 523
  'Not the Messiah' Oratorio 529
Gilmour, David 309
Gimson, Sally 373
Giovanni, Janine di 301

Gladstone, William 57
Glasgow 329–30
Glendinning, Victoria 366
Globe Theatre 30
Glucksmann, Lilly 517
Godfrey (BBC finance) 358
Gold, Jack 189–90
Golding, Ruth 153, 287
Goldman Sachs 422
Goldsmith, Jemima 473
Goldstone, John 218, 382, 417
Good Housekeeping 261–2, 412–13, 420
Goodison, Katherine 438
Goodwin, Fred 480, 495

Gordon, Ian 470
Gore, Al 97, 102, 392
Gore, Frederick 434
Gorkow, Alexander 507
Gormley, Antony 404
Gospel Oak Primary School 7, 123, 190, 239
Gotch, Corrine 30
Gough, Martin 292, 510
Grabsky, Phil 455
Grace, Nickolas 194–6
Grade, Michael 152, 315, 359
Graef, Roger 254, 291
Graham Norton Show (BBC) 201–2
Grandage, Michael 158
Grandparents' Association 443
Granger, Stewart 423
Grant, Linda 112
Grant, Sue 353
Gray, Rosie 247
Gray, Simon 323–4, 340, 359, 465, 469, 479
  possible *Hem's Chair* adaptor 61
  Quartermaine's Terms 312, 314, 317, 339, 352, 380
Grazia 374
Great British Village Shows (BBC series) 410
Great Treasures series (2005 series) 304
Grebenshchikov, Boris and Irina 214–15
Green, Jo 177
Greenwood, Cmdr Hilary (MP's uncle) 133
Greenwood, Judy (MP's cousin) 133, 259, 261, 410
Greenwood, Nigel (MP's cousin) 90, 133, 259, 260–1
Greenwood, Phoebe 261
Greenwood, Sarah (MP's cousin) 261
Greer, Germaine 476
Grierson Award 196–7
Griffin, Mike
  MP's driver 191, 291, 313, 342, 362, 377, 386
  Elsie hides under car 199
  early starts 213
  to Brighton 253
  to Whipsnade 280
  airport drive 310, 406
  in Oxford 403
Griffiths, Richard 284, 310
Groucho Club 33, 108, 359, 367
Grove, Trevor and Valerie 122, 262, 380
Guardian
  on Neil Diamond 12
  Christy on MP 42
  Amis on book tour 73
  TJ's work for 217
  Himalaya review 285

Index

MP's *Guardian* piece 322, 324, 420
East Sterling article 328
Tideland article 377
Spamalot review 386
New Europe review 421
podcast 526
Guest, Chris 115, 252
Guinness, Alec 335
Guinness, Sabrina 445
Gwangwa, Jonas 242

Hadrian 466
Hague, William 124
Halfway To Hollywood: Diaries 1980-1988
preparing 436, 474
initial edit 464
final text 503
audio recording 517
TJ reads 522
book signings 525, 535
publication day 525
Hall, Katori 521
Hall, Sara Jane 93–4, 95, 96–7, 116
Hall, Sir Peter 32, 359
Ham House 27
Hamann, Paul 16, 19, 41
Hambling, Maggie 261
Hamilton, Adrian 461–2
Hamlyn, Helen 502
Hammond, Richard 436
Hampstead Town Hall 214, 225
Hanbury-Tenison, Robin 85, 508, 513, 516
Hang Down Your Head and Die (1964 show) 314, 357
Hanks, Tom 200, 201
Hanson, Michele 120, 247
Harcourt, Johnny 345, 467–8
Hare, David 214, 269, 526
Harewood, David 521
Harris, Rolf 51–2
Harrison, Anouchka 61, 63, 64, 65, 74, 84, 102
Harrison, Dhani 134–6, 337
birthdays 31, 275
on George's wounding 51
on the press 54
on George's death 150
George's memorial service/ceremony 178–9
Olivia's 60th party 409
Harrison, George
Dhani's 21st 31
attacked by intruder 51, 98
recovering from attack 53
tells MP of attack 54

MP visits 55
stays with friends 56
buys TG ukulele 99
at Cirque de Soleil 102
Cooper and 133
ill health 133
Palins visit 134–6
death 149–50, 163
friends 173
new album 174
memorial service/ceremony 178–9, 200–1, 261
tribute evening for 196
claims by 'You don't remember me' woman 255
meets Olivia 275–6
early performance of 'Something' 337
MP inspired by singing 338
Olivia and 409
Olivia visits George's Garden at Chelsea 458
MP described as 523
Harrison, Olivia
Dhani's birthday 31, 275
intruder and 51, 98
character 54, 99
Cirque du Soleil 102
Palins visit 134–6
George's death 150
back to Friar Park 174
George's memorial service/ceremony 178–9
tribute evening for George 200
meets George 275–6
Concert for Bangladesh 337–8
60th birthday party 408–9
Palins take out for birthday 408
visits George's Garden at Chelsea 458
Harry Potter series 342, 375, 415
Harry, Prince 67
Hart-Davis, Adam 404
Hart, Romaine 111, 276, 360
Harvey, Lucy 351
Harwood, Ronnie 405
Hassan, Prince Sidi 402
Hatch, David and Mary 32, 177, 288
Hatchards 130, 171, 244, 372, 391
Hattersley, Roy 177–8
Hatton, Derek 445
Hawks, Tony 213
Hawthorne, Nigel 96
Hay, Jocelyn 315
Hayden, Benjamin 514
Hayes Fisher, John 431–2

Index

Hayward, Dougie 11
Healey, Denis 273, 416
Heap, Mark 359, 371
Heather (Will's American friend) 44, 51, 61, 533
Heffer, Simon 464
Heggessey, Lorraine 122, 200
Hegley, John 371
Heidi (friend of TJ) 378
Helene (family cleaner) 16
Helen's Trust 479, 491
Hell's Kitchen (ITV series) 311
Hemingway Adventure (1999 series)
  filming 1, 3
  America 6, 8, 9
  book 7, 10, 12, 13, 15, 21, 30, 39, 41, 45–6, 48, 130
  assembly of 14, 24
  viewings 17
  title for 18, 20
  Key West filming 20
  Cuba 24
  PBS and 35–6
  voiceovers for 35, 37
  publicity for 39–40, 42, 59–60, 68–71, 102
  reviews 41, 42, 43, 45, 47, 57
  viewing figures 42, 71–2, 154, 192
  Yushu Horse Fair 282
  paperback printing errors 511
Hemingway, Ernest 3, 4, 12, 22, 25, 70, 79, 327
Hemingway, Gregory 144
Hemingway's Chair (Palin) 60–1, 125, 157, 160, 178, 187
Hemming, John 402, 506, 512, 516, 517
Hemming, Sukie 402
Hendricks, John 15, 16, 68
Henry (cab driver) 402
Henshaw, Michael and Anne 427
Hensler, Philip 493
Hepburn, Katy 252
Herbert, Angela (MP's sister) 19
  depression and death 10, 84, 403, 517–18
  father and 65
  very much missed 226
  children and 279, 329–30
  funeral 464
Herbert, Camilla (MP's niece) 226, 279
Herbert, Esmé (MP's great-niece) 113, 300
Herbert, Eugene (MP's great-nephew) 113, 300
Herbert, Jeremy (MP's nephew) 10, 84, 113, 236, 248, 300
Herbert, Louisa 279
Herbert, Marcus (MP's nephew) 113, 279, 329–30
Herbert, Melanie 90, 113, 300
Herbert, Morag 279
Heroes (2005 play) 310
Herzog, Werner 509
Heseltine, Michael 29, 124, 289
Heslop, Stewart 113
Hewison, Robert 57, 116, 370
Hewitt, Patricia 373
Heyes, Bernard 225
Heyhoe Flint, Rachael 460
Hezbollah 379, 395
High Speed Link (HS1) 209–10
Highgate Literary and Scientific Institution 262
Higson, Charlie 23
Hill, Sarah 183
Hillman, Mayer 352
Himalaya with Michael Palin (2004 series)
  planning 210
  book 228, 229, 275, 279, 286
  Yushu Horse Fair 233
  filming 253
  insurance for 253
  viewings 257, 263, 271, 282, 285
  commentary 273, 277, 281
  hoardings for 280, 285
  Moody on 281
  previews 285
  publicity for 285, 289, 290, 525
  reviews 285, 287
  book sales 286, 290, 291, 293, 294
  book signings 286, 288, 289, 291, 292
  viewing figures 286
  interviews 293
  Book of the Year nominee 313
  wins TV and Film Book of the Year 313
  book publicity 320
  paperback sales 332
  Palace Theatre slideshow 344–5
  free book to every secondary school 366
  increase in tourism because of 387
  China bans 453
Hiro, Dilip 217
Hirst, Damian 162
Hislop, Ian 216
Hislop, Peter 222, 239, 241, 336, 459
Historic Chapels Trust talk 400
History Boys (2004 play) 269, 282, 284, 308
Hitler, Adolf 324
Hockney, David 261, 308, 449, 453
Hodgson, Brian 446
Hoëbeke (French publisher) 511
Hoffman, Heinrich 324

Index

Hogan, Lisa 464
Holland Park Comprehensive 100–1
Holloway, Julian 233
Hoon, Geoff 265
Hopper, Edward 269, 279, 449, 454–5
Hotel Adef, Oran 147
Howard, Trevor and Helen 130
Hughes, Lyn 411
Hughes, Robert 89–90, 342
Hughes, Simon 353
Human Face (BBC) 53, 85–6, 115
Humphrys, John 127, 314
Hungary 398
Hunt, Liz 421
Hunter, Leslie 75, 76, 81
Husain, Mishal 436
Husband, Tony 263
Hussein, Saddam 210, 217, 218, 219, 220,
    246–7, 395
Hutt, Prof Michael 466
Hynde, Chrissie 183–4

I.B. Tauris 230
Idle, Eric
    Road to Mars 26
    'doesn't want to play any more' 40–1
    friendship with MP 55
    Spamalot (musical) 166, 170, 196, 298, 299,
        320, 385
    MP reunites with 184, 185
    lunch with TG, MP and TJ 193
    tribute evening for George Harrison 200
    Vanity Fair photo shoot 245–6
    sends MP sheet music collection of
        Lumberjack Song 260
    in Top 50 comedian list 299
    Brian Musical 320, 342
    JC and 321
    calls JC 'doolally' 344
    MP on diary entries 361
    in France 379
    TJ on 384
    Spamalot West End opening 385
    MP worries about 392
    Spamalot animated movie 396, 398
    supper with TG and MP 413
    rejects involvement in *Monty Python:
        Almost the Truth* 470, 494
    Vanity Fair shoot 519
    Monty Python: Almost the Truth and 523
Ifans, Rhys 300
Ifield, Frank 119, 409
Ignatieff, Michael 38
Illy, Riccardo 95

The Imaginarium of Doctor Parnassus (2009
    film) 435, 484, 504, 526
Imperial War Museum (IWM) 214
In the Shadow of the Moon (2007 docu) 441
Independent 189, 315, 421, 513
Indian Ocean earthquake and tsunami (2004)
    297, 299, 300, 303, 309, 317
Ingleby-Mackenzie, Colin 233
Ingrams, Richard 94, 107, 301, 515
Innes, Neil 450, 458, 529, 536, 537
Innes, Yvonne 458, 537
Inshaw, David 449
Interiors, the World of magazine 148, 308
International Piping Championships,
    Glasgow 329
Iraq 214, 217, 218
Iraq War (2003–) 219–21, 230, 236, 246, 255,
    257–8, 264–5, 297, 389
Irons, Jeremy 1–2, 194–5, 386, 533
Islington Design Centre 15
Israel 158–9, 257, 378, 494, 495, 496, 507
Italy 3, 13, 95
Ivy, The 369–70
Izzard, Eddie 31–2, 312, 384

Jabberwocky (1977 film) 471
Jackson, Glenda 123
Jackson, Paul 52
Jacquemin, André 31
Jaffer, Ahmed E. H. 225
Jagger, Mick 73
James, Anne
    letters with MP 18, 156
    future plans 36
    Hemingway Adventure series 42
    lunch with MP 45, 62–3, 245
    MP's manager 67, 73
    Sahara series 74, 100, 101, 128, 157
    Full Circle and 101
    Sahara book bidding war 102, 104
    meeting at Orion 112
    MP's 'Himalaya' idea 208
    Himalaya budget 211
James, Clive 47
James I 307
James, Kath 319, 322
Janina (production) 99, 102
Jardine, Cassandra 187, 188
Jarman, Derek 105, 106, 120, 174
Jeans, Luke 3
Jellicoe, George, Lord 534
Jenkins, Simon 198
Joaquin (Chicago driver) 70–1
John Paul II, Pope 304, 416

Johns, Capt. W. E. 107
Johns, Sir Richard and Lady Elizabeth 61,
  199, 370
Johnson, Hugh 293, 401
Johnson, Lyndon B. 84
Johnston, Alan 450
Johnstone, Iain 26
Jonathan and Bernie (neighbours) 277, 417
Jones, Alison (née Telfer)
  supper with MP 8, 108, 119, 507, 522
  sees *Lenny* 31–2
  'ignites face' 99
  worried about TJ in hospital 166–7
  MacNaughton funeral 202
  Anna and 291, 302, 305, 310–11
  at Savile Club 452
  sees *Spamalot* 493
  paparazzi and 508
Jones, Anna (née Soderstrom) 378, 384
  TJ on 271
  Al and 291, 302, 305, 310–11
  French food and 382
  Nancy the puppy 387
  on Hammershoi women 389
  visits MP 389
  TJ's unstoppable socialising 399
  supper with MP 481
  daughter Siri 506, 522
Jones, Bill 318, 355, 450, 494, 512, 523
Jones, Nancy 138, 276, 452, 468, 475
Jones, Nigel 261
Jones, Simon 138, 276, 452, 468
Jones, Siri 523
Jones, Terry
  supper with MP 8, 302, 481, 487, 507, 522
  buys *How to Manage Your Mother* 11
  writing with MP 24
  calls JC 26
  sees *Lenny* 31–2
  Python script meetings 34
  JC and 38
  MP and 41, 108
  health issues 57, 64
  squash with MP 57
  'The Dog Who Saved the World' 64
  'Rat Tart' sketch 80
  gladiators and 88, 116
  TG's 60th 99
  BBC and 116
  Crusades 116, 402
  Life of Michael quotes 116
  Who Murdered Chaucer 116, 193
  evening with TG and MP 117–18, 175
  hip replacements 117–18, 155, 156, 378, 481

sees *Sahara* rushes 119
Python meeting 123
party for 159
gut blockage 166–7, 168
MP visits in hospital 166–7, 168
Spamalot discussions with MP 170
on a staging of *Life of Brian* 174
The Surprising History of Sex & Love 175
asks MP to ring Bennett 188
Peter Cook - A Posthumorous Tribute 190–1
lunch with TG, EI and MP 193
MacNaughton funeral 202
on Bush and English language 217
dinner with MP 217
Medieval Lives series 222
MP's 60th birthday 226
Vanity Fair photo shoot 245–6
River Café Christmas lunch 247
Ripping Yarns and 253, 264
writing books 262
fan club 264
Anna and 271, 355, 378, 399, 419
Al and Anna 291, 302, 305, 318
living at Water House 295
meets MP 310–11, 419
out with MP 318
Python meetings 320, 390, 423–4, 498
on *New Europe* 340
evening with MP 350–1
birthdays 355
Erik the Viking 355
on Helen 370
at Palins' 40th wedding anniversary 370
Barbarians 376
loves *Diaries* 379
on France 382
has cancer 384, 387
visits MP 389
EI and 392
Evil Machines 398
positive attitude 65th birthday 398
British Library with MP 399
Gormley encounter 404
on his libido 423
Richard II book 423
Henshaw and 427
Monty Python: Almost the Truth 450, 470, 512
TG 'Tribute' evening 484
Aardman visit with MP 488–9
sees *Spamalot* 493
Blair's 'despicable' education failure 496–7
daughter Siri 506, 523
paparazzi and 508
Vanity Fair shoot 519

watches *Mountaintop* with MP 521
becomes a dad again 522
Monty Python: Almost the Truth and 523
'Not the Messiah' Oratorio 529
drink with MP 536
Jones, Tim 138, 276
Jordan, Louise 479
Joseph, Stephen 125
Judith (curator) 502
Jules et Jim (1962 film) 460

Kabila, Joseph 'Baby' 127
Kahn, Nathaniel 276
Kancheli, Giya 236
Kane, Sarah 84
Kaplan, Robert 361
Kaplinsky, Natasha 409
Karzai, Mohammed 230
Katakis, Michael and Kris 4, 427–8, 495
Katz, Roger 130
Kay, John 437
Kay, Peter 359
Keane, Fergal 49
Keating, Roly 148
Keegan, Kevin 93
Kellaway, Richard 169
Kelly, Ellsworth 366
Keltner, Jim 201
Kennedy, Bobby 223, 498
Kennedy, Helena 466
Kennedy, John F. 372
Kent, Nic 88, 260, 314
Kent, Prince and Princess Michael of 372, 516
Kenwood House 6
Kermode, Mark 383, 484, 526, 528
Kew Gardens 362
Khalifa (driver) 149
Kielty, Patrick 388
Kieser, Bernard 12, 155
Kiley, Bob 367
King, Astrid 212, 268
King, Denis 119, 158, 212, 268
King, Jeremy 309
King, Martin Luther 521
Kingsley, Ben 224
Kington, Miles 445, 461
Kinnock, Glenys 108
'Kissing Jessica Stein' (2002 film) 256
Kitchen, Michael 27
Kitov, Stefan 340
Klein, Richard 338, 352, 355–6, 462, 486
Klimt, Gustave 415
Kline, Kevin 358
Kosovo 13

Kurkov, Andrey 419
Kurland, Norman and Deborah 235
Kwouk, Bert 429

La Clique (2009 show) 539
Lader, Philip and Linda 9, 10
Lady in the Van (2000 play) 74, 77, 148
Lahr, John 451–2
Lamarr, Mark 382
Lamb, Edward Buckton 303
Lamb, Irene 99
Lambton, Antony 534
Lamont, Norman 89
Lanesborough Hotel 454, 502
Larry Sanders Show 34
Lartigue, Jacques Henri 279
Last Day of World War One (*Timewatch* docu)
  425, 431, 447–8
The Last Emperor (1987 film) 390
Later . . . with Jools Holland (BBC) 198
The Late Show (TV show) 190
Latvia 420
Laurie, Hugh 177, 367–8
Lautrec, Toulouse 336
Law, Phyllida 434, 435
Lawrence, Thomas 501
Lawson, Mark 41, 322, 370, 526
Lawson, Nigella 237
LBC Radio 284, 428–9
Le Mesurier, John 143
Leach, Rosemary 35
Leathersellers 407
Lebanon 309, 377, 378, 395
Ledger, Heath 223, 435, 444, 446
Lee, Ralph 18, 28, 41
Leland, David 166, 196
Lendon, Ron, and Thelma 7
Lenon, Barnaby 512
Lenska, Rula 194–5
L'Etoile 283, 302, 485, 494
Lette, Kathy 118
Levi, Primo 48
Levinson, Al 81–2
Levy, Sherrie 11, 69, 71, 144, 367
Lewis, Jenny 378
Lewis, Martin 455, 531–2
Lewis, Roger 539
Lewis, Stephen 422
Lewis, Tony 235
Liam (architect) 465
Libya 114, 121, 149
Lieberson, Sandy 476, 484
Liebowitz, Annie 518
Life in Cold Blood (2008 TV series) 402

Index

Life of Michael: An Illustrated Biography of Michael Palin (Novick) 116
Lincoln, Andrew 339, 340
Lincoln, C. J. 451, 468
Lincoln's Inn Fields, Camden 362, 366
Lindsay, Robert 335, 367, 408
Lindley, Richard 514
Linnean Society 528
Linnell, Andrew 497, 498
Lipman, Maureen 25, 169, 268, 452
Live 8 concert (2005) 320–1
Liverpool City of Culture 362, 445
livery companies 407
Livingstone, Ken 71, 266, 367
Lloyd, John 176, 177
Lloyd Webber, Andrew, Lord 103, 344
Loach, Ken 266
local elections 374
Logan Hall, Glasgow 390, 466
Lolita (1997 film) 1–2
Lom, Herbert 429
Loncraine, Richard 12, 111, 399–400, 490
London Review of Books (LRB) 251, 269
Loose Ends (R4) 371
Lord, Pete 489
Lord's Cricket Ground 129, 179–80, 326–7, 366
The Love Show (theatrical docu) 111
Lu Wenxiang 231
Lucas, Sir Colin 399
Luff, Peter 190–1, 468
Lukacs, John 161
Lumley, Joanna 9–10, 454, 473
Lydia (Palins' neighbour) 306
Lynam, Des 26
Lynch, David 48
Lyne, Adrian 1

McCain, John 472, 481
McCarthy, John 118, 126
McCarthy, Mike 513, 514
McCartney, Paul 132, 201, 408, 432, 473
McCartney, Stella 281
McCormack, Mike 115, 125
McCourt, John 95
McDonald, Gus 103
McDonald, Trevor 58
McDougall, Peter 185
MacDowell, Andie 15
McEwan, Ian 38, 438
McGrath, Patrick 88
McGregor, Ewan 168, 313
MacGregor, Neil 371, 432
McGregor, Sue 45, 149

McGuinness, Martin 407
McInerney, Jay 35
MacInnes, Hamish 92, 304
McIntyre, Donal 228
McKellen, Ian 490
McKeown, Charles 257
Macklin, Charles 357
McLaren, Malcolm 174
MacNaughton, Ian and Eke 202, 207
McNeill, Mhairi 148, 211, 356, 449, 499, 510
McVeigh, Timothy 498
Madejski, Sir John 522
Madonna 164
Madrid bombings (2004) 256, 257
Magda (Bertolucci's amanuensis) 272
Magris, Claudio 95
Mahfouz, Naguib 476
Mail on Sunday (MoS) 163
Major, John 240, 532
Malcolm, Derek 111
Mallatratt, Stephen 125, 157, 160, 538
Mandelson, Peter 112, 354
Manet, Édouard 218, 291
Mangan, Lucy 421
Mardi Gras, New Orleans 360
Margaret, Princess 172
Margolis, Jonathan 74
Mark (PA) 28
Mark (photographer) 280
Markos (MP's hairdresser) 11, 56, 158, 265
Marks, Dennis 381
Marks, Harrison 108, 129
Marlow Meets (2009 art series) 453, 455
Marlow, Tim 449, 453, 455
Marozzi, Justin 171, 500–1, 510, 520
Marr, Andrew 456, 534
Martel, Yann 282
Martin, Angela 199, 280, 290, 316, 420
Martin, George 321
Martin, Giles 321
Martin, Michael 429
Martinez, Ursula 539
Marx, Ron 521, 523, 525
Mason, Nick 430
Masters, Jan 374–5
Mather, Victoria 371
Matisse, Henri 127, 148, 173
Matthiessen, Peter 175
Maunder, Tracy 60, 98, 164, 494–5
Mauritania 155
May Day rally (2002) 171, 172
Mayall, Rik 354
Mayo, Simon 524, 528
Mazower, Mark 345

Index

Meadow, Jeremy 307, 319, 328, 354, 358
Meakin, Nigel
  Ultimate Frisbee 5
  Sahara series 114, 193
  MP's 'Himalaya' idea 203
  wins BAFTA for *Sahara* 227
  back from *Himalaya* filming 241
  Himalaya series 257, 282
  MP's Brazil idea 333
  60th birthday party 341
  New Europe series 399, 420
  MP's birthday 406
Meakin, Peter 241, 406
Meakin, Rhian 341, 406
Meara, Canon 389
Medieval Lives (2004 docu series) 222
Medwin, Michael 233
Mellor, David 402
Mendes, Sam 433
Merchant, Stephen 382
Merton, Paul 357, 537
Merullo, Annabel 36
Mexico Gallery 260
Meyer, Lise 66, 289
Michael (Carlton School caretaker) 326
Michael, George 56
Michael (Molloy's partner) 433
Michael Palin and the Ladies Who Loved Matisse (2003) 148
Michael Palin and the Mystery of Hammershoi (2005)
  Montreal Arts Docs festival 356
  meets RA's Mary Anne Stevens 411
  cast/crew viewing 329
  filming 308–10
  idea for 202, 211
  MP's *Guardian* piece 321, 324
  RT coverage 321
Michael Palin Centre for Stammering
  raising funds for 3–4, 118, 174
  'Esther' docu 65
  Christmas party 294, 346
  American Stuttering Foundation and 393
  donations 407
  children helped at 413, 473, 518
  Ed Balls and 422, 428, 443, 469
  ex-stammerers 474
Michael Palin on the Colourists (2000) 75–7, 81, 82, 89, 96, 106, 110
Michael Palin's Iron Curtain (2001) 94, 95, 96–7, 116, 121
Michael Palin's New Europe (2007 series)
  idea for 334–5
  BBC meeting about *New Europe* idea 338

  recces 344, 358
  title for 347, 353, 356, 410, 411
  office opens 353
  itinerary meeting 366
  filming 375, 381, 383, 398, 406
  introduction idea 376
  book 380, 388, 395
  viewings 398, 412
  book completion 409
  book printed 412
  commentary 413, 414, 417
  typo in 414, 415
  audiobook 418
  media/ marketing conference for 418
  transmission date 418
  Observer article 420–1
  cast and crew screening 420
  no RT cover 420
  first episode goes out 421
  reviews 421
  viewing figures 421, 423, 424, 426, 439
  publicity for 422–3, 435, 444
  book signing tours 425, 428, 431
  publicity tours for 426
  book signings 432–3
  audience profile 432
  sales 439
  complaint about Yugoslav episode 451, 468, 469
  pulled in Australia 456
Michelangelo 370–1
Michigan 6, 8, 9
Midland Hotel, Bradford 448
Miliband, David 456, 466–7
Millennium Bridge 78, 91, 173
millennium celebrations 52
Millennium Galleries, Sheffield 64–5
Millennium Show (BBC) 49, 50
Millennium Wheel 46, 74
Miller, Jonathan 38, 153, 240, 374, 515
Miller, Keith 108–9, 180, 196
Miller, May 110
Miller, Rachel 38
Miller, Sarah 290, 299, 309, 397, 485
Milligan, Jane 286
Milligan, Spike 15, 120, 180, 286, 299, 321, 515
Mills, Michael 167
Mills, Roger 122–3, 145, 334–5, 376
  Sahara series 18, 63, 79, 107, 131, 173, 193
  critical of *Hemingway* series 45
  Sahara recce 99
  writes off Chad 100
  recceing the *Sahara* series 101–2
  BBC Health and Safety day 109

Index

Mills, Roger—contd
cricket with MP 129, 130, 179–80
MP's 'Himalaya' idea 201, 203
Pakistan recce 211
planning *Himalaya* 224, 239
Himalaya viewings 263
ill health 263
MP on nose 274
Himalaya viewings 285
MP's Brazil idea 333
'Silk Road' idea 332–3
MP's South America idea 334
prefers South America 335
New Europe idea 346
New Europe meetings 347, 381, 392, 418, 432
retiring 347
New Europe title 353
discusses *New Europe* with MP 355–6
on TJ's new relationship 355
Poland recce 357
New Europe commentary 406
New Europe and 420
reads piece in *Daily Telegraph Diary* 421
Poland episode, *New Europe* 425
JC and Alyce Faye 442
MP meets up with 450
runs geography quiz 460–1
diagnosed with Parkinson's 529
'Hairy Moments' talk 529
Mills, Susie 425
Milosevic, Slobodan 12, 13
Minghella, Anthony 305
Minogue, Kylie 442
Miriam (violinist) 225
Mirren, Helen 393, 401
Mirzoeff, Eddie 17, 20, 42, 101, 193, 361
Missionary, The (1982 film) 433
Mitchell, George 82–3
Mitchinson, John 36
Moby 198
Moir, Diana 346
Molloy, Dearbhla 433
Monkhouse, Bob 216
Monson, Professor 481–2
Montreal Arts Docs festival 356
Monty Python
organising 1, 384
  Las Vegas event 8, 9
  German shows 12
  wines 40
  group portrait 208
  autobiography 219–20, 234–5
  theme 243
  Vanity Fair photo shoot 245–6

The Brand New Monty Python Bok 252
Rémy Renoux's French show 305
pattern of 379
organising for future releases 382
website 417
case against ABC 463
income and copyright 475
Python-related plays/adaptations 487
Vanity Fair shoot 518–19
Monty Python: Almost the Truth (2009 TV docu) 450, 470, 494, 512, 523, 524
Monty Python and the Holy Grail (1975 film)
  DVD extra material 124
  Castle Anthrax 146
  video 232
  JC accents 257
  No. 6 best comedy film 349
  shown at Phoenix Cinema fundraiser 400
  Movie Connections 451
  Banks as extra 524
Monty Python sketches
  'It's Man at Shell Bay' 19, 28
  'Climbing the Uxbridge Road' 27
  'Seduced Milkman' 27
  'Bicycle Repair Man' 28
  'Silly Walk' 28
  'Spanish Inquisition' 66
  'Rat Tart' 80
  'Lumberjack Song' 200, 201, 530
  'Parrot Sketch' 240
  Camden girls and 243
  'Cheese Shops' 255
  'Dead Parrot' 255
  'Grimsby Fish Slapping Dance' 308
  'The Smuggler' 444
  'Déjà Vu sketch' 531–2
Monty Python's Flying Circus – At Last in French (2005 show) 305, 507
Monty Python's Flying Circus 167, 308, 414
Monty Python's Life of Brian (1979 film)
  Top 100 British Films 39
  rickshaws and screening of 40
  West End possibility 170, 174, 196, 320, 342
  preferences for Biblical films 259
  shown at Mountain Film Festival 316
  No.1 best comedy film 349
  film publicity biographies 353
  clips 395
  centurion and jailer sketch 413
Monty Python's The Meaning of Life (1983 film) 218, 527
Moody, Nicola
  Sahara series 117, 122, 125, 126, 128, 131
  watches *Sahara* series 160

Sahara viewing figures 191
reaction to *Sahara* 200
Himalaya and 208, 211, 281, 286
Mooney, Bel 389
Moore, Charles 508
Moore, Charlotte 536, 537
Moore, Dudley 164, 302
Moore, Louise 72, 102
Moore, Michael 213, 272
Moore, Roger 144
Moore, Simon 295, 310
Morgan, Eddie 528
Morgan, Rhodri 120
Morisot, Berthe 449
Morley, Sheridan 188
Morris, Ann 531
Morris, Chris 131, 132
Morris, Jan 48
Mortimer, Bob 23, 299
Morton, Samantha 223
Mosley, Nicholas 118
Moss, Kate 442
Mountain (BBC series) 418
Mountain Film Festival, Trento 316
Mountaintop (2009 play) 521
Moussa, Amr 530
Mowbray, Malcolm 207, 227
Mullan, Peter 168
Mumbai terror attacks (2008) 486
Munton, Sally 129
Murdoch, Rupert 165, 490
Murphy, Dervla 348, 372, 460
Murray, Andy 513
Murray, Braham 314
Murray, Gordon 31
Musa ('Michael Meets') 505, 513, 527, 533–4
Musgrove, Dr 280, 423
My Architect (2003 film) 276
My Favourite Programme (R4) 66

Nadal, Rafael 463
Năstase, Ilie 385
National Film and TV School (NFTS) 152
National Gallery 16, 34, 209, 229
National Portrait Gallery (NPG) 248, 324, 437
National Theatre 308, 526
Natural History Museum 496, 502
Natural History Museum, Oxford 57
Natural History Unit (BBC) 160
Naughtie, Jim 133, 459
Neal Street Restaurant 287, 305
Neil, Andrew 217
Neil (CBS) 266

Nepal 386–7, 446
Nettleton, John 538
Neuberger, Rabbi Julia 82
New Art Gallery, Walsall 55–6
New Zealand 426
Newby, Eric and Wanda 244, 245
Niccol, Andrew 15
Nicholas, Mark 327
Nicholas, Mike 170
Nicholls, Mike 341
Nicholson, Jack 227
Nicolo (cinematographer) 272
Nicolson, Nigel 513
Nicolson, William 291
Noël and Gertie (Morley) 188
Norden, Denis 414
Norman, Torquil 318
North America 220, 221
Northern Ireland 30, 35, 407, 500
Norton, Graham 201–2
Norwich City FC 7–8, 212–13
Norwich, J. Julius 274
Not Only But Always (2004 docu) 300, 301, 302
Novick, Jeremy 116
Nunn, Trevor 32
Nyqvist, Sven 420

Obama, Barack 439, 481, 501–2, 531, 533
O'Brien, Edna 69, 401
Observer, The 349, 413
Ockrent, Christine 310
O'Connor, Des 305
Oddie, Bill 354
Odedra, JJ 23
Odins 390, 423, 451
The Office Christmas special (2003) 247
O'Hanlon, Redmond 245
Okri, Ben 465
Old Bailey 354–5
Oldie, The 94–5, 107–8, 129, 301, 448
Oliver Twist (1999 TV series) 4, 7, 27
Olympic Games 322, 324, 404, 453, 469, 470–1, 531
Omar, Mullah 149, 151
'*On the Ropes*' (R4) 127–8
O'Neill, Terry 11
Open Book (R4) 506
Ordnance Survey 429–30
Orford, Suffolk 105
Orion Publishing Group 39, 103–4, 436–7
cover proposal 102, 155
Wellington House office 112
'Pythons' definitive history proposal 123

Orion Publishing Group—*contd*
  books sales 207, 332
  meetings at 397
  recordings at 399
  author party 401
  travel photo shoot 442
Orr, Chris 205–6, 207
Orr, Deborah 98
Other Side of Spike (TV docu) 515
O'Toole, Peter 180, 326, 447
Owen, David 502
Owen, Judith 360
Owl Bookshop 292
Oxford, John 447–8
Oxford Playhouse 403
Oxford University 459

Paisley, Ian 407
Pakistan 205, 211, 228, 232
Pakistan Society 307
Palestine 257, 495
Palestinian Film Festival 506–7, 509
Palin, Archie (MP's grandson) 365
  MP besotted with 368, 370, 380, 383, 390,
    394, 395
  MP looks after 381, 420
  early video appearance 390
  great-grandmother and 393
  begins to crawl 395
  MP entertains 398, 426
  into everything 401
  greets MP 407
  MP buys gifts for 425
  goes to Terracotta Warriors exhibition 432
  visits MP 433, 462
  gardening with Archie 437
  talks to Grandpa 437, 456, 464, 512
  favourite things in MP's study 448
  fax machine expert 451
  grandparents' delight 462
  Big Ben trip with MP 471–2
  Frisbees and 499
  MP reads to 501
  swine flu and 517
  becomes a big brother 519–20
  'Barney's dead' 530
  family Christmases 538
Palin, Edward (MP's father) 21, 65, 80, 403,
    457, 474
Palin, Edward (MP's great-grandfather) 136
Palin, Helen (MP's wife)
  playing tennis 8, 89, 112, 214
  playing badminton 11
  Tom goes 'missing' 14

  wedding anniversary 15, 168, 311, 454, 455,
    503
  chatted up by Barry Cryer 25
  sees eclipse 33
  fans and 35
  in hospital 43, 146
  family Christmases 50, 105, 296–7, 438
  family holidays 106, 444, 522
  cancels Paris weekend 111–12
  on MP's tweed coat 125
  helps MP with tent 141
  family birthdays 146, 407
  tennis fall 160
  60th birthday 183
  ill health 190, 348, 349
  New Year's Eve with MP 203
  praise for her beauty 215, 318
  visits old housekeeper 222
  MP's 60th birthday 225–6
  becomes catnapper 228
  Oak Village street party 231
  and MP's implants 237
  knee injury 247, 251
  working at CBS 266, 382
  mother has surgery 273, 274
  looking after neighbours' homes while
    away 277
  chocolate box error 289
  knee problems 295
  knee operation 300, 301–2
  recovering from surgery 306
  letters from MP 332
  reaction to fan letter 351
  becomes a grandmother 364
  40th wedding anniversary plans 367,
    369–70
  Archie and 380
  looks after Archie 380, 420
  visits Archie 383
  on MP's *Parkinson* 390
  cooks superb roast 400
  and MP's back 425
  encourages Bleasdale to have knee done
    445
  door kicked 455
  meets MP 457, 521
  family holiday 469
  Big Ben trip with Archie 471–2
  finalises will 475
  trick or treaters 480
  carol singers and 489
  recycling panic 489
  reporter at the door 508
  thumb operation 511

becomes a grandmother again 519

MP's grey hairs 524

Palin, Henry William Bourne 'Harry' (MP's great-uncle) 100, 169, 447

Palin, Mary (MP's mother) 21, 22, 105, 403

Palin, Michael

Venice Carnival mask 2, 3

buys boxing gear 5

rib injury 5, 10

Gospel Oak Primary School 7, 190, 239

writing/researching novels 8

Spitalfields house visit 10–11, 17

becomes a great-uncle 10

at the dentist 12, 155, 236–7, 292, 510

computer maintenance 13, 399–400

Tom goes 'missing' 14

wedding anniversary 15, 168, 311, 454, 455, 503

running injury 21–2, 24

Biggles in retirement idea 21

parents' grave 21, 119

watches football with JC 22, 23–4

recreates EH's skylight incident injury 23, 25

Soap Box Award 25

recycling centre visits 28, 223, 266, 350, 415, 477

on Northern Ireland 30, 35, 44, 92, 407, 500

sees eclipse 33

awarded CBE 45, 51–2, 53, 532

on the neighbourhood 48, 100, 126, 140–1, 152, 251, 270, 296, 298, 417–18, 455

stuck in lift 48

family Christmases 50, 105–6, 247, 248, 296–7, 438, 538–9

Playboy 20 question column 55

'Scottish Waste' ('Glasgow y Valencia') 58–9, 63, 65, 67–8, 71, 72, 79, 84, 87, 88, 90, 100, 477

has shoulder pain 59, 60

'one more big adventure' 62

body surfing 64

Cuban cigar incident 69

The Grim Reaper story idea 69

face massage 70

Mr Heeley's sex talks 72

faeces-sampling 79

singing fish from Pao 78

watches football 78, 80, 115, 140, 175, 212–13

BUPA medicals 79, 185–6, 280, 423

Belfast doctorate speech 82–3

watches cricket 82, 129, 179

on male kissing 83

in the sewer 86–7

'Yorkshireman of the Year' 93

on the railways 98

on passport 99–100

family holidays 106, 444, 469, 522

Oldie's Pin-Up page 107–8, 129

begins French course 107, 108

joy of children 108

BBC Health and Safety day 109

Women Painters idea 110

cancels Paris weekend 111–12

head measured for hat 112

ill health 112, 114, 115, 147, 241, 258, 282, 347

begins Sahara journey 113–14

re-familiarises himself with Spanish 113

injuries 122, 124, 160, 172, 339, 523, 525

letter-writing 124

in cricket commentary box 130, 327

has tent tantrum 141

Filofax losses 155–6

pension 163

'Buddha' series idea 166, 193

bids for jockstrap 169

on emails 169, 265, 298

'Aren't you Zoë Ball's dad?' 170

family birthdays 172, 183, 317, 406–7, 506

meets Helen 175, 330, 457, 521

'camels have three vaginas' evening 177

Radio Times cover 179, 237, 280, 321

'True Scotsman' kilt-wearer 184

'Michael Palin' train 186–7

takes European break 193

'Save the Plankton' sketch 196

stays at Windsor Castle 199–200

overcomes fear of singing in public 201

on chewing gum 203

60th birthday 214, 225–6

on Iraq 214, 218, 219, 220, 236, 257, 289, 366

in Birmingham to discuss new bag designs 216

takes a leaf out of Cliff's book 216

on new iMac 222

attic clearout 223

throws suitcases away 223

starts popping anti-malaria pills 226, 251

encyclopedia 'salesman' 230

Oak Village street party 231

selected for Social Trends Survey 232

Day of the Implants 236–7, 240

water leak debacle 237–8

Broadband drama 239, 241

on Concorde 241

on St Pancras station 259, 401, 434

Index

Palin, Michael—*contd*
carrying coffins 261
'Himalaya sickness' 263
worried about style of running 263
dead to Torontonians 265
experiences road rage 272
Gospel Oak gardens awards 277–8
humming ear 278
elephant encounter 280
background to running 281
mysterious eczema-like rash 282, 425
'We Love You, Michaels' ladies 285
chocolate box error 289
on disasters 299
in Top 50 comedian list 299
printer problems 306
Brasenose graduates' dinner 307
'Grimsby Fish Slapping Dance' DVD
    filming 308
BAFTA nominee 'goodie box' 311
BAFTA Special Award 311–12
Voice of the Viewer and Listener awards
    315
threatened by Brooks 316
London bombings and 322, 325
cricket with Parkinson 326–7
Stenhousemuir project 328–9, 329, 330–1
'great sewers of the world' offer 332
letters to Helen 332
throat problems 338–40, 345
inspired by George Harrison's singing 338
sees ENT man 345
twisted nose 345
trailed by Russian women 346
fan letters 351, 353
on East Anglian journalists 352
on gay men 353–4
'Michael likes talking' 353
No. 6 Top 20 Most Trusted Britons 354
crypt fans 355
watches swan family 356–7
receives two Valentine cards 357
becomes a grandfather 364, 368
besotted with Archie 365, 370, 380, 384,
    390, 393, 395
40th wedding anniversary plans 367,
    369–70
9th Greatest Explorer 367
Archie and 370, 407, 418, 448, 456, 462,
    499, 519
Voice of the Viewer & Listener awards 371
British Library 'Woolf' patron 373
has BBC programme medical 374
not a gardener 374

availability to open a Plum Museum 376
looks after Archie 380, 420
fans and 382, 459, 529
entertains Archie 383, 398, 426
on comedy of celebrity 396
testicle ache 397
finds 'be funny' approach difficult 399
Arctic Monkeys joke 401
supervising Archie 401
birthdays 406
'celebrate London' day 434
gardening with Archie 437
trips with Archie 441
'Python slips on banana skin' 445
knighthoods and 445–6
65th birthday 457
on retirement 457
fishmonger bangs on door 459
on the countryside 461
Hitler moustache on posters 463
talks to Archie on the phone 464
SOAS Honorary Fellowship 466
MRI scans 467–8, 469
aneurysm alert 468, 471, 481–2
Big Ben trip with Archie 471–2
accused of antisemitism 473–4
finalises will 475
offered Death programme 475, 476, 477–8,
    482
Palin for President 475
trick or treaters 480
books for restoration 483
Three Yorkshireman reunion 485, 494
carol singers and 489
recycling panic 489
knee problem 495
worried about statins 496
reading with Archie 501
'The Truth' novel 503, 515, 524
anxiety interview 505
on MPs' expenses 507
updates inoculations 507
reporter at the door 508
rabbi apologises to 517
worries about swine flu 517
'Archie 2 expected' 518
cricket jokes with JC 520
watches Sheffield Utd 522
tops BBC 'value for money' list 523
personal appearance reassessment 524
described as George Harrison 523
Mrs Betty Palin attire 527, 530
Saturday Night Live cocaine use 527
at Wig Specialities 527

Index

'taking Michael Palin to the toilet' 528
'Occasional Sparkle, Limited Appeal' list 537, 538
on changing face of bookselling 426
gifts for Archie 425
newsreaders and 409
sixth-former looks 421
visits Archie 417
voted 4th 'sexiest brain' 424

Palin, Rachel (MP's daughter)
cousin becomes father 10
on London bombing 17
at the BBC 18, 19, 528
Karen's mother comes to dinner 35
leaves home 41
away filming 44
family birthdays 55, 108, 146, 156, 336
re-edited Luther King film 67
'Great Speeches' 68, 71
borrow's HP car 71
meets Maggie Smith 77
'Conspiracies' filming 90, 98
family Christmases 105, 538–9
leaves BBC 137
sees Apocalypse Now Redux with MP 151
Warhol exhibition with MP 160
Pugh and 164
back to Gospel Oak Primary 190
watches Sahara with MP 192
director 222
MP's 60th birthday 226, 227
sees Waiting for Happiness with MP 242
Changing Rooms producer/editor 249, 255, 261, 277, 290, 297
sees Waiting for Guffman 252
Biblical film cutting 259
upset at Euro 2004 result 270
character 290
sees The Sea Inside with MP 295
car vandalised 296, 297–8
visits HP in hospital 302
Hell's Kitchen 311
London bombings and 322, 323
I'm a Celebrity 333, 342–3, 344, 345
back from Australia 347
free-fall jump 347
family lunches 379
sees Tideland Q&A screening 379
watches Frost/Nixon with MP 382
Great British Village Shows director 410
watches In the Shadow of the Moon with MP 441
family holidays 444
fly-on-the-wall docu 462, 464

watches 35 Rhums with MP 516
enjoys running 523

Palin, Rachel (née Winder) (MP's daughter-in-law)
MP visits 113, 368
meal with Pao 227
supper with MP 228
expecting baby 327, 510, 517, 519
becomes a mum 364
family lunches 379
as a parent 380
Archie and 383, 462
marries 394
visits MP 433
cross at Tom's ankle injury 510

Palin, Sarah 472, 481, 494

Palin, Thomas (Tom, MP's son)
is 'missing' 14
studio 37
travelling with MP 62
family Christmases 105–6, 538
meal with MP 113
family birthdays 145, 225, 287, 336
cooks for MP 173
back to Gospel Oak Primary 190
party banner by dyslexic 225
MP's 60th birthday 227
supper with MP 228
wants to leave music business 234
Urban Rock and 249
character 290
bike accidents 325–6
Carlton School 326
expecting baby 327
becomes a dad 364, 365
MP visits 368
in-laws on 375
family lunches 379
as a parent 380
Archie and 383
helps MP with computer problem 390
marries 394
brings Archie round 426
goes to Terracotta Warriors exhibition 432
visits MP 433
ankle injury 510
becomes dad again 519
Barney is run over 530
'Not the Messiah' Oratorio 530

Palin, Wilbur (MP's grandson) 519–20

Palin, William (Will, MP's son)
Spitalfields house 10–11, 17, 61
Ingres exhibition with MP 16
family birthdays 44, 146, 336, 484

Palin, William—*contd*
family Christmases 50, 105–6, 296, 538–9
offered Soane Museum job 59
lunch with MP 61, 437–8
walks with MP 80, 490
on Berlin 125
Hislop asks after 216
MP's 60th birthday 226
witty speaker reputation 249
Greenwood's funeral 260–1
Himalaya and 285
character 290
Cruickshank and 304–5, 348, 490
to Holburne Museum 317
London bombings and 323
Paul Smith and 331
leads the fight for Lincoln's Inn Fields 361, 366
MP visits 372
Soane tours 387
joins Travellers Club 387
Spitalfields' Society 387
Meets up with MP 513
enjoys running 523
'Not the Messiah' Oratorio 530
Palyn, George 307
Pamuk, Orhan 351, 381
Panorama (BBC) 258
Pao, Basil 3–4, 350–1, 457–8
on Southwold 21
photo books 25, 36
MP stays with 62
Sahara series 63, 131
singing fish for MP 78
meeting at Orion 112
Bertolucci and 113
works on *Sahara* book with MP 138–9, 155
'Buddha' series idea 166
Young Adam 168
MP's 'Himalaya' idea 201
MP's 60th birthday photos 227
arrives for *Himalaya* 240
meal with MP 254
Himalaya photos 255
evening with MP 272
MP meets up with parents 311
Hands: A Journey Around the World 333, 350
lunch with MP and TG 351
New Europe meetings 380
Palins meet 436
Chinese New Year party 446
Tate Britain with MP 482
Pao, Pat 139
Paris 5, 19

Park, Nick 489
Parker, Alan 189
Parkinson, Mary 473
Parkinson, Michael 190, 242–3, 281, 289, 326, 388, 473, 477, 488
Parkinson's disease 403
Parkinson's Disease Society Christmas Concert 434–5
Parris, Matthew 391
Parry, Bruce 422
Patten, Chris 459
Patterson, Dan and Laura 66, 289
Pattinson, Charlie 300, 316
Paul (maître d') 504
Paul Morrison Award (*Wanderlust*) 411–12
Pavarotti, Luciano 242–3, 485
Paxman, Jeremy 210, 371, 424–5
PBS (Public Broadcasting in America) 35–6
Peace Rally (2003) 209
Peach, Esmé 527, 533
Peacock, Christie 293
Peel, John 336
Pellegrinetti, Mary 514
PEN Writers In Prison 389, 405
Penguin Books 72, 102, 104
Penrose, John 264
Peploe, Clare 272
Peploe, Samuel 76, 81
Pepys, Samuel 435, 463, 466
Percy (nursery gardener) 374
Perle, Richard 220
Persia 344
Peru 175
Peter Cook - A Posthumorous Tribute 190–1
Peter Cook Foundation 188, 336, 337, 342
petrol protests 91
Pettet, Joanna 194, 195
Petty, Tom 54, 200, 201
Pevsner, Nikolaus 225, 293, 303
Phelan, Jacqui 391, 442–3
Phoenix Cinema 400
Phoenix Theatre 169
Picasso, Pablo 173, 266
Pickwick Papers (Dickens) 292, 435
Pile, Stephen 42
Pinter, Harold 58, 103, 380, 389, 416, 454
Pizza Express 379, 382, 460
Plimpton, George 70
Poland 96–7, 358, 360, 381, 399, 406, 425, 426, 525
Pole to Pole with Michael Palin (1992 series) 28, 156, 157, 223, 249
Pollock, Jackson 224, 454
Pompadour, Madame de 209

Index

Popham, Mike 176
Portal, Jane 432
Portillo, Michael 293
Powell, Nik 189
Powell, Tristram 58, 103–4, 227, 251–2, 416–17, 445–6, 476
The Power of Nightmares (BBC docu) 312
The Power of Yes (2009 play) 526
Pratt, Roger 484
Prescott, John 103, 373
Pringle, Bryan 504
Pringle, Craster 504
Pritchard, John
  MP meets up with 121, 450, 529
  Sahara series 193
  MP's 'Himalaya' idea 203
  BAFTA-nominated for *Sahara* 227
  back from *Himalaya* filming 241
  Acute Mountain Sickness 253
  New Europe meetings 392, 432
  MP's birthday 406
Private (2004 film) 495
Private Eye 176, 223, 336, 337, 419, 476
Privates on Parade (2002 play) 158
prosopagnosia 395–6
Proust, Marcel 465
Pryce, Jonathan 223–4, 295, 484
Pryce, Kate 223, 295
Psychologies Magazine 424
Pugh, David 164, 170, 174, 196, 310
Pujol, Joseph 49
Punch 223
Punch-Drunk Love (2002 film) 197
Purves, Libby 403
Puttnam, David 343–4, 485
Puttnam, Patsy 343
Python Night (30th anniversary docu) 18–19, 27–8, 31, 41, 384–5
Pythonland (2002 docu) 27, 28
The Python Years: Diaries 1969-1979 388–9, 430–1
  publicity interviews 371, 377
  hot off the press 375
  reactions to 379, 505
  reviews 384, 388, 419
  serialisations of 384
  sales 390, 392, 397, 436
  book signings 390

QI (BBC) 176
Quaid, Dennis 12
Quartermaine's Terms (1981 play revival) 312–14, 316, 338–40, 348, 352, 359, 366, 380
The Queen (2006 film) 393

Quick, Diana 537

Rachel (George and Olivia Harrison's assistant) 51, 56, 134, 150
Radio Times (RT) 30–1, 115, 179, 321, 340, 420
Ramsay, Allan 501
Ramsbotham, Peter 301
Randall & Hopkirk (Deceased) (2000 TV series) 23
Rankin 441–2
Rankin, Ian 282
Rantzen, Esther 65
Rattle, Simon 38
Rausing, Hans and Märit 9
Ravel's (local bistro) 256, 289, 356, 533
Raworth, Sophie 537
Ray, Satyajit 497
Reader's Digest 354
Real IRA bombings 120–1, 126
Redgrave, Corin 498–9
Redgrave, Vanessa 438
Reeves, Vic 23, 299, 383
Refugee Action 527
Reid, Travers 346
Renoux, Rémy 305, 507
Reynolds, Caroline 60, 61, 125, 160
Reynolds, Sir Joshua 501
Rhys Jones, Griff 312, 418
RIBA (Royal Institute of British Architects) 468, 497
Rice, Tim 473, 502
Richard & Judy (ITV) 464
Richard, Cliff 216, 354
Richard, Wendy 388
Richardson, Alex
  critical of *Hemingway* series 45
  in the sewer 128
  in the 'Sad Pub' 257
  ideas for new series 333
  New Europe editing 376, 399
  New Europe meetings 392, 432
  New Europe viewings 412
  MP meets up with 450
Rickman, Alan 425
Riddell, Mary 412
Ripping Yarns
  'Tomkinson's Schooldays' 65, 67, 84
  popularity of 67, 287
  DVD commentary 253, 264
  'Escape from Stalag Luft 112B' 264
  'The Curse of the Claw' 264
  'Whinfrey's Last Case' 264
  'The Testing of Eric Olthwaite' 477
  'Golden Gordon' 63, 362

Rippon, Angela 216
River Café 133, 173–4, 247
RNIB 450–1
Roar, Odd 345
Roberts, Gareth 47
Roberts, Jane 267
Robertson, Bruce 154
Robertson, Geoffrey 118
Robertson, Seona 466, 469
Robinson, Anne 264
Robinson, Mimi 374
Robinson, Peter 499
Robinson, Steve 240
Robinson, Sue 30
Robinson, Tony 49, 50, 51
Rochefort, Jean 96
Roddick, Andy 513
Rogers, Dafydd 174
Rogers, Richard, Lord 47
Rogers, Ruth 38, 133, 247
Romania 383, 385, 409
Ron the painter 116
Root, Jane 253
Rose, Wally 72–3
Rosenthal, Amy 268
Rosenthal, Greg 268
Rosenthal, Jack 61, 268, 314
Rosie (Mary Burd's friend) 259
Ross, Deborah 189
Ross, Jonathan 15, 40, 287, 422–3, 480, 486,
    523, 524
Rothschild, Jacob 235
Roven, Chuck 215
Rowley, David 375
Royal Academy (RA) 109–10, 255–6, 306–7,
    411, 449, 467
  exhibitions 2, 127, 291
Royal Albert Hall 200–1, 224, 507, 529–30
Royal Asiatic Society 446
Royal China, Queensway ('The Canteen')
    121, 175, 254, 436
Royal Court Theatre 84, 233
Royal Family 11, 29
Royal Geographical Society (RGS)
  Himalaya speech 366
  MP considers presidency 496, 497, 498
  MP presidency 496, 497, 505–6, 508, 510,
    513, 516, 531
  MP accepts presidency 498
  Special General Meetings 500–1, 505–6,
    512
  MP shown around by Rita 503
  'Michael Meets' 505, 513, 515, 527, 533–4
  'Beagle' campaign 506, 507, 508, 512, 514,
    516, 520, 529, 531
  MP first visit as President 510
  MP first council meeting as President 512
  first lecture introduction by MP 526
  MP introduces first lecture 526
  Monday night lectures 528, 534–5
  council meetings 535
  Children's Lecture 536
Royal Institute of British Architects (RIBA)
    284
Royal Opera House 194–6
Royal Television Society (RTS) 15–16, 283,
    409
Roylance, Brian, 'A Time to Live' 108
Rubens, Peter Paul 371
Rumsfeld, Donald 147, 203, 219, 265
Rushdie, Salman 38, 531
Ruskin, John 57
Russell, Ken 163
Russell, Shirley 163
Russia 352, 470
Rustin, Lena 294, 296, 346
Rustin, Ronnie 297
Ryan, Meg 12

Sachs, Andrew 480
Sacks, Jonathan 297
Sadler, Mick and Lulu 111
Saga magazine 377
Sahara with Michael Palin (2002 series)
  as project 18, 19, 65, 68, 74, 78, 80, 86
  as idea 62–3
  BBC and 92, 123
  Chad written off 100
  research 100, 131
  book 102, 103–4, 116, 117, 120, 126, 136,
    149, 155, 157, 158, 160, 240, 241
  progress 117
  title for 122, 126, 127, 128
  assembly viewing 128
  schedule 133
  filming 142–3
  fixer for 145
  viewings 146, 160
  likely popularity 154
  sold to America 157
  commentary 164, 172, 173
  clapperboard mix 189
  book signings 191–2, 199, 219–20
  viewing figures 191, 192–3
  wins TRIC award 210
  paperback 242, 251
  book is bestseller 249
  publicity for 278

Sainsbury's Magazine 274
St Alban 476
St Luke's Church 293
St Martin's, Gospel Oak 299, 303
St Pancras Almshouses 514
St Pancras International 259, 401, 434, 525
St Paul's Cathedral 355
Salgado, Sebastião 221
Salmon, Peter
    Cranham and 1
    Sahara series 19, 68, 80, 92
    Hemingway series 20, 39
    Harris and 51
    Space Travel idea for MP 62
    Stenhousemuir idea 327, 329
Salvoni, Elena (maître d') 429
Sam (Rachel's friend) 71
Sandler, Adam 197
Sarah (camel) 179
Sarah, Duchess of York 29
Sarah (Palins' neighbour) 277
Sarah (UNICEF) 343
Sargent, John Singer 497
Sarqui, Farooq 389
Saturday Night Live (US TV show) 360
Saunders, Maria 222
Saunders, Roger 34, 222, 353, 379
Savile Club 451, 452
Sayle, Alexei 213
Scardino, Marjorie 176
Scarfe, Gerald 341
Scarlett, John 502
Schama, Simon 80, 143
Schatz, Doug 220
Scholes, Paul 24
Scott-Irvine, Garry 353
The Sea Inside (2004 film) 295
Seberg, Jean 111
Secombe, Harry 120
Seinfeld, Jerry 34
Selborne, John, Lord 534
Sell, Colin 485
Sellers, Peter 187, 321
Seneca the Elder 391
Serbia 383
Serbs, the 383, 451
Serge (commercials producer) 254
Sergeant, John 240, 484
Serota, Nick 453
Serpentine Gallery 366
Service Commitment Awards, UCH 403–4
Severs, Dennis 342, 402
Sewell, Brian 198, 199
Shankar, Anoushka 190, 200

Shankar, Ravi 190, 200
Shannon, Dr 241
Sharman, Helen 402
Shearer, Harry 360
Sheekey's 123, 170, 193, 262, 413, 416
Sheeler, Charles 69, 356
Sheerness, Kent 387
Sheffield 46–7, 64–5, 186–7, 401–2, 511
Sheffield United FC 7, 53, 212–13, 369, 522
Shepherd, Cybill 70
Shepherd, Elaine 18, 41, 384
Shirley, Edwin 22
Shirley (Palins' neighbour) 277
Shrewsbury School 336, 354, 406, 422
Shu (China adviser) 230
Sibleyras, Gérald 310, 313
Sickert, Walter 113, 217–18, 336
Simmonds, Graham 98
Simon (Tom's friend) 234
Simpson, Alan 515
Simpson, John 148
Sinn Fein 30, 35
Sirhan, Sirhan 223, 498
Sissako, Abderrahmane 242
Skinner, Frank 36
Skirving, Archibald 501
Sloan, John 455
Sloman, Lynn 125
Slumdog Millionaire (2008 film) 497
Smiles, Ray 487
Smith, Arthur 94, 122
Smith, Delia 7, 212, 487, 537
Smith, Maggie 69, 74, 77–8, 214, 227
Smith, Paul 331
Snow, Jon 371, 403
Soames, Nicholas 464
Soane Museum 59, 153, 331, 366, 387, 483
SOAS University 466, 506–7
Social Trends Survey 232
Söderquist, Nina 493
Sofia Film Festival 340, 500
Sotheby's 434
Sotheran (rare book dealer) 368, 454
South America 333–4
South Bank Show (ITV) 385
Southwold, Suffolk 21–2
Spamalot (musical) 276–7, 344–5
    EI and 166, 170, 196, 298, 299, 320, 385, 386
    discussions with MP 170
    Pythons and 320, 493
    Beale as Arthur 335
    in America 341, 413
    South Bank Show on 385
    photos 385–6

Index

Palin, William—*contd*
  reviews 385
    West End opening 385–6
    animated movie 396, 398
Spankie, Sarah 397
Spectator 388, 508
Speight, Johnny 515
Spinal Tap 48, 349, 360, 430
Spitalfields' Society 387
Spitalfields Trust 438
Springsteen, Bruce 20
Stamp, Terence 194–6
Stanford's map shop 220, 245, 335, 341
Starr, Ringo 178, 201, 408–9
Station Agent (2003 film) 259
Steadman, Ralph 118
Steel, Mark 400
Stelios, Haji-Ioannou 309
Stenhousemuir 328–9, 329, 330
Stenhousemuir FC 330–1
Stephen, Jaci 16
Stephenson, Pamela 185
Stevens, Mary Anne 127, 411
Stewart, Dave 306
Stewart, Jackie 185
Stewart, Rod 242–3, 302
Sting 252, 309
Stoney, Heather 212
Stoppard, Tom 310, 341
Strachan, Alan 358
Strada 372, 516
Straight Story, The (1999 film) 48
Stratton, Michael 103–4, 277, 296
Stuart-Harris, Graham 65, 226, 370
Stuart-Harris, Margot 370
Stuart-Harris, Marjorie 65
Sturridge, Charles 155, 163
Stuttard, John 354
Suchet, David 37, 328
Sudjic, Deyan 309, 397
Summers, Julie 91
Sunday Times (ST) 241, 283
Sushrut (Indian environmentalist) 424
Sutcliffe, Thomas 285, 421
Swannell, John 208, 519
Swayze, Patrick 164, 524
Swinton, Tilda 168
Sykes, Eric 515
Sykes, Melanie 305
Syria 309

Taliban 145, 149, 151, 161
Talk Radio 26
Tatchell, Peter 219

Tate Britain 131–2
  Turner at 87
    MP has photo taken for exhibition 137
    exhibitions 163–4, 188, 336–7, 482
    MP films at 309
    Late at the Tate talk 449, 453, 455
Tate Modern 29–30, 87
  Blair visits 73
  exhibitions 151, 160, 173
  collection 186, 279, 350
  'Explore Tate Modern' 224
Taylor, Elizabeth 122
Taylor, Mary and Sebastian 7, 153
Tebbit, Lady Margaret 29
Television and Radio Industries Club
    (TRIC) Awards 210, 216
terrorism
  London 17, 18, 218, 322, 324–5, 326, 327
  threat of 210, 277
  plot to down airliners 379
  averted in London 412
  in Mumbai 486
Terry the Tarantula 179
Tewkesbury Floods (2007) 431
Thatcher, Margaret 29, 210, 240, 273, 490, 532
Theroux, Louis 152, 424
Thesiger, Wilfred 365
This Morning (ITV) 422
Thomas, Jeremy 168, 254, 262, 337, 484
Thomas, Michel 107, 108
Thomas, Rupert 148, 269, 308
Thompson, Barbara 403
Thompson, Emma 242–3, 435
Thompson, Mark 297, 405, 480
Thompson, Steve 463
Thomson, Alan 67
Thornberry, Emily 393, 428
Three Mills Island 22
Thubron, Colin 90
Tibet 197, 229, 233, 303
Tideland (2005 film) 306, 337, 377, 378, 379–80
Timbuktu 404
Time Bandits (1981 film) 179, 257
Times, The 352
Timlett, Ben 450, 494, 512, 523
Tinkley, Allen 8, 9
Titchmarsh, Alan 410, 481
Today (R4) 44–5, 137, 221, 345, 459
Today with Des and Mel (ITV) 305
Tóibín, Colm 506
Toksvig, Sandi 285
Tollan, Max 388
Tom Petty and the Heartbreakers 200
Tomalin, Claire 386

Took, Barry 165, 166, 167–8
Top Gear (BBC series) 310
Topping, Robert 525–6
Trafalgar Square 230, 248
Transport 2000 (T2000) 98, 115, 121, 125, 252,
     310, 342, 352
Transylvania 409, 433
Travel Bookshop 258
Travel Channel 347
Travellers Club 175, 387, 496, 534
Trees for London 98
Trench, The (1999 film) 37–8, 73
Trewin, Ion 274–5, 293–4, 319, 415–16
     'Scottish Waste' ('Glasgow y Valencia') 66,
        68, 74, 100
     lunch with MP 206
     Diaries and 271, 317, 354, 357, 361
     editing *Diaries* 279
     at Book Awards 313
     fundraising for local church 352
     Diaries lunch 436
     Alan Clark biography 525
Tribe (BBC series) 422
Trollope, Joanna 58
Truman Show, The (1998 film) 15
Tunisia 149
Turkey 366, 396
Turnbull, David 5, 17, 21, 42
Turner, J. M. W. 455, 501
Turner, Kathleen 66, 357
Tutt, Laura 22, 23, 85
Twentieth Century Theatre 258
Two Beards and a Blonde (2001 show) 119
Tynan, Kenneth 409

U2 252
Uganda 1, 3
Ukraine 378, 398
UKTV 347, 368
UNICEF 94, 144, 343
Union Club 416–17, 496
Untold Stories (Bennett) 337
Updike, John 35
Upstone, Robert 186
Urban Rock 249, 444
Uys, Pieter-Dirk 134

V&A 401, 431
V&P's (Italian restaurant) 274, 367, 375, 417,
     443, 468, 504
Vallance, Clem 78, 420
van Scheers, Robin 41
Vanity Fair 245–6, 518–19
Vasco and Piero's, Poland Street 274

Veling, Ranji 234, 246, 395–6
Venice 2, 4–5
Victor, Ed 430
Victorian morality 57
Vidal, Gore 177, 257, 274
Vincent, David 414
Vincent, Elmore 260
Viner, Brian 274
Viz magazine 412
Voice of the Viewer & Listener 315, 371
Vorderman, Carol 313
Vosburgh, Beryl 414
Vosburgh, Dick 119, 414

W (Head of Light Entertainment) 125
Wade, Laura 416
Wailes, Martha 17, 20, 22, 23, 36
Waite, Sir John 94
Waiting for Godot (Beckett) 367
Waiting for Happiness (2002 film) 242
'Waiting in the Wings' (Coward) 69
Wałęsa, Lech 381, 383
Walker, Alexander 321
Walker, Christine 283
Walker Gallery 455
Walker, Tim 518–19
Wall, Jeff 350
Wallace Collection 405–6, 510
Walmsley, Nigel 159, 487
Walter, Harriet 339, 340
Walters, Julie 445
Wanderlust magazine 356, 367, 411–12
Warren Hill Prison 363–4
Warren, Marcia 233
Watson, Emily 197
Watts, Annabel 188
Watts, John 133, 188
Wearing, Alison 68
Weatherill, Bernard, Lord 303
Weekend, The (1994 play revival) 233, 307, 328,
     354, 358
Weidenfeld & Nicolson (W&N) 206, 293,
     304, 332, 333, 414, 513
Weidenfeld, George 206, 304, 415–16, 513, 525
Weinstein, Bob 234, 246, 254, 262, 305
Weinstein, Harvey 215, 224, 234, 246, 254,
     272, 305
Wembley Stadium 22, 93
West, Rebecca 361
West, Sam 401, 416
West, Tim and Prue 319
Westminster Abbey 239–40, 359, 532–3
Westminster Cathedral 434–5
Westminster, Gerald, Duke of 450–1

Wexler, Mark 108
Weyden, Rogier van der 16
Wheeler, Charles 371, 372
Wheeler, Michael 57
Wheeler, Sara 530
Whicker, Alan 47
White, Michael 233
Whitehouse Cox 56
Whiteley, Richard 313
Whiteread, Rachel 350
White's Club 470
Who Murdered Chaucer (Jones) 116, 193
Who's Afraid of Virginia Woolf (2006 play) 357
Widdecombe, Ann 124, 171
Wilkinson & Eyre 362
Wilkinson, Chris 362
Wilkinson, John 303
Wilkinson, Tom 169
William, Prince 67
Williams, Alan 361
Williams, Nigel 158
Williams, Robbie 286, 442
Williams, Robin 223
Williams, Rowan 404
Williams, Simon 526
Wilmers, Mary-Kay 269
Wilson, A.N. 153
Wilson, Brian 184
Wilson, Harold 416
Wilson, Richard 66, 233, 307
Wilson, Woodrow 8
Wiltons 464
Wimbledon 321, 463, 513
Wind in the Poplars (Sibleyras) 310
Winder, Gordon and Clarice 375, 462
Windsor Castle 199–200
Winner, Michael 11, 288, 477
Winslet, Kate 433
Winston, Robert 537
Winstone, Pat 55, 389
Witchell, Nicholas 246

Wogan, Terry 266
Wolfe, Tom 456
Wolfowitz, Paul 219
Wolseley 251–2, 290, 307, 430, 485
Woman & Home 48
Woman in Black, The (2009 play) 157, 538
Wongchu Sherpa 386
Wood, Ron 361
Wood, Victoria 169
Woodall, Trinny 282, 304
Woods, Donald 138
Woods, Wendy 138
Woodward, Chris 317
Woolf, Leonard 19
Woolf, Virginia 19, 43, 48, 108, 198, 347, 373, 531
World Cups 93, 140, 175
Wright of Derby, Joseph 131–2, 137
Wright, Steve 125, 377, 435
Wright, Stuart Pearson 208, 264
Wyatt, Will 294, 424, 425
Wyeth, Andrew 499, 510
Wyndham's Theatre 267
Wynn-Jones, Mike 7, 212
Wynne, Steve 341

Xanto 405–6

Yelland, David 339
Yentob, Alan 16, 36, 247, 269, 290, 404–5, 430, 537
You Cannot Live as I Have Lived and Not End Up Like This . . . (Blacker) 406
Young Adam (2003 film) 168
Yugoslavia, NATO bombing (1999) 12, 13
Yule, Eleanor 93, 110, 200, 211, 308, 449, 510

Zimmerman, Paul 83
Zoob, Katti 376
Zsohar, Zsuzsanna 26, 30, 38, 42, 44
Zwack, Péter 376